Hand and Brain

*The Neurophysiology
and Psychology of
Hand Movements*

Edited by

ALAN M. WING
Medical Research Council
Applied Psychology Unit
Cambridge, England

PATRICK HAGGARD
Department of Psychology
University College London
London, England

J. RANDALL FLANAGAN
Department of Psychology
Queen's University
Kingston, Ontario
Canada

ACADEMIC PRESS
San Diego   New York   Boston   London   Sydney   Tokyo   Toronto

Front cover illustration: The hand in precision grip. For more details see Chapter 3, Figure 6. (Modified from Kapandji in Tubiana, 1981.)

This book is printed on acid-free paper. ∞

Academic Press
a division of Harcourt Brace & Company
525 B Street, Suite 1900, San Diego, California 92101-4495, USA
http://www.apnet.com

Academic Press Limited
24-28 Oval Road, London NW1 7DX, UK
http://www.hbuk.co.uk/ap/

Library of Congress Catalog Card Number: 96-5965

International Standard Book Number: 0-12-759441-8

PRINTED IN THE UNITED STATES OF AMERICA
98 99 00 01 02 03 EB 9 8 7 6 5 4 3 2 1

Contents

P A R T **2** The Motor Hand   33

3 Precision Grip in Humans: Temporal
and Spatial Synergies

**MARIE-CLAUDE HEPP-REYMOND, ERHARD J. HUESLER,
AND MARC A. MAIER**

4 Muscle Architecture Basis for Neuromuscular
Control of the Forearm and Hand

JAN FRIDÉN AND RICHARD L. LIEBER

5 Individuated Finger Movements: Rejecting
the Labeled-Line Hypothesis

MARC H. SCHIEBER

6 Multiple Hand Representations in the Motor Cortical Areas

ERIC M. ROUILLER

7 The Structure and Function of the Developing Corticospinal Tract: Some Key Issues

J. ARMAND, E. OLIVIER, S. A. EDGLEY, AND R. N. LEMON

P A R T 3 Hand Positioning in Reaching   147

14   Two Hands—One Action: The Problem of Bimanual Coordination

MARIO WIESENDANGER, OLEG KAZENNIKOV, STEPHEN PERRIG, AND PAWEL KALUZNY

15   Anticipatory Control of Grip Force in Rapid Arm Movement

ALAN M. WING

PART 5   The Sensorimotor Hand   325

16   Role of Primary Somatosensory Cortex in Active and Passive Touch

C. ELAINE CHAPMAN, FRANÇOIS TREMBLAY, AND STACEY A. AGERANIOTI-BÉLANGER

17 Proprioception and Its Contribution
to Manual Dexterity

LYNETTE JONES

18 Proprioceptive Mechanisms and the Control
of Finger Movements

ÅKE B. VALLBO AND JOHAN WESSBERG

Contributors

Numbers in parentheses indicate the pages on which the authors' contributions begin.

Stacey A. Ageranioti-Bélanger (329) Centre de Recherche en Sciences Neurologiques, Département de Physiologie, Université de Montréal, Montréal, Québec, Canada H3C 3J7

J. Armand (125) Centre National de la Recherche Scientifique, Laboratoire de Neurosciences Cognitives, 13402 Marseille Cedex 20, France

C. Elaine Chapman (329) Centre de Recherche en Sciences Neurologiques, Département de Physiologie, Université de Montréal, Montréal, Québec, Canada H3C 3J7

Scott Cooper (187) Department of Neurology, Columbia University, New York, New York 10032

S. A. Edgley (125) Department of Anatomy, University of Cambridge, Cambridge CB2 3DY, England

Andrew H. Fagg (243) Department of Computer and Information Sciences, University of Massachusetts, Amherst, Massachusetts 01003

J. Randall Flanagan (5, 415) Department of Psychology, Queen's University, Kingston, Ontario, Canada K7L 3N6

Martha Flanders (151) Department of Physiology, University of Minnesota, Minneapolis, Minnesota 55455

Jan Fridén (69) Department of Hand Surgery, Sahlgren University Hospital, S413 45 Göteborg, Sweden

Claude Ghez (187) Center for Neurobiology and Behavior, Columbia University, New York, New York 10032

Melvyn A. Goodale (15) Department of Psychology, University of Western Ontario, London, Ontario, Canada N6A 5CS

Patrick Haggard (5) Department of Psychology, University College London, London WC1E 6BT, England

Marie-Claude Hepp-Reymond (37) Brain Research Institute, University of Zurich, CH-8029 Zurich, Switzerland

Erhard J. Huesler (37) Brain Research Institute, University of Zurich, CH-8029 Zurich, Switzerland

Thea Iberall (243) Department of Computer Science, University of Southern California, Los Angeles, California 90089

Lorna S. Jakobson (15) Department of Psychology, Queen's University, Kingston, Ontario, Canada K7N 3P6

Marc Jeannerod (265) Laboratoire Vision et Motricité, INSERM U94, F-69500 Bron, France

Roland S. Johansson (381) Department of Physiology, Umeå University, S-90187 Umeå, Sweden

Lynette Jones (349) Department of Mechanical Engineering, Massachusetts Institute of Technology, Cambridge, Massachusetts 02139

Pawel Kaluzny (283) Laboratory of Motor Systems, Department of Neurology, University of Berne, CH 3010 Bern, Switzerland

Oleg Kazennikov (283) Institute for Problems of Information Transmission, Russian Academy of Sciences, Moscow, Russia 101447

Roberta L. Klatzky (431) Department of Psychology, Carnegie Mellon University, Pittsburgh, Pennsylvania 15213

Francesco Lacquaniti (213) Istituto di Fisiologia Umana, Università di Cagliari and Istituto Scientifico S. Lucia, I.N.B.-C.N.R., Rome, Italy

Susan J. Lederman (431) Departments of Psychology and of Computing and Information Science, Queen's University, Kingston, Ontario, Canada K7L 3N6

R. N. Lemon (125) Sobell Department of Neurophysiology, Institute of Neurology, London WC1N 3BG, England

Richard L. Lieber (69) Departments of Orthopedics and of AMES/Bioengineering, Biomedical Sciences Graduate Group, University of California and Veterans Administration Medical Centers, San Diego, California 92093

Marc A. Maier (37) Sobell Department of Neurophysiology, Institute of Neurology, London WC1N 3BG, England

John Martin (187) Center for Neurobiology and Behavior, Columbia University, New York, New York 10032

Ruud G. J. Meulenbroek (169) Nijmegen Institute for Cognition and Information, University of Nijmegen, 6500 HE Nijmegen, The Netherlands

E. Olivier (125) Sobell Department of Neurophysiology, Institute of Neurology, London WC1N 3BG, England

Yves Paulignan (265) Laboratoire Vision et Motricité, INSERM U94, F-69500 Bron, France

Stephen Perrig (283) Department of Neurology, University of Geneva, CH-1225 Chene-Bourg, Switzerland

David A. Rosenbaum (169) Department of Psychology, Pennsylvania State University, University Park, Pennsylvania 16802

Eric M. Rouiller (99) Institute of Physiology, University of Fribourg, CH-1700 Fribourg, Switzerland

Marc H. Schieber (81) Departments of Neurology, Neurobiology and Anatomy, Visual Science, Brain and Cognitive Science, and the Saint Mary's Brain Injury Rehabilitation Unit, University of Rochester School of Medicine, Rochester, New York 14642

Philip Servos (15) Department of Psychology, Stanford University, Stanford, California 94305

John F. Soechting (151) Department of Physiology, University of Minnesota, Minneapolis, Minnesota 55455

David C. Tong (151) Department of Physiology, University of Minnesota, Minneapolis, Minnesota 55455

François Tremblay (329) Centre de Recherche en Sciences Neurologiques, Département de Physiologie, Université de Montréal, Montréal, Québec Canada H3C 3J7

Åke B. Vallbo (363) Department of Physiology, Göteborg University, S-413 90, Göteborg, Sweden

Jonathan Vaughan (169) Department of Psychology, Hamilton College, Clinton, New York 13323

Johan Wessberg (363) Department of Physiology, Göteborg University, S-413 90, Göteborg, Sweden

Mario Wiesendanger (283) Laboratory of Motor Systems, Department of Neurology, University of Berne, CH-3010 Bern, Switzerland

Alan M. Wing (5, 301) Medical Research Council Applied Psychology Unit, Cambridge CB2 2EF, England

Preface

This book is about the sensorimotor control of the hand. It is concerned both with movements of the hand produced by the arm and with the shaping and manipulative abilities of the hand produced by movements of individual fingers. A major theme is the nature of coordination of the hand and of the arm both at the level of movements and in terms of muscle contributions. Hand function depends crucially on sensory factors. Indeed, the hand's role is often primarily sensory and hand movements enable active exploration which greatly increases the potential for extracting information from objects in the environment. This book therefore covers sensory as well as motor aspects of hand function, with contributions from a wide range of professionals in psychology, neurophysiology, engineering, and biomechanics, as well as the medical specialities of hand surgery and neurology.

Each chapter was written with advanced undergraduate readers in mind; there are copious illustrations, terms are defined, methods are explained, and a comprehensive index is complemented by a glossary. However, none of the authors let the tutorial nature of their presentations constrain their treatment to simplistic overviews. All have provided up-to-date and comprehensive coverage of their varied approaches to the neural control of the hand. The book will therefore not only provide a useful adjunct to undergraduate course-work, but will also serve the researcher seeking to update his or her knowledge in allied fields.

There are five sections to the book. Section 1 (The Hand in Action) serves to introduce issues that recur in later sections and provides a brief overview of some of the major methodologies that will be encountered. Section 2 (The Motor Hand) is concerned with movement elements, the coordination of muscles, and the description of the major structures and pathways in the central nervous system. Section 3 (Hand Positioning in Reaching) treats the nature of arm movement control that allows the hand to be positioned and oriented appropriately in space. Chapters in Section 4 (Hand–Arm Coordination in Reach and Grasp) describe the functional links between movements of the arm and of the fingers of the hand. Finally, Section 5 (The Sensorimotor Hand) reviews the sensory function of the hand and the relations between sensation, perception, and action.

Our thanks in producing this book go to all the contributing authors, but especially to Mario Wiesendanger for his continued support for the book project. Indeed, the motivation for the project came from a conference on the sensorimotor function of the hand that he organized with the assistance of Roland Johansson and Alan Wing and with the financial support of the Foundation Stefano Franscini, Eidgenössiche Technische Hochschule and the Schweizerische Akademie der Naturwissenchaftern. Thanks also to Sue Allison for her work with the figures, and to the staff of Academic Press for their editorial assistance on the production side.

Alan Wing, Patrick Haggard, Randy Flanagan
Cambridge, September 1995

The Hand in Action

A majority of tasks that people perform with the hand require differentiated movement of the digits. The fingers, and especially the opposable thumb, must frequently play varied and individual roles in order to create hand shapes for communicative gesture, environmental exploration, or grasping all manner of object shapes, or to apply and direct forces for manipulating, molding, or stabilizing hand-held objects with widely varying properties such as hardness and weight. The actions of the hand often are complemented by arm movements, for example, in positioning or orienting the hand to maximum advantage.

All this is possible in part because of the anatomical structure of the bones of the hand and arm and the many muscles, whose combined contractions flex some joints, extend others, and hold yet others in fixed position. However, no less important are the neural control systems embodied in the sensory and motor pathways of the nervous system and the integrative and coordinative structures of the brain and spinal cord. Somatosensory pathways bring information from skin and muscle, allowing subtle gradation of motor output with adjustment, for example, to cope with changes in the peripheral conditions under which movements are taking place. Vision is important in anticipatory tailoring of movement parameters to perceived attributes of the manipulandum such as shape. Or, visual cues may signal object properties (e.g., smooth texture indicates a slippery surface), which, on the basis of previous handling experience, call for different movement strategies.

In Chapter 1, Flanagan, Haggard, and Wing recount, in anecdotal fashion, the performance of an everyday task that embodies all the major themes that recur throughout later chapters. Indeed, the same issues may be found running through any textbook on motor control and, to that extent, this book will complement neuroscience courses on motor control. However, recognizing the diverse potential readership, Flanagan et al. not only outline the major issues in the psychology and neurophysiology of hand movement control, they also provide a brief description of some of the main methodological approaches encountered in the rest of the book.

The variety and subtlety of hand motor control demand considerable neural computational resources. The proportion of sensorimotor cortex devoted to hand function is considerably greater than that devoted to other body segments such as the lower limb. Interruption of cerebral blood supply (a cerebral vascular accident, CVA, or stroke) usually results in sudden onset of paralysis, or at least weakness (paresis), of the whole of one side of the body, opposite to the hemisphere affected by the CVA. In subsequent weeks and months, the hemiparesis often reduces in the leg and arm but it is common for there to be little improvement in the hand. This partly reflects the distribution territory of the middle cerebral artery but it also points to the specialized and complex nature of the neural machinery underlying hand function.

Although hemiparesis is a common consequence of a CVA, other problems may also arise. For example, it is quite common for there to be proprioceptive deficits of the hand associated with hemiparesis because the lesion extends over sensory and motor areas that are in quite close proximity. But, if the cortical lesion is more posterior, the result may be visual impairments without motor deficits. In some cases the visual deficit can be quite subtle, so that a patient may be able to visually recognize objects and yet be unable to successfully reach and grasp the object despite normal motor function. Such a deficit (referred to as optic ataxia) is discussed in Chapter 2 by Goodale, Jakobson, and Servos. Their general concern is with the transformations between vision and action that enable us to move to and grasp visually perceived objects. These authors provide evidence for two pathways geared toward perception and action. When faced with an object in the environment, we may want to extract information from it or act on it physically. Goodale et al. suggest the neural substrate underlying these contrasting behavioral functions may be quite distinct. They support their argument by a comparison of a patient with optic ataxia with another neurological patient who was able to use vision in reaching but had difficulty in making visual judgments about object attributes (which nevertheless clearly controlled action). This chapter is an excellent example of the insights to be garnered by combining psychology with neurophysiology in understanding brain function. It thus sets the goals that we hold for the book as a whole.

1

The Task at Hand

J. RANDALL FLANAGAN, PATRICK HAGGARD, AND ALAN M. WING

1. INTRODUCTION

Most of our actions are directed at objects in the world about us. Key components include our ability to perceive the qualities of an object and, having decided that it is appropriate to a task, to reach for it (with one or both hands), grasp and lift it, manipulate it or use it to act on some other object, and finally place it back down. While holding the object we can appreciate its attributes, confirming and extending the information available from vision. The incoming sensory information from the hand also serves a role in establishing the success of manipulative action, ranging from confirming the stability of the object in the hand's grasp to the provision of information about the relative motion of parts of the object.

This chapter is intended as an introduction to themes such as these, which are taken up in greater detail in the rest of the book. We start with a slightly tongue-in-cheek characterization of the manipulative functions of the hand. This serves the purpose of identifying many of the major issues that recur throughout the book. We then provide a brief summary of a number of the methods used to study neural control of hand function. Although not exhaustive, this section will help orient the reader to the variety of techniques that will be encountered later in the book. A glossary of important terms is provided at the end of the book in order to assist the reader with the wide range of specialist topics covered by researchers working in a variety of disciplines.

2. NEWTON'S APPLE

The ease with which healthy adults pick up, transport, and manipulate objects belies the complexity of the task from the point of view of neural control. Yet this complexity can become all too apparent when we observe the very young, the elderly, or people with neurological damage (e.g., following a stroke due to a cerebral vascular accident, CVA) attempting to perform a simple, everyday task such as pouring a drink. In order to illustrate the control issues involved in reaching, grasping, and manipulation, suppose we could join Sir Isaac Newton in the kitchen garden at Trinity College, Cambridge, where he is pondering the laws of motion in the comforting shade of an apple tree. Suppose further he is beginning to feel somewhat hungry, yet there are several hours to go before he will be able to assuage his appetite at high table in college that evening. At this point his attention is attracted by a shiny red object in the tree, the image of which strikes his retina.

Now, Sir Isaac's brain must solve the following problem; how can it translate the perceived location and shape of the object into a set of muscle commands that will bring his hand to the vicinity of the apple and shape it appropriately for grasping? Fundamental to this process is a *sensorimotor transformation* from a sensory frame of reference (or coordinate system) appropriate to the retina to a motor frame of reference in which commands to the muscles are specified (Chapter 8). This transformation might involve intermediate representations. For example, the apple could be represented in a coordinate system, which would take as input information about eye direction relative to the head and orientation of the head relative to the body. This representation might then be mapped onto an appropriate posture for the arm, defined by particular shoulder, elbow, and wrist angles and only subsequently transformed to specify corresponding levels of activity required in selected muscles.

Of course, it is unlikely that our eminent don would have been distracted from his meditations on integral calculus without first having identified the shiny red object as an apple. Thus, his visual system is not only required to identify object location. It must also provide information that allows object identification based on access to long-term memory. Presumably color, shape, and location in a tree allow our genius to figure out that the object affords eating. However, recent neuropsychological studies suggest that there are *separate visual systems* subserving cognition and action (Chapter 2). Thus, curiously, it is conceivable that, if Sir Isaac had brain damage resulting from a stroke he might be able to use visual information to recognize the apple, that is, perceive it in terms of being able to describe its attributes, but not be able to plan an accurate reach to grasp it!

Let us return to consider how Sir Isaac's central nervous system (CNS) would define a posture for the hand and arm so as to allow the apple to be grasped. Here, we encounter what has been termed the *degrees of freedom problem* (Chapter 9), which can be cast in terms of the following question. How is a specific posture to be selected from the large number of possible postures, any one of which would result in the hand encompassing the apple (even if some of them would leave our don looking rather inelegant)? Six numbers (degrees of freedom) are required to specify the location of a rigid object in three-dimensional space; three for position (x,y,z) and three for orientation (yaw, pitch, and roll). However, the joints of the arm allow 7 degrees of freedom; flexion–extension, abduction–adduction, and humeral rotation at the shoulder; flexion at the elbow; flexion–extension, abduction–adduction, and pronation–supination of the wrist. Thus, the arm with the hand fixed around an object has one surplus degree of freedom that allows some freedom of choice of elbow position.

The advantage of an extra degree of freedom (*kinematic redundancy*) is that it allows flexibility in selecting postures. Thus, even if there were a branch in front of the apple, Newton might still be able to achieve his goal of placing his hand on the apple by keeping his elbow out around the obstacle. The drawback to kinematic redundancy is that the brain must select among the alternative postures. What criteria or rules may be used to narrow down the options to any particular arm configuration? The problem is nontrivial considering just the shoulder, elbow, and wrist. It becomes an order of magnitude greater when we consider the further degrees of freedom contributed by the digits of the hand. These underlie our ability to grasp objects in many different ways employing all variety of grips (Chapter 12), but again this variety contributes to the issue of selection from multiple alternatives.

Thus far, we have considered only the final posture of the hand and arm. However, Newton will have to move his hand from some other position (maybe he had been using it to scratch his head as part of his cogitations). How should the path from initial to final position be chosen? One theoretical approach to movement control suggests that the brain is concerned only with end posture and that the path taken by the hand is merely a by-product of the commands associated with that change in posture. However, our ability to avoid obstacles between start and end points of a movement (and not only avoid collisions with the hand but also with the arm and particularly the elbow), suggests the brain plans a specific spatial path for the hand (and arm) through space. Again, the CNS must deal with a redundancy problem in that it must identify a particular path and associated kinematics (together defining a *goal trajectory*) from many that are possible. Moreover, in reaching to grasp there is the further question: how will *hand shape* develop and be coordinated with arm movement as the hand approaches the apple (Chapter 13)?

Once movement trajectories for the arm and hand have been planned,

Sir Isaac's motor system must determine the forces required to generate the desired motions. In movements involving several joints, this is a difficult problem because of mechanical interactions between limb segments. The motion of a given joint depends not only on the muscle forces acting on that joint but on the motions of other joints as well. Failure to allow for such interactions can lead to large discrepancies between intended and actual movement paths (Chapter 10). These errors could be compensated for by *feedback control* in which corrections are made on the basis of the moment-to-moment discrepancy between the intended and actual paths. However, feedback corrections are necessarily subject to sensorimotor transmission delays in the CNS, which create further problems. Therefore, some researchers have proposed instead that the CNS uses an *internal model* of the dynamics of the limb in order to compute the muscle forces necessary to realize planned trajectories. The advantage of such a control scheme is that if the CNS can specify accurate forces, there will be less need to monitor feedback.

Up to this point, we have considered only the reaching movement to the apple. However, much of the real action begins when Newton's illustrious hand contacts the fruit. The task then becomes one of establishing a *stable grasp*, plucking the apple from the branch, and then transporting it back for inspection and eating. Let us assume that, in order to pluck the apple, Sir Isaac grasps it with a precision grip using just the tips of the thumb and index finger. Because the apple is still attached to the branch, to prevent his fingers slipping over the surface as he pulls, Newton squeezes it. This increases the *grip force* at right angles to the surface of the apple and this, in turn, results in an increase in the friction between his skin and that of the apple, which counters the *load force* created by his pull.

To break the apple from the branch, Newton increases his pull and the rise in load force requires closely coordinated increases in grip force to prevent slipping. It might be assumed that past experience in handling apples, perhaps at the supermarket, would allow Newton to *predict* how hard he has to squeeze an apple for a given load force. However, if the apple is more slippery than he expects (perhaps because the Trinity undergraduates were earlier polishing the college apples as a class exercise in aesthetic appreciation), the grip force will be too low and the apple will start to *slip* from grasp. Fortunately for our natural scientist, this unexpected slip will likely stimulate mechanoreceptors in the skin (Chapter 19). The resultant afferent signal, following a path that probably takes in sensorimotor cortex, leads to a reflex increase in grip force with a delay sufficiently short to reestablish grasp before the fingers slip off the apple.

Generating force with the thumb and index finger to hold the apple in a stable grasp produces a variant on the degrees of freedom problem described earlier. Several muscles act on each digit (Chapter 4) and there is considerable redundancy in their contribution to increasing grip force. How should their relative contributions be determined? One way in which Sir Isaac's motor system might solve this problem is to reduce the number of individual elements that need to be controlled by exploiting coordinative *synergies* between muscles. That is, if subsets of muscles are constrained to act as a unit with a fixed relation between their levels and timing of activation, then the CNS could control these units rather than individual muscles (Chapter 3).

Having plucked the apple, Sir Isaac's grip must be directed to produce a frictional force to counter the force of gravity acting on the apple. At this stage his prior judgment of the apple's weight might help him select a grip force sufficient to prevent the apple dropping out of his hand. However, once the apple is detached from the tree, sensory information from cutaneous receptors will provide him with indications of grasp stability. Taken in combination with information about the level of effort required to hold the apple, this might lead him to revise his *weight estimate* (Chapter 20). With the apple free of the branch Newton can then begin to transport the apple toward him. This requires he first accelerate and then decelerate his hand. This creates *inertial forces*, which, in combination with the apple's weight, will tend to cause the apple to slip from grasp. So, as an addition to the trajectory planning required in moving the hand, transporting the apple implies preparing commands to the hand muscles to take account of the forces created by the kinematics of the planned path (Chapter 15).

Let us now imagine a different scenario and suppose that at the very moment Sir Isaac spots the object of his desire (or the apple of his eye), it starts to fall from the tree above him. Ever quick, he reaches to catch the apple. This *interception* task is considerably more complex than reaching for a static object, since it requires prediction of the path of the apple in time and space. Moreover, he also has to deal with the impact when the apple strikes his hand; here, he is assisted by reflexes probably involving sensorimotor cortex (i.e., *supraspinal reflexes*) that help stabilize the hand at the time of collision. Unlike fixed spinal reflexes that involve response only in the stretched muscle (Chapter 18), the anticipated collision means the supraspinal reflex triggers responses in both wrist flexors and extensors in a manner that contributes to absorption of the apple's impact (Chapter 11).

Whichever route brings the apple to hand, Sir Isaac now wants to inspect it in case some insect has gotten to it before him. Here he has a number of options. Holding the apple in one hand he may run the tips of the fingers of his other hand over it, seeking any softness or blemish in the otherwise smooth rounded form of the apple. This is termed *active touch*; through his own voluntary movements he picks up sensory information about the apple

(Chapter 21). By using active touch, Newton can extract richer sensory information than that obtained under passive touch conditions created, for example, by a colleague moving the apple for him while he rests his fingers on the surface. During active touch, cutaneous (and proprioceptive) sensory information is likely modulated by the CNS. This modulating, or *gating*, presumably enables Newton's brain to attenuate unwanted sensory information and enhance information that is important to the task at hand (Chapter 16).

Vision provides an alternative to touch for inspecting the apple. However, bringing all parts of the apple into view requires that Newton manipulate it to rotate it in his hand. If carried out without the help of the other hand, this involves *dexterous manipulation* with contrasting movements of several digits. For example, one strategy involves the application of force (or more accurately, torque) around an axis defined by the line between the thumb and index finger grip points. This torque can be supplied by movements of the ring finger. However, the fingers share a number of muscles in common (these are located in the forearm and attached by long tendons running over the wrist). Therefore, when commanding ring finger movement, Sir Isaac's motor system must compensate for the potential concomitant disturbance to the index finger (Chapter 5). Given the complexity of the underlying neural circuitry required to achieve this, it is perhaps not surprising that, as a preschooler, Izzy (as he was known to his friends at that time) could not achieve such dexterity. In fact, the fine finger control improves over a number of years and likely reflects the *development* of specialized neural connections in the spinal cord (Chapter 7). A further issue in such dexterous manipulation is the role of sensory feedback in controlling the induced motion. This includes information from receptors not only in the skin but also in muscles and joints (Chapter 17).

On inspecting the apple, Sir Isaac discovers a blemish in the form of a small hole in the apple and suspects that there may be an unwelcome visitor in it. He therefore takes out his handy Swiss pocketknife (presented by a visiting scholar) to investigate. The functional use of a tool requires *bimanual coordination* whereby the apple is supported in one hand and operated on by the other. Bringing the hands together and working on the apple requires that movements in one hand be precisely matched by complementary moves of the other to preserve their relative positions (Chapter 14). The cost of an error in such skill is a cut (which makes laboratory study of such tasks difficult to get past today's ethical committees!). Such coordination of the two hands calls on additional neural resources including the supplementary motor area (Chapter 6). With deft use of the blade, Newton uncovers a worm. He puts down the knife and pulls the worm out, which requires a particularly sensitive precision grip so as not to squash it, then proceeds to enjoy the fruits of his labor.

3. METHODS USED IN THE ANALYSIS OF THE MOTOR FUNCTION OF THE HAND

Our extended example in the previous section illustrates certain key problems in hand movement control, and these recur throughout this book. In particular, the issues of coordination of multiple degrees of freedom and of sensory guidance are to be found in both behavioral and neurophysiological studies. While tasks (and the subjects performing them) vary widely, the common underlying theme is how does the brain control complex movement for effective goal-oriented action.

The research described in this book includes a wide range of methods, from several different scientific disciplines, which have contributed to our understanding of the relations between brain activity and hand function. Some of these methods may be unfamiliar to some readers, and we now briefly review a few of the principal methods that have been used to study manual dexterity. These are: kinematic recording, recording patterns of muscle activity using electromyography, the tracing of neural connections using specialized chemicals, electrophysiological recording from single neurons in the brain, magnetic stimulation of the brain, and functional brain imaging.

In recent years, optical tracking systems have been developed that allow simultaneous quantitative measurement of the trajectory in three-dimensional space of several points on the moving limb. These systems have allowed researchers to study the coordination between different parts of the body during a single movement, as, for example, between the preshaping of the hand and the movement of the arm when grasping an object. However, there is no a priori guarantee that the kinematic information recorded directly reflects the neural program that the brain uses to control movement. Therefore, researchers have often suggested that measures that appear consistently under a wide variety of conditions reflect the underlying neural control (the so-called argument from invariance). Alternatively, kinematic recording can be used in conjunction with measurement of forces and a biomechanical model of the limb to infer torques acting around joints, which some researchers take to be more directly relevant to understanding muscle action.

When a muscle contracts, it produces a low-voltage electrical signal that can be recorded with electrodes placed on the surface of the skin over the muscle and suitable high-gain amplification. The recording is known as the *electromyogram* (EMG). The relation between the magnitude of the EMG and muscle tension is somewhat controversial, but it does allow comparisons between the amount of activity in an individual muscle under different circumstances. Problems can arise if comparisons are made of EMG amplitude across different muscles, because differences in signal level can arise from factors such as the distance of the electrodes from the muscle. However, the temporal pattern of muscle contraction, for example, the times at which each of a pair of muscles increases its level of activity, may be compared. This timing information can provide useful clues to the various neural pathways contributing to a muscle contraction. Different pathways having different lengths and numbers of synapses from a known stimulus site will produce muscle responses at correspondingly different latencies.

An understanding of the relations between hand and brain is obviously helped by an understanding of the neural pathways carrying afferent information from hand to brain, and efferent information from brain to hand. Several chapters in this book report anatomical studies that have traced these pathways in monkeys, in order to model their structure and function in humans. The *anatomical tracing* techniques are simple to describe, but technically demanding to carry out. They involve injecting small quantities of a chemical (called the tracer or label) at a known location in the nervous system of an animal, which is often identified by electrophysiological recording (see below). The tracer is then transported away from the injection site throughout the neuron, as part of the cell's normal metabolic transport processes. Depending on the tracer used, this transport may be orthodromic (same direction as the nervous impulse) or antidromic (opposite direction). After a suitable interval, the animal is sacrificed and slices of neural tissue are reacted with further chemicals. Microscopic examination can then reveal sites to which the original tracer has been transported. Tracing studies not only tell us where neurons project, but also what sort of connections they make. Many corticospinal cells, for example, branch in the spinal cord to synapse on motoneurons of different muscles. The physiological contribution of each branch may be unclear, but the consistency of the anatomical finding in tracing studies suggests that this distributed feature of neural control of the hand may be involved in precisely tuning the coordination of the fingers.

While anatomical studies tell us that a neural pathway exists, *electrophysiological recording* from single neurons in the brain tells us more about what the pathway does, since it reveals what aspects of the sensory or motor task the particular neuron is specialized for. The method involves inserting a fine electrode into the brain of an animal with the aim of penetrating a single neuron, and recording the individual neural impulses in that neuron during the task being studied. Single unit studies of the sensory system typically examine the tuning of a neuron by systematically varying the parameters of a stimulus delivered to the animal, and plotting the amount of firing as a function of the appropriate stimulus parameters.

Most single unit studies of the motor system have correlated the discharge pattern with physical parameters such as force or direction of movements made by trained animals or even with motor unit discharge patterns (obtained from EMG recorded with fine wire electrodes in the muscle rather than using the surface electrodes referred to earlier). A complication of working with the motor system is that behavior must be controlled so as to obtain an appropriate range of movement parameters. Moreover, control conditions must be run to check that environmental stimuli are not the source of the observed neural firing patterns. However, a benefit of studying the motor system is that, in principle, the role of the single unit may be studied by direct stimulation while recording effects on motor unit discharge of relevant muscles. (There is now a noninvasive procedure for stimulating cortical tissue; transcranial magnetic stimulation of the brain. TMS involves creating a strong localized transient magnetic field near the scalp, which induces current flow in underlying neural tissue.).

For obvious ethical reasons, invasive physiological recording of brain activity is only rarely possible in humans, for example, when neurosurgical procedures require electrodes be placed on or in brain tissue for functional assessment purposes. In the last century considerable progress in understanding the function of various areas of the human brain came from correlating behavioral deficits associated with information about the underlying neural lesions (e.g., due to a CVA) derived from postmortem examination. Such studies were often made difficult because patients survived for quite long periods following their initial illness and possibly incurred further brain damage. In the second half of this century, this methodological difficulty was alleviated by the development of X-ray techniques (computed tomography, CT) that provided high-resolution images allowing living brain tissue to be differentiated from areas of lower-density tissue associated with brain lesions.

Recently, the endeavor of mapping function onto brain regions has received a considerable boost from new brain scanning procedures capable of providing images of normal brain function. These procedures differentiate areas according to their metabolic activity, which in turn is determined by neural signal transmission levels. One of these (positron emission tomography, PET) relies on the detection of decay of radioactive particles (using a radioactive marker previously introduced through the blood). This procedure requires relatively long periods (several minutes) of sustained activity (e.g., repetitive finger movements) to build up a picture in which elevated activity of the relevant area (finger region of primary motor cortex) emerges from background levels of activity in other areas. In contrast, the technique of functional magnetic resonance imaging (fMRI), which has the advantage of not requiring the use of radioactive markers, can build up a picture over relatively short periods of 10 s. Both procedures obviously have important medical applications, but they are also significant for allowing behavior to be mapped onto concurrently active regions of the brain.

2

The Visual Pathways Mediating Perception and Prehension

MELVYN A. GOODALE, LORNA S. JAKOBSON,
AND PHILIP SERVOS

1. INTRODUCTION

The higher primates, especially humans, are capable of reaching out and grasping objects with considerable accuracy. Vision plays a critical role in the control of this important skill. Only recently, however, has there been much investigation of the organization of the visual pathways mediating the control of the different components of manual prehension. Accumulating evidence from both neuropsychological studies of patients and electrophysiological and behavioral work in the monkey suggests that these pathways, particularly at the level of the cerebral cortex, may be quite distinct from those underlying what we traditionally think of as visual "perception." In this chapter, we review some of this evidence. The chapter is based on material previously covered in detail in Goodale (1993a, 1993b) and Jakobson and Goodale (1994).

2. TWO VISUAL SYSTEMS IN PRIMATE VISUAL CORTEX?

Beyond primary visual cortex (V1) in the primate brain the ascending visual pathways within the cerebral cortex project to a complex mosaic of interconnected areas, each of which contains visually sensitive neurons with rather different response properties (for review, see Felleman & Van Essen, 1991; Zeki, 1993). Despite the high degree of interconnectivity between the different cortical visual areas, work on the monkey has revealed that there are two main streams of projections emanating from primary visual cortex and projecting to different cortical regions (Ungerleider & Mishkin, 1982): a *ventral* stream, which leaves V1 and projects via a series of cortico-cortical projections to the inferotemporal cortex; and a *dorsal* stream, which projects from V1 to the posterior parietal cortex. A simplified diagram of these two streams of projections is presented in Figure 1.

Ungerleider and Mishkin (1982) proposed that anatomical separation of the cortical visual projections into two distinct streams reflects a fundamental division of labor in visual processing. According to their original account, the ventral stream plays a special role in the visual identification of objects, while the dorsal stream is responsible for localizing objects in visual space. This "Two Visual Systems" model of cortical visual processing was one of the most influential accounts of visual function throughout the 1980s, and is still regarded as an important organizing principle for a wide variety of visual phenomena in visual neuroscience and cognitive psychology. In this chapter,

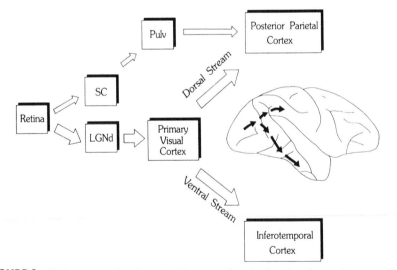

FIGURE 1   Major routes whereby retinal input reaches the dorsal and ventral streams. The diagram of the macaque brain (right hemisphere) on the right of the figure shows the approximate routes of the cortico-cortical projections from the primary visual cortex to the posterior parietal and the inferotemporal cortex, respectively. LGNd: lateral geniculate nucleus, pars dorsalis; Pulv: pulvinar; SC: superior colliculus.

however, we argue that Ungerleider and Mishkin's original distinction between object vision and spatial vision (or *what* vs. *where*) fails to capture the essential difference between the functions of the ventral and dorsal streams of processing. We introduce a recent proposal by Goodale and Milner (1992; Milner & Goodale, 1993), which invokes instead the distinction between visual perception and the visual control of skilled action and, in so doing, puts greater emphasis on differences in the output requirements of the dorsal and ventral streams. As we shall see, according to this account, both streams process information about object characteristics, such as size, orientation, and shape, and both process information about spatial location. Each stream, however, uses this visual information in different ways. Transformations carried out in the ventral stream permit the formation of perceptual and cognitive representations that embody the enduring characteristics of objects and their spatial relations with each other; those carried out in the dorsal stream, which utilize instantaneous object features that are organized within egocentric frames of reference, mediate the control of goal-directed actions.

3. THE NEUROPSYCHOLOGICAL EVIDENCE

3.1 Dissociations in the Processing of Object Size, Orientation, and Location for Perception and Prehension

The initial evidence for this reinterpretation of the functional distinction between the dorsal and ventral streams came from a series of recent investigations of visually guided behavior in neurological patients in which damage appeared to be largely confined to one stream or the other. Traditionally, of course, work with such patients has been offered as part of the evidence for Ungerleider and Mishkin's (1982) original Two Visual Systems model. Thus, patients with damage to the superior portions of the posterior parietal cortex (which is thought to be a region within the human homolog of the dorsal stream in the monkey) often show *optic ataxia*. That is, they are unable to use visual information to reach out and grasp objects in the hemifield contralateral to the lesion, and make large directional errors. At the same time, such patients often have no difficulty recognizing or describing objects that are presented in that part of the visual field. Conversely, patients with *visual form agnosia*, following damage to the occipitotemporal region (which is thought to correspond to the monkey's ventral stream), are unable to recognize or describe common objects, faces, drawings, or abstract designs, even though they often have no difficulty using vision to avoid obstacles as they move through the world. On the face of it, these clinical observations certainly appear to support the what-versus-where dichotomy originally proposed by

Ungerleider and Mishkin (1982): a ventral stream supporting object vision but not spatial vision, and a dorsal stream supporting spatial vision but not object vision. When the behavior of these patients is examined more closely, however, a different picture emerges.

3.1.1 Optic Ataxia

Consider the patients with optic ataxia following parietal damage. As was just indicated, the fact that they have difficulty reaching toward objects has often been interpreted as a deficit in spatial vision—a kind of disorientation that makes it impossible for them to localize an object in visual space. The problem with this interpretation, however, is that in many patients the disorientation shows effector specificity. Thus, in some patients, the deficit shows up when one hand is used but not the other (Bàlint, 1909; Perenin & Vighetto, 1988). Even when reaching is impaired, whichever *hand* is used, several patients with optic ataxia can direct their *eyes* accurately toward targets that they cannot accurately reach for (Ratcliff & Davies-Jones, 1972; Riddoch, 1935). Such results show clearly that in no sense can the misreaching in optic ataxia be attributed to a loss of *the* sensory representation of space in such patients. Indeed, as we shall see later, these observations suggest that there are *multiple* spatial codings, each controlling a different effector system.

Observations in several laboratories have also shown that some patients with optic ataxia not only have difficulty reaching in the right direction, but they also show deficits in their ability to position their fingers or adjust the orientation of their hand when reaching toward an object, even though they have no difficulty in verbally describing the orientation of the object (Perenin & Vighetto, 1988). Other clinical reports suggest that patients with damage to the posterior parietal region can also have trouble adjusting their grasp to reflect the size of an object they are asked to pick up. Such deficits were observed, for example, in a patient (VK) who was recovering from Bàlint's syndrome, in which bilateral parietal lesions had resulted in a profound disorder of spatial attention, gaze, and visually guided reaching (Jakobson, Archibald, Carey, & Goodale, 1991). While VK was able to identify line drawings of common objects with little difficulty, her ability to pick up objects remained grossly impaired. Unlike neurologically intact subjects, for example, the size of her grasp was only weakly related to the size of the objects she was asked to pick up and she often opened her hand as wide for small objects as she did for large ones. Moreover, compared to normal control subjects, VK took much longer to initiate and execute her movements and also made a large number of adjustments in grip aperture as she closed in on the target. Similar deficits have also been observed in another patient (RV) with bilateral lesions in the occipitoparietal region (Goodale, Murphy, Meenan, Racicot, &

Nicolle, 1993). (It is important to note that the grasping deficits in patients like RV and VK cannot be explained by motor weakness or by a problem in the selection of appropriate hand postures. Both patients showed normal finger tapping and hand-strength scores in the hand used for grasping and neither patient was apraxic [i.e., they could follow instructions such as "Show me how you eat soup with a spoon"]. In short, the deficit was visuomotor, not motor, in nature.)

Such studies suggest that it is not only the spatial location of the object that is apparently inaccessible for controlling manual prehension in such patients, but the intrinsic characteristics of the object as well. These data, like the effector-specific deficits in localization, make it clear that one cannot explain the behavior of these patients by appealing to disorientation or spatial vision deficits. In fact, in at least one way, the spatial vision of some of these patients is demonstrably intact, since they can often describe the relative location of objects that they cannot pick up (Jeannerod, 1988). These dissociations between visual perception and the visual control of skilled movements, which cut across both object vision and spatial vision, are not easily accommodated within the original Ungerleider and Mishkin (1982) framework. Such dissociations are consistent, however, with the proposal put forward by Goodale and Milner (1992).

As Goodale and Milner (1992) point out, the visual control of prehension requires more than spatial location information; it also requires information about the size and orientation of the goal object. After all, we do not reach to locations in space but to objects! Thus, if the dorsal stream is important in the mediation of such actions (as Goodale and Milner propose) then the deficits in the visual control of grasping shown by VK and other patients with posterior parietal lesions are exactly what one would expect to see. It should be emphasized, however, that not all patients with damage in this region have difficulty shaping their hand to correspond to the size and orientation of the target object. Some have difficulty with hand postures, some with controlling the direction of their grasp, and some with foveating the target. Indeed, depending on the size and locus of the lesion, a patient can demonstrate any combination of these visuomotor deficits (for review, see Milner & Goodale, 1995). Different subregions of the posterior parietal cortex, it appears, support different visuomotor components of a skilled act.

3.1.2 Visual Form Agnosia

If patients with optic ataxia can identify objects that they cannot pick up, can patients with visual form agnosia pick up objects that they cannot identify? Goodale, Milner, Jakobson, and Carey (1991) studied the behavior of one such patient (DF) who developed a profound visual form agnosia following

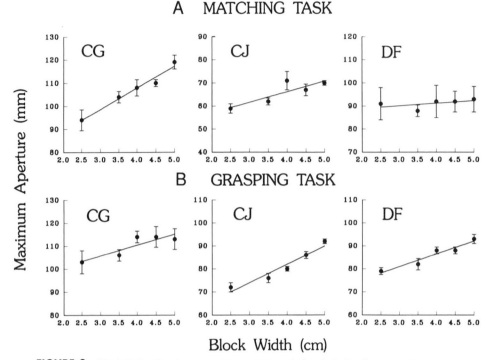

FIGURE 2 The relationship between object width and thumb–index finger aperture on a matching task and a grasping task for the patient DF and two age-matched control subjects (CG and CJ). When DF was required to indicate how wide the block was by opening her finger and thumb, her matches were unrelated to the object width and showed considerable trial-to-trial variability. When she picked up the block, however, the size of her grasp was well correlated with the width of the block.

carbon monoxide poisoning. Although MRI brain scanning revealed a pattern of widespread damage consistent with anoxia, most of the damage was evident in areas 18 and 19, with area 17 apparently remaining largely intact (Milner et al., 1991). Despite her profound inability to recognize the shape, size, and orientation of objects, DF showed strikingly accurate guidance of hand and finger movements directed at these very same objects. Thus, when she was presented with a pair of rectangular blocks of the same or different dimensions, she was unable to distinguish between them. (Pairs of blocks were selected from two sets of five blocks, each with a surface area of 25 cm² but with dimensions ranging from 5 × 5 cm to 2.5 × 10 cm.) When she was asked to indicate the width of a single block by means of her index finger and thumb, her matches bore no relationship to the dimensions of the object and showed considerable trial-to-trial variability (see Figure 2A). In contrast, when she was asked simply to reach out and pick up the block, the aperture between her index finger and thumb changed systematically with the width of the object as the movement unfolded, just as in normal subjects (see Figure 2B). In other words, DF scaled her grip to the dimensions of the object she was about to pick up, even though she appeared to be unable to perceive those object dimensions.

A similar dissociation was seen in DF's responses to the orientation of stimuli. Thus, when presented with a large slot that could be placed in one of a number of different orientations, she showed great difficulty in indicating the orientation of the slot either verbally or even manually by rotating a hand-held card (see Figure 3A). Nevertheless, when she was asked simply to reach out and insert the card, she performed as well as normal subjects, rotating her hand in the appropriate direction as soon as she began the movement (see Figure 3B).

Findings such as these are difficult to reconcile with Ungerleider and Mishkin's (1982) idea that object vision is the preserve of the ventral stream of projections, for here we have a patient in whom a profound loss of object perception exists alongside the ability to use object features such as size and orientation to guide skilled actions. Such a dissociation, of course, is consistent with Goodale and Milner's (1992) proposal that there are separate neural pathways for transforming incoming visual information into representations for action and representations for perception.

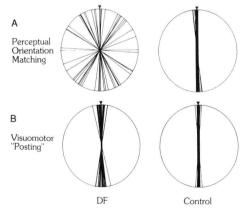

FIGURE 3   Polar plots of the orientation of the hand-held card when DF and a control subject were each asked to rotate the card to match the orientation of the slot (A) or to post the card into the slot (B). The orientation of the card on the visuomotor task was measured at the instant before the card was placed in the slot. In both plots, the actual orientations of the slot have been normalized to vertical.

3.2 Dissociations in the Processing of Object Shape for Perception and Prehension

So far, we have presented evidence to suggest that the visual perception of an object's size, orientation, and location may depend on neural mechanisms that are independent from those involved in using these same object features for the control of manual prehension. But the size, orientation, and location of an object are not the only features that control the parameters of a grasping movement. To pick up an object successfully, it is not enough to orient the hand and scale the grip appropriately and direct the grasp in the correct direction; the fingers and thumb must also be placed at appropriate opposition points on the object's surface. Computation of these grasp points must take into account the surface boundaries or shape of the object. In fact, even casual observations of grasping movements suggest that the posture of the fingers and hand are remarkably sensitive to object shape. But does the visual analysis of object shape for grasping, like the related analyses of object size and orientation, depend on neural mechanisms that are relatively independent of those underlying the perceptual identification of objects? To answer this question, the ability of the patient DF to discriminate objects of different shape was compared with her ability to position her fingers correctly on the boundaries of those same objects when she was required to pick them up (Goodale, Meenan et al., 1994). In addition, DF's performance on these tasks was compared to that of patient RV, mentioned earlier, who had developed optic ataxia after strokes, which left her with large bilateral lesions of the occipitoparietal cortex, with no involvement of the temporal cortex.

The shapes that were used to compare the discrimination and grasping abilities of DF and RV were based on the templates used by Blake (1992) to develop algorithms for the control of grasping in two-fingered robots working in novel environments. These shapes were chosen because they have smoothly bounded contours and an absence of clear symmetry. Thus, the determination of stable grasp points requires an analysis of the entire contour envelope of the shape. In the Goodale, Meenan, et al. (1994) experiment, the shapes were made from wood, were painted white, and were designed so that they could be picked up using the index finger and thumb in a precision grip. DF and RV were first presented with a series of pairs of these shapes (on a black background) and they were simply asked to indicate whether the two shapes were the same or different. As Figure 4 illustrates, their performances on this discrimination task were strikingly different. DF hovered just above chance and she seemed quite unable to distinguish one shape from another; in contrast, RV achieved scores well above 80% correct. In other words, whereas DF apparently failed to perceive whether two objects had the same or different outline shapes, RV had little difficulty in making such a discrimination.

Quite the opposite pattern of results was observed when DF and RV

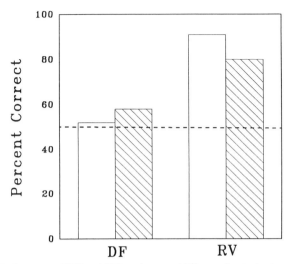

FIGURE 4 Performance of DF and RV on the same/different discrimination tests. The open bars show performance on the task in which the relative orientation of the two shapes on the same trial was identical; the hatched bars show performance on the task in which the relative orientation of the twin shapes varied between same trials. The control subject (not shown) scored perfectly on both tests although she took longer when the two shapes on the same trials were presented at different orientations. The dotted line indicates chance performance. (From Goodale, M. A., Meenan, J. P., et al., 1994.)

were asked to pick up the shapes. Even though DF had failed to discriminate between these different objects, she had no difficulty in placing her finger and thumb on stable grasp points on the circumference of these objects when any one of them was placed in different orientations in front of her. In fact, the grasp points she selected were remarkably similar to those chosen by a neurologically intact control subject (see Figure 5). In addition, DF showed the same systematic shift in the selection of grasp points as the control subject when the orientation of the object was changed. Moreover, there were other similarities between DF's grasps and those of the control subject: the line joining the two grasp points tended to pass through the center of mass of the object; these grasp lines often corresponded to the axes of minimum or maximum diameter of the object; and finally, the grasp points were often located on regions of the object boundary that would be expected to yield the most stable grip—regions of maximum convexity or concavity (Blake, 1992; Iberall, Bingham, & Arbib, 1986).

RV's grasping was different from DF's (see Figure 5); RV often chose unstable grasp points and she stabilized her grasp only after her finger and thumb made contact with the object. Thus, despite her apparent ability to perceive the shape of an object, RV was unable to use visual information about object shape to control the placement of her finger and thumb as she attempted to pick up that object. Once she had made contact with the object, however, her manipulation of it appeared essentially normal. This suggests that, despite her problems in visuomotor control, she was able to use tactile and haptic information to control the placement of her fingers. It was only her visuomotor performance that was disturbed. In order to quantify differences between the performance of RV and DF (and the control subject), the shortest distance between the grasp line (connecting opposing grasp points) on each trial and the object's center of mass was measured. As Figure 6 illustrates, whereas DF and the control subject did not differ on this measure, both differed significantly from RV, who often chose grasp lines that were some distance from the object's center of mass.

These findings provide clear evidence that the visual control of prehension is sensitive to the shape (as well as the size, orientation, and spatial location) of the goal object and that this analysis appears to depend on neural systems that are independent of those underlying the visual perception of object shape. The pattern of deficits and spared visual abilities in DF and RV in this study (together with the results of the earlier work reviewed in the previous section) is consistent with the idea that the human homolog of the ventral stream may be specialized for the visual perception of objects in the world, while the dorsal stream is specialized for the visual control of skilled actions directed at those objects (Goodale & Milner, 1992). But at

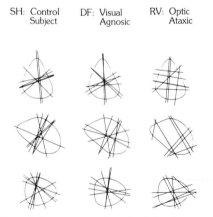

FIGURE 5 The grasp lines (joining points where the index finger and the thumb first made contact with the shape) selected by the optic ataxic patient (RV), the visual form agnosic patient (DF), and the control subject (SH) when picking up three of the twelve shapes. The four different orientations in which each shape was presented have been rotated so that they are aligned. No distinction is made between the points of contact for the thumb and finger in these plots. (From Goodale, M. A., Meenan, J. P., et al., 1994.)

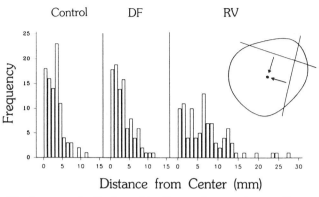

Distance from Center (mm)

FIGURE 6 The frequency distributions of the distances between the grasp lines and the center of mass of the shape for DF, RV, and the control subject for all twelve shapes. The inset shows how those distances were calculated for two different grasp lines. (From Goodale, M. A., Meenan, J. P., et al., 1994.)

least two important questions remain to be addressed. Why should the brain have developed two different visual systems, one for perception and one for action? What are the important differences in the kinds of transformations that each of these systems carries out on incoming visual information?

4. DIFFERENT TRANSFORMATIONS FOR DIFFERENT PURPOSES

Consider first the task of the perceptual system. Its fundamental task is to identify objects and their relations, classify those objects and relations, and attach meaning and significance to them. Such operations are essential for engaging in social interactions, exchanging information with others, accumulating a knowledge base about the world, and choosing among different courses of action. In short, perception provides the foundation for the cognitive life of the animal. As a consequence, perception tends to be more concerned with the enduring characteristics of objects (and their relations) so that they can be recognized when they are encountered again in different visual contexts or from different vantage points. To generate these long-term representations, perceptual mechanisms must be object based; that is, constancies of size, shape, color, lightness, and relative location need to be maintained across different viewing conditions. Some of these mechanisms might use a network of viewer-centered representations of the same object (e.g., Bülthoff & Edelman, 1992); others might use an array of canonical representations (e.g., S. Palmer, Rosch, & Chase, 1981); still others might be truly "object centered" (Marr, 1982).

Whatever the particular coding might be, it is the identity of the object, not its disposition with respect to the observer that is of primary concern to the perceptual system. This is not the case for the visuomotor mechanisms that support actions directed at that object. In this case, the underlying visuomotor transformations have to be viewer centered; in other words, both the location of the object and its disposition and motion must be encoded relative to the observer in egocentric coordinates (e.g., retinocentric, head-centered, or shoulder-centered coordinates; see Soechting et al., Chapter 8). (One constancy that must operate, however, is object size; in order to scale the grasp during prehension, the underlying visuomotor mechanisms must be able to compute the real size of the object independent of its distance from the observer.) Finally, because the position and disposition of a goal object in the action space of an observer are rarely constant, such computations must take place de novo every time an action occurs (for a discussion of this issue, see Goodale, Jakobson, et al., 1994). In other words, action systems do most of their work on-line; perceptual systems do most of their work off-line. To summarize then, while similar (but not identical) visual information about object shape, size, local orientation, and location is available to both systems, the transformational algorithms that are applied to these inputs are uniquely tailored to the function of each system. According to Goodale and Milner (1992), it is the nature of the functional requirements of perception and action that lies at the root of the division of labor in the ventral and dorsal visual projection systems of the primate cerebral cortex.

5. EVIDENCE FROM MONKEY STUDIES

5.1 The Dorsal Stream

Electrophysiological studies of the dorsal and ventral streams in the monkey lend considerable support to the distinction outlined above (for a more detailed account of the electrophysiology, see Goodale 1993a; Milner & Goodale, 1993). For example, in sharp contrast to the activity of cells in the ventral stream, the responses of cells in the dorsal stream are greatly dependent on the concurrent behavior of the animal with respect to the visual stimulus. In fact, while it is difficult to record any visually driven activity in the dorsal stream of anesthetized monkeys, recordings from alert monkeys have revealed a rich array of cells whose activity is affected by both visual stimulation and motor activity. Separate subsets of visual cells in the posterior parietal cortex, the major terminal zone for the dorsal stream, have been shown to be implicated in visual fixation, pursuit and saccadic eye movements, visually guided reaching, and the manipulation of objects (Hyvärinen & Poranen, 1974; Mountcastle, Lynch, Georgopoulos, Sakata, & Acuña, 1975). In reviewing these studies,

R. A. Andersen (1987) has pointed out that most neurons in these areas "exhibit both sensory-related and movement-related activity." For example, many cells in the posterior parietal cortex have gaze-dependent responses; in other words, where the animal is looking determines the amplitude of the cell's response to a visual stimulus (e.g., R. A. Andersen, Asanuma, Essick, & Siegel, 1990; R. A. Andersen, Essick, & Siegel, 1985). Modulation by gaze direction is important because it permits the computation of the spatial (head-related) coordinates of the stimulus independent of retinal location.

Recent work by Duhamel, Colby, and Goldberg (1992) has also shown that some cells in the posterior parietal cortex (in area LIP, the lateral intra-parietal sulcus) appear to shift their receptive field transiently just before the animal makes a saccadic eye movement, so that stimuli that will fall on that receptive field after the eye movement is completed will begin to modulate the cell's activity before the eye movement occurs. In addition, many cells will respond when an eye movement brings the site of a previously flashed stimulus into the cell's receptive field. Taken together, these results suggest that networks of cells in the posterior parietal cortex anticipate the retinal consequences of saccadic eye movements and update the cortical representation of visual space to provide a continuously accurate representation of the location of objects in the world. The egocentric spatial coding generated by these cells and the gaze-dependent cells described earlier would be of value only over short time spans, since every time the animal moved its head, eyes, or body, the representation would be updated. This kind of short-term coding could provide critical information about the location of a goal object for calibrating the amplitude and direction of a reaching movement, but not for the long-term storage of information about the allocentric (or relative) location of that object with respect to other objects in the world.

Many of the well-known motion-sensitive cells in the dorsal pathway seem remarkably well suited to providing inputs for continually updating information about the disposition and structural features of objects in ego-centric space (e.g., Newsome, Wurtz, & Komatsu, 1988; Saito et al., 1986). Also, a subset of these cells seem quite capable of monitoring limb position during manual prehension (Mountcastle, Motter, Steinmetz, & Duffy, 1984), while motion-sensitive cells in the temporal lobe have been reported not to respond to such self-produced visual motion, although they do respond to moving objects (Hietanen & Perrett, 1993).

In a particularly interesting recent development (Sakata, Taira, Mine, & Murata, 1992; Taira, Mine, Georgopoulos, Murata, & Sakata, 1990), some cells in the posterior parietal region that fire when the monkey manipulates an object have also been shown to be sensitive to the intrinsic object features, such as size and orientation, that determine the posture of the hand and fingers during a grasping movement. These cells are not tied to a particular spatial or retinal location; indeed, many do not have a definable receptive field. Nevertheless, they are visually driven, responding selectively to the size and/or orientation of the object. Thus, these manipulation neurons are tied both to object properties and to the movements of the hands and fingers that are appropriate for those properties. The route by which the visual information required for the coding of the object shape reaches the posterior parietal cortex is at present unknown. It is unlikely, however, that the shape coding in manipulation cells is dependent on input from the higher-level modules within the ventral stream that support the perception of object qualities. Evidence against this possibility is that monkeys with profound deficits in object recognition following inferotemporal lesions are nevertheless as capable as normal animals at picking up small food objects (Klüver & Bucy, 1939), at catching flying insects (Pribram, 1967), and at orienting their fingers in a precision grip to grasp morsels of food embedded in small oriented slots (Buchbinder, Dixon, Hyang, May, & Glickstein, 1980). In short, these animals behave much the same way as the patient DF described earlier: they are unable to discriminate between objects on the basis of visual features that they can clearly use to control their grasping movements.

Many of the neurons in the dorsal stream receive visual inputs both from the geniculostriate pathway and from the superior colliculus, via the pulvinar and/or the lateral geniculate nucleus (Gross, 1991). These inputs would be classified as largely broad-band or magnocellular in origin (with high temporal and low spatial resolution) (Livingstone & Hubel, 1988). The dorsal stream also sends extensive projections to the superior colliculus. Area LIP, for example, projects strongly to the intermediate and deep layers of the superior colliculus, which are intimately involved in oculomotor control (C. Asanuma, Andersen, & Cowan, 1985; Lynch, Graybiel, & Lobeck, 1985). Many regions in the posterior parietal cortex, including area LIP, also send extensive projections to nuclei lower in the brain stem, especially those in the dorsolateral region of the pons (e.g., Glickstein, May, & Mercier, 1985). These pontine nuclei, which are closely linked with the cerebellum, have been implicated in the subcortical organization of skilled visuomotor behavior (Glickstein & May, 1982). The pattern of downstream projections from the dorsal stream suggests that one way this processing stream may mediate the control of skilled actions is by modulating more phylogenetically ancient brain stem networks.

The posterior parietal region is also strongly linked, in a reciprocal fashion, with those premotor regions of the frontal cortex directly implicated in oculomotor control, reaching movements of the limb, and grasping actions of the hand and fingers (e.g., C. J. Bruce, 1990; C. J. Bruce & Goldberg, 1984; Cavada & Goldman-Rakic, 1989; Gentilucci & Rizzolatti, 1990; Petrides & Pandya, 1984). In addition, there are projections from the posterior parietal cortex to various regions in the striatum (Cavada & Goldman-Rakic, 1991). Recent work by Graziano and Gross (1993) has shown that neurons in those regions of the striatum receiving dorsal-stream inputs not only show visuomotor properties but also code space in body-centered coordinates. Thus, in addition to its connections with subcortical motor regions, the dorsal stream appears to be intimately connected with a number of telencephalic structures involved in motor control.

5.2 The Ventral Stream

In contrast to the dorsal stream, the primary source of visual input to the ventral stream comes from the geniculostriate pathway; input from the superior colliculus (via the pulvinar) appears to be of little importance in determining the receptive field characteristics of cells in this stream (Gross, 1991). The geniculostriate input to the ventral stream is about equally divided between magnocellular (high temporal and low spatial resolution) and parvocellular (low temporal and high spatial resolution) channels (Ferrera, Nealey, & Maunsell, 1992). Unlike the cells in the posterior parietal cortex, visually sensitive cells in the inferotemporal cortex, the major terminus of the ventral stream, are unaffected by anesthesia and the ongoing behavior of the animal. Many of the cells in this region and in neighboring areas of the superior temporal sulcus also show remarkable categorical specificity (Gross, 1973), and some of them maintain their selectivity irrespective of viewpoint, retinal image size, and even color (Hasselmo, Rolls, Baylis, & Nalwa, 1989; Hietanen, Perrett, Oram, Benson, & Dittrich, 1992; Perrett et al., 1991). Cells in the anterior region of the inferotemporal cortex also show a columnar arrangement (much like the columns in the primary visual cortex) in which cells responsive to similar visual features of objects are clustered together (Fujita, Tanaka, Ito, & Cheng, 1992). In addition, cells in the inferotemporal cortex and the adjacent regions of the superior temporal sulcus typically have exceptionally large receptive fields that most often include the fovea and usually extend across the vertical meridian well into both half-fields, a feature that is consistent with the idea that these cells generalize their response across the visual field and code the intrinsic features of an object independent of its location (Gross, 1973).

Cells in the ventral stream, far from providing the "real-time" information needed for guiding action, specifically ignore changing details. Such observations are entirely consistent with the suggestion that networks of cells in the inferotemporal cortex, in sharp contrast to the action systems in the dorsal stream, are more concerned with the enduring characteristics of objects than they are in the moment-to-moment changes in the visual array. The object-based descriptions that the ventral stream delivers would appear to form the basic raw material for recognition memory and other long-term representations of the visual world. In line with this idea is the observation that the responsivity of cells in the ventral stream can be modulated by the reinforcement history of the stimuli employed to study them (Richmond & Sato, 1987; Sakai & Miyashita, 1992). Indeed, it has recently been suggested that cells in this region might play a role in comparing current visual inputs with internal representations of recalled images (Eskandar, Optican, & Richmond, 1992; Eskandar, Richmond, & Optican, 1992), which are themselves presumably stored in other regions, such as neighboring regions of the medial temporal lobe and related limbic areas (Fahy, Riches, & Brown, 1993; Nishijo, Ono, Tamura, & Nakamura, 1993).

Unlike the dorsal stream, the ventral stream has no significant projections to either the superior colliculus or the pontine nuclei (Baizer, Desimone, & Ungerleider, 1993; Glickstein et al., 1985; Schmahmann & Pandya, 1993). There are, however, strong reciprocal connections between the inferotemporal cortex and the amygdala, a structure that has few if any connections with the posterior parietal cortex (Baizer et al., 1993). The amygdala, a limbic structure lying deep in the temporal lobe, has been implicated in the mediation of social and emotional reponses to visual signals in both monkeys and humans (Adolphs, Tranel, Damasio, & Damasio, 1994; Brothers & Ring, 1993; Kling & Brothers, 1992). The inferotemporal cortex also projects heavily to the perirhinal and parahippocampal cortices and other regions of the medial temporal lobe that appear to be important for storing information about objects in memory, while the projections from the posterior parietal cortex to these regions are not nearly so prominent (Suzuki & Amaral, 1994). Thus, the ventral stream shows none of the evidence for direct modulation of subcortical visuomotor systems evident in the dorsal stream; instead, the ventral stream appears to be connected quite directly with neural mechanisms that are critically involved in associative learning, long-term memory, and social behavior.

6. SEPARATE STREAMS FOR PERCEPTION AND ACTION

In summary, then, the monkey work converges rather well on the neuropsychological studies described earlier. Both sets of evidence suggest that different transformations are carried out on the information that reaches the ventral and dorsal streams of visual projections in primate cerebral cortex—differences that reflect the requirements of the different output systems served by the two streams (Goodale & Milner, 1992). To reiterate this distinction once more: the ventral stream delivers the perceptual and cognitive representations underlying (visual) knowledge of objects and events in the

world, and the dorsal stream, which utilizes the moment-to-moment information about the location and disposition of objects in egocentric frames of
reference, mediates the on-line (visual) control of goal-directed actions. Of
course, the dorsal and ventral streams work in a highly integrated fashion in
the behaving organism and there is considerable anatomical evidence for a
complex interconnectivity between the two streams (for review, see Milner &
Goodale, 1995). What needs to be done now is to investigate in detail the
differences in the processing characteristics of these two functional systems
and the way in which they work together to control behavior.

PART 2

The Motor Hand

The classic paper of Lawrence and Kuypers (1968) perhaps marks the beginning of a period that has seen an explosion of interest in the neural control of the hand. They found that bilateral lesions of the pyramidal tract, or corticospinal tract as it is now more often called, whose fibers descend from the primary motor cortex (M1) to synapse directly with lower motor neurons in the spinal cord, produced a permanent deficit in precise independent finger movements in monkeys. In contrast, weakness of the arm also associated with the lesion rapidly disappeared and the animals soon recovered fast and accurate positioning of the hand. Their study thus seemed to pinpoint the neural substrate of manual dexterity.

Lawrence and Kuypers's work indicates a special contribution of the pyramidal tract and M1 to independent finger actions. However, it does not resolve an issue on which there has been considerable debate, namely, whether the activity of cells in the motor cortex represents movements (i.e., flexible patterns of coordinated voluntary action), or just muscles. On one hand, anatomical studies reveal that the hand motor neurons lie only one synapse away from the cerebral cortex, suggesting that the corticospinal tract is simply the "final common path" (Sherrington, 1906) relaying neural commands to the muscles. On the other hand, neurophysiological studies of the properties of corticospinal neurons in the M1 suggest that they represent complete actions, such as different kinds of grip, rather than the contraction of individual muscles.

Many researchers have investigated what the code that the cortex uses for specifying voluntary movements might be. The chapters in this section give a broad sampling of recent work, and highlight three important aspects of the cortical representations of hand movement. First, the cortical computations must be complex because the mechanical actions of the hand musculature are complex. Second, the cortex must control groups of hand muscles, making them work together as synergies to perform dexterous actions such as grasping. Third, physiological and anatomical studies show that the various motor cortical areas may be arranged in a hierarchy, with anterior areas such as the Supplementary Motor Area (SMA) representing more abstract, higher-level aspects of hand movement than the primary motor cortex itself.

The material in these chapters shows that the classical view of voluntary control of dexterous hand movements, which emphasized the final common path function of the motor cortex, requires revision. For example, Penfield's early work (Penfield & Rasmussen, 1950) on stimulating the exposed motor cortex in patients undergoing brain operations led to a way of thinking about the cells of the motor cortex as analogous to the strings of a marionette. These strings could be pulled by a homunculus (a little man in the head—perhaps equivalent to Descartes's soul) to produce voluntary actions of the set of muscles to which they projected. We now see that the homuncular analogy is inappropriate for the neural control of the hand. A genuine understanding of the relation between brain and hand must take account of the hierarchical organization of several different representations of the hand muscles, projecting in a many-to-many fashion onto the numerous muscles of the human hand.

Functional hand movements, as when grasping an object, require simultaneous activity in several different muscles in the hand, which work together as a synergy. The brain might control the synergy using a set of quantitative rules that define certain parameters of activity in the participating muscles. However, the synergies must be organized in a flexible fashion, since different grips require a different distribution of activity across the same set of muscles. The research described by Hepp-Reymond, Huesler, and Maier in Chapter 3 attempts to discover the quantitative rules underlying some grip synergies by correlating the activity of different muscles during grip tasks. If a pair of muscles work together in a tight synergy, there should be a high correlation between their levels of activity. Hepp-Reymond et al. found that correlations of overall muscle activity, as measured by surface EMG, were generally low. Thus, the brain uses quite variable combinations of muscle activity to perform the same hand movement. This suggests a hierarchy of control, with the control of the synergy being specified at a higher level in the brain than the level at which the activity of the participating muscles is specified. However, the results also showed that correlations were more common between single motor units in separate muscles. They infer that motor units in different muscles may receive common drive from the cortex, implying divergent central control.

Hand movements are caused by muscles pulling on tendons to produce rotation around joints. Muscles in the forearm contract to rotate the hand around the wrist joint, while finger movements can be produced either by muscles in the forearm (extrinsic to the hand) or by intrinsic muscles in the hand itself. Fridén and Lieber's Chapter 4 discusses how the anatomical organization of hand muscles relates to their function in dexterous movement. As surgeons faced with the practical problem of restoring hand function, they explore the effects of muscle length changes caused by surgically transferring a tendon so that a muscle with better function can substitute for a weaker muscle. They show that physiological changes take place at the sarcomere level, which suggests that the fibers of hand muscles are optimized for precise production of fine forces at the fingertip. These analyses have implications for designing tendon transfer operations, which restore as much manual dexterity as possible.

In Chapter 5, Schieber provides a clear example of how the marionette analogy of hand movement control has been replaced by the concept of a distributed, many-to-many mapping between cells in the motor cortex and the muscles of the hand. Schieber shows that movements of a single finger are not produced by activity in a labeled line (i.e., marionette string) in the motor cortex. Instead, moving a single finger requires contracting several muscles, many of which function as fixators to prevent the major muscle contraction from moving additional fingers. A similar multiple representation applies in the primary motor cortex: recordings from cells in monkeys trained to carry out single finger movements showed that many cells are active when the monkey moves any one of a number of digits. This result implies that a given cortical area represents more than one digit.

Lawrence and Kuypers's classic lesion study demonstrated that the corticospinal tract is essential for dexterous hand movement. The two remaining chapters in this section confirm the role of the corticospinal tract in hand control by correlating the anatomical development of corticospinal fibers in young monkeys with the development of the animal's fine motor skills. In Chapter 6, Rouiller uses tracing techniques to compare the connectivity of neurons in the SMA and the M1. He provides evidence that neurons in the SMA make direct connections to spinal motoneurons responsible for hand movement and concludes that there are parallel corticospinal pathways from the SMA and the M1. This suggests that the SMA may be directly involved in controlling movement execution together with the M1 and may not be concerned only with movement preparation. Stimulation and lesion studies have provided some evidence that the SMA is particularly important in the control of bilateral actions. This might lead one to expect both ipsi- and contralateral corticospinal connections from the SMA. However, Rouiller shows that the balance of projections is similar to the M1 and hence predominately contralateral. This suggests that to the extent that the SMA plays a key role in bimanual tasks, that role might be subserved by pathways other than the direction of the corticospinal route (e.g., cortico-cortical projections).

In Chapter 7, Armand, Olivier, Edgley, and Lemon focus on the development of cortico-motoneuronal connections from the primary motor cortex and review data from a number of species. An important idea is that developing skill is associated with progressive refinement of an initial excess of connections referred to as exuberant arborization. In particular, the ability to make fractionated or relatively independent finger movements seems to be associated with the selective elimination of excessive connections, to leave many-to-many cortico-motoneuronal connections, which are nevertheless focused on independent movement of a particular digit. They also discuss the relatively new technique of transcranial magnetic stimulation (TMS) for noninvasive investigation of cortico-motoneuronal connections.

3

Precision Grip in Humans

Temporal and Spatial Synergies

**MARIE-CLAUDE HEPP-REYMOND,
ERHARD J. HUESLER, AND MARC A. MAIER**

1. INTRODUCTION

1.1 The Concept of Synergy

One of the major issues in motor control is whether the central nervous system (CNS) is concerned with the control of each individual muscle or whether it combines muscles into groups or synergies and exerts control over each group as a unit rather than over the constituents of the group. The concept of synergy has a long history and is still subject to various interpretations. Basically, synergy means acting together, without any presupposition as to the source of the coupling. Synergistic processes can either have a common source or drive, or be merely based on spatial or temporal coincidences. Two prominent scientists in the field of motor control have clearly outlined the large span of possible definitions of the word synergy.

Sherrington, in *Integrative Action of the Nervous System* (1947), assumed that muscle synergies are laid down in the spinal cord (Beevor, 1904), the reflex arc being at the basis of synergic muscle grouping. In his terms: "The reflex-arc is the unit mechanism of the nervous system when that system is regarded in its integrative functions. . . . Coordination, therefore, is in part the compounding of reflexes" (p. 7). The Sherringtonian concept of synergy is clearly linked to low-level neural elements only one step away from the muscle. An alternative view of synergy stressing higher-level neural processes is that of Bernstein (1967) who, in contrast to the anatomical-morphological concept of Sherrington, proposed a functional, operational definition. In his view, a synergy is a "higher level organising principle of movements" and is not tied to any particular muscle grouping. Gelfand, Gurfinkel, Tsetlin, and Shik (1971), in the spirit of Bernstein, emphasize the problem of the control of many degrees of freedom: "Synergy is a class of movements having similar kinematics. . . . For realization of a movement it is necessary to control a small number of independent parameters although the number of muscles participating to the movement may be large" (p. 332). This definition can include almost any movement, such as locomotion, scratching, grasping. Accordingly, the CNS groups several variables into functional synergies, each synergy being controlled by a single central command. Thus, the components that build up a synergy are constrained to act as a single unit, leading to a simplification of the central command to the musculature.

Although the Sherrington and Bernstein perspectives on synergy differ widely on the implementation, that is, low-level control of muscles grouped within a reflex versus high-level control of kinematic parameters, both predict similar consequences on the muscular level: a specific constant task or movement should be produced by a fixed, that is, invariant, muscle activation pattern. However, extending this issue to systems with excess degrees of freedom (as in most natural multijoint movements), it is evident that a constant movement can be achieved with variable muscle activation patterns. If, in such systems, muscle groups with spatially and temporally coherent activation patterns are observed for a given movement, then the existence of fixed synergies, implying hardwired linkages, would be supported (W. A. Lee, 1984).

Several experimental findings on the anatomical-physiological level speak in favor of fixed synergies. Divergent corticospinal axons in the spinal cord, demonstrated anatomically by Shinoda, Yokata, and Futami (1981) and physiologically for the cortico-motoneuronal (CM) system of the wrist muscles by Fetz and Cheney (1980) and of the finger muscles by Lemon, Mantel, and Muir (1986; see Lemon, 1993), are crucial evidence that some muscle coupling could be centrally organized, possibly in a fixed manner. These findings suggest that the primary motor cortex controls some kind of spinal functional units that may be constituent parts of specific motor acts. Thus, the divergence onto different motoneuron pools has given strong support for the concept of a common drive of central origin. The idea of common drive, first formulated and tested by Sears and Stagg (1976) for intercostal motoneurons and subsequently applied to synchronization between motor units (MUs) of a single finger muscle by De Luca, LeFever, McCue, and Xenakis (1982a), has since been supported by others for pairs of MUs located within one muscle or in two separate muscles (Bremner, Baker, & Stephens, 1991a, 1991b, 1991c; Datta & Stephens, 1990; Nordstrom, Miles, & Türker, 1990). Most of these investigations reported substantial common inputs, and several findings, based on clinical observations in deafferented patients, suggest that their origin is more central than peripheral (J. R. Baker, Bremner, Cole, & Stephens, 1988; Datta, Farmer, & Stephens, 1991).

On the operational-functional level, fixed muscle synergies have been found, mainly in human postural responses to forward and backward sway. During stance perturbation in the sagittal plane, a fixed temporal sequence of activation of the muscles, first at the ankle, then the knees, followed by the trunk, is characteristic of the maintenance of postural stability (Nashner, 1981). If the biomechanical support conditions are changed so that it is not possible to develop torque at the ankle, forward or backward sway elicits a different synergy, also quite stereotyped and termed the hip strategy (Horak & Nashner, 1986). Although a variety of activation patterns have been described for whole body posture maintenance (see also Moore, Rushmer, Windus, & Nashner, 1988), the view is still held of a given perturbation eliciting the same stereotyped pattern of muscle activity—one fixed synergy tailored to each task context, ultimately leading to a large variety of synergies.

However, the question arises, then, whether there is a specific synergy for each and every variation of the task. In extremis, this would lead to no computational simplification at all for the CNS and thus be similar to independent control of each muscle. The alternate hypothesis, that fixed muscle synergies may be preserved under varying conditions, has been tested in the control of the human arm by several investigators. Their goal was to find out whether spatial and temporal muscle couplings would be so stable that they would be resistant to changes in the direction of torque production (Buchanan, Almdale, Lewis, & Rymer, 1986; Buchanan, Rovai, & Rymer, 1989) or in the experimental conditions, such as pseudorandom perturbations compared to intentional movements (Soechting & Lacquaniti, 1989). No consistent patterns of muscle coactivation could be disclosed in these investigations. In their words, "the type of fixed synergies with muscles always working together appears to be an exception rather than the rule" (Buchanan et al., 1989, p. 1211). In an excellent review, Macpherson (1991) suggested a way out of the dilemma by asking whether synergies can be flexible and how. This concept suggests that, within a redundant muscle system, a limited set of synergies can be tuned to certain varying task demands. The tuning would be a matter of learning, requiring modifiable rather than hardwired neuronal linkages.

A clear case of flexible synergies is given by studies in cats that have demonstrated variable activity in the neck muscles for head movements in various directions (Keshner, Baker, Banovetz, & Peterson, 1992). Each muscle displayed a peak of activation in a well-defined direction, but the axes of maximal activation differed between reflex and voluntary responses. These findings for the head-neck system, with more muscles than degrees of freedom in the joints, indicate that a given head movement is generated by various activation patterns of the effectors. These patterns are relatively constant in individual cats but not necessarily similar across all animals. The stability in individual cats may be achieved through learning and practice.

Since the hand presents several biomechanical features similar to those of the head-and-neck system (more muscles than joints), we wondered whether its control, in particular that of grasping behavior, requires muscle synergies and, if so, whether these synergies are fixed or flexible.

1.2 Precision Grip: Biomechanics and Muscle Activity

The complex structure of the hand and wrist consists of 27 bones. Thirty-nine muscles located either in the forearm (extrinsic muscles) or in the hand itself (intrinsic muscles) move the digits and the wrist (MacKenzie & Iberall, 1994; Tubiana, 1981). The number of muscles exceeds the number of degrees of freedom provided by the joints, resulting in a biomechanically over-specified system (Hogan, 1985). Many hand muscles also control more than one joint, such as the long finger flexors. These muscles have therefore no single action on the fingers they are attached to, but, on the contrary, can participate in a variety of actions (e.g., Ranney & Wells, 1988, for the lumbricals). Furthermore, Schieber (1993; see also Chapter 5) has also indicated the possibility that some muscles, like the flexor digitorum profundus (FDP), can have separate functional subdivisions. Given this peripheral complexity, it is interesting to ask whether the CNS can use muscle synergies to simplify the control of hand and finger movements.

The tip-to-tip pinch between thumb and index finger, often used in fine manipulation, and called precision grip (Napier, 1956, 1960; A. H. Schultz, 1968), is an extreme case showing this complexity and redundancy of the muscular system, since at least 15 muscles have a direct or indirect contribution in exerting force, for example, to hold a small object (Figure 1). In fact, the pinch grip requires the stabilization of three joints in each finger, which can be considered as a biomechanical 4-bar linkage system (Chao, An, Cooney, & Linscheid, 1989). It also requires that the compression force, that is, the static equilibrium, as well as the specific archlike position, be maintained between thumb and index finger (Figure 2). According to biomechanical constraints (Chao et al., 1989), the extrinsic muscles with tendons spanning all four links are best suited for providing a continuous output force,

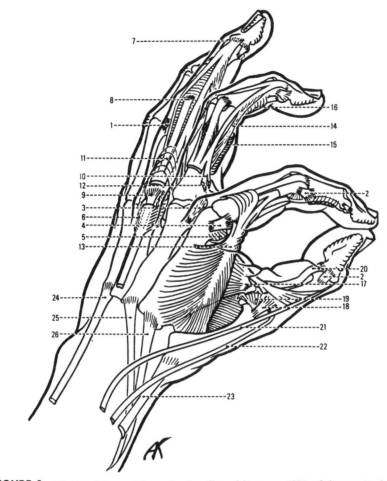

FIGURE 1   The hand in precision grip. 1: collateral ligament (CL) of the proximal inter-phalangeal (PIP) joint; 2: CL of the PIP joint; 3: CL of the metacarpophalangeal (MCP) joint; 4: CL in the MCP joint; 5: accessory fibers of CL of the MCP; 6: expansion of the common extensor; 7: distal insertion of the extensor digitorum; 8: insertion of the middle extensor tendon; 9: deep expansion; 10: expansion of the interosseus to the lateral band of the extensor digitorum; 11: interosseus hood; 12: lumbrical tendon; 13: first dorsal interosseus with its complete system of insertion and the tendon of the first lumbrical; 14: retinacular ligament; 15: flexor pully on the first phalanx; 16: distal pully on the second phalanx; 17: adductor pollicis; 18: medial CL of the MCP joint of the thumb; 19: accessory CL; 20: flexor pollicis longus tendon; 21: extensor pollicis longus tendon; 22: extensor pollicis brevis tendon; 23: abductor pollicis longus tendon; 24: extensor carpi ulnaris tendon; 25: extensor carpi radialis brevis tendon; 26: extensor carpi radialis longus tendon. (Reproduced with permission from Kapandji, in Tubiana, 1981.)

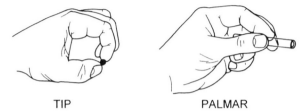

TIP   PALMAR

FIGURE 2   Two types of prehension, after Schlesinger (1919). According to Napier (1956), the tip and palmar grip both are precision grips.

whereas the intrinsic muscles can adjust and modulate grip force by stabilizing the metacarpal and phalangeal joints and counteracting rotational moments.

One of the first detailed descriptions of the functions of the muscles of thumb, index, and middle finger during pinch grip was given by J. R. Close and Kidd (1969). Their descriptions were based on simultaneous recordings of finger motion and corresponding electromyographic (EMG) activity in six to eight muscles. They noted that in the pinch there was coactivation of many muscles, even those not directly implicated in flexion of index finger or of thumb. This observation was confirmed by Long, Conrad, Hall and Furler (1970). In monkeys, Hepp-Reymond and Wiesendanger (1972) also showed antagonist coactivation during force generation in precision grip.

According to A. M. Smith (1981), the clearest examples of coactivation of antagonist muscles are found in the prehensile repertoire of primates. Various classifications of grasping behavior in human and nonhuman primates have been proposed, the most simple one suggesting two main classes: power grip and precision grip (Napier, 1956, 1960). In the former, all the fingers are active in grasping an object against the palm with usually large forces. In contrast, in precision grip, smaller forces are exerted at the tips of the index finger and thumb, requiring another pattern of stability and muscle activation. A further distinction was made by Landsmeer (1962) and Long et al. (1970) between fine manipulatory finger movements and static pinches. This led to a contrast between isotonic dynamic actions and isometric tonic contractions using different patterns of muscle activation. Long et al. (1970) came to the conclusion that, in tip-to-tip pinch, the extrinsic muscles provide the main compression force, being assisted by the intrinsics such as the 1st dorsal and palmar interossei (1DI, 1PI) through their metacarpophalangeal (MCP) flexion component. Among the thenar muscles, they suggested that the flexor pollicis brevis (FPB) provides compression force by metacarpophalangeal flexion of the thumb, the adductor pollicis (AdP) provides direct compression forces, and the opponens pollicis (OPP) provides metacar-

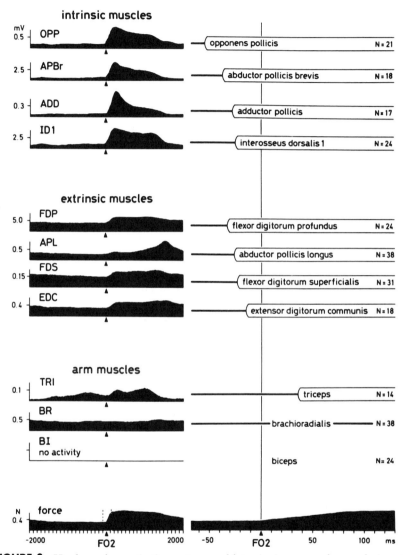

FIGURE 3 Hand muscle coactivation patterns and latencies in one monkey producing step force increases. Mean rectified, integrated EMG activity (one experimental session per muscle) (*left panel*). Representative mean force curve (*bottom line*). FO2: onset of force increase from the first to the second force level. Time scale: ± 2 s. Mean differences between EMG activity increase and FO2 and mean force curve around FO2 on an enlarged time scale (*right panel*). (After Rufener & Hepp-Reymond, 1988.)

pal rotation to maintain the most efficient position for the development of pinch force by the extrinsic muscles. In contrast, the long finger flexors play the major role during fine manipulation.

The most extensive investigation published to date on the muscle activity in the grip is that of A. M. Smith and Bourbonnais (1981) who recorded the activity of 24 muscles in the monkey, leading to a series of important observations (A. M. Smith, 1981). During static hold of a submaximal force between index finger and thumb, the majority of the finger muscles were active, some of them during the hold phase, some during the preceding ramp increase in force, and some during both phases. The time of onset of activation differed in the various muscles so that the muscles were recruited successively. In general, the upper arm muscles were not modulated with the exerted force. A small pilot investigation, in monkeys trained to exert grip force in a step-tracking paradigm requiring two consecutive forces, reproduced some of the observations of Smith and Bourbonnais and revealed some new aspects such as the fine-graded modulation of intrinsic and extrinsic muscle activity (Rufener & Hepp-Reymond, 1988). It demonstrated clearly the coactivation of anatomical antagonists (such as the extensor digitorum communis, EDC), even in a low force range, and only a random activation of the proximal muscles such as biceps and triceps (Figure 3).

Chao et al. (1989) also addressed the problem of the organization of grip and the control of grip force. Their quantification of thumb muscle forces, based on a biomechanical model, was expressed in terms of the percentage of the maximal voluntary contraction exerted for various types of pinch and grasp. The authors came to the conclusion that in precision grip three functional classes of thumb muscles can be distinguished. Group I muscles respond accordingly to increase in load, group II muscles are active only when force reaches a certain range, and group III muscles comprise antagonist muscles, counterbalancing the applied load and providing joint stability. According to their data, in the tip pinch, the flexor pollicis longus (FPL), the AdP, 1DI, and OPP may be put into group I, the extensor pollicis longus (EPL) and abductor pollicis longus (AbPL) into group II, and finally the abductor pollicis brevis (AbPB) and extensor pollicis brevis (EPB) into group III.

1.3 Rationale of the Present Investigations

Although a number of studies of grasping behavior have described the EMG activity in groups of muscles recorded simultaneously, no quantitative assessment of the muscle participation and muscle coupling in the production of grip force has been attempted in order to answer the fundamental question: Does muscle coactivation in the grip imply the presence of synergies, or is this presence the result of pure spatiotemporal coincidences?

To address this issue, synergies should be assessed quantitatively in spatial, temporal, and scaling terms (W. A. Lee, 1984). Spatial implies the stable coactivation of a group of muscles, temporal the synchronization of their activity. Scaling means that spatial or temporal synergies are conserved and may covary with modulations of task parameters, such as force. No investigations so far have tried to tackle the question of muscle linkage in these three terms. In this chapter we now present the results of such an investigation.

Interpreting the term synergy in a restrictive sense, that is, a group of muscles acting together, we have attempted to assess quantitatively the muscle synergies during fine-graded control of force in the precision grip, an everyday task. The experimental conditions intentionally reduced the complexity of the natural grasping behavior, limiting it to a static grip on a passive object. The basic assumption was that under such controlled conditions, the source of the muscle coactivation patterns described by several groups could be approached more easily than with complex multijoint movements, such as the closing of hand and fingers. Furthermore, this approach may shed some light on the important problem of how the CNS controls force in a system with a large number of active muscles. Our earlier investigations on the central control of precision grip have repeatedly disclosed cortical and subcortical neurons whose firing patterns correlate with the resultant grip force (Anner-Baratti, Allum, & Hepp-Reymond, 1986; Hepp-Reymond, Huesler, Maier, & Qi, 1994; Hepp-Reymond, Wyss, & Anner, 1978; A. M. Smith, Hepp-Reymond, & Wyss, 1975; Wannier, Maier, & Hepp-Reymond, 1991). Only part of the task-related neurons displayed patterns similar to those of the active muscles. The others had either unexpected patterns or showed negative correlations between their firing rate and force. The latter was also true for a sample of identified CM units (Maier, Bennett, Hepp-Reymond, & Lemon, 1993). In view of the large number of muscles involved in the grip, an organization into synergies may make this complex system more controllable and account partly for the cortical cell activity and its various relations to exerted grip force.

Our experimental situation allowed us to assess the existence of synergies in the three required terms mentioned above: *spatial* by correlating the activity of two simultaneously active muscles, *temporal* by cross-correlating the muscle activity in pairs of muscles under stationary conditions, and *scaling* by computing the correlations at the three force levels separately, after testing the force-related behavior of the muscles. The main issues and analytical approaches are schematically outlined in Figure 4, which displays a hypothetical situation and the possible outcome of the analyses. Both global muscle activity and MU activation patterns have been investigated. Thus, the present investigation illustrates some key methods in motor neuroscience (see also Wing, 1992) and raises the issue of how the brain achieves the

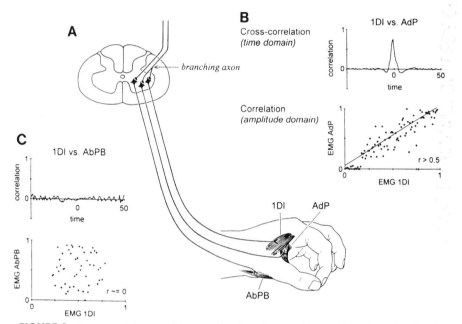

FIGURE 4   Synopsis of theoretical issues and analytical approaches. (A) Example of three hand muscles active in precision grip and their respective innervation (AbPB, abductor pollicis brevis; AdP, adductor pollicis; 1DI, first dorsal interosseus). In this example, AdP and 1DI receive a common input (branching axon), while AbPB is individually innervated. (B) Synchronous activation of AdP and 1DI in the time domain is reflected as a peak in the cross-correlation function; coactivation of the two muscles in the amplitude domain is shown by the covariation of the EMG amplitudes in the scattergram (correlation coefficient r is statistically significant). (C) In this hypothetical example, AbPB and 1DI are not correlated, either in the time or in the amplitude domain.

incredibly complex task of coordinating the many degrees of freedom afforded by the biomechanics of the hand. Basically, the outcome of this investigation fails to provide evidence of constant common drive of the kind that would be expected from hardwired synergies.

2. RECORDING EMG DURING FORCE PRODUCTION

The activity of 15 muscles was recorded in 6 right-handed subjects over a number of sessions. The experimental setup, task, EMG, and force recording procedures are described in detail in Maier and Hepp-Reymond (1995a). Briefly, the subjects sat comfortably in front of a video screen that continuously displayed three target force levels as horizontal lines. The subject grasped a fixed, but individually adjusted, manipulandum with the palmar tips of thumb and index finger of the right hand, 10 mm apart in opposition (Figure 5). A cast fitted to each subject's hand guaranteed the same hand posture over several sessions. A cursor provided instantaneous visual feedback of the grip force and displayed the force trace produced over time on the screen. Two pairs of strain gauge force transducers measured the one-dimensional force of the thumb and index finger separately. The two force components were added electronically, yielding the resultant grip force displayed on the screen.

Subjects generated three consecutive isometric ramp-and-hold force steps of 1 N each. For the first block of 20 to 25 trials the hold forces were 1, 2, and 3 N. A single trial lasted 15 s during which the subject had to match the target forces displayed on the screen as accurately as possible (Figure 5). In each session, a second block of trials was performed with lower force levels of 0.5, 1.5, and 2.5 N.

Intramuscular EMG activity was recorded from up to eight intrinsic and/or extrinsic finger muscles simultaneously. The following muscles were recorded from: Thumb: abductor pollicis brevis, opponens pollicis, flexor

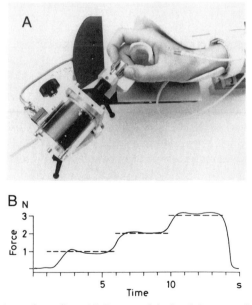

FIGURE 5 Experimental paradigm. (A) Posture of the hand during performance of the task. The hand and wrist rest in an individually fitted cast that stabilizes the wrist. (B) Schematic time course of the isometric force produced during the task. Stippled lines represent predrawn target forces; the solid line is applied force. (Maier & Hepp-Reymond, 1995a. © 1995 Springer-Verlag.)

pollicis brevis, adductor pollicis, extensor pollicis brevis, extensor pollicis longus, flexor pollicis longus, abductor pollicis longus. Index finger: 1st dorsal interosseus, 1st palmar interosseus, 1st lumbrical (1LUM), extensor digitorum communis, extensor digitorum proprius (EI), flexor digitorum superficialis (FDS), flexor digitorum profundus. Thumb force, index finger force, and total force as well as the EMGs were recorded on tape for later analysis.

We now address the following five issues:

1. Are the patterns of muscle activation in static precision grip within a group of muscles constant? (Section 3)
2. Can muscle synergies in the precision grip be identified in spatial and scaling terms? (Section 4)
3. Can any fixed temporal relationship be shown within muscle pairs? (Section 5)
4. Can more robust and frequent muscle coupling be shown at the MU level? (Section 6)
5. How does MU synchronization relate to temporal coupling and co-activation at the global EMG level? (Section 7)

The main findings will be simplified here for the sake of clarity and the reader can consult Maier and Hepp-Reymond (1995a, 1995b) for more details.

3. CONSTANCY OF MUSCLE ACTIVATION PATTERNS

To obtain a global measure of muscle activation, the multiunit EMG signals were full-wave rectified and smoothed off-line by a moving analog averager (time constant 200 ms). EMG signals and forces were digitized at 100 Hz, stored, and analyzed on a laboratory computer (Figure 6). For each trial mean EMG amplitude during generation of static force was calculated at each force level (2- to 3-s segments). Correlations between EMG amplitude and force were calculated over all the trial data points. For the 15 muscles recorded in groups of 4 to 6 in several sessions, three main observations were made on the basis of this quantitative analysis.

With respect to the relation between muscle activity and force, three main functional classes of muscles could be established following Chao et al. (1989). The present data suggested the following distribution of the 15 muscles among the three classes. The intrinsic muscles (1DI, 1PI, 1LUM) and the long flexors of the index finger (FDP, FDS) as well as two intrinsic thumb muscles (AdP, FPB) fulfilled the requirements for primary muscles. In almost all sessions and subjects, they showed significant correlations with force. The other thenar muscles (OPP, AbPB) and the extrinsic thumb muscles (FPL, EPL, EPB, AbPL) may be described as secondary, since they

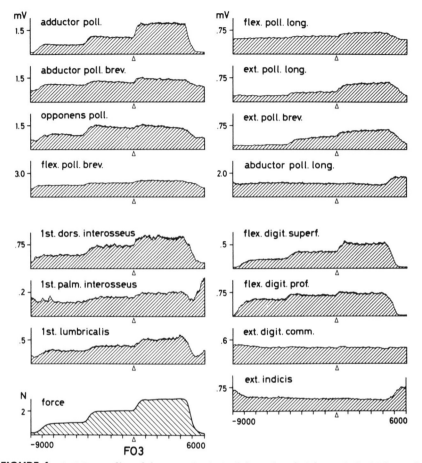

FIGURE 6 Activity profiles of the seven intrinsic (*left panel*) and eight extrinsic (*right panel*) muscles of one subject, recorded over five experimental sessions. The EMG is full-wave rectified, smoothed and averaged over 20 trials. Averaged force curve (*left bottom line*). All graphs aligned on the onset of force increase from the second to the third force level (FO3). Display time: 15 s. Force in newtons (N) and muscle activity in millivolts (mV).

had significant correlations in almost 50% of the sessions and may be more reliably activated at higher forces. The long extensors of the index finger (EDC, EI) showed almost no correlation with force in this low range and could be classified as tertiary muscles (see also Figure 6).

It is interesting in the present data that the intrinsic muscles obviously played a major role in the generation of small and finely graded forces in the grip, these forces reaching about 10% maximal voluntary contraction (MVC) at the highest force level. This finding differs from the often-quoted conclusions of Long et al. (1970) and is probably due to the low force range in the present study, which requires less stabilization and force to counter the action of the long finger flexors, thus freeing the intrinsic muscles for precise force regulation. The findings are in agreement with data of Kilbreath and Gandevia (1993) but challenge those of Chao and collaborators (1989) who

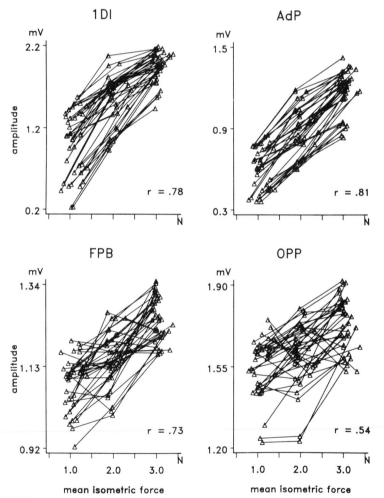

FIGURE 7   Scatter diagram of EMG activity as a function of force for four intrinsic muscles recorded simultaneously. △ represents a single trial measurement at a given force level. Data points belonging to the same trial are connected. r, Linear correlation coefficient; $n = 114$ for each muscle, corresponding to 38 trials.

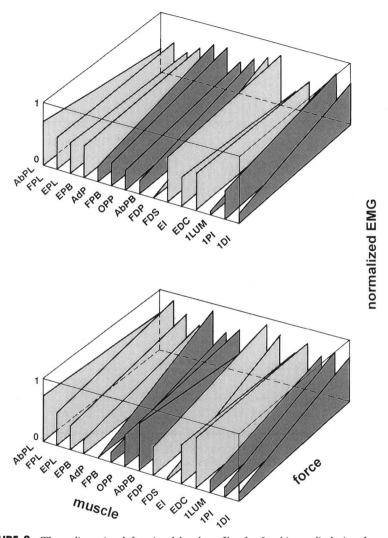

FIGURE 8 Three-dimensional functional hand profiles for 2 subjects, displaying for each muscle the mean normalized EMG activity as a function of force. X-axis: muscles; Y-axis: force (0–3N); Z-axis: mean normalized EMG (0–1 maximally). Shading is dark for intrinsic muscles, light for extrinsic muscles.

concluded from their biomechanical analysis of the hand, in particular of the thumb, that the extrinsic muscles generally are the main force producer, although the intrinsic muscles produce more force during tip pinch than during power grip.

Another important finding was intraindividual constancy, revealed by the second block of 20 trials requiring less force at the three levels. For 76.5% of all tested cases, the correlations were similar in both blocks, and the comparison of the means did not reveal any significant difference between the two data sets.

The third feature of the data was a striking and unexpected degree of intertrial variability in the force-related muscle activity (Figure 7), although the subjects produced the required isometric force with great accuracy, in the mean to within 4% at the 3-N level. Using multiple regression, it could be demonstrated that the large trial-by-trial EMG scatter observed could be explained by nonrandom variations of activity in the majority of the muscles, regardless of their contribution to grip force. Thus, even muscles with weak relations to force were activated in a nonrandom fashion and played an active, though grip-force-independent role in the present experimental situation.

The relation between EMG activity and force is displayed in a schematic manner in Figure 8 for 2 subjects and the 15 muscles averaged over several sessions. Visual comparison of these two functional hand profiles reveals consistent trends for most muscles, but also some important interindividual differences. The last observation suggests that no strict rule exists in the way muscles are used to generate grip force in this experimental situation. The only obvious and coherent data across all 6 subjects were the predominant participation of the intrinsic muscles discussed above. These different profiles indicate that specific biomechanical features of the individual hand may play a nonnegligible role in the way muscles are used to generate and maintain grip force. However, changes between sessions for a single subject also suggest that other unknown peripheral or central factors, as well as individual learned strategies, may modulate the muscle activity in this redundant multimuscular system.

4. MUSCLE SYNERGIES IN THE AMPLITUDE DOMAIN

To test whether the EMG activity of a particular muscle covaries with that of another muscle, correlations were computed over trials between the EMG activity of two muscles recorded simultaneously, at each force level separately, that is, in three different, but related, steady conditions. The criterion for synergic activation in the amplitude domain was the presence of significant correlation coefficients for at least two of the three force levels.

Data were obtained in 82 of the 105 possible muscle combinations yielded by permutation of the 15 muscles. Each of the 82 muscle combinations was tested in at least one subject and more than half of them in several subjects (up to 4) and several sessions (maximum 12 in one case only).

The first finding was that some clear coupling between muscles could be detected, but rarely over all three force levels. Of the 82 different muscle combinations tested, 46 (57%) showed either coactivation or trade-off in at least one of the subjects. Following the definition of Sirin and Patla (1987), the term coactivation synergy was used for positive (Figure 9) and trade-off for negative correlations (Figure 10). Of the significant correlations found, 83% were classified as coactivation and only 11% as trade-off. For some rare muscle combinations, the type of synergy differed among subjects (AdP–AbPB, AdP–EDC, OPP–EDC). The proportion of synergies found among the various types of muscle combinations was almost similar (56% intrinsic–intrinsic, 68% extrinsic–extrinsic, and 53% extrinsic–intrinsic).

The second important finding was that, across individuals, stable linkages in muscle pairs were quite rare. Of the 46 muscle combinations tested in more than one subject, 33% met the criterion for synergy and only 13% (i.e., six muscle combinations) were present in all the subjects tested. Figure 11 shows in a triangular matrix the distribution of these synergies, the ones found in all subjects being indicated by a dark background. These six stable, and maybe fixed, muscle combinations belonged mainly to functional or anatomical synergists and the majority consisted of intrinsic muscles.

A third, unexpected finding was the rarity, within individuals, of stable synergies, when the data sets obtained for the first and second block of trials were compared. In the second block requiring slightly less force, the most

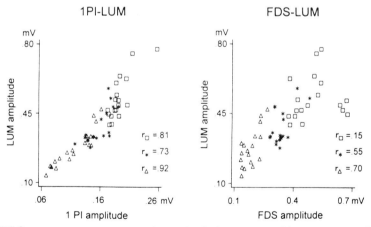

FIGURE 9   Coactivation synergies in the amplitude domain assessed by pair-wise correlations between the EMG activity of three muscles recorded simultaneously. Correlation coefficients r are calculated at each force level separately ($n = 18$) and are significant everywhere except for FDS–1LUM at the 3-N level. △, data points at 1-N level; *, 2-N level; □, 3-N level.

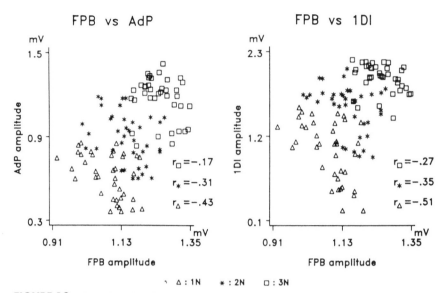

FIGURE 10 Examples of trade-off synergy for two pairs of muscles recorded simultaneously (same session as Figure 7). $n = 38$ per force level. (Same display type as Figure 9.)

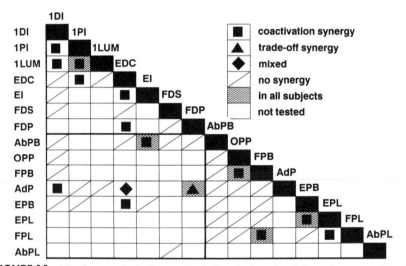

FIGURE 11 Muscle synergies in the amplitude domain (cases involving at least two subjects). The triangular matrix displays all possible pair-wise combinations of the 15 muscles. Symbols explained in the figure.

frequent muscle coupling was obtained in pairs of intrinsic muscles. From the 82 muscle combinations tested, only 24 displayed stability across both experimental blocks. Moreover, when the 20 muscle combinations with synergies in at least two subjects were considered, only two (1PI–1LUM, FDP–EDC) showed stability within individuals.

This lack of stability, at the both inter- and intraindividual levels, obviously puts the existence of fixed synergies into question. In the present data it was impossible to find any common denominator for either the interindividual or the intraindividual cases of stability. Even the 1DI–AdP synergistic coupling was not found in all the subjects and was often unstable over time, confirming observations of J. M. M. Brown and Bronks (1988). Furthermore, the majority of the synergies were not observable over the three force levels, suggesting non-force-related processes in the linkage, such as nonspecific covariation of the level of activation in several muscles.

5. MUSCLE SYNERGIES IN THE TIME DOMAIN

The existence of linkage between muscles in the time domain was established by cross-correlating two simultaneously recorded EMGs. To this end, EMG segments of 2.1 s duration were selected from the hold phase at each force level, after full-wave rectification, low-pass filtering with 100-Hz cutoff, and digitizing at 500 Hz. A Fast-Fourier Transform (FFT) was performed on each segment of data and cross-correlations computed following the method described in Press, Flannery, Teukolsky, and Vetterling (1988). Muscle activity was considered synchronous if the size of the cross-correlation peak was above four standard deviations of the total signal. The size of the peak was expressed as a percentage of the height of the respective autocorrelations. Peaks occurred on average at time zero with a range of ± 8 ms (Figure 12).

The frequency of occurrence of temporal synergies, that is, of significant synchronization for at least two force levels, was even lower than that of synergies in the amplitude domain described in the previous section. In fact, synchronization occurred in only 21 of the 82 muscle combinations tested, the majority involving pairs of intrinsic muscles. Seven muscle combinations, all between intrinsic muscles, displayed interindividual stability, since they were found in all the subjects in whom they were tested (Figure 13). Some of these pairs could be predicted from their common biomechanical action, such as the OPP–FPB and the 1DI–AdP pairs. In addition, some may be expected from the descending cortical command and their divergence into several motoneuron pools, like the 1DI–AdP pair. The other synchronized combinations mainly consist of functional agonist muscles (1PI–1DI, 1DI–1LUM, AbPB–OPP).

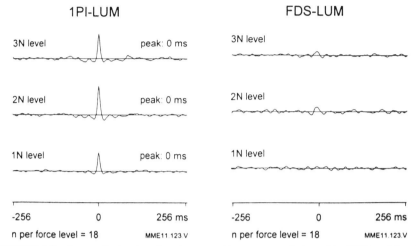

FIGURE 12   Synergy in the time domain assessed by cross-correlation of the EMG activity of the same muscle pairs as in Figure 9. The cross-correlograms were calculated at each force level over a period of 512 ms with a temporal resolution of 2 ms and averaged over 18 trials. Strong synchronization may be observed between 1PI and 1LUM at all three force levels, whereas there is weak synchrony in the FDS–1LUM pair at the higher forces only.

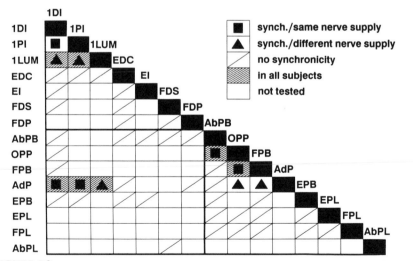

FIGURE 13   Synchronization between muscle pairs (cases involving at least two subjects). Symbols explained in the figure.

The simultaneous occurrence of muscle synergies in both the amplitude and time domains was quite rare and was restricted to cases of coactivation synergy. In other words, synchronization was never found in pairs that showed trade-off. Only 11 muscle combinations showed coincidence of synergies in the amplitude domain and synchronization between their constituent muscles. The majority of these combinations consisted of two intrinsic muscles acting on a single digit and innervated by the same peripheral nerve. For 5 of the 11 combinations, simultaneous occurrence was found in at least two subjects.

6. TEMPORAL SYNERGIES AT THE MOTOR UNIT LEVEL

The strongest evidence for fixed synergistic coupling between muscles is the short-term synchronization of the activity of two MUs located in different muscles. Synchronization can be disclosed by cross-correlation analysis of the two MU firing patterns. Common input is then revealed by the presence of a significant peak of short duration around time zero.

From a selected sample of muscle pairs analyzed at the multiunit EMG level, synchronization of their constituent MUs was investigated with two objectives in mind. The first was to test whether temporal coupling in MU pairs would be more prominent, frequent, and robust than at the multiunit level. The second aim was to check whether MU synchronization can account for the synergies discussed above, for those not only in the temporal but also in the amplitude domain.

To decompose the multiunit EMGs (analyzed in the previous section) into their constituent MUs, specialized computer software was used (ARTMUP, automatic recognition and tracking of motor unit potentials; Haas & Meyer, 1989). This package employs a three-stage algorithm. In the first phase, segments with high activity are automatically selected within the EMG signal. In the next phase, a cluster analysis detects and classifies isolated MU potentials according to seven shape parameters (such as maximal positive peak amplitude, peak-to-peak amplitude). Finally, overlapping and superimposed potentials are detected and all potentials verified for plausibility (Figure 14). The MUs obtained were characterized with regard to their modulation of firing rate during the task. The great majority of the MUs showed positive correlations between force and firing frequency, four MUs (in AbPB, FDS, and AbPL) exhibited negative correlations between frequency and force, and another four MUs showed no frequency modulation with force. The mean firing frequency was around 7 Hz, while the range varied between 5 and 14 Hz.

For cross-correlation analysis, 93 MUs were selected, belonging to 44 of

A
EMG-data

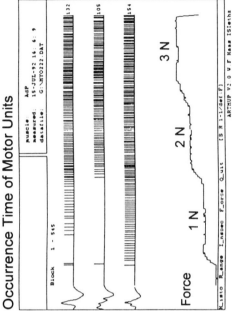

B
Occurrence Time of Motor Units

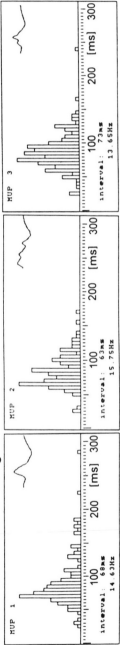

C
Inter-Potential-Interval Histogram

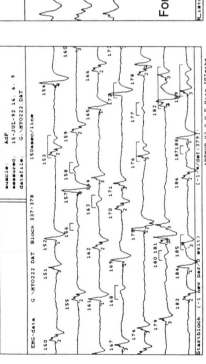

the muscle pairs discussed in the previous sections. Cross-correlation was performed on 166 MU pairs separately for each force level, yielding a maximum of three correlograms per MU pair. The data presented here are based on a total of 312 cross-correlograms acquired from 59 MU pairs with one, 68 with two, and 39 with three cross-correlograms, each containing a minimum of 200 counts per MU. All the cross-correlation peaks that fell within ±20 ms of time zero were tested for significance.

The statistical significance of the synchronization peaks was determined by computing the cumulative sum derivative (CUSUM) taken with a limit of 3 standard deviations (Figure 15). The CUSUM derivative technique allows detection of changes in otherwise noisy histograms. By integrating the differences between bin count and mean bin count in the control period, subtle changes in the cross-correlogram can be made visible and delimited. The theory of stochastic point processes is used to approximate the variance of the CUSUM and to set limits for significant synchronization (Davey, Ellaway, & Stein, 1986). To compare the cross-correlation peaks of different MU pairs in this study and with data reported by other groups, the peaks were described in terms of relative peak amplitude (k, Sears & Stagg, 1976) and relative mean peak amplitude (k', Ellaway & Murthy, 1985).

Significant MU synchronization between intermuscular MUs was found in 86 of the 312 cross-correlations, corresponding to 75 of the 166 analyzed pairs. In general, the synchronization peaks, as quantified by the indices were quite small, reflecting relatively weak temporal coupling between the 75 significant MU pairs (k = 2.19 ± 0.50, k' = 1.70 ± 0.30). These values are, however, in the range of those reported previously (Bremner et al., 1991a, 1991b, 1991c; Harrison, Ironton, & Stephens, 1991; Nordstrom, Fuglevand, & Enoka, 1992; Schmied, Ivarsson, & Fetz, 1993; Schmied, Vedel, & Pagni, 1994). The synchronization of MU pairs located in two separate muscles was significantly weaker than that of intramuscular pairs (Huesler, Maissen, Maier, & Hepp-Reymond, 1995).

Synchronization was found for all three force steps in only one MU pair (1DI–1PI). The strength of synchronization did not increase systematically

---

FIGURE 14 Decomposition of the global EMG of adductor pollicis (AdP) into its constituent MU potentials by ARTMUP (see text). (A) EMG data after segmentation, cluster analysis, and detection of superposed potentials. EMG activity at the 2-N level during 1.05 s displayed on seven lines from top to bottom. Numbers corresponding to the detected signal segments (*above*) and classified MU potentials (*below*). Square brackets denote not completely decomposed segments. (B) Spike trains of three discriminated MUs and respective total force trace in one trial. Time scale: 15 s. (C) Inter-potential-interval histograms of the three MUs with wave form depicted (*top right*). Interval: statistical mode of the histogram and its reciprocal value, that is, firing rate.

with force but was rather inconsistent. Moreover, MU synchronization appeared to be closely related to the recruitment threshold of each of the MUs within a pair. Of the 86 significant cross-correlogram peaks, the majority ($n = 59$) occurred at a force level at which both MUs were recruited, either at that level ($n = 32$) or at the recruitment level of the MU with the higher threshold ($n = 27$). That is to say, the probability of synchronization in the majority of the MU pairs declines in excess of the recruitment thresholds of the MUs.

An interesting feature of MU synchronization was related to the location of the MUs in the hand muscles (Table 1). The proportion of synchronization was the same for the pairs of MUs located in two extrinsic as for those located in two intrinsic muscles (approximately 50%). According to the two indices, k and k', the synchronization strength was stronger between MUs that both belonged to extrinsic muscles than between MU pairs in intrinsic muscles. The weakest estimates of synchronization as well as the lowest frequency of occurrence (34%) were obtained for MU pairs located in intrinsic/extrinsic muscle combinations.

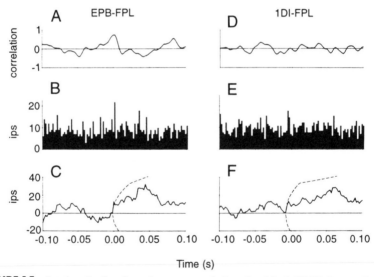

FIGURE 15   Synchronization shown by cross-correlation of multiunit EMGs (*top panel*) and of single MU pairs (*center panel*) with their respective CUSUM (*bottom panel*). (A,B,C) EPB–FPL pair: corresponding synchronized behavior at multiunit and MU level (518 and 501 MU potentials, respectively; k = 2.54, k' = 2.54). (D,E,F) 1DI–FPL pair: significant synchronization at MU level (593 and 648 MU potentials; k = 1.86, k' = 1.70), but without synchronization of the multiunit EMGs. Time in s; binwidth, 2 ms; ordinate, counts transformed into impulses per second (ips) = counts/(binwidth × number of triggers). Dotted line in C and F: ±3 *SD* of CUSUM. CUSUM test in (C) clearly significant, in (F) significant only in the first bin.

TABLE I Frequency of Occurrence and Strength of MU Synchronization between Muscle Pairs as a Function of Muscle Location

	Muscle pair location		
	Extrinsic/extrinsic	Intrinsic/intrinsic	Extrinsic/intrinsic
Frequency[a]	48% (21)	52% (87)	34% (58)
k[b]	2.78 ± 0.64	2.13 ± 0.39	1.93 ± 0.30
k'[b]	1.95 ± 0.35	1.70 ± 0.28	1.55 ± 0.18

[a]Frequency of occurrence as a percentage of MUs tested; total number in parentheses.
[b]Strength of MU synchronization in terms of normalized peak amplitude, k, and area, k'.

7. RELATION BETWEEN MOTOR UNIT SYNCHRONIZATION AND MUSCLE COUPLING

Since the global EMG signal comprises the sum of all its MU potentials in the vicinity of the recording electrode, overlap between synchronization at the multiunit and single MU level was expected. This assumption was tested at each force level separately. A total of 101 multiunit cross-correlograms, 45 with significant synchronization, were compared with their constituent single MU cross-correlations (Figure 16).

The first important observation was that the whole MU pool did not need to be synchronized in order to produce temporal coupling at the global level. Either one MU pair with strong synchronization or weaker coupling of several MU pairs could induce global muscle synchronization. Thus, synchronization of one MU pair is necessary but not sufficient to establish global temporal coupling.

Secondly, MU synchronization was disclosed in 50% of globally non-synchronized muscle pairs. This observation testifies to the greater sensitivity of detecting synchronization at the MU level, insofar as asynchronous firing of MUs can mask the signal of the synchronized ones. Furthermore, this also demonstrates that significant MU synchronization is restricted to a selected number of MU pairs. The same comparison between MU synchronization and muscle coupling in the amplitude domain led to similar conclusions.

Finally, the simultaneous occurrence of MU synchronization together with global coupling in the amplitude and time domains could be observed in 9 of the 11 muscle combinations mentioned above (Section 5). This occurred mainly in pairs of intrinsic muscles: 1DI–1PI, 1DI–AdP, 1DI–FPB, 1LUM–1PI, 1PI–AdP, and AdP–OPP. These three types of linkage were also seen in a pair of extrinsic synergist muscles (EPB–EPL, Figure 16) and, unexpectedly, in two pairs of one intrinsic and one extrinsic muscles (AdP–FDS, FDS–

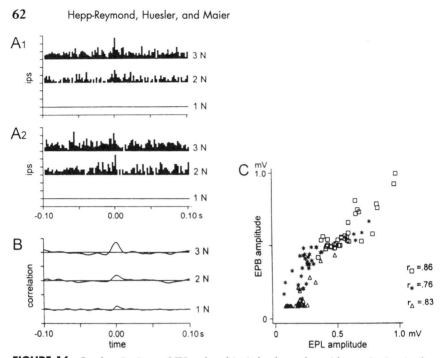

FIGURE 16 Synchronization at MU and multiunit level together with coactivation in the amplitude domain for one muscle pair (EPL–EPB) displayed over three force levels. (A1, A2) Synchronization of two MU pairs, EPL MU1–EPB MU1 (A1), EPL MU1–EPB MU2 (A2). The peaks are small but all exceed three *SD* in the CUSUMs (not shown). Cross-correlation was not computed at the first force level because both MU1 and MU2 of the EPB were not active at this level. One interval on the ordinate is 10 impulses per second (ips). (B) Multiunit synchronization significant on the 2-N and 3-N level. One interval on the ordinate corresponds to a correlation coefficient of .25. (C) Significant coactivation synergies (*p* < .001) for all three force levels displayed as in Figure 9, with 34 data points per force level.

OPP), although they are neither synergists, nor do they share the same biomechanical actions.

8. DISCUSSION

It is known from earlier studies that a large number of extrinsic and intrinsic hand muscles participate in precision grip. In our investigation, almost all of the 15 muscles linked to either thumb or index finger were not only activated but also scaled their activity with the production of increasing grip force. These muscles could be classified functionally according to their activation patterns and their force scaling. In contrast to previous assumptions, the activity of many intrinsic muscles was clearly related to force production, whereas the long finger flexors had a rather less important function. This pattern was quite consistent across subjects and is probably specific for the low grip forces required (~10% maximal voluntary contraction [MVC]). Thus, in broad terms, a global spatial synergy, that is, the reliable and patterned activation of task-related muscles, was a common finding. However, this description does not tell us whether the CNS uses muscle synergies to produce grip force or whether it activates and controls each muscle independently. To tackle this question, the statistical relation between coactive muscle has to be addressed. This may provide evidence of muscular interdependence, speaking in favor of synergies, or independence, indicating their absence. The experiments reviewed in this chapter employed various measures to assess the occurrence of synergies in the amplitude domain and the time domain, and their characteristics.

8.1 Are There Fixed Muscle Synergies in Precision Grip?

The present data disclosed synergistic coupling in the amplitude domain, but only in about one third of the muscle combinations tested. Coactivation, that is, positive correlation between the EMG amplitudes, was the dominant pattern of synergy, whereas trade-off, that is, negative correlation, occurred in less than 15% of the cases. Even fewer synergies were identified in the time domain analyses. Synchronization at the global EMG level occurred in about 25% of the tested muscle combinations. At the single MU level a higher amount of synchronization (45%) was found in the restricted sample tested. Single- and multiunit synchronization generally showed coincidence but this overlap was not complete. This clearly depends on the relative distribution of synchronous MUs within the muscle and on the strength of the common drive, which, as estimated by other investigations, can vary and also appears modifiable (Bremner et al., 1991a, 1991b, 1991c; Dietz, Bischofberger, Wita, & Freund, 1976; Schmied et al., 1993).

For grip functionality, it is important to ask whether mechanically linked muscles preferentially show muscle synergies, in either the time or the amplitude domain. Indeed, the present observations suggest that the most prevalent muscle combinations with synchronization were those with clear synergistic-like, task-related mechanical action (Figures 11 and 13). In the amplitude domain, stable synergies appeared sometimes also in combinations of mechanically uncoupled or weakly coupled muscles and, in contrast to synchronization, also between anatomical antagonists. Thus, the majority of synergies were confined to grip-related, functional synergists, including some anatomical antagonists.

A fixed muscle synergy should, in principle, show coupling in the amplitude and time domain and reveal synchronization between some of the constituent MUs. Furthermore, a fixed synergy should be invariant with slight changes of task conditions. It might be argued that amplitude and time domain synergies need not necessarily occur together, since different mechanisms may underlie their appearance. Our data seem to indicate that this is indeed the case since coincidence of both types of synergies was not the rule. Only in two muscle combinations (FPB–OPP, 1PI–1LUM), was the coincidence found in all subjects. Somewhat surprising was the existence of synchronization between two muscles in the absence of any correlation between their activation levels. Why is synchronization only rarely coupled with synergy in the amplitude domain? In principle, strong enough synchronous variation of the firing rate of two muscles should produce a covariation of EMG activity. Theoretically, and supported by the present data, both types of muscle synergies do not need to occur concurrently. On one hand, covariation in the amplitude domain can be based on an asynchronous increase of firing rate of MUs, by some general enhancement of excitation. On the other hand, MU pairs can be synchronized without any concomitant global muscle coupling, since synchronization, for example, of one MU pair, can be detected, although other nonsynchronized MUs produce non-covarying EMG signals.

The evidence for the existence of fixed synergies during force production in precision grip is rather weak. In the amplitude domain, interindividual stability was rare. It remains an open question whether the few muscle combinations with stable synergistic activation should be considered as being fixed. Six muscle combinations showed coupling in all subjects and might therefore be considered as fixed muscle synergies. However, in the second block, with slightly lower forces, only one of those combinations (FPB–OPP) still exhibited coupling, indicating a high task specificity, probably due to their common flexion action across the MCP joint of the thumb. One would have expected only minor changes between the two consecutive blocks, since the task, specifically the joint configuration, remained identical with the exception of slightly lower target forces. It is therefore quite unlikely that synergies in the amplitude domain were fixed and that biomechanical relations per se may be a strong and frequent source of coupling.

In the time domain, interindividual, stable multiunit synchronization was found in seven muscle combinations, and, in five of those, synchrony occurred in every session (Maier & Hepp-Reymond, 1995b). The muscle combinations with common synchronization formed three clusters: one between intrinsic index finger muscles (1DI–1LUM, 1PI–1LUM), another between thenar muscles (FPB–OPP, OPP–AbPB), and a third one between the thumb adductor and intrinsic index finger muscles (AdP–1DI, AdP–1PI, AdP–1LUM). However, two points speak against their fixed nature: first, most of them did not show synchrony on all three force levels, as was also demonstrated for MU pairs; and second, the synchrony was not strong enough to produce a concomitant covariation of the EMG amplitudes. These findings raise questions with regard to the mechanism of synchronization.

In conclusion, the variability of the synergies between subjects and between the two experimental blocks suggests that the CNS does generally not rely, or quite rarely relies, on fixed synergies for the production of force in the precision grip. However, the amount of synergy found in the amplitude and time domain also leads us to reject the concept of fully independent control of the active muscles. Thus, we are left favoring the existence of flexible synergies and we turn to consider possible mechanisms.

8.2 Source of Flexible Synergies

Kirkwood and Sears (1978) suggested that a repertoire of muscle synergies could be generated by synchronous occurrence of excitatory postsynaptic potentials evoked in motoneurons by synaptic input from branches of common presynaptic fibers (see Figure 4). The cortico-motoneuronal system could provide the substrate for common input. It is well established that direct cortico-motoneuronal connections between pyramidal tract cells and spinal motoneurons innervating hand and forearm muscles are essential for the execution of independent finger movements and can terminate in more than one motoneuronal pool (for reviews, see Hepp-Reymond, 1988; Lemon, 1993). Further support for a strong central influence has been provided by clinical observations (J. R. Baker et al., 1988; Datta et al., 1991; Davey, Ellaway, Friedland, & Short, 1990; Farmer, Swash, Ingram, & Stephens, 1993), indicating that short-term synchronization depends on intact cortical systems and is little affected by peripheral input.

In primates, the size of the muscle field for CM units facilitating intrinsic hand muscles is smaller than for CM cells to wrist muscles (Buys, Lemon, Mantel, & Muir, 1986). This probably reflects the importance of the CM system for fractionated finger movements. Muscle fields reflecting either an anatomical or a functional relationship among intrinsic or extrinsic hand muscles in the precision grip were disclosed. Anatomical synergists, such as AdP–FPB, and functional synergists, such as AdP–1DI, seemed to be linked preferentially. This fits well with the present observation that the most prevalent muscle combinations with synchronization were those with clear synergic-like, task-related biomechanical action. Thus, functional synergies (predominantly synchronization) could, to a certain extent, be determined by the distribution and weights of the CM connections.

Of course, other descending systems to the spinal apparatus sharing some properties with the CM system should be considered, too, such as the rubro-motoneuronal projections that directly impinge onto motoneurons of distal muscles and also display divergence at the spinal level (Mewes & Cheney, 1991). In addition, cortico- and rubrospinal connections to spinal interneurons, as opposed to motoneurons, might provide another source of control. And finally, mechanisms of presynaptic synchronization at the cortical level could also take part.

Nevertheless, if we assume that the corticospinal system, in particular the CM system with its divergence at spinal level, is primarily responsible for muscle synergies, the question arises: why are fixed synergies so rare and how can such a hardwired system generate flexible synergies? Several sources could play a role in adapting synergies to the behavioral goal.

First, variations in the descending command could be responsible. Johansson, Lemon, and Westling (1994) demonstrated that the excitability of motor cortex, measured by EMG responses to transcranial magnetic stimulation, changed during performance of a precision grip task under different load conditions. This effect was mediated by cutaneous afferents responding to the alteration in load. Furthermore, Schmied et al. (1993) provided convincing evidence that the amount of MU synchronization is modifiable, depending on visual and auditory feedback. Thus, even if there were a hardwired spinal system, descending commands varying from trial to trial could break up and adapt fixed synergies, this effect being subject even to voluntary interference.

Second, the effect of the descending command onto the motoneurons could be subject to variation that differs among elements of a synergy. K. M. B. Bennett and Lemon (1994) showed that the strength of postspike facilitation produced by CM cells in hand muscles changed during a precision grip task, depending on the level of target muscle activity. This could have been achieved by changes in the number of recruited MUs for a given facilitated muscle, thus indicating that the CM connections are not of fixed nature. Such a feature would endow the CM system with flexibility. Alternatively, these kinds of changes could have been brought about by changes of motoneuron excitability, caused, for example, by cutaneous afferents, being known to change recruitment order (Garnett & Stephens, 1980). Moreover, rather than heavily depending on the monosynaptic CM connections, the descending command may primarily activate spinal interneuronal circuits (segmental as well as propriospinal interneurons), the flexibility of which could produce variable but synergistic motoneuronal activity (Kirkwood & Road, 1995).

Presynaptic inhibition of Ia terminals could be another source of modulation. This was indirectly investigated in humans by Meunier and Pierrot-Deseilligny (1989). Decreasing presynaptic inhibition was found to increase Ia afferent input to synergists, thus enhancing the stretch reflex. Increasing presynaptic inhibition decreased Ia input to antagonists muscles and thus enhanced coactivation. This mechanism effectively modulates the interplay between the reciprocal organization of the stretch reflex and the coactivation of antagonist muscles. The corticospinal system could convey and modulate this kind of inhibition (Burke, Gracies, Meunier, & Pierrot-Deseilligny, 1992). Nielsen and Kagamihara (1992) also showed that the Ia inhibitory action is reduced during cocontraction of antagonist muscles, and they attributed this effect to central commands.

Finally, spinal circuits can introduce flexibility to a greater extent than previously assumed, specifically for forearm motoneurons (Hultborn & Illert, 1991), and the fusimotor system clearly has the potential to modulate synergies by enhancing or lowering, or even gating, specific groups of afferents to synergistic motoneuron pools (Gandevia & Burke, 1992).

In conclusion, the data support the idea that the corticospinal, specifically the CM, system produces task-dependent and flexible muscle synergies during precision grip. Peripheral mechanisms, mediated by muscle and cutaneous afferents could support and adapt the central control of flexible functional muscle synergies in the spinal network, via complex Ia connections, presynaptic inhibition, or specific fusimotor drive.

8.3 Conclusions

The results summarized in this chapter indicate that the control of movement parameters of a clearly specified task does not dictate a unique and deterministic synergistic muscle activation pattern. On the contrary, the CNS appears to control the task performance and the biomechanical redundancy of the hand by using flexible short-term synergies, predominantly for muscle combinations with task-related, synergic mechanical action. The variable muscle synergies observed do not explain the behavioral consistency and accuracy of grip force production.

For grip formation, kinematic invariances have been established for the points of contact between thumb and index finger during dynamic opening and closing of the grip (Cole & Abbs, 1986), and also for the regulation of safety margins, that is, the ratio between grip force and load (tangential) force when subjects grasp and lift an object with precision grip (Johansson & Westling, 1984b; see also Chapter 19). Invariances have also been described in bimanual activity (Wiesendanger et al., Chapter 14) as well as control of equilibrium during postural perturbations (Macpherson, 1988). However, no one has been able to relate the behavioral invariance to parallel invariance at the EMG level, that is, to fixed muscle synergies.

A basic assumption is that movement specification in systems with redundant degrees of freedom poses a computational problem for the CNS. According to a considerable number of investigations, including the present one, there is no good evidence at the muscular level for any fixed pattern, despite the kinematic invariances. In consequence, one might further ask whether there are other ways or levels to simplify movement control. For example, Macpherson (1991) has suggested that, within a hierarchical control scheme, learned high-level and task-dependent motor strategies may produce flexible (low-level) synergies. However, this primarily relocates, rather than answers, the question. In contrast, one might even conclude that there is no need for the CNS to simplify movement control. Rather than looking for ways of simplification in a top-down approach one should perhaps focus on the cooperation of loosely defined descending commands with on-line corrective regulation from peripheral systems. This might more easily explain the variability as well as the adaptability of the motor system.

4

Muscle Architecture Basis for Neuromuscular Control of the Forearm and Hand

JAN FRIDÉN AND RICHARD L. LIEBER

1. SKELETAL MUSCLE ARCHITECTURE

Studies of skeletal muscle anatomy have previously emphasized fiber type differences between muscles (e.g., R. I. Close, 1972), but architectural differences can be functionally more significant. For example, it is believed that fast skeletal muscle fibers are slightly stronger and shorten approximately twice as fast as slow skeletal muscle fibers (Bodine, Roy, Edlred, & Edgerton, 1987; R. I. Close, 1972). However, muscles of different architecture, but similar fiber type, may differ in strength and speed by factors of ten or twenty (Gans, 1982; Lieber & Blevins, 1989; P. L. Powell, Roy, Kanim, Bello, & Edgerton, 1984; Roy, Bello, Powell, & Simpson, 1984; Sacks, & Roy, 1982; Wickiewicz, Roy, Powell, & Edgerton, 1983). Thus, in terms of functional properties, skeletal muscle architecture plays a greater role than fiber type distribution.

Architecture is defined as the arrangement of muscle fibers relative to the axis of force generation (Gans, 1982). The most important architectural properties are muscle fiber length and physiological cross-sectional area (PCSA). This is because muscle excursion and velocity are directly proportional to muscle fiber length, while isometric muscle force is directly

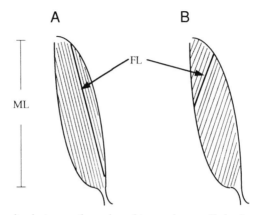

FIGURE 1 Generalized picture of muscle architectural types. Skeletal muscle fibers may be oriented along the muscle's force-generating axis (A) or at a fixed angle relative to the force-generating axis (B). These figures represent idealized views of muscle architecture and probably do not adequately describe any single muscle. ML, muscle length; FL, fiber length.

proportional to muscle PCSA. Because of these direct structure–function correlations, studies of muscle architecture provide insight into muscle functional properties. This can be illustrated by studying two different muscles with dramatically different designs but identical muscle fiber types (Figure 1). Both muscles have approximately the same amount of contractile material (mass), but the arrangement of this material is quite different. The muscle in Figure 1A has relatively long fibers that extend almost the entire length of the muscle and are parallel to the muscle's force-generating axis. This is the classic parallel-fibered muscle. In contrast with this is the muscle in Figure 1B, which has short fibers relative to the muscle that are tilted by about 30° to the muscle's force-generating axis. This is the classic pennated muscle.

The intrinsic length-tension and force-velocity properties of the two muscles in Figure 1 are the same, that is, the properties of the composite sarcomeres are identical. It is the arrangement that imparts the functional differences between the two muscles. The muscle with longer fibers has a greater absolute working range than the muscle with shorter fibers. This is because, for a given length change, the sarcomeres in muscle A lengthen less, the length change being distributed over a greater number of sarcomeres. However, muscle A generates a lower tension than muscle B because muscle A contains a much smaller PCSA. In other words, muscle A is designed for excursion, while muscle B is designed for force production. This basic concept of architectural differences between muscles in the hand and forearm has immediate implications for an understanding of hand function and may be particularly relevant when attempting to replace lost motor function by transposition of intact muscle by surgical tendon transfer.

The architectural designs of the forearm and intrinsic hand muscles were recently described by Lieber, Fazeli, and Botte (1990) and Lieber, Jacobson, Fazeli, Abrams, and Botte (1992). Architectural differences, and therefore functional specialization, were found both between and within functional muscle groups (i.e., wrist movers were architecturally different from digital flexors and extensors, and some wrist movers differed from each other). In a study by Lieber et al. (1992) it was demonstrated that muscles in the forearm differ with respect to muscle architecture (Table 1). Generally, the digital extensors were similar in design, being characterized as relatively long-fibered, small PCSA muscles. The digital flexors were characterized as relatively long-fibered muscles with intermediate PCSA. However, 2 muscles of similar mass, pronator teres (PT) and brachioradialis (BR) stood out as being quite different from an architectural point of view. In fact, BR and PT provide a concrete example that equal muscle mass does not necessarily imply equal function. It has been demonstrated that muscle PCSA (i.e., physiological not anatomical CSA) is proportional to maximum tetanic tension (P. L. Powell et al., 1984), while muscle fiber length (not muscle length) is proportional to muscle velocity or excursion. PT has a larger PCSA than BR and should generate approximately 10 kg of tetanic tension compared to BR's 3 kg (assuming a muscle specific tension of 2.2 kg/cm^2; P. L. Powell et al., 1984). Thus, PT would be well suited to tasks requiring large forces. The architectural differences between PT and BR are illustrated in Figure 2.

The intrinsic muscles of the hand are of paramount importance in efficient hand function. Electromyographic studies have provided insights into the unique functions of the intrinsic hand muscles (Backhouse & Catton, 1954; Long, 1968; see also Chapter 3 by Hepp-Reymond et al.). However, few investigators have characterized architectural and functional properties of the intrinsic muscles (Jacobson, Raab, Fazeli, Abrams, & Botte, 1992). An understanding of muscle architectural specialization has significant implications for surgical procedures involving muscle and tendon transfer, biomechanical modeling, prosthesis design and analysis of normal function.

In their study of architectural design of the human intrinsic hand muscles, Jacobson et al. (1992) found that the lumbrical muscles provided several extreme examples of architectural adaptation (see Table 2). The fibers of these muscles extend 85 to 90% of the muscle length. This is the highest fiber length/muscle length ratio in the upper limb. It is interpreted as a high excursion design. The result is that lumbrical muscles have a flat and broad length-tension curve that would allow relatively constant contractile force over a long range of fiber lengths, depending on the position of the flexor digitorum profundus (FDP) tendon. It is likely that lumbrical muscle fiber

TABLE I Comparisons between Arm Muscle Force and Excursion

Force muscle	Cross-sectional area (mm²)	Excursion muscle	Fiber length (mm)
PT	413	BR	121
FCU	342	ECRL	76
ECRB	273	FDP M	68
ECU	260	FDS I(C)	68
FDS M	253	FDP R	65
FDP M	223	FDP I	61
FDP S	220	FDS M	61
FPL	208	FDP S	61
PQ	207	FDS R	60
FCR	199	EDC M	59
FDS I(P)	181	EDC I	57
FDP I	177	EDQ	55
FDP R	172	EDC S	53
FDS I(C)	171	PL	52
FDS I(D)	163	EDC R	51
FDS R	161	FCR	51
ECRL	146	ECU	51
BR	133	EIP	48
EDC M	102	ECRB	48
EPL	98	FPL	45
EDC R	86	EPL	44
PL	69	FCU	42
EDQ	64	FDS S	42
EIP	56	FDS I(D)	38
EDC I	52	PT	36
FDS S	40	FDS I(P)	32
EDC S	40	PQ	23

Note. Muscles include: the extensor digitorum communis to the index, middle, ring, and small fingers (EDC I, EDC M, EDC R, and EDC S, respectively); the extensor digiti quinti (EDQ); the extensor indicis proprius (EIP); extensor pollicis longus (EPL); the flexor digitorum superficialis muscles (FDS I, FDS M, FDS R, and FDS S); the flexor digitorum profundus muscles (FDP I, FDP M, FDP R, and FDP S); the flexor pollicis longus (FPL); pronator quadratus (PQ); palmaris longus (PL); pronator teres (PT); brachioradialis (BR); extensor carpi radialis brevis (ECRB); extensor carpi radialis longus (ECRL); flexor carpi winaris (FCU); extensor carpi ulnaris (ECU); flexor carip radialis (FCR); proximal (P); central (C); distal (D).

length facilitates active muscle contraction, even during FDP contraction, by allowing the lumbrical origin to move without large changes in sarcomere length. If the lumbrical muscle fibers were shorter, FDP excursion could stretch lumbrical sarcomeres to the point where they were unable to generate active force. Additionally, Jacobson and co-workers demonstrated that adductor pollicis (AdP) was the intrinsic muscle with the largest PCSA, that is, generating the highest maximum isometric tension. Generally, the intrinsic muscle PCSAs are the lowest of all measured in the upper limb, with the exception of those muscles that have no extrinsic synergists. AdP and the first dorsal interosseus (1DI) are the primary muscles contributing to key pinch grip, which can be used to generate high forces. Also, 1DI abducts against the cumulative flexion forces of the flexor pollicis longus (FPL), flexor pollicis brevis (FPB) and opponens pollicis (OPP) in opposition and during key pinch. These muscles also function to maintain key pinch during forearm release of the object.

Skeletal muscles demonstrate a remarkable degree of architectural specialization, which appears to be well suited to each muscle in order that it might perform its task. Since the two most important architectural parameters are fiber length and PCSA, these have been plotted on a scattergraph in Figure 3. Since fiber length is proportional to excursion and PCSA is proportional to muscle force, these graphs can be used to understand the functional

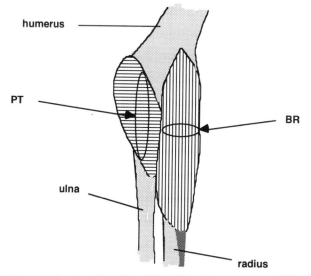

FIGURE 2 Schematic drawing of brachioradialis (BR) and pronator teres (PT) of the left arm. BR with its long fibers arranged at a small pennation angle has a PCSA that is only one third of PT with short fibers that are more highly pennated. Ellipses superimposed on muscles represent the PCSA in that muscle region. (Redrawn from Lieber et al., 1992, Fig. 7, p. 794.)

TABLE II Architectural Properties of Hand Intrinsic Muscles

Muscle	Muscle mass (g)	Muscle length (mm)	Fiber length (mm)	Pennation angle (deg)	Cross-sectional area (cm²)	FL/ML ratio
AbDM	3.320 ± 1.67	68.40 ± 6.5	46.20 ± 7.2	3.90 ± 1.3	0.890 ± 0.49	.680 ± .10
AbPB	2.610 ± 1.19	60.40 ± 6.6	41.60 ± 5.6	4.60 ± 1.9	0.680 ± 0.28	.690 ± .09
AbPL	9.960 ± 2.01	160.40 ± 15.0	58.10 ± 7.4	7.50 ± 2.0	1.930 ± 0.59	.360 ± .05
AdP	6.780 ± 1.84	54.60 ± 8.9	34.00 ± 7.5	17.30 ± 3.4	1.940 ± 0.39	.630 ± .15
1DI	4.670 ± 1.17	61.90 ± 2.5	31.70 ± 2.8	9.20 ± 2.6	1.500 ± 0.40	.510 ± .05
2DI	2.650 ± 1.01	62.80 ± 8.1	25.10 ± 6.3	8.20 ± 3.1	1.340 ± 0.77	.410 ± .13
3DI	2.010 ± 0.60	54.90 ± 4.6	25.80 ± 3.4	9.80 ± 2.8	0.950 ± 0.45	.470 ± .07
4DI	1.900 ± 0.62	50.10 ± 5.3	25.80 ± 3.4	9.40 ± 4.2	0.910 ± 0.38	.520 ± .11
EPB	2.250 ± 1.36	105.60 ± 22.5	55.00 ± 7.5	7.20 ± 4.4	0.470 ± 0.32	.540 ± .13
FDM	1.540 ± 0.44	59.20 ± 10.4	40.60 ± 13.7	3.60 ± 1.0	0.540 ± 0.36	.670 ± .17
FPB	2.580 ± 0.56	57.20 ± 3.7	41.50 ± 5.2	6.20 ± 4.5	0.660 ± 0.20	.730 ± .08
1LUM	0.570 ± 0.019	64.90 ± 10.0	55.40 ± 10.2	1.20 ± 0.9	0.1120 ± 0.028	.850 ± .03
2LUM	0.390 ± 0.22	61.20 ± 17.8	55.50 ± 17.7	1.60 ± 1.3	0.0790 ± 0.038	.900 ± .05
3LUM	0.370 ± 0.16	64.30 ± 8.9	56.20 ± 10.7	1.10 ± 0.8	0.0810 ± 0.036	.870 ± .07
4LUM	0.230 ± 0.11	53.80 ± 11.5	50.10 ± 8.4	0.70 ± 1.0	0.0630 ± 0.026	.900 ± .05
ODM	1.940 ± 0.98	47.20 ± 3.6	19.50 ± 4.1	7.70 ± 2.9	1.100 ± 0.43	.410 ± .09
OPP	3.510 ± 0.89	55.50 ± 5.0	35.50 ± 5.1	4.90 ± 2.5	1.020 ± 0.35	.640 ± .07
2PI	1.560 ± 0.22	55.10 ± 5.0	25.00 ± 5.0	6.30 ± 2.2	0.750 ± 0.25	.450 ± .08
3PI	1.280 ± 0.28	48.10 ± 2.9	26.00 ± 4.3	7.70 ± 3.9	0.650 ± 0.26	.540 ± .08
4PI	1.190 ± 0.33	45.30 ± 5.8	23.60 ± 2.6	8.20 ± 3.5	0.610 ± 0.23	.520 ± .10

Note. Values represent mean ± standard deviations. Abbreviations: abductor digiti minimi (AbDM); abductor pollicis brevis (AbPB); abductor pollicis longus (AbPL); adductor pollicis (AdP); dorsal interosseus muscles (DI1–DI4); extensor pollicis brevis (EPB); flexor pollicis brevis (FPB); lumbrical muscles (LUM1–LUM4); opponens digiti minimi (ODM); opponens pollicis (OPP); and palmer interosseus muscles (PI2–PI4). (Reproduced with permission from Jacobson et al., 1992.)

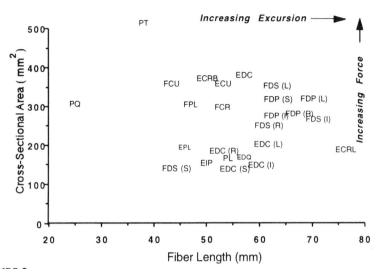

FIGURE 3   Scatter plot of fiber length versus PCSA for forearm muscles. Muscles that cluster together in this graph are architecturally similar. (Reproduced with permission from Lieber et al., 1992, Fig. 6, p. 793.)

specializations of each muscle. Muscle architecture has a dramatic influence on muscle force-generating properties. Muscle force is proportional to PSCA, while muscle speed (or excursion) is proportional to fiber length.

2. FUNCTIONAL CONSEQUENCES OF ALTERED MUSCLE FIBER LENGTH

By using intraoperative laser diffraction measurement of the extensor carpi radialis brevis muscle (ECRB) sarcomere lengths before and after surgical tendon lengthening in patients with lateral epicondylitis, Fridén and Lieber (1994) established the *in vivo* length-tension relationship of the ECRB as well as the magnitude of the corresponding muscle shortening following tendon release. To predict the effects of ECRB lengthening on joint strength, two pieces of information are required: the relation between ECRB sarcomere length and tension and the moment arm of ECRB at the wrist joint. The latter has recently been reported by Jacobson et al. (1992) and can be used directly. In order to determine the relation between sarcomere length and tension, it is important to know the lengths of the actin and myosin filaments within ECRB and the physiological sarcomere lengths over which ECRB operates. These data were recently presented by Lieber, Loren, and Fridén (1994) based on measurements of *in vivo* sarcomere length (see Figure 4).

They demonstrated that, physiologically, the ECRB operates in the range of 2.5 µm to 3.6 µm. Given the measured actin filament length of 1.30 µm and myosin filament length of 1.66 µm, these data suggest that the muscle operates primarily on the plateau and descending limb of its sarcomere length-tension curve (Figure 5).

Following ECRB surgical tendon lengthening by 9 mm, sarcomere length decreases by 0.3 µm (Fridén & Lieber, 1994). Thus, the physiological operating range of the ECRB after lengthening will be from 2.2 µm to 3.3 µm. Since the relationship between sarcomere length and tension is linear throughout the descending limb of the length-tension relationship, it is clear that in this case ECRB shortening actually results in muscle strengthening over most of the physiological range. It is easy to demonstrate that, since

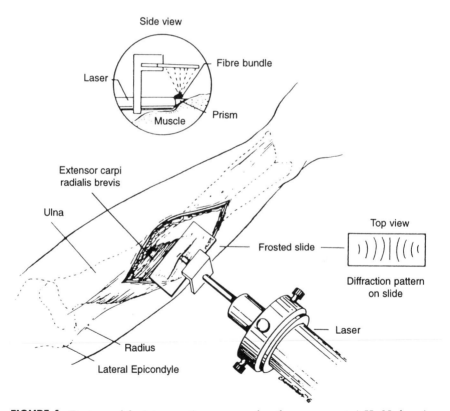

FIGURE 4   Device used for intraoperative sarcomere length measurement. A He-Ne laser is inserted beneath a fiber bundle and aligned normal to the transmitting face of the prism for optimal transmission of laser power into the muscle. Diffraction spacing is measured manually using calipers. (Reproduced with permission from Lieber et al., 1994.)

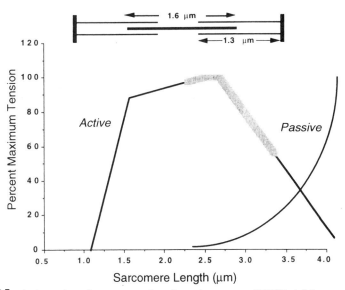

FIGURE 5   Active and passive sarcomere length tension curves of ECRB. A 0.3-μm sarcomere length decrease results in a 25% increase in active muscle force and a 25% decrease in muscle passive tension. Shaded line represents the distribution of measured ECRB sarcomere length. (Redrawn from Fridén & Lieber, 1994, Fig. 4, p. 273.)

tension is maximum in the ECRB at a sarcomere length of 3.8 μm, tension in the descending limb of this length-tension curve in Figure 4 decreases at the rate of 77% maximum tension/μm. Stated the other way around, 0.3 μm of sarcomere shortening corresponds to a 22% increase in muscle force. Since the strength of active muscle force represents the multiplication of muscle force times the wrist joint moment arm (Lieber & Boakes, 1988), wrist extensor strength can be predicted as a product of muscle force and wrist moment arm.

Recently we compared sarcomere length changes in the two architecturally different wrist extensors, the extensor carpi radialis longus (ECRL) and ECRB during wrist joint rotation in 3 patients using the method in Figure 4. We found a significant difference between the slopes of the sarcomere length-joint angle relationships. The slope for ECRB relationship was about 50% greater than that of ECRL, which is about the same proportion as the ratio between fiber lengths—ECRL fibers (76 mm) are about 50% longer than ECRB fibers (48 mm). These data suggest that the moment arm of the two muscles at the wrist joint are approximately equivalent. As a result, we would predict that ECRL would generate active force over a greater range of motion than would ECRB. This type of fiber length disparity between synergists is not unprecedented. For example, the rabbit tibialis anterior (TA) and extensor digitorum longus (EDL) have approximately the same moment arm at the ankle joint but have muscles fibers that are significantly different in length. Thus, it appears that the musculoskeletal system may be matched such that high-gear and low-gear muscles are juxtaposed in order to permit generation of a significant joint moment at a variety of angular velocities.

It is interesting to speculate regarding the long-term effect of surgical procedures that alter sarcomere length. It is likely that adaptation of the number of sarcomeres in series would occur as described by Williams and Goldspink (1973) for immobilization of the cat soleus muscle. Their demonstration of sarcomere number regulation, which tended to return sarcomere length to optimum, provides a compelling reason to believe that sarcomere number could stabilize postoperatively to produce the original sarcomere length range. The time course of this adaptation could be determined from external wrist torque measurements using a musculoskeletal model similar to that developed by Zajac and colleagues for the human lower limb (Delp et al., 1990; Hoy, Zajac, & Gordon, 1990). Obviously, this information would improve our understanding of the design and plasticity of the human musculoskeletal system.

3. IMPLICATIONS FOR TENDON TRANSFER

Treatment of the spinal cord injured patient remains one of the great challenges of medical rehabilitation engineering. A common surgical procedure directly intervening with hand function is tendon transfer. That means moving the insertion site of a muscle to a new location to substitute for lost or impaired function. Tendon transfers can restore lost function, correct flexion contractures, and improve cosmesis (Keenan, 1987). In addition, new transfers are now possible in conjunction with the use of neural prostheses (functional electrical stimulation), which promise even greater functional restoration than was previously obtainable.

Surgical tendon transfers in the upper extremity are commonly used to restore lost function after trauma, stroke, and neuromuscular disease. Traditional guidelines used to decide which specific donor muscle should be used for a particular tendon transfer consider morbidity caused by loss of the donor muscle, muscle availability, route of transfer, and functional synergy and the surgeon's experience and preference. Less attention has been paid to the specific contractile characteristics of the donor muscles themselves or the specific length at which the muscle should be attached. Brand, Beach, and Thompson (1981) presented a description of forearm muscle work capacity based on muscle mass and fascicle length measurements. Lieber and and

Brown (1992) developed a quantitative model for muscle property comparison. Such anatomical studies on cadaveric specimens do provide insights into muscle function, but it is even more desirable to obtain intraoperative data from living human tissue that could be applied to tendon transfer procedures.

What are the consequences of tendon transfer? If the surgical procedure moves the muscle insertion so that muscle fiber length increases, we would immediately observe an increased moment arm. As the joint rotates, the amount of sarcomere length change per joint angle rotation increases. Thus, muscle force changes over a narrower range of motion. As a result of increased moment arm, active range decreases, and the joint angle at which muscle force is maximum changes. Since the joint angle corresponding to maximum muscle force is now even farther from the angle at which the maximum moment arm occurs, a torque (strength) decrease would occur simply because the angles at which optimal muscle and joint properties occur are different. In other words, weakness can be observed because of a change in muscle fiber length, not just a change in the muscle's ability to generate tension. In the long term, the muscle will add sarcomeres and compensate for the increased moment arm. As more sarcomeres are added, three events will take place: (1) active range of motion will increase; (2) torque will increase; and (3) joint angle at which maximum strength occurs will shift. If this complete adaptation does not occur, it is obviously important to transfer donor muscles that are architecturally similar to the muscles whose function they are replacing.

The physiological and biomechanical rationales for many tendon transfers are not clear. The normal torque generating system must be understood before rational decisions can be made regarding surgical procedures that involve it. It is clear that skeletal muscle architecture, neural drive, muscle moment arm, and tendon properties are the central components of the torque generating system and that interaction between them results in the particular shape of the torque profile. However, questions remaining are: How should muscle force and excursion of donor muscles be matched to their intended function? When a muscle is surgically transferred, at which sarcomere length should the muscle be set? Does the neuromuscular system adapt following transfer? If so, how should this adaptation be exploited during rehabilitation? Is spastic muscle qualitatively different than normal muscle? Does spastic muscle represent a model of overuse or disuse?

5

Individuated Finger Movements

Rejecting the Labeled-Line Hypothesis

MARC H. SCHIEBER

1. INTRODUCTION

Individuated finger movements—those in which one or more fingers move relatively independently of the movement or posture of other fingers or more proximal parts of the arm—underlie our ability to manipulate objects, and to express cognitive output in acts like typing or playing musical instruments. Control of such finger movements often is tacitly assumed to be exerted via labeled lines from the brain to each finger (Figure 1). Each finger is assumed to be moved by its own set of flexor and extensor muscles, and in turn each set of muscles is assumed to be controlled from a somatotopically distinct region of the primary motor cortex (M1). This labeled-line hypothesis suggests that control of the primate hand is analogous to control of a robotic hand via separate software channels, servo amplifiers, and motors for each digit.

But as I review here, recent studies indicate that the primate hand is controlled quite differently. Whenever any given finger is moved, many different muscles are active, some muscles acting to move that finger and other muscles acting to stabilize other fingers. Externally observable movement

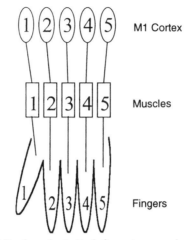

FIGURE 1 The labeled-line hypothesis. Each finger is assumed to be flexed and extended by its own muscles, which in turn are assumed to be controlled from somatotopically arranged and spatially separate regions of the primary motor cortex (M1).

results from the net effect of tension generated by all the active muscles. In M1, activity occurs throughout the hand area no matter which finger is moved. These findings challenge the labeled-line hypothesis, suggesting instead that movement of any given finger is controlled by a network of neurons distributed throughout the M1 hand area. Via its connections with the spinal cord, this network activates the combination of muscles needed to produce the intended finger movement. This distributed control system for the fingers, though initially appearing more complex than a labeled-line mechanism, may permit efficient generation of an extensive movement repertoire.

2. PERFORMANCE OF AN INDIVIDUATED FINGER MOVEMENT TASK

To study how the nervous system generates individuated finger movements, rhesus monkeys (*Macaca mullata*) were trained to flex and extend each digit of the right hand and the right wrist in response to visual cues (Schieber, 1991). A monkey placed its right hand into a manipulandum that separated the digits into different slots. At the end of each slot, each fingertip lay between two microswitches, one of which the monkey closed by flexing that digit, the other by extending. The wrist could also flex and extend. The monkey viewed a panel of light-emitting diodes (LEDs) that informed him continuously which switches were open or closed, and, at pseudorandom intervals, instructed him which switch to close within 700-ms to obtain a reward. If the monkey closed any other switch during the reaction time, movement time, or during a 500-ms final hold period, that trial was aborted without reward. Strain gages mounted on the microswitch lever arms provided a continuous analog signal representing the position of each finger. Trials requiring either flexion or extension of different fingers or of the wrist were presented in a pseudorandom rotation.

Figure 2 shows typical examples of the finger movements made by a monkey in performing this task. Digits are referred to in the figure by number: 1 for the thumb through 5 for the little finger, and W for the wrist. During some movements, such as thumb flexion, little motion occurred in any digit other than the thumb. During other movements, however, some of the noninstructed digits moved considerably. When the monkey was required to flex his middle finger, for example, the index and ring fingers flexed somewhat as well. During still other movements, some digits actually moved in the wrong direction; for example, as the monkey flexed his little finger, the

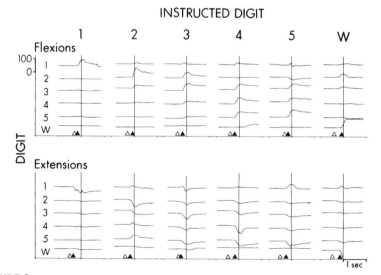

FIGURE 2   Finger movements in single trials. Each frame shows 6 vertically stacked analog traces representing the simultaneous motion of digits 1 (thumb) through 5 (little finger) and of the wrist (W) during a single instructed movement trial. From left to right, successive frames show trials in which the monkey was instructed to move digit 1 to 5 or the wrist. In each frame, an open triangle above the time base marks illumination of the red instruction/trigger LED; a solid triangle, the onset of motion in the instructed digit; a vertical line, the time of switch closure. Data for each digit have been normalized on a 0–100 scale: 0 being extension switch closure; 100, flexion switch closure. (Modified with permission from Schieber, 1991.)

index finger actually extended. Each simultaneous trajectory of all five fingers and the wrist therefore will be described as an instructed movement of a given digit in a given direction, recognizing that each instructed movement may involve some motion of noninstructed digits. For brevity, an instructed movement can be referred to by the number of the instructed digit and the first letter of the instructed direction (f for flexion; e for extension). In spite of the movement of noninstructed digits, in each instructed movement the instructed digit moved more than any other digit. Hence movements 1f through 5f and Wf involved a systematic progression of which digits moved, from the more radial to the more ulnar digits, and then the wrist.

3. THE EXTRINSIC FINGER MUSCLES AND THEIR ELECTROMYOGRAPHIC ACTIVITY

Why should the monkeys move their noninstructed digits so much, when theoretically moving the instructed digit alone would provide optimal task performance? In part, the answer to this question may lie in the structure of the extrinsic finger muscles. The fingers are flexed and extended primarily by the long extrinsic muscles, whose bellies lie in the forearm and whose tendons pass across the wrist to insert on the digits. Unlike most muscles elsewhere in the body, several of these muscles give off multiple insertion tendons. In humans, four extrinsic muscles give off only a single tendon to a single digit: flexor pollicis longus (FPL), extensor pollicis longus (EPL), extensor indicis proprius (ED2), and extensor digiti quinti proprius (ED5); whereas three larger muscles each give tendons to all four fingers: flexor digitorum profundus (FDP), flexor digitorum superficialis (FDS), and extensor digitorum communis (EDC). In the macaque, however, EPL is the only extrinsic extensor or flexor that gives a tendon to a single digit. FPL is not separate from FDP, which gives tendons to all five digits. The macaque homologs of ED2 and ED5—extensor digiti secundi et tertii proprius (ED23) and extensor digiti quarti et quinti proprius (ED45)—each give tendons to two digits. And FDS and EDC each give tendons to all four fingers. Given the multitendoned structure of the extrinsic muscles, the reverse question arises: How can these muscles produce movement of one digit without producing equivalent motion of other digits?

One possible answer would be that the intrinsic muscles of the hand, rather than the extrinsics, could be responsible for flexing or extending only one finger at a time. Each intrinsic muscle—interosseus, lumbrical, or (in macaques) contrahentes—originates in the palm, passes the metacarpophalangeal joint (MCP) volar to its axis of rotation, and then inserts dorsally on the extensor apparatus of a single finger. Intrinsics thus can contribute to flexion of the MCP joint and to extension of the proximal and distal interphalangeal joints (PIP and DIP) of each finger. Rather than controlling the overall flexion and extension of the digits, therefore, the intrinsic muscles act mainly in controlling the configuration of a given digit's phalanges at the MCP, PIP, and DIP joints, and in controlling abduction/adduction motion about the MCP joint (Basmajian, 1978; Brandell, 1970; J. R. Close & Kidd, 1969; Landsmeer & Long, 1965; Leijnse et al., 1992; Long, 1968; Long & Brown, 1964; Long et al., 1970; Spoor, 1983). The intrinsic muscles are unlikely to account for individuation of flexion and extension finger movements.

A second possible answer would be that each multitendoned finger muscle, though nominally a single muscle, might have multiple functional subdivisions, with a different subdivision serving the tendon to each finger. Although anatomically a single muscle, functionally the nervous system could turn these different subdivisions on and off like different muscles. This would provide a set of functionally different muscles for each digit, as conceived of in the labeled-line hypothesis. Indeed, recent studies of a number of feline monotendoned muscles have shown that a single muscle (as defined by gross anatomy) may contain a number of neuromuscular compartments, each of which consists of a separate pool of motor units whose muscle fibers are clustered in a distinct region of the muscle belly (Chanaud, Pratt, & Loeb, 1991; English, 1984; English & Weeks, 1987; Loeb, 1989). Electromyographic (EMG) studies have demonstrated that the neuromuscular compartments in a single muscle can be differentially activated, indicating that the motoneuron pool for these muscles functionally contains more than one subpool.

One indication of neuromuscular compartmentalization can be branching of the muscle nerve outside the muscle belly; a separate primary muscle nerve branch then enters each compartment of muscle fibers. Examination of the innervation of macaque multitendoned finger muscles suggested such branching only for FDP, whose muscle nerve divides into separate branches for the radial, ulnar, and accessory regions of the belly (Serlin & Schieber, 1993). Because of the tendon structure of the macaque FDP, however, these different regions do not act on single digits. The radial region, FDPr, flexes digits 1, 2, and 3, and the ulnar region, FDPu, flexes digits 3, 4, and 5. The other multitendoned finger muscles receive multiple nerve twigs whose muscle fiber territories likewise do not serve single tendons. A second indication of functional subdivisions can be found in differential EMG activity recorded from different regions of the muscle. EMG studies in monkeys performing the individuated finger movement task provided evidence of functional subdivisions in FDP, but not in other muscles (Schieber, 1993; 1995). Recordings from FDPr showed marked EMG activity during instructed movement 2f and moderate activity during 3f, but none during 4f or

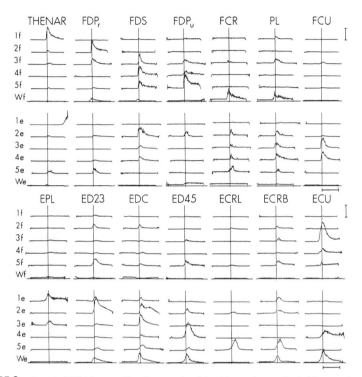

FIGURE 3 A typical EMG recording from each of the 14 muscles studied. All examples shown are from monkey K. Horizontal calibration bar represents 1 s. The vertical calibration bar represents different numbers of arbitrary integrated EMG units for different recordings: Thenar, 1000; FDPr, 1000; FDS, 500; FDPu, 500; FCR, 250; PL, 500; FCU, 750; EPL, 250; ED23, 1000; EDC, 1000; ED45, 1000; ECRL 750; ECRB 1000; ECU, 1000. (Reproduced with permission from Schieber, 1995.)

5f. Recordings from FDPu showed marked activity during 5f, moderate activity during 4f, little during 3f, and none during 2f. These differential patterns of EMG activity indicate that the macaque FDP contains at least two functional subdivisions, though neither subdivision acts on only one finger. Still, available evidence of functional subdivisions in the multitendoned muscles is inadequate to account for individuation of flexion and extension finger movements.

Consider, therefore, a third possible answer: that different movements in which one finger moves more than others could be produced by different combinations of activity in a set of multitendoned muscles. This possibility was explored by recording EMG activity from 14 muscles: thenar; flexor digitorum profundus, radial region (FDPr); flexor digitorum profundus, ulnar region (FDPu); flexor digitorum superficialis (FDS); flexor carpi radialis (FCR); palmaris longus (PL); flexor carpi ulnaris (FCU); extensor pollicis longus (EPL); extensor digiti secundi et tertii (ED23); extensor digitorum communis (EDC); extensor digiti quarti et quinti (ED45); extensor carpi radialis longus (ECRL); extensor carpi radialis brevis (ECRB); and extensor carpi ulnaris (ECU). All of these are forearm muscles that act on the fingers or wrist, except for the thenar muscles, which were included to account for thumb flexion, during which no forearm muscle was active.

Figure 3 shows examples of typical EMG recordings from each of these muscles during each of the twelve instructed movements. For each muscle, a column shows a stack of 12 histograms of EMG activity during the 12 different instructed movements, the 6 flexions above (1f to Wf) and the 6 extensions below (1e to We). Each histogram was compiled in 10-ms bins from the pulse frequency representation of integrated EMG activity recorded during 8 to 13 correctly performed trials of that instructed movement, with data aligned at the onset of movement in the instructed digit (vertical line), and smoothed with a 20-ms moving window. Inspection of the column for each muscle shows that most muscles were active during more than one instructed movement. Conversely, inspection of the row for each instructed movement shows that most instructed movements involved activity in multiple muscles.

EMG activity during three instructed movements (1f, 3f, and 5f) is described in more detail as examples. During 1f, the thenar muscles were active, and all 13 of the other muscles were silent. Hence the thumb flexed with little movement of other digits. During 3f, three flexor muscles were active: FDPr, FDS, and FDPu. This could have put the greatest total tension on digit 3. But contraction of these multitendoned muscles would also have tended to flex digits 2, 4, and 5, which in fact did flex to some extent during 3f. ECRB and ECU also were active during 3f, presumably to stabilize the wrist against the flexing torques produced by FDPr, FDS, and FDPu. During 5f, FDS and FDPu were active, but not FDPr. This could have put the most flexing tension on digit 5, with some flexing tension also exerted on digits 4, 3, 2, and the wrist. To prevent excessive flexion of these digits, the monkey apparently activated ED23 and ED45. The contraction of ED23 could have produced the extension of digit 2 seen during 5f. The observed movements of both instructed and noninstructed digits during different instructed movements thus might be accounted for by different combinations of activity in multitendoned muscles.

The possibility that different combinations of multitendoned muscle activity might produce the observed finger movements was explored further with a simple model based only on each muscle's recorded EMG activity, and its anatomical connections to the fingers and/or wrist (Schieber, 1995). Each digit's motion (or lack thereof) was quantified as the slope of the relatively linear trajectory formed by plotting the position of that digit as a function of the position of the instructed digit during a given instructed movement ($S_{i,j}$, Schieber, 1991). This slope was close to 0 if the digit remained still during the movement, and closer to 1 the more the digit moved. The slope of any digit for any movement should be the result of the activity in all the muscles ($b = 1$ to q) that act on that digit. Therefore, the slope of the ith digit during the jth instructed movement ($S_{i,j}$) was modeled as the sum of the EMG activity change in each muscle during a given movement ($A_{b,j}$), weighted by a constant that represented the coupling of each muscle to each digit ($C_{b,i}$), which was the same for all movements.

$$S_{i,j} = \sum_{b=1}^{q} C_{b,i} \times A_{b,j}$$

In the model, each muscle was allowed to affect only those digits upon which it can act mechanically *in vivo*. Experimental data were available for the motion slopes ($S_{i,j}$) and the EMG activity changes ($A_{b,j}$), but not for the coupling constants ($C_{b,i}$). These constants therefore were iteratively adjusted with a simple gradient descent algorithm to optimize the fit of the slopes calculated by the model to the slopes derived from experimental data.

With constants optimized, the values calculated by the model fit the data quite well (Figure 4). The model calculated that during 1f, thenar muscle activity will flex the thumb, but other digits will remain still. During 3f, the model calculated that activity in FDPr, FDS, and FDPu will flex digits 2 through 5, but digit 3 will flex the most. During 5f, the model calculated that activity in FDPu and FDS will flex digit 5 more than digit 4 (whose flexion is checked by ED45), and that contraction of ED23 will extend digit 2. Errors in the model's fit of the data varied from small differences in the amplitude of the slope calculated for particular digits during a given movement, equivalent to a few degrees or a fraction of a millimeter of actual finger movement (e.g., digit 4 during 3f), to a discrepancy in the direction of movement of a given finger (e.g., digit 5 during 2e). Such errors might indicate that the finger movements are affected by activity in muscles not included in the present study.

Nevertheless, the simplicity with which the model provided a satisfactory overall fit to real finger movements supports the notion that these individuated movements of different fingers were produced largely by different combinations of activity in the multitendoned extrinsic finger muscles. Production of individuated movements by the model (or by the real muscles) requires that different muscles have different actions on the various digits. But the muscles that flex and extend the fingers need not provide independent motors for each digit as assumed in the labeled-line hypothesis, which should therefore be rejected (see Figure 9). Instead, most digits are moved by a set of muscles, many of which simultaneously affect multiple digits.

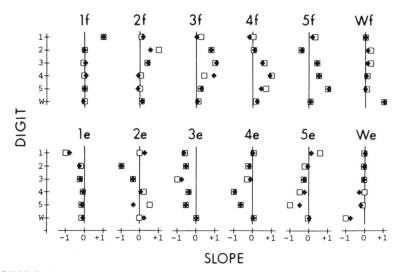

FIGURE 4 Fit of slopes ($S_{i,j}$) computed by the model (♦) to slopes derived from experimental data (□) for each digit (i) during each instructed movement (j). In the model, each muscle (h) was allowed to affect only those digits upon which it can act mechanically *in vivo*. A muscle's contribution to the slope of a particular digit during a given instructed movement then was computed as that muscle's EMG activity change during the movement ($A_{h,j}$) multiplied by a weighting constant specific for that muscle–digit coupling ($C_{h,i}$). These constants, which were the same for all 12 instructed movements, were iteratively adjusted to optimize the fit between the slopes computed by the model and the target values derived from experimental data. (Reproduced with permission from Schieber, 1995.)

A system of multitendoned muscles actually provides certain control advantages. Most finger movements made by primates (including humans) are not isolated movements of a single digit. Perhaps the most frequent use of the fingers, for example, is grasping an object with the whole hand. Grasping is used dozens of times per day by any individual. For a monkey holding a tree branch, or for a painter holding a brush in one hand and a ladder with the other, grasping must not fail. A system that produces this fundamental mode of finger movement with one or two large muscles driven by a simple control system might be more reliable than a system with several slim muscles whose coordinated action requires a complex controller acting over several channels. Besides a reliability advantage, the simpler control system would use fewer control resources for a frequently performed, fundamental movement. When less frequent, but more highly individuated finger movements are needed (e.g., when monkeys groom single hairs, or when the painter relaxes by playing the piano), additional muscles would be called into play via additional control resources, combining with the fundamental mode to sculpt the grasp into a highly individuated movement (Schieber, 1990).

4. NEURON ACTIVITY IN THE PRIMARY MOTOR CORTEX

M1 is an essential part of the brain for the production of individuated movements. Deficits of individuated movements are the first to appear and last to recover when lesions affect M1 in humans (Twitchell, 1951). In macaques, after experimental lesions of M1, or lesions of its projection in the corticospinal tract, almost all motor functions recover rapidly except for relatively independent finger movements, which may never return to normal (Hamuy, 1956; Lawrence & Kuypers, 1968; Travis, 1955a).

The labeled-line hypothesis predicts that movements of different fingers are controlled from spatially separate parts of M1. This concept is derived largely from summary drawings, like the homunculus of Penfield (Penfield & Rasmussen, 1950), or the simiusculus of Woolsey (Woolsey et al., 1951), which show a motor map of the contralateral body parts laid out on the M1 cortex, including a different region of M1 cortex for each digit. Such a detailed somatotopic organization of M1 suggests that neurons located laterally in the M1 hand region should be preferentially related to thumb movements, and that neurons located medially should be preferentially related to movements of the little finger.

Experimental studies have indicated, however, that the somatotopy of M1 is not as spatially segregated as might be suggested by the homunculus or simiusculus (reviewed in Schieber, 1990). These studies provide evidence of (1) *convergence* of output from large, overlapping cortical territories onto single muscles, and (2) *divergence* of output from any given cortical site to multiple muscles. *Convergence* of cortical output is evident from studies in which electrical stimulation (either surface stimulation or intracortical microstimulation) at numerous points distributed over a large expanse of M1 evoked movement of the same body part, contraction of the same muscle, or even action potentials in the same motor unit (P. Andersen, Hagan, Phillips, & Powell, 1975; D. R. Humphrey, 1986; Kwan, MacKay, Murphy, & Wong, 1978; Leyton & Sherrington, 1917; Penfield & Boldrey, 1937; Sato & Tanji, 1989; Uematsu et al., 1992; Woolsey, Erickson, & Gilson, 1979; Woolsey, 1951). *Divergence* of output from single M1 neurons to multiple muscles has been shown both anatomically and physiologically. Anatomically, intracellular horseradish peroxidase staining has demonstrated terminal ramifications from single corticospinal axons in the spinal motoneuron pools of multiple muscles (Shinoda et al., 1981). Physiologically, spike-triggered averaging has demonstrated facilitation of EMG activity in more than one muscle at monosynaptic latencies following the spikes of single M1 neurons (Buys et al., 1986; Cheney & Fetz, 1980, 1985; Cheney, Fetz, & Palmer, 1985; Fetz & Cheney, 1980; Lemon et al., 1986). In addition to convergence and divergence of M1 outputs, extensive horizontal *interconnections* between subregions within the M1 hand area have recently been demonstrated (Huntley & Jones, 1991). Convergence, divergence, and interconnections within the M1 hand area would tend to diminish the somatotopic specificity of control from M1.

However, the labeled-line hypothesis still could hold at the cortical level if all the convergence, divergence, and intrinsic interconnections of M1 were arranged such that when neurons in one discrete subregion of the M1 hand area were activated, certain muscles would contract, others would be inhibited, and the result would be movement of one finger. Activation of another subregion of M1 would produce movement of another finger, and so forth. Single neuron recordings in the M1 hand area of monkeys trained to perform the visually cued individuated finger movement task, however, failed to support this hypothesis (Schieber & Hibbard, 1993). Figure 5 shows the activity of two different M1 hand area neurons during each of the 12 visually cued individuated finger movements. These two neurons discharged during different numbers of instructed movements. Neuron K13409 discharged consistently only during instructed movement 2e. Neuron K11301 discharged during some of the instructed movements, but not during others.

To determine whether a given neuron was related to an instructed movement, for each trial the neuron's spike count in 10-ms bins was smoothed with a 50-ms moving window, and a Kolmogorov-Smirnov test ($p < .05$) was used to evaluate differences between the distributions of counts per bin during a 500-ms control period preceding movement and each of three test periods: the premovement period, the movement period, and the total reaction period. A neuron was considered consistently related to the instructed movement if its discharge during any one of the three test periods was significantly different from control in 90% or more of the correctly performed trials. If so, the neuron's firing frequency change was computed as the peak (or trough) during the total reaction time plus movement time of the average histogram minus the firing frequency averaged over the control period.

This statistical analysis confirmed significant and consistent discharge of K13409 only during movement 2e, and of K11301 during 9 of the 12 instructed movements: 3f, 4f, Wf, 1e, 2e, 3e, 4e, 5e, and We. Figure 6 shows the distribution in two monkeys (K and S) of the number of M1 neurons that discharged in a significant and consistent manner during different numbers of instructed movements. Although many neurons in each monkey were related to just one or two instructed movements, many neurons were also related to four, five, six, or more. The fact that single M1 neurons could be related to so many instructed movements made it unlikely that separate regions of the M1 hand area would be differentially activated during movements of different fingers.

Somatotopically arrayed regions of M1 for the different fingers were further sought by examining the activity in different mediolaterally located electrode penetrations. If the thumb were controlled from the most lateral portion of the M1 hand area, and the little finger from the most medial, then

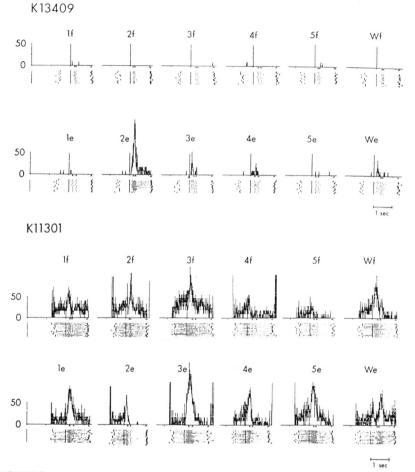

FIGURE 5 Activity of two M1 neurons during each of the 12 instructed finger movements. In each frame, the dot raster below shows the neuron's discharge during 10–13 successful trials of the indicated instructed movement, aligned at the onset of the instruction signal (vertical line); the histogram above is formed as the average of these rastered data (binwidth 10 ms). Tick marks in each raster line indicate (1) movement onset in the instructed digit, (2) end of movement, and (3) reward delivery; carat marks beneath each histogram indicate the average time of these events. (Data for neuron K11301 is redrawn with permission from Schieber & Hibbard, 1993. Copyright © 1993 AAAS.)

lateral electrode penetrations should record more neurons related to thumb movements and medial penetrations should record more neurons related to little finger movements. Figure 7 shows the locations at which electrode penetrations in monkey K passed through the M1 hand area. Penetrations A and B were typical electrode penetrations down the anterior bank of the

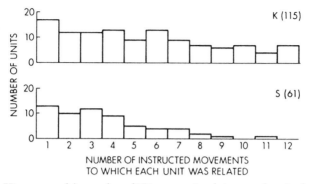

FIGURE 6 Histograms of the number of M1 neurons (totals in parentheses) related to different numbers of instructed movements in monkeys K and S. (Redrawn with permission from Schieber & Hibbard, 1993. Copyright © 1993 AAAS.)

central sulcus. Figure 8 shows the significant activity changes for each of the neurons recorded in these two penetrations. Also shown is the depth at which successive neurons in each penetration were recorded, to indicate that cortex along the entire anterior bank of the central sulcus was sampled. No predominance of activity related to thumb movements (1f and 1e) was evident in the neurons recorded in the most lateral penetration, A. Nor was activity related

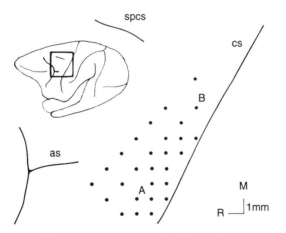

FIGURE 7 Location of electrode penetrations in the M1 hand area of monkey K. The left hemisphere region enlarged for the figure is indicated by the rectangle in the inset (*upper left*). Solid lines represent: cs, the central sulcus; as, the spur of the arcuate sulcus; spcs, the superior precentral sulcus. Calibration bars at lower right indicate medial (M) and rostral (R). Activity of single neurons from two selected penetration locations, A and B, is summarized in Figure 8.

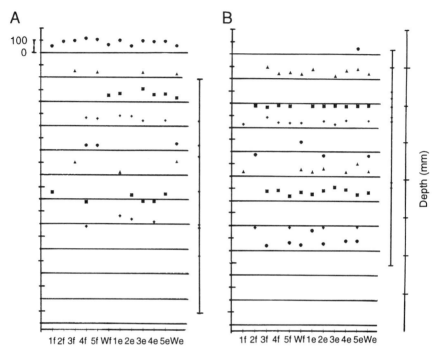

FIGURE 8 Stacked displays of neuronal activity from two penetration locations, A and B (see Figure 7), selected to provide a lateral to medial sampling of the M1 hand area in monkey K. Each tier in a stack represents the firing frequency changes of a single neuron during each of the 12 instructed movements to which that neuron's discharge was significantly and consistently related. Successive tiers in a stack represent the activity of different neurons recorded at successive depths at the penetration location, indicated by diamonds on the vertical bar to the right of each stack (scale, *far right*). In each penetration, neurons related to various subsets of the 12 instructed movements were found. Although penetration A was more lateral, no preponderance of neurons related to thumb movements (1f, 1e) was observed. Conversely, though penetration B was more medial, no preponderance of neurons related to movements of the little finger or wrist (5f, 5e, Wf, We) was observed.

to little finger movements (5f and 5e) predominant in the neurons recorded medially in penetration B. Instead, neurons related to any of the 12 instructed movements were found at any mediolateral recording site. And conversely, neurons related to any given finger movement were spread throughout the M1 hand area.

Even though neurons active during any given finger movement were found spread throughout the hand area, the possibility remained that bulk of neuronal activity occurred in different, somatotopically arranged regions during movement of different fingers. This possibility was examined by calculating the centroid of significant firing frequency changes for the population of recorded M1 neurons during each instructed movement (Schieber & Hibbard, 1993). Rather than being spread somatotopically, the centroids for the 12 movements all were clustered together near the middle of the M1 hand area. Though the M1 hand area extended for 8 to 9 mm along the central sulcus, the centroids were spread over only 2 mm. When the coordinates of the centroids for the 10 finger movements (wrist movements excluded) were projected on a line tangential to the central sulcus, a significant somatotopic spread was detected only in monkey K (Spearman's rank correlation coefficient, $r_s = 0.69$, $n = 10$, $p < .05$).

Neuron recordings in monkeys thus demonstrated that individuated movements of different fingers involve overlapping populations of neurons distributed throughout the M1 hand area. In humans, similar overlap in the M1 territory controlling different fingers is suggested by recent positron emission tomography studies of regional cerebral blood flow. These studies indicate that, although a shift in the locus of peak activity occurs when

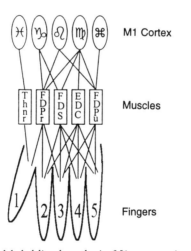

FIGURE 9 Rejecting the labeled-line hypothesis. M1 neurons (symbols) can no longer be viewed simply as "upper motor neurons" that control a given muscle or movement. Though some M1 neurons project to only one muscle, other M1 neurons have projections that diverge to multiple muscles. Conversely, many multitendoned muscles receive converging input from cortical neurons distributed over large territories that overlap extensively. When individuated finger movements are performed actively, many M1 neurons discharge during a number of different finger movements. Neurons active during movements of different fingers are not spatially segregated into somatotopically organized regions within the M1 hand area. Different individuated finger movements thus appear to be produced by different combinations of activity in a spatially distributed population of M1 neurons.

humans move their thumb versus their index finger (Grafton, Woods, & Mazziotta, 1993), the entire territory activated is similar during index finger abduction or middle finger flexion/extension versus opening/closing of the whole hand (Colebatch, Deiber, Passingham, Friston, & Frackowiak, 1991; Remy, Zilbovicius, Leroy-Willis, Syrota, & Samson, 1994). In both humans and monkeys, then, activity appears throughout the entire hand area no matter which finger is moved.

Thus the cortical level of the labeled-line hypothesis, in which separate regions of M1 cortex control each finger, should also be rejected (Figure 9). Though some M1 neurons may be active during movement of one particular digit, many other M1 neurons participate in controlling movements of more than one digit. Different individuated finger movements appear to be produced by activity in spatially overlapping populations of M1 neurons. Control of any particular finger movement involves a neural network distributed throughout the M1 hand area.

5. DISCUSSION

Given that (1) multiple muscles are activated in most individuated finger movements, and (2) each muscle is represented in a wide M1 territory that overlaps with the territories of other muscles, one might have predicted that the M1 hand area would show distributed activation during any individuated finger movement. But why should somatotopic representation in M1 be so diffuse, while other cortical maps are comparatively precise? In the primary somatosensory cortex (S1), for example, the fingers are mapped in an orderly somatotopic arrangement, with a distinct zone representing the glabrous skin of each digit (Kaas, Nelson, Sur, Lin, & Merzenich, 1979; Pons, Wall, Garraghty, Cusick, & Kaas, 1987).

The body surface is a two-dimensional sheet, however, and therefore can be mapped in a point-to-point fashion onto the two-dimensional cortical surface of S1. In contrast, the bodily movements controlled by M1 occur in three-dimensional space, and therefore cannot be mapped simply onto a two-dimensional cortical surface. Moreover, the "mapping" in M1 might be a problem of even higher order than representing three dimensions in two. Consider the possibility that activation of each muscle might be represented as a dimension in a q-dimensional space, where q is the number of muscles. Different points in this q-dimensional muscle space then would represent the different combinations of muscle activity needed to produce various movements. M1 neurons would need to activate each muscle to the coordinate appropriate for achieving an intended movement. Though some M1 neurons might activate only one muscle, others might activate several muscles in fixed proportion, which could be represented as yet another dimension. In this entirely speculative scheme, although the resulting movements would occur over time in three-dimensional space, the controlling computations would take place in an imaginary space of much higher dimensionality. Such a space could not be simply mapped on the two-dimensional surface of the cerebral cortex.

Furthermore, the point-to-point map of the body surface in S1 is based in part on the likelihood that contiguous points on the sensory surface will receive similar stimulation at the same time. For example, when a complex object is palpated with the fingers, a pair of receptors at adjacent locations on the middle finger is more likely to receive similar stimuli at any instant than is a pair consisting of one receptor on the middle finger and a second receptor on the ring finger. Correspondingly, in the normal S1 cortex, layer IV neurons with receptive fields covering both the middle and ring fingers are not found. But if the skin surfaces of the middle and ring fingers are joined surgically such that receptors on the middle and ring finger skin are more likely to receive similar simultaneous stimulation, then neurons with receptive fields bridging the surfaces of the two fingers appear in S1 (Allard, Clark, Jenkins, & Merzenich, 1991). These findings suggest that some efficiency of neural processing is gained by representing inputs with a high likelihood of simultaneity together in the cortex.

For M1 the problem is quite different. Generating an extensive repertoire of movements requires that numerous different combinations of simultaneous muscle activity all be represented. If processing efficiency is highest when different output elements of M1—whether muscles, body parts, or movements—with a high likelihood of simultaneity are represented close together, then intermingling representations of M1 output elements might provide the most efficient representation of numerous possible combinations. Suppose, for example, that FDPr was represented next to FDS, but not next to EDC. Then the neural processing for a movement that combined activation of FDPr and FDS might be quite efficient, but the processing for a movement that combined FDPr and EDC would be correspondingly inefficient. The greatest overall efficiency for both movements might be had in an intermingled representation of FDPr, FDS, and EDC. If all possible combinations are equally likely, then segregating the representations of FDPr, FDS, and EDC might produce no gain in overall efficiency, and perhaps even a net loss. Intermingling M1's representations of numerous different output elements might thus be well suited for efficient generation of an extensive movement repertoire.

The fact that the somatotopy of M1 is not as discrete as that of S1 does not mean that M1 has no somatotopic organization. The degree of somatotopic segregation of M1's representation of different body parts correlates roughly with their mechanical separation, however. In primates and humans, the face is represented laterally, the lower extremity medially, and the upper extremity in between. Each of these major body parts has dozens of muscles whose activity can be combined in numerous different ways to produce different movements. But since these major body parts are largely (though not entirely) mechanically independent, individuated movements within a particular major body part can be controlled with relatively little concern for the movement of other major body parts. Correspondingly, perhaps, representations of major body parts overlap little in M1.

In primates and in humans, the distal portion of each extremity is most densely represented caudally in M1, and the proximal portion rostrally. Movements of the distal and proximal portions of a given extremity are more mechanically interdependent, however, and M1 outputs to distal and proximal parts of the limb correspondingly show substantial overlap and/or intermingling. Within the macaque hand, movements of different fingers rely on the the same set of muscles, and M1's representations of these different muscles and finger movements are extensively intermingled. What about M1's representation of the hand in humans? As described above, the muscles of the human hand potentially provide a greater degree of independence for digits 1, 2, and 5 than that found in the macaque hand. It might not be surprising, therefore, to find somewhat more somatotopic separation of these digits in the human M1. Nevertheless, generation of any given finger movement is likely to involve distributed activation of neurons spread throughout the M1 hand area.

ACKNOWLEDGMENTS

The author wishes to thank M. Hayles for editorial assistance and B. Forgash for help in preparing the manuscript. This work was supported by Grant R01-NS27686 from the National Institute of Neurologic Disorders and Stroke, USA.

6

Multiple Hand Representations in the Motor Cortical Areas

ERIC M. ROUILLER

1. INTRODUCTION

Four principal regions of the cerebral cortex are commonly recognized as contributing directly to the control of hand movements: the primary motor cortex (M1 or area 4); the supplementary motor area (SMA or mesial part of area 6); the premotor cortex (PM or lateral part of area 6); and the cingulate motor areas (CMA or areas 23 and 24). Further subdivisions of SMA, PM, and CMA have been proposed on the basis of either functional or morphological criteria, or both. For instance, SMA has been divided into a rostral part and a caudal part (M. Wiesendanger, 1986), more recently referred to as pre-SMA and SMA-proper (Matsuzaka, Aizawa, & Tanji, 1992; Tanji, 1994) or area F6 and area F3, respectively (Luppino, Matelli, Camarda, Gallese, & Rizzolatti, 1991; Luppino, Matelli, Camarda, & Rizzolatti, 1993; Matelli, Luppino, & Rizzolatti, 1991). In PM, two major regions are generally distinguished from each other (Boussaoud & Wise, 1993a, 1993b; D. R. Humphrey & Tanji, 1990; Kurata, 1991, 1994): the dorsal PM (PMd) and the ventral PM (PMv). In CMA, three subareas have been proposed (Dum & Strick, 1991). The aim of the present chapter is to illustrate how neuro-anatomical methods, used in combination with electrophysiology to identify various motor cortical areas, may be used as a basis to investigate their contrasting functions in monkeys. The chapter first overviews previous studies available in the literature, followed by a summary of a new experiment

Hand and Brain
Copyright © 1996 by Academic Press, Inc. All rights of reproduction in any form reserved.

aimed to establish the pattern of connectivity of the hand representations of M1 and SMA with the cervical motoneurons.

A large zone of M1 is involved in the selection of distal muscles of the contralateral forelimb, as shown by intracortical microstimulation (ICMS) that can evoke movements of the fingers or the wrist (H. Asanuma & Rosén, 1972; Donoghue, Leibovic, & Sanes, 1992; D. R. Humphrey, 1986; Sato & Tanji, 1989; Sessle & Wiesendanger, 1982). These data showed that there is a representation of muscles and movements, which is not continuous as one would expect from the classical homunculus view. On the contrary, there are multiple representations of each muscle and of each type of movement. In other words, when moving a stimulating electrode in the hand area of M1, the same muscle can be activated at various foci separated from each other by zones related to other muscles. Similarly, a given movement (e.g., flexion of the thumb) can be evoked by stimulating several distinct cortical foci, inter- mingled with other foci whose stimulation evoke different movements (e.g., extension of the thumb, movements of other fingers). A similar picture of primate motor cortex has been derived from spike-triggered averaging of electromyographic activity (see Lemon, 1988 for review), showing that "clus- ters of output neurones can facilitate the same muscle and each muscle is represented many times over in the cortex." This arrangement is believed to subserve the control of complex muscle synergies, such as those involved in coordinated movements of the fingers (see Hepp-Reymond et al., Chapter 3; Schieber, Chapter 5).

Electrophysiological and neuroanatomical investigations have demon- strated the existence of additional hand representations in nonprimary motor areas. Thus, in SMA-proper, a distal hand representation has been found. However, it appears spatially restricted, whereas the representation of more proximal forelimb muscles is more prominent (Kurata, 1992; Luppino et al., 1991, 1993; Macpherson, Marangoz, Miles, & Wiesendanger, 1982; M. Wies- endanger, 1986). The precise balance between the distal and proximal repre- sentation of the forelimb in SMA remains controversial (Mitz & Wise, 1987; Tanji, 1994). Nevertheless, the earlier idea that SMA comprises mainly a representation of proximal and axial muscles should be discarded given con- sistent observations of widespread activity in SMA elicited by movements limited to the hand (Ikeda, Lüders, Burgess, & Shibasaki, 1992, 1993; Kristeva, Cheyne, & Deecke, 1991; Lang, Cheyne, Kristeva, Beisteiner et al., 1991; Okano & Tanji, 1987; Tanji, 1994; Tanji, Okano, & Sato, 1988; Thaler, Rolls, & Passingham, 1988). At present it is unclear whether there is also a hand representation in pre-SMA, because there is difficulty in eliciting move- ments with ICMS in this region (Matsuzaka et al., 1992; M. Wiesendanger, 1986). The distinction between pre-SMA and SMA-proper is justified, how- ever, by a number of differences regarding corticocortical connections, sen- sory inputs, and neuronal activity related to the preparation, programming, and execution of movements (see Tanji, 1994, for review; Halsband, Matsuzaka, & Tanji, 1994).

At least one, possibly two, hand representations have been identified in CMA (Dum & Strick, 1992; Luppino et al., 1991; Morecraft & Van Hoesen, 1992; Muakkassa & Strick, 1979). In PM, it has been suggested that there are several hand/arm representations, one to two in PMd and two in PMv (Gentilucci et al., 1988; Kurata & Tanji, 1986; Maier, de Luca, Herrmann, & Hepp-Reymond, 1992; Muakkassa & Strick, 1979; Rizzolatti et al., 1988; Rizzolatti, Scandolara, Matelli, & Gentilucci, 1981a, 1981b). In the other commonly used nomenclature defined by Rizzolatti and collaborators, PMd includes the area F2 caudally and F7 rostrally, while in PMv a distinction is made between F4 caudally and F5 rostrally (Gentilucci et al., 1988; Matelli, Luppino, Fogassi, & Rizzolatti, 1989; Matelli et al., 1991; Rizzolatti, et al., 1988).

The topographic distribution of multiple hand representations has been visualized neuroanatomically by plotting the location of corticospinal (CS) neurons projecting to the cervical cord (C5 to T1). This involves injection of a retrograde tracer in the region of the spinal cord containing the motoneuron pools associated with the distal muscles of the forelimb (Dum & Strick, 1991; He, Dum, & Strick, 1993; Hutchins, Martino, & Strick, 1988; Macpherson, Wiesendanger, Marangoz, & Miles, 1982; Martino & Strick, 1987; Figure 1). Counting CS neurons thus identified revealed that about 50% of them originated in M1 (Dum & Strick, 1991). In the nonprimary areas, the proportions of CS neurons ranged from 12 to 19% in SMA, 12 to 21% in PM, and 17 to 21% in CMA, as determined in two monkeys (Dum & Strick, 1991). A subset of CS neurons in M1 send axons to the pool of distal motoneurons where they establish direct contacts with motoneurons, as demonstrated in an elegant intracellular recording and staining study by Lawrence, Porter, and Redman (1985). Such direct corticomotoneuronal (CM) connections are believed to be a prerogative of primates, which provides them with the ability to perform independent, finely controlled movements of the fingers (Armand, 1982; Bortoff & Strick, 1993; Kuypers, 1981; Lawrence, 1994; Lemon, 1993; Maier et al., 1993; Porter & Lemon, 1993; see also Armand et al., Chapter 7).

Assuming a classical hierarchical organization of the motor system, it might be supposed that the hand representation of M1 is mainly concerned with the selection of the appropriate muscles to perform the desired movement, whereas non-M1 hand representations would be more concerned with attention, selection, preparation and programming of hand movements, essentially for complex tasks (Tanji, 1994, for review; Wise, 1985). In this perspective, the hand representations in SMA, CMA, and PM would exert their influence on motor cortical outflow indirectly, mainly via their dense projection to the hand representation of M1 (Porter, 1990). However, the presence of CS neurons in most non-M1 hand representations suggests that

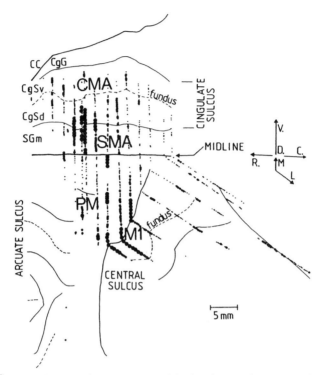

FIGURE 1 Unfolded cortical representation of the distribution of corticospinal neurons in the left hemisphere, after injection of a retrograde tracer (CB=cholera-toxin B subunit) in the contralateral hemicervical cord. Labeled neurons are represented by individual dots when they were isolated, whereas moderate and dense clusters of stained neurons are represented by medium- and large-size filled circles, respectively. R, rostral; C, caudal; V, ventral; D, dorsal; M, medial; L, lateral. M1, primary motor cortical area; PM, lateral premotor cortical area; SMA, supplementary motor cortical area; CMA, cingulate motor cortical area. Note the presence of retrogradely labeled corticospinal neurons in CMA, SMA, PM, and M1. CC, corpus callosum; CgG, cingulate gyrus; CgSd, dorsal bank of cingulate sulcus; CgSv, ventral bank of cingulate sulcus; SGm, medial wall of frontal gyrus. Data derived from retrograde tracing studies (Rouiller, Babalian et al., 1994. Copyright © 1994 Springer-Verlag).

they may also act more directly on the cervical motoneurons controlling hand muscles, in parallel to the CS neurons in M1. A crucial question then is whether CS neurons in non-M1 hand representations make direct CM contacts, as has been shown for the CS neurons located in M1. Later in this chapter this issue is addressed experimentally to investigate whether the hierarchical view is correct. However, first we review a number of studies that have differentiated the functions of the various motor cortical areas. These data were derived from observations on human beings, such as functional imaging of brain function when performing a motor act or by assessing motor deficits in patients. Other data originate from various experimental approaches performed in subhuman primates (monkeys), including recording of single neurons when performing a motor task, observations of motor deficits associated to a surgical lesion or reversible inactivation of a given motor cortical area, as well as neuroanatomical experiments aimed to establish connectivity in the motor pathway.

2. FUNCTIONAL SPECIALIZATION OF SMA AND M1

2.1 SMA and Bimanual Control

Several lines of evidence derived from early electrical stimulation (Penfield & Jasper, 1954) and lesion studies (Travis, 1955b) suggest that SMA is a bilaterally organized motor area. One specific function proposed for SMA was the control of bimanual movements (see Halsband et al., 1993; M. Wiesendanger, 1993; M. Wiesendanger, Wicki, & Rouiller, 1994). Skillful bimanual performance, as in knitting or playing a musical instrument, requires precise coordination of both hands in space and time. The execution of such bimanual skills is impaired by mesial frontal cortical lesions, with or without encroaching on the corpus callosum (see M. Wiesendanger, 1993, for review). Callosal transections alone do not significantly affect learned bimanual

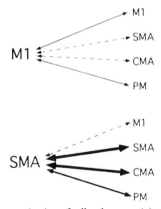

FIGURE 2 Summary of the organization of callosal connectivity of the hand representations of M1 and SMA (*left*) with the motor cortical areas of the opposite hemisphere (*right*). CMA, cingulate motor areas; PM, premotor cortex. Dashed lines indicate sparse projections (e.g., M1 with SMA and M1 with CMA). For the other connections, three grades of line thickness represent light (thin line), moderate (medium line), and dense (thick line) projections, respectively. The hand representation of M1 is modestly connected to the opposite motor cortical areas, as compared to the hand representation of SMA. Data derived from anterograde and retrograde tracing studies (Rouiller, Babalian et al., 1994).

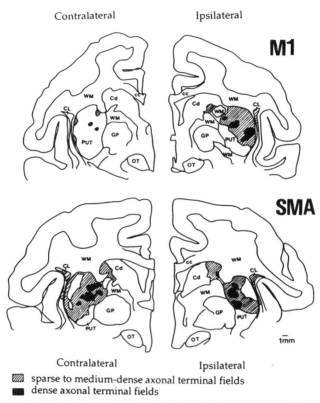

Contralateral   Ipsilateral

☒ sparse to medium-dense axonal terminal fields
■ dense axonal terminal fields

FIGURE 3   Corticostriatal projection originating from the hand representation of M1 (*top*) or from the hand representation of SMA (*bottom*). As a result of BDA injection in the hand representation of the right M1 or SMA, the location of corticostriatal axon terminals were plotted, distinguishing dense axon terminals (black zones) from sparse to medium-dense axon terminals (hatched zones). As illustrated here for a representative frontal section, the projection to the putamen and caudate nucleus originating from M1 is mainly ipsilateral, whereas the projection originating from SMA is clearly bilateral. (Wiesendanger, Rouiller, Kazennikov, and Perrig, in press)

skills (Preilowski, 1975). It is therefore possible that mesial cortex may exert a hierarchically superior role (supramotor coordinating structure) for bimanual action. This is referred to as the bimanual hypothesis (see Wiesendanger et al., Chapter 14). The above clinical data are consistent with data from monkeys, showing that unilateral lesions of the mesial cortex, including SMA, induce obligatory bimanual movements (C. Brinkman, 1984; C. Brinkman & Porter, 1979; J. Brinkman, 1981).

In searching for possible anatomical bases for bimanual coordination, we recently established with a neuroanatomical study that the hand representation of SMA has a strong callosal interconnection with the non-M1 motor cortical areas of the opposite hemisphere. In contrast, the hand representation of M1 exhibited only weak callosal projections (Rouiller & Babalian, et al., 1994). The topology and density of the callosal connectivity of the hand representations of SMA and M1 are summarized in Figure 2. Greater bilateral connectivity of the SMA hand area, as compared to that of M1, is also found in the corticostriatal projections. The SMA hand area sends dense projections to the striatum on both sides, while the hand area of M1 projects mainly to the ipsilateral putamen and caudate nucleus (Figure 3; see also Jürgens, 1984; Künzle, 1978; Leichnetz, 1986; McGuire, Bates, & Goldman-Rakic, 1991; Withworth, LeDoux, & Gould, 1991). In this context, one might speculate whether the more bilateral SMA projections might be linked to a different pattern of corticospinal projection; thus, the proportion of CS axons directed to the ipsilateral cervical cord is significantly higher when originating from the hand area of SMA than from the hand area of M1. This question is also addressed experimentally later in the chapter.

2.2 Subcortical Inputs to SMA and M1

The motor cortical areas receive inputs from the basal ganglia and the cerebellum via the thalamus. On the basis of comparisons of the spatial distributions of pallidothalamic and cerebellothalamic terminal fields in the thalamus as well as the zones of origin of thalamocortical projections, it has been postulated that M1 and SMA receive segregated subcortical inputs, from the cerebellum and the basal ganglia, respectively (Ghez, 1991; Schell & Strick, 1984). Such a segregation of subcortical inputs to M1 and SMA has been taken as anatomical support for their functional differentiation in the control of movements.

The idea that there is segregation of subcortical inputs to M1 and SMA was based on indirect comparisons of data derived from tracer experiments carried out in separate series of animals. Recently, we reexamined this hypothesis using a multiple tracer approach in the same animal (Rouiller, Liang, Babalian, Moret, Wiesendanger, 1994). Briefly, two retrograde tracers were injected in the hand representations of M1 and SMA, initially defined by intracortical microstimulation, in order to label the corresponding thalamocortical neurons. In addition, two anterograde tracers were injected in the output nuclei of the cerebellum (cerebellar nuclei) and the basal ganglia (globus pallidus) in order to label the cerebellothalamic and pallidothalamic terminal fields, respectively. This protocol was conducted in three monkeys. The spatial distributions of the four markers were then studied in four adjacent sections of the thalamus.

The spatial distribution of the various markers in the thalamus formed complex mosaics that transgressed cytoarchitectonic boundaries. Thus, the location of pallidothalamic and cerebellothalamic terminal fields, as well as

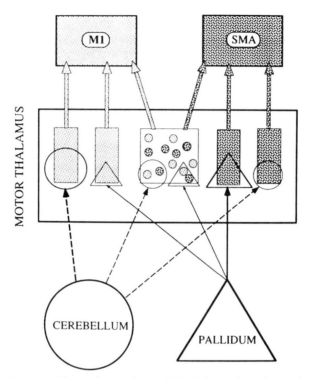

FIGURE 4 Summary of how subcortical, transthalamic inputs from the cerebellum and the basal ganglia reach in a mixed fashion the hand representations of M1 and SMA (see text for a detailed description). In the motor thalamus, rectangles represent the territories projecting to the hand representations of M1 (two leftmost rectangles) or SMA (two rightmost rectangles), determined by retrograde neuroanatomical tracing; in addition, territories in the thalamus were found to contain mixed, adjacent clusters of neurons projecting to one or the other hand representations (small circles in the square). Derived from anterograde neuroanatomical tracing conducted in the same animal, circles and triangles illustrate how cerebellothalamic and pallidothalamic projections may have access to the territories projecting to the hand representations of M1 and SMA.

the location of the clusters of thalamocortical neurons projecting to M1 and SMA, did not fall really within one or the other of the thalamic nuclei. The data are summarized in Figure 4. In the motor thalamus, there were subregions containing neurons projecting to the hand representation of M1 and not to the hand representation of SMA (two leftmost rectangles in the middle part of Figure 4). Correspondingly, there were subregions containing neurons projecting to the hand representation of SMA and not to M1 (two rightmost rectangles in the middle part of Figure 4). In addition, there were subregions containing mixed (adjacent) clusters of neurons projecting either to the hand representation of M1 or to the hand representation of SMA (square in the middle of Figure 4). Note that only rare neurons in this zone were double-labeled, indicative of a divergent projection to both M1 and SMA, in line with a previous report (C. Darian-Smith, Darian-Smith, & Cheema, 1990).

The spatial distribution of the pallidothalamic and cerebellothalamic terminal fields are represented in Figure 4 by triangles and circles, respectively. An important observation was the absence of overlap of these two projections in the thalamus. However, given the overlap of the thalamic zones projecting to the cerebral cortex, it appeared that cerebellothalamic terminal fields overlapped territories projecting to the hand representation of M1 (as expected), but also territories projecting to the hand representation of SMA. Correspondingly, the pallidothalamic terminal fields overlapped territories projecting to the hand representation of SMA (as expected) but also territories projecting to the hand representation of M1. It can be concluded that the hand representations of M1 and SMA receive mixed subcortical inputs, via the thalamus, from the basal ganglia and the cerebellum. This conclusion is consistent with reports of pallidal inputs to M1, based either on transneuronal retrograde tracing using viruses as marker (Hoover & Strick, 1993) or on double-labeling data (Inase & Tanji, 1995). The existence of cerebellar inputs to the hand representation of SMA has been proposed before on the basis of a transneuronal retrograde tracing approach, using WGA-HRP at high concentration (R. Wiesendanger & Wiesendanger, 1985). Mixing of cerebellar and pallidal inputs in the hand representations of M1 and SMA is also consistent with previous electrophysiological data (Jinnai, Nambu, Tanibuchi, & Yoshida, 1993; Nambu, Yoshida, & Jinnai, 1988, 1991).

Although these projections are mixed, it is significant that, in quantitative terms, cerebellothalamic terminal fields overlapped more thalamic territories projecting to M1 than to SMA (circle larger on the left than on the right, in the middle part of Figure 4). Correspondingly, pallidothalamic terminal fields appeared to overlap more territories projecting to the hand representation of SMA than to M1 (triangle larger on the right than on the left, in the middle part of Figure 4). In conclusion, subcortical inputs from the cerebellum and the basal ganglia to the hand representations of M1 and SMA are mixed, but with a predominance of cerebellar inputs to M1 and of pallidal inputs to SMA.

2.3 Functional Specialization Reflected by Activity of Single Neurons

As illustrated above for the hand representation of SMA, anatomical data based either on experimental lesions and/or tracing of connections are useful methods to address the question of the functional specialization of a motor cortical area. However, they need to be complemented by data derived from functional methods. Among them, recording of single unit activity has proven to be an appropriate method for investigating the possible contribution of various motor cortical areas or subcortical motor structures to different aspects of voluntary movement control. An enormous amount of data is available in the literature related to the neuronal activity reflecting motor control, and therefore only a few particular aspects will be briefly reviewed here. In particular, the activity of single neurons has been shown to be associated with coding of *force* or its first derivative (Evarts, 1968; Georgopoulos, Ashe, Smyrnis, & Taira, 1992; Hepp-Reymond & Maier, 1991; Maier et al., 1993; Wannier et al., 1991: in M1 and PM), the *direction of intended limb movements* (Caminiti & Johnson, 1992; Caminiti, Johnson, Burnod, Galli, & Ferraina, 1990; Caminiti, Johnson, Galli, Ferraina, & Burnod, 1991; Caminiti, Johnson, & Urbano, 1991; Georgopoulos, Kalaska, Caminiti, & Massey, 1982; Georgopoulos, Kettner, & Schwartz, 1988; Kalaska & Crammond, 1992; Schwartz, Kettner, & Georgopoulos, 1988: in M1, PM, and in the parietal cortex), *limb velocity* (A. R. Gibson, Houk, & Kohlerman, 1985: in the red nucleus), *target position* (G. Alexander & Crutcher, 1990b: in M1 and SMA), detailed *movement trajectory* (Hocherman & Wise, 1990: in M1, PM, and SMA), and the *order of sequential movements* (Mushiake, Inase, & Tanji, 1990; Tanji & Shima, 1994: in SMA). Some of these associations are already reflected in the preparation phase, that is, before the actual movement (G. Alexander & Crutcher, 1990a; Chen, Hyland, Maier, Palmeri, & Wiesendanger, 1991; Fetz, 1992; Kurata, 1989; Matsuzaka et al., 1992; Mushiake, Inase, & Tanji, 1991; Shima et al., 1991; Tanji et al., 1988; Wise, 1985; Wise, di Pellegrino, & Boussaoud, 1992).

In the context of the postulated specialization of SMA for the control of bimanual movements, single unit data recorded in our laboratory from monkeys performing a bimanual task showed some degree of specialization. Neurons influenced by movement of the ipsilateral hand were more numerous in the hand representation of SMA than in M1 (Kazennikov et al., 1996). In line with this observation, previous data already suggested that, in contrast to M1, a majority of neurons in secondary motor areas are not only related to contralateral movement execution but also participate in ipsilateral and bilateral movements (Tanji et al., 1988). However, a restricted subregion of the hand representation of M1 has been characterized as an output zone specialized for bilateral hand movement (Aizawa, Mushiake, Inase, & Tanji, 1990).

Neuronal activity was studied in SMA-proper, pre-SMA, M1, and PM in monkeys performing arm movement sequences prompted by either external or internal cues (Halsband, Ito, Tanji, & Freund, 1993; Halsband et al.,

1994). This study confirmed that PM neurons were more active when the sequence of movements was visually triggered. In contrast, SMA neurons were more active when the sequential motor task was internally generated. In this respect, preSMA appeared to occupy a position intermediate between SMA-proper and PM. Activity in pre-SMA was more related to externally cued movements during the premovement period, but a clear relationship to internally cued movements was found during movement. In contrast to non-primary motor areas, neurons in M1 showed no preferential relationship to external or internal cues to action.

There is evidence that lateral PM (PMd and PMv) is involved in dealing with the selection and guidance of movements based on visual information (Wise, 1985). In line with this, both PMd and PMv receive projections providing visual information, originating from the prefrontal cortex or, more directly, mainly from parietal visual or polysensory areas (see Boussaoud, di Pellegrino, & Wise, in press, for review). In PMd, a recent study demonstrated the presence of neurons whose activity reflected the direction of upcoming limb movement but varied with eye position (Boussaoud, 1995).

In PMv, many neurons in area F4 responded to visual stimuli presented in the space around the animal. Their receptive fields were not coded retinotopically but rather in body-centered coordinates, possibly providing a stable frame of reference for visually guided movements (Fogassi et al., 1992). However, these data were challenged by the observation of a large proportion of neurons in PMv that were influenced by gaze (Boussaoud, Barth, & Wise, 1993). It has been suggested that the area F4 contains a representation of proximal movements (Gentilucci et al., 1988). In contrast, the rostral part of PMv, the area F5, appeared to be mainly a representation of distal movements (Rizzolatti et al., 1988). Neurons in F5 have firing properties reflecting more specific goal-related motor acts rather than single movements made by the animal. For instance, some neurons were active specifically in relation to precision grip movements, while others were active in relation to finger prehension, and a third class of neurons in relation to power grip movements (Rizzolatti et al., 1987,1988). Some neurons in F5 were not only active in relation to such movements performed by the monkey, but also in a similar manner when the same movements were performed by the experimenter while the monkey observed the scene (di Pellegrino, Fadiga, Fogassi, Gallese, & Rizzolatti, 1992).

2.4 Functional Specialization Revealed by Transient Inactivation

The traditional approach of making a permanent surgical lesion of a structure in order to assess the behavioral deficit has provided important information on brain function in general. However, this approach has a number of disadvantages making the interpretation of the data sometimes uncertain, including difficulty in controlling the location and extent of the lesion, presence of long-term plastic changes induced by the lesion, the development of compensatory strategies, and limited use of the same animal. Techniques of regional reversible inactivation by pharmacological or cooling methods have been introduced in order to eliminate (or at least minimize) these difficulties. Reversible inactivations allow assessment of immediate deficits without the need for postoperative recovery delay, which can permit long-term plastic changes. The absence of such changes can be checked in terms of the disappearance of the deficits as soon as the action of the cooling or pharmacological agents is removed (performance should return to normal). A major advantage of the technique is the possibility of inactivating, in separate sessions, various motor structures in the same animal. This is extremely important when experiments are conducted in subhuman primates, whose training for complex motor tasks can represent a considerable time investment.

Inactivation in monkeys of the midline cerebral cortex (essentially SMA) by local cooling has demonstrated that the neuronal discharge patterns in the hand representation of M1 associated with the performance of a wrist movement are only lightly modulated by SMA activity. Moreover, performance of the task was not affected by SMA inactivation (E. M. Schmidt, Porter, & McIntosh, 1992). Pharmacological reversible inactivation has allowed identification of the respective contribution of the two major subdivisions of PM, namely PMd and PMv (Kurata & Hoffman, 1994): PMd was found to be more important than PMv for the preparation of a forthcoming movement, whereas PMv was more involved in the execution of visually guided movements.

2.5 Functional Imaging of Motor Activity

Specialization of a brain region for a particular information processing operation can be investigated using techniques of functional imaging. In humans, regional cerebral blood flow (rCBF) measured with positron emission tomography (PET) has allowed reexamination of the somatotopic map of M1, SMA, and CMA (see, e.g., Grafton, Woods, Mazziotta, & Phelps, 1991; Matelli et al., 1993; Paus, Petrides, Evans, & Meyer, 1993), as well as functional differentiation between M1 and SMA. For example, Roland, Larsen, Lassen, and Skinhoj (1980) compared rCBF when subjects performed a simple finger movement (activity in M1 only), a complex finger movement (activity in M1 and SMA), or mental planning of a complex finger movement (activity in SMA only). Measurements of rCBF showed a significant increase of activity in PM, SMA, and the superior parietal association cortex in relation to movement selection (Deiber et al., 1991): the activation was larger in

SMA when the movement selection was triggered with internal cues as compared to external cues. Comparison of simple versus complex finger movements showed in the latter case a significant rCBF increase in SMA and the ipsilateral primary motor and somatosensory areas (Shibasaki et al., 1993). A study of the functional anatomy of visually guided finger movements with rCBF in humans showed that SMA contributes in part to the sequencing of movements, while the parietal cortex plays a role in the integration of the spatial attributes during selection of movements, (Grafton, Mazziotta, Woods, & Phelps, 1992).

In the context of motor learning, rCBF has allowed the topography of distinct fields in M1 and PM to be related to the execution or preparation of reaching movements and to visuomotor learning (Kawashima, Roland, & O'Sullivan, 1994). Further, rCBF data showed more prominent activation in the lateral PM and the parietal association cortex during new learning, while SMA (and the basal ganglia) were more activated during performance of the prelearned sequence (Jenkins, Brooks, Nixon, Frackowiak, & Passingham, 1994), in general agreement with previous reports (Roland, Meyer, Shibasaki, Yamamota, & Thompson, 1982; Seitz & Roland, 1992). Distinct stages have been recognized during motor learning on the basis of rCBF data: association areas are preferentially activated in early stages of motor learning while cerebello- and striatomotor-cortical loops are preferentially activated in later stages (see Halsband & Freund, 1993, for review).

Using functional magnetic resonance imaging, which provides better spatial resolution than rCBF, multiple hand representations were observed in the mesial cortex (SMA and CMA) of humans performing sequential finger movements (Tyszka, Grafton, Chew, Woods, & Coletti, 1994), with differential activation depending on whether the movement was imagined or really executed.

A segregation of the movement-activity taking place in M1 and SMA has been postulated on the basis of magnetic and electric fields measurements (see Lang, Cheyne, Kristeva, Lindinger, & Deecke, 1991, for review). In particular, selective activation of SMA was observed in musicians tapping bimanually different rhythms (Lang, Obrig, Lindinger, Cheyne, & Deecke, 1990).

3. EXPERIMENTAL INVESTIGATION OF THE CORTICOSPINAL CONNECTIVITY OF THE HAND REPRESENTATIONS OF SMA AND M1

Given the above review, an unresolved question is whether the hand representations in nonprimary motor cortical areas can directly address hand motor neurons. In this section, we consider an experiment in which the mode of apposition of CS axons originating in the hand representation of M1 is compared with that from the hand representation of SMA. The experimental work was based on a neuroanatomical tracing method (double-labeling) under electrophysiological guidance. The same data serve to address a second question formulated around the bimanual hypothesis: what is the anatomical basis for the greater bilateral representation of the hand motor function in SMA compared to M1? More precisely, do CS axons originating from SMA project more densely to the ipsilateral cervical cord than the CS axons coming from the hand representation of M1?

3.1 Methods

Two monkeys were anesthetized with ketamine (5 mg/kg body weight) injected intramuscularly. The hand representations of M1 and SMA were identified by intracortical microstimulation (ICMS), eliciting contralateral hand movements (Macpherson, Marangoz et al., 1982; Rouiller, Babalian et al., 1994; Rouiller, Liang et al., 1994; Sessle & Wiesendanger, 1982). Then, under pentobarbital anesthesia (30 mg/kg body weight), the anterograde neuroanatomical tracer BDA (biotinylated dextran amine; 5% in distilled water; see Veenman, Reiner, & Honig, 1992) was injected in low-threshold ICMS sites (Figure 5), in M1 (monkey 1) or in SMA (monkey 2). A total volume of about 10 µl was distributed at six to seven points along three distinct ICMS electrode penetrations.

Over the next three weeks, ICMS was repeated in daily sessions using a rectangular metallic chamber chronically implanted for consistency of stimulation. These sessions served to better define the borders of the hand representations in M1 or in SMA and also to ensure the BDA would be transported anterogradely along the CS axons all the way down to the cervical cord. In a last session, ICMS was repeated at the sites where BDA was injected, in order to precisely identify the contralateral hand muscles activated. Then, under ketamine anesthesia, massive injections of the retrograde neuroanatomical tracer CB (cholera-toxin B subunit, 0.5% in distilled water; see Ericson & Blomqvist, 1988; Liang & Wan, 1989; Luppi, Sakai, Salvert, Fort, & Jouvet, 1987) were made in the intrinsic hand muscles, in extrinsic extensors and flexors of the fingers as well as in extensors and flexors of the wrist (approximate total volume 100 µl; Figure 5). Following a survival time of 4–6 days to allow the retrograde transport of CB to the cervical motoneurons, the animal was reanesthetized with a lethal dose of pentobarbital and perfused through the heart with 300 ml saline followed by 4000 ml fixative (4% paraformaldehyde in 0.1M phosphate buffer, pH 7.4). The brain and the spinal cord were dissected, postfixed for 3–4 hours and soaked in 10% and 30% sucrose solutions in phosphate buffer for 2 and 6 days, respectively.

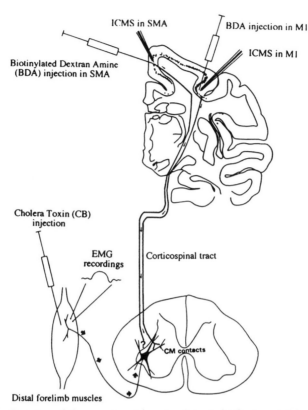

FIGURE 5 Overview of the experimental protocol to study the connectivity of CS axons originating from the hand representation of M1 or SMA with cervical motoneurons controlling distal forelimb muscles. The hand representation in M1 or SMA was defined by intracortical microstimulation (ICMS), where the anterograde tracer biotinylated dextran amine (BDA) was injected by pressure. The retrograde tracer cholera-toxin B subunit (CB) was injected in the muscles of the contralateral forelimb activated by the ICMS. Sections of the cervical cord were treated to visualize the two tracers in order to determine to what extent the CS axon terminals overlap the motoneuronal pools.

The two hemispheres and the cervical cord were cut into sections (50 μm thick) in the frontal stereotaxic plane on a freezing microtome and seven series of sections were collected separately. Sections were treated to demonstrate the presence of the tracers as previously described in detail for CB (Rouiller, Liang et al., 1994) and BDA (Rouiller, Babalian et al., 1994; Rouiller, Moret, & Liang, 1993). Among the seven series of sections, one was Nissl-stained, a second was reacted for CB, a third for BDA, whereas two to three additional series were reacted for both BDA and CB. The latter sections were first treated to demonstrate BDA, using nickel intensification in order to obtain a black reaction product in CS axons, followed by CB immunohistochemistry without nickel intensification in order to obtain a brown reaction product in motoneurons. As previously shown, CB provides a relatively extensive labeling of the motoneuronal dendrites in addition to a dense staining of the soma (Liang, Moret, Wiesendanger, & Rouiller, 1991; Rouiller, Liang, Moret, & Wiesendanger, 1991).

3.2 Results

EMG recordings   Prior to injection of CB in the distal muscles (see Section 3.1), ICMS was performed at the location in SMA where BDA was injected in monkey 2. Muscle activity (EMG) recordings were derived from two silver wire electrodes placed on the skin above the left wrist extensors, while ICMS was applied to the distal hand representation of the right SMA (monkey 2). EMG responses were averaged over 200 stimulations in SMA, consisting of three consecutive pulses (0.2 ms duration) separated from each other by 3 ms, and presented once every second. Intensities tested ranged from 10 to 150 µA. A typical EMG recording is shown in Figure 6, where a slight modulation (facilitation) of the ongoing EMG activity was visible at 30 µA. The facilitation was more pronounced at higher intensities, with a progressively decreasing latency. At 140 µA, the latency of the facilitation was about 10 ms, which is consistent with a close relationship of the distal hand representation of SMA with the effectors. Although suggestive, these latency measures do not unequivocally demonstrate CM connectivity, as recently discussed by Babalian, Liang, and Rouiller (1993). A major difficulty here is the large variability in CS axons diameter, thus corresponding to a wide range of conduction velocities. Definitive evidence of CM contacts between CS axons originating from SMA and cervical motoneurons depends on neuroanatomical data presented in the following.

Retrograde labeling of cervical motoneurons   CB-labeled motoneurons in the cervical cord are illustrated in the photomicrograph of Figure 7 and in the camera lucida reconstructions in Figures 8 and 9. They were located in the ventral horn, forming longitudinal columns extending from C5 to T1. In individual cross-sections, the motoneurons were located laterally in the ventral horn. Their general location was consistent with a previous description of the distribution of motor columns in macaque monkeys (Jenny & Inukai, 1983): motoneurons labeled with CB in the present study were found at the cumulated locations where Jenny and Inukai found labeled motoneurons after injections of horseradish peroxidase (HRP) in forearm muscles acting on the wrist (C5 to T1), or in forearm muscles acting on the hand (C8 to T1), or in hand muscles acting on the thumb and index finger (C8 to T1).

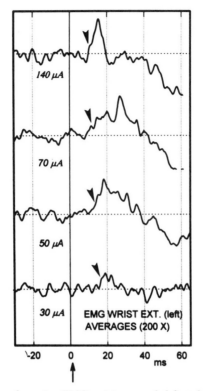

FIGURE 6 Modulation of ongoing EMG activity, recorded from left wrist extensors, in response to stimulations delivered to the hand representation of the right SMA (arrow). The four traces are the EMG responses, each averaged from 200 stimulations, to four different intensities (30, 50, 70, 140 µA). Facilitations of the ongoing EMG activity are indicated by arrowheads.

In the present work, after injection in distal muscles, CB labeled densely the soma of corresponding motoneurons, as well as the proximal dendrites. Further away from the soma, the dendritic labeling progressively decreased, fading away at a distance of 700–800 µm.

Anterograde labeling of CS axons   As a result of injection of the anterograde tracer BDA in the hand representation of M1 (monkey 1) or SMA (monkey 2), the CS axons were labeled anterogradely all the way down to the cervical cord. Therefore, the CS axons could be observed at various levels along the pyramidal tract, in particular at the pyramidal decussation. Immediately below the decussation, the respective proportions of decussated (contralateral CS projection) or undecussated (ipsilateral CS projection) axons

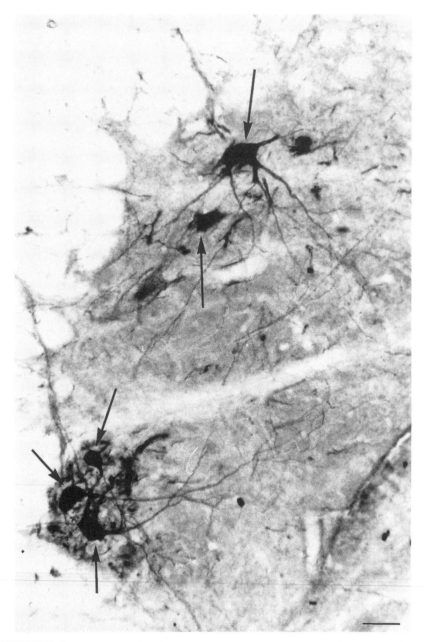

FIGURE 7 Photomicrograph of the left hemicervical cord in the zone of the group of motoneurons labeled after injection of CB in extensors and flexors of the wrist and fingers of the left forelimb in monkey 2. The soma (arrows) and proximal dendrites were densely labeled (visible in the original as brown reaction product), while distal dendrites progressively faded. Scale bar = 50 μm. (This section appears on the left of the reconstruction in Figure 9).

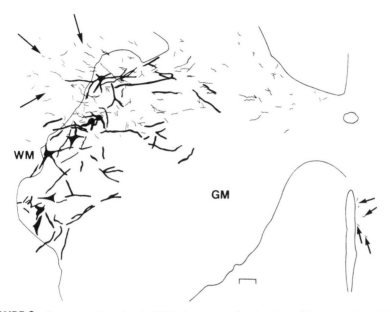

FIGURE 8   Reconstruction of an individual transverse hemisection of the cervical cord (level C8-T1) in monkey 1, showing CB retrogradely labeled motoneurons (thick lines) and anterogradely BDA-labeled CS axonal portions (thin lines). CB was injected in distal muscles of the left forelimb whereas BDA was injected in the hand representation of the right M1. Scale bar = 100 μm. Note that the somata of motoneurons are restricted to the lateral zone of the gray matter. CS axons in the opposite ventral funiculus are indicated by small, thin arrows. Thick arrows point to CS axons in the white matter, in the lateral funiculus. GM, gray matter; WM, white matter.

were established (Table 1). Although the total number of axons labeled after BDA injection was higher in monkey 1 (M1 injection) than in monkey 2 (SMA injection), the proportion of undecussated axons was comparable for both monkeys (5.3 and 6%, respectively). These data suggest that the bilateral distribution of CS axons immediately below the pyramidal decussation is comparable whether they originate from M1 or SMA.

The BDA reaction product appeared black, and was therefore easily distinguishable from the brown labeling of motoneuronal dendrites. In the white matter at C5 to T1 (the levels where motoneurons were labeled with CB), the BDA-labeled CS axons were found mainly in the lateral funiculus (contralaterally with respect to the injected hemisphere). A few labeled axons were also observed in the ipsilateral lateral funiculus (not shown) and in the ipsilateral ventral funiculus (Figures 8 and 9). From the white matter, some of the CS axons entered the gray matter, where their diameter decreased abruptly. The general distribution of the labeled CS axons in the gray matter (contralateral to the

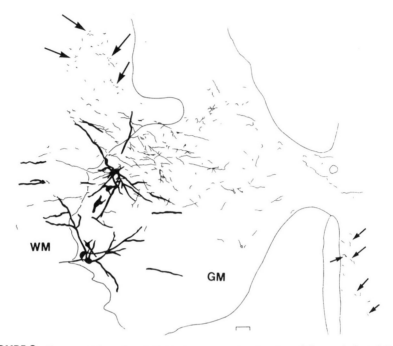

FIGURE 9 Reconstruction of an individual transverse hemisection of the cervical cord (level C8-T1) in monkey 2, showing CB retrogradely labeled motoneurons (thick lines) and anterogradely BDA-labeled CS axonal portions (thin lines). CB was injected in distal muscles of the left forelimb, whereas BDA was injected in the hand representation of the right SMA. Scale bar = 100 μm. Note that the somata of motoneurons are restricted to the lateral zone of the gray matter. Several stem axons are visible in the white matter (upper left zone, thick arrows), in the lateral funiculus. Small thin arrows point to CS axons in the opposite ventral funiculus. GM, gray matter; WM, white matter.

TABLE I   Bilateral Distribution of Corticospinal Axons in Two Monkeys as a Function of Motor Cortical Area of Origin.

	Number of axons ipsilaterally	Number of axons contralaterally	% of Ipsilateral CS axons
M1	170	3025	5.3
SMA	130	2030	6.0

Note. On the basis of biotinylated dextran amine (BDA) injection in the hand representation of M1 (monkey 1) or SMA (monkey 2), the number of labeled CS axons on each side was estimated immediately below the pyramidal decussation. The volume of BDA injected in M1 was 10.5 μl in seven sites along three penetrations; the volume of BDA injected in SMA was 9 μl in six sites along three penetrations. The injected zones were identified as part of the hand representation by intracortical microstimulation.

cortical injection), as seen on an individual transverse section, is shown in Figures 8 and 9. The general distribution of CS axonal ramifications in the contralateral cervical cord was surprisingly similar in the two animals. The CS axonal terminal arbors were focused to the Rexed laminae V–X, thus including the lateral motor nuclei of lamina IX. The projection to the medially located lamina VIII was, however, sparse in both monkeys.

At higher cervical levels (above C5), there was also in both animals a dense projection to the contralateral gray matter, directed mainly toward laminae VI and VII. In addition, on the ipsilateral side, there was a medium-dense projection terminating principally in the medial part of the spinal gray matter (lamina VIII), arising from the two ipsilateral funiculi (ventral and lateral), as well as from axons coming from the other side and crossing the midline. It seemed that this ipsilateral CS projection directed to the lamina VIII at upper cervical levels was slightly denser after injection in SMA (monkey 2) than in M1 (monkey 1). This difference is not due to a higher number of CS axons in the ipsilateral ventral and lateral funiculi after injection in SMA but rather to a more extensive ramification of the CS axons originating from SMA than those coming from M1. The ipsilateral projection, directed to the lamina VIII, is still present at lower cervical levels (C5 to T1), but it was less dense than in the upper cervical cord.

Overlap between CS axonal arbors and distal motoneurons   As illustrated in Figures 8 and 9, there is a relatively large region of overlap between the CS axon terminal zones and the motoneurons, particularly if one takes into account the relatively wide extension of their dendrites. The region of overlap covers the Rexed lamina IX (containing the motoneuronal cell bodies), as well as the more medially located lamina VII. Comparing monkey 1 and monkey 2, it appeared that the zone of overlap between CS axons and motoneurons had a roughly comparable extent for the two animals.

Corticomotoneuronal (CM) contacts   Visual examination of the sections at high magnification (1000×) allowed cases of close apposition between BDA-labeled CS axons (black) with either the soma or a dendrite of a CB-labeled motoneuron (brown), to be identified in both monkeys. Several cases of close apposition between a CS axon originating from the hand representation of M1 (monkey 1) with the soma or the dendrite of a motoneuron were observed, confirming the data reported by Lawrence et al. (1985). The new finding in the present study is that close appositions were observed between motoneurons and CS axons originating from the hand representation of SMA (monkey 2). An axosomatic apposition is illustrated in Figure 10A and B. Close apposition between another CS axon originating from SMA (monkey 2) with a motoneuronal dendrite is illustrated in Figure 10C. As mentioned above, the same types of apposition were observed in monkey 1 for CS

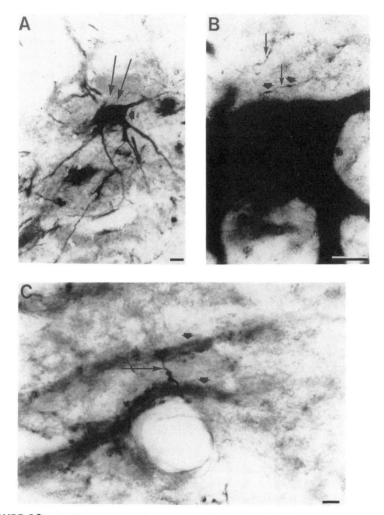

FIGURE 10 (A) Photomicrograph showing a CB retrogradely labeled motoneuron (thick arrow) in monkey 2 (see also Figure 7) with its proximal dendrites (brown reaction product) and BDA anterogradely labeled CS axonal arbors (thin arrows). Note the very thin diameter of the CS axons. Scale bar = 20 μm. (B) High magnification of the motoneuron shown in (A) with the two CS axons (arrows) near the soma. Note the presence of two boutons *en passant* on one CS axon (arrowheads). Scale bar = 10 μm. (C) Axodendritic apposition between two CB-labeled dendrites (oriented roughly horizontally, large arrowheads) and a BDA-labeled CS axon oriented perpendicularly (thin arrow), with boutons *en passant*. Scale bar = 5 μm.

axons originating from the hand representation of M1 (not shown). Although quantification of these data is not reliable, the probability of finding cases of close apposition was roughly comparable for the two monkeys, that is, for CS axons originating from M1 or SMA. Axodendritic appositions appeared more frequent than axosomatic appositions.

3.3 Discussion of Experimental Results

The present study allowed confirmation in monkeys, at light microscopic level, of the presence of close appositions between boutons on CS axons originating from the hand representation in M1 and motoneurons of the cervical cord. Corticomotoneuronal contacts for CS axons originating in M1 have been previously reported in Lawrence et al.'s (1985) outstanding work in which CS axons and motoneurons were labeled intra-axonally and intra-cellularly, respectively. The present study provides evidence that such cor-ticomotoneuronal contacts are not the sole prerogative of CS axons originating from M1: there are also close appositions between cervical motoneurons and CS axons originating from the hand representation of SMA. These data argue against a strict hierarchical organization of the motor system and are therefore consistent with the notion that M1 and SMA provide two separate motor output pathways. Therefore, SMA may be in a position to contribute to the control of hand movements, in parallel with M1. This is in line with observations that neurons in SMA are not only active during the preparation of hand movements, but also in relation to the execution of the movements itself (Chen et al., 1991; Halsband et al., 1994; M. Wiesendanger & Wise, 1992).

Although the probability of observing cases of close apposition between CS axonal ramifications and motoneurons was comparable for M1 and SMA, their number appeared relatively low. This is consistent with the observations of Lawrence et al. (1985) that "each main collateral of a CS axon establishes very few synaptic contacts, and possibly only one, with the dendrites of recipient motoneurons." However, quantification of appositions was difficult in the present material. First, only a relatively low number of CS axons were labeled with BDA (Table 1). Similarly, only a relatively small number of motoneurons were labeled. In addition, although the injections of BDA in the cortex and CB in the muscles were performed under electrophysiological control (ICMS), it is not certain whether the matching was optimal between BDA-labeled CS neurons and CB-labeled motoneurons. In particular, the cortical injection may not have been in the part of M1 and SMA with most CS projections to the injected muscles and/or the CB injection in the muscles may not have been where most end plates are located.

Another limitation of the present study is the partial labeling of the motoneuronal dendritic trees, restricted to a distance of about 800 μm. In a recent study in the rat, in which motoneurons associated to distal forelimb muscles were labeled intracellularly (Babalian et al., 1993), we have shown that the dendrites of motoneurons extend profusely, in particular in the medial direction, nearly reaching the midline of the spinal cord. It is therefore likely that the dendrites of motoneurons in monkeys also extend a long distance, and that only the proximal portion of the dendrites were visualized in the present material. This reflects the fact that filling of the motoneuron is more efficient intracellularly than by injecting the tracer in the corresponding muscles (Babalian et al., 1993; Liang et al., 1991). Consequently, it is likely that the number of close appositions observed in the present material was underestimated, since possible contacts with distal dendrites escaped detection. Another difficulty was the extremely thin diameter of some CS axonal arbors in the gray matter, at the limit of the resolution of the light microscope. For that reason, future analysis of such material at EM level is needed, in particular to confirm that the appositions observed here correspond to synapses. Ideally, a quantitative analysis of corticomotoneuronal contacts would involve an experiment in which a large number of CS axons would be labeled by BDA injections in the cortex, followed in a second step by intracellular filling of motoneurons, for which connection with the injected cortical sites had been demonstrated by intracellular responses to pulses delivered to the cortex.

The hand area of SMA is more bilaterally related to the effectors than the hand area of M1, as determined by electrical stimulation, lesion, and behavioral studies (e.g., C. Brinkman, 1984; Penfield & Jasper, 1954; Travis, 1955b; M. Wiesendanger, 1993). The present data indicate that the anatomical basis of the bilateral organization of the hand area of SMA does not derive from corticospinal projections, since the trajectories and distribution of CS axons originating from the hand areas of SMA or M1 were similar. There was only a slight difference with respect to the density of the ipsilateral projection directed to the lamina VIII (mainly at upper cervical levels): it was denser when originating from SMA than from M1. However, it is unlikely that this small difference contributes significantly to the more bilateral relationship with the effectors of SMA than with M1. More important are the significant differences between SMA and M1 observed for other efferent projections. For instance, the hand area of SMA is densely connected to the opposite frontal cortex in contrast to the hand area of M1, which is only sparsely connected with the other hemisphere (Gould, Cusick, Pons, & Kaas, 1986; Jürgens, 1984; McGuire et al., 1991; Rouiller, Babalian et al., 1994). Similarly, the corticostriatal projection originating from SMA is bilateral, whereas that from M1 is essentially ipsilateral (Jürgens, 1984; Künzle, 1978; Leichnetz, 1986; McGuire et al., 1991; Withworth et al., 1991; Figure 3 in this chapter).

4. GENERAL CONCLUSIONS

A survey of the literature related to multiple hand representations in motor cortical areas fails to show they have contrasting localized function. There is no definitive evidence that a particular motor function is associated with any one hand representation. On the contrary, various properties appear to be distributed across several hand representations, indicating that they operate in a cooperative mode. In other words, the hand representation of M1 and the nonprimary hand representations might be concerned with different but overlapping aspects of motor control, as reviewed by Georgopoulos (1994). The present study provides an anatomical basis for such a possible co-operation between the hand representations of M1 and SMA in their address-ing motor units, as both hand areas give rise to close appositions with the motoneurons of the hand muscles (in this line of thinking, see also the comparison of movement related potentials recorded from M1 and SMA: Ikeda et al., 1992).

Despite some overlap in function, hand representations in different mo-tor cortical areas do show some degree of functional specialization, some-times correlated with particular connectional properties. For instance, there are indications of a specialization of the hand representation of SMA for bimanual coordination, the sequencing of complex movements, and trigger-ing of movements based on internal cues. However, clear evidence for a specialization limited to a single area is lacking, in part because other related areas have not been investigated for the same property.

Sometimes, evidence for a functional specialization established with one method has been challenged on the basis of another approach. For instance, rCBF data suggested that SMA is involved predominantly in the control of well-practiced motor acts, as opposed to new motor sequences (Jenkins et al., 1994). This is in contrast to single unit data in SMA of monkeys, showing a marked decrease of premovement activity of single neurons in relation to a given motor task when it became overtrained (Aizawa, Inase, Mushiake, Shima, & Tanji, 1991). However, a subsequent lesion of M1 restored pre-movement activity changes in SMA, interpreted by the authors as a use-dependent reorganization of the neuronal activity in SMA (Aizawa et al., 1991). This suggests that single unit and rCBF data may not reflect the activity of the same populations of neurons. With single unit recordings, only a limited number of neurons are investigated, possibly with a bias of sampling toward a restricted subpopulation of neurons (probably the large neurons). rCBF appears to be a more general marker of activity but, of course, with a limited spatial and temporal resolution, as compared to single unit record-ings. A source of variations in the interpretation of rCBF data might be related to the use of several subjects providing an average measure. Another risk of misinterpretation of rCBF data is the definition of a threshold used to distinguish active from nonactive regions, maybe leading to an oversim-plification of the distribution of activity in the brain in relation to a given motor task. The existence of multiple cortical areas, devoted to a given modality, is a general principle of organization of the cerebral cortex, found in motor and sensory systems. The idea of cooperative operation of multiple cortical areas presents an advantage in terms of functional plasticity. One can imagine that cooperating areas may progressively substitute for the role of a related dysfunctional area, and do so more easily if functions are widely distributed rather than restricted to highly specialized, functionally unique areas.

ACKNOWLEDGMENTS

The author thanks M. Wiesendanger, O. Kazennikov, A. Babalian, and X. H. Yu for their participation in experimental sessions. Thanks are due to V. Moret for histology and A. Schwartz and J. Corpataux for taking care of the monkeys in the animal room. The experimental work was supported by the Swiss National Science Foundation (Grants No 3130–025138, 31–28572.90), the Roche Foundation (Basle, Switzerland), and the CIBA-GEIGY Jubiläums-Stiftung (Basle, Switzerland).

7

The Structure and Function of the Developing Corticospinal Tract

Some Key Issues

J. ARMAND, E. OLIVIER, S. A. EDGLEY, AND R. N. LEMON

1. INTRODUCTION

Abnormal development of descending motor systems is associated with a variety of movement disorders, yet we know little about how these systems develop. Given the importance of the corticospinal system for normal sensorimotor function of the hand, it is of special relevance to study this system. In primates, some corticospinal neurones establish a monosynaptic linkage between the primary motor cortex and spinal motoneurones, particularly those innervating hand and finger muscles. Comparative studies performed in different species of adult primates suggest that these neurones, called cortico-motoneuronal (CM) cells, are probably essential for the ability to perform relatively independent finger movements (Armand, 1982; Bortoff & Strick, 1993; see Lemon, 1993; Heffner & Masterton, 1975, 1983; Kuypers, 1981).

Among the numerous descending pathways projecting to the spinal cord, the corticospinal tract is the least mature at birth and undergoes dramatic

Hand and Brain

changes during the first postnatal days or months, depending on the species. Therefore, since skilled finger movements also develop postnatally in the primate, it is of great interest to determine which features of the corticospinal system are critical for these movements and particularly whether the development of CM connections is a prerequisite for the performance of relatively independent finger movements, as originally suggested by Kuypers (1962).

A large number of anatomical, physiological, and neurochemical changes occur before the corticospinal system reaches its full maturation. The sequence in the development of the corticospinal system is not different from that of the other descending pathways in the CNS (see Barkovich, Lyon, & Evrard, 1992). Thus, the initial stage would consist of corticospinal axons growing down the spinal cord. There is then a short "waiting period" after which collaterals enter the gray matter. The last process in the development of descending pathways is the myelination of their axons. In some species, experimental evidence also exists that during the development of the corticospinal system an excessive number of axons and synapses are formed, the excess being progressively eliminated. These exuberant corticospinal projection axons may originate from cortical areas additional to those giving rise to the corticospinal projections in the adult and may have an aberrant pattern of projection in the spinal cord (see Section 2).

Some of these changes in the corticospinal system can be employed as useful indicators to assess its maturation at different phases of development. We review a number of issues related to the development of the corticospinal system, including interspecies differences in the maturation of the corticospinal system and aberrant or exuberant projections (Section 2). The pattern of projections of the corticospinal fibers within the spinal gray matter is also considered (Section 3) and an important distinction made between corticospinal projections to the motoneurone pools and functional cortico-motoneuronal connections (Section 4). Growth in diameter of corticospinal axons and their myelination are discussed with respect to age-related changes in conduction velocity (Section 5). The use of noninvasive brain stimulation as a means of investigating corticospinal development in humans and macaque monkey is discussed (Section 6), as well as the question of the constancy of the central motor conduction time during childhood (Section 7). Finally, we examine whether changes in these different features of the corticospinal system can be related to the development of skilled finger movements (Section 8).

We refer to a number of new studies that have given useful insights into corticospinal development in different species, including humans (Alisky, Swink, & Tolbert, 1992; Eyre, Miller, & Ramesh, 1991; Khater-Boidin & Duron, 1991; Kudo, Furukawa, & Okado, 1993; K. Müller, Ebner, & Hömberg, 1994; K. Müller & Hömberg, 1992) and our own recent investigation of corticospinal development in the macaque monkey (Armand, Edgley, Lemon, & Olivier, 1994).

2. WHAT CAN WE LEARN FROM THE DEVELOPMENT OF THE CORTICOSPINAL SYSTEM IN DIFFERENT SPECIES?

The corticospinal tract is present in most mammals, although there are major differences in its origin, course, termination, and function (Armand, 1982; Heffner & Masterton, 1975, 1983; Kuypers, 1981; Nudo & Masterton, 1988; Phillips, 1971). Quite apart from these differences, direct comparison of corticospinal development across species is rendered difficult by the marked contrast in their developmental timetables (Passingham, 1985). In the developing corticospinal system, as in many others, exuberant cortical areas of origin, transient corticospinal fibers and aberrant spinal projections have been reported to occur in various mammals. The subsequent elimination of axon collaterals and possibly cell death may provide clues as how the adult pattern of connectivity is progressively organized.

Marsupial   In the opossum, the existence of transient corticospinal projections has been associated with an increased number of cells of origin in pouch young with estimated postnatal age varying between 42 and 62 days, as compared to the adult animal (Cabana & Martin, 1984). These cells are located in the same cortical areas as in the adult, as well as in additional areas. In the spinal cord, these transient corticospinal projections gave rise to an increased termination density, but in the same bilateral regions of the gray matter as in the adult (Cabana & Martin, 1985). These projections are eliminated by the time of weaning. No transient projections are observed to spinal levels below the thoracic segments, which is as far as the adult tract reaches.

Rodent   In the 3-day-old hamster, the corticospinal tract has been reported to contain twice as many axons as in the adult (Reh & Kalil, 1982). The major decline in axon number during the second postnatal week is not accompanied by cell death in the sensorimotor cortex (Reh & Kalil, 1982). At 5 days, when corticospinal axons invade the cervical gray matter, their cells of origin are already found in discrete sensorimotor areas almost identical to those in the adult (Kalil, 1985). The supernumerary corticospinal fibers are thus regarded as axon collaterals of sensorimotor neurones that are eliminated during development. The supernumerary fibers do not seem to terminate in the spinal gray matter, since the ingrowth of corticospinal terminations has been described as a progressive invasion of the gray matter to reach the adult pattern of termination, rather than the result of selective terminal elimination (Reh & Kalil, 1981). At the midthoracic level in the rat, the numbers of fibers increase between birth and the beginning of the second postnatal week, when there are 50–70% more corticospinal axons than in the adult. By postnatal day 10, the numbers of corticospinal fibers decrease to the adult value (Adams, Mihailoff, & Woodward, 1983; Joosten, Gribnau, & Dederen, 1987; Mihailoff, Adams, & Woodward, 1984; Schreyer & Jones, 1982, 1988b; Stanfield & O'Leary, 1985). These additional corticospinal axons have a more widespread cortical origin extending from the frontal to the occipital pole (D'Amato & Hicks, 1978; Leong, 1983; Schreyer & Jones, 1988a). Most of these transient corticospinal fibers have been shown to be axonal collaterals of neurones whose final targets were supraspinal (Stanfield & O'Leary, 1985; Stanfield, O'Leary, & Fricks, 1982). Early work show that transient spinal axon collaterals do not grow into the spinal gray matter (Joosten et al., 1987) or form connections with spinal neurones (Schreyer & Jones, 1988b). However, Curfs, Gribnau, and Dederen (1994), using horseradish peroxidase (HRP) gels implanted in the sensorimotor cortex and longer survival times, have recently demonstrated the presence of transient corticospinal projections to all parts of the spinal gray matter between postnatal days 4 and 10, before restriction to the adult pattern of termination.

Carnivore   In the ferret (Meissirel, Dehay, & Kennedy, 1993), the relative area of cortex that gives rise to fibers projecting to the medullary pyramid is 70% larger in neonates than in adults. However, the transient fibers originating in cortical areas, which in the adult make no contribution to the adult corticospinal tract, do not pass beyond the pyramidal decussation. In the cat, the extent of the cortical origin of corticospinal neurones has been reported to be the same in the 20-day-old and adult animals (I. C. Bruce & Tatton, 1981) and some preliminary observations indicate that the same is true in 1-day-old kittens (J. Armand, B. Kably & P. Buisseret, unpublished observations). Despite this, exuberant corticospinal terminations have been described during the period of formation of terminal arborization (2–5 postnatal weeks) (Alisky et al., 1992; Thériault & Tatton, 1989). During the 4th and 5th postnatal week, a diffuse labeling was observed bilaterally in all parts of the gray matter. At 6–7 weeks after birth there was selective elimination of the transient ipsilateral projections to the dorsal horn and the dorsolateral part of the intermediate zone and the bilateral projections to the ventral horn (Alisky et al., 1992), leaving an adultlike pattern of termination. This selection of mainly contralateral terminations appears to have a cortical correlate, since the cells of origin that were initially bilateral gradually changed to a more unilateral pattern between the 4th and 7th week (Girard, Bleicher, & Cabana, 1993).

Primate   In the monkey, corticospinal neurones have the same cortical origin at 5 months as in the adult (Biber, Kneisley, & LaVail, 1978). Armand et al. (1994) have further demonstrated that the corticospinal fibers originating in the motor cortex hand area project to the same regions of the spinal gray matter in neonate and adult macaque monkey, although with differential densities. In the neonate, corticospinal terminals were not found in aberrant regions such as the ventral motoneuronal cell groups.

In summary, there is good evidence for the existence of aberrant corticospinal projections during the postnatal period in many species, and their existence has been correlated with a more widespread cortical area of origin in opossum, rat, and ferret. However, these supernumerary fibers do not always project as far as the adult corticospinal axons, and the existence of functional terminations within the spinal gray matter is not proven. In the opossum, these transient terminations were found in the same regions of the spinal gray matter as in the adult, whereas in cat they first invaded the whole gray matter bilaterally, and then were selected into the adult pattern of termination. In contrast, in nonhuman primates, from birth to adulthood, corticospinal fibers originate from the same cortical areas and are present in their target area within the spinal gray matter, although their density increased during the first postnatal months, especially within the group of dorsolateral motoneurones. However, these results may simply reflect the relatively advanced stage of the tract at birth in primates (Passingham, 1985), so that exuberant areas of origin and aberrant pattern of terminations may exist at earlier (fetal) stages of the development.

Our current knowledge thus does not allow us to assume a common mechanism for corticospinal development in these different species. Studies of rodents have provided much useful information and have yielded some of the key principles that govern the development of the corticospinal system. However, pronounced differences between rodents and primates in the structure, function, and developmental timetable of the corticospinal system question the applicability of these findings to primates, including man.

3. ARE THERE CORTICO-MOTONEURONAL PROJECTIONS TO THE HAND MUSCLE MOTONEURONE POOLS IN THE NEONATAL PRIMATE?

Kuypers (1962) used degeneration techniques to study the development of the corticospinal tract in the macaque. After large lesions in the motor cortex, the Nauta technique was used to visualize the terminals of degenerating corticospinal axons. In a neonate he found that these fibers had reached all levels of the spinal cord white matter and that there were terminals within the spinal intermediate zone, but not in the motor nuclei. The only exceptions to this were a few degenerating fibers present at the dorsal margins of the lateral motor nuclei at C8. This is where the motoneurones supplying the intrinsic hand muscles are located (Jenny & Inukai, 1983); it is unclear whether these were fibers of passage or genuine terminals. Kuypers noted an "almost adult pattern" of terminal labeling (i.e., including labeling in the dorsolateral motor nuclei supplying the hand muscles) was found in an 8-month-old animal.

The sensitivity of degeneration methods is surpassed by that of modern tracers. Armand et al. (1994) reinvestigated corticospinal development in the macaque using anterograde transport of WGA-HRP (wheat germ agglutinin conjugated to HRP). Multiple injections of 10% WGA-HRP were made within the hand region of the primary motor cortex in animals at different stages of development. Injections were specifically targeted to reach the depths of the rostral bank of the central sulcus, where most of the hand representation lies. After 72 hours, the animals were killed, frozen sections of the spinal cord were cut, and sensitive histochemical procedures used to visualize the transported WGA-HRP. Because of the importance of CM projections for hand function, the study of Armand et al. (1994) concentrated on the pattern of termination among the dorsolateral motoneurones at the C8-Th1 level, which supply hand and finger muscles (Jenny & Inukai, 1983). The gray matter of these segments had denser terminal labeling than that at any other spinal levels.

In the adult, terminal labeling was particularly heavy in the dorsolateral part of the intermediate zone ,and, although less dense, was also present throughout the dorsolateral group of motoneurones (Figure 1D). There was no labeling of the ventral motoneurones, which supply more axial motoneurones.

The labeling observed in the 5-day-old monkey was very weak (Figure 1A). Faint labeling was present among the dorsolateral motor nuclei, densest along the dorsal margin as reported by Kuypers (1962). Fainter and more scattered labeling was also present in the center of the motor nuclei. No labeling was observed among the ventral motoneurones. Some of the fine axons supplying this terminal labeling entered the gray matter directly through the lateral edge of the intermediate zone toward the motoneurones, as in the adult cases (see Bortoff & Strick, 1993). In the 2½-month-old monkey there was heavy labeling within the intermediate zone of the spinal gray matter, which formed a distinctive ring around the dorsolateral motor nuclei, and this dense labeling extended into the most dorsal motoneurones (Figure 1B), in contrast to a more diffuse labeling among the others. In the 11-month-old monkey, labeling was similar to the 2½-month-old animal, with further encroachment of fibers into the lateral group of motoneurones (Figure 1C). However, this labeling was less extensive and intense than in the adults (compare Figures 1C and D).

In summary, although there is evidence for small numbers of fine cor-

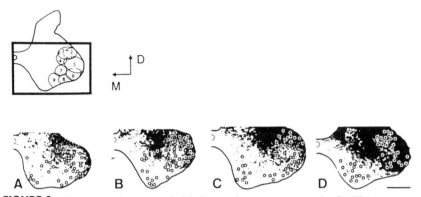

FIGURE 1   Corticospinal anterograde labeling in the gray matter at the C8-Th1 junction at different ages: at 5 days (A), 2½ months (B), 11 months (C), and in the adult (D). The black frame in the top diagram indicates the region of gray matter represented below, and also shows the distribution of motor nuclei innervating nine selected hand and arm muscles. M, medial; D, dorsal. 1, first dorsal interosseus; 2, lateral lumbrical; 3, adductor pollicis; 4, abductor and flexor pollicis brevis; 5, flexor digitorum profundus and superficialis; 6, extensor digitorum communis, abductor and extensor pollicis longus; 7, flexor carpi ulnaris; 8, extensor carpi ulnaris; 9, triceps brachii. (Inset modified from Jenny & Inukai, 1983.) In A–D, the distribution of corticospinal terminal labeling obtained from digitized paratungstate-tetramethyl benzidine (TMB)-reacted sections is shown (black stipple). Circles indicate the locations of counterstained motoneurones. Scale bar = 500 μm.

ticospinal axons reaching the hand motoneurone pools at birth, these projections are sparse even by comparison with the 2½-month-old monkey. This conclusion is supported by another recent anatomical study in a newborn macaque by Stanfield and Asanuma (1993) who confirmed, with a different technique, that corticospinal terminals were "virtually absent" around the lateral motoneuronal pools. Additionally, our study also indicates that, even at 11 months, the labeling in the ventral horn was not yet as dense as in the adult. The significance of these results is discussed in the next section.

4. ARE FUNCTIONAL CORTICO-MOTONEURONAL CONNECTIONS PRESENT IN THE NEONATAL PRIMATE?

Demonstration of functional cortico-motoneuronal *connections* is far more difficult than is the demonstration of cortico-motoneuronal *projections* described above. On one hand, the demonstration of corticospinal projections within the motor nuclei of the ventral horn does not prove that they are making functional contact with motoneurones. On the other hand, it must be remembered that the dendritic tree of many spinal motoneurones extends far beyond the boundaries of the motor nuclei, and as a consequence, corticospinal terminals in the intermediate zone could still make monosynaptic connections with motoneurone dendrites (Porter & Lemon, 1993, p. 124). Changes in the dendritic morphology of immature spinal motoneurones may also be important (Dekkers, Becker, Cook, & Navarrete, 1994; Goldstein, Kurz, Kalkbrenner, & Sengelaub, 1993). Thus, light microscopic (LM) methods are of limited use in addressing problems of functional connectivity.

Electron microscopic (EM) and electrophysiological methods could be used to demonstrate functional CM connections, but neither is straightforward. We know little about the ultrastructure of the primate CM synapse in the adult, let alone anything about its development. In the only available report known to us, Ralston and Ralston (1985) have reported that, in the monkey, anterograde labeling of corticospinal axons from the motor cortex results in labeling of synaptic terminals within the motor nuclei. These authors found labeled synaptic terminals of both the presumed excitatory (S type) and inhibitory (C type) variety. However, all electrophysiological studies of CM synapses to date have indicated that they have only excitatory actions, and it has been concluded that the inhibitory actions exerted by the corticospinal tract are mediated via inhibitory interneurones. But this conclusion is secure only for corticospinal neurones with rapidly conducting axons (see Porter & Lemon, 1993, p. 155). It is clear that further detailed ultrastructural studies of the termination of developing corticospinal axons upon identified motoneurone are needed.

The use of electrophysiological approaches to prove the existence of a monosynaptic connection requires intracellular recording from the target motoneurones. The monosynaptic origin of the excitatory postsynaptic potential (EPSP) is indicated when the segmental delay between the arrival of the tract volley and EPSP onset is too short to involve more than one synapse (see Phillips & Porter, 1977, pp. 143–146), and/or when the EPSP has the appropriate properties (fixed size, shape, and latency and ability to faithfully follow trains of stimuli). This approach is effective for EPSPs generated by rapidly conducting fibers (Porter & Lemon, 1983, pp. 165–166), but there are serious difficulties in establishing the monosynaptic origin of long-latency, slowly rising EPSPs. This problem is well illustrated by the long-running debate over the possible existence of CM synapses in the rat (Babalian et al., 1993), which remains unresolved. Thus it may be difficult to obtain conclusive electrophysiological evidence for the development of direct CM connections.

An alternative approach is to use either direct stimulation of the corticospinal tract in the pyramid (Edgley, Eyre, Lemon, & Miller, 1990; Lemon et al., 1986) or of the motor cortex (Felix & Wiesendanger, 1971) or noninvasive electrical or magnetic stimulation of the motor cortex (Edgley et al.,

1990; Flament, Goldsmith, & Lemon, 1992; Flament, Hall, & Lemon, 1992; Ludolph, Hugon, & Spencer, 1987). The latter technique has been extensively used in humans (Rothwell, Thompson, Day, Boyd, & Marsden, 1991), where the short latencies of EMG responses evoked by transcranial magnetic stimulation (TMS) have been taken as an indication of CM action. The CM origin of such responses has been confirmed in both monkey (Edgley et al., 1990) and humans (Baldissera & Cavallari, 1993; Gracies, Meunier, & Pierrot-Deseilligny, 1994).

One must first question whether or not EMG responses can be elicited in young primates; the second issue is whether such responses are mediated by the CM system. We shall consider the evidence for monkey and man separately.

In the *monkey*, Felix and Wiesendanger (1971), using surface anodal stimulation of the motor cortex, were unable to elicit short-latency responses in hand and forearm muscles in a 7-week-old monkey (under barbiturate anesthesia), although responses were obtained in a 10-month-old. In a longitudinal study, Flament, Hall, and Lemon (1992) applied TMS to 2 young macaques sedated with ketamine. A large circular coil and a stimulator of maximum output 1.5 Tesla was used. No responses could be elicited in hand muscles before 4 and $5\frac{1}{2}$ months, respectively. In a second longitudinal study, Flament, Goldsmith, and Lemon (1992) found that responses in hand muscles were first elicited about one month earlier than in foot and tail muscles. We have since confirmed the absence of hand muscle responses to TMS in a newborn monkey and in a $2\frac{1}{2}$-month-old animal. Some responses were obtained in a 3-month-old monkey when facilitation of EMG activity was provided by cutaneous stimulation (Olivier, Lemon, Edgley, & Armand, 1994).

When responses to TMS do appear in the infant monkey, the low conduction velocity of the corticospinal tract and peripheral nervous system make it difficult to be certain that the responses obtained are monosynaptic in origin. In the monkey, when clear responses to TMS were evoked in the 1DI muscle at around 4 to $5\frac{1}{2}$ months, they had a mean latency of about 16 ms (Flament, Goldsmith, & Lemon, 1992; Flament, Hall, & Lemon, 1992). This compares to 11 ms in the longer conduction path of the adult. These longer-latency responses in the infant monkey could be mediated either by slowly conducting CM cells, or by indirect pathways, with more rapidly conducting axons. This could include reticulo- or rubrospinal pathways, or propriospinal pathways activated by the corticospinal system (Lundberg, 1979). It may be significant that in all species studied, descending pathways originating from the brain stem develop in advance of the corticospinal tract (Cabana & Martin, 1984; Kudo et al., 1993; Langworthy, 1933; Weidenheim, Kress, Isaak Epshteyn, Rashbaum, & Lyman, 1992).

In *man*, the presence or absence of EMG responses to TMS in the neonate is still a matter of debate. Responses generally have high thresholds. Koh and Eyre (1988) and K. Müller, Hömberg, and Lenard (1991) found that TMS did not elicit EMG responses in the relaxed human baby, although they report that the age at which this is first possible is at 6 years and at 13 months, respectively. This result may mean that the connections mediating these responses are weak, since there is evidence that the capacity of TMS to elicit a response in a relaxed muscle is a good indication of the strength of the connections involved. In the adult, proximal muscles with relatively weak CM connections must be actively contracted for short-latency responses to TMS to be obtained; this is not true of distal muscles, which have stronger connections (E. Palmer & Ashby, 1992a; Rothwell et al., 1991; see Porter & Lemon, 1993, pp. 186–193). However, it is worth noting that Khater-Boidin and Duron (1991) found that percutaneous electrical stimulation of the motor cortex systematically elicited EMG responses in thenar muscles in full-term newborn infants. However, because electrical stimulation of the scalp can stimulate fiber systems deep within the brain, it is possible that these responses were not mediated by the corticospinal system (Burke, Hicks, & Stephen, 1990; Edgley et al., 1990; Rothwell et al., 1994).

In contrast to the situation in the relaxed infant, Eyre et al. (1991) found that TMS did elicit relatively long-latency responses in actively contracted hand muscles, even in neonates. This group has recently claimed that CM connections are present at birth, on the basis of the time course of the TMS-induced facilitation of the myotatic reflex in biceps (Conway, Eyre, Kelly, de Kroon, & Miller, 1992). In the human neonate, EMG responses to TMS recorded from actively contracted muscles have latencies of around 26 ms in biceps brachii and 32 ms in the hypothenar muscles (Eyre et al., 1991). These latencies compare to adult values for the same muscles of about 10 ms and 19 ms, respectively. Eyre et al. (1991) reported a rapid decrease in the latency of the evoked responses during the first 2 years after birth and then, from the age of 4 years, total EMG response latencies progressively increase. The long duration of the central motor conduction time (CMCT) in neonates (see Section 6) makes it difficult to assess whether or not the responses evoked by TMS are mediated monosynaptically.

Mention should also be made of the work of Stephens and his group, who have studied in detail the ontogeny of the cutaneomuscular reflexes evoked by electrical stimulation of the digital nerves and recorded in intrinsic hand muscles (Evans, Harrison, & Stephens, 1990). They have demonstrated that the most likely origin of the later, so-called E2, component of this reflex originates from a transcortical loop through the motor cortex. This E2 component is not present in newborn infants, and does not appear until around 4 years of age. It is possible that the E2 component is not present because of the immaturity of the corticospinal connections with hand muscle motoneurone pools.

In summary, no conclusive evidence exists for functional CM connections in neonates. In adult human subjects, the short latency of EMG responses to TMS has been taken as evidence of CM origin; in human neonates these responses are either absent or have long latencies, and could be mediated either by immature, slow-conducting corticospinal fibers or by other pathways. In the newborn macaque monkey, EMG responses to TMS are not present. Absence of responses to TMS in the monkey could simply reflect the difficulty of exciting the immature corticospinal neurones (see Section 6) or it might indicate more fundamental differences in the development of functional connections to spinal motoneurones in human and monkey. At present, it would appear that TMS is unlikely to provide the answer to our question.

5. HOW DOES THE AXON DIAMETER OF THE CORTICOSPINAL NEURONS CHANGE DURING DEVELOPMENT AND HOW IS THIS RELATED TO CONDUCTION VELOCITY?

A number of closely related structural parameters are known to determine the conduction velocity (c.v.) of central and peripheral axons in the adult (see Paintal, 1978; Waxman, 1978). These include the axon diameter, myelin thickness, and internodal length, which are linearly related to conduction velocity. It is of considerable interest to monitor changes in c.v. of corticospinal axons during development because of recent studies that have attempted to relate those changes to the functional maturation of the motor system (K. Müller & Hömberg, 1992) (see Section 7).

Myelination of the corticospinal tract is for the most part a postnatal process in all species that have been studied to date. The rat and hamster are born with the tract in an undeveloped state, with fibers reaching the medullary decussation at birth and on the third postnatal day, respectively (Gribnau, De Kort, Dederen, & Nieuwenhuys, 1986; Reh & Kalil, 1981; Schreyer & Jones, 1982). Corticospinal axons have reached all levels of the spinal cord before myelination begins (Schreyer & Jones, 1982). There then appears to be a wave of myelination and growth of axon diameter, which produces a continuous increase in the c.v. of the whole tract. The largest axons appear to be myelinated first (M. A. Matthews & Duncan, 1971; Reh & Kalil, 1982).

In the cat and monkey, and in man, corticospinal fibers reach all levels of the spinal cord before birth (Alisky et al., 1992; Kuypers, 1962; Thériault & Tatton, 1989). In the kitten, Oka, Samejima, and Yamamoto (1985) followed increases in the c.v. of corticospinal axons during the first month of life by measuring the latency of antidromic responses evoked in corticospinal neurones by stimulation of the tract at the medullary level. At birth, the fastest axons were calculated to conduct at 0.7 m/s, compared to 15 m/s 1 month later. In humans, T. Humphrey (1960) concluded, on the basis of material from aborted human fetuses, that the corticospinal tract reached sacral levels of the cord at a gestational age of only 29 weeks. There is no myelination of the corticospinal tract at this time (Brody, Kinney, Kloman, & Gilles, 1987; Langworthy, 1933), although the process has begun in other descending pathways (Weidenheim et al., 1992). Myelination of the cranial part of the tract in man could take from two to three years (Yakolev & Lecours, 1967). Brody et al. (1987) examined the degree of myelination in postmortem brains of a large number of infants (see Figure 2). They found that myelination of the tract was still far from complete by the end of the second postnatal year. In their sample, 50% of the brains showed a mature pattern of myelination of the pyramid by around 15 months; a mature pattern of myelination within the corticospinal tract at the cervical level was observed in 50% of the sample by about 20 months of age.

In human neonates, the conduction velocity of corticospinal axons in the spinal cord has been estimated at about 10 m/s; this value compares to conduction velocity of about 50–70 m/s found in adults (Khater-Boidin & Duron, 1991). Recent data of Eyre et al. (1991) on CMCT actually suggest that maximum fibers diameter and conduction velocity of corticospinal axons

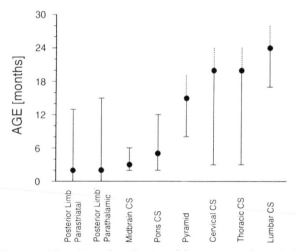

FIGURE 2   Rostrocaudal gradient of myelination of the corticospinal tract in humans. Solid circles indicate median values of the postnatal age at which infants attain degree 3 of myelination ("mature myelin") for different levels of the corticospinal (CS) tract. The vertical bars give the 10th and 90th percentile values for age. The vertical dotted lines indicate that the exact 90th percentile is not known but is greater than 24 months. (Redrawn from Fig. 4 of Brody et al., 1987.)

could continue to increase until 14 or 16 years of age. A similar protracted development of other central pathways has been reported (Pujol, Vendrell, Junque, Marti-Vilalta, & Capdevila, 1993).

Our recent study of conduction velocity in the macaque monkey (Armand et al., 1994) suggests that full myelination of corticospinal neurones in the spinal cord may not be complete until well into the second year of life. Corticospinal volleys were excited by single stimuli delivered to the medullary pyramidal tract (PT) via implanted tungsten electrodes (Edgley et al., 1990) in one neonate, a $2\frac{1}{2}$ and 11-month-old infant, and one adult macaque. Antidromic potentials were recorded from the ipsilateral motor cortex and orthodromic corticospinal volleys were recorded from the surface of the spinal cord at a cervical and at a low thoracic level. The distance between recording sites was carefully measured, and used to estimate the c.v. of the fastest corticospinal fibers between the two levels. Another estimate of c.v. (and the only one that could be obtained in the neonate) was derived from antidromic potentials, recorded from the motor cortex and activated by stimulation of the spinal cord at the same levels.

These experiments revealed striking changes in c.v. over both the cranial and the spinal courses of the macaque corticospinal tract. Figure 3 illustrates antidromic potentials evoked from the medullary PT and recorded from the motor cortex in adult and in 11- and $2\frac{1}{2}$-month-old monkeys. The peak of the earliest part of this response (indicated by an arrow) had a latency of 1.05, 1.13, and 2.32 ms, respectively. Since all of the PT electrodes were implanted at the same level in the medulla, these latency differences must represent a decrease in conduction time within the brain. Moreover, since the macaque brain reaches its adult size as early as 2–3 months and body weight 0.7 kg (Holt, Cheek, Mellits, & Hill, 1975), the latency changes must reflect an increase in c.v. of the fastest conducting PT fibers over their cranial course. This was especially marked from $2\frac{1}{2}$ to 11 months.

Figure 4 shows the changes in c.v. estimated over the spinal course of the corticospinal tract. The c.v. of the fastest fibers increased from 7.8 m/s in the 5-day-old monkey, to 28.4 m/s in the $2\frac{1}{2}$-month-old monkey, and then to 54.8 m/s in the 11-month-old monkey. In the adult, the c.v. was 72.6 m/s. This value accords with velocities reported in adults (Edgley et al., 1990: 66–72 m/s; Ludolph et al., 1987: 67 m/s). Note that, compared to the marked difference between the 11-month-old and adult animals, in the c.v. within the spinal cord for corticospinal axons, there was hardly any difference in the latency of the cortical antidromic potentials excited from the PT electrodes (see Figure 3). This observation is in agreement with a rostrocaudal maturation of the corticospinal tract in man (Brody et al., 1987, see Figure 2; Langworthy, 1933).

The time constant of the exponential fitted to the four data points plotted in Figure 4 is 8 months. The equation predicts that a c.v. of 66 m/s (the

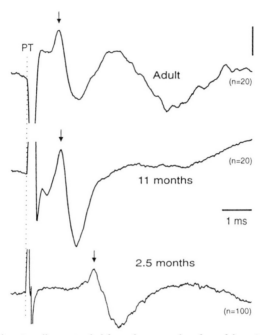

FIGURE 3 Antidromic volleys recorded from the exposed surface of the primary motor cortex to stimulation of the pyramidal tract (PT) in adult and in 11- and 2½-month-old monkeys. Stimulation strengths were 100, 200, and 200 μA, respectively. n = number of sweeps contributing to averaged traces. Scale bar = 20 μV (10 μV in the 2½-month-old monkey). The cathodal PT electrode was located at the stereotaxic level P6. The dotted line indicates the onset of PT stimulation; the positive peak of the antidromic response is indicated by an arrow in each case. (Modified from Armand et al., 1994.)

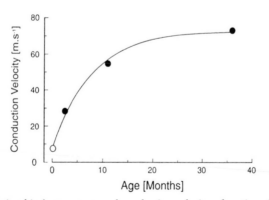

FIGURE 4 Relationship between age and conduction velocity of corticospinal axons in the spinal cord. In three monkeys (●), this was estimated by the difference between the latencies of orthodromic volleys excited by PT stimulation and recorded at two spinal levels. In the 5-day-old monkey (○) this value was calculated using antidromic cortical volleys evoked by stimulation of the dorsolateral funiculus (DLF) at two spinal levels. The line shows the exponential fitted over the data point ($y = 73.0 - 64.9 \exp(- .125x)$, $r = .99$). (Modified from Armand et al., 1994.)

lowest adult value found in adult macaque monkeys by Edgley et al., 1990)
would not be reached until about 16 months of age.

Axon growth and myelination not only change the conduction velocity of
the tract axons during development, but also determine their maximal discharge frequency and therefore their information carrying capacity. This is
an important feature of the system, since corticospinal neurones are known to
fire at high frequencies during voluntary movement (Porter & Lemon, 1993
pp. 212–214). It might also be critical to the interpretation of results obtained with TMS, since this is known to elicit repetitive discharge in adult
corticospinal neurones (see Sections 5 and 6 below). Poorly myelinated fibers
have long refractory periods, and a limited capacity for transfer of high-
frequency information (W. I. McDonald & Sears, 1970; Paintal, 1978). Armand et al. (1994) found that antidromic cortical volleys excited by stimulation of the dorsolateral funiculus of the spinal cord (DLF) could follow short
trains of high-frequency stimulation (300 Hz) in a neonatal monkey. These
volleys were conducted at around 8 m/s, so failure to conduct repetitively is
unlikely to be significant for these axons. This is in keeping with observations
on peripheral axons with c.v. of around 10 m/s, which have been shown to
follow stimulation rates of 300 Hz (see Paintal, 1978). However, repetitive
activation may be affected in the vast majority of developing axons that have
much slower conduction velocities.

Most studies of the development of the corticospinal axons have concentrated on the fibers at the pyramidal level where they are easy to identify and
to measure. However, more detailed studies of the corticospinal tract at
different spinal levels are needed. This is because many fibers leave the
corticospinal tract as it passes through the medulla (Kuypers, 1958). In rodents, corticospinal fibers can be readily distinguished from other fiber systems because they travel deep in the dorsal funiculus. In carnivores and
primates it will be necessary to distinguish corticospinal fibers from others
within the cord by using, for example, anterograde tracers injected into the
cortex. We still need to know more about the proportion of fibers present in
the medullary corticospinal tract that finally reach the cord. D. R. Humphrey
and Corrie (1978) found that 75% of 236 motor cortex pyramidal tract
neurons (PTNs) reach the C3-C4 level in the monkey; they found a somewhat higher proportion of fast (82%) than slow fibers (68%) reaching the
cord. In a study in the cat, Relova and Padel (1991) reported that only 48% of
axons in the pyramid reach the cord; the mean conduction velocity of cor-
ticobulbar neurones is only 34 m/s, compared to 78 m/s for corticospinal
neurones. In the adult rat, whereas 58% of corticospinal fibers in the pyramid
are unmyelinated (diameter range: 0.05–1.21 μm), at midthoracic level only
46% of fibers are unmyelinated (Leenen, Meek, Postjuyma, & Nieuwenhuys,
1985; Schreyer & Jones, 1988b).

There appears to be a significant decrease in the proportion of unmyelinated fibers in the adult medullary corticospinal tract as we traverse the phylogenetic scale from rodent, to cat and to macaque. In the rat, 58% of the fibers are unmyelinated (Leenen, Meek, & Nieuwenhuys, 1982; Leenen et al., 1985), 25% in the hamster (Reh & Kalil, 1982), and 8–12% in the cat (Thomas, Westrum, Devito, & Biedenbach, 1984). In the macaque monkey, Ralston and Ralston (1985) found less than 1% of corticospinal fibers to be unmyelinated. However, at the EM level, it is possible for unmyelinated fibers to be mistaken for astrocytic processes (Ralston, Milroy, & Ralston, 1987), and this raises some doubts about counts of unlabeled fibers at the EM level, all of which have realized much larger numbers than those reported for the same species at the LM level (Porter & Lemon, 1993, pp. 81–82). We need to understand much more about these fine unmyelinated fibers in the adult, because this might provide important clues as to their function in the neonate, in which they make up almost the entire tract.

In summary, in all species studied so far, the myelination of corticospinal axons is a postnatal process clearly protracted with respect to that of the other descending pathways. This period of myelination far outlasts that in which the spinal gray matter receives corticospinal innervation. In primates, corticospinal axons seem to be myelinated over their cranial before their spinal course. In the spinal cord, myelination of the corticospinal tract follows a rostral-to-caudal gradient. Based on estimates of their conduction velocity, myelination and increase in diameter of corticospinal axons can be described by an exponential function. However, these conclusions are based on the assumption that the relationship between axon diameter and conduction velocity remains constant during development.

6. IS TRANSCRANIAL MAGNETIC STIMULATION A GOOD TOOL FOR STUDYING CORTICOSPINAL DEVELOPMENT?

Transcranial magnetic stimulation (TMS) has yielded a wealth of knowledge of the corticospinal system in man (see Rothwell et al., 1991). However, as with any noninvasive method, there are some uncertainties and difficulties, some of which confound accurate interpretation of the results obtained. These difficulties should ultimately be resolved by experiments designed to illuminate the action of TMS on the central nervous system.

A key question remains whether or not PTNs are excited directly or transsynaptically by TMS. There is good evidence in the anesthetized monkey that TMS can excite PTNs at or close to the cell body (Edgley et al., 1990, 1992). A recent study by S. N. Baker, Olivier, and Lemon (1994) has shown that this is also the case in the conscious monkey, and that the size of the direct volley excited by TMS can be altered by changes in cortical excitability. Edgley et al. (1992) found that most PTNs showed both direct and indirect (presumed transsynaptic) responses to TMS, and it has long been considered that it is the temporal summation of these descending volleys that leads to the excitation of the target motoneurones (Day, Dressler et al., 1989; Day et al., 1987). It should be stressed that, under appropriate conditions, a single volley is sufficient to excite a target motoneurone (Day, Dressler et al., 1989; E. Palmer & Ashby, 1992a).

In the anesthetized monkey, TMS does not evoke direct responses in most of the corticospinal neurones with slowly conducting axons (<30 m/s; S. A. Edgley, J. A. Eyre, S. Miller, & R. N. Lemon, unpublished observations), and given that neonatal axons may conduct much more slowly than this, it must be questioned whether, at birth, these elements are excitable by currently available intensities of TMS. This issue could be resolved by direct recording from the corticospinal tract. But, in general, it would come as no surprise to find that the maturation of the cortical neuropil, and of the corticospinal neurones themselves must also influence their sensitivity to external stimuli (I. C. Bruce & Tatton, 1980; Pascual, Fernandez, Ruiz, & Kuljis, 1993; Zecevic, Bourgeois, & Rakic, 1989).

If a corticospinal volley is evoked by TMS, the EMG response that results from it occurs after a certain delay including a central and a peripheral conduction time. Given the large changes in body size that occur during development, it is more appropriate to concentrate on the central delay. In most human studies, the central motor conduction time has been estimated by subtracting, from the latency of EMG response to TMS recorded in a given muscle, the latency of the responses excited by magnetic stimulation over the cervical spines. The latter is thought to excite the peripheral motor axons as they leave the vertebral column (Plassman & Gandevia, 1989), and thus gives an estimate of the peripheral conduction time. Subtraction of this value allows the central motor conduction time to be calculated.

We can assume that a number of different delays contribute to the CMCT. These comprise delays at the cortical level (e.g., any differences due to indirect vs. direct activation of the tract cells), the conduction time within the corticospinal tract itself, and spinal delays (the synaptic delay plus the amount of temporal summation needed to reach firing threshold for the motoneurone, that has already been referred to above). Obviously, changes in CMCT during development cannot be attributed to changes in any single one of these delays, and are therefore not directly comparable to changes in axonal conduction velocity studied in animal experiments. The contribution of these delays may vary in different studies and in different subjects, and this may explain why such a wide range of values for the central motor conduction time in normal adults have been reported, although the standard deviation of data obtained within each study is generally small (see Table 1 in Rothwell et al., 1991).

In summary, TMS has been a valuable tool for investigating corticospinal development. However, there are uncertainties as to how TMS acts upon cortical neurones, and whether or not the EMG responses it evokes are mediated solely by the corticospinal tract. Of course, these difficulties also apply to the adult, but are compounded in the very young by our lack of detailed knowledge concerning the maturation of the tract.

7. DOES THE DEVELOPMENT OF THE CORTICOSPINAL TRACT PROVIDE EVIDENCE FOR A PRINCIPLE OF CONSTANT CENTRAL MOTOR CONDUCTION TIME?

In their pioneering TMS study of motor conduction time in over 450 subjects, aged from 32 weeks gestation to 55 years, Eyre et al. (1991) found that the central motor conduction time dramatically decreased during the first two years. The adult value of CMCT was reached between 2 and 4 years and then remained remarkably constant during childhood and adolescence. A consistent value for CMCT, of around 5 ms, was derived from responses to TMS in both the biceps and hypothenar muscles following stimulation applied over the motor cortex and cervical enlargement. Since the conduction distance between the vertex and C7 increases linearly between 2 and 16 years (see Figure 5 of Eyre et al., 1991), their finding implies that the conduction velocity of corticospinal neurones increased proportionally over this period of time. Therefore, the conclusion of this study is that the maturation of the corticospinal system, as estimated by the conduction velocity of the fastest corticospinal neurones, is not reached before about 16 years of age (Figure 5).

K. Müller et al. (1991, 1994), using the same approach, claimed that their findings did not support those of Eyre et al. (1991) because they found that CMCT reached an adult value between 8 and 10 years. They concluded, first, that the maturation of the corticospinal system is reached at this age and second, that their data did not support the "constancy hypothesis." The first conclusion would appear flawed because, even if CMCT reached an adult value at 8–10 years, the increasing conduction distance between the cortex and C7 during adolescence implies that the conduction velocity of corticospinal axons must also rise in order to keep CMCT constant (see above). As far as the constancy of CMCT during childhood is concerned, a careful analysis of data published by K. Müller et al. (1994) reveals they do not really differ from those of Eyre et al. (1991). Indeed, they considered that CMCT reached the adult value when it fell within the range of mean + 1 SD of measurements obtained in adult subjects. This is a restricted criterion and if the 95% or 99% confidence limit of the adult value (+ 1.96 SD or + 2.58 SD, respectively) is used, their results are actually close to those reported by Eyre

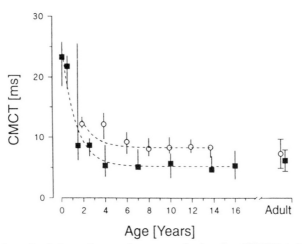

FIGURE 5   Age-related change in central motor conduction time (CMCT) in humans. Solid squares indicate median CMCT values and vertical bars the 10th and 90th percentile for different ages (redrawn from Fig. 2F of Eyre et al., 1991). Data published by K. Müller et al. (1994; their Fig. 2) are shown by the open circles; original data have been collected into 2-year bins for comparison with those of Eyre et al. (1991). The mean adult value (+95% confidence interval) is also given for comparison (Heald, Bates, Cartlidge, French, & Miller, 1993; K. Müller et al., 1994). The lower dashed line shows the exponential fitted over the data of Eyre et al. (1991) ($y = 5.2 + 21.2 \exp(-.81x)$, $r = .97$). The upper dashed line gives the exponential fitted over the reduced data of K. Müller et al. (1994), using the same time constant ($\tau = 1.25$ year, $y = 7.22 + 27.2 \exp(-.81x)$, $r = .77$).

et al. (1991). Indeed, Figure 5 shows that the data of K. Müller et al. (1994) do suggest that CMCT is constant after 3 or 4 years of age.

Most of the differences between the data of K. Müller et al. (1994) and Eyre et al. (1991) can be explained by their different methodological approach: K. Müller et al. (1994) recorded EMG responses from relaxed muscles, whereas Eyre et al. (1991) recorded responses during ongoing background contractions. This probably explains why K. Müller et al. (1991, 1994) could not evoke any EMG response before 1 year and why, when they did obtain a response, its latency was always slightly longer than those of Eyre et al. (1991) (see Figure 5). Analysis of data of Khater-Boidin and Duron (1991) obtained with percutaneous electrical stimulation confirms the dramatic decrease of CMCT during the first 2 years after birth and the fact the adult value of CMCT is reached by 3–4 years.

In summary, there are no real discrepancies between the results reported in these three different studies: they are consistent with rapid exponential decrease of CMCT during the first 2 years and adult value is reached by 3–4 years. Eyre et al. (1991) have suggested that, if this general rule applied to all corticospinal fibers (not just the largest/fastest fibers), the constant central conduction time would help to provide stability of timing in movement command signals throughout the developmental period. The exponential decrease in CMCT during the first 2 years is compatible with changes in diameter of largest corticospinal axons in the pyramid, which increases from 1 to 7 μm during that period of time (Verhaart, 1950).

8. ARE THERE DIFFERENT MATURATIONAL TIMETABLES FOR AXON MYELINATION, SYNAPTIC CONNECTIONS, AND MOTOR FUNCTIONS?

Let us now reconsider the original suggestion of Kuypers (1962) and Lawrence and Hopkins (1976) that maturation of CM connections is essential for the performance of relatively independent finger movements (RIFM). Lawrence and Hopkins hand-reared two unoperated infant monkeys from birth. They were tested on a variety of tasks, including the retrieval of small food morsels from a modified Klüver test board. The earliest signs of reaching in the control animals were at 3–4 weeks of age. Reaching was inaccurate and grasping of food rewards was part of a rather gross whole arm and hand movement. The retrieval of food was clumsy and, when successful, was achieved by closure of all digits around the reward; release of the food at the mouth was often achieved with difficulty. Smooth reaching occurred in the third month and the first signs of RIFM were present in the second to third month. The control animals were judged to have fully mature RIFM at 7–8 months of age. Hinde, Rowell, and Spencer-Booth (1964) have observed that infant monkeys first begin to groom other monkeys at around 6 months of age. RIFM are a quintessential requirement for grooming (see Porter & Lemon, 1993 p. 104).

The successful use of the hand for skilled movements depends on a large number of different factors. Kuypers always insisted that the CM system was essential for the capacity to perform RIFM. In this way he stressed the CM system was a necessary but not a sufficient factor: it was not only the presence of the CM connections, but the manner in which these connections were used by the motor system that ultimately determined the motor behavior observed in the developing animal. It can be argued that the influence of important factors contributing to the execution of RIFM, such as the use of tactile feedback, visuomotor coordination, and, at higher levels of organization, the impact of experience, mimicry, and culture, cannot be expressed unless the motor pathways linking the cortex to the final common path are developed.

If this model is correct, it would be unlikely that RIFM could be produced before the establishment of CM connections. In the human neonate, Watts, Eyre, Kelly, and Ramesh (1992) tested 20 children on a board similar to that used by Lawrence and Hopkins (1976). They reported that most children could winkle out small chocolate morsels from the board at an age at which the CMCT measurements would indicate that the corticospinal system is immature. These authors argued that, if the formation of CM connections is an essential prerequisite for this motor capacity, the rapid fall in conduction time cannot represent the formation of these connections. The same group has since suggested that, in man, CM connections are present at birth (see above).

In the macaque monkey CM projections to the hand are weak at birth, but are already clearly present at $2\frac{1}{2}$ months, at which time RIFM were first reported to be present by Lawrence and Hopkins (1976). It is therefore still possible to argue that the establishment of CM connections could precede the onset of RIFM. However, the earliest signs of responses to cortical stimulation (3 months is the earliest we have seen such responses) certainly lag behind these developments, suggesting that functional connections may not yet be operating at this age. Measurement of the c.v. of the fastest corticospinal fibers shows that, rather than there being a sudden change in conduction over the corticospinal pathway at a particular age, there is an exponential increase in c.v. over the first 16 months of life. Clearly, the capacity to perform a precision grip is present long before the c.v. of the fastest fibers reaches an adult value. The system is functional before full myelination of axons is achieved. Thus, the different measures of development all seem to mature along different timetables. The lack of any obvious parallels in the maturation of structure, function, and behavior may reflect the crudeness of the measures being used.

Finally, we must not ignore the maturation of the motor behavior itself. The precise onset of RIFM is extremely difficult to define; finger movements in monkeys of 3 months of age are still slow and inaccurate, and cannot be compared with that of older animals. The maturation of motor skill does appear to be closely linked with central motor conduction delays. K. Müller and Hömberg (1992) found that there were significant relationships between CMCT, measured in relaxed subjects aged 2 to 13 years, and speed of finger tapping and of aiming movements and the time to complete a peg-transportation test. Thus, slow maturation of precise, skilled finger movements may be associated with prolonged structural and functional changes, but we shall need more sophisticated approaches at all levels to determine the causal relationships between them.

ACKNOWLEDGMENTS

We thank the Wellcome Trust and the CNRS-Royal Society Exchange Scheme for financial support. We thank Rosalyn Cummings and Jeremy Skepper for their expert assistance.

PART 3

Hand Positioning in Reaching

Over the last 15 years interest in the control of multijoint movement has blossomed. This has been made possible by new three-dimensional spatial tracking techniques and developments in mathematical analysis tools. Previously, psychologists had studied hand positioning tasks requiring multijoint arm movement, but they typically did not record movement trajectories and restricted analysis to the hand's spatial and temporal variability at the end of movement. Physiologists concerned with characterizing muscle activity did look at kinematics but restricted the movements to a single joint.

The shift to studying the kinematics of multijoint movement has introduced several theoretical issues specifically associated with the motion of a chain of linked segments. These issues may be expressed as problems faced by the CNS in hand positioning tasks such as reaching:

1. How does the CNS represent target position in space preparatory to goal-directed movement and how is this representation translated into an appropriate set of joint angles for shoulder, elbow, and wrist (the sensorimotor transformation problem)?

2. Once a target arm posture is specified, how is a specific trajectory to that posture selected from the many that are possible (the motion planning problem)?

3. How are the joint torques (or muscle forces) that will achieve the desired trajectory determined (the inverse dynamics problem)?

Each of the chapters in this section addresses one or several of these fundamental problems.

Soechting, Tong, and Flanders (Chapter 8) are concerned with contrasting two possible reference frames that might be used to represent target position in controlling reaching movements. In one, it is assumed that the position of the hand is represented in an intrinsic frame of reference fixed to the forearm; in the other, hand position is taken to be represented directly in an extrinsic frame of reference fixed to the vertical. Soechting et al. assess these alternatives by examining systematic errors in matching the orientation of a visually presented rod with another rod held in the hand at a number of different locations. They reasoned that if people represent objects in an intrinsic frame of reference, they should make predictable matching errors when their forearm orientation does not correspond to the orientation that would be required to grasp the reference rod. The authors find only partial support for this hypothesis and conclude that, in this task at least, people use a frame of reference that is intermediate between one fixed to the forearm and one fixed to the vertical. They go on to suggest that the people may be able to select different frames of reference depending on task demands and context.

In Chapter 9, Rosenbaum, Meulenbroek, and Vaughan examine a hand positioning task involving motions of the hip, shoulder, and elbow. In general, any one of an infinite set of possible combinations of hip, shoulder, and elbow angles may be used to reach a given hand position in space. This flexibility allows us, for example, to reach around objects or to approach them in a way that is appropriate for the kind of grasp we wish to make. However, it forces the brain to solve the computational problem of which of the infinity of possible combinations to choose. Rosenbaum and colleagues develop a theory in which an optimal posture is determined by a set of cost functions. In particular, they propose there is a travel cost related to joint angular changes as well as a spatial cost related to hand position in extrinsic space. Thus, they have included cost functions in both intrinsic (joint) and extrinsic (hand) frames of reference. A key idea is that the CNS can select a weighted combination of different cost functions depending on the demands of the task. It is interesting to speculate that the intermediate frame of reference identified by Soechting et al. results from such a trade-off between cost functions.

Although the focus of Rosenbaum et al.'s chapter is on posture, these authors do propose a means of planning trajectories between initial and final postures (a joint-based strategy). Other trajectory planning strategies are possible, but, regardless of which strategy applies, the CNS is then faced with the problem of determining the forces required to realize the trajectory plan. This issue is taken up in the chapter by Ghez, Cooper, and Martin (Chapter 10) who examine how cats coordinate reaching with the paw in the presence of torques created by motions of the various segments of the forelimb. When reaching around an obstacle to grasp a food morsel, complex interaction torques are generated at the shoulder and elbow joints so that the forces acting on one joint depend on the motions of other segments. If uncorrected, these tend to make the hand deviate from the desired path of approach to the target. Analysis of the EMG patterns shows that the motor system compensates for these dynamic interactions by introducing counteracting muscle torques. Ghez et al.'s findings emphasize both the complexity of hand positioning and the need for distributed activity over muscles acting at several joints.

In Chapter 11 Lacquaniti also uses biomechanical analyses to identify features of motor behavior that reflect the neural control of coordinated hand and arm movement. When subjects catch a ball that falls vertically into the hand, both predictive and reactive mechanisms are used to produce appropriate catching action. The predictive component involves a model of the ball's flight together with an internal model of the current position and movement of the arm. The reactive component uses visual information about the ball's approach to control the stiffness or impedance of the arm measured at the hand. The impedance of the hand must be precisely matched to the ball at the time of impact, so that the ball neither bounces out of the hand (as it would if the impedance were too high) nor knocks the hand out of the way (as it would if the impedance were too low). Lacquaniti's comprehensive measurements of the hand's response to perturbations during catching suggest that the CNS switches reflex pathways on and off to continuously modulate the impedance in the time just before and after impact.

8

Frames of Reference in Sensorimotor Integration

Position Sense of the Arm and Hand

JOHN F. SOECHTING, DAVID C. TONG,
AND MARTHA FLANDERS

1. INTRODUCTION

We make implicit use of frames of reference whenever we define spatial relations. For example, when someone says, "The book is on my right," we understand that it is located to the right of the speaker's midsagittal plane. This is true even if we are standing to the speaker's right and her head and gaze are directed toward us (i.e., the book is in her left visual hemispace). Now, if the speaker says, "I'm going to move my hand to the right," we would probably guess that her intent was to move the hand in a direction perpendicular to her forearm (or perhaps perpendicular to the plane of her arm). Furthermore, if the speaker looks at and reaches for the book, her hand may move rightward while her gaze shifts to the left. Thus, not only are frames of reference used to define spatial relations, but we use a multiplicity of them, sometimes all at the same time: the location of the book was defined in a frame of reference fixed to the trunk, while the direction of hand motion was defined in a frame of reference fixed to the arm, and the direction of gaze in a frame of reference fixed to the head. In this review, we will try to show that we make use of frames of references not only cognitively, when we describe our actions, but that they are also explicit in the neural processing that underlies the planning and production of movements.

What exactly is a frame of reference? The term derives from classical mechanics, where it was realized a long time ago that Newton's laws of motion were valid only in an inertial frame of reference, for example, one that was fixed to the earth. To generalize, imagine a three-dimensional wire frame that is attached to some object, for example, the earth, the head, the trunk, or the upper arm. All measurements are now made with respect to this imaginary frame. For example, we could define distance as the length from one of the corners of the frame, and direction as the angles with the sides of the frame. Motion is defined by the change in this distance and direction with time.

We make use of frames of reference (implicitly or explicitly) whenever we make measurements during an experiment. For example, suppose we are interested in studying arm movements. We may place reflective markers on various anatomical landmarks such as the shoulder, elbow, and wrist and film the motion of these markers using video cameras. Since the cameras are stationary with respect to earth, we are describing the motion in an inertial frame of reference. For purposes of illustration, we may generate a stick figure diagram, connecting the various markers and superimpose the stick figures for each frame (Figure 1A). Typically, markers in individual frames are shifted so that one of the markers (such as the shoulder) is aligned in each frame (Figure 1B; see also Pozzo, Berthoz, & Lefort, 1990). What we have now done is describe the motion in a different frame of reference—one fixed

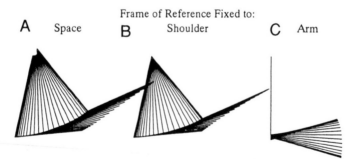

FIGURE 1 Arm movements described in three different frames of reference. The stick figure diagrams illustrate motion of the shoulder, elbow, and wrist joints for a movement that was about 45° upward and forward. (A) shows the movement described in a frame of reference fixed in space. In (B), the frame of reference translates with the shoulder, and in (C), the frame of reference translates and rotates with the upper arm. Note that the movement involves flexion at the shoulder and extension at the elbow.

to the shoulder. This may be purely a matter of convenience in that it makes it easier to illustrate some aspect of the motion. For example, in Figure 1C the motion of the forearm relative to the upper arm is depicted by choosing a frame of reference fixed to the upper arm.

Is the choice of a particular frame of reference purely a matter of convenience or does it actually have some significance in terms of neural processing leading to the production of some overt behavior? More specifically, does it make sense to ask the question: In what frame of reference is a particular behavior elaborated? We believe the question does make sense, and we try to illustrate why by two examples.

The first concerns the vestibuloocular reflex (VOR), which acts to stabilize gaze when the head is rotated. The afferent input to this reflex arises from semicircular canal afferents that sense rotation of the head in an inertial frame of reference. The axes of this frame of reference coincide with the planes of each of the semicircular canals (Simpson & Graf, 1985) and are fixed to the head. Normally, the head's frame of reference is aligned with a frame of reference fixed in space, so that vertical to the head (i.e., perpendicular to the horizontal canals) corresponds to vertical in space (aligned with gravity). But, when the head is tilted, the canal axis and the gravitational vertical will no longer be in alignment. So there are two possibilities for the output of the VOR. The resulting eye movements could also be controlled in the frame of reference of the canal afferents, with axes aligned with the head. However, if gaze is to be stabilized in a frame of reference that remains fixed in space, one would expect the VOR to be organized in a gravitational frame of reference. Angelaki and Hess (1994) have recently concluded that, in fact, the VOR is controlled in an inertial frame of reference aligned with gravity. They based this conclusion on the observation that the axes of eye rotation during the postrotatory nystagmus remain fixed in space even when the head is suddenly tilted.

As a second example, consider our sense of self-motion. Vestibular afferents contribute to this sense and consequently one might expect that our sense of self-motion is also expressed in an inertial frame of reference. However, motion of the visual surround also elicits a sense of self-motion (Berthoz, Pavard, & Young, 1975) even when we are stationary in an inertial frame of reference. Does this mean we sense motion in two different frames of reference—one an inertial one and another that is fixed to the visual surround? In fact, we sense motion in neither one, but in a frame that is a compromise between the two and perhaps reflects proprioceptive and tactile cues as well (Lackner & Graybiel, 1981). In short, we sense motion in a frame that is intermediate to the more veridical ones we might use to measure the motion of objects on earth.

2. NEURAL FRAMES OF REFERENCE

Neural activity underlying these behaviors can also be thought to encode information in particular frames of reference. We have already mentioned that vestibular afferents encode head rotational (and translational) accelerations in an inertial frame whose axes are aligned with the head's axes. Muscle stretch receptors can be thought to encode the orientation of one limb segment in a frame of reference that is attached to the segment's proximal neighbor (see Figure 1C). (Stated more simply, stretch receptors can encode the angle between adjacent segments.) The rods and cones of the visual system encode the location of a source of light in a frame of reference that is fixed to the retina.

Whereas the frame of reference in which peripheral afferents encode information can be deduced from the receptors' anatomy, the frame of reference used by central neurons to encode information may be neither as clear nor as consistent. To cite one example, motor cortical neurons are tuned to the direction of an upcoming arm movement (Georgopoulos, Kalaska, Crutcher, Caminiti, & Massey, 1984). Each neuron fires maximally for movements in a particular direction (the "best direction"). How is the "best" direction defined? First of all, Georgopoulos, Caminiti, Kalaska, and Massey (1983) showed that it was defined relative to the starting position of the hand. Neural discharge did not depend on the posture of the hand at the end of the movement, but on the change of the posture that was produced by the movement. Caminiti et al. (1990; Caminiti, Johnson, Galli et al., 1991) further showed that this frame of reference was fixed to the arm and that the axes of this frame of reference rotated when the initial posture of the arm changed. They explored arm movements from three different initial locations and found that the directional tuning of motor cortical neurons depended on the initial location. On average, the best directions rotated with the arm. If a change in starting location required an arm rotation of about 20° about the vertical in a clockwise direction, the best direction also rotated about 20° in a clockwise direction. That is to say, the best direction did not change when direction was measured in a frame of reference fixed to the arm.

However, this was true only in an average sense for the entire population of neurons. Taken one by one, the frame of reference for the coding of movement direction in single neurons was neither fixed in space, nor was it fixed to the arm, but it was different for every neuron. This example illustrates what appears to be a general property of how information is processed in the central nervous system. Namely, this processing is distributed in nature with every neuron encoding information in a slightly different manner and in a slightly different frame of reference. Taken to its logical conclusion, one might infer that there are as many frames of reference as there are neurons, leading one to question the utility of this concept. It may well be that the question of neural frames of reference is ill posed unless it is framed in terms of the behavior of neural populations.

If information in a neuronal population can be viewed as being encoded in a particular frame of reference, then the transfer of information from one population to another can be thought of as a mapping from one frame of reference to another. We have already discussed the VOR and have mentioned that this reflex maps head rotational signals in a head-fixed frame of reference to one that is fixed in space. We have also mentioned that muscle stretch receptors, which are thought to be important for limb position sense (McCloskey, 1978), encode limb orientation in a frame of reference that is fixed to limb segments. As we will show shortly, arm orientation appears to be sensed in a frame of reference whose axes remain horizontal and vertical, fixed in space. If so, a mapping from an arm-fixed frame of reference to one that is fixed in space (or to the trunk) is implied. More generally, we have discussed the problem of planning an arm movement to a spatial target as requiring a series of such transformations from one frame of reference to another (Flanders, Tillery, & Soechting, 1992).

In this brief introduction, we have tried to demonstrate that the question "Is a particular behavior expressed in a definable frame of reference?" is a valid one. However, the answer may not always be an obvious one in that the frame of reference may not turn out to be the one we might chose *a priori*. For example, the frame of reference in which we sense motion reflects a compromise among the various sensors that contribute to our sense of motion (e.g., vestibular and visual) and consequently the frame of reference for motion sensing is intermediate to the ones of the various sensors. Furthermore, behavior generally results from distributed processing by a neural population, and when one tries to extend the question down to the level of single neurons, one may find that the information provided by neural activity in each neuron is expressed in a different frame of reference.

We now examine in some detail the question of how information about the posture of the arm and hand is sensed and presumably encoded.

3. POSITION SENSE OF THE ARM

Even in the absence of vision, we have a sense of the static posture of our limbs. The source of this sense has been investigated extensively and has been thought at various times to arise primarily either from joint afferents (Skoglund, 1973) or from muscle stretch receptors (Gandevia & McCloskey, 1976; McCloskey, 1978), the latter being the generally accepted point of view at present. Cutaneous afferents most likely contribute as well (Edin & Abbs,

1991) and our sense of limb position reflects the contribution of a multiplicity of sources (see Jones, Chapter 17). Since most of these afferents sense changes in posture of one limb segment with respect to another, it seems reasonable to expect that position sense could be defined more precisely as a sense of joint angles. From the perspective we established in the Introduction, the position of one limb segment would be expressed in the frame of reference of its proximal neighbor. Thus, the posture of the wrist would be defined relative to the forearm, the posture of the forearm relative to the upper arm, and that of the upper arm relative to the trunk.

When we first began to study pointing movements of the arm (Soechting & Lacquaniti, 1981), we made an observation that caused us to question this assumption. At the end of movements that always began with the elbow near 90° (see Figure 1), introspectively we had a poor sense of whether we flexed or extended our elbow to get to the target (Figure 1C). However, we seemed to have a much better sense of whether the forearm was inclined upward or downward at the end of the movement (Figure 1B). In other words, it appeared that we sensed the posture of our forearm in a frame of reference that was fixed in space rather than in a frame of reference fixed to the upper arm.

To test this more precisely, we presented subjects with a task in which they had to match the posture of the left and right forearms in these two different frames of reference, and we verified our suspicion: subjects were able to match forelimb orientation (in a spatial frame of reference) much better than they were able to match elbow joint angle (Soechting, 1982). Both arms were in parasagittal planes, the left upper arm was always vertical, whereas the right upper arm's orientation varied from trial to trial and subjects had to align the left forearm's orientation or joint angle with that of the right forearm. This observation was confirmed by Worringham, Stelmach, and Martin (1987). In their experiments, the inclination of the two upper arms always differed by 20°. In one experiment, later replicated by Darling (1991), both arms were in parallel parasagittal planes. They also obtained similar results when the two arms were in vertical planes that were perpendicular to each other. Soechting and Ross (1984) extended the analysis to a matching task in which the right arm was not always in a vertical plane, while motion of the left forearm was restricted to the sagittal plane. We, too, came to the same conclusion: the posture of the forearm is sensed in a frame of reference that is fixed in space, one of the axes of this frame of reference being vertical. We also suggested that another of the axes was horizontal and perpendicular to the frontal plane of the trunk. Thus, the posture of the forearm was defined by two angles: the angle of forearm elevation, defining the forearm's angle with a vertical axis, and the angle of forearm yaw, defining the forearm's angle with the sagittal plane. Based on results with a similar experimental approach, the posture of the upper arm appeared to be defined in the same frame of reference as was the posture of the forearm.

We now digress briefly to take up a technical point. How does one determine whether performance on one task is better or worse than the performance on another task? In the initial experiment, Soechting (1982) measured the root mean square (r.m.s.) error in matching angles and found that the r.m.s. error was significantly lower when subjects matched forearm elevation than when they matched forearm flexion. The r.m.s. error can be split up into two components: a constant error, which is defined as the average error if repeated measures are taken, and the variable error, defined as the standard deviation of the constant error. These two sources of error reflect two different aspects of the performance: the variable error provides a measure of the uncertainty in the performance, whereas the constant error provides a measure of biases in the performance.

The variable error and constant error can be independent measures. In fact, Worringham et al. (1987) found that variable errors were about the same when subjects matched forearm orientation and when they matched joint angle. However, the constant errors were substantially different: the constant error in matching joint angle was much larger. In fact, the constant error in matching elbow angle (about 17° in both experiments) was close to the difference in inclination of the two upper arms (20°), suggesting that the subjects were in fact matching forearm orientation, contrary to the instruction.

In the experiments described below, we were unable to obtain repeated measures because the posture of the arm varied randomly from trial to trial. In those experiments, we developed a measure that is comparable to constant error. We used linear regression methods to fit the data with polynomials (Soechting & Flanders, 1989) and we defined the r.m.s. difference between this polynomial fit and the perfect performance to be the persistent error.

If one asks subjects to perform a task in a frame of reference that is not normally used for that task, one might expect that their performance would reflect a bias toward a performance in the natural frame of reference. This would be reflected in the constant error, which should be proportional to the degree of misalignment of the two frames of reference. This is in fact what has been found in the task of matching elbow angles of the two forearms. As noted before, the constant error found by Worringham et al. (1987) was close to the 20° misalignment of the two frames of reference. Qualitatively, Soechting (1982) found that the persistent error increased with the angle of upper arm flexion, in agreement with this prediction.

The results of the experiments we have just summarized are consistent with the conclusion that the posture of the arm is represented in a spatial frame of reference whose axes are vertical and horizontal. However, they do not exclude other possibilities. In every case, the trunk was also vertical and thus it is also possible that the frame of reference is aligned with the trunk's axis rather than the vertical. Furthermore, the possibility remains that forearm posture is defined in a frame of reference that is intermediate to one fixed in space (or to the trunk) and to one that is fixed to the upper arm. Since Worringham et al. (1987) found a strong bias to matching forearm orientation when subjects were instructed to match elbow angle, but not vice versa, this possibility appears remote, but it may be useful to revisit that particular question as well.

When the posture of the arm is defined by yaw and elevation angles, simple algorithms that map a desired hand path in space (such as a circle or an ellipse) into the arm's motion arise (Soechting & Flanders, 1991; Soechting & Terzuolo, 1986). We have also been able to deduce an algorithm whereby a point in space, initially defined in a retinotopic frame of reference, can be mapped into the posture of the arm that would place the hand at that location (Flanders et al., 1992).

4. POSITION SENSE OF THE HAND

Our more recent investigations (Flanders & Soechting, 1995; Soechting & Flanders, 1993) have concerned the frame of reference in which the posture of the distal portion of the arm is represented. Our results suggest that hand orientation is defined neither in a frame of reference that is fixed in space nor in one that is attached to the forearm but in one that is intermediate to those two. The initial clue was provided by experiments in which we asked subjects to align a grasped rod with a similar rod that was presented visually.

4.1 Visual Matching of Grasped Rod Alignment

In a first series of experiments, we presented the rod to the subjects at random locations in the workspace and at random orientations. More specifically, we varied the slant, which we defined as the angle the rod made with the vertical and its tilt, defined as its rotation in the frontal plane (Soechting & Flanders, 1993). We defined slant to be positive when the top of the rod was slanted away from the subject. We asked subjects to remember the rod's location and orientation, to close their eyes, and to move their arm to place a grasped rod at the same location and orientation. In some experiments, the subjects grasped the rod with a power grip (i.e., its orientation could be changed only by rotation of the wrist) and in other experiments they used a precision grip (in which the rod's orientation could be changed also by finger movements). The results were comparable for the two experimental conditions.

Subjects were reasonably accurate on this task. In Figure 2A, we show the persistent error in matching the rod's slant as a function of the target's slant and elevation (its location above or below the plane of the shoulder). (These

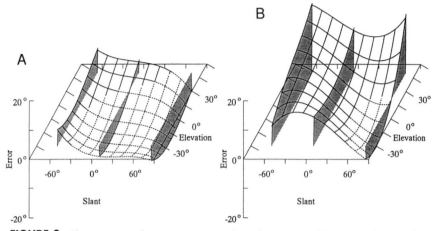

FIGURE 2 Slant errors under two experimental conditions. (A) subjects were instructed to match the location and orientation of a rod from memory. (B) Subjects were instructed to match only the rod's orientation while the rod was in view. Slant is defined as the angle the rod makes with the vertical. If the top of the rod points away from the subject, slant is defined to be positive. The errors are plotted as a function of the rod's elevation (angular distance above or below a horizontal plane through the shoulder) and slant. Note that subjects make appreciably larger errors when asked to estimate orientation only and the rod is in view. (Adapted from Soechting and Flanders, 1993.)

errors were computed by means of regression analysis and represent our estimate of constant error at each location and orientation.) The error depended also on the target's tilt, distance, and azimuth (location relative to the parasagittal plane through the shoulder), but these effects were not as pronounced nor as informative. As shown in Figure 2A, the error varied with the slant angle, with small positive errors for negative angles and negative errors at positive angles. Thus, subjects tended to orient the rod closer to the vertical than they should have. The r.m.s average of the error was about 9°.

We wanted to determine whether subjects processed information about target orientation separately from the information about the target's location. Therefore, we also asked subjects to match only the target rod's orientation, keeping their arms at their sides (upper arm vertical, forearm horizontal) and their eyes closed. In this task we found errors that were comparable to those we found when subjects were asked to match both target location and orientation. In fact, neither persistent nor variable errors were significantly different. Since there were, nevertheless, consistent trends in the errors that we found under both experimental conditions, we then set out to see if we could determine their origin. One possibility (Goodale & Servos, 1992) was that they arose because we forced subjects to remember the rod's location and orientation and their memory could be faulty. To test for that possibility, we performed a control experiment in which we also asked subjects to match only the rod's orientation with their arms at their sides, but now with the rod in view. We expected, at worst, to find errors that were comparable to those we had found in the other experimental conditions. To our surprise, the persistent errors were in fact larger ($p < .01$) when they could see the target and did not have to rely on memory.

Figure 2B shows how the error in slant varied with the target's slant and elevation under this last experimental condition. As in Figure 2A, there was a tendency for the error to be negatively correlated with the slant error, but the major trend evident in Figure 2B is the dependence of the persistent error on the elevation of the target rod. When the target was above the plane of the shoulder (positive elevations), subjects tended to make positive slant errors, that is, they tended to rotate the top of the cylinder farther away from them than they should have.

In the experiment just described, we had varied the target's slant as well as its tilt angle. To begin to understand the source of the errors somewhat better, we then performed another experimental series in which the rod was constrained to rotate in the sagittal plane (i.e., we varied only the slant angle, keeping tilt constant). The results were comparable to those shown in Figure 2B (cf. Fig. 11A of Soechting & Flanders, 1993). In this last experiment, we asked subjects, after they had matched only target orientation with vision, to match its location as well as orientation in the absence of vision, that is, to replicate the initial experiment (Figure 2A). The results were comparable to those shown in Figure 2A. So the errors made in the presence of vision did not induce subsequent errors when the task was performed in the absence of vision.

Clearly, forcing subjects to dissociate information about target location from information about target orientation when the object is in view introduced large, consistent errors that were not present under other conditions. It could be argued that these differences in performance resulted because the two tasks were processed by different neuronal pathways (more specifically, the ventral and dorsal streams; see Goodale et al., Chapter 2). Such an interpretation would be based on the differential deficits observed in patients on a variety of perceptual and motor tasks (Goodale, Jakobson, Milner et al., 1994; Goodale et al., 1991). However, there are two other possible explanations that can account for this phenomenon and that do not require us to invoke the possibility that anatomically distinct parts of the brain are involved differentially in the sensorimotor processes for quite similar motor actions. It is possible that subjects misperceive the orientation of the target because they do not compensate fully for the angular elevation of the direction of gaze. Alternatively, the errors could result because subjects use a frame of reference more closely aligned with the forearm rather than one that is fixed in space to determine hand orientation.

Figure 3 illustrates schematically how failure to compensate for gaze direction could lead to the observed errors. For a bar (heavy solid line in Figure 3) located in the midsagittal plane on the visual horizon (the primary gaze direction), the line of sight is perpendicular to the vertical bar (and parallel to the horizontal bar). If the location of the object is above or below the horizon, vertically and horizontally oriented objects will no longer be perpendicular or parallel to the line of sight. The solid bars denote what would be perceived to be vertically and horizontally oriented objects if subjects were to persist, nevertheless, in defining orientation relative to the line of sight. The dashed lines indicate the true vertical and horizontal at all three locations.

Now, if subjects held the rod vertically (with their arm at the side) whenever they perceived the rod to be oriented vertically, they would make positive errors when the target was above the visual horizon and negative errors whenever it was below the horizon. While this prediction does not match precisely the errors described in Figure 2B, the general trend is in agreement.

Similar errors would also result if subjects defined the orientation of the rod relative to the forearm's orientation (i.e., in the forearm's frame of reference). In this instance, the geometry is somewhat more complicated, but the

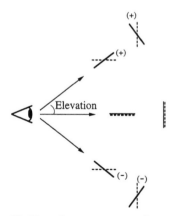

FIGURE 3 Expected errors if subjects do not compensate for gaze direction in judging object orientation are shown by the heavy solid lines at three different elevations. Correct performance on the task of setting a line vertically or horizontally is indicated by the dashed lines at the same three locations. As indicated schematically, failure to compensate would produce positive errors at positive elevations and negative errors at negative elevations in Figure 2B.

argument is similar to the one we just developed. When the target is above the plane of the shoulder, the forearm would be inclined upward from the elbow. For the sake of argument, assume its orientation parallels the upward-pointing arrow in Figure 3. Now, if a subject grasped the upper rods (solid bars) in Figure 3, they would be either perpendicular or parallel to the forearm. If subjects reproduced the same orientation of the hand when the arm was at the side with the forearm horizontal, they would hold the rod vertically or horizontally (dashed lines) and they would tend to make positive errors. Analogously, for targets below the shoulder, the forearm would be inclined downward, and one would expect negative errors according to this argument.

Thus, both hypotheses are in accord qualitatively with experimental observations. To distinguish between them we conducted several other experiments. In the first series of experiments, we evaluated how a subject's perception of rod orientation was affected when the rod's elevation, azimuth, and distance from the subject were varied. Subjects stood erect and were asked to align a luminous cylindrical rod vertically or horizontally at each of 18 locations. The rod was attached to the shaft of an electrical motor (rotating at 6 °/s), which the subjects controlled by means of a three-position switch. Given the orientation of the experimental setup, the rod was always constrained to rotate in a sagittal plane. At each location we evaluated the subjects' ability to orient the rod in the dark and in the presence of visual cues provided by the laboratory environment (light), with two trials per location for each condition. Subjects were encouraged to continue to adjust the orientation of the rod until they were well satisfied it was horizontal or vertical, even if this required them to reverse the direction of the motor several times.

In order to more fully describe the influence of object elevation on the perception of orientation, we performed a second series of experiments in which we restricted the location of the rod to points lying in the midsagittal plane and changed the location within this plane randomly from trial to trial. In each trial subjects were again asked to rotate the rod until it appeared to be vertical. For each of the five subjects who participated in this second experiment, we obtained at least 70 trials, with rod elevation ranging from $-45°$ to $30°$. One of these five subjects had also participated in the first series of experiments.

The results from both sets of experiments rule out the possibility that subjects failed to compensate adequately for changes in gaze direction in their perception of object orientation. In both experiments, the subjects made small errors, in the direction opposite to what would have been predicted by the initial hypothesis. Figure 4 shows results from one representative subject for six positions in the midsagittal plane in the first experiment. Each panel of the figure shows the orientations to which the subject rotated the luminous

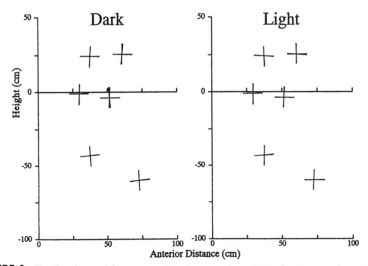

FIGURE 4 Results obtained from one subject instructed to orient a luminous rod vertically or horizontally in the dark (*left*) and in the light (*right*). Height and anterior distance are measured relative to a point between the two eyes. The midpoint of each line represents the location of the center of the rod in the midsagittal plane, and the orientation of the line represents the subject's estimate of the vertical and horizontal directions at that location. In the dark, errors are negative at positive elevations, and positive at negative elevations.

rod so that it appeared vertical or horizontal. There were two trials for each experimental condition.

While this subject was able to orient the rod repeatably, she did not orient it veridically to the vertical or the horizontal in the dark. In particular, for the two locations well below eye level ($-45°$), the vertical estimates are slanted consistently with the top toward the subject (positive errors, Figure 3), while the horizontal estimates also show positive errors (proximal end slanted downward). The average error for these estimates was $3.4° \pm 0.7°$ for the vertical and $5.4° \pm 1.3°$ for the horizontal. When the rod was located above eye level ($20°$), the errors were generally negative: $-3.2° \pm 2.1°$ for the vertical and $-0.7° \pm 0.9°$ for the horizontal. The dependence of the orienting error on the elevation of the rod was statistically significant ($p < .01$), with a regression coefficient of -0.11 ± 0.03 (*SE*) for the vertical and -0.08 ± 0.01 for the horizontal.

The results illustrated in Figure 4 are representative of the results obtained in all four subjects. A linear regression analysis of the combined data for all four subjects showed a statistically significant dependence of the error in estimating vertical and horizontal on rod elevation ($p < .01$), with regression coefficients of -0.12 ± 0.02 for the vertical and -0.09 ± 0.03 for the horizontal. The errors for estimating horizontal and vertical are comparable to each other, for a given spatial location of the rod. One can account for the errors if one assumes that subjects overestimated the amount of gaze angle elevation relative to the horizontal plane. The errors we found are exactly opposite in sign to the prediction illustrated schematically in Figure 3.

In the second series of experiments, gaze elevation was varied over a wider range ($-45°$ to $30°$). Results from 2 of the 5 subjects who participated in this experiment are presented in Figure 5. The line interpolating the individual data points represents the fit of a cubic polynomial to the data. The coefficients for the polynomial were obtained using multiple regression analysis, retaining only those coefficients that differed significantly from 0 ($p < .05$). For one of the 5 subjects, the errors in estimating the vertical orientation of the rod did not depend significantly on gaze elevation. The results for the other 4 subjects were in agreement with the results obtained in the first series of experiments. Subjects tended to make positive errors in orienting the rod when it was located below eye level, and negative errors when it was above eye level. At eye level, there was a small bias toward negative errors.

The error in estimating the vertical did not vary linearly with gaze elevation, however. Over the range of $\pm 25°$, the errors tended to be small,

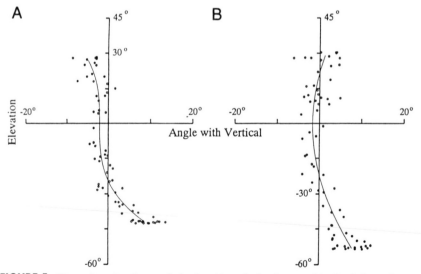

FIGURE 5   Errors in estimating vertical orientation of a luminous rod in the dark are dependent on the gaze elevation. Each panel (A and B) shows results from one subject. Each individual data point is the result from one trial at the indicated elevation (plotted along the vertical axis). The solid lines interpolating the data points are the best fit of a polynomial to the data.

increasing sharply at lower and higher elevations. Results similar to those presented in Figure 5A were obtained in two other subjects. The results from the fourth subject (Figure 5B) were also generally comparable, especially for locations below eye level. At positive elevations, there was considerable variability in the individual data points, which showed positive as well as negative errors. The polynomial fit for this subject indicates, however, that the errors tended to reverse from negative to positive at elevations above 25°.

Results from these two experiments tend to rule out the explanation that the errors subjects made in aligning the rod with visually perceived targets arose because they misperceived the orientation of the target. Two other series of experiments did provide support for the alternative hypothesis, namely that subjects tended to perform this task in a frame of reference that tends to be aligned with the forearm. In the first experiment, subjects matched only the orientation of the rod (similar to the experiment illustrated in Figure 2B), except that in some trials the forearm was extended and in other trials the forearm was flexed. (Recall that in the experiment shown in Figure 2B the forearm was perpendicular to the upper arm.) If the forearm is more extended, one would expect the persistent errors to be more positive, and if the forearm is more flexed, one would expect them to be more negative. The experimental results (cf. Fig. 12 of Soechting & Flanders, 1993) were in qualitative agreement with this prediction. However, the effect was much smaller than one would have predicted if subjects used a frame of reference fixed to the forearm. If that were the case, one would expect the change in persistent error to be equal to the change in the forearm's inclination. The effect we obtained was only about 1/6 of the predicted one, a 60° change in elbow angle leading to a 10° change in persistent error.

4.2 Orienting a Grasped Rod According to Verbal Instruction

A second series of experiments (Flanders & Soechting, 1995) was also consistent with the idea that subjects represent the orientation of the hand in a frame of reference that is intermediate to ones fixed in space and fixed to the forearm. In these experiments we avoided the problem of visually induced errors by giving subjects verbal instructions. We asked subjects to orient the grasped rod either vertically, horizontally, or at a 45° angle in the spatial frame of reference. In other trials, we asked them to orient the rod perpendicularly to the forearm, either in a vertical or horizontal plane. They were instructed to achieve this task with their eyes closed, at the end of an active or passive movement. For passive movements, the experimenter moved the subject's hand to random locations in the workspace whereas for active movements, we presented the subjects with a point target and asked them to move their hand to that location. In these experiments, we were not particularly interested in their accuracy of pointing but used this device to achieve a variety of forearm orientations.

When subjects were asked to align the grasped rod with the direction of gravity or perpendicularly to it, they made small errors that showed only slight trends with changes in arm posture. This was true both when the arm was moved actively and when it was transported passively by the experimenter. However, the results were substantially different when we asked subjects to slant the rod at ±45° with the vertical. Figure 6A shows how the persistent error depends on the azimuth and elevation of the hand's location when subjects tried to orient the rod at +45°. The error is negatively correlated with the hand's elevation. This is precisely what one would predict if the subjects had tried to orient the rod at 45° relative to the forearm. We obtained similar results when subjects tried to orient the rod at −45° with the vertical, namely a negative slope in the error with hand elevation. However, when we asked subjects to orient the rod perpendicularly to their forearm, we obtained the opposite trend (Figure 6B). The persistent error had a positive correlation with the hand's elevation, as one would expect had the subjects tried to align the rod with the gravitational vertical. Thus, in both instances (Figure 6A and 6B) we obtained consistent errors, suggesting that subjects were attempting to perform the task in the frame opposite to the one they were instructed to use.

We also conducted a more quantitative analysis of these persistent errors. In each trial, we measured the forearm's orientation (in the spatial frame of reference) and computed the degree to which the errors shown in Figure 6 were correlated with the forearm's orientation. This analysis showed that in fact the subjects did try to comply with the instruction. If we define a contin-

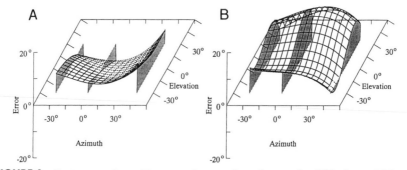

FIGURE 6   Slant errors when subjects were instructed to orient a rod at 45° in the spatial frame of reference (A) and perpendicularly to the forearm (in the frame of reference of the forearm) (B). Note that in both instances, slant error depends on the elevation of the hand relative to the shoulder, but the trends are of opposite sign. These results suggest subjects performed both tasks in a frame of reference intermediate to the spatial one and the one fixed to the arm.

uum between the reference frame fixed in space and the one fixed to the forearm, subjects' performance shifted by about 25% from the spatial reference frame to the one fixed to the arm when they were asked to orient the rod in space. The performance shifted about 20% from the forearm's frame of reference to the spatial one when they were asked to orient the rod relative to the forearm. In other words, they were about 75 to 80% correct.

This result has two implications. First, subjects use a frame of reference that is intermediate to one fixed in space and one fixed to the forearm to define the hand's orientation. A similar conclusion has been reached by Carrozzo and Lacquaniti (1994) based on subjects' performance in a visuo-kinesthetic matching task. Second, this intermediate frame of reference is labile—subjects are able to shift it toward one fixed in space or toward one fixed to the arm, depending on the task. The results of our studies on hand orientation are thus in contrast to the previously described studies concerning the frames of reference of the proximal arm. As we have already mentioned, there is strong evidence that the orientation of the proximal arm is defined in a spatial frame of reference and it is open to question whether or not subjects are capable of changing the frame of reference for defining proximal arm posture.

It is possible that if one were to devise a clever enough experiment, one might yet uncover evidence for shifting frames of reference for the proximal arm. However, it is also possible that the difference between how posture of the proximal and distal limb segments is encoded reflects differences in their function. As many investigators (cf. Hollerbach, 1988) have observed, the arm serves as a platform for the hand or, stated in other words, as a link between the trunk and the hand. As we have discussed elsewhere (Flanders & Soechting, 1995; Soechting & Flanders, 1991, 1993), the spatial transformations between object location and arm orientation appear particularly simple when arm orientation is defined in a spatial frame of reference. With regard to the hand, there may well be advantages in having a greater degree of flexibility in defining the hand's orientation. Sometimes, it is both useful and important to define it in a spatial frame of reference, for example, when one holds a full cup of coffee. At other times, it may be more useful to define the orientation of the hand relative to the forearm, for example when one holds a screwdriver. (The arm is stiffest along the axis of the forearm [Mussa Ivaldi, Hogan, & Bizzi, 1985] and the range of wrist rotation is greatest when arm pronosupination can contribute.)

5. CONCLUSION

In this survey, we have tried to demonstrate that it is possible to determine experimentally the frame of reference in which a particular behavior is expressed. As we noted in the Introduction, different aspects of the same behavior may be expressed in different frames of reference, and thus the problem of sensorimotor integration may be viewed as one of defining a series of transformations between different frames of reference. Such transformations lend themselves naturally to so-called black-box models of neural processing. The contents of each box consist of a set of parameters (such as angles, distances, or velocities) defined in a particular frame of reference, and the mapping from one box to another is defined by simple mathematical operations such as addition, multiplication, or filtering. Such simple black-box models are, of course, not new; for example, they have proven useful for a long time in understanding the control of eye movements (cf. Robinson, 1981, 1985). In the field of oculomotor control, it has even proved possible to associate many of these black boxes with specific neural structures.

However, as we also mentioned in the Introduction, in general it is more appropriate to view neural processing as being distributed in nature. If that is true, then one can associate the output of a population of neurons only with a particular black box, the parameters being encoded by each neuron being different. If one accepts the aim of understanding behavior at the level of single cells, then one may begin to wonder about the utility of the concept of frames of reference extended to the single-unit level.

Despite the daunting nature of the aim, we nevertheless believe that there is some hope. One can entertain the possibility that the reference frames that are expressed at the behavioral level will impose some constraints on how information is encoded in individual neurons, or, alternatively, some constraints in the patterns of connectivity among the neurons at any one structural level and between structural levels. Such an approach has actually proved successful in understanding how visually derived spatial information is encoded. R. A. Andersen and Zipser (1988) have shown that posterior parietal neurons' discharge depends both on a visual target's location in a retinotopic frame of reference and the eye's position in a head-centered frame of reference. By means of a neural network model, they showed that a population of such neurons could be used to encode target location in a head-centered frame of reference, that is, this neural population could achieve the transformation between two frames of reference. Perhaps it is not overly optimistic to hope that in the near future the sensorimotor transformations underlying arm and hand movements can be understood similarly.

ACKNOWLEDGMENT

The authors' work was supported by Grants NS-15018 and NS-27484 from the United States Public Health Service.

9

Three Approaches to the Degrees of Freedom Problem in Reaching

**DAVID A. ROSENBAUM,
RUUD G. J. MEULENBROEK,
AND JONATHAN VAUGHAN**

1. INTRODUCTION

How easy it is to take for granted the capacity to pick up objects and manipulate them, to gesture, to use one's hands to support one's weight, to soothe a child by stroking his or her hair. We use our hands in almost all that we do. So central to our lives is the use of our hands that some anthropologists view the development of tool use as the single most important force behind human evolution (A. Wallace, 1964). Our everyday conversation is likewise filled with metaphors for prehension. We grasp what others say, point to others' ideas, get a grip on ourselves, and so on. One has the sense that the hand, as Kant once observed, is the window to the mind. No wonder that students of mental function have long been attracted to the study of manual performance.

To fully appreciate how hands are controlled, one must do more than stand in awe of their achievements. A more analytical approach is needed. The approach taken here focuses on computations. It has become widely accepted that the brain can be understood not just in terms of its physical

Hand and Brain

makeup but also in terms of the computations it performs. Similarly, hand function can be understood not just in terms of the anatomy and physiology of the upper extremity but also in terms of the computations that allow hands to maneuver as they do. Computational analyses rely on abstract descriptions, which can be valuable when one recognizes that the problems faced by the manual control system may be faced by other systems as well. When such common problems are recognized, computational analyses of hand function can inform, and in turn be informed by, computational analyses of functions involving other parts of the body. Computational analyses can also be implemented in artificial control systems, most notably robots, so they can have practical as well as theoretical benefits.

2. THE DEGREES OF FREEDOM PROBLEM

Consider the simple act of reaching for a rigid object. How many descriptors are needed to characterize the object's position in space? The answer is six. The object's center of mass has an x, y, and z value, and the object also has a pitch, roll, and yaw. Now consider the ways the arm and hand can be configured when holding the object steadily. Ignoring the variations in force that can be produced as the object is held, and ignoring the paths that can be followed on the way to the grasp, the number of static postures that can be used to hold the object if the object is entirely within reach is infinite. This follows from the fact that more descriptors characterize the actor's position in space than characterize the object's position in space. The number of descriptors needed to characterize the actor's position in space is the minimal number of mechanical degrees of freedom (df) that characterize the human body. Considering just the joints, there are about 100 mechanical dfs (Turvey, 1990). The arm, excluding the fingers, has seven mechanical dfs: three at the shoulder, two at the elbow, and two at the wrist. Without even considering the fingers, then, we see that more dfs characterize the positions that the arm can adopt than characterize the position that the object can adopt. Hence, infinitely many arm postures can be adopted to take hold of the object, provided again that at least one part of the object is entirely within the workspace (the region that can be reached). If we now consider the movement that brings the hand and arm to the grasp position and treat the movement as a series of hand positions, each of which can be expressed as one of an infinite number of postures, then the number of ways that the object can be statically grasped is seen to be even smaller than the number of ways that the hand can be brought to that final grasp position.

 The ability to reach for an object with infinitely many postures is a blessing for the actor because, if some joints can no longer move, it may still be possible to reach the object with the dfs that remain. As long as there are at least as many dfs in the body as in the object, it is possible to reach the object. The presence of excess dfs is also beneficial from the standpoint of obstacle avoidance. If an obstacle lies between the actor and the object, it helps to have a posture that allows the actor to reach around the obstacle to take hold of the object.

What then is the problem with having alternative methods of reaching for an object? The problem is to understand how particular, adaptive reaches are selected. Nicolai Bernstein (1967), the Russian scientist who first discussed this issue, called it the "degrees of freedom problem." It has become the focus of much work in motor control research (e.g., Jordan & Rosenbaum, 1989; Turvey, Fitch, & Tuller, 1982).

In this chapter, we review three approaches to the degrees of freedom problem. The first two approaches, which Bernstein advocated, focus on ways that the number of dfs within the body might be smaller than would be supposed by listing ways that individual effectors can behave anatomically. These two approaches are reviewed here in Sections 3 and 4. The third approach, which has only recently come to the fore in motor control research, emphasizes the satisfaction of costs. We review this approach in Section 5.

Before we turn to the review, we wish to offer two caveats. First, because this is a tutorial, we have tried to provide a set of illustrations rather than an exhaustive review. Our aim is to give a sense of the approaches that have been taken rather than to explicate in detail any one of them. Second, this chapter is strongly worded. We subscribe to the idea, which might be viewed as radical, that cost containment is the only way to solve the df problem. This perspective differs from the one that was promoted by Bernstein and his disciples (e.g., Kugler, Kelso, & Turvey, 1980; Turvey, 1990), who focused almost entirely on effector coupling (synergies and coordinative structures) and biomechanical constraints.

3. COUPLING

Let us return to the fact that the arm (minus the hand) has seven dfs. It would simplify the control of the arm if some of these dfs were functionally eliminated, particularly if the number of dfs of the arm equaled the number of dfs in the task description. Suppose a task to be performed were fully characterized by two dfs. An example would be "Bring the tip of the right index finger to location (x, y) in the sagittal plane." If the number of dfs of the arm could be reduced to two, the df problem would be eliminated for this task. The method for reducing the dfs considered in this section is exploitation of effector coupling. If two independent elements of a system are coupled, then their number of dfs reduces from two to one. Hence, in general, for a system with n dfs that must satisfy a task involving m dfs ($m < n$), coupling of at least $n - m$ elements will eliminate the df problem.

Is there sufficient coupling to have this effect? There certainly are linkages between the effectors. For reviews, see Heuer (in press) and Turvey (1990). One well-known example is the asymmetric tonic neck reflex: when a baby faces to one side, the elbow on that side of the body flexes, whereas the elbow on the opposite side of the body extends (McGraw, 1943). Such interactions among the head and arms indicate that, even at an early age, effectors that are potentially independent from an anatomical standpoint are, in fact, interdependent. Many neonatal and postneonatal reflexes have this property (see Rosenbaum, 1991).

Coupling of the limbs is not seen only in infantile, reflexive behavior; it is also seen in adult voluntary movement. Many acts involving the two hands illustrate the coupling. A familiar example is the outcome of attempting to pat one's head with straight up-and-down motions while rubbing one's stomach with circular motions, or attempting to draw a circle with one hand while drawing a square with the other. Although these are fanciful tasks, they reveal striking interactions between the limbs, the understanding of which has been a major aim of behavioral neurophysiology, starting at least with von Holst (1939). Von Holst observed that if a human adult oscillates one arm at some frequency and tries, at the same time, to oscillate the other arm at some other frequency, the movements of the two limbs show considerable interaction. Many studies have confirmed the robustness and generality of these effects, and impressive mathematical tools have been brought to bear to characterize the interactions in terms of nonlinear, coupled oscillators (e.g., Fuchs & Kelso, 1994). Bimanual interactions also appear in discrete (one-shot) movements. When people reach with two hands for two spatial targets, the time taken by one hand to reach a given spatial target can be dramatically affected by the difficulty of the reach that must be performed with the other hand (Kelso, Southard, & Goodman, 1979; see also Wiesendanger et al., Chapter 14).

There are also linkages within the arm. As shown by Kots and Syrovegnin (1966), subjects found it easier to flex the wrist and elbow simultaneously or to extend the wrist and elbow simultaneously than to extend the elbow while flexing the wrist or to flex the elbow while extending the wrist. Similarly, Haggard and Wing (1991) found that when the arms of human subjects were pulled back by a mechanical device as the subjects reached forward to grab an object, the tips of the thumb and index finger were drawn toward each other, as if the two fingers were returning to positions they had occupied before. All these observations indicate that there is intersegmental coupling within the arm as well as between the arms.

What do these results imply about the df problem? Classically, they have

been taken to suggest that linkages between effectors reduce or even eliminate the df problem. Is this conclusion correct? If coupling eliminated the df
problem for a task described by n dfs, it would be impossible to perform a task
described by more than n dfs. The fact that a person can perform a task in
different ways (e.g., to adopt an extreme posture when reaching for a target
when an obstacle is in the way) indicates that actors are not rigidly constrained by linkages that might otherwise be postulated to explain why they
can perform the task in a particular way. If linkages are activated according to
task demands, as argued by some (e.g., Kugler et al., 1980), then the problem
remains of how those linkages, and not others, are activated. Some tasks
might be performed in only the ways that rigid linkages permit, but this
amounts to saying that the df problem can be solved when the df problem
does not arise, which is uninteresting.

The second reason why coupling does not solve the df problem is that it
is a teleological fallacy to suppose that if linkages help reduce dfs, they exist
for this purpose. Consider the fact that when one sneezes, one's eyes close.
This is a linkage in the classical sense; it occurs reliably and is not due to
simple muscular or skeletal connections. However, it is hard to believe that
the coupling exists for the purpose of making it easier to decide what to do
with the eyes when a sneeze is coming on.

It is not really known why some linkages exist and others do not. To take a
well-known example (Schöner & Kelso, 1988), oscillating the two index fingers
gives rise to interesting interactions. For example, when the fingers oscillate in
an antiphase manner at a slow pacing frequency and then are made to oscillate at
a higher frequency, they tend to fall into phase, but if the fingers oscillate in an in-
phase manner at a slow frequency and then speed up, they do not fall into the
antiphase mode. This and other phenomena led Kelso and his colleagues to draw
on the mathematics of dynamical systems to model the observed interactions
(Fuchs & Kelso, 1994). They obtained impressive fits to their data, and their
results were provocative because their equations found expression in other
biological and physical systems. The drawback of the approach, however, is that
we don't know why the kind of dynamical system that characterizes two-finger
oscillation characterizes this form of behavior and not others. As one of us
observed elsewhere (Rosenbaum, 1991), the analysis doesn't explain why people
don't start to hop when they run faster.

There is a further aspect of neural coupling that bears on the view that
coupling serves to reduce dfs. As emphasized by Bernstein (1967), when people
learn new tasks they often freeze joints, thereby reducing the dfs to be
controlled, but then with practice, they free up these joints and capitalize on the
interplay between them. The control of pistol shooting provides an example.
Novice shooters lock the wrist, attempting to stabilize the gun as much as
possible, but more advanced shooters loosen the wrist so that inadvertent
lowering or raising of the gun barrel that occurs when the elbow or wrist bends is

compensated for by counterrotation of the other joint (see Tuller, Turvey, & Fitch, 1982). Thus, dfs are freed up as pistol shooters become more experienced. Freeing up dfs also occurs when people learn to throw with the nonpreferred hand (P. V. McDonald, van Emmerik, & Newell, 1989). These phenomena show that coupling of effectors may have more to do with refining the way tasks are performed than with selecting particular movements.

4. BIOMECHANICAL CONSTRAINTS

Let us turn now to another kind of constraint that has been emphasized in connection with the df problem. This is the biomechanical constraint. Biomechanical constraints can limit movement choices. They do so by eliminating movements that are impossible, such as those that take joints beyond their ranges of motion or that demand forces that are physiologically impossible. They also limit movement choices by eliminating the need for detailed planning of movements that can in fact occur. In throwing, for example, one need not specify what the arm must do at each instant, because transfer of momentum from the upper arm to the forearm and hand can allow the forearm and hand to be flung forward during the throwing motion (R. M. Alexander, 1991; see Rosenbaum & Krist, in press, for review). Similarly, muscle activity in the lower leg may be unnecessary when the leg swings forward during locomotion because transfer of angular momentum from the upper leg can propel the lower leg forward (McMahon, 1984), obviating detailed planning of the lower leg's trajectory (Thelen, Kelso, & Fogel, 1987). In much the same way, the viscoelastic properties of muscles can eliminate the need for detailed planning of limb trajectories. Target forces for opposing muscles and/or associated reflex thresholds can be established that define equilibrium positions that, in principle, imply complete trajectories to goal positions (Bizzi & Mussa-Ivaldi, 1989; Feldman, 1986).

These are just some of the ways that biomechanical constraints can limit action choices. Because biomechanical constraints can have this effect, they can, strictly speaking, help reduce the df problem. On the other hand, biomechanical constraints can rarely eliminate the df problem entirely, as demonstrated by the fact that one can perform the same task in different ways at will. As long as these alternative actions are biomechanically possible, it is obvious that biomechanical constraints have not eliminated them.

5. COST CONTAINMENT

If coupling and biomechanical constraints do not allow particular movements to be selected, how do the selections occur? We believe that movements are selected on the basis of cost containment. In our view, actors attempt to minimize (or at least satisfy) costs relevant to the tasks they perform. We will elaborate this view in this section, but first wish to comment on its historical place.

Cost containment has only recently gained acceptance in the motor control community. As an indication of this state of affairs, an influential review of the field, published less than 20 years ago (E. Saltzman, 1979), made no mention of cost containment as a strategy for dealing with the df problem. Even recent discussions that had the df problem as a primary focus failed to mention the cost containment approach (Turvey, 1990). For our purposes, it is not especially important why cost containment has only recently received attention. Perhaps the reason is that the concept is still undergoing rapid change. For example, as seen below, our notion of cost containment differs from that of others because we think it is unlikely that any single cost will be found for motor performance. This is not because we think the tools for finding a single putative cost are too blunt. Instead, we believe that an essential part of planning and controlling physical behavior is the capacity to specify in a flexible manner what costs should be contained. In our view, when a task is given by an external agent (e.g., an experimenter or a coach), the actor must elaborate the task description until the df problem vanishes. The way the actor does so, in our view, is to assign weights to the costs that are potentially relevant to performance. The heart of our approach, then, is that the actor redefines the task until there is no ambiguity about how it should be performed.

5.1 The Search for a Single Cost

If one peruses the recent motor control literature, one finds a number of authors who have attempted to identify a single cost that the motor system, by default, tries to minimize. For example, Stein, Oguztoreli, and Capaday (1986) compared several different cost candidates for muscle movement, and W. L. Nelson (1983) did the same for the kinematics of the hand in violin bowing and of the jaw in speech production. In neither study was it possible to identify a single winning cost.

Other authors who have looked for a single default cost, and whose ideas we want to examine now in some detail, are Hogan (1984), Flash and Hogan (1985), and Uno, Kawato, and Suzuki (1989). Hogan and Flash were struck by the observation that subjects making point-to-point hand movements in the horizontal plane spontaneously produced straight or nearly straight hand paths. They were also struck by the fact that the tangential velocity of the hand (i.e., the instantaneous rate of change of position of the hand) was usually well described by a bell-shaped curve (Morasso, 1981). This set of outcomes was obtained even if the path of the arm in joint space was highly curved or nonmonotonic (i.e., one or more joints reversed angular direction). Flash and Hogan argued that the observed behavior suggests that the motor system behaves as if it strives for maximally smooth movement of the hand through extrinsic space (i.e., minimization of the mean squared jerk of the hand in its extrinsic spatial path from the start to the finish of the movement). Flash and Hogan's model accurately predicted much of the data concerning the kinematics of the hand as it moves through the horizontal plane on its way to specified target locations.

Despite the success of Flash and Hogan's model, Uno et al. (1989) expressed concern over the fact that Flash and Hogan's hypothesized cost (minimum jerk) neglected dynamics. They were disturbed by the fact that, for Flash and Hogan, it would not matter if the actor had to move the hand horizontally from one point to another with or without a horizontal load pulling on the hand. In an experiment, Uno et al. showed that such a load had a dramatic effect on the hand paths that subjects followed. The result led Uno et al. to propose that a different cost is minimized—the rate of change of torque. Uno et al. showed that data that could be explained with the minimum jerk model could also be explained with the minimum torque change model, but not vice versa.

An issue that has arisen in the debate between Uno et al. and Flash and Hogan is why hand paths are not always straight, as they should be if they are planned as straight lines in external space (as supposed by Flash and Hogan). From a dynamics perspective like the one espoused by Uno et al., curved trajectories are expected as long as the curvature can be rationalized in terms of torque-change minimization. However, Wolpert, Ghahramani, and Jordan (1994) argued that curved hand paths are not necessarily incompatible with planning straight-line motions in external space, provided external space is perceived as curved. They presented evidence consistent with this viewpoint. Using a visual adaptation procedure in which objectively straight lines were made to appear curved, Wolpert et al. studied the way subjects changed their visually guided hand paths. They inferred from their data that the hand paths subjects perceived as straight were in fact slightly bent. We do not find the statistics from this study convincing, however. Furthermore, a student at the University of Massachusetts, Richard Gobeil, and one of us (DAR) performed an informal study, which led to the opposite conclusion from the one reached by Wolpert et al. In Gobeil's study, subjects attempted to draw lines (with the right hand) with the eyes either open or closed. When the subjects performed the task in the eyes-open condition, their lines were much straighter than when they performed the task in the eyes-closed condition. This result contradicts the hypothesis that the source of hand path curvature is visual.

Given all these conflicting outcomes and interpretations, can it ever be established whether Flash and Hogan or Uno et al. are correct? We think not, because the answer to the question of what cost is minimized (or satisfied) will always be task dependent. One really does not need to resort to laboratory experiments to recognize that there are some tasks for which it is crucial to plan with respect to extrinsic spatial coordinates and others for which it is not. An architect drawing lines on a blueprint will obviously care more about making straight lines in extrinsic space (on the blueprint) than will a person doing jumping jacks in the gym. The fact that the architect and the exerciser can be the same person indicates that one actor can plan in different ways at different times. Similarly, a violinist may make legato bow strokes when playing one piece of music, or spiccato bow strokes when playing another. The legato strokes will be smooth, but the spiccato strokes will be jerky; whether the strokes are smooth or jerky depends on what the violinist wants to communicate.

These observations imply that the best one can hope to show in a debate like the one between Flash and Hogan and Uno et al. is that Flash and Hogan are correct in some circumstances and that Uno et al. are correct in others. This may seem like an unsatisfactory state of affairs. The problem remains of defining the circumstances that favor the Flash–Hogan solution or the Uno et al. solution.

5.2 Differential Weighting of Costs

We have already indicated what we believe to be the solution to this problem. The solution we envision is a system that can emphasize different costs depending on the task to be performed. At least two steps are needed to implement such a system. First, possible costs must be identified, and second, those costs must be differentially weighted. Thus, if a task is defined as a weighted sum of $i = 1, 2, \ldots, n$ costs, each of which has a corresponding weight, w_i, then one must define all the n costs in order for the weights to be assigned to them, and for the task, T, to be finally defined as a weighted sum of the costs:

$$T = \sum_{i=1}^{n} w_i c_i .$$
(1)

It is convenient to have the weights take on values from 0 through 1 and sum to 1, because then the weight assigned to each cost reflects the emphasis given to it.

How can this scheme be put to use? Recently, it was implemented in a model of the planning of reaches (Rosenbaum, Loukopoulos, Meulenbroek, Vaughan, & Engelbrecht, 1995; Rosenbaum, Engelbrecht, Bushe & Loukopoulos, 1993). In the next section we briefly describe the model. A more complete description is given in Rosenbaum et al. (1995).

6. POSTURE-BASED PLANNING

When different costs are emphasized in planning, one must be clear what the costs apply to. In our model, costs apply to proposed goal postures. Goal postures are proposed, in our model, after spatial targets are identified and before movements to the goal postures are created.

6.1 Reasons for Postures

We have several reasons for proposing that motor planning includes consideration of postures. First, a major insight into motor control, coming initially from Feldman and his colleagues (Asatryan & Feldman, 1965; Feldman, 1986) and then from Bizzi and his colleagues (Bizzi & Mussa-Ivaldi, 1989), is that the nervous system may define target limb positions by specifying equilibrium points for the muscles. An equilibrium point is a set of muscle lengths for which muscle tensions balance out (sum to zero) or for which muscle stretch receptors stop triggering corrective muscle responses because of centrally set reflex thresholds. In principle, when an equilibrium point is specified and the starting point is known, the trajectory to the equilibrium point comes for free, making detailed planning of the trajectory unnecessary. A further advantage of equilibrium point control is that when an equilibrium point is specified, muscle lengths and joint angles associated with the equilibrium point are both implied (Shadmehr, 1993). This means that if one wishes to specify a whole-body vector of joint angles (a goal posture), the set of muscle lengths needed to achieve that goal posture is implied as well (although the muscle forces are not). Hence, specifying a goal posture when a starting posture is known implies that all the muscles in the body can continuously change their starting lengths to their goal lengths.

A second reason for believing that postures are selected before movements are planned is that it makes sense to assume that the units used for planning can be affected by learning. Findings from memory-for-movement tasks show that people are poor at remembering movements but are good at remembering positions. For example, in an experiment by Laabs (1973), when subjects moved the hand over a particular distance and direction and then the hand was moved by the experimenter to a new starting position, subjects had a hard time reproducing the distance or direction they just covered, but they found it easy to go back to the position to which they had just moved. Getting to this position from the new starting position demanded a different movement from the one just performed, which suggests that the movement that was just carried out was not stored, whereas the final position was. (For an excellent review of the memory-for-movement task, see Smyth, 1984.)

A third reason for proposing that goal postures play a central role in motor planning is that choices of possible movements have been shown, in rating studies (Rosenbaum, Vaughan, Jorgensen, Barnes, & Stewart, 1993), to be related to the evaluations that postures receive but not to the evaluations that movements receive. These ratings were obtained in studies involving the end-state comfort effect. This is a strong tendency for subjects to reach out and take hold of an object in an uncomfortable posture (e.g., with an under-hand grip) so that, after the object has been moved to another location, the terminal posture is comfortable (e.g., an overhand grip). When subjects evaluated the relative ease of making movements that would bring the hand to an overhand or underhand posture in the first object-grabbing motion or in the object-placing motion, the ratings they gave failed to predict the preferences they showed. However, when subjects evaluated the relative comfort of the overhand or underhand postures in the first object-grabbing position or in the second object-placing position, these ratings accurately predicted subjects' preferences. Thus, the evaluations of the postures better accounted for the factors that subjects took into account in their grip choices than did the evaluations of the movements.

A fourth and final reason for our emphasis on posture planning is mainly pragmatic. The dimensions along which postures vary are not controversial; they are just the mechanical degrees of freedom of the joints. By contrast, the dimensions along which movements vary are manifold. They can include times, distances, directions, peak velocities, and so forth. Although in principle any of these factors might actually be used in planning movements, it is difficult to determine in advance which factors actually are used. Hence, for ease of modeling, as well as the other reasons given above, we hypothesize a posture-based planning stage prior to a movement-based planning stage.

6.2 Finding a Goal Posture

If a goal of planning a reach is finding a goal posture, how is the goal posture found? A first hypothesis, which can be quickly dismissed, is that the brain stores all possible postures. The problem with this view is that there are an infinite number of locations to which the hand, or any point along the limb segment chain (any contact point), can be directed. Furthermore, as noted earlier, for any location within the workspace there are an infinite number of postures that can allow a contact point along the limb segment chain to reach that location.

A more reasonable possibility is that the brain stores just a few postures, or posture representations, and relies on these representations to derive new postures. A method for deriving new postures is to take a weighted sum of the stored postures, where the weights assigned to the stored postures reflect their judged effectiveness for achieving the task to be performed. The minimal number of stored postures that is needed is $2n$, where n is the number of mechanical dfs of the joints and 2 is the number of values at the ends of each df's range of motion (the minimum and maximum value of each df).

The basic functioning of our system is shown in Figure 1. (A) shows a stick figure with just 3 dfs (a bendable hip, shoulder, and elbow) as well as a spatial target to be reached. (B) shows three possible stored postures. Stored posture 1 is not very excited in this situation, whereas stored posture 2 is very excited, and stored posture 3 has an intermediate level of excitement. One reason why stored posture 2 is more excited than stored posture 1 is that the

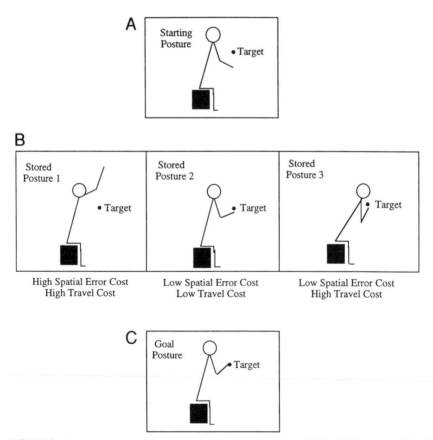

FIGURE 1 Basic workings of the posture-based planning system. (A) A stick figure capable of bending at the hip, shoulder, and elbow, along with a spatial target to be reached for. (B) Three hypothetical stored posture representations, with the level of their spatial error cost and travel cost indicated beneath each subpanel. (C) A goal posture.

hand (the contact point for this task) is much closer to the spatial target than is the hand for stored posture 1. Thus, one cost affecting the excitation of each stored posture is its spatial error cost—the distance in extrinsic spatial coordinates between the contact point and the spatial target to be reached. For convenience, we express this distance as the Euclidean distance between the contact point and the center of the spatial target. We assume that this distance can be computed through forward kinematics (i.e., elementary trigonometry operating on the lengths of the limb segments and joint angles).

Stored posture 3 is less excited than stored posture 2 even though its hand comes as close to the spatial target as does the hand of stored posture 2. The reason for the difference in the excitation levels of stored postures 2 and 3 is that the estimated cost of moving from the starting posture to stored posture 3 is greater than the estimated cost of moving from the starting posture to stored posture 2. We call this the travel cost. The travel cost of a stored posture depends on the angular displacements that each of its joints (or more generally, each of its dfs) must undergo to bridge the gap in joint space between the starting posture and the stored posture; the contribution of each joint's displacement is weighted by that joint's expense factor, which is a free, but empirically estimable, parameter.

Because we wish to find a single goal posture by taking a weighted sum of the constituent stored postures, it is necessary to transform the total costs of the stored postures into weights. We do this by passing the total costs of all the stored postures through a Gaussian filter, which yields a maximum value when the input total cost equals zero, and which has a standard deviation that is directly proportional to the minimum total cost of any stored posture. The weight assigned to each stored posture is its Gaussian value divided by the sum of the Gaussian values of all the stored postures. The advantage of making the standard deviation of the Gaussian directly proportional to the minimum total cost of any stored posture is that if there is a stored posture that is ideally suited for the task (i.e., its total cost equals zero), the standard deviation of the Gaussian goes to zero and the ideal stored posture is given a weight of 1; thus, only that stored posture determines the goal posture. Otherwise, all the stored postures contribute, but the weight assigned to any given posture depends on how well suited to the reaching task the best-suited stored posture is. We call this method Gaussian averaging, and we adopt it because it allows for either adoption of the best stored posture when there is a perfect stored posture or a weighted sum when there is none. Neurophysiological studies have shown that the brain uses both a winner-take-all strategy (C. D. Saltzman & Newsome, 1994) and a weighted sum strategy (Erickson, 1984; Georgopoulos, 1991) in decision making. Both methods are allowed by Gaussian averaging.

It is important to make two additional comments about the derivation of a weighted sum for defining a goal posture. First, it is possible to take a weighted sum of stored postures because postures can be viewed as vectors in joint space; the dimensions of the space are the mechanical dfs of the joints. Second, an additional process must be invoked to counteract a problem that arises when postures are combined to generate a goal posture. The problem arises from the fact that a weighted sum of postures, all of which permit a contact point to come to a spatial location, may nonetheless turn out to be a posture that does not permit the contact point to reach that same spatial location. In robotics, this is called the convexity problem (Craig, 1986); the term refers to the fact that the region of posture space containing postures that bring a contact point to a given spatial location may be convex but, paradoxically, the average of the region may lie outside the region, thus making the average posture one that does not permit the contact point to reach the spatial location. The convexity problem is a well-known difficulty with posture averaging (Bullock, Grossberg, & Guenther, 1993). To compensate for the convexity problem in our system, we allow for a feedforward correction process where, after a goal posture is found that is too far from a spatial target, another goal posture is found that is designed to bring the contact point to a spatial location on the opposite side of the spatial target. The idea is to capitalize on biases that arise when stored postures are linearly combined, just as a marksman may compensate for biases in shooting by deliberately aiming for a target that is displaced from the true target by the mirror image of the bias. Adding the feedforward correction process to our model provides an experimentally testable index of planning time: the greater the number of feedforward correction cycles, the longer the planning time should be.

6.3 Bridging the Gap between the Starting Posture and the Goal Posture

The final component of our theory permits movement from the starting posture to the goal posture. The method is simple interpolation. For convenience, we assume that the default movement is a straight line in joint space from the starting posture to the target posture. This is tantamount to saying that biological action follows the Principle of Least Action (Fox, 1987). Also for convenience, we assume that the angular velocities of the joints are bell-shaped functions of time. This amounts to saying that each joint is driven by a sinusoidal torque generator. A number of studies have provided evidence consistent with the latter assumption (Abrams, Meyer, & Kornblum, 1989; Bock, 1994; Flanagan & Ostry, 1990; Lacquaniti & Soechting, 1982; Soechting & Lacquaniti, 1981), although departures from exact bell shapes have been observed depending on speed–accuracy requirements (see Bullock & Grossberg, 1988, for review) and the direction of motion (Flanagan & Ostry, 1990). Departures from straight-line trajectories through joint space have also been observed, but the capacity to vary the curvature of the path through joint space has also been viewed as a useful way to generate trajectories that avoid obstacles or permit production of desired hand paths (Hollerbach & Atkeson, 1987).

6.4 Some Outcomes of the Model

In this section we discuss how our model performs, emphasizing those aspects that bear on the allowance for differential cost weighting. The aspects of the model's performance that will be discussed here have been demonstrated with simulations involving a computerized stick figure with 3 dfs (a bendable hip, shoulder, and elbow, permitting movement in the sagittal plane). A more complete review of the model's achievements appears in Rosenbaum et al. (1995).

One feature of the stick figure's performance is that it can bring different contact points along the limb-segment chain to any reachable location in the workspace (Figure 2). It is possible to reach with a contact point at the wrist, for example, by assigning spatial error costs to stored postures based on the distance between the spatial target to be reached and the location the wrist would occupy if each of the stored postures were adopted. Similarly, it is possible to reach with a contact point at the elbow or at the shoulder, or indeed at an arbitrary point between two joints, by assigning spatial error costs to stored postures based on the distance between the spatial target to be reached and the locations those contact points would occupy. A tool can also be used for reaching because, as long as its length and angle of attachment to the body are known, forward kinematics can be used to determine where a

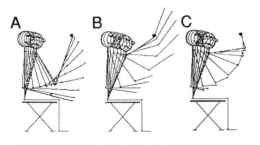

FIGURE 2   Simulations of reaching with a hand-held tool (A), with the elbow (B), and with an amputated limb (C). (From Rosenbaum et al., 1995. Copyright © 1995 by the American Psychological Association. Reprinted with permission.)

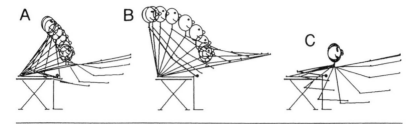

FIGURE 3 Simulations of adaptation to increased expense of elbow rotation (C) and hip rotation (B) compared to reaching with normal joint expenses (A). The starting posture and the location of the spatial target (in front of the knee) are the same in all three panels. (From Rosenbaum et al., 1995. Copyright © 1995 by the American Psychological Association. Reprinted with permission.)

contact point along the tool will be in relation to the spatial target; those stored postures that best permit the tool to come close to the spatial target are assigned most weight.

Another basic feature of performance that becomes possible with the differential cost-weighting approach taken in our model is the capacity for adaptation to changes in joint mobility. Biological actors are resilient. When a person's elbow is suddenly injured, the person continues to complete everyday tasks but in different ways than before, typically with more hip movement than usual or with more shoulder movement than usual. Joints compensate for reduced mobility of other joints immediately, without the need for extensive training. The challenge is to explain how they do so.

Our model provides a possible way of explaining the compensation. As seen in Figure 3, simulations relying on our planning system display instant adaptation to sudden changes in the mobility of the joints. These simulations were achieved by having the stick figure adopt the same starting posture and supplying it with the same spatial target, but giving it expense factors for individual joints that were either normal or higher than normal. The normal values were determined in an experiment with human subjects who reached for spatial targets in the sagittal plane and for whom hip, shoulder, and elbow expense values were estimated by minimizing discrepancies between predicted and observed postures (Vaughan, Rosenbaum, Loukopoulos, & Engelbrecht, 1995). In the simulations, when the elbow's expense factor was increased above normal the stick figure immediately compensated by bending the shoulder and hip more than normal, and when the hip's expense factor was increased the stick figure immediately compensated by bending the shoulder and elbow more than normal. In both cases, the compensation occurred because more weight than usual was assigned to the stored postures that required rotation of joints with relatively low expense factors.

7. CONCLUSIONS

In this chapter we have tried to show that differential cost weighting provides a promising new way to explain the impressive range of behaviors that actors achieve. We have tried to demonstrate this point both didactically and through a review of our model. Although our modeling work has mainly involved simple reaching, we believe the approach can apply to other behaviors as well. For example, we have already simulated handwriting, creating a stick figure like the one described here that can write, even producing essentially the same graphic output with different effectors (Meulenbroek, Rosenbaum, Thomassen, & Loukopoulos, 1994; Meulenbroek, Rosenbaum, Thomassen, Loukopoulos, & Vaughan, in press). We have also modeled walking, treating locomotion as a cyclic transition between postures (Rosenbaum et al., 1995). In principle, our model can also extend to grasping and other forms of hand movements, because postures of the hand, like postures of the arms, torso, and legs, can be evaluated and combined to form goal postures. One way to model the planning of reach-and-grasp movements is to specify goal postures involving the arm, hand, and fingers. Thus, well-known relations between transport of the hand and opening and closing of the fingers during reach-and-grasp movements (Paulignan and Jeannerod, Chapter 13) can, in principle, be modeled in terms of two successive goal postures, the first involving an intermediate arm position with the fingers spread apart, and the second involving a final arm position with the fingers closer together. Grip and load forces (see Wing, Chapter 15) might also be modeled in terms of goal postures, because postures can include forces as well as joint angles or muscle lengths, and because forces can be specified by designating spatial targets for the fingers or hand that are inside or past the object to be grasped, the depth of the virtual target determining the force to be applied (Bizzi, Hogan, Mussa-Ivaldi, & Giszter, 1992; Vaughan, Rosenbaum, Moore, & Diedrich, 1995). Of course, more work is needed to elaborate and evaluate these claims, but a successful theory based on flexible weighting of costs now seems within reach.

ACKNOWLEDGMENTS

This work was supported by Grant SBR-94–96290 from the National Science Foundation, a University of Massachusetts BRSG Faculty Research Grant, a Research Scientist Development Award from the National Institute of Mental Health, the Dutch Organization for Scientific Research (NWO Stimulans Premie), the Royal Netherlands Academy of Science, and the Hamilton College Faculty Research Fund.

10

Kinematic and Dynamic Factors in the Coordination of Prehension Movements

CLAUDE GHEZ, SCOTT COOPER,
AND JOHN MARTIN

1. INTRODUCTION

In reaching for an object, the transport and grasp phases are conceptualized as being represented in the nervous system by distinct motor "schemata" (Arbib, 1985; Arbib, Iberall, & Lyons, 1985; Jeannerod, Arbib, Rizzolatti, & Sakata, 1995) that are organized by different aspects of the visual scene (see Iberall and Fagg, Chapter 12). At a kinematic level, transport mainly reflects information about object location relative to the initial position of the hand (Ghez, Gordon, Ghilardi, & Sainburg, 1994; Ghilardi, Gordon, & Ghez, 1995). The characteristic straightness of hand paths (Morasso, 1981) and the bell-shaped velocity profiles that scale with distance (Atkeson & Hollerbach, 1985) indicate that extent and direction are substantially preplanned (Ghez, Gordon, Ghilardi, Christakos, & Cooper, 1990; Ghez et al., 1994). The kinematic features of grasp, on the other hand, depend primarily on the shape and orientation of the object (Arbib et al., 1985). Preparation for grasp is initiated during transport and preshapes the hand to the contours of the object before reaching it (Jakobson & Goodale, 1991; Paulignan, MacKenzie, Marteniuk, & Jeannerod, 1990; Paulignan, MacKenzie et al., 1991). Like the straight hand paths and the scaled velocity profiles of the reach phase, hand preshaping underlines the importance of prediction in organizing the kinematic details of prehension. Taken as a whole, analyses of hand trajectories and reaching errors in humans support the idea that planning takes place in a neural representation that preserves the spatial relationships of hand and target as well as the location of potential obstacles that could constrain hand path.

How the nervous system controls the forces (i.e., movement dynamics) used to generate the kinematic events is less well understood. Transformation of intended hand movements into suitable commands to rotate joints against loads requires a coordinate system suitable for encoding the magnitudes of joint rotations, torques, or muscle actions. This is referred to as an intrinsic coordinate system to distinguish it from the extrinsic coordinates encoding the spatial locations of hand and objects. A significant problem facing analyses of the transformation from one coordinate system to the other is the complex nature of the biomechanical task of governing multijoint motions through muscle actions.

In isolated single-joint movements the relationships between observable changes in position and the forces needed to produce them are relatively straightforward. As a result, the function of muscle activation and of neural control in coordinating antagonists can be understood intuitively from a few basic physical principles. Simple Newtonian mechanics prepare us to appreciate the importance of agonist and antagonist muscles in first accelerating and then in braking the mass of the limb, and for reciprocal neural mechanisms to coordinate these actions. Further insight into how such mechanisms are likely to be used is gained by knowing that the mechanical response of a muscle to a burst of action potentials that trigger contraction is relatively slow: force continues to increase well after electrical activation is over, and decays over a still longer time course. Since the duration of the force rise may be as long or longer than a reaction time, antagonist activation appropriate to decelerate or reverse a trajectory at a given location requires anticipatory or predictive mechanisms in addition to more automatic segmental circuits (J. Gordon & Ghez, 1987a, 1987b).

In controlling the motions of a multiarticulated limb, however, muscle contraction acts in concert with additional forces, that vary during movement in still more complex ways. At rotating joints, the actions of these forces are expressed as torques. Gravitational torque depends on the spatial orientation of the limb relative to gravity as well as on the position of each joint. Gravity can assist or resist a given movement and movement plans need to consider this. A more complex problem for neural control is that motion at each joint produces forces that are transmitted to all the other joints of the linked mechanical system as interaction torques. These torques are not only dependent on limb configuration but they vary with velocity and acceleration (both angular and translational). Children are amused by the effects of these torques in playing with articulated mechanical snakes and seeing that movements they impose on the tail are transmitted down the entire chain of linked segments. The limb is similar: movements at the shoulder—or even the trunk and body—are transmitted down to the hand. In a seminal report, Hollerbach and Flash (1982) demonstrated through simulations that to produce the canonical straight hand paths of two-joint reaching movements, the nervous system had to take account of these torques. If it did not do so, substantial path distortions would occur. In recent studies we have shown that proprioception provides critical information for controlling interaction torques and allows subjects to calibrate learned internal models of the properties of their limb (Ghez, Gordon, & Ghilardi, 1995; Ghez & Sainburg, 1995). Without proprioception, as in severe cases of large-fiber sensory neuropathy, this does not occur, causing profound trajectory disturbances and errors in aimed hand movements (Sainburg, Ghilardi, Poizner, & Ghez, 1995; Sainburg, Poizner, & Ghez, 1993). Experiments in cats also show that inactivation of interpositus nuclei of the cerebellum, which also receive proprioceptive information from the limb, produces trajectory errors attributable to uncompensated interaction torques (Cooper, 1995; Cooper, Martin, & Ghez, 1993; Martin, Cooper, Hacking, & Ghez, 1994). Similar lack of compensation has now also been documented in cases of human cerebellar ataxia (Bastian, Mueller, Martin, Keating, & Thach, 1994).

Interaction torques between digit segments have been shown to influence movement of the digit as a whole (Cole, 1990). However, the influence of shoulder and elbow motions on the hand during prehension, has not, we believe, been examined. Because of the long length of the lever arm, the forces produced by shoulder and elbow movements on the joints of the hand are likely to be large. The present report examines the organization of prehension in the cat, an animal with natural speed and great skill in catching prey with its paws. Feline prehension is a particularly attractive model for studying multijoint limb control, since a vast body of information concerning the spinal circuitry responsible for mediating cortical and brain-stem commands is available in this species (Baldissera, Hultborn, & Illert, 1981). Moreover, the pioneering work of Alstermark, Lundberg, and colleagues has demonstrated that transport and grasp are mediated by different spinal interneuronal systems (Alstermark, Gorska, Johanisson, & Lundberg, 1987; Alstermark, Isa, Lundberg, Pettersson, & Tantisira, 1991; Alstermark, Isa, & Tantisira, 1991; Alstermark, Lundberg, Norrsell, & Sybirska, 1981). C3-C4 propriospinal neurons are critical for the former and have recurrent collaterals feeding into cerebellar control circuits, while segmental neurons mediate the latter.

After briefly describing our experimental approach, we show that in the cat the paths of the distal points of the limb are comprised of relatively straight segments. Our kinematic analysis of joint motions indicates that these result from precisely coordinated motions at multiple forelimb joints (Martin, Cooper, & Ghez, 1995). Moreover, cats adapt the angulation of distal joints to the changes in orientation of the target, a response similar to hand preshaping in primates. Through an analysis of the interplay of torques acting at the different joints, we then show how neural control mechanisms also anticipate the interactions transmitted to distal segments. Overall, our chapter stresses the importance of predictive mechanisms, and the discussion presents speculations about higher level integration and internal representations for behavior are alluded to.

2. METHODS

Cats were trained to retrieve a small piece of meat with their paw from a narrow food well placed horizontally in front of them at a comfortable distance (see Gorska & Sybirska, 1980; Martin et al., 1995). In the absence of restraints, reaching involves a complex series of head, body, and limb movements that may vary substantially from trial to trial according to the initial posture and other variables, including individual style. To avoid having to evaluate the effects of head and body motions on reaching, we restrained the cats in a hammock (Alice Chatham, Inc.), which allowed only about 1 cm of torso movement. For further standardization, the cats were trained to apply a force exceeding a set level on a sensor placed under the reaching paw for 1–2 s prior to reaching for the baited food well. In order to assess the kinematic and dynamic strategies used by the animals, we varied the height, distance, and inclination of the food well within their comfortable workspace.

Qualitative features of the movements were assessed by examining single fields ($\frac{1}{60}$th s) of videotaped movements (1 ms shutter speed; Panasonic camcorder AG450). For kinematic quantitative analyses, however, we used the MacReflex (Qualysis, Inc.) video digitizing system, which computed the x and y coordinates of the centroids of retroreflective markers, recorded in the sagittal plane at 100 Hz. These markers were attached to the skin of paw tip (taken as the distal phalangeal segment of the 4th digit), metacarpophalangeal joint (MCP), and wrist. Since the skin over the shoulder and elbow is highly mobile, we used an orthopedic pin implanted in the humerus, which protruded from the skin, to obtain better estimates of these points. An outrigger attached to the pin was aligned with the humerus and had retroreflective markers over the glenohumeral joint and the lateral epicondyle (axis of rotation of elbow). Analyses were restricted to reaches that remained close to the imaging plane. Finally, electromyograms (EMGs) were recorded from bipolar wire electrodes inserted percutaneously into selected wrist and elbow muscles identified by electrical stimulation. Raw EMG signals were filtered (300–1000 Hz), rectified, bin integrated (Ghez & Martin, 1982), and acquired at 100 Hz. Signals from strain gauges, EMGs, and photodiodes sensing entry of paw into the food well were recorded on a second Macintosh computer equipped with A/D converters (National Instruments). Both sets of data were combined for analyses.

The torques responsible for the recorded motions were computed from equations of motion of a planar four-segment limb (Cooper, 1995). Segment lengths were measured for each animal and segment masses were obtained from published data for cats (Hoy & Zernicke, 1985). As in the work of Smith, Zernicke, and colleagues (J. L. Smith & Zernicke, 1987), we have subdivided the numerous terms of the equations of motion into four torques. However, we chose to compute motions and torques in terms of joint angles (see Cooper, 1995, for the four-segment case; see Sainburg et al., 1995, for the two segment case) rather than in terms of segment angles in space (e.g., Hoy & Zernicke, 1985, 1986). Unfortunately, because the terms comprising individual torques are not the same for segment and joint-based computations, the resulting values cannot be directly compared. Thus, in order to avoid confusion we have used a somewhat different terminology to identify torque components and to reflect these computational differences (see below and Appendix).

3. RESULTS

3.1 Kinematic Features of Reaching in the Cat

3.1.1 Neural Planning Subdivides Paw Transport into Differentially Controlled Movement Segments

In approaching the kinematic analysis of complex movements, it is important to begin by identifying elementary components whose control may be subject to different task variables or specific constraints (such as distance or accuracy). For example, in drawing movements, Viviani and co-workers suggested that such components could be distinguished by path curvature and movement speed (i.e., tangential velocity) (Lacquantiti, Terzuolo, & Viviani, 1983; Viviani & Cenzato, 1985; Viviani & McCollum, 1983; Viviani & Schneider, 1991). Thus, in many tasks, hand paths can be divided into relatively straight segments (i.e., where curvature is low) joined at bends where speed falls to local minima. Such segmentation is present in two-dimensional reaching movements as well, when obstacles are present (Abend, Bizzi, & Morasso, 1982) or when a new target is presented during movement (Flash & Henis, 1991; Paulignan, MacKenzie et al., 1991). Similar segmentation occurs in feline prehension movements (Figure 1) where wrist and paw tip paths consist of two relatively straight segments joined at a bend. The paw is first rapidly raised to a location in front of the target (lift phase), then it is directed into the food well (thrust phase) (Figure 1A).

Spatial trajectories during these phases are governed two different spatial features of the task. The location of the bend joining the two wrist paths segments varies with the position of the food well, as can be seen in Figure 1B (arrows) where target height is varied. This via-point, through which the wrist passes without stopping, therefore represents an implicit target of the lift phase of movement. During this phase, wrist speed has the bell-shaped profile typical of reaching movements as in human reaching (see above) and peak speed scales with the distance moved (Figure 1C). As is shown here, the duration of lift does not increase with distance but remains approximately constant (termed isochrony by Viviani and co-workers; Viviani & Cenzato, 1985; Viviani & McCollum, 1983). This tight regulation of duration has been

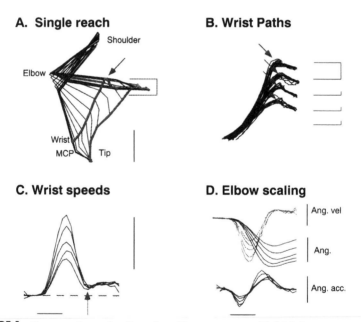

FIGURE 1   Segmentation and scaling of reaching movements. (A) Stick figure representation of a single movement to a target 14 cm above the footplate. The paths of the paw tip and wrist are shown in gray. Metacarpophalangeal (MCP), elbow, and shoulder paths are not shown. (B) Wrist paths for reaches to targets located 8, 11, 14, and 17 cm above the footplate. Gray arrows mark the approximate location of the end of the lift phase on paths, which corresponds to the gray arrow on the ensemble averages in (C). (C) Ensemble averages of wrist speed for reaches to targets located at heights of 8, 11, 14, 17, and 20 cm. Arrow marks the approximate transition from lift to thrust. (D) Ensemble averages of elbow joint angle, angular velocity, and angular acceleration to the same targets as shown in (C). Scale bars: (A) 5 cm; (C) 100 ms, 1 m/s; (D) 50°, 1000°/s, 20,000°/s/s.

reported for isometric responses in cats and humans (Ghez & Vicario, 1978; J. Gordon & Ghez, 1987a) and for the segments of continuous drawing movements (Viviani & McCollum, 1983; Viviani & Schneider, 1991), but in human reaching some prolongation in movement time is more common (e.g., Atkeson & Hollerbach, 1985; J. Gordon, Ghilardi, Cooper, & Ghez, 1994). During thrust, both path angle and movement speed are largely independent of the spatial location and distance of the target. While wrist speed may show a second small peak, more commonly, as shown for a different experiment in Figure 1C, a clear peak may not be evident. Closeup views of single video fields ($\frac{1}{60}$th s) show that the paw usually avoids the walls of the food well during thrust and that the claws extend in preparation for grasp (see Fig. 6A in Martin & Ghez, 1993). Thus, the lower speed during thrust is likely to reflect a form of speed–accuracy trade-off (Fitts, 1954).

These simple spatiotemporal movement segments resulted from the combined rotations of all forelimb joints. The distance covered by the paw during lift resulted mainly from flexion of the elbow. The duration of this movement was independent of target height over the range of distances examined. Isochrony resulted from the proportional scaling of both velocity and acceleration (Figure 1D), a strategy referred to as pulse-height control (Ghez, 1979, 1983; J. Gordon & Ghez, 1987a; J. Gordon, Ghilardi, Cooper, & Ghez, 1994) or speed sensitive (Corcos, Gottlieb, & Agarwal, 1989).

Angular changes at other joints (shoulder and wrist and MCP) were more complex. For example, the shoulder is initially retracted (i.e., extended) and later protracted (i.e., flexed). The retraction acted to linearize the paw path early during lift rather than to transport the paw to the target, while the protraction brought the paw closer to the target and contributed significantly, together with elbow extension, to the thrust. It is interesting to note that wrist paths often become markedly bowed during inactivation of localized regions in the anterior interpositus nucleus of the cerebellum because the animal fails to retract the shoulder during lift. This causes, in turn, large systematic end point errors (Cooper, 1995; Cooper et al., 1993). Thus, linearity of the end effector path can entail monophasic trajectories at some joints and biphasic ones, with direction reversals, in others.

3.1.2 Anticipatory Adjustments and Adaptation of Distal Joint Angles to Spatial Demands

In primate prehension, the shape of the object to be grasped determines the spatial orientations of hand and digits at the time of contact. Therefore, the motions producing the required end effector configurations have to be initiated earlier. This applies to feline prehension as well. For example, the orientation of the paw segment has to match the angle of the food well prior to entry. When the food well is oriented horizontally, the wrist needs to be almost fully extended for the paw to enter and traverse the length of the well.

However, because flexion (i.e., plantar flexion) occurs early in lift (see below for the origin of this phenomenon), the wrist needs to be extended subsequently (i.e., dorsiflexed) before thrust.

Figure 2 shows the time course (A) and spatial organization (B) of both wrist angle and wrist angular acceleration. By representing these variables as variations in a gray scale directly on the wrist path it can be seen that the wrist flexes initially during lift and then extends as the via-point is approached. The similarity in wrist angle during thrust for the different target locations is evident by the similar shading of the paths during thrust at the different heights (Figure 2A, *right*). The light grayband (black arrow in Figure 2B,

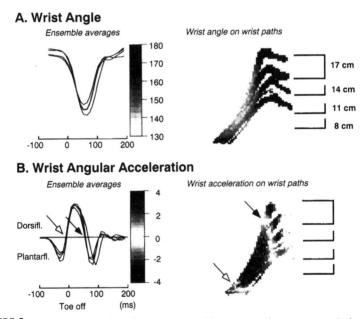

FIGURE 2   Spatial control of reaching. (A) Ensemble averages of wrist joint angle for reaches to targets 8, 11, 14, and 17 cm above the footplate are shown to the left. Wrist angle is represented as a gray scale on wrist paths on the right. (B) Ensemble averages of wrist joint angular acceleration (*left*) and wrist acceleration represented as a gray scale on wrist paths (*right*). For paths shown on right, the movement variable (either wrist joint angle or joint angular acceleration) was transformed into a gray scale that was used to plot successive points on the path. The shade of each point in the path corresponded to the shade that represented the amplitude of the wrist angle (A) or acceleration (B) when the joint was at that location. In order to increase the sensitivity of the display in (B), we have plotted the absolute value of the acceleration (i.e., both positive and negative acceleration values) with the same gray scale. The interval between the open and closed arrows on the ensemble average is shown on the paths to the right. Gray scale calibrations for the path plots in (A) and (B) are shown in relation to the ensemble averages. Scale bars: (A) °/s; (B) °/s/s × 10,000.

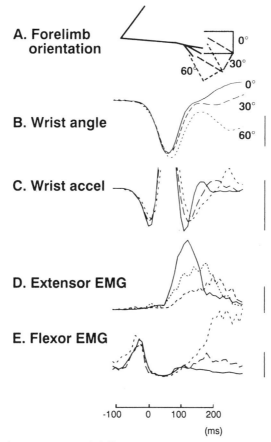

FIGURE 3 Reaching to targets with different orientation angles. (A) Limb segments from the video field immediately preceding tube entry showing that the wrist and MCP joint angles are progressively more flexed as target orientation was increased from 0 to 60°. (B, C, D, and E) Ensemble averages of wrist angle, angular acceleration, wrist (and digit) extensor EMG, and wrist flexor EMG. In this task, we adjusted slightly the height of the target so that the maximal height of the wrist path was approximately the same for targets of different orientations. Scale bars: (B) 20°; (C) 20,000°/s/s; (D and E) 500 arbitrary units.

right) shows that the wrist is decelerated over a short distance near the via-point to achieve the required near-horizontal wrist angle needed for target entry.

As shown in Figure 3, wrist and MCP angles at target entry depend on the orientation of the food well. In particular, flexion of the wrist increases with the inclination of the food well. Accordingly, EMG activity increases in wrist and digit flexor muscles and decreases in extensors. These reciprocal changes in distal muscle activity consistently begin well before target entry, reflecting the same predictive control seen in primate preshaping. This adaptation of distal joint angles to the inclination of the food well without changes in the early phase of lift, indicates that kinematic and EMG changes occurring late in the reach are fundamentally independent of those occurring earlier.

In sum, path segmentation has been taken to reflect the operation of central planning mechanisms (e.g., Hogan, 1988; Morasso, 1981)) in two-joint human reaching movements. Similar arguments apply here for cat fore-limb movements: the paths show two quasi-linear segments that are defined by spatial coordinates of starting points, via-points, and end points. The motions of the different joints function not only to linearize paths, which would otherwise be curved (Cooper, 1995), but also to prevent collisions or contact with obstacles. As is the case of preshaping in primate prehension, these joint angle changes need to be implemented in advance of the goal. Time series and path displays of kinematic variables show the remarkable degree of precision with which this spatial control is achieved.

4. DYNAMIC INTERACTIONS AFFECTING DISTAL MOTIONS DURING PREHENSION

As we noted in the introduction, it is difficult to deduce the role of neuro-muscular events in controlling movement from records of angular changes at the joints alone. This is because muscle contraction acts in concert with a variety of other time-varying forces. One approach to compute the different forces producing recorded motions of joints is based on the d'Alembert principle, which views acceleration as a state of equilibrium between multiple torques—derived from Newtonian mechanics—that sum to zero. As noted in Methods, we have chosen to compute the terms of the equilibrium equation for each joint as torques acting directly to rotate the individual joints, rather than acting on the centers of mass of the limb segments (see also Appendix). The main reason for selecting this coordinate frame is that it corresponds more directly to those of muscle actions and proprioceptive inputs than would a system of coordinates for coding segment angles in space.

Unfortunately, regardless of the coordinate system that is used, in a linked system of four joints the resulting equations are highly complex (e.g., in a joint-based system, at the elbow they include some 79 individual terms). Different approaches for grouping terms into functionally meaningful components have been used by different investigators (see Appendix). For our approach (Cooper, 1995) we identify three categories of torque that reflect the dimensions and masses of the segments. These are illustrated schematically, together with the effects of muscle action (a fourth torque term, described below), for the elbow joint in Figure 4. The first two torques contribute to both single and multijoint movements and are described in the upper part of the figure. First, in movements that are not confined to the horizontal plane, such as those studied here in the cat, the weight of the limb segment produces a gravitational torque. The magnitude of this torque depends on the spatial orientation of the segments attached to the joint. It is, however, also affected by the configuration of the distal segments (not illustrated). Second, the inertial load carried by the joint, which we term self-torque, represents the resistance of the forearm (and the distal segments attached to it) to being accelerated or decelerated. This torque must be overcome by agonist muscles at movement onset and resisted by antagonists at the end of movement, to counter the tendency for forearm inertia to resist the decrease in velocity. The self-torque therefore represents a move-ment-dependent torque that varies inversely with angular acceleration but that is scaled by the combined moments of inertia of the forearm and paw segments. Since, in rotating, the elbow moves both of those segments, self-torque is dependent on the angles of the distal joints. For example, flexion of the wrist, which occurs at the beginning of lift (Figure 1A and Figure 3), reduces the self-torque that muscles must overcome to accelerate the elbow into flexion.

A third variety of torque arises from the motions of all linked segments, the interaction torque, and is unique to multijoint systems. Three types of interaction have been distinguished according to whether they vary with the accelerations, velocities, or the product of accelerations and velocities of the linked segments. Although we have not distinguished them in the analyses presented below, it is useful to consider them individually to appreciate when, during movement, a particular effect may dominate. The actions of these torques are illustrated schematically in the boxed part of Figure 4A. Accelera-tion-dependent torque tends to bring the joint toward 90° and is therefore dependent on limb configuration. Thus, in the example illustrated in Figure 4A (*left*), when the elbow angle is greater than 90°—as happens at the begin-ning of lift—acceleration of the shoulder into extension (white arrow) causes flexion at the elbow (black arrow). The velocity-dependent interaction torque is termed centrifugal torque. Centrifugal torque pulls a rotating mass, in this case the forearm, away from its center of rotation. Here, rotation of the shoulder generates a centrifugal torque that extends the elbow. Since this torque is proportional to velocity, it is significant later in movement and, indeed, reaches its peak when acceleration-dependent torque crosses zero (dotted line at b in Fig 4B). Finally, for completeness, it should be noted that the proximal joint is also subject to a Coriolis torque, which is proportional to the product of the angular velocities at each joint.

After the effects of gravity, self-, and interaction torque are considered, there remains an unaccounted for (or "residual") quantity for the equilibrium equation to sum to zero. This residual torque includes the effects of

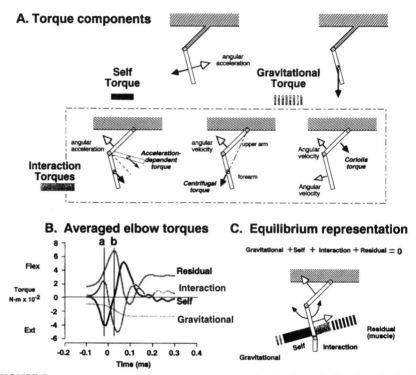

FIGURE 4   Dynamic analysis of elbow motion. (A) (*top*) Explanation of self- and gravitational torques acting at the elbow for single-joint movement (flexion). For the self-torque (*left*), open arrow indicates direction of acceleration driving motion and solid arrow the direction of the self-torque opposing motion. For the gravitational torque (*right*), solid arrow shows the direction of torque. The three torques comprising the interaction torque are shown within the dashed rectangle. From left to right, acceleration-dependent torque, velocity-dependent centrifugal torque, and Coriolis torque. Open arrows indicate the direction of the angular acceleration and velocity and the solid arrows the direction of the particular interaction torques. For the acceleration-dependent torque, the black forearm segment and arrows show that the torque acts to flex the forearm when elbow angle is greater than 90°; the gray forearm segment and arrows show that the torque acts to extend the forearm when elbow angle is less than 90°. (C) The magnitudes of the four torques acting on the joint at peak elbow flexor acceleration (corresponding to vertical line labeled a in [B]) are depicted as a stacked histogram. Open arrows show direction of elbow flexor acceleration and shoulder extensor acceleration. Black arrows show directions of positive (interaction and residual) torques contributing to accelerating the limb, and negative (self- and gravitational) torques that resist motion. (Gravitational, light gray; self-, black; interaction, dark gray, residual, black and white.) (B) Ensemble averages of residual (dashed black), interaction (solid gray), self- (black), and gravitational (dashed gray) torques. Solid vertical line at (a) is at peak elbow flexor acceleration and at (b), peak flexor residual torque.

muscle contraction. It is sometimes referred to as generalized muscle torque (GMT) (J. L. Smith & Zernicke, 1987). Similarly, in other publications we have used the term muscle torque for its descriptive value. The term residual torque may, however, be preferable to recall that it also includes complex time-varying elastic and viscous effects resulting from soft tissue deformation and, if the paw is in contact with the force plate, ground reaction force. Finally, it is important to realize that the values of the residual torque do not vary with the coordinate system. Thus, while interaction and self-torques differ in segment and joint coordinates, residual torque remains the same.

4.1 Torques at the Elbow and Shoulder during Reaching

Figure 4B shows the averaged time course of gravitational, self-, interaction, and residual torques at the elbow for a series of typical reaching movements. The solid vertical line at (a) marks the peak extensor self-torque and corresponds to the peak flexor acceleration (not shown). Since torques depend on the spatial orientation and configuration of the limb, which are not apparent in time series, we have found it useful to depict them as a stacked bar histogram directly on the stick figure (4C). By placing individual components appropriately on either side of the segment, taken as the zero line, the torques that accelerate or resist motion in a particular direction can be readily appreciated. It can be seen that at time (a) in (4B), the elbow is accelerated into flexion by the combined contributions of the interaction and residual torques and resisted by gravitational and self-torques (although this was not illustrated in Figure 4 for simplicity, ground reaction forces contribute to residual torque until toe-off). The interaction torque arises principally from the extensor acceleration of the shoulder as depicted schematically in Figure 4A by the white arrow. However, from the time series plots, it can be seen that the elbow flexor residual torque substantially outlasts this flexor interaction torque from the shoulder. Indeed, EMG recordings indicate that flexor muscles continue their activity to counter both the developing extensor interaction torque and the extensor gravitational torque. A corresponding synergy also operates at the shoulder, where extension is assisted by interaction torque arising from elbow flexion (not shown).

The reversal in direction of elbow acceleration (at the zero-crossings of elbow acceleration and self-torque; solid line, b) and the beginning of thrust (with its elbow extension) occur because the shoulder has now begun to flex and produces an extensor interaction torque. Elbow residual torque peaks at the reversal but remains flexor at the beginning of thrust, and, following a transient extensor phase, can be seen to remain flexor during the latter period of the record, corresponding to the end of the thrust phase. EMG recordings have shown that elbow flexor muscles are active before toe-off and remain active for the duration of reach. While elbow extensors are also active before toe-off (as well as earlier during stance), they are silenced during flexor acceleration. Extensor activity resumes at the time when residual torque becomes extensor. Thus, dynamic analysis shows that during lift, elbow joint motion is produced by both active control signals to flexors and by the actions of interjoint mechanical interactions. During this phase, forelimb inertia and gravity both act to resist flexor motion. The direction of elbow movement reverses, however, because of an interaction produced by the change in the direction of shoulder motion, rather than by a direct action of elbow muscles. This is similar to what occurs for two-joint reversal movements in humans (Sainburg et al., 1995).

4.2 Regulation of Distal Joint Angles in Preparation for Target Entry and Grasping

We have seen earlier (Figure 3) that the wrist undergoes a triphasic sequence of angular changes: flexion (i.e., plantar flexion)—extension (dorsiflexion)—flexion, leading to the maintained orientation of paw with the food well. The play of torques responsible for this is illustrated in Figure 5. The wrist is initially flexed by the combined action of interaction and gravitational torques arising as the forearm is lifted from the force plate (see especially [a] in 5C). Residual torque during this period is extensor, and therefore limits the degree of wrist flexion. However, as the interaction torque reverses from flexion to extension at (b), the synergy with residual torque accelerates the wrist into extension. We have found that this reversal in the direction of wrist motion frequently occurs during the brief interval in which residual and interaction torques are both extensor. Finally, at (c), wrist residual torque switches toward flexion to counter the extensor self- and interaction torques at end of lift.

In order to determine the relationship of wrist residual torque to muscle activation patterns, we recorded EMGs in wrist (and wrist-digit) flexor and extensor muscles (Figure 6). Early during the reach, activity of wrist flexor and extensor muscles was reciprocal. Flexor muscles were active during stance but became silent just before toe-off and wrist extensor muscles were silent during stance and became active just before toe-off. These EMG recordings confirm the biomechanical analysis indicating that wrist flexion occurs principally because of the dynamic effects of interaction and gravitational torque.

The time course of EMG activity after toe-off, where this torque is free of ground reaction forces, parallels the residual torque. Wrist extensor muscles remain active for most of the lift and thrust phases (Figure 6). However, this extensor action is modulated by the phasic reciprocal activation of wrist flexors corresponding to the period when flexor residual torque

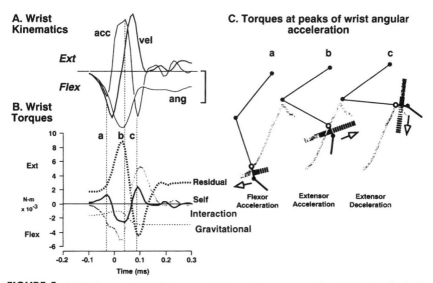

FIGURE 5 Wrist kinematics and torques. (A) Ensemble averages of wrist joint angle (ang), angular velocity (vel), and angular acceleration (acc). (B) Ensemble averages of residual (dashed black), interaction (solid gray), self- (black), and gravitational (dashed gray) torques. (C) Torques represented on stick figures at peak wrist angular flexor acceleration (a), extensor acceleration (b), and extensor deceleration (c). Open arrows show direction of acceleration (or deceleration). Scale bar: (A) 30°, 200°/s, 10,000°/s/s.

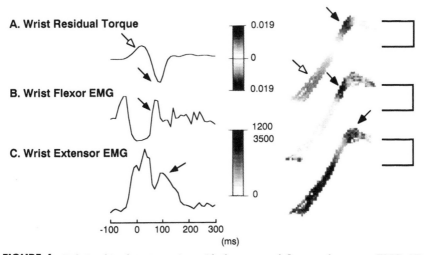

FIGURE 6 Relationships between wrist residual torque and flexor and extensor EMG. (A) Ensemble average of wrist residual torque is shown (*left*); torque is represented as a gray scale of absolute torque value directly on wrist paths (*right*). Interval between open and solid arrows on the ensemble average is shown on the paths. (B and C) As in (A) but for wrist flexor and extensor EMG, respectively. Solid arrows on ensemble averages point to EMG peak values and mark the locations of these EMG responses on the paths. Scale bars: (B) 1200 arbitrary units; (C) 3500 units.

transiently decelerates joint motion, as seen in Figure 5C(c). Then, during thrust, wrist angle is regulated by the steady cocontraction of wrist extensors and flexors, while residual torque remains near zero (see also Figure 3).

Although our prehension task explicitly demands that the paw reach a specific location with the limb in a particular configuration, dynamic interactions may vary. We therefore asked how the animals were able to achieve consistent kinematic outcomes when interaction torques varied. Since animals reach for higher targets through increasing elbow excursions and scaled elbow velocities and accelerations, the subsequent decelerations prior to the via-point (see Figure 1D) produce increasing extensor interaction torques at the wrist. Is this reflected in increasing amounts of wrist extension or is wrist angle regulated through variations in flexor residual torque? The ensemble averages of interaction torques and residual torques in Figure 7 (A, B) show reciprocal changes in interaction and residual torques for reaches to targets at four different heights. Scatter plot of residual torque (♦) against interaction

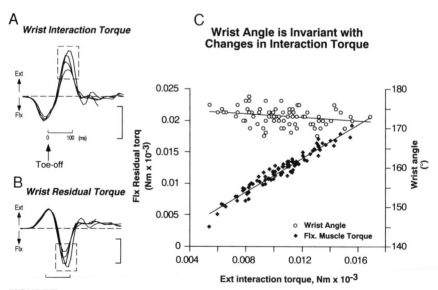

FIGURE 7   Compensatory relationship between wrist flexor residual torque and extensor interaction torque. (A) Ensemble averages of wrist interaction torque for reaches to four target heights (8, 11, 14, and 17 cm above footplate). Region enclosed by dashed rectangle corresponds to the peak extensor interaction torque, where peak values were marked on individual trials in (C). (B) Similar to (A) but for wrist residual torque. Region enclosed by dashed rectangle corresponds to the peak flexor residual torque. (C) Plots of the relationships between peak extensor interaction torque and peak flexor residual torque (♦; $r = .96$, $n = 39$, $p < .001$) and wrist joint angle (○; $r = .39$, $n = 39$, $p < .05$). Note that the absolute values for residual torque are plotted. Scale bars: (A,B) 0.001 Nm $\times 10^{-3}$).

torque (C) shows that this holds for individual responses as well: flexor residual torque increases with extensor interaction torque. Wrist joint angle, however, remains relatively constant (○). Thus, variations in interaction torques are countered by linear increases in wrist residual torque. Although residual torque reflects both viscoelastic forces and active muscle contraction, we saw earlier that animals adapt wrist angle to the orientation of the food well through changes in activation of flexor muscles. Consequently, these findings suggest an important contribution of feedforward mechanisms in regulating wrist angle through variations in residual torque.

Do animals also control distal joint angle indirectly by varying proximal joint motions to produce varying interaction torques? If this were so the animals would, for example, increase the angle of their wrist angle to enter a more inclined food well by reducing the deceleration of their elbow, and perhaps the earlier acceleration as well. In experiments conducted in 2 cats trained to reach into food wells at three different inclinations (as in Figure 3, but with small adjustments in the height of the food well made to maintain wrist height the same for the different planes of the food well aperture), we were unable to find any evidence of this: there were no systematic variations in proximal joint motions to account for differences in paw angle. Thus, variations in wrist angle at target entry were independent of interaction torque acting on the wrist. These results indicate that animals tend to rely on the timed contraction of distal muscles during the later phase of movement to control the kinematics of distal joints rather than exert this control indirectly through proximal muscles.

5. DISCUSSION

The present findings emphasize the crucial role played by predictive mechanisms in prehension, both in planning the kinematic organization of the movement and in controlling the dynamics of joint motions. At a kinematic level, neural planning mechanisms appear to break down the task of retrieving a morsel of food into relatively simpler components with specific spatial goals that are defined in extrinsic space. These findings conform with the notion of schemas proposed by Arbib (Arbib et al., 1985). Viviani (Viviani & McCollum, 1983) suggested that such units of behavior might be evident in the quasi-linear and isochronous (i.e., constant duration) paths segments. This is demonstrably the case for the prehension movements examined here: lift and thrust were influenced by different spatial variables, controlled by different rules, and apparently involved the paths of different limb points (wrist during lift and tip or claw during thrust). These and other results suggest further that the overall tempo of the movement components is specified by the nervous system quite early as it establishes the movement plan.

Indeed, the scaling factor that relates target distance or height to movement extent (here the via-point of the wrist) in visual space is dependent on a general tempo for the different movement segments.

It is interesting that the locus on the limb whose path is planned most explicitly may not be the same for different movement components: while during thrust path planning needs to focus on the paw tip (or the claw), for lift it seems to focus on the wrist (see also illustrations of linear path segments of different points of the forearm in human reaching in Paulignan, MacKenzie, et al., 1991). This is less surprising when it is recalled that under unconstrained conditions, the motions of limb segments for prehension are associated with motions of the body itself with distinct kinematic or dynamic functions. For example, locomotion may be necessary to bring the object within reach and anticipatory postural adjustments to prevent loss of balance. How these aspects of motor behavior are integrated has not been studied in detail, but it is likely that their planning involves the paths of different parts of the body (e.g., body or head) and different coordinate systems (e.g., allocentric, object, head, shoulder, or hand centered). Informal observations of such naturalistic behaviors in humans and cats show that the paths of the body when reaching for an object are, much as hand paths in two-joint movements, typically formed of straight line segments. It should be noted, however, that path linearity, like isochrony of a given movement segment, should be regarded as a strategic, and therefore optional, default solution to a spatial problem. We believe that this solution is chosen because it simplifies other aspects of motor planning (Ghez, Hening, & Gordon, 1991; J. Gordon, Ghilardi, Cooper, & Ghez, 1994; J. Gordon, Ghilardi, & Ghez, 1994). The nervous system can obviously direct hand movements in other ways as well, as for curved brushstrokes in painting, or for top spins in tennis or Ping-Pong.

The spatiotemporal demands of prehension tasks require parallel planning and execution of several movement components. For example, work in both human and subhuman primates (see Jeannerod, 1988; Jeannerod et al., 1995, for reviews) has emphasized how the planning of reach and grasp are governed by different aspects of the visual information about the target. Target distance and the locations of obstacles are critical in planning the kinematics of the reach, while object properties such as shape and orientation are critical for the grasp. The execution of these two components of prehension occurs in parallel. For example, digit span is adjusted (according to learned scaling factors and safety margins) before the target is reached, avoiding the need for the hand to stop before grasping. The conformation of wrist and paw angles to the inclination of the food well during reach indicates that similar principles apply to prehension in the cat.

The explicit spatial demands of prehension tasks are, however, associated with implicit dynamic demands. Indeed, the analyses of joint torques and

EMG patterns presented here show that muscle action is organized, not only to propel the limb and thus to overcome inertial and other loads. It is also adapted to exploit or to counter "reactive forces" (Bernstein, 1967), which develop during movement as needed to produce the planned paw path. Thus, elbow flexors lifting the paw are assisted by interaction torques from the concurrent shoulder extension and by the reduced inertial load at the elbow resulting from the change in wrist configuration. The exquisite nature of this integrated control is most evident at the wrist. Here, residual torque (produced by muscle action) variously counteracts or assists interaction torques resulting from motions at other joints and is controlled to achieve the appropriate wrist angle. This control is not, however, without constraints: while the animals adapted residual torques at the wrist to interaction torques produced by motions at proximal joints, they did not vary the motions of proximal joints to change these interactions. This could reflect the temporal precedence of the kinematic plan for reach over that for thrust segment. More importantly, however, our findings indicate that the control of joint dynamics through variations in muscle activation bridges the boundaries of movement segments defined by end-effector paths or the joint trajectories.

It has been suggested that the loads imposed by interaction torques during reaching might be countered automatically, simply by stiffness of the joints, as the hand traverses a planned equilibrium trajectory (e.g., Hogan, 1984; Mussa-Ivaldi et al., 1985). A discussion of the concept of equilibrium control is beyond the scope of this paper. However, it may be noted that a significant attraction of the original notion of end point control, which gave rise to it, was that it provided a relatively simple mechanism for compensating for variant loads (Feldman, 1974; Holmes, 1939; Polit & Bizzi, 1979). As such, it appeared to be a simplifying strategy that might preclude the need for complex computations of inverse dynamics. More recently, however, it has become clear that additional anticipatory neural processing mechanisms are needed to accommodate these and other variant loads if accuracy is to be achieved. Thus, in human subjects, such dynamic effects are countered by specific feedforward strategies requiring the learning of internal models of the limb, rather than simply by variations in joint stiffness (Sainburg et al., 1993, 1995; Shadmehr & Mussa-Ivaldi, 1994). In particular, we showed that, during intended hand movements, proprioceptive information is critical for controlling the interaction torques at the elbow that arise from shoulder motions (Sainburg et al., 1995). These distal effects of proximal motions during reaching movements are adapted to specific kinematic tasks through practice and depend critically on learning (Ghez & Sainburg, 1995; Sainburg & Ghez, 1994, in press). Much the same is likely to be the case for the wrist effects studied here, since our cats needed several days of practice to learn to adjust their wrist angle to the inclination of the food well.

The work of Smith, Zernicke, and colleagues has demonstrated that interaction torques can also be controlled directly through spinal mechanisms. Those authors found that during the paw-shake reflex in spinal cats, muscle action at the ankle functioned primarily to accelerate the paw segment, whereas knee muscles countered interaction torques arising at the ankle (Hoy & Zernicke, 1986). They went on to show that this compensatory action was mediated through reflex pathways triggered by ankle proprioceptors and acting, heteronymously, on hip muscles (Koshland & Smith, 1989a, 1989b; J. L. Smith & Zernicke, 1987). The more varied kinematic requirements of the hand and digit tasks associated with proximal movements may require greater intervention by supraspinal circuitry when activity depends on learning and related adaptive mechanisms.

In sum, it is important to recognize that the higher levels of the motor systems no more contract muscles than an orchestra conductor produces sounds. Instead, it may be useful to view higher planning mechanisms as choreographer and conductor, deploying individual performers, each with its own properties, and setting the tempo at which the score of schemas is to be played. From this perspective, muscle and reactive forces are not fundamentally different agents for the nervous system. Rather, they are both embedded in learned internal representations of the dynamic properties of the limb (Ghez et al., in press; Ghez & Sainburg, 1995), of surrounding objects (Vicario & Ghez, 1984), and of their potential interactions.

6. APPENDIX: INTRODUCTION TO JOINT TORQUES BY SCOTT COOPER

6.1 Explanation of Movement-Dependent and Interaction Torques

Given a description of the motion of an object and its mass, the inverse dynamic problem is to find the force that produces that motion. Any solution to this problem must be based on the fundamental equation of classical or Newtonian mechanics:

$$\mathbf{F} = \mathbf{ma} \tag{1}$$

To a first approximation, the joints of a human or cat limb permit rotation of limb segments relative to each other. One can therefore employ the angular equivalent of Newton's equation (Euler's equation):

$$\mathbf{T} = \mathbf{I\alpha} \tag{2}$$

Where α is angular acceleration, I is moment of inertia, and $\mathbf{T}$ is torque. (The form given above is for motion in a plane; in three dimensions, $\mathbf{T}$ and α are vectors, I is a matrix, and there is an additional term $\varsigma \times \mathbf{I}\varsigma$ (where ς is angular velocity and x indicates a vector cross product). The most commonly used approach to solve this is based on d'Alembert's Principle by setting acceleration equal to zero, and then fixing up the equation by adding a term to make the results come out right.

$$\mathbf{F} + \{-m\mathbf{a}\} = 0 \tag{3}$$

Note that this equation describes an equilibrium in which all forces sum to zero. The term $\{-m\mathbf{a}\}$ is an inertial or fictitious force (it is easy to see that it has units of force). What is really being done here is to describe the system in a new frame of reference, one that is moving with the object. Newtons's laws do not apply in accelerating frames of reference and $\{-m\mathbf{a}\}$ is the discrepancy. The essential point of d'Alembert's principle is that once we have added the correcting term, we can forget about the fact that the frame of reference is accelerating, and proceed to analyze it as if it were not. Despite its name, a "fictitious" force is very real. Automobile airbags exist to protect drivers against the fictitious force that hurls them into the steering wheel in an accident.

When a muscle exerts a force, the opposing inertial force is made up of contributions from the inertia of all segments being moved by the muscle, that is, all those distal to the joint where the muscle acts. The linear acceleration of each segment's center of mass contributes a force $\{-m\mathbf{a}\}$, and the segment's angular acceleration contributes a torque $\{-I\mathbf{\alpha}\}$. The forces $\{-m\mathbf{a}\}$ can be expressed as torques by multiplying by the appropriate moment arms, which, in general, are dependent on limb configuration. Together with the torques $\{-I\mathbf{\alpha}\}$, they are then called movement-dependent torques (MDTs). There are three types of MDTs acting at any given joint: those proportional to the angular acceleration of a particular joint (acceleration-dependent torque), those proportional to the squared angular velocity of a particular joint (centrifugal torque), and those proportional to the product of the angular velocities at two different joints (Coriolis torque). Here, we refer to MDT as the sum of all MDTs acting at a joint. The force that must be supplied, by muscle contraction, muscle viscosity, tendon and ligament stretch, and the like, together with gravity and ground reaction force, is, by d'Alembert's principle, equal and opposite to MDT. An important conclusion follows from this, namely, that the movement-dependent torque at one segment depends on the motion of all the segments. This is because (1) force of inertia at a given joint depends on the acceleration of all segments distal to it, and (2) acceleration of a given segment depends on the movement at all joints proximal to it. Movement-dependent torques can be viewed as loads that must be opposed by muscle contraction in order to produce an intended movement, or as torques that produce movement if not opposed. They can be plotted as a function of time, measured, and analyzed exactly like ordinary torques. This approach has two advantages.

First, fictitious forces or torques often provide a useful way of thinking about the mechanics of the limb movement. For example, if the shoulder flexes with constant angular velocity, the elbow tends to extend; conversely, flexing the elbow requires more force from the biceps if the shoulder is flexing with constant angular velocity than if the shoulder is stationary. It is natural to speak of an extensor centrifugal torque at the elbow. This is equivalent to describing the motion of the elbow in a frame of reference that rotates with the shoulder. The same behavior could be described in a stationary frame of reference without recourse to a centrifugal torque, but the description would be more complex, and no more accurate.

Second, analysis of MDT gives quantitative expression to the fact that the nervous system, in specifying the degree of contraction of a muscle that crosses a particular joint, must take into account not only the intended motion of that joint, but also the motion of all the other joints of the limb. The effect of these motions is represented as interaction torques that perturb the motion of the joint, and for which the muscle must compensate. Individual MDTs corresponding to motion of different joints may correspond to components of motor planning that are dependent on anatomically separate proprioceptive pathways related to those different joints.

6.2 Approaches to the Analysis of Movement-Dependent Torques

The researcher who undertakes to analyze movement-dependent torques confronts two decisions: (1) in what coordinate system should MDTs be computed, and (2) how should they be classified. The results of the analysis will differ according to the choice of coordinate system and classification scheme. There are no "correct" answers to these questions, and various laboratories have answered them differently. We feel strongly, however, that any author who analyzes movement-dependent torques needs to state explicitly how he or she has resolved the questions and why. In what follows, we discuss the issues of coordinate system and classification scheme, and attempt to justify our method of analysis.

6.3 Choice of Coordinate System

Suppose one wishes to compute MDT at the knee joint. For didactic purposes, consider a three-segment limb composed of thigh, leg, and paw segments, with hip, knee, and ankle joints. It is then necessary to devise a formula giving knee MDT as a function of the motion of the whole limb. That motion could be described in any of an infinite number of coordinate systems. Two approaches are used most widely.

One approach is to measure the angle of each limb segment relative to an external reference (say, a vertical plumb line) and express MDT as a function of those angles and their time derivatives ("segment angle coordinates"). However, muscle torque cannot then really be defined in the usual way as the torque due to muscles acting at a given joint. This is because the motion of a segment is the product equally of muscles acting at its proximal and distal end. One solution is to define muscle torque acting on a given segment as torque due to muscles acting at the segment's proximal joint (Hoy & Zernicke, 1985). Muscle torque at the distal joint then becomes part of MDT due to motion of more distal segments. This is reasonable except that it involves an arbitrary decision to accord special status to the proximal rather than the distal joint. Alternatively, muscle torque can also be defined as torque due to muscles acting at the segment's proximal and distal joints. This quantity, while perhaps more mathematically rigorous, is rather far removed from a conventional physiological view of muscle action.

The principal advantage of segment angle coordinates is that the expression for MDT is much simpler, and the number of individual MDTs smaller than with joint angle coordinates. Another advantage is that all MDTs are proportional either to the angular acceleration or to the squared angular velocity of a particular limb segment: in other words, there are no Coriolis torques. On the other hand, segment angle coordinates have certain disadvantages. Notably, they are inconsistent with an analysis of limb kinematics in terms of joint motions. If one wishes to compare limb kinematics with MDTs, one must describe the kinematics in the same coordinate system as the torques. Thus, if MDT were computed in segment angle coordinates, kinematics would have to be described as the rotation of limb segments relative to an external reference, rather than in terms of joint rotation as is usually done. If joint angle kinematics are compared with segment angle MDT (or vice versa) situations can arise in which motion occurs without corresponding torques or torques without corresponding motion.

A second approach is to measure the angle of hip, knee, and ankle joints, and express MDT as a function of those angles and their time derivatives ("joint angle coordinates"). We have chosen to adopt this joint-based coordinate system on the grounds that it corresponds more closely to conventional anatomical and physiological schemes for describing limb motion and muscle action. In addition, we suspect that joint angles may correspond better than segment angles to the coordinate system in which the nervous system actually perceives limb position, since it is an intrinsic rather than an extrinsic coordinate system. Joint angles are reflected in spindle afferent activity from uniarticular muscles, while there is no receptor that can directly measure segment angle relative to an external reference.

6.4 Classification Scheme

The expression for MDT is composed of a number of terms, each of which can be regarded as a separate torque. Alternatively, groups of terms can be summed and each sum treated as a separate torque. When the number of terms is large, as in our four-segment, joint-coordinate limb model, this is virtually mandatory in order to make sense of the data; even when the number of terms is not unmanageably large, such clustering of terms is a powerful conceptual tool. We present below a schema for grouping torques; it is not the only possible system, but it illustrates the principal characteristics according to which limb torques can be classified.

1. *Interaction torque* at a joint is that portion of MDT that is determined by the motion of other joints, and thus represents the sum of all interjoint interactions affecting that joint. By excluding MDT due to motion of the same joint, we define a quantity that corresponds to the idea of "interaction torque."

2. *Self-torque* at a joint is that portion of MDT that is dependent on the motion of that joint and no others. When motion is expressed in joint coordinates, the self-torque depends only on angular acceleration, and thus has a simple, intuitive interpretation: it represents the limb's inertial resistance to acceleration. It should be noted, however, that when motion is expressed in segment coordinates, self-torque depends on angular velocity as well, making interpretation more difficult.

Note that all the segments distal to the joint where self-torque acts contribute to this resistance, and that their contributions depend on joint angles, that is, on limb configuration. This is what distinguishes self-torque from the "net" torque of Zernicke and colleagues (apart from a factor of $[-1]$).

3. *Gravitational torque* represents the torque on the joint due to the weight of segments distal to it.

4. *Residual torque*, also called generalized muscle torque (Hoy & Zernicke, 1986; J. L. Smith & Zernicke, 1987) or simply muscle torque (Sainburg et al., 1995), represents muscle contraction, tendon and ligament stretch, joint capsule deformation, and external forces acting on the limb, if any (e.g., ground reaction force). Since it cannot be computed directly, it is computed from the other torques using the d'Alembert principle (see above), which states that torques must all sum to zero.

6.5 Additional Considerations

1. *Joint of origin.* Torques comprising interaction torque can be subdivided according to the joint on whose motion each depends. This is potentially useful because selective lesions of the peripheral nervous system or of somatotopically organized parts of the central nervous system or other manipulations might be used selectively to deprive the nervous system of infor-

mation about the motion of particular joints (e.g., Koshland & Smith, 1989b). Acceleration-dependent and centrifugal torques can easily be classified in this manner; Coriolis torques are more difficult to classify, since they depend on the motion of two different joints.

2. *Acceleration versus velocity dependence.* Movement-dependent torques can be further subdivided according to whether they are acceleration dependent or velocity dependent (centrifugal and Coriolis). This can be useful because acceleration- and velocity-dependent torques dominate at different times during a movement. In a movement that starts and ends at rest, for example, acceleration peaks at the beginning and end of the movement, while velocity peaks about midway. We have previously exploited this fact to analyze limb mechanics during the first instant of movement initiation (J. Gordon, Ghilardi, Cooper, & Chez, 1994).

3. *Dependence versus independence on limb configuration.* The expression for most torques can be further subdivided into terms that include sines or cosines of joint angles, and terms that do not. The former are configuration-dependent components, while the latter are configuration independent. Self-torque has a configuration-dependent component, and this, arguably, might be considered an interaction torque, since it depends on the angles of joints other than the one where it acts. We have left it a part of self-torque, however, because it does not depend on the motion of those joints but rather on their static position.

ACKNOWLEDGMENTS

We are grateful to Stephen Strain for assistance in deriving dynamic equations and to Tony Hacking for expert technical assistance and figure preparation. We are also indebted to Ming Hong for carrying out the initial experiments using food wells at different inclinations. Supported by NIH Grant NS31391

11

Neural Control of Limb Mechanics for Visuomanual Coordination

FRANCESCO LACQUANITI

1. INTRODUCTION

Visuomanual coordination involves a complex integration of multisensory information in the context of cognitive representations about the task variables (see Georgopoulos, 1986; Jeannerod, 1991; Poulton, 1981; Wing, Turton, & Fraser, 1986). Internal representations of the physical properties of both the external object to be acted upon and of the effector limb are used by the brain to build a reference model of a forthcoming dynamic interaction. These internal representations are accessed by the action system in feedforward mode with respect to predictable targets, but they can be updated using peripheral information to produce adapted responses (Ghez et al., 1990). Reference models can be construed as internal images that allow a simulated, virtual exploration of the environment and an anticipatory adaptation of the motor responses to environmental changes before they actually occur. In this way visuomotor coordination exploits on-line information about both target and limb to trigger anticipatory responses and tune automatic reactions evoked by contact with the object. The existence of considerable flexibility in the fit between the properties of the environment and the properties of the action system of the organism makes the specific solutions highly context dependent.

Hand and Brain
Copyright © 1996 by Academic Press, Inc. All rights of reproduction in any form reserved.

Object prehension and manipulation require a fine-grained control of limb mechanics. Mechanics dictates modes of interaction and represents the interface between the neural commands and the environment. Thus, the study of the modulation of the mechanical behavior of a limb can reveal the laws and strategies of neural control of movement and posture. Considerable conceptual advances have recently been made in this field, mainly spurred by a renewed interest in the experimental study of natural, unconstrained motor behavior, and the quantitative correlation between neural activity and mechanical behavior of the limb. In this chapter I illustrate these issues by considering one specific case of visuomanual coordination, namely that involved in catching. Interceptive tasks such as manual catching are common motor behaviors in everyday life. Their study can help in understanding how the brain solves the computational problems of visuomotor coordination. What are the sources of perceptual information about an approaching object? How is that information processed in the brain? What are the basic motor programs used to intercept the object? How are these basic programs modified according to specific task demands, such as those involved in parametric changes of the object properties (mass, velocity, etc.)? These are some of the issues addressed in this chapter.

2. ANTICIPATORY RESPONSES IN CATCHING TASKS UNDER VISUAL GUIDANCE

Catching a moving ball represents an ideal paradigm to study adaptive visuomanual coordination. The preplanned dynamic interaction with an object in motion requires that the physical parameters of the impact on the hand be accurately predicted. Time, location, and momentum of the impact must be estimated, and limb kinematics and kinetics accordingly controlled. Thus, the hand must be placed so as to intercept ball trajectory, and limb rigidity must absorb ball momentum. Subjects cannot self-pace the modulation in time of these variables, but must comply with timing constraints imposed from outside. The role of cognitive set and expectation about the anticipated properties of the forthcoming impact can be directly addressed by modifying experimental variables such as height of fall or mass of the ball.

Most of the initial studies on catching behavior were aimed at addressing questions related to information processing theories (Alderson, Sully, & Sully, 1974; Sharp & Whiting, 1974, 1975; Whiting & Sharp, 1974). They mainly focused on the issue of the amount of information necessary to make a decision. One question concerned the critical time interval for processing visual information on ball flight in order to catch successfully (Whiting & Sharp, 1974). In a paradigm that obscured vision at various times during ball flight, best performance was found when the ball was visible for a period of

240 ms at about 300 ms from contact with the hand. This period of time is necessary to foveate the ball and then track it to integrate visual information. A similar visual exposure at a time less than 300 ms prior to contact cannot be adequately processed to produce an appropriate motor response under such conditions. These studies clearly indicated that not only the duration of the time window for visual exposure but also its timing relative to contact are crucial variables.

The nature of the visual processing involved in catching has been investigated mainly within the conceptual context of affordances, as developed by J. J. Gibson (1966). Affordances are determined by the fit between the properties of the environment and those of the organism's action system. In particular, the optic flow field (i.e., the field of the instantaneous velocities of each point of the image on the retina) can represent the primary visual source from which to compute the time-to-contact. One can decompose mathematically the optic flow field and its spatial derivatives under rotation invariance (Koenderink, 1986). The 0th-order invariant is translation. The first-order invariants are divergence (dilation), rotation, and deformation. In normal physiological conditions all elementary components are present in the optic flow field. Overall components can be derived by integrating the elementary local components over parts of the visual field (Koenderink 1986). Optic flow is thought to be processed centrally by the short-range motion analyzers that rely on directionally sensitive motion-detecting units. Thus, many neurons in areas MT and MST of the temporal lobe are selective to different combinations of the optic flow components, including translation and dilation (Duffy & Wurtz, 1991). The nature of the operations performed neurally to extract optic flow components and solve structure-from-motion problems is unknown, but is thought to involve geometrical solutions akin to linear filters operating on the velocity field (Koenderink, 1986).

D. N. Lee (1980) proposed a strategy that does not rely on computing the distance from the target and the velocity of the target, but simply compares on-line retinal information with a preset threshold. For an object in uniform motion (i.e., moving at constant velocity) orthogonal to the projection plane of a stationary eye, the time-to-contact is directly specified by the optical variable τ, defined as the inverse of the rate of dilation of the retinal image. Lee hypothesized that motor responses are geared to a specific τ margin, in other words, they are initiated once the dilation rate of the retinal image has reached a preset value. It has been suggested that the τ strategy is used in several visuomotor tasks. Direct tests of the hypothesis have been carried out, for example, for the long jump (D. N. Lee, Lishman, & Thomson, 1982) and running over irregular terrain (W. H. Warren, Young, & Lee, 1986). In the case of the task of ball catching, the τ-margin hypothesis has been tested by Savelsbergh et al., in a task that required catching a ball thrown from in front (Savelsbergh, Whiting, & Bootsma, 1991; Savelsberg, Whiting, Burden, & Bartlett, 1992). They compared catching a small ball, a large ball, and a ball that deflated on approaching, shrinking from large to small. They found that subjects adjusted amplitude and timing of hand aperture to the apparent size of the ball (i.e., the pattern of relative expansion of the retinal image). Savelsbergh et al. also studied the time of onset of electromyographic (EMG) activity in a number of arm muscles and found that these were independent of approach speed, depending only on time-to-contact.

In the case of uniform motion there is an exact correspondence between time-to-contact and τ. The study of behavior when an object accelerates allows a more stringent test of the τ hypothesis, because τ now gives an erroneous estimate of the real time-to-contact. D. N. Lee, Young, Reddish, Lough, and Clayton (1983) have suggested that the control of timing actions may have not evolved beyond a first-order level, that is, a level that involves measuring the rate of dilation of the retinal image. This avoids the problem of computing higher order time derivatives of visual motion. According to this hypothesis, the visuomotor system relies on the information provided by the dilation rate of the retinal image; it assumes then a constant velocity approach of the target and gears the motor responses to the preset τ margin. When the approach is uniformly accelerated, as during free fall, the optical variable τ overestimates the time-to-contact. Under such conditions, the τ hypothesis makes the specific prediction that the longer the duration of flight of a free-falling ball (i.e., the higher the drop of a ball accelerating under gravity), the earlier the time of initiation of the anticipatory motor responses (see Figure 1).

This prediction has been tested in a series of studies (Lacquaniti, Carrozzo, & Borghese, 1993a; Lacquaniti & Maioli, 1989a, 1989b) that addressed the role of anticipatory responses associated with catching free-falling balls using the apparatus shown in Figure 2. Heights of fall were 0.2, 0.4, 0.8, 1.2, and 1.6 m. (The corresponding flight times were 202, 286, 404, 495, and 571 ms). Balls of identical-external appearance but different mass were used (in the range from 0.2 to 0.8 kg, in 0.2-kg steps). EMG was recorded from the elbow and wrist flexors and extensors. It was found that the anticipatory EMG responses were comprised of early and late components (Figure 3). Early responses were produced at a roughly constant latency (about 130 ms) from the release of the ball. This latency corresponds to a visual reaction time for a highly compatible stimulus–response relation. These early components last less than 50 ms and therefore cannot affect directly the grasping action except for the lowest drops. However, they are theoretically relevant to two physiological problems. First, these responses are most likely related to covert cognitive processes involved in motor preparation, such as those associated with cerebral event-related potentials (e.g., the so-called CNV, Contingent Negative Variation, and the Readiness Potential). Second, it was

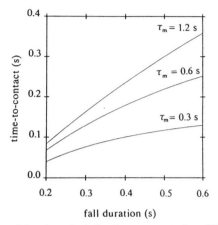

FIGURE 1   Predictions of the τ hypothesis for visuomotor reactions. The equation $t_c = \tau_m + d$ $- (\tau_m^2 + d^2)^{\frac{1}{2}} - \partial$ predicts the value of the time remaining before contact (time-to-contact, t_c) at which anticipatory responses would be triggered under the assumption of an approach of the visual target at a constant velocity, where d is the duration of fall and ∂ is a fixed visuomotor delay. τ_m represents a preset margin value of the optical variable τ. Three curves corresponding to the indicated values of τ_m have been plotted. Values of τ_m below 0.3 s have not been considered because they would predict times-to-contact shorter than those experimentally observed (onset time of EMG anticipatory activity at $\approx$150 ms prior to contact). (Adapted from Lacquaniti et al., 1993a.)

observed that the amplitude of the early EMG responses was inversely proportional to the height of fall. Therefore, these responses correspond to a readiness reaction that already incorporates an estimate of the duration of fall. The shorter the time available for the preparation to contact, the larger the size of the population of α-motoneurones that are recruited within this reaction time.

The major buildup of EMG activity occurred in the form of late anticipatory responses whose latency increased with the height of fall. However, the onset time computed relative to the time of contact varied little. In addition, this onset time did not depend on the mass of the ball. These results, therefore, afford a direct test of the τ hypothesis for accelerated motion. Given a fixed visuomotor delay, the τ hypothesis predicts that the time-to-contact should increase substantially with increasing height of fall (see Figure 1). Thus, if the visuomotor responses were geared to τ, they should start at earlier (longer) time-to-contacts the longer the drop, irrespective of the specific value of τ margin used by the brain. However, except for the wrist extensors, the onset and duration of the EMG anticipatory responses with respect to the time of impact (corresponding to the time-to-contact) did not change systematically with height of fall (Figure 4). In sev-

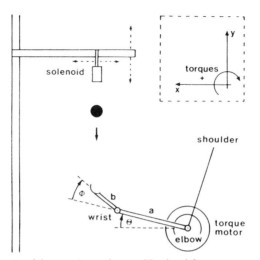

FIGURE 2 Schematic of the experimental setup. Hand and forearm were strapped to a 2-degrees-of-freedom electrogoniometer, which measured elbow (θ) and wrist (Φ) angles. Elbow joint was aligned with the shaft of a torque motor, which constantly applied a torque equal to and opposite that of the gravitational torque on the goniometer. The hand was fully supinated, and subjects wore a stiff glove. The ball was dropped by an electromagnet from variable heights. (Adapted from Lacquaniti & Maioli, 1989a.)

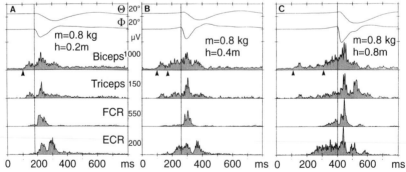

FIGURE 3 Effect of ball mass (m) and height of fall (h). Ensemble averages from 1 subject. The vertical lines denote the time of impact. Traces from top to bottom correspond to elbow angle (θ), wrist angle (Φ), rectified EMG activity of biceps, triceps, flexor carpi radialis (FCR), and extensor carpi radialis (ECR). The indicated scales apply to all panels of each experiment. The computed time of onset of the early and late anticipatory responses of biceps are indicated by the arrowheads. (Adapted from Lacquaniti & Maioli, 1989a.)

eral instances one can note a small incisure in the modulation of anticipatory activity just prior to impact.

The observations on early and late EMG responses taken together indicate that motor responses are not timed according to τ, but instead are based on a rather accurate estimate of the actual time-to-contact (Lacquaniti et al., 1993a). This parameter can be computed by means of estimates of the instantaneous velocity of the target $v(t)$, fall distance h, and acceleration of gravity g: $t_c = \sqrt{2h/g} - v(t)/g$. Gravity acceleration may be internalized from lifelong exposure and is also measured by our vestibular apparatus. It is important to note that when the path of the ball trajectory is at an angle from the line of sight, more than one component of the optic flow can contribute to determine time-to-contact. In some cases the component due to translation of the retinal image outweighs the dilation component. Also, eye movements may contribute to the estimate of time-to-contact (Sharp & Whiting, 1975).

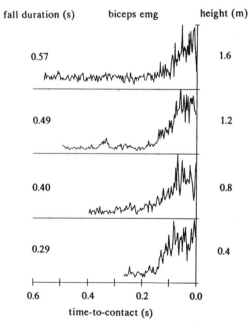

FIGURE 4   Time course of the EMG anticipatory responses for the biceps muscle. The traces correspond to the results obtained at the indicated heights of fall. The corresponding duration of fall is reported on the left. For the sake of comparison, the EMG traces have been scaled to their maximum and aligned relative to impact time. The time axis indicates the time remaining prior to impact (time-to-contact). The time to onset relative to the impact and the time course of biceps responses do not change systematically with height of fall. (Adapted from Lacquaniti et al., 1993a.)

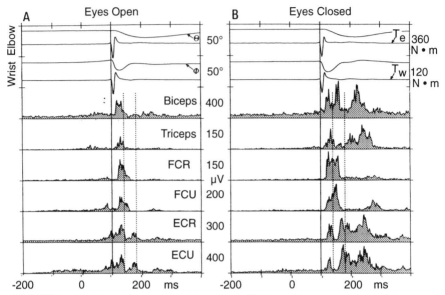

FIGURE 5   Catching with eyes open (A) or closed (B). Ensemble averages obtained from one subject in an experiment in which a 0.4-kg ball was dropped from 0.8 m at t ≈ −400 ms and hit the hand at t = 0 ms. Traces plotted from top to bottom correspond to elbow angle (θ) and torque (T_e), wrist angle (Φ), and torque (T_w), rectified EMG activity of biceps, triceps, flexor carpi radialis (FCR), flexor carpi ulnaris (FCU), extensor carpi radialis (ECR), and extensor carpi ulnaris (ECU). Calibration bars for θ and Φ are in the middle, those for T_e and T_w are on the right. The two dotted vertical lines (at t = 40 and 80 ms after impact) delimit the time windows for the short-, medium-, and long-latency responses to impact. (Adapted from Lacquaniti & Maioli, 1989b.)

Sequences of saccades alternated to smooth pursuit can be used to track the target. Thus, the summation of the efferent copy of the command encoding eye velocity and of the retinal velocity error may provide a signal proportional to target velocity.

The anticipatory responses observed during catching bear a superficial resemblance to the pattern of muscle activity beginning at a fixed interval of time prior to landing from a fall or jump (Greenwood & Hopkins, 1976; McKinley, Smith, & Gregor, 1983; Melvill Jones & Watt, 1971). The latter are not contingent on vision, since other sensory cues (mostly vestibular) along with planning can effectively substitute for visual cues in eliciting anticipatory responses during landing, in cases where the height of jump is known in advance. Sensory substitution leads to invariant motor responses when vision is suppressed even in the case of postural control during anteroposterior translation of the body (Berthoz, Lacour, Soechting, & Vidal, 1979).

No such substitution can take place during catching. When blindfolded subjects are provided with advance information about the height of drop and an auditory cue signals the time of ball release, they are able to reach a perceptual estimate of the expected duration of fall, as demonstrated by the fact that they can easily detect randomly interspersed cases of inaccurate timing of the auditory cue. However, as shown in Figure 5, they are unable to produce anticipatory muscle responses consistently (Lacquaniti & Maioli, 1989b). This clearly demonstrates that the estimate of fall duration is completely separate from the estimate of instantaneous time-to-contact, which is necessary to trigger consistent anticipatory responses. Thus, the latter needs to be controlled by dynamic on-line information rather than static information.

3. PARAMETRIC TUNING OF THE RESPONSES

On-line visual information may not suffice per se to plan adequate motor responses. It must be integrated and interpreted within the cognitive constructs pertinent to the specific context of a given visuomotor behavior. Internal representations are used by the brain to build a reference model of a forthcoming dynamic interaction. Reference models include a model of the mechanical plan to be acted upon, that is, the musculoskeletal apparatus of a given body segment, and a model of the external loads to be expected. These models are able to predict the dynamic characteristics of the mechanical interaction and can then be used to adjust parametrically the neural controller so as to produce the desired responses.

Coming back to the catching task, we have already discussed the importance of spatiotemporal constraints for planning a successful catch. We must add that, in order to intercept the trajectory of the ball at the right time, a priori knowledge on the most likely path and law of motion (e.g., linear motion uniformly accelerated by gravity during free fall, parabolic projectile motion during ballistic throws, etc.) is presumably used in conjunction with visual on-line information. This is demonstrated by the observation that visuomotor actions performed under stroboscopic light, which disrupts information on target velocity, may be preserved under conditions in which the law of motion is predictable (e.g., free fall).

In catching, the impulsive impact is characterized by the change in momentum associated with the collision between ball and hand. This depends on the momentum of the ball and limb just prior to impact and on the coefficient of restitution at the contact point (which is related to the elasticity of the physical bodies at contact). In catching (but not in hitting), the limb is generally quasi-stationary prior to contact. Thus, predictive analysis mainly concerns the ball's momentum (but see later). Figure 6 shows that the mean

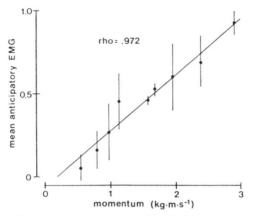

FIGURE 6 Linear relation between the mean amplitude of late anticipatory responses (computed over the 50-ms interval preceding ball impact) in biceps and the theoretical momentum of the ball at impact time. Data points correspond to the mean values (± 1 *SD*) of the (normalized) results from four experiments. (Adapted from Lacquaniti & Maioli, 1989a.)

amplitude of late EMG anticipatory responses during catching scales linearly with the expected momentum of the ball at impact (Lacquaniti & Maioli, 1989a). This was demonstrated using a factorial design, which involved the independent experimental manipulation of height of fall and mass of the ball. Thus, other kinematic or kinetic parameters could be excluded as putative control elements. In addition, it has been shown that, when the mass of the ball is unexpectedly changed, subjects scale their responses to the expected momentum, thus corroborating the contention that momentum rather than terminal velocity represents the control parameter.

The prediction of ball momentum depends on a cognitive operation performed on the basis of hybrid information. Information on instantaneous velocity of the ball is available through vision. However, considering the presence of a visuomotor delay of about 100 ms, that anticipatory responses begin some 150 ms prior to contact and that there is centrally preset reversal of proprioceptive responses some 60 ms prior to contact (see Section 5), one may guess that about 200 ms is the period over which subjects must extrapolate in the forward direction to estimate the velocity of the ball at impact. That subjects do extrapolate rather than just using past information (frozen at 200 ms prior to contact) is demonstrated by the following observation. It is a frequent finding that subjects move their hand just prior to impact. However, the specific strategy that is adopted varies from one condition to another: subjects raise their arm toward the falling ball in some cases, while they lower their arm in other cases (Lacquaniti, Borghese, & Carrozzo, 1992). Consequently, the relative time of impact will be earlier relative to the stationary condition in the former case, resulting in a relatively smaller ball momentum at impact; in the latter case, the impact time will be delayed, resulting in a greater ball momentum. The linear regression between mean EMG amplitude and momentum at impact indicates that subjects do estimate the true, expected terminal momentum.

As for the other term in the expression for momentum, the ball's mass is presumably estimated based on an internal model of the ball's properties. Linear scaling with momentum suggests that the power law scaling that applies to lifting different weights (Stevens, 1975) does not apply to a dynamic action such as catching. Estimate of inertial mass is more pertinent in this case. Experiments conducted under microgravity have indicated that mass discrimination differs from weight discrimination, pointing to different cognitive and perceptual substrates (Ross, Brodie, & Benson, 1986).

Although the pattern of anticipatory responses is set from the very first trial of each catching session, the amplitude of the mechanical oscillations of the limb evoked by the impact is significantly larger in the first trial than in the following ones. This then suggests that a scheme of adaptive control involving a reference model is in operation. According to this scheme, an internal model of the dynamic interaction that is expected to occur at impact is built on a priori knowledge and available on-line information (such as visual cues to the velocity of the ball and the limb). The response of this model to the perturbation is compared with the actual response of the limb to produce an error signal. This error is subsequently used to calibrate the parameters of the neural controller of the plan and to update the internal model. Thus, if the model does not accurately predict the desired performance, possibly because of a faulty estimate of the properties of impulsive impact, kinesthetic and cutaneous information obtained with the first trial can be used to correct the estimate.

4. FUNCTIONAL ORGANIZATION OF REFLEX RESPONSES TO HAND PERTURBATIONS

The hand is the end effector of the multijointed arm. In a multijointed limb the net reflex response of a given muscle to a load perturbation results from the complex, state-dependent interaction at spinal and supraspinal levels of inputs from that same muscle (autogenic inputs) and from other muscles acting on the same or different joints (heterogenic inputs, see Jankowska, 1992). Thus, the classical description of the operation of the stretch reflex, as derived from single-joint studies, may not be applicable to multijointed motion. In the latter case, reflex activation of a given muscle can be preceded by an increase, a decrease, or no change in the muscle length (Gielen, Ramaekers, & van Zuylen, 1988; Lacquaniti & Soechting, 1986; Smeets & Erkelens, 1991). In general, the reflex responses will depend on the angular motion at several limb joints. This bears important consequences for the functional significance of the reflex. Previously, emphasis was placed on parameters of a single muscle (i.e., muscle length, its rate of change) as both the input and the controlled variables of the reflex loop. Attention is now directed to variables, such as net joint torques, that are more global and reflect the dynamical state of whole limb motion (Gielen et al., 1988; Lacquaniti & Soechting, 1986; Smeets & Erkelens, 1991).

A load perturbation applied to a limb evokes electromyographic responses that are often fractionated in multiple components (see Figure 5B). It has been found that early responses of monoarticular muscles are correlated with the changes in angular position and velocity at that joint (Dietz, 1992; Gielen et al., 1988: Lacquaniti & Soechting, 1986). However, there is an important nonlinearity in such reponses, because their gain is deeply affected by the direction of the simultaneous angular motion at the other coupled joints (Lacquaniti & Soechting, 1986). Early responses of biarticular muscles, instead, are related to the angular motion at both joints (Lacquaniti & Soechting, 1986). However, this behavior is not simply accounted for on the basis of autogenetic negative feedback of the changes in muscle length signaled by muscle spindles. In general, early responses of both mono- and biarticular muscles seem to depend on the interaction at the spinal level of auto- and heterogenic feedbacks, probably related to the diverging patterns of connections (Jankowska, 1992).

Late muscle responses evoked by load perturbations to the upper limb are related instead to changes in net torque at one or more joints of the limb (Lacquaniti & Soechting, 1986). The relationship between late reflex responses and net torque is similar to that observed for voluntary contractions. Similar organizational principles may then underlie both voluntary and reflex control of the limb (Koshland, Gerilovsky, & Hasan, 1991). It has recently been argued that late reflex activation in muscles that are not stretched by the perturbation is not appropriate to counteract changes in joint position (Koshland et al., 1991). However, there are strong indications that the sign and magnitude of late reflex responses are appropriate to oppose changes in joint torque (Gielen et al., 1988; Lacquaniti & Soechting, 1986).

The possible contribution of transcortical pathways to late components of the stretch reflex has been examined in a series of studies involving both normal and neurological subjects (Capaday, Forget, Fraser, & Lamarre, 1991; P. B. C. Matthews, 1991; E. Palmer & Ashby, 1992b; Thilmann, Schwarz, Tipper, Fellows, & Noth, 1991). A cortical contribution seems more important for the reflexes of hand muscles than for those of other muscles. Cerebellar participation in corrective reactions has been demonstrated in the monkey by recording the changes in simple spike discharge of Purkinje cells during predictable pulls at a hand-held object (Dugas & Smith, 1992). Preparatory and late reflex responses have been found in the cerebellum that parallel the changes in EMG activity.

It is known that the amplitude of proprioceptive reflexes is task dependent (for a review, see Dietz, 1992). Recent studies have looked into the mechanical implications of such task dependency. The gain of long-latency stretch reflexes and stretch-evoked stiffness on hand muscles has been found to be larger during a task involving position control than during a force-control task (Akazawa, Milner, & Stein, 1983; Doemges & Rack, 1992). In sum, because the relations between the multiple inputs and outputs that define the behavior of the stretch reflex are not fixed but depend on the state of the system, their functional interpretation cannot be accomodated simply within the classical framework of time-invariant servocontrol. Rather, the operation of the reflex circuits is best understood within the context of adaptive control, that is, a control process capable of estimating and modifying state and output variables on the basis of internal models of expected behavior.

5. PROSPECTIVE CONTROL OF REFLEX RESPONSES IN CATCHING

In catching, prospective control involves precise modulation of proprioceptive reflexes. It has been shown (Lacquaniti et al., 1991, 1992) that the direction of myotatic responses transiently reverses with a precise timing. Short-latency responses evoked by unpredictable load perturbations applied to the elbow joint (using the torque motor shown in Figure 2) obey the law of reciprocal innervation of antagonist muscles at any time during the trial, except during a limited time interval centered on the time of ball impact. During that interval (from about 60 ms prior to impact up to about 60 ms after impact), the pattern of the responses consists of a substantial coactivation of both stretched and shortening muscles (see Figures 7, 8). This time window overlaps with the grasping phase of catching, involving flexion of the fingers around the incoming ball. Grasping starts about 30 ms prior to contact and ends some 50 ms after contact (Alderson et al., 1974; Lacquaniti & Maioli, 1989b). The overall margin of error for the timing of the grasp action is about ±20 ms from the optimum time. Timing errors outside these limits result in unsuccessful performance, because the ball either rebounds or falls off the hand. Human subjects consistently time their grasp action within the range of about 14 ms around the optimum time.

Since the changes in stretch reflexes begin before impact, they must be

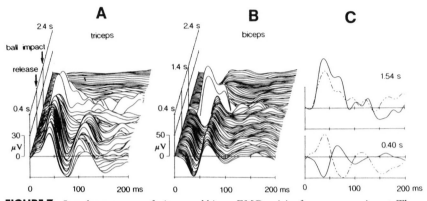

FIGURE 7   Impulse responses of triceps and biceps EMG activity from one experiment. These responses were obtained by cross-correlating the EMG activities with the pseudorandom perturbations. (A and B) Each trace is the EMG response at the time indicated by the oblique scale, time being measured from the onset of the perturbations. As plotted, the responses represent the average contribution to the motor output by a 20-ms torque pulse tending to flex the elbow and occurring 0–200 ms before. The vertical lines denote the time of release (1 s) and impact of the ball on the hand (1.55 s). (C) The impulse responses of biceps (solid line) and triceps (dashed line), obtained at 0.4 s (*bottom*) and at 1.54 s (*top*), are superimposed. Note the reversal of biceps responses around impact time. (Adapted from Lacquaniti et al., 1992.)

generated within the central nervous system (CNS). It may then be hypothesized that the reversal and coactivation of reflex responses is set centrally by switching between alternative spinal pathways, namely from the pathways of reciprocal inhibition to those of coexcitation and coinhibition of antagonist α-motoneurone pools (Lacquaniti et al., 1991). As far as the patterns of spinal connections of Ia and Ib afferents are concerned, it is now well established that there exist two main systems working in parallel in the cat (see Jankowska, 1992). The first corresponds to the classical Ia reciprocal inhibition circuit. This circuit is mediated by inhibitory interneurones in lamina VII of the spinal cord that receive convergent modulation from multiple primary afferents, Renshaw cells, and supraspinal centers. It has subsequently been demonstrated that there exists an additional system mediated by lamina VI interneurones classified as Ib interneurones. About 50% of them, however, also receive convergent inputs from Ia afferents. Thus peripheral signals on changes in muscle length and on changes in muscle tension are combined at a premotoneuronal level. In turn, Ib interneurones participate in both widespread coexcitation of antagonist α-motoneurones, as well as nonreciprocal inhibition. The excitability of these interneurones, as with lamina VII Ia inhibitory interneurones, is extensively modulated by descending tracts (including corticospinal and rubrospinal systems).

Evidence on the existence in man of extensive patterns of cross-connections is emerging from recent studies. Reciprocal Ia inhibition has been demonstrated between flexor and extensor muscles of the wrist and elbow (Baldissera, Campadelli, & Cavallari, 1983; Day, Marsden, Obeso, & Roth-

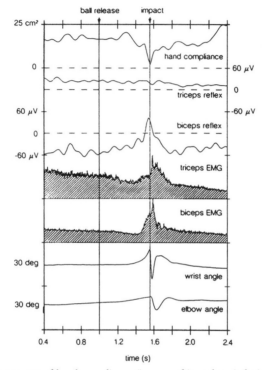

FIGURE 8 Time course of hand compliance (inverse of impedance) during catching. Pseudorandom pertubations were applied continuously to the elbow joint by a torque motor during each trial starting with time 0 s. The ball was released 1 s later and hit the hand at 1.55 s. The pseudorandom sequence was shifted by one element from trial to trial until all elements were shifted. In the figure, the bottom four traces are plotted from the ensemble average of all trials. In the average, the effect of the motor perturbations cancels out. The EMG traces have been scaled to their maximum. EMG and kinematic data of single trials were cross-correlated with the pseudorandom perturbations, thus eliminating the activity uncorrelated with these perturbations (such as the activity related to catching). The traces labeled "biceps reflex" and "triceps reflex" correspond to the mean amplitude (over the 20–60-ms interval) of the EMG responses obtained by cross-correlation. Note the reversal of the direction of the reflex response in biceps around impact time. The trace labeled "hand compliance" corresponds to the variance of the mechanical oscillations of the hand in the vertical direction induced by the torque pulses (the mechanical oscillations were obtained by cross-correlation with the measured changes in hand position). Note the minimum in hand compliance around impact. (Adapted from Lacquaniti & Maioli, 1992. © 1992 with kind permission from Elsevier Science—Sara Burgerhartstraat 25, 1055 KV Amsterdam, The Netherlands.)

well, 1984; Katz, Penicaud, & Rossi 1991). Connections among muscles acting at different joints have been also shown: thus, stimulation of Ia afferents from wrist muscles excites biceps motoneurones at a latency compatible with monosynaptic linkage and inhibits triceps motoneurones with disynaptic linkage (Cavallari & Katz, 1989). In addition, extensive convergence from a number of descending and peripheral inputs onto a propriospinal-like system has now been demonstrated in humans (Burke, Gracies, Mazevet, Meunier, & Pierrot-Deseilligny, 1992).

Switching between different spinal pathways does not necessarily imply that one or more pathways become active at the expense of complete gating of the alternative pathways. Rather, it is likely that the operation of such pathways can coexist functionally. However, their respective gains are centrally modified, shifting the overall balance more toward one response mode or another. In this respect, then, the behavior of the system is comparable to that of the VOR, in which adaptive and learning properties are accompanied by suitable changes in the synaptic weights of parallel neural pathways. However, the reversal of the stretch reflex occurs on a much faster time scale than that usually observed for the adaptive changes in the VOR.

The highly accurate timing of the reversal of the stretch reflex during catching indicates that it must depend on a predictive, feedforward control scheme relying on precise information on time-to-contact. There are at least two different schemes of implementation of the switching, both reminiscent of analogous adaptive or optimal switching in automatic control of robot manipulators (Åström & Wittenmark, 1989). The first scheme is called gain scheduling and involves a preprogrammed change in the response of the feedback loop the timing of which is decided in feedforward mode relative to a forthcoming, completely predictable event. The second scheme for the switching between two different operating states involves a network that changes synaptic weights so as to optimize some performance criterion. As explained in a subsequent section, one such criterion might be the maximization of limb impedance (which determines resistance to limb position perturbations; see next section) during the preplanned mechanical interaction with an object. Indeed, Figure 8 shows that hand compliance (inverse of impedance) was transiently minimized at the time of the impact of the ball with the hand during catching. This minimum overlapped in time with the reversal of biceps reflex.

6. LIMB MECHANICS

A perturbation such as the dropped ball that tends to displace the limb from its reference position is resisted by restoring forces that are due to the intrinsic viscoelastic properties of muscles and to muscle contractions of reflex and nonreflex origin. The mechanical interaction between a limb and the environment is concisely characterized by the impedance of the limb, which describes the dynamic relation between force and displacement. The hypothesis has been put forth by a number of authors that limb impedance is a variable controlled by the human brain (e.g., Bizzi et al, 1992; Feldman, 1980; Hogan, 1985; Houk & Rymer, 1981; A. M. Smith, 1981). Impedance control may afford a unified treatment of diverse problems implied in motor control, such as planning unconstrained trajectories of a limb and control of contact forces with the external environment during constrained motion (cf. Bizzi et al., 1992).

Let us first introduce some basic notions about impedance. Mechanical impedance represents an extension to the field of mechanics of the definition of electrical impedance. In general, an impedance relates an input flow variable to an output effort variable. For electrical circuits, input flow is current and output effort is voltage. For a mechanical circuit, input flow is motion and output effort is force. Linear or angular dimensions are used depending on the nature of the degrees of freedom of the system. Thus, one can define the mechanical impedance of a translatory system as the relation between its linear displacement and the resulting force. Similarly, the impedance of a rotary joint relates angular motion and torque. Mechanical impedance, just as electrical impedance, includes static and dynamic components. Static components reflect force contributions that are due to changes in position, while dynamic components reflect force contributions that are due to changes in the time derivatives of position (velocity, acceleration, etc).

If we restrict our attention to a single degree of freedom (it does not matter whether translatory or rotary), its impedance can be parameterized in terms of different static and dynamic scalar terms, depending on the mechanical elements that are included in the circuit. A typical example of a mechanical system is one comprising a spring, a dashpot, and a mass. If we deal with ideal linear elements, then the general form of the circuit equation is:

$$f = m\ddot{x} + c\dot{x} + k(x - x_0) \tag{1}$$

where f is an external driving force (time varying in the most general case), x, $\dot{x}$, and $\ddot{x}$ are the position, velocity, and acceleration, respectively, of the point-mass m; c and k are the viscosity and stiffness coefficients, respectively, and x_0 is the resting length of the spring (i.e., the shortest length at which force is exerted).

The definitions of mechanical impedance given above can be applied to physiological systems that are relevant for motor control research. According to macroscopic models of muscle behavior, a component of muscle elasticity lies in series with the contractile apparatus, and depends on the same mechanism to generate tension (i.e., formation of cross-bridges). A second elastic component is in parallel, and depends on connective tissues and membranes. The contractile machinery is also associated with a viscous resistance. In general, muscle stiffness and viscosity exhibit a complex nonlinear behavior, which depends on muscle length, its rate of change, recruitment, and firing rate of motor units (Houk & Rymer, 1981). However, for sufficiently small input perturbations, muscle behavior can be linearized to Equation (1). In addition, it is well established that the behavior of the closed-loop system, that is, of reflexive muscle, is much more linear (Houk & Rymer, 1981). In human physiology, we are generally concerned with the overall behavior of rotary joints, such as the elbow or wrist. Since the muscles generally act in parallel on a rotary joint, the overall effect of all agonist and antagonist muscles is obtained by summing all individual contributions of stiffness and viscosity.

Stretch reflexes also contribute to the net viscoelastic behavior of a joint. Although the neural circuits underlying the operation of stretch reflexes are highly complex and only partially understood (see Section 4), it is generally agreed that some important components of these reflexes reflect the afferent signals from the muscle spindles, signals that are closely related to changes in length and rate of change of length (see Vallbo and Wessberg, Chapter 18). Thus, phenomenologically, the simplest form of behavior of stretch reflexes in humans is adequately described by an equation similar to Equation (1), describing viscoelastic behavior, but incorporating a feedback delay. In sum, the combination of intrinsic viscoelastic properties of active muscles and the operation of stretch reflex loops endow the overall neuromuscular system with the characteristics of an impedance, the parameters of which can be determined experimentally. These parameters are not constant, but depend on the operating point of the system. The importance of the determination of the mechanical parameters is that their modulation reflects the nature of the neural control processes.

The mechanical properties of multi-jointed systems present new problems to be addressed (Hogan, 1985). Limb stiffness, viscosity, and moment of inertia (the rotary equivalent of mass) are not simply scalar quantities, as in the single-joint case, but have a directional character. In multijointed movements the relation between force and displacement is a vector field, with the direction of force generally not coincident with the direction of displacement. Vectorial entities can be encoded in the CNS in different reference frames (Soechting & Flanders, 1992; see also Soechting et al., Chapter 8). Thus, the impedance of a multijointed limb could be represented in the reference frame fixed to the limb segments, using as coordinates the angular positions of the participating joints. Limb impedance could also be represented in an earth-fixed reference frame describing the position of the limb end point: in the case of the arm, the Cartesian coordinates of the hand. These two frames of representation have a different status vis-à-vis the problem of impedance control. The output of neural control is muscle activity that modulates directly muscle stiffness and viscosity, and therefore joint impedance. However, one might hypothesize that the goal of impedance control in manipulative tasks needs to be expressed in hand coordinates. This then raises the problem of transformation of an intended impedance expressed in hand coordinates into the actual impedance controlled in joint or muscle coordinates. This is not a trivial problem, because hand impedance does not depend solely on the pattern of muscle activity but also depends on the geometrical configuration of the limb (Hogan, 1985). In other words, the same pattern of muscle activity may result in very different values of hand impedance depending on the values of the joint angles. Thus, in order to modulate hand impedance according to desired results, the CNS must be endowed with an internal model of limb geometry (Ghez et al., 1991; Lacquaniti et al., 1992). Internal models behave as predictive estimators of an expected relation between motor output and environment. Thus they allow bidirectional mapping between motor space, defined in joint or muscle coordinates, and task space, defined in earth- or object-fixed reference frames. Adaptive modulation of limb impedance represents experimental evidence for this mapping.

7. ADAPTIVE CONTROL OF HAND IMPEDANCE

In contrast to most current artificial manipulators, humans possess an extraordinary ability to modulate limb impedance according to task requirements. Direct evaluation of the time-varying changes of the coefficients of angular stiffness and viscosity has been performed during catching (Lacquaniti et al., 1992, 1993b). The temporal modulation of these coefficients was complex (Figure 9). Different coefficients changed with different time courses. In addition, changes in viscosity did not parallel changes in stiffness. Finally, some interindividual variability was also present. However, all these factors could be correlated to specific underlying mechanisms. The changes in the direct coefficients of angular stiffness tended to covary with changes in the coupling coefficients (describing the mechanical interaction between arm segments) from trial start up to about 30 ms prior to impact time. The latter changes could be correlated qualitatively to parallel changes in net muscle activity preceding impact. In cases in which muscle activity built up prior to impact, the coefficients of angular stiffness increased relative to their baseline levels. Correspondingly, in cases in which muscle activity was reduced prior to impact, angular stiffness dropped. This parallelism in time between stiff-

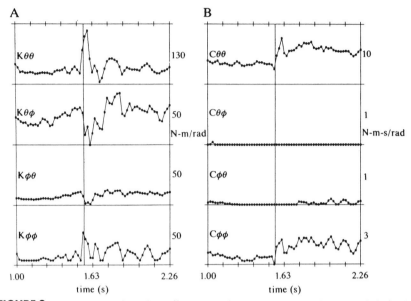

FIGURE 9   Time course of angular stiffness (A) and viscosity (B) in 1 subject. Symbols for the stiffness coefficients: $K_{\theta\theta}$ and $K_{\Phi\Phi}$ are the direct terms, relating elbow torque to elbow angle and wrist torque to wrist angle, respectively: $K_{\theta\Phi}$ and $K_{\Phi\theta}$ are the cross-coupling terms, relating elbow torque to wrist angle and wrist torque to elbow angle, respectively. Viscosity coefficients are defined similarly, but they relate joint torques to angular velocities. Each tick mark on the time axes corresponds to 126 ms. (Adapted from Lacquaniti et al., 1993b.)

ness and muscle activity conforms with observations on the relation between static stiffness and mean muscle activity (Kearney & Hunter, 1990; Mussa-Ivaldi et al., 1985).

The major changes in angular stiffness occurred over a time interval roughly centered on impact (about 30 ms before up to 100 ms after impact; see Figure 9). In this period there was a complete dissociation between the direction of changes of the direct terms of stiffness, which peaked transiently, and the corresponding direction of changes of the coupling terms, which dropped transiently. These changes around impact time can be accounted for by parallel changes in the behavior of stretch reflex responses. As reviewed above, catching involves a transient reversal of the direction of stretch reflex responses centered on impact, leading to coactivation of antagonist muscles (Lacquaniti et al., 1991). This reversal is consistently correlated in time with the peaks in the direct terms of stiffness and viscosity. Reflex coactivation most likely contributed to these peaks, because joint torques produced by contraction of antagonist muscles subtract but stiffnesses and viscosities add.

The complex temporal modulation of angular impedance during catching implies the existence of distinct neural control processes acting separately on different components of the angular impedance. This has far-reaching consequences. There are two main aspects that need to be discussed: (1) differential control of direct and coupling terms of angular stiffness, and (2) differential control of angular stiffness and viscosity.

The differential control of direct and coupling terms of angular stiffness is functionally significant because it effectively stiffens elbow and wrist joints and decouples their respective angular motions from one another, right at the time of the mechanical interaction between the limb and the ball. Simulation studies have shown that decreasing the magnitude of coupling stiffness terms does lead to an improved stabilization of limb posture under specific mechanical conditions (Lacquaniti & Soechting, 1986). Thus, it reduces overall limb oscillations when the direction of angular motion resulting from an external perturbation is opposite at the two joints.

Neural control also differentially affects angular stiffness and viscosity, as indicated by the fact that the time course of viscosity changes did not parallel that in stiffness during catching. The direct terms of angular viscosity increased prior to impact, whereas the viscosity coupling terms remained close to zero throughout. The different time course of viscosity and stiffness changes implies that the overall damping (i.e., the ratio of viscosity and stiffness that indicates the oscillation tendency) is not maintained constant. This contrasts with the behavior under stationary conditions (Kearney & Hunter, 1990), but is in agreement with other observations carried out on single-joint systems under time-varying conditions (D. J. Bennett, Hollerbach, Xu, & Hunter, 1992; Lacquaniti, Soechting, & Terzuolo, 1982). Differential control of static (elastic) and dynamic (viscous) components of limb impedance is important, because it affords the possibility of affecting different parameters of the motor response (e.g., steady-state error, transient oscillations, settling time) to a variable extent, depending on changing requirements of the task. The main functional significance of the modulation of angular stiffness and viscosity during catching is represented by control of impedance at the hand. Object prehension and manipulation involve the specification of position and contact forces at the interaction point (Jeannerod, 1984; Johansson, 1991). One possible solution is offered by the control of the dynamic interaction between the hand and the object (Bizzi et al., 1992). Explicitly planning and controlling a desired interaction involves the problem of coordinate transformation of limb impedance (Lacquaniti et al., 1992; Mussa-Ivaldi et al., 1985). The coordinate transformation required to convert intended hand impedance into actual muscle and joint impedance depends critically on the availability of accurate internal models of the mechanical properties of the limb (see above).

The series of studies on catching have provided evidence that net impedance at the hand is accurately tuned for the dynamic interaction with the falling ball. The (time-varying) matrices of coefficients expressing stiffness and viscosity in the Cartesian coordinates of the hand have been computed (Lacquaniti et al., 1993b). From these matrices, the vector components that determine the resistance provided by the hand to a virtual displacement in the vertical direction, that is, along the direction of ball fall, have been extracted (Figure 10). The changes in these components of hand resistance are due to the combined effect of the changes in the angular stiffness and

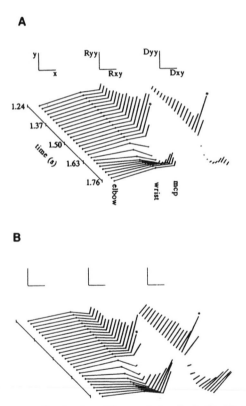

FIGURE 10 Time course of end-point stiffness and viscosity in 2 subjects (A and B, respectively). Stick diagrams depict the geometry of the limb at 20-ms intervals, starting from 0.31 s before impact (*top*) up to 0.21 s after impact (*bottom*). Impact time is denoted by the asterisk. Limb end point corresponds to the third metacarpophalangeal joint (MCP), where impact occurs. Thick lines to the right of the limb end point represent the vectors $[\mathbf{R}_{xy}\mathbf{R}_{yy}]$ of hand stiffness and the vectors $[\mathbf{D}_{xy}\mathbf{D}_{yy}]$ of hand viscosity. Each tick mark on the time axes corresponds to 130 ms. (Adapted from Lacquaniti et al., 1993b.)

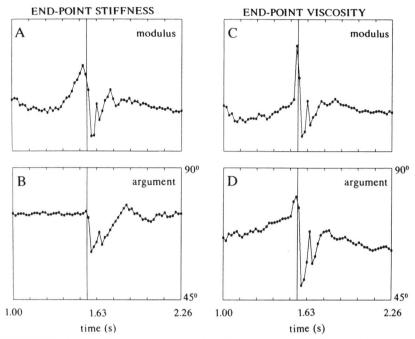

FIGURE 11 Average time course of end-point stiffness and viscosity. The modulus of hand stiffness and viscosity are plotted (A and B, respectively). Scale is arbitrary because in each experiment the modulus was normalized to the maximum before averaging. The argument of hand stiffness and viscosity are plotted (B and D, respectively). A 0° argument corresponds to a horizontal vector pointing outward from the hand, whereas a 90° argument corresponds to a vertical, upward vector (see Figure 10). Each tick mark on the time axes corresponds to 126 ms. (Adapted from Lacquaniti et al., 1993b.)

viscosity at the elbow and wrist joints, and of the simultaneous changes in the geometrical configuration of the limb during catching. As a consequence, the time course of the changes in hand impedance does not parallel that of any single term of angular impedance, nor does it parallel the time course of changes in limb geometry. Indeed, it is an important point that changes in both limb geometry and angular impedance were somewhat variable among experiments, whereas the changes in hand impedance were consistent.

It is precisely the modulation of hand impedance that appears to be finely tuned to impact time (Figure 11). The magnitude of hand resistance vectors increased consistently prior to impact, albeit with a different time course for hand stiffness and viscosity. The magnitude of hand stiffness and viscosity at impact time was either maximum or close to maximum. Also prior to impact, the direction of the viscosity vectors rotated closer to the vertical, indicating that a relatively larger component of reactive forces is exerted in the direction of the expected perturbation.

Hand stiffness and viscosity appear to be controlled by the CNS independently of limb position in the catching task (Lacquaniti et al., 1993b). This can be shown by correlating their changes with those of the equivalent inertia at the hand. The latter reflects directly the geometrical configuration of the limb. It was found that the degree of correlation between the orientation of the vectors of hand viscosity and the orientation of the vectors of hand inertia was variable during the task. Initially the two sets of vectors were closely aligned; around impact time, however, viscosity vectors rotated closer to the vertical than inertia vectors, whereas the former moved farther away from the vertical relative to the latter during the final stage of catching. This contrasts sharply with the results obtained under conditions of stationary maintenance of posture, when the hand impedance covaries with the changes in limb geometry (Mussa-Ivaldi et al., 1985). The changes in hand impedance are poorly correlated with the changes in hand position during catching. In fact, the largest variation of hand impedance coincides with limited and variable changes in hand position prior to impact.

The results on catching lend support to the hypothesis that all components of limb impedance, that is, stiffness, viscosity, and inertia, can be controlled in parallel by the CNS. Such parallel control is optimally suited to modulate the overall mechanical behavior of the limb according to task needs, by decoupling inertial contributions from viscoelastic contributions. Parallel control does not imply that there is no exchange of information between the corresponding channels. Quite the contrary, an essential prerequisite for this type of control is that each channel "knows" about the other and can modify its output accordingly. Thus, as we have argued above, hand stiffness and viscosity are mechanically determined by limb geometry and the only way they can be tuned according to task needs is by taking into account the changes in the geometrical configuration. The converse is also true: constraints arising from muscle activation patterns and biomechanics are taken into account in planning a specific sequence of geometrical configurations of the limb aimed at the interaction with an object (cf. Jeannerod, 1991; Lacquaniti et al., 1982).

The transient maximization of hand impedance in world coordinates implies that the CNS is able to represent internally the intended hand impedance and to transform it into appropriate patterns of activation of the relevant muscles. This coordinate transformation requires an internal model of limb geometry. The results summarized above can then be interpreted as indicative of the fact that muscle activity is modulated on the basis of an internal model of limb geometry. It is conceivable that, in the course of the ontogenesis of the brain processes involved in the construction of motor acts, an isomorphism emerges epigenetically between the internal models of the body and space, on one hand, and limb movement and its perception, on the other hand. The notion that the brain is endowed with fairly accurate internal models of limb geometry is well established and has long been subsumed under the neurological rubric of Body Scheme (cf. Gurfinkel & Levik, 1979). The Body Scheme is largely inborn and stable, but model parameters, such as the estimate of mass and length of the individual limb segments, can be recalibrated adaptively. A recent study has demonstrated that proprioceptive information is essential to maintain an adequate internal model of the mechanical properties of the upper limb (Ghez et al., 1990). Deafferented subjects (whose sensory impairments were due to large fiber neuropathies) were unable to compensate for workspace anisotropies in limb inertia and produced pointing errors that were direction dependent. Vision of the limb could partially correct these movement errors.

The role of internal models of limb geometry for the control of movement also emerges from other pointing studies. Thus, Lacquaniti et al. (1982) showed that arm kinematics was unchanged when a pointer was used that doubled the effective length of the forearm. This indicates that the transformation of target location from the world coordinates into the angular coordinates of the joints incorporates information on the effective length of the limb segments. Finally, Flanders and co-workers (1992) have studied an arm pointing task in three dimensions. When pointing was performed to a remembered target in the absence of vision, there were significant errors in distance only. These errors were accounted for by the specific nature of the transformation performed from the world coordinates of the target (as internally represented using visual information) to the intrinsic joint coordinates of kinesthetic representation of arm orientation. Again, these sensorimotor transformations imply accurate internal representations of limb geometry.

ACKNOWLEDGMENTS

This work was partially supported by grants from CNR, Ministero della Sanita, and EEC.

PART 4

Hand–Arm Coordination in Reach and Grasp

While the excess degrees of freedom produce a computational problem for hand positioning, this problem is even greater in reach-to-grasp movements because there is shaping of the hand to be coordinated with hand transport by the arm. Since each finger has a number of joints and the thumb is opposable, there are many different alternative hand shapes that could be used to produce a stable grasp on most objects.

The degrees-of-freedom problem for grasping may be solved by choosing an optimal placing of the fingers. Indeed, people do typically constrain their grip configurations to a small number of consistent patterns, which Iberall and Fagg (Chapter 12) describe in terms of opposition space between virtual fingers. A virtual finger is a grasp surface that may comprise one or more digits or the palm. An opposition space is defined by two or more virtual fingers that allow an object to be grasped. Iberall and Fagg show how neural networks can use the virtual finger concept as a useful task-level abstraction in planning grasps. The configuration of virtual fingers to grasp an object is quite straightforwardly related to the shape of the object, and neural networks then offer an attractive method for solving the optimization problem of how to configure the actual digits so that the virtual fingers produce appropriate opposition forces on the object.

Paulignan and Jeannerod (Chapter 13) review several studies of the relation between arm movement subserving hand transport and grasp configuration or aperture during movements to reach out and grasp an object. Research on such movements has concentrated on two questions: (1) whether the two components of prehension are controlled by separate visuomotor channels in the brain and (2) whether these pathways interact by sharing information about the progress of each component during the ongoing movement. They review a number of previous experiments from which they conclude that the concept of two independent visuomotor channels may be preserved. While there is now evidence that perturbations to one channel can lead to modifications in the other, the authors suggest that this can be explained in terms of reprogramming of the movement rather than the operation of a single program that allows sharing of information between channels.

In Chapter 14, Wiesendanger, Kazennikov, Perrig, and Kaluzny focus on the issues of hierarchical control and motor equivalence in the coordination of bimanual movements. They examine a task in which a monkey opens a drawer with one hand to retrieve a food morsel with the other. They show that the temporal variability of bilateral events is lower than the variability within each limb and, moreover, that the variability decreases as the movement progresses toward the goal. The authors suggest that this reflects the actions of a high-level central controller that coordinates the lower level pattern generators driving each limb. They also suggest that there may be mutual interactions between these lower level elements. Thus, the motor system appears to harness sets of muscles to produce a desired synergy in a remarkably flexible way, apparently with few limits on what grouping of body parts may be incorporated into a single synergy.

The previous chapters consider coordination of hand and arm in moving toward an object. In contrast, Wing (Chapter 15) examines hand–arm coordination when moving an object held in the hand. In particular, he considers the problem of how precision grip forces must change when moving an object in the face of varying load forces due to arm movement. A precision grip with the tips of the thumb and index finger on opposing sides of an object requires a grip force normal to the object surfaces in order to develop frictional force sufficient to counteract gravitational and inertial load forces. Wing reviews a series of studies that show that the motor system controls grip force adjustments with considerable precision, and in remarkable synchrony with voluntary arm movements, suggesting an anticipatory coordination between the two actions. He argues that similarities between anticipatory modulation of grip force and anticipatory postural adjustments in standing balance suggest there are common underlying neural mechanisms for the maintainance of stability in the face of voluntary movement.

12

Neural Network Models for Selecting Hand Shapes

THEA IBERALL AND ANDREW H. FAGG

1. INTRODUCTION

The simple task of grasping objects has been studied for centuries by scientists and engineers who have tried to understand and duplicate the versatility of the human hand. With its 31 muscles, over 25 degrees of freedom, and high sensibility, the hand has an extensive capacity for interacting with objects. Schlesinger (1919) identified hand surfaces and shapes that combine with object characteristics to name possible ways that the hand, in effect, creates tools for prehension. Napier (1956) noted the power and precision capabilities of the human hand, suggesting that these relate to the power and precision requirements of tasks. MacKenzie and Iberall (1994) define prehension as the application of functionally effective forces by the hand to an object for a task, given numerous constraints. They state that the functional demands on a posture are to apply forces to match the anticipated forces in the task (stable grasp), impart motion to the object (manipulate), transport the object, and gather sensory information about the state of the interaction with the object. In effect, different postures of the hand present different degrees of available force, motion, and sensory information. One of the challenges, then, is to understand the mechanisms involved in selecting the posture that best matches the requirements and the constraints of the presented task.

One approach to this problem is the construction of mathematical models of the neural processes involved in the selection of a hand posture. As a pattern recognition problem, it is an ideal candidate for using neural networks. Results from neuroanatomical and neurophysiological experiments offer a set of constraints as to the flow of information through such a computational architecture. Neural regions implicated in certain activities can be modeled by artificial network topologies. Weight matrices in artificial neural networks represent the synaptic connections between neurons. An especially useful tool in this domain is the use of learning algorithms, which specify how these weight matrices modify the behavior of individual neurons of a model in order to satisfy some set of constraints. For example, it is possible to use behavioral information to specify the computations to be performed by a neural network as a whole, but it is the learning algorithm that determines the behavior of the individual neurons. Adaptation occurs as synapses are modified, and networks learn to associate a set of outputs to a given set of inputs. These neural firing patterns can then be compared to what is seen in experiments in real biological systems.

In what follows, we first discuss a high-level language for describing grasp plans, then using that language examine several experimental studies pertaining to the selection of hand configurations, and finally show how these data may be studied through the use of neural models.

2. A LANGUAGE FOR DESCRIBING HAND SHAPES

2.1 Opposition Space and Virtual Fingers

In observing how subjects grasped different sized mugs, Arbib et al. (1985) noted that different numbers of fingers were used, depending on the length of the mug handle. Yet, the task remained basically the same: a finger was placed on top of the handle, one or more fingers were placed inside the handle, and, if available, fingers were placed against the outside of the handle. They suggested that each of these functions was being performed by a *virtual finger* (VF) as the method of applying the force. A VF is an abstract representation, a functional unit, for a collection of individual fingers and hand surfaces applying an oppositional force. Real fingers group together into a VF to apply a force or torque opposing other VFs or task torques. As seen in Figure 1A, the index finger can be a VF, as can the thumb. In Figure 1B, all four fingers form one VF, the palm another. When a real finger maps into a VF, its physical characteristics map into abstract state variables that can describe the VF. Anatomical joint configurations, range of motion, finger size, and palm size contribute to kinematic components of VFs such as lengths, widths, and orientations. Biomechanical considerations of the intrinsic and extrinsic hand muscles, tendons, ligaments, and skin surfaces contribute to the force compo-

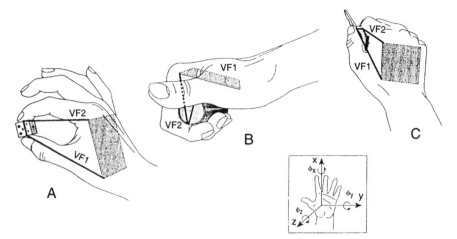

FIGURE 1   Prehensile postures consist of combinations of three basic ways that the hand can provide oppositions around objects. The opposition occurs between two hand surfaces, or virtual fingers (VF), relative to a hand coordinate frame placed on the palm (see inset). (A) Pad opposition occurs along an axis generally parallel to the palm. (B) Palm opposition occurs along an axis generally perpendicular to the palm. (C) Side opposition occurs along an axis generally transverse to the palm. (From MacKenzie & Iberall, 1994, © 1994 with kind permission from Elsevier Science—NL, Sara Burgerhartstraat 25. 1055 KV Amsterdam, The Netherlands.)

nents of VFs such as orientation of the applied force at the grasping surface and its strength. Properties of cutaneous mechanoreceptors such as location, morphology, receptive field size, innervation density, and adaptation characteristics contribute to the sensory components of the grasping surface of VFs such as sensitivity and resolution.

In prehension, at least two forces are being applied in opposition to each other against the object's surfaces. Iberall et al. (1986) used the term *opposition* to describe three basic directions (or primitives) along which the human hand can apply forces, relative to a hand coordinate frame placed on the palm (see inset, Figure 1). A prehensile posture then consists of combinations of these primitives, which are as follows:

1. *Pad opposition*: occurs between hand surfaces along a direction generally parallel to the palm (Figure 1A). This usually occurs between volar surfaces of the fingers and thumb, near or on the pads. An example is holding a needle or small ball. This is the x axis in the inset in Figure 1.

2. *Palm opposition*: occurs between hand surfaces along a direction generally perpendicular to the palm (Figure 1B). Grasping a large hammer or screwdriver are examples of palm opposition. This is the z axis in the inset in Figure 1.

3. *Side opposition*: occurs between hand surfaces along a direction gener-ally transverse to the palm (Figure 1C). As an example, one holds a key between the volar surface of the thumb and the radial sides of the fingers. Of course, it can occur between the sides of the fingers, as in holding a cigarette. This is the *y* axis in the inset in Figure 1.

The Opposition Space model suggests that, in prehensile postures, the hand is applying oppositional forces around an object or against task forces and torques along three general directions, either alone or in combinations. An *opposition space* is the collection of oppositions and the VFs used. It can be described in both physical terms (e.g., amount and orientation of force vec-tors, innervation density of grasping surface) and abstracted terms (e.g., types of oppositions, VF mappings). In pad opposition, the hand can exert small forces, impart fine motions, and gather precise sensory information to match the accuracy and manipulation requirements of the task. (For a discussion of precision manipulation in microsurgery see Jones, Chapter 17.) Pads on the finger distal palmar surfaces are highly specialized for prehension in that they provide friction, epidermal ridges, sticky self-lubricating excretions, and an ability to comply with (instead of be displaced by) touched objects. In addition, receptors having small and well-defined receptive fields are especially dense in the finger pulps. In palm opposition, the hand can match or create larger forces while still ensuring a stable grasp, using the arm and wrist to provide grosser motions. Greatest gripping forces are generated using the extrinsic flexors with their greater mechanical advantage, with due consideration to the wrist posture and size of object. In addition, for smaller objects such as medium sized cylinders, shearing forces tend to pull the object into the grasp and normal forces tend to be larger than for larger objects. However, this increased power is at a cost of the loss of skin sensitivity under heavy loads. In side opposition, the thumb pad is brought against the object in opposition to the radial side of a finger. As a bridge between power and precision grasps, this posture offers a medium range of forces while still offering some availability of sensory information due to the thumb pad being in contact with the object and some ability to impart motions to the object (as in turning a key).

Importantly, the hand can assume these oppositions in combinations. As Napier (1956) pointed out, some postures exhibit multiple characteristics. For example, a pad opposition in the radial fingers works in combination with a palm opposition in the ulnar fingers. The pad opposition occurs between the thumb (VF1) and the index and middle fingers (VF2). At the same time, the palm opposition occurs between the palm (VF1) and the ring and little fingers (VF2). This creates a grasp that combines the dexterity and sensitivity of the three radial digits using the distal pulps, with the strength of the other two fingers in a powerful opposition to the palm.

2.2 Opposition Space and Behavioral Experiments

The Opposition Space model may be used in behavioral experiments for measuring human performance. For example, Newell, Scully, Tenebaum, and Hardinman (1989) performed grasping studies in adults and children, asking them to grasp cubic objects ranging in width from 0.8 to 24.2 cm. Newell et al. studied the number of fingers used by the subjects in opposition to the thumb and noted that the number of fingers used in VF2 in opposition to the thumb (VF1) increased with object size. As expected, a VF2 of one finger was used in opposition to the thumb at very small object sizes, and a VF2 of all four fingers was used in opposition to the thumb for larger cubes (for the largest objects, two hands were used). For intermediate objects, there were preferred grip patterns of two or three fingers in opposition to the thumb. Further, the frequency curves and patterns of hand use were similar for adults and children when plotted against the object/hand ratio.

Similar studies were performed by Iberall, Preti, and Zemke (1989) who asked subjects to place cylinders (8 cm in diameter) on a platform using pad opposition. The cylinders varied in length from 3 to 11 cm. The platform varied in width between two sizes: very narrow, making the task a precision task, or wide, making the task less precise. No instructions were given on how many fingers to use in VF2 as it opposed the thumb (VF1). Of the fifteen finger combinations possible, seven combinations were used, with the size of VF2 ranging from one to four fingers. The combinations of fingers observed were: index alone (I), middle alone (M), index and middle (I–M), middle and ring (M–R), index and middle and ring (I–M–R), middle and ring and little (M–R–L), index and middle and ring and little (I–M–R–L). It was also observed that 60% of the grasps used a VF2 of one or two fingers. More fingers were used in VF2 as cylinder length increased, which supports the findings of Newell et al.

2.3 Biological Evidence for Opposition and Virtual Finger Size Coding

The Opposition Space Model can be used to examine biological results. Rizzolatti (1987; Rizzolatti et al., 1988) has studied grasping-related activity in a subarea of the macaque inferior premotor cortex referred to as F5. During movement preparation and execution, many neurons code for the specific opposition that is made by the monkey, but do not respond during axial or proximal movements made in the absence of distal movements. A neuron that codes for a precision grip (pad opposition) made by either the contralateral or ipsilateral hand is shown in Figure 2. Other neurons have been observed to be active during the execution of a palm opposition or side opposition. Additional groups of neurons within F5 are responsive to other motor acts involving the hands. These include neurons that fire while the

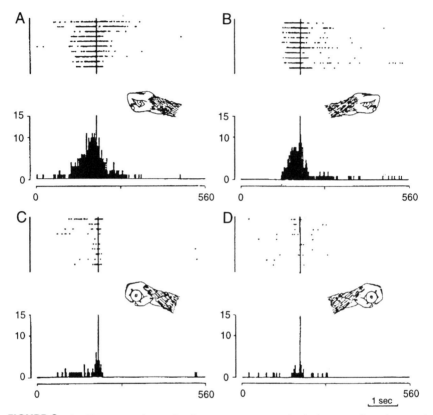

FIGURE 2 An F5 neuron that codes for precision grip in both the contralateral (A) and ipsilateral (B) hands. The neuron does not respond significantly to a palm-opposition type grasp. The histograms are centered at the point where the monkey made contact with the object. (From Fig. 4 of Rizzolatti, et al., 1988.)

monkey is grasping with the hand and mouth, as well as neurons that are active when the monkey is tearing an object.

What we see within F5 appears to be rather distinctive groups of cells, each of which codes for a functionally different opposition that the monkey makes. This is the case even when different grasps make use of overlapping muscle groups. The language of opposition spaces is thus useful in describing what is happening at the F5 level in that it captures to some degree these fundamental divisions of activity.

In terms of VF representations in cortical areas, physiological studies done in the somatosensory and motor cortex have found neurons responding to multiple finger representations. For example, Strick and Preston (1982) found multiple representations of digits in receptive fields of neurons in the motor cortex of the squirrel monkey. Interestingly, combinations of fingers were observed, such as receptive fields corresponding to the index–middle fingers, index–middle–ring fingers, and index–middle–ring–little fingers.

2.4 The Role of Neural Modeling

Information processing in artificial neural networks involves the interactions of a large number of simple processing elements, or units, that can either inhibit or excite each other. Thus, they honor general neurobiological constraints, but using simplifying assumptions, are motivated by cognitive phenomena and are governed primarily by computational constraints (Churchland & Sejnowski, 1988). Each unit has an activation state and units are connected together through synapses in some pattern of connectivity. Weight matrices represent the synaptic connections. Rules govern how information is propagated and how learning occurs in the network. The processing units can represent individual neurons or else concepts (that can either be individual cells themselves or groups of cells). More important, the issue for these models is how a computation is performed without regard to at what level it is working.

This chapter concentrates on several neural network models for the planning of grasp configurations following the Opposition Space model. In particular, the network models will concentrate on computing the number of fingers, selecting the opposition, and selecting a hand opening size to be used in a grasp posture. While we do not suggest that these algorithms are the ones used in the central nervous system, the models presented offer a style of computation that is brain-like. Wherever possible, we offer ties between our models and results from the neurosciences.

3. NEURAL NETWORKS FOR SELECTING FINGERS

In grasping an object, the number of fingers to be used in VF2 in the grasp must be determined. For this computation, the human brain takes into account an extensive range of object, task, environmental, anatomical, and biomechanical constraints (MacKenzie & Iberall, 1994). As a starting place for modeling the CNS, simple neural networks can be constructed that learn to associate a few of these constraints, such as object or task characteristics, to the number of fingers to be used in VF2. Iberall et al. (1989) constructed simple networks to determine a real finger mapping for VF2 in pad opposition. Two of the networks are seen in Figure 3. Both networks have three layers of processing units. Tasks, defined in terms of task difficulty and cylinder length, were presented to the input layer of the network in Figure 3A.

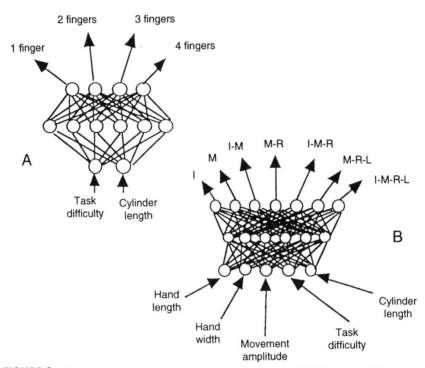

FIGURE 3   Networks modeling virtual to real finger mapping. (A) Using task difficulty and cylinder length as inputs, the network computes the size of VF2. (B) Using task difficulty, cylinder length, hand length, hand width, and movement amplitude as inputs, the network selects which real fingers constitute VF2. I, index finger; M, middle finger; R, ring finger; L, little finger. (From Iberall et al., 1989.)

The coding for these inputs matched the experimental paradigm: tasks had two states (easy, hard) and cylinders ranged in size between 3 and 11 cm in length. The output of this layer o_i was projected through a set of weights w_{ij}, representing the strength of connection between neuron i in the input layer and neuron j in the next layer. The activation level (a_j) of the neurons in this next layer, the hidden layer, is computed by

$$a_j = f \left[\sum_i (oi \star w_{ij}) \right]$$

where $f(\ )$ is a nonlinear function, typically the sigmoid: $f(x) = \dfrac{1}{1 + e^{-x}}$.

The output of the hidden layer neurons was then projected through another set of weights to an output layer, where the weighted activation values were also computed. The output of the output layer represented the number of fingers to use in VF2.

In Figure 3B, another network topology was explored. In this case, the second network had five inputs and seven outputs. Added to the inputs were additional constraints to associate with VF2 size, the subject's hand length, hand width, and the distance the hand had to travel. In terms of the outputs, each output unit represented one combination of fingers, for example, the index finger alone (I), the middle finger alone (M), the index and middle fingers combined (I–M).

Initially, the networks designed by Iberall et al. did not know how to associate task and object properties with the number of fingers in VF2, but adaptation of the values of the weights allowed such an association to occur. This was accomplished using a supervised adaptation rule, which uses a training signal that contains some measure of the desired behavior of the network. A training set is presented for learning, containing a collection of input/output pairs that identifies to the network what the output should be for a given set of inputs. In this case, the training set was constructed using averaged data collected from the subjects reaching for the cylinders. Iberall et al. used a supervised adaptation rule called the generalized delta rule (Rumelhart, Hinton, & Williams, 1986), which changes the values of the weights from the hidden layer to the output layer as follows:

$$\Delta w_{ij} = \alpha(t_{pi} - o_{pi}) \, o_{pj}$$

where i refers to units in the output layer and j refers to neurons in the hidden layer and Δw_{ij} is the weighting of the connection from the ith hidden unit to the jth output unit. The actual output o_{pi} for a particular input/output pair p is subtracted from the desired output t_{pi}. The constant α is the learning rate. The values of the weights connecting the input layer to the hidden layer are updated as follows:

$$\Delta w_{jk} = \alpha o_{pj}(1 - o_{pj})o_{pk} \sum_i (t_{pi} - o_{pi})w_{ij}$$

where k refers to units in the input layer. Training pairs were presented to the network in thousands of trials until the error between the computed output and the desired output is reduced to zero (or at least very close to zero), indicating that the network learned which fingers to use given the inputs. An error cutoff of .05 was used to indicate that the network had converged on a solution.

In order for the networks to learn the desired associations, the training set was repeatedly presented to the network. For the network in Figure 3A with two inputs and four outputs, it took 2072 of these repetitions to converge on a solution (total error .004). For the network in Figure 3B, it took 3000 cycles to converge (total error .001). The higher number of cycles is likely due to the greater complexity of the second network; in other words, there were more computations to perform on each cycle and thus convergence was not as quick.

Such networks, using experimental evidence to provide a training signal, offer insight into neural processing. Following the results of Strick and Preston (1982), the units in the output layer of the network in Figure 3B may be at the motor cortical level. This style of computing offers a compact representation for associating object and task characteristics to the selection of fingers in VF2. Importantly, after so many learning trials, it generalizes the problem, so that it may respond to novel situations. An example of this generalization ability is presented in the next section.

4. NEURAL NETWORKS FOR LEARNING HAND POSTURE

Having considered VF mapping onto digits, we now consider the factors influencing the selection of opposition type. The commonality between the next three models is their recognition of object properties and task parameters.

4.1 Learning To Select an Opposition

In the high-level planning of prehensile movements, we first transform object and task requirements into a selection of the appropriate set of oppositions, which are further elaborated by computing the VF parameters. Iberall (1988) used a simulated neural network to choose an opposition for a given set of task requirements. As seen in Figure 4A, an adaptive multilayered network of simulated neurons was constructed. The network consisted of four input units (bottom row), four hidden units (middle row) and one output unit (top row). Supervised learning, the generalized delta rule, was used to train the network. A given task (surface length, object width, amount of force, and task precision) was presented to the input layer. The training set was drawn from data points compiled from experimental and observational data. These data were coded relative to the hand's size and force capabilities, and grasp postures were characterized by the chosen opposition. An opposition was chosen by summing up weighted activation values of the hidden units, each of which depend on a weighted sum of activation from the input units. This computed mapping was then compared to the desired mapping in the training set. If there was a difference, the weights were adjusted between the input units, hidden layer, and output units in order to reduce this difference.

An error cutoff of .05 was used to indicate that the network learned the training set. It took 833 repetitions of the training data to converge on a solution. An important tool for understanding the behavior of a network is to

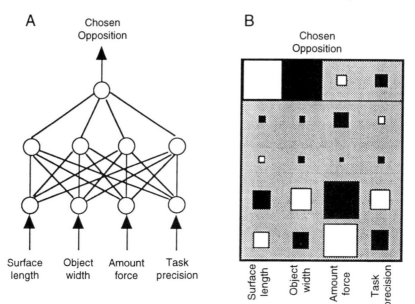

FIGURE 4 Choosing an opposition space from task and object properties using neural networks. (A) Network architecture showing four input units, four hidden units, and one output unit. (B) Weights between network elements. Black squares are negative weights, white squares are positive weights. The size of the square is proportional to the magnitude of the weight. Grey is threshold. The columns show the weights from the inputs to the hidden layer. The topmost row represents the weights from the hidden layer to the output unit. (From MacKenzie & Iberall, 1994, © 1994 with kind permission from Elsevier Science—NL, Sara Burgerstraat 25. 1055 KV Amsterdam, The Netherlands.)

examine the values stored in the weights. A matrix of these weights can be constructed, as seen in Figure 4B. The bottom row represents the weights connecting the input units to the leftmost hidden unit, the next row represents the weights to the second hidden unit, and so on. The top row represents the weights connecting the hidden layer to the output unit. An analysis of the weight matrix indicated that the first two hidden units had a large influence, whereas the other two hidden units had a moderate influence.

One of the significant advantages of neural network models is their ability to generalize. In analyzing how the network generalized the input/output space, Iberall noted that the network learned to use palm opposition when the forces were large. With higher precision requirements in the task, the network chose pad opposition. Also, there was a tendency toward using palm opposition when the length of the object increased, particularly when the forces were increasing as well. These results mirror behavior that has been observed in human prehension.

4.2 Combining Human Examples and Optimality Criterion

Uno, Fukumura, Suzuki, and Kawato (1993) developed a five-layer neural network for mapping object and task properties into an appropriate hand shape (Figure 5). Inputs are presented to this network on the left and outputs are seen on the right. Two hidden layers are present. The center third layer in this five-layer network is a storage layer for storing an internal representation (an encoding) of the inputs. Human performance data is used to initially train the network (learning phase) so that it stores representations of hand shapes used for given object shapes. This training is then combined with an optimality criterion to select the hand shape given a novel condition (optimization phase), in other words, reading out the optimal hand shape from its storage.

The inputs to the network are a two-dimensional visual image of the object and a corresponding hand configuration executed by the human, as sensed by a VPL DataGlove (VPL, Inc., California). The DataGlove had 16 sensors recording 13 flexor/extensor joint angles and 3 abduction/adduction angles. Two types of hand postures are used: palm opposition and pad opposition. During the learning phase, the network is trained using the generalized delta

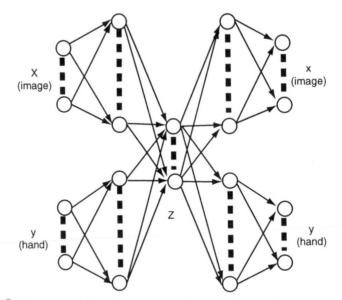

FIGURE 5 Neural network for objects and hand postures. During the learning phase, two-dimensional visual images of objects and DataGlove sensory data representing hand postures are presented to the network on the left (input layer). During the optimization phase, an optimal posture is chosen based on a criterion function. (From Uno et al., 1993.)

rule in supervised learning to autoassociate the combination of visual input and observed human behavior. In other words, given this pair of inputs as the teacher, the network learns to generate as output the same information as seen at its inputs. Because the third layer is small relative to the size of the input vector, the representation at this level must be compact (i.e., the network is forced to use only the essential qualities to represent each different situation). Such a representation will allow the network to generalize when confronted with a novel situation.

During the recall (or optimization) phase, the network inputs are initialized with the image of the current object and a canonical hand configuration. The output of the network is connected back into the input layer (hand configuration subvector only), and the network is allowed to perform several cycles of input-to-output computations. Because the network has been trained to autoassociate certain visual/hand configuration pairs, when it reaches one of these states, it is guaranteed to stay there. It is at this point that we say that the network has converged on a solution, and halt the search process.

However, choosing the correct hand posture based solely on the visual input is an ill-posed problem, since there are many possible solutions. Therefore, during the optimization phase, Uno et al. introduce a criterion function that further biases the direction of search. For palm opposition, the criterion function is defined as

$$C_1(y) = \frac{1}{2}\sum_i y_i^2$$

where y_i is the ith joint angle of the simulated hand. $C_1(y)$ is therefore minimized when the hand is flexed as much as possible. For pad opposition, the criterion function is defined as

$$C_2(y) = \sum_{i \in MP,CM} y_i^2 + \sum_{j \in IP} (1.0 - y_j)^2$$

where the metacarpophalangeal joints (MP) of the fingers and the carpometacarpal joint (CM) of the thumb are flexed as much as possible, and the interphalangeal joints (IP) of all five digits are stretched as much as possible.

The third layer of neurons was examined in order to compare their response properties to those observed in area F5 of the monkey (see Figure 6). Uno et al. observed that the level of neuronal activity increases with object size. This can be seen in the figure for both cylinders and spheres. Activation patterns for the same object class were similar, indicating an encoding for objects. In the figure, the activation pattern for cylinders is different than that for spheres. In terms of oppositions, as seen in Figure 6, the neuronal activa-

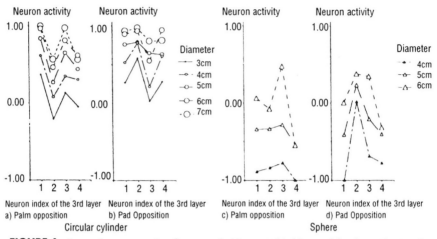

FIGURE 6 Internal representation for grasped objects, at third layer of five-layered network. (A) Grasping different size cylinders in palm opposition. (B) Grasping different size cylinders in pad opposition. (C) Grasping different size spheres in palm opposition. (D) Grasping different size spheres in pad opposition. (From Uno et al., 1993.)

tion patterns are different, depending on the opposition used, again indicating an encoding for opposition.

4.3 Reinforcement Learning for Grasp Planning

Another approach can be used to acquire the mapping from object and task parameters to hand configuration in robotics research. Rather than learning to exactly mimic human grasp plans, the planner actually learns by observing the results of executing its own plans. Note that there is still a teacher involved in the process—instead of telling the robot exactly what to do, the teacher tells the robot only how well it did in performing its task. In this way, it is possible to construct plans that are best oriented toward the actuation and sensing capabilities of the robot. This is a property that is not necessarily achievable when only mimicking human performance, since underlying the human behavior may be a program that relies on sensory feedback that is not available to the robot. When this happens, the robot is unable to distinguish situations in which different motor decisions must be made.

The high-level performance measure of how well the robot did, referred to as the reinforcement feedback signal, is typically given in the form of a scalar score. In the case of the grasping task, this score measures two elements: the success and the efficiency of the executed grasp (described below in more detail). Based on this feedback information, the reinforcement learning algorithm (Barto, Sutton, & Anderson, 1983; Sutton, 1988) adjusts the connection strengths of the artificial neural network so as to maximize the success and the efficiency of the grasps.

The neural architecture (as shown in Figure 7) has been adapted from the work on primate visual-motor conditional learning (Fagg & Arbib, 1992) and the work on reinforcement learning for reactive control of a mobile vehicle (Fagg, Lotspeich, Hoff, & Bekey, 1994). The visual and task information that is input into the model is represented as an activity pattern across a set of neurons (V). For the example described below, a total of 11 neurons are used: 3 represent object type (cylinder, cube, and plate), 3 represent length (short, medium, long; note that this is a discrete representation), 3 for diameter (narrow, medium, wide), and 2 for task requirements (manipulability and stability). In the monkey, this visual information is provided by subregions of the posterior parietal cortex (PPcx); task information can be derived from a number of different regions including prefrontal cortex (PFcx), and pre-supplementary motor area (preSMA).

This information is projected through a set of synapses (W) to a feature

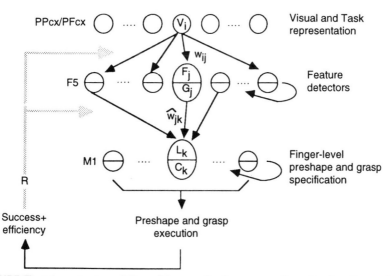

FIGURE 7 Schematic view of the architecture for the grasp configuration learning model. Visual parameters (hypothesized to be provided by posterior parietal cortex, PPcx) and task requirements (from prefrontal cortex, PFcx) are combined at the feature detector layer (inferior premotor subarea F5). The activated feature detectors in turn select a hand configuration by specifying how individual fingers will behave during the preshape and grasp (primary motor cortex, M1). This program is executed and then evaluated by a teacher. The evaluation (R) is used to update the interlayer connection strengths.

detector layer (F/G), in which each neuron represents some higher order feature of the original description (e.g., a feature detector representing cylinder and manipulability would receive connections from the corresponding input neurons). The activity level of the feature detector unit (F) is computed according to the following equation:

$$F_j = \sum_i (V_i \star w_{ij}) + \text{Noise}_j$$

where

F_j is the activity level of feature detector unit j
V_i is the activity level of input unit i
w_{ij} is the strength of connection from input unit i to feature detector j
$Noise_j$ is a random signal that is injected into feature detector j

These feature detector units then interact through a local competition mechanism to contrast-enhance the incoming activity pattern. For this version of the model, the implementation is a one-pass local-maximum operation: a neuron produces a nonzero output if and only if it is the most active neuron within a small neighborhood. The output of the feature detector units (G) is computed as follows:

$$G_j = \begin{cases} F_j & \text{if } F_j = \max_{j-N \leq l \leq j+N} \{F_l\} \\ 0 & \text{otherwise} \end{cases}$$

where

- G_j is the output of unit j
- N defines the size of the region of competition. Note that we have implicitly assumed that the neurons are arranged in a linear array.

The active feature detectors then vote for the configuration to be imposed upon the hand by passing activation to the output units (L):

$$L_k = \sum_j (G_j \star \hat{w}_{jk}) + \text{Noise}_k$$

where:

L_k is the activity level of output unit k
$\hat{w}_{jk}$ is the strength of connection from feature detector unit j to output unit k
$Noise_k$ is a random signal that is injected into output unit k

The configuration specifies which fingers will be actively participating in the grasp and how the fingers should be positioned during the actual execution of the preshape and grasp. As this model is designed to drive the Belgrade/USC Hand (Bekey, Tomovic, & Zeljkovic, 1990), the index–middle and the ring–little finger pairs are considered single entities to be controlled. The output (C) consists of seven separate subvectors, each specifying a different detail of the grasp configuration. Three of the subvectors (each consisting of two units) specify the participation of the thumb, I–M fingers, and R–L fingers in the grasp, respectively. One subvector (also consisting of two units) determines whether the thumb will be abducted or not. The three remaining subvectors (each consisting of three units) determine the degree of flexion (small, medium, and large) during preshape of the thumb and of the I–M finger and R–L finger pairs, respectively.

For each subvector, a winner-take-all circuit computes the single most active unit of the set:

$$C_k \begin{cases} 1 & \text{if } L_k = \underset{m \in S(k)}{\text{Max}} \{L_m\} \\ 0 & \text{otherwise} \end{cases}$$

where

$S(k)$ is the set of units that are in the same subvector as unit k
C_k indicates whether configuration bit k is a winner

It is this resulting pattern of activity (C) that is used by the execution system. The execution of the preshape and grasp is handled by a hardwired (nonneural) program. After execution of the specified grasp, a teacher evaluates the performance of the system. There are two elements to this evaluation: success and efficiency. Success tells us whether or not the grasping movement was able to pick up the object. If the robot is unable to accomplish this, then a reinforcement signal of $R = -0.1$ is given by the teacher. If the grasp is successful, then a positive reinforcement signal ($R = 1.0$) is given, but discounted if the grasp is inefficient. A grasp is considered inefficient if the fingers preshape to a larger extension than is necessary for the presented object. The discount factor is set such that if the system produces a preshape of maximum possible aperture for a narrow cylinder, a reinforcement of 0.4 is given (assuming success).

This type of feedback scheme differs in one important way from the models already presented. In each of those models, error is defined by the network's performance relative to the human behavior. However, in this reinforcement learning algorithm, the error is defined more abstractly—relative to the success of the behavior in accomplishing the defined task. Thus, this latter scheme will favor motor programs that tend to be more successful (which we implicitly assume are those programs that are better oriented toward the robot's sensing and actuation abilities). One should also note that the use of the efficiency term in this model is similar to Uno's technique of minimizing joint angles during his optimization phase.

The reinforcement signal is used by the learning algorithm to update the connection strengths in the projections from the visual/task representation to the feature detectors (w), and from the feature detectors to the action units ($\hat{w}$), with the goal of ultimately maximizing the level of reward that is received. The adjustments to the connection strengths are done using a Hebbian/Anti-Hebbian learning algorithm, as follows.

The system is presented with a certain input, for which a grasp plan is computed by the network and then executed. Suppose, on one hand, that the teacher gives a positive reinforcement signal for the system's performance on the trial. In this case, we would like to ensure that the next time the system is presented with the same input, the same plan is output. This is accomplished by updating the connection strengths as follows. First, to ensure that the same set of feature detectors is activated, the connection strengths from active input units (V) to active feature detectors (G) are increased (thereby increasing their response level the next time). Second, in order to increase the active feature detectors' support of the selected grasp plan, the connection strengths from the active feature detectors (G) to the active output units (C) are increased.

On the other hand, suppose that negative reinforcement is given. This could be due to the fact that either the wrong set of feature detectors was selected or the specified grasp plan was incorrect. Since we do not know which is the case, both are assumed. Thus, the connection strengths from the input units (V) to the feature detectors (G) are reduced, thereby giving other feature detectors an opportunity to become active next time. In addition, the support of the active feature detectors for the specified configuration is reduced, which allows other configurations to be tried.

These rules are captured in the following connection strength update equation:

$$\Delta w_{ij} = \alpha R V_i G_j w_{ij}$$
$$\Delta \hat{w}_{jk} = \alpha R G_j C_k \hat{w}_{jk}$$

where

Δw_{ij} and $\Delta \hat{w}_{jk}$ are the changes to the connection strengths
α is a learning rate parameter
R is the teacher's reinforcement signal

During the training process, the system was presented with a sequence of situations selected from six possibilities. The presented object was a cylinder of one of three widths. In addition, the task requirement could be either manipulability or stability. The experiments were performed in simulation. Evaluation of the grasps was accomplished by checking that the fingers were opened wide enough to clear the object and that the task requirements were suitably satisfied. If manipulability was a requirement, the system was expected to generate a pad opposition grasp configuration (with the thumb opposing the fingertips). If stability was required, then the system had to have produced a palm opposition in order to be considered successful. The protocol randomly presented the system with one of the six possible situations. However, if the system failed to grasp the object, then the same situation was presented until a successful grasp was obtained.

For the results presented below, the system required 2500 trials before its performance peaked. After training, all grasps were successful but not all were completely efficient. Of the 80 feature detector units, only 18 achieved significant response levels. Figure 8 shows the postlearning response curves of five of these as a function of the situation that is presented. Units A–D are all selective for a pad opposition, although C and D are also selective to some degree for the width of the object. Unit E is selective for palm opposition. These grasp-specific neurons, similar to those reported by Rizzolatti et al. (1988) in area F5, resulted from the learning process and the system's interac-

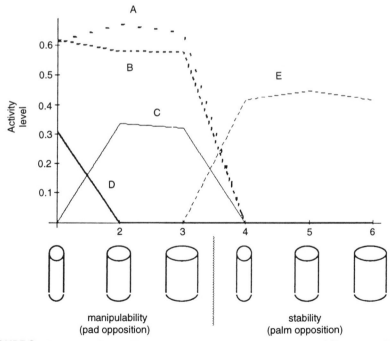

FIGURE 8 Responses of several feature detector units (A–E) given the six different situations. All units are selective for either pad or palm opposition.

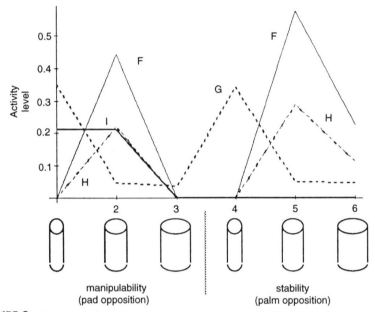

FIGURE 9 Responses of four additional feature detector units (F–I) from the same experiment. Units F, G, and H are selective for the width of the cylinder. Unit I is selective for small and medium cylinders for pad opposition.

tion with its environment, even though the architecture did not inherently contain these concepts.

In addition to grasp-selective cells, other types of units were also seen in this experiment. Figure 9 demonstrates several such cells. Cells F and H are selective for objects of medium width regardless of the grasp type that is made. Cell G is selective for small objects, but does show some activity for the other situations. In all, nine units demonstrated purely opposition-related activity, where only four showed object size selectivity. The remaining five showed selectivity either to exactly one situation or to an arbitrary combination of multiple situations. To date, only opposition-specific activity has been observed in F5 (due to experimental design); the other responses seen in the model stand as predictions to be examined in future experiments. However, within an anatomically related area (the posterior bank of the anterior interparietal sulcus or AIP), Sakata has seen activity that may be loosely interpreted as grasp specific (Taira et al., 1990), as well as activity that is specific to the size of objects (H. Sakata, personal communication, 1994).

Finally, it is important to note that the firing pattern of some cells did not follow a simple symbolic rule such as fire during all oppositions. Rather, these cells responded to a combination of several different input dimensions. Despite this apparent difficulty of placing symbolic labels on these cells, their interaction with other cells in the feature detector layer was able to yield a correct and consistent grasp plan.

5. CONCLUSIONS

In this chapter, we have been interested in understanding how humans and monkeys construct grasp plans in the face of both functional and object-specific constraints. The language of opposition space and virtual fingers provides a high-level language for describing such plans. Different hand postures offer different capabilities, and the selection of a posture is an important computation performed by the central nervous system. In order to model this selection, the five networks presented in this chapter offer examples of a neural style of processing. All involve computations performed through the interactions of a large number of simple processing elements, or units, that had an activation state and were connected together through synapses in some pattern of connectivity. Units either excited or inhibited each other, and synaptic connections were represented by weight matrices. While honoring general neurobiological constraints, they all used simplifying assumptions.

The use of neural models allows us to explore the implementation of planning processes, while incorporating experimental results from behavioral, anatomical, and neurophysiological studies. A modeler incorporates these results into artificial neural networks, making design decisions about the network topology, connectivity, the coded representation, and the learning algorithms. Two networks were presented to demonstrate the selection of fingers in VF2. They both were three-layered networks that learned to associate object and task characteristics to VF2 size using a supervised learning algorithm called the generalized delta rule. In the first case, an output represented the width of the VF, while in the second case, the output represented specific finger combinations. The output of either of these networks could possibly be at the motor cortical level, where evidence of multiple representations of the hand has been identified. In terms of the selection of an opposition for the posture, three approaches were demonstrated. The first one, a three-layered network, learned to associate object and task characteristics to oppositions using the generalized delta rule. The second one used the generalized delta rule in a five-layered network that learned to associate object and hand shapes, developing an internal representation for this association on its middle layer. The third model used reinforcement learning in a three-layer network to associate object and task characteristics to hand configuration, also using a middle layer to store the association. In both of these latter networks, it was shown that the activation of the units in the middle layer demonstrates an internal representation for an opposition. Such an internal representation has been observed in a premotor cortical area.

Neural learning algorithms provide us with a mechanism for taking high-level behavioral constraints and deriving a low-level neural structure, which we believe can be used in understanding the biological implementation of these programs. Furthermore, learning techniques can begin to tell us something about the development of the programs in the biology as the systems mature. In addition, these techniques can be applied to building flexible and robust control systems for robots, a process that has the potential for shedding even more light on our understanding of biological systems.

ACKNOWLEDGMENTS

The reinforcement learning model has been implemented in NSL (Neural Simulation Language; Weitzenfeld, 1991), which is available via anonymous ftp from yorick.usc.edu. More information may be obtained by contacting Alfredo Weitzenfeld (alfredo@rana.usc.edu). The finger selection model and the opposition selection model were implemented using Michael Jordan's network simulation system. This work has been supported in part by grants from the University of Southern California Graduate School, School of Engineering, and Computer Science Department, the National Science Foundation (IRI-9221582), and by the Human Frontiers Science Program.

13

Prehension Movements

The Visuomotor Channels Hypothesis Revisited

YVES PAULIGNAN AND MARC JEANNEROD

1. INTRODUCTION

Due to its high number of degrees of freedom, the primate hand can perform highly complex movements. However, although in our everyday life we are able to grasp a broad variety of objects with different shapes and sizes, a basic description of prehensile activities of the hand can be made in such a way as to reduce this apparent complexity. By looking at the function of the hand as a whole, Napier (1956) concluded there exist only two types of prehension movements. "The object may be held in a clamp formed by the partly flexed fingers and the palm, counter pressure being applied by the thumb lying more or less in the plane of the palm. This is referred to as the power grip. The object may be pinched between the flexor aspects of the fingers and the opposing thumb. This is called the precision grip." Although two types of grip is probably too limited a number, it stresses the general idea of a reduction of degrees of freedom, among the many possible ones.

The history of experiments made on grasping movements is tightly linked with that of motion analysis technology. Napier was able to make qualitative descriptions of object grasping using photographs of the hand. But such a technique gives information about only the static, and not the dynamic, aspect of the movement. Using high-speed cinematographic film, Jeannerod (1981) was able to describe two major components for grasping movement; the transportation of the hand to the vicinity of the object to be grasped and the formation of a particular posture for the fingers. One of the most important observations was that adopting the finger posture anticipates the real grasp and occurs during the hand transport before tactile information from the target is available.

More recently, the advent of computerized motion analysis in normal and brain-lesioned human subjects, together with the use of neurophysiological techniques in behaving monkeys, have made it possible to describe the pattern of hand movement during object-oriented actions, and to identify some of the brain mechanisms involved in their control. Trajectory, final precision of the movements, coordination of digit movements, reaction and movement time and also variability are the parameters currently in use to gain insight into the organization of prehension movements control.

Given the large body of new data generated by these techniques, it appeared useful to reappraise Jeannerod's (1981) original hypothesis (see also Jeannerod & Biguer, 1982). Do current data support the existence of "visuomotor channels activated in parallel by a specific visual input and controlling a specific part of the arm musculature" (Jeannerod, 1981, p. 155)? More specifically, does "processing of the spatial properties of [an] object result in activation of proximal muscles [e.g., at the shoulder joint]" while "processing of its intrinsic properties feeds into muscles of more distal segments [e.g., fingers]"?

2. BACK TO THE VISUOMOTOR CHANNELS

Plurality of visuomotor mechanisms in prehension reflects in part the organization of sensory systems. Although objects are perceived as phenomenal entities, sensory systems are known to detect features, not objects (Jeannerod et al., 1995). Objects have to be split into basic visual features, or properties, like size, shape, or texture, each of which is assumed to activate a specific visual mechanism. Such intrinsic properties constitute the identity of an object. In addition, when object perception is considered in the behavioral context, another set of properties emerges. Objects have a specific orientation, distance from the body, and location in the frontal plane : these are extrinsic properties.

Both intrinsic and extrinsic properties of objects are essential attributes for governing actions directed toward them, especially if one assumes that the different properties of an object are matched by specific mechanisms that generate motor commands appropriate to each property. These mechanisms can be conceived as specialized input–output structures that simultaneously operate for extracting a limited number of parameters from the visual world and for producing corresponding responses. The visuomotor channel hypothesis further specifies that the movement as a whole is represented by a single program governing the integrated aspect of the action, or in other words the activation and coordination of the components. Accordingly, the combined action of the musculoskeletal segments related to the act of prehension, in addition to their differential involvement in independent channels, would be governed by a specific set of rules, hierarchically higher than those of the channels, and coordinating the activity of the channels in the time domain. Interactions between the two components of prehension have been conceptualized by Arbib (1981) in a model that stresses both separate activation of each component by specific visual pathways and coordinated output. The notion of uniqueness of the program is thus in theory not incompatible with that of parallel visuomotor channels. Finally, the hypothesis predicts that error-correcting mechanisms (using visual feedback, or other reafferent sources) should also be channel specific. Error signals issuing from a given aspect of the movement (e.g., inadequate finger preshaping relative to object size) would be detected only by the channel specialized for the processing of the relevant visual cue and for generating the proper correction.

3. KINEMATIC DESCRIPTION OF NORMAL PREHENSION MOVEMENTS

Testing the degree of independence of each component with respect to the other is critical for evaluating the validity of the hypothesis. For example, the proposed model implies that changing the object location should not affect grip formation, and modifying the object size should not perturb transport of the hand. Such experiments require a careful description of the two components. The kinematics of the transport component can be described by recording arm movements. The measures should not be contaminated by finger movements, which pertain to the grip component. For movements of constant amplitude and directed to targets at different directions in space, Morasso (1981) found invariant velocity profiles only for the hand displacement. The shoulder and the elbow have angular motions markedly different depending on the movement goal. Thus, in order to describe the arm movement, the point chosen must be as distal as possible. This argument justifies the use of the wrist to characterize the transport component.

   The channel encoding object properties is responsible for the formation of a grip, which involves opening the fingers large enough to match the object size. This component may be characterized by the size of the grip. If the subjects are instructed to use precision grip, the manipulation component can be characterized by the distance between the thumb and fingertips or the angle made by the digits at the carpometacarpal joint.

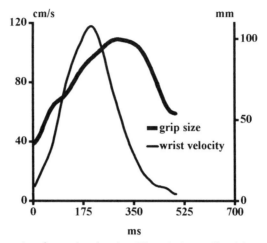

FIGURE 1 Kinematics of normal prehension. The velocity profile of the wrist and the amplitude of the grip are shown as a function of time in a normal prehension movement. The object is
a dowel (1.5 cm in diameter), located 30 cm from the subject and 20° to the right of its body
midline.

The kinematics of normal grasping (Figure 1) are described in the basic
observations of Jeannerod (1981, 1984, 1986). The transport component is
characterized by an asymetrical velocity profile with a single peak. When the
target distance increases, the maximum velocity is higher. This result was
confirmed in other studies (Chieffi, Fogassi, Gallese, & Gentilucci, 1992;
Gentilucci et al., 1991; Gentilucci, Chieffi, Scarpa, & Castiello, 1992). During the deceleration phase the velocity decreases rapidly up to a point (peak
deceleration) and then decreases less rapidly or even increases once again.
Peak deceleration occurs at around 70–80% of movement time (Jeannerod,
1981, 1984, 1986). The grip size pattern described by Jeannerod was also
confirmed. The fingers open to a maximum grip size and then close around
the object. The maximum grip size is larger than the real size of the object.
The peak aperture of the grip occurs consistently after the velocity peak of
the wirst with a delay of 100–120 ms, that is, around the time of peak
deceleration.

4. THE EFFECTS OF VARYING OBJECT LOCATION
ON PREHENSION MOVEMENTS

There are two ways to study the effects of changes in object location on
prehension movements. In one the target object is maintained stationary at

different spatial locations; in the other it is displaced in a stepwise fashion during the movement.

4.1 Systematic Changes in Object Location

Several experiments have been made on grasping stationary objects located at different distances or directions from the subjects. (Chieffi et al., 1992; Gentilucci et al., 1991, 1992; Paulignan, MacKenzie et al., 1991). In these studies no effect of distance was found on grip size. These results are thus in favor of an independence of the respective components. However, by using the simultaneous presentation of objects having different locations and sizes, Jakobson and Goodale (1991) showed that when the distance to be covered by the hand was longer, the fingers opened wider (see below). These authors concluded that there exists a single program governing the two components. This contention is not fully supported by their data, due to the small amplitude of the effects. The difference in maximum grip size for the same object at different distances was very small (104 mm vs. 99 mm), in fact close to the limits of precision of the Watsmart system used to analyze the movements (about 1 mm; Marteniuk, Leavitt, MacKenzie, & Athenes, 1990).

Another explanation of Jakobson and Goodale's results was that the larger finger opening resulted from a compensatory mechanism aimed at correcting errors of the grasp or transport. As stated by Chieffi and Gentilucci (1993, p. 471) "Only if the grasp were shown to vary as a function of possible transport errors would it be possible to maintain that finger opening planning depends on transport planning." Chieffi and Gentilucci presented to the subjects objects of three different sizes (from 1 to 6 cm) located at two distances (7 and 17.5 cm) from the starting position of the fingers. They observed, as did Jakobson and Goodale (1991), a small increase in maximum grip size in relation to augmentation of movement amplitude. If the two components were the expression of the same program, the transport errors, due to variability of wrist trajectory, should be corrected by adjusting the grip size. Chieffi and Gentilucci compared the rate of increase in grip size and the increase in wrist variability. When distance was the tested factor, a significant correlation was found only for the smaller object. They concluded that "this result cannot be interpreted in favour of the dependence of the grasp on extrinsic properties. If extrinsic object properties played a role, the effect of distance should have been present for all objects . . . " (Chieffi & Gentilucci, 1993, p. 476).

Instead of presenting static objects, it is also possible to analyze prehension movements in a situation where the object position changes continuously during the subject's movement. Chieffi et al. (1992) presented objects moving in the sagittal plane toward the subject. The objects were randomly presented at four velocities. When the velocity increased the subject grasped the object nearer the starting position. The amplitude and the time to the velocity peak of the wrist were lower when the object was faster. No effect of object speed was found on the grip size. In a second experiment objects of different sizes and velocities were used. Again the grip size was not influenced by object velocity. Finally, no difference was observed in grip size between grasping stationary and moving objects. Thus, continuously changing the object position at different speeds does not affect the component concerned by the size of objects.

Most data obtained in studying the effects of systematic changes in object location are thus in favor of the independence of the components of prehension movements. When the data seem to show apparent coupling between components, a more detailed analysis shows that transport and grasp are not dependent on each other.

4.2 Step Changes in Object Position

According to the visuomotor channels hypothesis, the error correcting mechanisms should also be channel specific. In other words, modifying the spatial location of the object during the movement should not affect the grip formation.

In order to perturb object position, Paulignan et al. (1990) presented subjects with three identical objects (10 cm high, 1.5 cm in diameter) placed at 10°, 20°, and 30° from the body midline. It was possible to illuminate one object at a time. Changing instantaneously the illumination from one object to another was perceived as a displacement of the object. Subjects were instructed to reach and grasp the illuminated dowel. Two conditions were used: one in which an object was illuminated until the subject grasped it, and a second one in which, in 20 of the 100 trials, the light was unexpectedly shifted from the central dowel to one placed to the right (30°) or to the left (10°). The perturbation occurred at the onset of the movement, due to the release of a start switch. The remaining 80 trials, in which no perturbation occurred, served as control trials.

Analysis of the wrist kinematics showed that the motor system reacted to the perturbation as soon as 100 ms after the object location had changed (Paulignan et al., 1990; Paulignan, MacKenzie et al., 1991). This time lag was measured on the acceleration profile. The velocity profile of the wrist showed a double peak pattern. The second velocity peak, of a lower amplitude than the first, corresponded to the observed reorientation of the hand to the new target location. This result shows that the mechanism responsible for hand transport reacts within a short time when confronted with an unexpected error message.

Contrary to the prediction, however, the other component was also affected by the perturbation (Figure 2). The change in grip size showed a double peak pattern in 80% of the perturbed movements. In the trials where a double peak was present on the grip size curve, these peaks consistently lagged the velocity peaks of the transport. This led the authors to compute the correlation between these associated peaks. If the prehension movement is governed by a unique program, a high correlation should be observed. When a perturbation occurs the new velocity peak produced must have the same relation with the second peak of grip aperture as for a normal movement. In fact, no significant correlation between the different peaks could be found. In addition, the percentage of movements with a double peak was only 80%. In the remaining 20% there was only an inflexion point, which implies that the fingers did not close but only stopped opening. Thus the grip response was variable: in some trials an active closure process took place and in others only a pause in the actual program occurred. If the two components had been the expression of a simple program such variability would not have been expected. A better explanation is that when a perturbation occurs the double peak pattern reflects coordination between two separate channels. Considering that the response of the size channel consists in producing a grip depending on object size, the perturbation has no effect because its maximal size is of the same amplitude as in control trials, although the amplitude of velocity peak is affected.

In an earlier experiment Gentilucci et al. (1992) had used the perturbation paradigm with three identical spheres of 4 cm in diameter. The perturbation of object location was made along the subjects' sagittal axis, from the nearest position (15 cm from the subject) to the other two (27.5 or 40 cm). Perturbation of object position produced two submovements on the transport component. The time to peak acceleration occurred earlier on the perturbed trials than on control trials. Neither the time to peak nor the amplitude of the acceleration peak was influenced by the amplitude of the perturbation. Thus, the first part of the transport component was not dependent on movement amplitude. Because the time and the amplitude of acceleration peaks in control trials were affected by the movement amplitude, the authors concluded that the perturbation produced an interruption of the initial movement. They also observed a double peak in the grip curve versus time. However, the maximal amplitude of the grip was not affected by the perturbation. Again, if one considers that the role of the manipulation channel is to produce a posture adapted to the object, there is no effect of the perturbation on this component. Concerning the presence of two peaks on the grip curves in perturbed trials, the authors postulated that the presentation of two objects in the perturbed trials might require two motor plans. "Since the two plans were in succession it is not surprising that the first grip

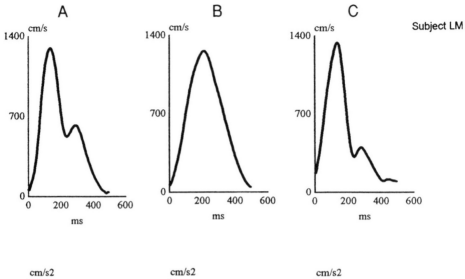

A   B   C   Subject LM

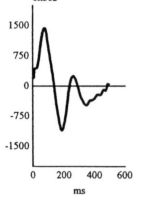
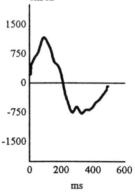
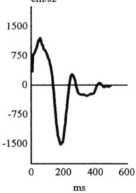

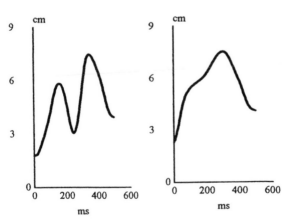
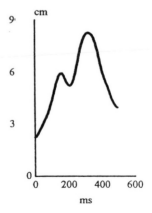

was interrupted and a second grip was reprogrammed. Therefore the observation of a double pattern of finger aperture/closure is not sufficient to demonstrate the hypothesis of a temporal coupling between the beginning of the two components" (Gentilucci et al., 1992, p. 80).

By analyzing the blocked trials, the same authors found a coupling between the two components. The onset time and the duration were the same for the two components. Moreover, the beginning of finger closure corresponded to a fixed threshold of wrist velocity. If this coupling corresponds to a genuine property of the system, it should persist in the perturbed condition, that is, the reorganization should begin at the same time for the transport and the grasp. The second submovement occurred much later in the grasp than in the transport component, the time lag between the two being 240 ms. A time lag was also observed by others. Paulignan, MacKenzie et al. (1991) observed a 100-ms time lag between the transport and the grasp responses to the perturbation. The differences between delays observed in different experiments are not in favor of a rigid temporal coupling between the two components.

The experiments on step changes in object location do not provide enough arguments to invalidate the visuomotor channel theory. In addition, the observed double peak in grip size could be due to the presentation of two objects. Indeed, when only one is presented (Chieffi et al., 1992; Haggard, 1994), this pattern is not present. The double peak could reflect a simple disruption of the necessary coordination between the components if, as Gentilucci et al. (1992) have suggested, the grip closure is triggered by a certain threshold of wrist velocity. Further experiments are needed to test these two explanations. The delay for the transport component response to visual perturbation is short: 100 ms (Paulignan, MacKenzie et al., 1991); 150 ms (Gentilucci et al., 1992). The existence of different response times for the two components in response to perturbation of object location does not fulfill the criterion for a unique program governing the two components.

5. THE EFFECTS OF VARYING OBJECT SIZE ON PREHENSION MOVEMENTS

When the size of the object changes, the hand configuration for placing the fingers on the object can be very different, corresponding to different preci-

FIGURE 2   Effect of step changes in object position on prehension movements. Two perturbed trials in which the target shifted from 20° to 10° and from 20° to 30° are shown, respectively, in (A) and (C); (B) is a control trial. The upper and middle rows give the velocity and acceleration profiles of the transport component; the lower row shows the time course of the distance between the thumb and index finger. (Redrawn from Paulignan, Mackenzie et al., 1991.)

sion requirements. When, for example, a subject grasps a small cup or a large mug the number of fingers involved changes. Depending on the size of the handle and the estimated weight, one, two, or three fingers will participate in the grasp. But these fingers have the same functional role and behave as a single finger, hence the concept of a virtual finger (Arbib et al., 1985; see Iberall and Fagg, Chapter 12). When more fingers are used, the size of the corresponding virtual finger changes but the functional type of grip remains the same.

The first systematic study of object size on grip formation was made by Jeannerod (1981) showing that the maximum grip amplitude is proportional to the object size. This result was confirmed by numerous studies (Bootsma, Marteniuk, MacKenzie, & Zaal, 1994; Castiello, Bennett, & Stelmach, 1993; Gentilucci et al., 1991; Jakobson & Goodale, 1991; Marteniuk et al., 1990; Marteniuk, MacKenzie, Jeannerod, Athenes, & Dugas, 1987; Paulignan, Jeannerod, MacKenzie, & Marteniuk, 1991; Servos & Goodale, 1994; Servos, Goodale, & Jakobson, 1992; Zaal & Bootsma, 1993). It was shown to appear in 13-month-old children (von Hofsten & Rönnqvist, 1988). Marteniuk et al. (1990) have shown that, for objects from 1 to 10 cm in diameter, an increase of 1 cm for the object corresponds to an increase of 0.77 cm in maximum grip size. A similar value was found by others (Bootsma et al., 1994; Paulignan, Jeannerod et al., 1991).

Experiments in which object size is changed from trial to trial or during the movement can answer the question of whether grasping objects of different sizes has an effect on the other component, that is, the transport of the hand.

5.1 Systematic Changes in Object Size

Marteniuk et al. (1990) have demonstrated an effect of object size on the transport component. Movement time was longer for small objects. This lengthening corresponded to an increase in duration of the deceleration phase. Thus, the final positioning of the hand took longer when the object was smaller.

Jakobson and Goodale (1991) have also presented stationary objects of different sizes and placed at different distances. They found that when the object size increased, the duration of the movement was longer in contrast to the result of Marteniuk et al. (1990). There was also an effect on the spatial path; the hand went higher for a larger object. They concluded that a higher order system is responsible for the integration of the components of a prehension movement. Although significant, the observed differences were small. For example, considering the hand elevation, the values were 56 mm (small object), 57 mm (middle object), and 60 mm (large object).

Gentilucci et al. (1991) have studied the prehension of objects of different size (a cylinder 6 cm in diameter and 5.5-cm height, and a sphere of 0.5 cm in diameter). The two objects were grasped differently; a precision grip for the smaller one, and a whole-hand prehension for the larger one. The latter was defined as "a flexion of all fingers around an object in such a way as to form a ring around it" (Gentilucci et al., 1991; Rizzolatti et al., 1988). The authors observed an effect of the object size on the transport component. When the size increased, the movement time shortened, and the peak velocity increased. The effect on movement time mainly comprised a decrease of the time spent after the deceleration peak.

In the above three experiments the tested objects differed in terms of the difficulty of the task, which is proportional to the target area: the smaller the surface of the object, the higher the precision requirements for finger positioning, in accordance with Fitts's law (Fitts, 1954). In the Marteniuk et al. (1990) experiment the surface of the object ranged between 7.98 and 79.8 cm². The difference was much larger in the case of Gentilucci et al. (1991), where the values varied from 0.79 to 94.2 cm². In the experiment of Jakobson and Goodale, the surface available to place the fingers on the object varied from 10 to 25 cm². These experiments have thus tested more than the effect of object size alone. Increasing the diameter of a cylinder not only affects the grasp, but also the transport of the hand because of the differences in precision requirements for the fingers' motions. Zaal and Bootsma (1993) conducted an experiment in which they compared movements directed at cylinders of different sizes and at oblong objects having the same surface area for positioning the fingers. Changing object size alone had no effect on the transport component. This has been confirmed recently (Bootsma et al., 1994).

5.2 Step Changes in Object Size

The visuomotor channel hypothesis predicts that if the size of the object changes during the movement, the transportation of the hand should not be affected by the perturbation. This prediction was tested in two experiments.

In order to perturb the size of the object, Paulignan, Jeannerod, et al. (1991) presented to subjects two concentric dowels. The inner dowel was 10 cm high and 1.5 cm in diameter. The outer dowel was 6 cm high and 6 cm in diameter. Due to the size and curvature of the objects, the contact surface was not the same for the two objects (18.8 cm² and 73.4 cm² for the small and the large object, respectively). Each trial began with illumination of the small or the large object (40 control trials for each one). In 20% of the trials (perturbed trials) a perturbation occurred; the light was unexpectedly shifted from the initial target to the other one. The shift was produced by the release of a start switch at the onset of the movement. Due to low level of ambient light, the appearance was that of an instantaneous change in dowel size.

In most subjects, the profile of change in grip size during the movement in perturbed trials (small to large object) was marked by a discontinuity: grip size increased up to a first peak, then stopped increasing, and finally increased again up to a second peak before decreasing until contact with the dowel. Kinematic analysis revealed that the first peak corresponded to the maximum grip aperture observed in control trials directed to the small object. The second peak in grip size occurred later in time (475 ms after movement onset), and its amplitude corresponded to the size of grip observed in control trials for the large object. In some subjects, the second peak was the only one observed. The double-peak pattern in grip size, when present, was clearly visible on the curve of grip velocity. On this curve, the time of occurrence of the first grip velocity peak had the same value as in small control trials. This first velocity peak was followed by a second one corresponding to the reopening of the grip. The time between the two peaks, where grip size velocity was the lowest, thus represented the earliest sign of corrective finger movements aimed at grasping the large dowel. This important landmark was located at a mean time of about 330 ms following movement onset. The mean movement time in perturbed trials where object size increased was lengthened by about 175 ms with respect to the small control trials.

During this experiment no significant changes were found in the time values of the wrist kinematic landmarks with respect to their control trials. Time to peak velocity and time to peak deceleration were within the same range in both cases. This shows that the wrist kinematics were not affected by the perturbation, at least during the first 300 ms following movement onset. The movement time increase in perturbed trials was therefore likely to be due to the lengthening of the low velocity phase following peak deceleration.

Another experiment concerning the perturbation of object size was made by Castiello et al. (1993). These authors were interested in the effects of changing the size of the object and the type of grasp, arguing that during natural prehension a small object will be grasped by a precision grip and a big one by a whole-hand prehension. The definition of a whole-hand prehension needs clarification. The definition given by Gentilucci et al. (1991) implies contact with the palm. The definition proposed in Castiello et al. (1993) is different. It implies "a grasp which involves the use of all the digits but without emphasis on the production of power," "all fingers opposing the thumb," that is, a precision grip implying all the fingers (see Napier's definition at the beginning of this chapter).

In Castiello et al.'s experiment, the large object was 8 cm high and 8 cm in diameter. The small one was 2 cm high and only 0.7 cm in diameter. Thus, the surface available for positioning the fingers on the object was very different for the two objects. Several conditions tested the effect of changing object size, or the type of grasp, or both. When subjects had to shift from the precision grip/small object to the whole-hand prehension/large object, the transport phase was affected, particularly the deceleration peak. The problem is to know which factor is responsible for such an effect. It can be due to object size but also to the type of grasp.

The above experiments show how difficult it is to produce a pure change in object size. When this is the case, however, the transport component is unaffected by the size of the object. A recent study (Bootsma et al., 1994) controlling precisely the object size and width confirms this result. When these two parameters were changed simultaneously, the area available for placing the fingers became a factor affecting the transportation of the hand.

6. TIME AND ACCURACY CONSTRAINTS

In this section we consider the question, What effects do accuracy constraints imposed on prehension movements have on the coordination between grasp and transport components when the temporal parameters of the movements are systematically varied?

6.1 Systematic Changes of Movement Time

Wing et al. (1986) asked subjects to grasp objects with a precision grip at two different speeds: a normal speed (chosen by the subject) and a fast speed (as fast as possible without knocking or dropping the object). The movement amplitude was 28 cm. The movement time values obtained were 376 ms for the fast and 735 ms for the normal condition. When the subject used the faster speed the fingers opened wider. These data were confirmed by S. A. Wallace and Weeks (1988) who studied two movement durations (200 ms and 400 ms) and by S. A. Wallace, Weeks, and Kelso (1990). The interpretation of Wing et al. (1986) postulates the existence of an error-correcting mechanism where the grasp component takes into account the transport errors. When movement speed increases, the variability of muscle force impulses increases (R. A. Schmidt, Zelaznik, & Frank, 1979). Thus, the movement variability is higher. The augmentation of maximum aperture could be a compensatory mechanism for the increase in transport variability. In theory, the shorter the movement time, the higher the transport variability and the larger should be the maximum aperture. But in this case, as suggested Chieffi and Gentilucci (1993), the effect on grasp aperture must be correlated to wrist variability in order to correspond to a compensatory mechanism.

6.2 Systematic Changes of Accuracy Requirements

The best way to understand how precision can be manipulated is to first define what this parameter means in prehension. Pointing movements toward a target do not require the subject to achieve the goal with a zero velocity. Consequently, the spatial accuracy requirements will be defined by the target geometric properties in a plane, namely the surface of the target.

During natural grasp the definition of precision requirements is more complex. First, many objects require an accurate grasp because they are fragile or unstable. The importance of such a parameter was underlined by Marteniuk et al. (1987) who showed a lengthening of the deceleration phase for a fragile object. These properties can be permanent for these objects or they can be context dependent (when a stable object is placed in an unstable position). Second, the area available for placing the fingers depends on object size and affects the transport component. When the area where the fingers are positioned on the object is smaller, the movement time is longer (Bootsma et al., 1994; Bootsma & Van Wieringen, 1992; Castiello et al., 1993; Jakobson & Goodale, 1991; Marteniuk et al., 1990; Zaal & Bootsma, 1993), principally due to an increase of the deceleration phase, where the finger closure occurs. Thus, in a prehension movement, the hand displacements must be controlled in a three-dimensional space rather than in a plane, as for pointing. In most cases, the hand velocity must be equal to zero at the time of contact in order to avoid object displacements.

S. A. Wallace and Weeks (1988) studied the effect of changing precision constraints on this aspect of prehension movement. They asked subjects to grasp a dowel mounted on a joystick that allowed measurement of object displacement. In a first experiment they imposed precision constraints by giving the subjects limits for object displacement. Three levels were tested, with a small, middle, and high movement tolerance, respectively. When the tolerance was small the movement time was longer and the amplitude of velocity peak lower. In a second experiment the tolerance and the objects size were varied. In this case the transport component was sensitive to the tolerance alone. Accurate grasp implies that at the time of fingers contact, the different forces applied to the object are distributed in a manner compatible with a stable grasp. These forces correspond to what Napier (1955) and then Arbib and colleagues defined as the opposition space (Iberall et al., 1986). Namely, for a precision grip, it is possible to define an opposition axis along which the forces exerted on the object by the fingers must be applied to have opposite directions in order to ensure a stable grasp.

7. THE VISUAL CONTROL OF MOVEMENT GUIDANCE

The role of vision in movement guidance was studied by Paulignan, Jeannerod, et al. (1991) and Paulignan, MacKenzie, et al. (1991) using cylinders of variable diameter as graspable objects. The positioning of the fingers around a cylinder does not represent in itself an important constraint, because there is an infinite number of possibilities for the fingers to contact the object. Yet, as Paulignan et al. observed during their experiments, the final position of the fingers on the cylinders presented very low spatial variability. A similar result was obtained by Jakobson and Goodale (1994) and Goodale et al. (1993). They showed that for an object with a complex shape, the subjects chose particular points on the surface to place the fingers. This high degree of precision in the positioning of the fingers implies a fine control of hand displacements toward its final position.

Morasso (1981) suggested that the point used to visually guide the arm should be as distal as possible. This distal point will thus be the more relevant to describe the transport component. One possible candidate could be the center of the wrist (Arbib et al., 1985), in which case the motor system has to calculate a vector between the object and the wrist. Another possibility, as proposed by Wing and his colleagues, is that the thumb is used as the distal point, instead of the wrist. They showed that during the prehension of an object, the thumb contributed little to grip formation (Fraser & Wing, 1981; Wing & Fraser, 1983; Wing et al., 1986), because the distance between the

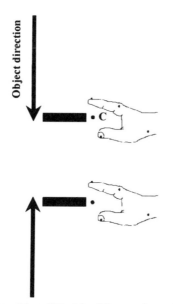

FIGURE 3   Grasping moving objects: Principle of the experiment. Transport of the hand could be controlled by guiding the displacement of the center of gravity of the grip (C) until it corresponds to the location of the center of the object. When the object motion is parallel to the finger opening–closing movement, the line of approach of C is the same, thus the pattern of finger displacement should not be affected by the object's movement direction. (*Top*) the object is moving downward (*bottom*) the object is moving upwards.

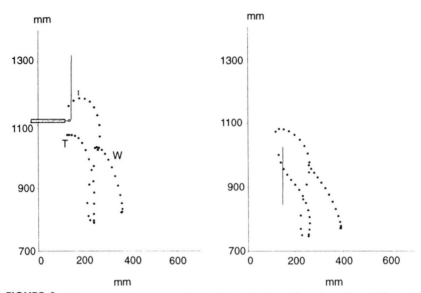

FIGURE 4   Finger movement pattern during the prehension of moving objects. The points represent the spatial path of the thumb (T), index (I), and wrist (W) in a vertical plane. The object displacement is also represented (solid line; diagram on left, downward movement; diagram on right, upward movement). The pattern of finger movements depends on object direction.

thumb and a line going through the wrist and the center of the target was constant during prehension. The tip of the thumb is indeed a distal point of the arm, and its transport will be affected by the area of contact available on the object. However, Paulignan et al. showed that, during the experiments in which the size or the location of the object was perturbed, the thumb played an active role in the grip formation. As the rate of these perturbations was low (10% for each condition), this effect could not be due to an alternative strategy used by the subjects in the perturbed trials.

Alternatively, visual control of hand transport could involve guiding the grip center of gravity until it corresponds to the location of the object center. In order to test this hypothesis, Paulignan and Gentilucci (1996) recorded the grasping of objects moving perpendicularly to the hand's line of approach. For a precision grip using only two fingers, the thumb and the index, the center of the opposition axis ("C" on Figure 3) will be guided to the object's center of gravity. When the object motion is parallel to the finger opening–closing movement, the line of approach of C is the same, thus the pattern of finger displacement should not be affected by the direction of the object movement. A robot arm was used for presenting objects. Two main conditions were defined depending on the object's movement direction: upward and downward. As the result showed (Figure 4), the contribution of each finger to grip formation was tightly dependent on the object's movement direction, contrary to the prediction of the hypothesis.

None of these hypotheses is thus satisfactory for explaining how prehension movements are guided by vision. Knowing the answer to this question would be important, because the only way to optimally characterize the transport component is to use the point of the limb that is controlled as a descriptor. Looking at the wrong point will give only a biased image with more variability, which can mask the existence of correlation and coordination between the components.

8. CONCLUSION

The aim of this chapter was to analyze evidence for or against the visuomotor channel hypothesis (Jeannerod, 1981). The point was to determine whether or not there are valid arguments against the existence of parallel processing for the action of grasping an object. Testing this model implies, first, describing the two components with the correct parameter. It also implies that the experiments in which the object properties are changed during the movement are sufficiently selective, that is, that only the object location or the object size are changed, for example. As mentioned earlier, there is a difficulty here because changing object size can also affect the area available for positioning the fingers, a factor that has implications for the transport component.

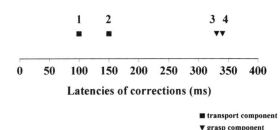

FIGURE 5   Comparison of corrections obtained for different types of perturbations. These data represent a compilation of experiments made by different groups. The squares represent the responses of the transport component to perturbations of object location or arm movement. The triangles represent the responses of the grasp component to perturbations of object size. Key: (1) Paulignan, MacKenzie, et al., 1991; (2) Gentilucci et al., 1992; (3) Paulignan, Jeannerod, et al., 1991; (4) Castiello et al., 1993.

In experiments in which the object location was changed, there was no effect on the maximal grip aperture. The double peak pattern observed on the grip curve might be due to the presentation of two different objects. Indeed, when grasping a single moving object, no such a pattern was observed. When a pure change in object size was produced, there was no effect on the kinematics of the transport component, but there was an effect on movement time, due to a disruption of the coordination. Moreover, a comparison between the corrections observed in response to the different types of perturbations provides strong arguments in favor of the parallelist hypothesis (Figure 5). In the experiments in which the perturbation affected the spatial position of the object, changes in transport kinematics could already be detected within 100–150 ms following the perturbation (Castiello, Paulignan, & Jeannerod, 1991; Gentilucci et al., 1992; Paulignan, MacKenzie et al., 1991). This early correction sharply contrasts with the effects of perturbations in object size where the grip changes occurred in 330–340 ms (Castiello et al., 1993; Paulignan, Jeannerod et al., 1991). This difference between the two types of corrections is a somewhat counterintuitive finding, since the inertial properties (the musculoskeletal mass) of the systems respectively involved in correcting for position or size perturbations would lead to the expectation that fingers should react at least as fast as the arm. The fact that this did not occur means that the limiting factor for the speed of corrections to size perturbations must be looked for at the central stage of visuomotor processing, rather than at the execution level.

These results suggest that the two components of prehension are controlled by distinct pathways and that these pathways are selectively activated when perturbations are applied to either one or the two components. The neurophysiological basis for this type of organization has been fully reviewed in several papers (Jeannerod, 1994b; Jeannerod et al., 1995; Jeannerod & Rossetti, 1993). Although the two mechanisms for preshaping and for transporting the hand, respectively, lie close to each other in the posterior parietal cortex, they can be dissociated by lesions. Jeannerod, Decety, and Michel (1994) described a patient who, following a parietal lesion, was specifically impaired for grasping objects. Whereas the transport component was normally accurate, the finger grip grew up to a maximum size so that there was no longer any relation of grip size to object size. This pathological deficit resulted in awkward grasps where the fingers did not close in time around the object, and the object was bumped by the palm of the hand. This is an illustration of the modular organization of object-oriented behavior, in which actions result from the combination and coordination of several subactions, each with an identifiable and separate neural substrate.

14

Two Hands—One Action

The Problem of Bimanual Coordination

**MARIO WIESENDANGER, OLEG KAZENNIKOV,
STEPHEN PERRIG, AND PAWEL KALUZNY**

1. GENERAL OUTLINE

Human skills typically require the cooperation of both hands. The precision in this spatial and temporal bimanual cooperation raises the question of how the two brain hemispheres cope with the problem of bimanual coordination. There is no simple answer to this question because the demands differ according to the task requirements and because coordination seems to be primarily constrained by the environment itself. For example, it is obvious that swimming in the butterfly style requires a strong coupling of both arms, which move symmetrically during the entire cycle. But consider a bimanual act that is object related, such as grasping an orange with one hand and peeling it with the other hand. In this instance, the labor is divided among the two hands, one stabilizing the object, the other manipulating it. Such an asymmetric division of labor obviously needs separate controls. In yet another bimanual skill, like typewriting, the task also requires to a large extent independent manipulations. Playing a musical instrument, like the piano, is a particularly skillful bimanual motor performance. It is most likely that the individuated finger movements of each hand are controlled by the respective contralateral hemisphere via the cortico-motoneuronal component of the pyramidal tract. And yet the individuated finger movements are also subject to controls of an entire phrase of music; to the phrase (and not to single notes) the artist will consciously attend and put into it all his or her interpretation of the music.

Clearly then, in all skillful bimanual performances, the impression is that of a unified single act, with the two hands differing in their contributions and yet being bound together for achieving the goal in a smooth and coordinated fashion. These simple phenomenological considerations indicate that the hands may work independently as components of a performance that is, however, orchestrated at a higher level for goal achievement (*Bewegungsmelodie*). This kind of reasoning emerged early in this century and led to the proposition that sensorimotor centers, that is, motor and association cortical areas, are responsible for a general movement plan or program, a term introduced by the neurologist von Monakow (1914). The individual components (muscles, articulations) that make up the action are selected and executed unconsciously and variably from trial to trial, whereas the goal remains invariant and is consciously selected. Since the time of Hughlings Jackson, neurological doctrines emphasizing hierarchical organization, and the discovery of severe motor disorders that arise, not out of a paralysis of the motor apparatus, but rather from faulty programming (Liepmann, 1920; von Monakow, 1914) brought strong support for the hierarchical hypothesis of purposeful motor control. Neurological patients suffering from apraxia have difficulties in putting together movement components into a purposeful act. For example, patients with dressing apraxia typically display a bimanual deficit in buttoning. These higher order deficits were thus interpreted as an expression of a faulty superordinate movement plan, which is required for invariant goal achievement (Bernstein, 1967).

The principle of motor equivalence is intimately associated with the above concept of invariant goal achievement and was also born out of observations made in brain-lesioned patients or animals. It is based on the following common observation as described by Lashley (1930) in his discussion of motor equivalence: "when habitually used motor organs are rendered nonfunctional by removal or paralysis, there is an immediate spontaneous use of other motor systems which had not previously been associated with or used in the performance of the activity." As an example of such a transfer, he mentions "the shift from writing with finger movements to movements of the arm or even with a pencil held in the teeth, still preserving the characteristics of individual chirography." In other words, the concept of motor equivalence has the meaning of invariant goal achievement with variable means. The hierarchical view underlying the concepts of goal invariance and motor eqivalence entered the psychological literature under various terms, all denoting a superordinate constraining of movement components into a unified purposeful motor act: coordinative structure (Bernstein, 1967; Easton, 1972; Kugler et al., 1980; Turvey, 1977), higher unit of performance (Welford, 1968), generalized motor program (R. A. Schmidt, 1988), or coordinated control program and motor schema (Arbib, 1990).

The prevailing view until the early 1980s was that neural processing starts with goal definition, followed by programming of the strategy, and terminates with a release of the motor command. However, this hierarchical and serial model has since been seriously questioned, particularly if considered with a strict temporal order of preparatory and executive processes (e.g., Kelso & Tuller, 1981). The bulk of experimental evidence suggests that many motor centers of the brain are activated in a largely overlapping time span and that the various structures are engaged cooperatively and in parallel in producing purposeful motor output (see M. Wiesendanger, 1990, and M. Wiesendanger & Wise, 1992, for further discussion). The significance of parallel processing is commonly viewed as an expression of functional specialization in sensorimotor subareas or of a divison of labor. With respect to motor control, division of labor has also been advocated for the two hemispheres; this is expressed in the clear-cut task-dependent specialization of the hands (e.g., MacNeilage, 1990).

Another aspect of bimanual coordination discussed in the neurological and psychological literature deals with tapping and rhythmic behavior in general. It is a common experience that bimanual tapping, in phase or in phasic alternation, can be easily performed, whereas out of phase movements are difficult, requiring extensive practice. Newborn babies have a strong tendency to move both arms together. As skills are developing and hands are being used independently, rhythmic simultaneous movements of the two arms are still important elements of many natural acts. Descriptively, this has been termed assimilation effect (Marteniuk, MacKenzie, & Baba, 1984). Locomotor rhythmic activity is not limited to the lower limbs, but involves also the trunk and the arms (for arm swing) and it is well established that such rhythms are based on spinal networks generating coordinated rhythms via intersegmental and commissural connections (Grillner & Wallén, 1985). The pattern generators can be modulated by sensory inputs and descending systems from the brain stem and from higher motor centers, which, in part, distribute their fibers to both sides of the spinal cord (e.g., the bilaterally distributing pathway originating in the reticular formation; Kuypers, 1981). Any model of bimanual coordination has therefore also to consider the implication of coupling of the two arms, say in ball catching, by low-level neural pattern generators (Figure 1), which may be usefully involved in simultaneous or antiphase rhythmic activity of the arms (Kelso, Putnam, & Goodman, 1983; Kelso et al., 1979).

By way of summary, Table 1 shows the three concepts that have been

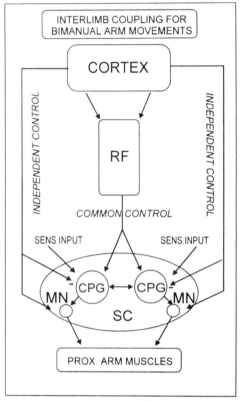

FIGURE 1   Proposed model of neural circuitry implicated in common and independent controls of the hands. RF, reticular formation with bilaterally projecting descending fiber system; SC, spinal cord segment; CPG, central pattern generator; SENS.INPUT, segmental somatosensory influence on central pattern generators; MN, motoneuron. Note that activation of independent controls automatically inhibits the CPG.

TABLE I   Proposed Organizing Principles for Goal-Directed Movement

Organizing principle	Behavioral consequence
(1) Assimilation effect	Neural coupling devices for initiating simultaneous multilimb movements.
(2) Division of labor	Parallel processing, specialized subareas, hemispheric specialization.
(3) Hierarchical organization	Goal invariance, motor equivalence.

discussed in the past and that may be considered as organizing principles for purposeful, goal-directed movements. Previously these organizational principles or rules have been discussed separately. In the present account, we discuss experimental paradigms involving both forelimbs with the aim of examining whether the three rules can be demonstrated and assessed objectively. In particular, we explore the novel question whether the principles that have heterarchic (1, 2) as well as hierarchic (2, 3) elements coexist in the same movement paradigm. Our experiments addressing these issues were conducted in healthy human subjects performing Task I involving measurement of simple bimanual reaction time (RT), Task II involving bimanual unloading, and Task III involving a more natural pull-and-grasp action. In addition, experiments with monkeys trained to perform a similar bimanual pull-and-grasp Task III are also included. The review is organized in the order of the above three principles.

2. ASSIMILATION EFFECT

We have measured how well the hands are temporally coupled in movement initiation in three experiments utilizing the different Tasks I, II, and III. It will be shown that movement initiation is indeed fairly well synchronized, including even the asymmetric and more natural pull-and-grasp Task III.

2.1 Bimanual RT Paradigm (Task I)

In this study by Kaluzny, Palmeri, and Wiesendanger (1994) human subjects were asked to exert as quickly as possible small quasi-isometric force pulses with the index fingers against two force transducers. The force signals and the EMG bursts from the two interossei muscles were used to measure RTs. The go-signal was a lateralized weak electrical pulse applied to the middle finger of the right or the left hand. It had been found before that in unimanual performance the right and left hands may be consistently asymmetric in RT. The aim of the experiments was to test whether any asymmetry would persist or disappear with bimanual performance. Figure 2 illustrates a representative result obtained in 1 subject (out of 10 investigated subjects).

For the present purpose, only bimanual results are presented as histograms of EMG latencies of the first dorsal interosseus muscle. In Figure 2A, the response histograms of the left and right interossei muscles are plotted in separate histograms. The scatter of the left- and right-hand responses is large in comparison with the histogram of the paired right–left differences of bimanual RTs shown in (B). The distribution is centered around zero ms and has a narrow scatter. This means that the RTs of the two fingers covary, as is also apparent from the high correlation coefficient (C). Significant departures from zero were observed in some individual subjects, but the differences were always small (less than 10 ms) and in both directions. In a similar bilateral RT study, Di Stefano, Morelli, Marzi, and Berlucchi (1980) found that, when proximal arm movements were tested, the synchronization was better than for distal hand movements. This was explained by the anatomical findings in monkeys that proximal (but not distal) muscles are controlled by both hemispheres, thus ensuring "a yoked movement of both limbs."

2.2 Synchronization in a Bimanual Unloading Task (Task II)

The goal of this experiment by Kaluzny and Wiesendanger (1992) was to study how well postural stability can be maintained in distal hand muscles in the face of an intervening perturbation generated by the subject's own opposite hand. The experimental setup is shown in Figure 3A. It was shown before that for a proximal task (like that of a waiter unloading plates from the supporting hand), postural stability is well maintained (Hugon, Massion, & Wiesendanger, 1982); but it was suggested (Dufossé, Hugon, & Massion, 1985; Paulignan, Dufossé, Hugon, & Massion, 1989) that the bilateral postural stabilization mechanism was a prerogative of proximal effectors. The outcome of the present distal task was, however, very similar to that obtained in the proximal task: a suppression of tonic postural EMG activity in the load-bearing index finger preceded unloading produced by the opposite active finger. This resulted in a far smaller positional disturbance than one can

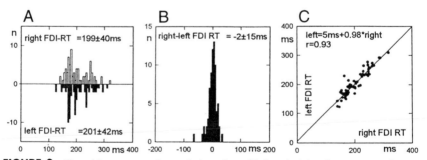

FIGURE 2 Time histograms and correlation plot of left and right electromyographic responses recorded from the first dorsal interosseus (FDI) muscle in a bimanual reaction time (RT) task. (A) Comparison of left and right RTs with means and *SD*. (B) Histogram of paired differences with mean and *SD*. Note smaller scatter, centered around zero, in comparison to the larger scatter in the individual hand responses. (C) Linear correlation between paired right and left responses. The high correlation coefficient provides a measure of the covariation and coupling of the two hands.

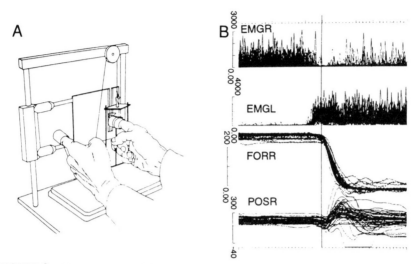

FIGURE 3   (A) Apparatus used for the unloading experiment. The right index finger is unloaded, via a pully system, by an active upward abduction of the left index finger. (B) Recorded variables. EMGR and EMGL, activity of first dorsal interosseus muscle of the right and left hand, respectively; FORR, force traces of the unloaded right index finger; POSR, position traces of unloaded right index finger (100 superimposed traces from an individual subject). Note the near synchronous activity increase in the left hand and the deactivation in the right hand. (From experiments of Kaluzny & Wiesendanger, 1992).

see with a passive (i.e., external) unloading. The suppression roughly coincided with the EMG activity burst of the opposite index finger (Figure 3B). This is clearly a more complex situation because the synchronization concerns phasic activation in one hand and suppression of activity in the other hand. On average, the suppression slightly lagged behind the burst of the active hand. In a trial-by-trial analysis, the right–left intervals were more variable than in the first RT experiment. This may have been caused partly by a less precise measure of the onset of an activity decrease. The observed variability in bimanual synchronization is unlikely to be a disadvantage for stabilization, since a few milliseconds would not be critical because of the inertia of the mechanical system.

2.3 Initial Bimanual Synchronization in a Pull-and-Grasp Task (Task III)

In this task, right-handed subjects performed a reach-and-pull movement with the left arm and a reach-and-grasp movement with the right arm (for full details, see Kazennikov et al., 1996; Perrig et al., 1996). As shown in Figure 4, the two hands converge at the open drawer where the right hand

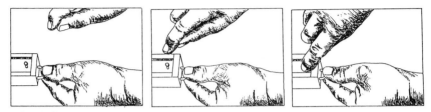

FIGURE 4 Bimanual pull-and-grasp task performed by a human subject, with the right hand approaching the drawer, which is about to be pulled open by the left hand (drawings made from digitized video recordings). The subjects have to remove, with the precision grip, a small rod from the drawer. Sensors signal contact of left hand with the drawer handle, entry of the right index finger into the drawer, and drawer displacement. (From unpublished experiments of Perrig, Kazennikov & Wiesendanger.)

has to pick up a small rod with the precision grip. No other particular instruction was given to the subjects and they were free to move at their ease after an acoustic signal. The goal-oriented asymmetric movement sequence was the most complex of the three tasks but was performed promptly and without difficulties. It can be considered as a bimanual skill similar to many

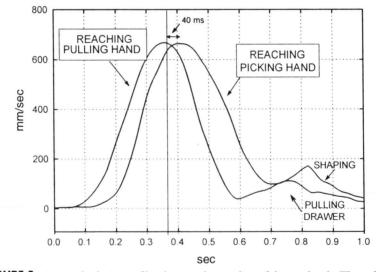

FIGURE 5 Averaged velocity profiles showing the coupling of the two hands. Three-dimensional trajectories of the left thumb and the right index finger were recorded by a movement analyzing system (passive markers reflecting infrared pulses, ELITE-system) and digitized for obtaining velocity signals.

purposeful everyday skills of human subjects. At this point, we are concerned only with the question of bimanual initiation of the task, coming back later to the question of end-point (goal) synchronization. The degree of coupling was assessed by measuring in each trial movement onset of the left and right hand (lift-off from the two touch-sensitive start platforms), as well as on the basis of velocity profiles. Frame-by-frame inspection of video recordings already indicated that most subjects tended to move both hands at about the same time, but with a short phase advance of the left hand. A minority of subjects chose a different strategy by moving more sequentially (e.g., waiting to move the right picking hand until the left hand had reached the handle of the drawer). On the average, movement onset of the right hand followed that of the left hand by 56 ± 49 ms (grand mean of all subjects). The coupling of the two hands in movement initiation was further assessed by means of the correlation coefficients (movement onset right vs. movement onset left); the grand mean for all subjects was $r = .7513 \pm .236$.

With regard to velocity profiles the tendency was, for the majority of subjects, to synchronize both arms for reaching. Figure 5 illustrates averaged velocity profiles of the left and right hand paths. The velocity peak of the left hand was selected in each trial for aligning the corresponding right-hand velocity profile. In this subject the right–left peak interval was 40 ms. The population histogram of all subjects showed a broad distribution centered near zero (grand mean $= 49 \pm 145$ ms).

In conclusion, a tendency for common movement initiation of the two limbs could be confirmed for all three experiments. For the complex pull-and-grasp task, this was somewhat surprising, since the picking hand may be expected to wait until the drawer is opened. It thus appears that simultaneous initiation is a relatively robust principle used even in asymmetric tasks. However, it was also clear that the temporal coupling always allowed for considerable variability (and thus probably also flexibility), particularly in the asymmetric Tasks II and III. These observations are in line with the concept of a common command or of an assimilation effect which was interpreted by Marteniuk et al. (1984) as being caused by neural cross-talk between separate streams of commands to each hand. If the intensity specifications for the two hands differ (different distances or masses), the two separate commands need to be adjusted by the postulated neural cross-talk. Viewed from the premise that for many bimanual skills the two hands need independent controls, the idea of a neural device for conditional coupling (i.e., flexible intervening of coupling if useful for the particular task) is plausible. Such a hypothetical neural device may operate at a relatively low, possibly spinal level. As pointed out by Marteniuk et al. (1984), "perhaps the development and learning of bimanual skills involves the elimination (insulation) or incorporation of neural cross-talks, depending on the task requirements." The term neural cross-talk is, however, nebulous with respect to known neural circuits. Neural stepping oscillators, known to exist in the spinal cord of vertebrates, would be good candidates also for nonlocomotor rhythmic activity or for entraining quasi-simultaneous actions.

3. DIVISION OF LABOR AND HAND SPECIALIZATION

If goal coding by higher neural structures for achieving a unified bimanual motor act does exist, one should expect that the task assignment for the individual hands would be an integral part of this goal coding and therefore be consistent. It is a fact that human subjects specialize in the use of hands in many skills. In right-handers, the left hand usually is the postural hand, whereas the right is used for fine manipulation. As commented by Mac-Neilage (1990), the left hand provides postural support for a grasped object and at the same time spatial reference for the right hand, which manipulates the object. Hand preferences can be demonstrated also in nonhuman primates who frequently exhibit consistent hand choices for object-oriented bimanual actions (Fagot & Vauclaire, 1988; MacNeilage, 1990). We have trained 8 monkeys on the bimanual pull-and-grasp task. Of these, 6 monkeys spontaneously chose the left hand for pulling and the right hand for picking the food from the drawer, 1 monkey clearly preferred the right hand for pulling, and 1 monkey changed between the left and the right hand. Of the 20 human subjects who participated in the bimanual pull-and-grasp task (Task III adapted for human use), all subjects also chose the left hand for pulling and the right hand for grasping the object. All 20 subjects scored as right-handers (test of Oldfield, 1971). But from 5 additional subjects who were not included in the study for various reasons, 3 spontaneously chose the right hand for pulling, one of them scored as an ambidexter, the 2 others as right-handers.

The asymmetry of roles played by the two hands, observed for human subjects and monkeys alike, is considered to reflect a specialization of brain function in motor control. It has been suggested that the left hemisphere in right-handers exerts a hierarchically superior role over both hands. It is thus possible that the left hemisphere is determining their respective roles in skilled bimanual movements (e.g., Kimura & Archibald, 1974). As mentioned in the introduction, evidence for superordinate controls in executing bimanual movements comes from patients with unilateral lesions of the parietal association cortex and the mesial frontal cortex. With parietal lesions of the dominant hemisphere, patients often fail to use their hands properly for buttoning clothes, or for eating with fork and knife, and so on (Hécaen, 1978); with mesial frontal lesions, patients sometimes develop bizarre bimanual disorders, such as intermanual conflict and alien hand syndrome (for review, see M. Wiesendanger et al., 1994). It is important to note that these bimanual deficits may occur without paresis or tonic changes contralaterally to the lesion.

In monkeys with unilateral lesions of the mesial frontal cortex, we failed to find evidence for selective, that is, truly specific bimanual deficits, but bimanual actions were transiently disturbed due to a clear contralateral deficit in manipulations. For example, monkeys failed to retrieve food morsels wedged into holes of a perspex plate, a manipulandum used by Mark and Sperry (1968) for testing bimanual coordination. In order to be successful, the monkey has to push down the food with a finger and to grasp the extruded morsel from below the plate. In our monkeys, the failure was, however, clearly due to a difficulty in pushing down the food with the hand contralateral to the lesion; the grasp with the ipsilateral hand was normal (to be published elsewhere; see M. Wiesendanger et al., 1994, for a preliminary account). It was reported that lesions of the posterior parietal cortex in monkeys also produced deficits limited to the contralateral arm and hand (Faugier-Grimaud, Frenois, & Stein, 1978; Lamotte & Acuna, 1978). The question of possible bilateral controls of these cortical areas (as inferred from human pathology) needs, however, more detailed and quantitative investigations.

In conclusion, a consistent division of labor with respect to goal-directed bimanual movements appears to exist in both subhuman primates and in human subjects. The question is not settled whether one hemisphere is superior to the other in controlling both hands (hierarchic control) or whether each hemisphere specializes for certain job assigments (division of labor). Evidence for the former assumption comes from human studies. The bulk of evidence from lesion studies in subhuman primates points to contralateral rather than higher order bimanual deficits. However, the issue remains to be studied further.

4. HIERARCHICAL ORGANIZATION

4.1 Goal Invariance

In this section we describe results obtained in 3 monkeys that had been taught to perform the bimanual pull-and-grasp task. They were not trained to perform as fast as possible, but were highly motivated and ran fast to pick up small pieces of a cookie with the precision grip. A large amount of data on the temporal structure of this bimanual task was collected following an extensive training, resulting in consistent performance (Kazennikov et al., 1994).

The task was similar to the pull-and-grasp task of human subjects described above (Task III). In short, the task consisted in reaching separately through a left and a right window, which opened simultaneously at trial onset. In all 3 monkeys, the left arm was leading and reached out to grasp the handle of a spring-loaded drawer which was pulled open while the right arm aimed toward the baited drawer to pick the food (Figure 6). Frame-by-frame analysis of video sequences indicated that entrance of the index finger into the food well occurred at the moment the drawer was fully opened. In order to test this more precisely, a number of sensors were used to measure the timing of left-hand and right-hand events in the bimanual synergy (left hand: movement onset, touch drawer handle, drawer completely opened; right hand: movement onset, index finger enters food well of drawer). All these discrete events were entered for each trial into a laboratory computer, together with the analog signal of the drawer displacement. The variability of the left- and right-hand events as well as paired left–right differences were examined on a trial-by-trial basis and the results from many sessions were pooled together for each of the monkeys.

Similar to the results obtained in human subjects, movement onset was well coupled between the hands, but with a somewhat larger delay of the right hand, which followed the leading left hand. In this section, the focus of interest is, however, on the bimanual coordination in reaching the goal, that is, grasping the food morsel from the opened drawer. We therefore limit the

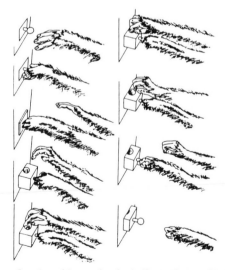

FIGURE 6 Monkey performing a bimanual task, similar to that used in human subjects (drawings obtained from video recordings). Note sequential synergy with synchronization of drawer opening by left hand and picking of the food morsel by the precision grip of the right hand.

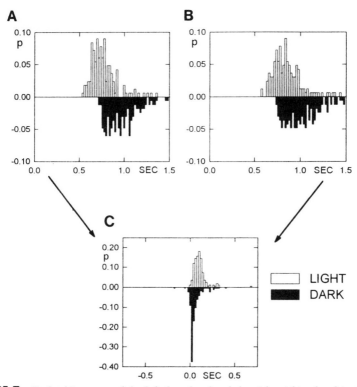

FIGURE 7 Goal achievement of the left draw hand and the right picking hand in the task illustrated in Figure 6. Histograms with open bars are from results obtained when vision of the workspace was available to the monkey; histograms with solid bars are from results obtained when vision was excluded (complete darkness). Note that for both conditions the scatter in timing of the left- and right-hand events defining goal reaching was large, whereas the scatter of the paired right–left differences of these events was small. As is evident from the histograms in (A) and (B), the loss of vision considerably slowed down performance. In spite of this, the synchronization and scatter in goal reaching was even improved in the dark (95 ± 76 ms in light condition, and 43 ± 71 ms in dark condition). Linear correlation of the paired right and left goal-related events (not shown) remained also very high in dark condition (r = .92 in light condition, r = .94 in dark condition). (From experiments of Kazennikov et al., 1994.)

discussion on the bimanual end-point control. It turned out that in all 3 monkeys the paired differences for the two events defining goal achievement (i.e., drawer fully opened by left hand and entering of the right index finger into the food well) were near zero (65 ms, grand average). The degree of synchronization of this event pair and its variance were as good as or even better than synchronization and its variance at movement onset. This is remarkable, since the timing variance of the individual hand components was considerably increased as the movement sequence progressed toward the goal. The essence of this point is shown in Figure 7, which is a rather impressive illustration of the concept of goal invariance achieved in spite of variable means. This result means that the right and left components of the synergy covary in order to achieve the end-point invariance; this can also be demonstrated by the high correlation coefficient for end-point events ($r = .923$, grand average). These correlation coefficients were in fact significantly higher than those calculated for the initial event pairs of left and right movement onset ($r = .75$). The same picture emerged in parallel experiments performed on human subjects who had no long-term training before task performance and who also received no particular instruction how to perform the task.

The conclusion from this experiment is that temporal invariance for goal achievement is a consistent rule that can be assessed quantitatively, both in "overtrained" monkeys and in human subjects that had not practiced the task over prolonged time. The left–right synchronization and the correlation of the goal-related components were at least as precise as or usually even more precise than the parameters defining task initiation.

4.2 Motor Equivalence

By manipulating constraints imposed on the pull-and-grasp Task III, we succeeded in demonstrating also the rule of motor equivalence. Results obtained in monkeys and also in human subjects will be used to make the point. The first pertinent question we asked was whether the end-point control was essentially guided by vision or by somatosensory signals generated by one or the other limb. Alternatively, well-trained monkeys may rely mainly on a memorized motor plan. In fact, it can hardly be doubted that implicit memory was an important factor in the present task, since the manipulated object was in a constant position relative to the body, and since the drawer movement was constrained in its path and extent. Nevertheless, the performance was characterized by significant trial-by-trial variability of the individual hands in the spatial and temporal domain. As mentioned in the previous section, this variability of the hands, together with the intermanual goal invariance, are already an expression of motor equivalence (invariant goal with variable means). It was further predicted that changing constraints would not affect goal invariance. Three task conditions were changed in order to test this prediction: vision, additional loading of the drawer, and cutaneous sensibility of the pulling hand. Note that the changed conditions occurred in blocks of trials and not unpredictably.

Effect of removing visual guidance: When the monkeys were exposed to complete darkness, the highly motivated animals continued to perform the task without hesitations. Analysis of the time structure revealed that the various events were delayed in the no-vision condition and that variability increased. However, despite these changes in the left and right hands, intermanual synchronization was unchanged or sometimes even improved in the dark, as illustrated in Figure 7 for one of the monkeys. The timing of the goal-related events was very high for all three monkeys ($r = .92$) and remained so in total darkness. The same behavior was observed in human subjects performing the pull-and-grasp task.

Effect of unimanual loading: When additional constant loads were imposed on the pulling hand, the pull phase was consistently prolonged, resulting in a delay of the left hand in reaching the goal. One could expect that the unperturbed right hand arrives too early and that synchronization and correlation at the end point deteriorates. This was, however, not the case, even when the same experiment was performed in complete darkness. Thus, load-induced changes occurring in one hand were adjusted in the first few trials by an equal prolongation of the nonloaded hand. Analogous findings were obtained in human subjects tested with increased loads and without vision. Subjects were more variable in their (unconscious) adjustments; for example, some slowed down for the whole trajectory, others moved slowly at the beginning of reaching, and still others when approaching the goal.

Effect of unimanual cutaneous nerve block: This experimental condition was limited to 5 human subjects. Normal performance was compared with that when cutaneous sensation of the thumb and index finger used to pull open the drawer was abolished by reversible nerve block. The anesthesia concerned touch and moderate pressure sensibility and to a large extent also pain sensibility. During anesthesia, reaching the handle of the drawer was often not precise (misreaching) and grasping it for pulling was grossly abnormal with frequent slips. The deficit further increased when subjects were also blindfolded. This resulted in a massive left-hand delay in reaching the goal, that is, pulling the drawer completely open. Despite this gross temporal change, goal achievement was perfect in that the unperturbed hand was immediately adjusted in its timing to meet in synchrony with the perturbed hand at the goal.

In conclusion, the three conditions explored for the natural bimanual skill clearly established the presence of motor equivalence, a term used long ago by Lashley (1930) indicating invariant goal achievement with variable means. Of particular interest was the preservation of goal invariance when the changed constraints had a direct influence on one limb only (increased pulling time when the drawer load was increased or when cutaneous sensation was impaired). Goal invariance in this case means that the opposite nonperturbed limb had to adjust its timing for maintaining bimanual synchronization. When asked, all subjects reported that they were not aware that they had adjusted the timing of the nonperturbed arm. Renewed interest in the concept of end-point control has arisen because of the potential insight it could provide in goal coding by the higher sensorimotor control centers of the brain (see, e.g., Abbs & Cole, 1987). In this context, the latter authors also discussed the necessity of many biological systems to be flexible "for achievement of many different motor objectives or the same objective under different contexts or task conditions" (p. 19).

5. SUMMARY AND CONCLUDING REMARKS

The exquisitely well coordinated bimanual actions that make up many everyday skills of human beings and to some extent also of higher monkeys and hominids are a great challenge for scientists interested in the mechanisms of motor behavior. Probably due to the complexity of the problem, the underlying neural mechanisms that rule the behaviorally expressed coordination are virtually unknown. One potentially promising approach is to first elaborate quantitatively as far as possible the rules that govern the behavior of the two hands and arms. In this review, results of investigating some simple and some more complex bimanual movements performed by subhuman primates and human subjects are discussed in the attempt to demonstrate that quantitative criteria for bimanual coordination, at least in the temporal domain, can indeed be established.

Two modes of coordination were tentatively distinguished, the first concerning bilateral whole-limb coordination, used especially for bilateral initiation of many skills and for bilateral rhythmic behavior. It is argued that the coupling of the two limbs may occur at a relatively low level, possibly implicating spinal pattern generators. Bilaterally linked pattern generators of locomotor rhythms have been identified in the vertebrate spinal cord (Grillner & Wallén 1985). It is therefore conceivable that other bilateral actions, in addition to locomotion, make use of the pattern generators.

A second, more complex coordination concerns purposeful and goaloriented bimanual synergies and is implicated in the temporal and spatial coordination of both hands for goal achievement. This coordination is sometimes also referred to as end-point control. The presence of a goal-related coordination appeared as a temporal goal invariance, contrasting significantly in its lower variance as compared to that of the constituent unimanual components. Typical of this goal-related coordination was its insensitivity to changes of the task conditions (vision, loading, exclusion of cutaneous sensibility), that is, an emergence of motor equivalence, meaning that goal remains invariant when the right- and left-arm components vary. It was furthermore shown that the necessary adaptive changes occur automatically and are not perceived consciously. Finally, there is suggestive evidence that cortical networks in the parietal and frontal association areas and perhaps also the interhemispheric commissure, the corpus callosum, are essential for goal coding.

In his kinematic chain model, Guiard (1988) makes a distinction of an initial and a final control phase of bilateral arm coordination, the first phase being performed by "macrometric proximal organs," corresponding to the reaching movements in our complex bimanual task. This is then followed by the final or "micrometric distal" phase, which is directly related to the goal and which does the fine tuning of the object-related bimanual coordination. However, it is doubtful whether the proximal component is sequentially chained together with the distal component. EMG recordings in many proximal and distal muscles in our monkey task revealed a high degree of temporal overlapping of activity in proximal and distal muscles. Therefore, the chain model is, in our opinion, not an adequate model. The question, however, remains how the very precise and robust bimanual end point or goal achievement is controlled. The fact that exclusion of one sensory channel (vision, cutaneous sensation of left pulling fingers) does not abolish end-point control may be due to a combined multisensory control whereby sensory channels may substitute for each other.

In summary, the study of a complex bimanual and goal-oriented synergy revealed deterministic behavior in goal achievement, whereas looking at right-hand or left-hand constituents, a more probabilistic behavior was found. We therefore suggest that the examined bimanual and goal-directed synergy has the connotation of a system characterized by its temporal invariance in spite of the variability of its components (the individual hands). Weiss (1969) in fact used the property of variance reduction to define a system. The essential point of the theory is that the system imposes coordination of the constituent parts (and not vice versa). This concept of macrodeterminism or downward causation merits a renewed interest in attempts to construct models of complex systems. It is doubtful that one will ever be able to understand this system's behavior solely on the basis of detailed analysis of its individual components; they appear to be too complex and too probabilistic in their behavior. Rather, the emphasis should be directed to the question of how the system's rules are imposed downward on the components. It is interesting to note that this situation is typical for biological systems in general. Weiss (1969) strongly emphasized the layered organization in biology. In his view, a system can be defined as an ensemble whose variance is smaller than the sum of variances of its constituent parts. Furthermore, he argued that biological systems having this property are found at the molecular and up to the behavioral level of organization.

The other important issue of our study is that coupled whole-limb movement initiation which is likely to be controlled at a lower level, can be observed in the same asymmetric and goal-oriented synergies characterized by end-point control. We therefore suggest that, in the overall control of complex synergies, low-level pattern generators may be usefully included as building bricks of the synergy. The presence of assimilation effects, division of labor, and end-point control in the same task, as observed in our study, thus argues for combined heterarchic and hierarchic organizational principles.

ACKNOWLEDGMENT

A. Palmeri, M. Corboz and U. Wicki participated in the early stages of these experiments. This research was supported by the Swiss National Science Foundation (Grants No. 31–27569.89 and 31–36183.92).

15

Anticipatory Control of Grip Force in Rapid Arm Movement

ALAN M. WING

1. INTRODUCTION

With his observation that spinal mechanisms alone could not provide the forms of muscle synergy that promote the arm "from a simple locomotor prop to a delicate explorer of space" Sherrington (1906) was emphasizing the specialized nature of motor control of the hand. There are in this book many examples of manual dexterity that appear to support a distinction between fine manipulative movements, primarily involving the distal musculature, and gross postural movements, subserving balance with major involvement of the proximal muscles. This distinction is also to be seen in didactic divisions in the field of motor control between studies of voluntary movement and research into posture and locomotion. This chapter qualifies this contrast in proposing that fine motor control over the digits, when maintaining the geometric position of an object in the hand as it is moved by the arm, serves a postural function.

However, this is not to say that the hand and arm should be considered a dumb "prop." Rather, in providing a stabilization function when moving a grasped object, the hand reflects generalized, high-level, planning components of motor control that are sensitive to, and make allowance for, dynamic disturbances created by voluntary movement. In this chapter evidence of

Hand and Brain
Copyright © 1996 by Academic Press, Inc. All rights of reproduction in any form reserved.

anticipatory modulation of grip force subserving stable grasp is reviewed. It is argued that the anticipatory control of grip force is analogous to anticipatory components of posture control evident in maintaining standing balance. In both cases coordinated muscle responses provide anticipatory stabilization in the face of self-induced, equilibrium-disturbing forces. The nature of the stabilization implies the operation of motion planning based on internal modeling of load kinematics and dynamics.

2. LIFTING OBJECTS

A natural starting point for a review of the grasp function of the hand is the definition of phases of lifting provided by Johansson and Westling (1984b). The traces in Figure 1 show the forces acting during precision grip (using opposed thumb and index finger) of the instrumented apparatus shown on the left. The vertical force developed by the arm muscles acting on the apparatus produces a *load force*, which starts at zero (at the start of the trial the apparatus rests on the table) and rises to equal the weight of the apparatus. This is shown at the top of the figure. The next trace shows a horizontal *grip force* between thumb and finger pressing on the vertical plates. With the digits in contact with the object, the grip force begins to rise first and is then joined by the rise in load force. When the load force matches the weight of the apparatus it rises from the table as shown by the third trace, which indicates

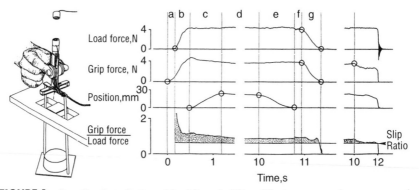

FIGURE 1   Coordination of grip and load force in lifting. The instrumented apparatus on the left allows load force, grip force, and position to be recorded during various phases of lifting (a, preload; b, loading; c, transitional; d, static; e, replacement; f, delay; g, unloading). On the right is shown the effect of relaxing grip force while the object is still held above the surface; the slip ratio is defined by the point at which the object slides from grasp. (Reproduced with permission from Johansson & Westling, 1984b. Copyright © 1984 Springer-Verlag.)

position. After a small overshoot, grip force settles at a steady level in the holding phase until the object is set down.

2.1 Grip Force and Object Stabilization

The functional significance of the grip force in Figure 1 is that it allows the development of a *frictional force* that opposes the load force. If the frictional force is large enough, it prevents the apparatus from slipping under the effects of gravity when it is in the air (phases c, d, e). Or, if the apparatus is still in contact with the supporting table, the frictional force prevents the hand slipping off, leaving the apparatus behind (phases a, b, f, g). A larger load force due to a heavier object requires a greater grip force. If grip force is gradually relaxed when holding the object off the table, there comes a point (shown on the right of Figure 1) when the object will slip. The ratio of the grip force to the load force (bottom trace) at which slipping occurs, which is termed the *slip ratio*, depends on the coefficient of friction for the surfaces in contact. This depends, in turn, on a number of factors including surface roughness. When holding an object with a rough surface between thumb and finger a given load can be met by a smaller grip force than would be required for a smooth surface. Thus, for example, the slip ratio for grip surfaces covered in sandpaper is lower than for surfaces covered with silk.

The grip force that people use when holding an object in the air is generally only slightly greater than the minimum required for a given surface to prevent slip. It thus makes sense to speak of a *safety margin*, which may be defined as the ratio of the excess grip force to the minimum grip force that just prevents slipping (Westling & Johansson, 1984). If grip force drops during steady holding of an object, so that slip does occur, sensory receptors in the skin are activated and these result in a reflex increase in grip force with a latency of 75 ms (Johansson & Westling, 1987a). This is about twice the latency of the most rapid spinal reflex in intrinsic hand muscles (P. B. C. Mathews, 1984) and it is likely that the additional time involves supraspinal pathways, possibly including sensorimotor cortex (for further discussion of sensory factors in grasp, see Johansson, 1991 and Chapter 19).

2.2 Coordination of Grip Force and Load Force during Loading

We now turn to consider the coordination between grip force and load force, evident in their parallel increase in the loading phase of lifting (b in Figure 1). The mass of the object determines the load force and, in combination with the frictional conditions, the minimum grip force required to keep the grip force/load force ratio above the slip ratio in static holding (phase d). However, the grip force/load force ratio must exceed the slip ratio at all times, including during the loading phase. In principle, this could be achieved in any number of ways, which might even include an entirely sequential approach in which the increase in grip force and the increase in load force follow one another in succession. However, except for the brief preload phase (a), increases in load force occur in parallel with increases in grip force (Johansson & Westling, 1984b). We now consider two experimental manipulations that allow the relation between grip force and load force to be examined in more detail and that demonstrate the anticipatory nature of the force increases.

In an experiment described by Johansson and Westling (1988a), three different object masses were used in different blocks of trials. Figure 2 shows grip force and load force in the lift phase for a number of lifts by a single

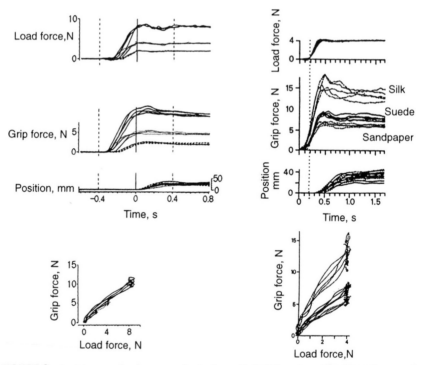

FIGURE 2   Anticipatory development of grip force. (*Left*) When the subject has prior experience of the weight to be lifted (200, 400, 800 g), the rate of rise of grip force depends on weight (Johansson & Westling, 1988a, copyright © 1988 Springer-Verlag; 15 superimposed lifts by a single subject synchronized by movement onset). (*Right*) When different grip surfaces are used with a fixed weight (400 g) the rate of rise of grip force is least for sandpaper, moderate for suede, and highest for silk (Johansson & Westling, 1984b, copyright © 1984 Springer-Verlag; 16 superimposed lifts by a single subject synchronized by load force onset).

subject. Although the different object masses required different levels of grip force, the time to attain these was approximately constant. That is, the rate of rise of grip force varied systematically with mass. Load force rates also changed systematically with mass and these changes were matched so that the grip force/load force relation not only remained approximately linear, but had the same slope across different masses (Figure 2, lower left). Comparison of the rise of grip force and load force across conditions reveals that the force rates diverged from the very outset. This implies anticipation of final force levels, that is, load force and grip force rates were programmed in advance on the basis of past experience. This was confirmed in other experimental conditions in the same study in which object weight changed unexpectedly between trials. On such trials, load force and grip force rates initially corresponded to those for the weight as experienced on the previous trial (Johansson & Westling, 1988a).

Alterations in grip surface affecting friction require changes in grip force without affecting load force. The question then arises whether such changes affect the form of the grip force/load force function or whether it remains linear with changes only in slope. Johansson and Westling's (1984b) study included a comparison of the effects of changes in grip surface. Data from a series of lifts by a single subject of the test object with grip surfaces covered in sandpaper, suede, or silk are shown on the right of Figure 2. With a smooth surface such as silk, which requires a higher grip force in steady holding, the rate of rise of grip force was higher than with a less slippery, rough surface such as sandpaper. The grip force rise rate for suede, which is intermediate in roughness, lay between those for silk and sandpaper. Load force rates were unaffected by the frictional conditions. The grip force/load force functions (Figure 2, bottom right) reveal similar, near-linear functions that differ primarily in slope.

The differences in grip force rise rate with grip surface were present from the outset, suggesting an anticipatory basis, as for the differences in grip force rise rates due to object mass. This idea received support from observations by Johansson and Westling (1984b) on the effect of changing grip surfaces pseudorandomly in a series of lift trials (Figure 3). When grip surfaces were changed between trials, on the first trial after a change in surface, the rise in grip force initially followed a course appropriate to the previous surface and was only modified some 100 ms after contact. However, on the next trial with the new surface, the grip force rise rate was set correctly from the outset. This was true of both surface-induced increases (Figure 3A) and decreases (Figure 3B) in friction.

The anticipatory nature of grip force development in lifting thus applies to both object mass and surface texture. But is grip force driven directly by object information in both cases? Where there is variation in load force

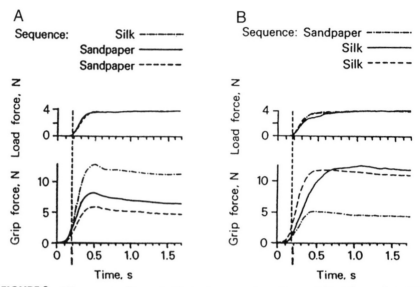

FIGURE 3 Adjustment to changes in friction between grip surfaces and skin. The graphs in (A) and (B) each represent a sequence of three consecutive trials selected from series of lifts of a 400-g object with pseudorandom changes of grip surfaces. The sequence silk, sandpaper, sandpaper (A) results in a decrease in the rate of rise of grip force; the sequence sandpaper, silk, silk (B) results in an increase in grip force rise rate. Average data based on 162 trials from 9 subjects. (Reproduced with permission from Johansson & Westling, 1984b. Copyright © 1984 Springer-Verlag.)

geared to object mass, it may be that grip force is determined indirectly on the basis of the planned load force. One way to examine this possibility would be to determine whether trial-to-trial variation in grip force, or more particularly in the initial rate of rise of grip force, is correlated with variation in the initial rate of rise in load force (with object properties held constant). Force rise rates might be positively correlated because trial-to-trial variation in the target load force function (e.g., a subject might vary the duration of load force rise) would be mirrored in the grip force function (e.g., rise rate) selected to match the load force function. However, if such a linkage did operate, the positive correlation between grip force and load force would be likely to be less than one because of peripheral variation due to noise in the separate motor output channels to hand and arm (cf. Wing, 1992). In contrast, if grip force and load force are independently specified, zero correlation of initial rise rates would be expected. In this case, grip force rise would have to be sufficiently ahead of the rise in load force for the safety margin to be retained in the face of variations in grip force rise rate.

The form of the grip force/load force functions in Figure 2 suggests that, within a condition, the initial rates of rise of grip force and load force are positively correlated. This is consistent with the hypothesis that grip force may be geared to planned changes in load force. Further support for this idea comes from a lifting experiment conducted by Kinoshita, Ikuta, Kawai, and Udo (1993) who asked subjects to vary lifting speed. They showed that, in the loading phase, grip force rates were closely related to load force rates. Moreover, Johansson, Riso, Häger, and Backström (1992) described a paradigm in which subjects were asked to freely vary their pull on a fixed manipulandum (a so-called passive object; see Johansson, Chapter 19). Illustrative data in their report indicate a close correspondence between grip force and load force (with a slight lead of grip force increases over load force increases). Such correspondence indeed suggests that the grip force function is planned in relation to planned changes in load force. In the next section we consider a development of the lifting paradigm that allows further investigation of the dependence of grip force on load force.

3. MOVING AN INERTIAL LOAD HELD IN PRECISION GRIP

In Johansson and Westling's lifting experiments described above, subjects raised the apparatus shown on the left of Figure 1 one or two centimeters above the table surface, held it steady for a short period, and then replaced it. However, suppose subjects had been asked to make an arm movement and carry the apparatus (appropriately designed to allow this—see Figure 4) some appreciable horizontal distance. Such a movement, taking perhaps a third of a second and transporting the object, say, 30 cm, would involve periods of acceleration then deceleration with magnitudes that would be of the same order as the acceleration due to gravity. This would result in appreciable inertial forces acting on the object in addition to the force of gravity (see Figure 4). If, in static holding, there is only a small safety margin in the level of grip force used to prevent slip due to the force of gravity, the additional forces due to accelerating and subsequently decelerating an object pose a real threat to its stability in the hand. The increase in load force could result in the safety margin being exceeded and the object slipping.

Given there are supraspinal reflexes that can raise grip force in response to slip, it might be thought that such reflex mechanisms could compensate for load force elevated by one's own movement. However, feedback-driven corrections would result in problems with rapid movement of a small object, since the hand could slip right off the object in the time it takes for long-loop reflexes to have an effect. It therefore seems reasonable to expect anticipa-

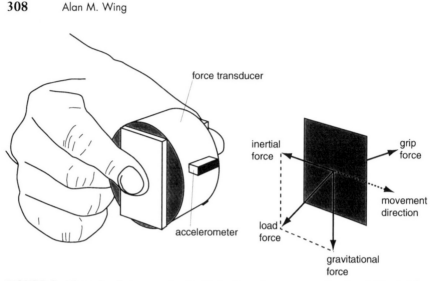

FIGURE 4 Measuring forces associated with horizontal movement of an inertial load. The accelerometer allows inertial load force to be determined as the product of the mass with the acceleration due to linear motion at right angles to the grip force sensed by the force transducer. If slip is to be avoided, the product of grip force and the coefficient of friction between the digits and the force transducer must exceed the magnitude of the resultant of the gravitational force and the inertial force.

tory adjustments of grip force for changes in load force arising from arm kinematics. A series of experiments conducted in the motor control laboratory at the Applied Psychology Unit showing this to be the case will now be reviewed.

3.1 Horizontal Movements

Illustrative acceleration, load force, and grip force traces obtained when a subject moved the apparatus shown in Figure 4 in a horizontal straight line 30 cm from right to left (toward body midline) at a slow or moderate speed are shown in Figure 5. Before and after the movement, the load force simply reflects gravity acting on the mass of the object and the grip force is clearly above the slip ratio indicated by the horizontal arrow. However, associated with the movement, as documented in Flanagan, Tresilian, and Wing (1993) and Flanagan and Wing (1993), there is a clear rise in grip force just prior to the rise in load force. Faster movements associated with higher accelerations, and therefore with larger load forces, are associated with higher peak grip forces. Because the rise in grip force associated with voluntary movement occurs simultaneously or just before movement onset, it may be identified as anticipatory. The increase in peak grip force with peak load force in the faster movements suggests the grip force rise is intended to compensate for increases in load force that the subject expects will be associated with arm movement.

The effect on grip force of an unexpected abrupt application of an external force, which approximately doubled the load force due to gravity alone, is shown on the right of Figure 5. In this case the subject was simply asked to maintain the position of the force transducer. Note that the load force application itself does not appreciably alter the grip force, since the axes of force application are orthogonal to those of grip force and there is no biomechanically induced cross-talk. The perturbation to the load induces an increase in grip force after a delay of some 70 ms, sufficient time for a supraspinal reflex involving sensorimotor cortex (see Cole & Abbs, 1988). Although fast, this delay stands in strong contrast to the simultaneous elevation of grip force and load force in voluntary movement.

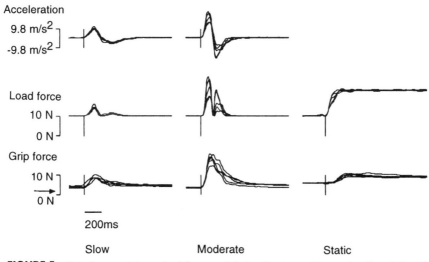

FIGURE 5 Grip force anticipates load force modulation due to arm kinematics. Slow (*left*) and moderate (*middle*) 30-cm horizontal right-to-left arm movements produce brief periods of horizontal acceleration followed by deceleration. The load force traces immediately below are determined by the absolute value of the product of the object mass (0.26 kg) with the resultant of the (time-varying) horizontal acceleration and the (constant) acceleration due to gravity (9.8 m/s/s). The grip force traces rise with or slightly ahead of the load force traces and reach a peak synchronous with the peaks in load force. This synchronicity may be contrasted with a static holding condition (*right*) in which a horizontal load (measured with a second force transducer, top traces) was applied at an unpredictable time and resulted in grip force increases (bottom traces) after a delay of 70 ms. (Illustrative data from a single subject; 5 trials aligned on load force onset.)

3.2 Knowledge of Object Mass and Movement Kinematics

The modulation of grip force in anticipation of load force implies that the nervous system has access to information concerning both the object mass and the kinematics of the forthcoming movement, since changes in either of these would require different grip force. Information about object mass may arise from various sources. Experiments have shown that grip force in lifting depends on cues available in advance of holding the object. Thus, visually or haptically perceived size (A. M. Gordon, Forssberg, Johansson, & Westling, 1991a, 1991b, 1991c) and cues identifying common objects (A. M. Gordon, Westling, Cole, & Johansson, 1991) influence the development of grip force in lifting. These effects on grip force in lifting may be mediated by subjective estimates of mass that subjects could then also use in the prediction of inertial loads in subsequently transporting the object.

Errors in estimating object mass may result in setting inappropriate load and grip force targets prior to lifting. By unexpectedly increasing object weight during a series of lifting trials, Johansson and Westling (1988a) were able to examine the effect of underestimation of object mass, which resulted in lift-off failing to occur at the expected time. The failure of the expected sensory feedback caused a series of probing coordinated increases in grip force and load force until the object rose successfully off the support. On the next trial the force rates were reprogrammed to this new weight implying there had been an updating of sensorimotor memory. In the context of moving an object, such updating could also be significant for anticipation of inertial loads due to arm movements.

In static holding, the muscular effort required to generate sufficient load force with the arm to keep the object raised against gravity might also give cues to mass (see Flanagan, Chapter 20). In this regard it would be interesting to know how people cope with moving objects in space. Under conditions of microgravity there is no experience of weight in the grasp and hold phase that precedes object transport and this means that important cues by which mass might be inferred prior to movement would be missing. In planning movement under microgravity conditions, there might therefore be greater reliance on visual and/or memory cues to an object's mass. In addition, there might be overgripping to reduce the consequence of an erroneous judgment of mass. Alternatively, the hand might initially be moved more slowly than normal to allow more time for feedback-based adjustments to grip force.

Visual cues may also be important in defining distribution of mass through an object. Goodale et al. (see Chapter 2) describe the case of a neurological patient who had lost the normal ability to locate the center of mass from visual cues. This ability is likely to be important in determining grip points that straddle the center of mass. Using such points with precision grip avoids introducing torques about the grip axis that would tend to turn the object during lift and also during subsequent transport movements. However, unexpected torques experienced while lifting the object might lead to revised estimates of object mass distribution that would be pertinent to subsequent transport.

Regarding information about movement kinematics, data on point-to-point hand movements indicate that people select a trajectory that minimizes the rate of change of acceleration, which is termed jerk (Flash & Hogan, 1985). This suggests that grip force modulation might be based on load force computed from the estimate of object mass and the form of the acceleration function planned for the forthcoming movement. However, others have argued that the nervous system is not directly concerned with movement kinematics. For example, under the equilibrium point hypothesis (Feldman, 1986, Flanagan, Feldman, & Ostry, 1992) it is assumed that movement from one position to another is based on setting the central drive to the agonists and antagonists to levels appropriate to the desired end posture. Details of the movement trajectory are not planned, but arise as a consequence of system dynamics. In such accounts of hand trajectory formation it might be assumed that information about kinematics of the forthcoming movement, necessary for determining the required modulation of grip force, is derived from an internal, forward model of the consequences of a change in equilibrium point (Flanagan, Tresilian, & Wing, 1996).

3.3 Vertical Movements

Earlier, modulation of grip force with changes in the horizontal component of load force was described. It was noted that grip force increases with the initial rise in load force at the onset of arm movement. The question may then be asked whether the grip force increase is timed in relation to the onset of movement or whether the rise in grip force is associated specifically with the expected rise in load force. This question may be answered by looking at vertical movements. Load force is given by the product of the object's mass with the vector sum of the acceleration due to arm motion and that due to gravity. Thus, upward movement leads to an immediate rise in load force, whereas downward movement causes an initial decrease in load force (until the arm's downward acceleration exceeds that due to gravity).

The traces in Figure 6 were obtained by asking a subject to make vertical straight line movements of about 30 cm. As observed by Flanagan and colleagues (Flanagan et al., 1993; Flanagan & Wing, 1993) the traces show that grip force rises immediately with upward movement but is delayed (or even shows a small decrease) in downward movement until the load force rises appreciably above the baseline in the later deceleration phase of the movement. When the downward movement is made more rapidly (Figure 6, right-

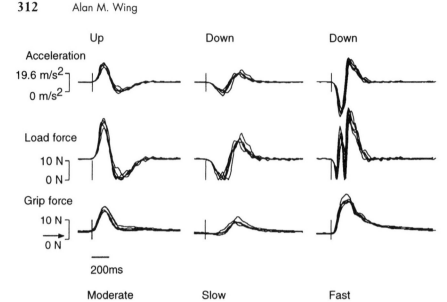

FIGURE 6   Initial rise of grip force is associated with load force onset rather than movement onset. Acceleration and load force (upper two sets of traces) and grip force (bottom set of traces) for moderate upward (*left*) and slow downward (*middle*) movements, and fast downward movements (*right*). In the fast downward movement the negative-going segment of the acceleration exceeds the acceleration due to gravity. This results in an onset of load force that is nearer movement onset than in the slow downward movement and there is an associated earlier rise in grip force. (Illustrative data from a single subject; 5 trials aligned on load force onset.)

hand side), an appreciable load force is developed in the initial phase and the grip force trace may then be seen to rise earlier (and to higher values in the deceleration phase). This implies that the timing of the grip force increase is associated with the load force rise and not simply with the onset of arm movement.

The late rise in grip force evident in slow downward movement is interesting because it shows that grip force adjustment is scheduled according to the load force function rather than according to onset of the arm movement. It is also important because it implies the underlying anticipatory process is sensitive to the cancellation of forces due to arm movement and gravity. The necessary information about the direction of the force of gravity relative to the planned movement probably stems from a combination of vestibular and proprioceptive cues such as those that contribute to postural reflexes in standing (Dietz, 1992). In addition, the experience of weight during the static holding phase prior to moving the object may be important. With cues to object mass, and information about the kinematics of the planned movement (in particular, the acceleration and deceleration), the subject is in a position to predict the load forces associated with accelerating and decelerating the arm in a point-to-point movement and to determine how these might interact with the force due to gravity. However, it may be noted that in vertical movements the decreases in load force below that due to gravity do not result in grip force dropping appreciably below baseline for static holding. A second point to note is that grip force modulation in moderate vertical upward movement (Figure 6, *left*) is, if anything, less than that in moderate horizontal movement (Figure 5, *middle*). Yet, peak load force in the upward movement is appreciably higher. It thus appears that grip force is not a simple linear function of total load force and it may be that it is determined according to different rules for different movement directions.

4. GENERALITY OF ANTICIPATORY MODULATION OF GRIP FORCE

The finding that grip force modulates with load force arising from movement kinematics is robust. For example, Flanagan et al. (1993) observed a strong positive correlation across subjects between the durations of grip force and load force rise. The durations were also strongly correlated over trials within subjects (who were instructed to make repeated moves of similar amplitude and duration); typical values were greater than .9. There was also a reliable positive correlation of maximum grip force and maximum load force, though this was usually less than the correlation of the onset times; a typical value was .6.

A notable characteristic of grip force adjustment for phasic modulation of load force is that grip force drops back quickly toward the baseline, albeit with a longer time course than that of the load force modulation. If subjects are asked to make repeated cyclic movements between two points it might be thought that the grip force would settle at a steady, elevated level throughout the movement sequence. However, this turns out not to be the case. Figure 7 shows illustrative data from an experiment (Flanagan & Wing, 1995) in which subjects were asked to make repeated up-and-down movements between two points. The traces show persisting modulation of grip force in phase with load force. The reduction of grip force between load force peaks in cyclic movement suggests the central nervous system attaches some importance to maintaining a low grip force. This idea is reinforced by the observation that the grip force/load force ratio (bottom trace in Figure 7) exhibits a minimum that is stable over cycles. The traces on the left were produced with smooth grip surfaces, those on the right, with rough surfaces. The minimum grip force/load force ratio during cyclic movement clearly reflects the different slip force for the two surfaces.

One might speculate that the apparent regulation of minimum grip force is motivated by a goal of keeping down energy demands. However, one difficulty for this view is that the reduction of grip force is not simply due to passive relaxation of the agonists but also involves antagonist activity (Flanagan, Lemon, & Wing, unpublished observations). An alternative view, which deserves further research, is that the compliant grip resulting from a low grip force is advantageous for the sensory appreciation of the object and its dynamic attributes. A further possibility is that grip force is maintained at a low level to facilitate subsequent manipulation of object position in the hand.

The grip force adjustments associated with load force variation are not limited to the precision grip between thumb and index finger used in the above studies but apply to a range of grips (Flanagan & Tresilian, 1994). For example, modulations of grip force with load force were observed when subjects were asked to make vertical movements of the force transducer when it was provided with special surfaces requiring outward-directed grip force (Figure 8, *left*). In this configuration, decreases in inward-directed grip force secure increases in frictional force to compensate for load force increases. Despite the use of an unfamiliar grip with changed roles for the participating muscles, there was clear anticipatory modulation in grip force, similar to that seen in Figure 6.

Further evidence of the generality of the processes responsible for grip force modulation was obtained by asking subjects to hold the force transducer with a grasp defined by the index fingers of two hands with the remain-

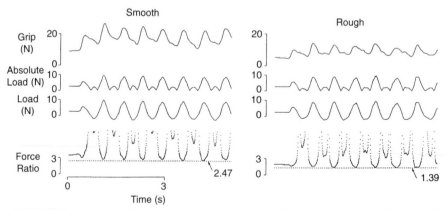

FIGURE 7 Persistence of grip force modulation with load force modulation in cyclic vertical movements. The grip surfaces of the apparatus in Figure 4 were covered in smooth satin (*left*) or rough sandpaper (*right*). The upper trace shows grip force, the middle trace, load force. The lowest trace shows the grip force/load force ratio. (Illustrative single trial data from one subject; reproduced with permission from Flanagan & Wing, 1995. Copyright © 1995 Springer-Verlag.)

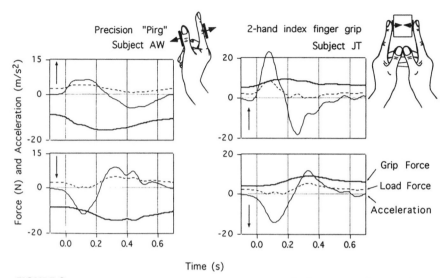

FIGURE 8   Generality of anticipatory grip adjustments: A grip that reverses the normal geometric relations in precision grip ("pirg") results in grip force modulation with load for upward (*above left*) and downward (*below left*) movement similar to modulation with normal precision grip. Two-handed grip (*right*) also demonstrates coupling of load and grip force. (Illustrative single trial data from one subject; reproduced with permission from Flanagan & Tresilian, 1994.)

ing fingers clasped to keep the hands together (Figure 8, *right*). In vertical movements the relations between grip and load force functions were again similar to those in Figure 6. This is remarkable considering the change in effectors and the different neural pathways involved in bilateral action. Such generality of grip force modulation across different forms of grasp (effector invariance) suggests that the underlying anticipatory processes may be relatively high level since they are not specified in terms of any particular skeletomuscular configuration. On the other hand, two observations suggest the modulation is not directly accessible to conscious control. First, it has been noted (Flanagan et al., 1993) that subjects are not generally aware of anticipatory modulation of grip. Second, people are not usually able to suppress the modulation; although they adopt strategies such as stiffening or overgripping, these only reduce and do not completely eliminate the modulation (Flanagan & Wing, 1995).

5. ALTERED LOAD FORCE REGIMES

So far in this chapter the load forces that have been considered have been inertial; they have been determined by the acceleration and deceleration of the hand and the mass of the object. Are people sensitive to, and able to predict, load forces arising from other sources and following different physical laws? An experiment in which grip force was monitored while subjects were asked to make rapid 20- to 30-cm horizontal movements of a manipulandum subjected to contrasting load force regimes suggests they are (Flanagan & Wing, 1996). Three conditions were run; in the first the load was purely inertial, in the second it was viscous (load proportional to velocity), and in the third it was spring-like (load proportional to distance from the start position). The loads were developed using a computer controlled linear motor with a manipulandum that avoided any gravitational component to the load force (see Figure 9, *left*).

The three sets of traces in Figure 9 show systematic differences in grip force function as a function of the type of load force. Anticipatory modulation of grip force for the twin-peaked load force function produced by the acceleration and deceleration of the inertial load is seen on the left. After 20 trials of pushing and pulling this load the viscous load was introduced. Initially, subjects' movements were somewhat slowed. However, after 10 or so trials, movement time was restored to normal. At this point, as can be seen

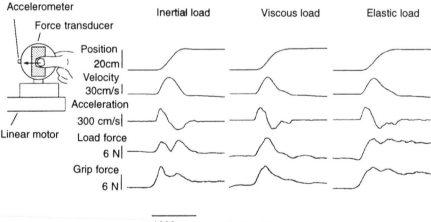

1000 ms

FIGURE 9 Sensitivity of grip force function to contrasting load force functions. Grip force (bottom trace) was recorded during horizontal movements of the load cell in Figure 4 mounted on a linear motor whose motion was computer controlled to simulate an inertial (*left*), viscous (*middle*), or spring load (*right*). The different kinematics (upper traces) and load dynamics (the load force was measured with a second force transducer) associated with each load result in contrasting grip force functions. (Illustrative single trial data from one subject; data from Flanagan & Wing, 1996.)

in the middle set of traces, the load force had become a single peaked function and the grip force exhibited a a maximum halfway through where, under the inertial load, there had been a local minimum. Grip force now clearly coincides with peak velocity. Finally, after changing to the spring load, a grip force rise was obtained (see the traces on the right) that matched the form and time course of the continuous rise in load force. Thus, anticipatory grip modulation is not limited to inertial loads but can be adapted to a variety of contrasting load force regimes. This finding reinforces the idea that subjects are aware of kinematics of the forthcoming movement. Either the forthcoming movement is planned in these terms or the consequences of movement commands are modeled to determine expected kinematics (see Section 3.2).

6. ANTICIPATING ENVIRONMENTAL INTERACTIONS

As mentioned earlier, anticipatory modulation of grip force is not specific to a particular form of grasp but exhibits effector invariance. In the work reviewed so far the anticipation has related to the consequences of one's own movement, which depend on movement kinematics and attributes of the load such as mass of the object. However, the load may also depend on external forces. Thus, in the case of gravity, the load is different depending on whether movement is vertical or horizontal and grip force modulation changes accordingly. Gravity represents a constant background force and so there is considerable opportunity to learn its consequences (Lackner, 1990). It is therefore important to note that the sensitivity of grip force to external forces extends to impulsive loading. Thus, Johannsson and Westling (1988b) showed that subjects will raise grip force in anticipation of the collision resulting from a ball dropped onto a platform held with a precision grip. The question then arises as to the relation between modulations of grip force driven by such an externally governed predictable load and load forces arising from one's own movements.

Consider the task of keeping a ball bouncing by cyclic vertical movements of a hand-held paddle. Each upward stroke with the paddle will generate inertial load forces that would be expected to induce anticipatory increases in grip force. In addition, at the point of collision, there will be an extra load force due to the impact of the ball. If there is anticipatory modulation of grip force for the collision, it might be thought that this would be integrated with the grip force modulation for load force arising from arm kinematics. However, a recent experiment by Wing, Flanagan, and Tresilian (1996) has demonstrated that there is independent modulation of grip force for load forces arising from collisions superimposed on load forces arising from cyclic movement. This is illustrated in Figure 10. Load force and grip

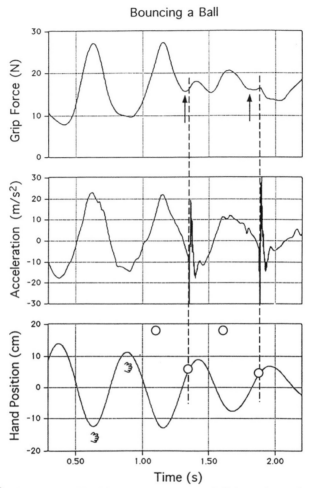

FIGURE 10 Anticipation of load force due to collision. A ball dropped onto the apparatus in Figure 4 during cyclic up-and-down movements (position trace at the bottom) bounced twice producing sharp impulsive increments in acceleration (middle trace) that are anticipated by modulations of grip force (top trace). (Illustrative single trial data from one subject.)

force traces obtained while a subject bounced a ball on the side of a force transducer (*right*) are compared with those obtained when simply moving the force transducer up and down at the same frequency (*left*). In both cases modulation of grip force is evident with the periodic up-and-down movement of the transducer. On the right, superimposed on this periodic effect, just prior to the sudden load elevations due to the collision of the ball with the bat, there are clear grip force increases. These occur in various phases relative to the periodic modulation of grip force, which appears unaffected by the collisions. Thus, the modulation of grip force for predictable own motion is kept separate from grip force adjustments that compensate for expected collision with an approaching object.

7. WHOLE BODY MOVEMENT

Until now the focus of this chapter has been on anticipatory modulation of grip related to load forces resulting from arm movements. However, it is interesting to note that one of the tasks studied by Flanagan and Tresilian (1994) caused loading of a hand-held object as a result of whole body motion. Subjects were asked to jump up to, or down from, a chair while keeping their arm and hand in a fixed position relative to the body. Figure 11 shows modulations of grip force with the fluctuations in load force. Again, grip force was elevated when load force rose. The jumping motion produced a distinct low-load middle phase prior to landing that allowed a particularly clear dip in grip force to be seen.

The focus of the jumping task analysis was on the anticipatory adjustments to grip force, which served to stabilize the object in the hand during the load forces induced by the jump. However, it is important to appreciate that the task would have induced destabilizing forces, not only on the hand-held object, but also on body posture as a whole. For example, the upper limb supporting the object away from the body would have experienced forces

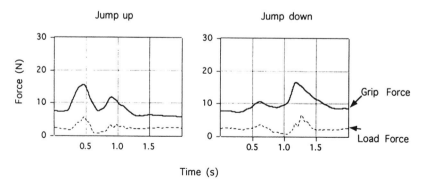

FIGURE 11 Grip force modulates with load force created by jumping up to (*left*) or down from (*right*) the seat of a chair. (Illustrative single trial data from one subject; reproduced with permission from Flanagan & Tresilian, 1994.)

tending to disturb its posture relative to the trunk. Thus, it is reasonable to suppose that the jump would have induced compensatory activity of the shoulder, elbow, and wrist muscles of that arm. Indeed, it is likely that the forces generated by the leg muscles in a jump would disturb the posture of most of the body segments. This raises the question whether the mechanism responsible for the anticipatory modulation of grip force might be associated with anticipatory processes underlying more widespread postural adjustment.

A number of studies have detailed anticipatory whole body postural adjustments associated with rapid arm movements. Moving the arm imposes forces that tend to destabilize not only the hand-held obect but also the position of remote body segments. Bouisset and Zattara (1981, 1987) have documented subtle postural adjustments to the trunk and lower limbs just prior to the onset of a rapid arm movement. They and others (for a review, see Massion, 1992) have argued that these anticipatory adjustments serve the role of minimizing the impending disturbance to posture due to the upcoming focal movement. It is thus interesting to ask about the relation between whole body anticipatory postural adjustments and grip force adjustments associated with rapid movements of the arm. To what extent might grip force and whole body postural adjustments be driven by related brain mechanisms?

Wing, Flanagan, and Richardson (1996) have examined this issue by measuring grip force and ground reaction forces associated with horizontal load forces developed when using precision grip to push or pull on a manipulandum attached to a linear motor that simulated a dynamic inertial or a static load. The question was whether posture and grip would exhibit similar trial-to-trial fluctuation immediately prior to arm movement. Figure 12 shows average data from the four experimental conditions for a single subject. Clearly just prior to the rise in load force, there were marked changes in grip force and in ground reaction force; on average the onset of grip force increase was 59 ms ahead of load force onset, while change in the vertical moment occurred 32 ms before load force onset. If grip force and postural adjustments reflect a common preparatory process (or at least shared information about the upcoming arm action), they should be correlated. The average (4 subjects, 4 conditions) correlation between grip force and vertical moment onset times was .4, while that between the maximum rates of change of grip force and vertical moment was .6, both values being statistically significant.

Links between stabilization functions of the hand and body posture have been noted before, but in tasks calling for reactive rather than anticipatory modulation of motor behavior. Thus, Traub, Rothwell, and Marsden (1980) showed that perturbation of arm posture by a pull at the wrist when the hand was placed with the fingers encompassing but not touching a free-standing object (a sherry glass) led to a grab reflex with thumb muscle EMG latency of 50 ms. At the time, this work was important for pointing to the operation of

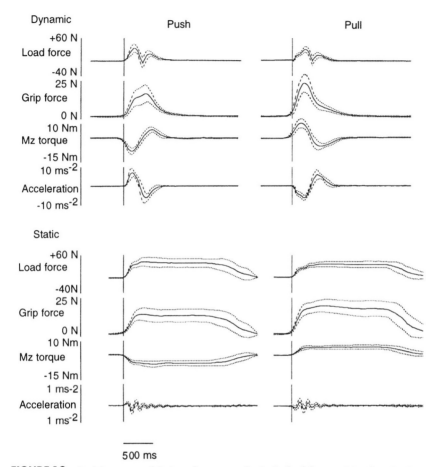

FIGURE 12   Anticipatory modulation of posture and grip for load forces arising from horizon-tal pushing (*left*) or pulling (*right*) of the load cell in Figure 4 mounted on a linear motor simulating an inertial (*top*) or static (*bottom*) load (see Figure 9, *left*). Mean functions from 20 trials (the dotted lines indicate one standard deviation on either side) show changes in grip force and ground reaction force (middle two traces) slightly leading load force changes (top trace). The bottom trace shows the resulting apparatus acceleration (or vibration in the static condition; note the change in vertical scale). (Data from one subject; 20 trials in each condition aligned on load force onset; data from Wing, Flanagan, & Richardson, 1996.)

long-loop reflexes acting at points remote to the stimulus (the authors sug-gested perturbation-induced muscle length change would have been concen-trated at the shoulder and so distant from the hand muscles). These so-called heterogeneous reflexes were shown to be finely tuned to context so that the elicited response could change depending on preexisting conditions. For example, Traub et al. noted that if the perturbation was given with the glass already held in the hand, no further elevation of hand muscle activity was observed, that is, there was no superimposed grab response.

Similar context dependence of heterogeneous postural reflexes was demonstrated by Marsden, Merton, and Morton (1981). They showed that right arm postural responses elicited by perturbations to the trunk are changed depending on whether a low inertia object held in the hand is to be stabilized in space or whether a massive object is being held that affords reliable support. Wing, Flanagan, and Richardson's (1996) result might thus be considered as an extension of a previously demonstrated principle of coordinated multisegment responses to postural perturbation. However, an important difference is that the earlier work involved reactive mechanisms triggered by imposed perturbations. The importance of the new findings is that they show that there is coordination of anticipatory adjustments across upper and lower limbs based, presumably, on predictions of the destabilizing effects created by the voluntary movement of the arm.

8. CNS MECHANISMS

What neural bases might underlie anticipatory adjustments of grip force? A number of other chapters in this book discuss central nervous system (CNS) mechanisms subserving sensorimotor function of the hand. However, the focus of these chapters is on concurrent control of movements of the fingers. This leaves open the question as to what brain regions contribute to anticipatory adjustments of grip force without overt finger movement. A more general issue is whether CNS mechanisms contributing to anticipatory modulation of grip are also involved in anticipatory postural adjustments.

A number of research groups working on hand trajectory control have suggested that cerebellar circuits use information about upper limb dynamics in preparing muscle commands that will allow desired movement of the hand to be achieved despite interaction torques that arise between arm segments during movement (Hollerbach & Flash, 1982; see Ghez et al., Chapter 10). Thus, Kawato, Furukawa, and Suzuki (1987) have proposed that the cerebellum uses an inverse dynamic model that receives the desired trajectory as input and provides the required joint torques as output. Miall, Weir, Wolpert, and Stein (1993) have argued that the cerebellum controls movement by using a forward model of upper limb dynamics to determine movement consequences of muscle commands; the commands are then subject to modification using rapid internal feedback. In both approaches, peripheral feedback is considered to be important for modifying the internal model as well as allowing closed-loop guidance where the model is inaccurate. In this regard it is interesting to note that patients with peripheral sensory neuropathy produce arm movements that are uncoordinated due to failure to allow for interaction torques (Sainburg et al., 1993). Even though the cerebellum may use predictive control it is nevertheless dependent on sensory feedback for up-to-date information about current movement conditions. Sainburg et al. observed that vision greatly improved performance in deafferented patients. It thus seems likely that their patients' problem lay with a lack of information, such as initial limb configuration, required by the cerebellar model rather than with a failure of the internal model itself.

If the cerebellum plays a role in forward modeling of hand motion planning, it might be expected that anticipatory grip force adjustments should also be abnormal in cerebellar patients, to the extent that grip force is predicated on an internal dynamic model. Some support for the suggestion that the cerebellum contributes to anticipatory grip force adjustment comes from a study by F. Müller and Dichgans (1994). They observed a lack of coordination of grip and load forces when patients with degenerative cerebellar disorders carried out a lifting task using a precision grip. The grip force used by the patients failed to show the normal monotonic increase with load force. Furthermore, over trials, the patients did not adapt their grip force rise rates to match different loads. Although they were able to adjust grip force rates to some degree, they did so significantly less efficiently than control subjects and Müller and Dichgans concluded that this represented a failure of anticipatory parameterization. In future research it will be important to determine whether the observed grip force impairment in cerebellar patients extends to the anticipation of load forces induced by arm kinematics. Kawato (1992) has proposed that different regions of the cerebellum may control other motor functions such as posture and locomotion on a similar basis to upper limb movements (see also Kawato & Gomi, 1992). Another interesting question is therefore whether differently localized cerebellar lesions produce dissociated impairment of anticipatory postural adjustments and grip force adjustments.

Finally, it will be of interest to determine whether any groups of patients with lesions of the cerebral cortex exhibit impaired anticipatory grip force adjustment. While forward modeling of dynamics may primarily involve the cerebellum, it would seem reasonable to suppose any such modeling mechanism would take as input information about object physical attributes and about the desired movement in a coordinate system encoding all relevant kinematic parameters. Jakobsen and Goodale (1994; see also Goodale et al., Chapter 2) have suggested a role for parietal cortex in coding visual information about object shape important for grasping. It may be that this area also codes attributes such as mass distribution and surface roughness that are relevant to setting an appropriate grip force. With regard to kinematics,

Kalaska (1991) has proposed that superior parietal cortex may provide a neuronal representation of movement kinematics for kinesthetic perception and movement control. His data were based on single unit recordings in primates; further research is needed to determine whether neurological patients with lesions in this area exhibit deficits in anticipatory adjustment of grip force, which may be attributed to impaired representation of kinematic information.

9. CONCLUSIONS

The theme of this chapter is that there is anticipatory modulation of the grip force developed by the digits of the hand to compensate for the otherwise destablizing effects of load forces that act on hand-held objects during voluntary arm movement. With stabilization of the object in the hand the geometric relations between hand and object are preserved; this may be termed a postural function. Notwithstanding the evolution of the hand's important role in object manipulation and the existence of attendant control processes, a primary postural function remains. Thus, in voluntary arm movements there are important parallels between anticipatory modulation of grip and anticipatory postural adjustments.

Since the adjustments to grip force are anticipatory, it is interesting to suggest that their detailed study may make a significant psychological contribution with regard to the understanding of movement planning processes. Of course, this point applies equally to anticipatory postural adjustments; thus, ground reaction forces might be used to index the anticipatory adjustments associated with the upper limb movement. However, difficulties arise in attempting this approach because the ground reaction forces are mechanically affected by the progress of the focal arm movement. Explicit models of whole body posture are being developed; however, these embody many assumptions and they are insensitive to subtle differences in dynamic loading of the arm. In contrast, the force used in grasping an object in a precision grip orthogonal to the line of motion is unaffected by the arm movement and so offers a direct window on the nervous system's plans for arm motion.

PART 5

The Sensorimotor Hand

The hand is richly endowed with cutaneous receptors, particularly in the glabrous (nonhairy) skin near the tips of the digits. The receptors transducing mechanical events send neural impulse patterns up the dorsal columns of the spinal cord to the primary somatosensory cortex area immediately posterior to the central sulcus. The somesthetic function of this area was established in the early part of this century by electrical stimulation. The stimulation produces paresthesias that are referred to specific peripheral loci. The best known work of this kind was, of course, that of Penfield and Rasmussen (1950) who dramatically demonstrated the particularly large area of cerebral cortical tissue devoted to the hand's sensory capacities. Lesions in this area can occur as a result of stroke and result in impaired appreciation of touch (e.g., poor 2-point discrimination, tactile localization).

Cortical processing of sensory information moves from simple topographic representation of local sensory events in the primary receiving areas toward the extraction of behaviorally relevant features based on inputs converging from several downstream sources. To the extent that salience and task dependence are determined by behavioral factors such as attention, motor set, and motivation, it is important that these factors can operate and be appropriately manipulated. An important step forward in studying the functions of primary sensory cortex was the move away from recording in anesthetized animals to the use of chronic single neuron recording techniques in behaving animals.

Chapter 16 by Chapman, Tremblay, and Ageranioti-Bélanger considers the response of single neurons in primary sensory cortex of monkeys trained to discriminate surface texture (an object attribute important, e.g., in determining the grip force required in precision grip). Work in their lab had previously shown that the activity of sensory cortical neurons is reduced (gated) if stimulation is applied when an animal is making a voluntary movement. Such gating may be viewed as reducing the overall information processing load. However, it is paradoxical in that discrimination performance is generally better if there is active movement of the digits over the surface. In a new study Chapman et al. found that an appreciable number of sensory cortical neurons are not subject to gating during an active texture discrimination task. They speculate that these might be the neurons particularly relevant to the texture decision.

As pointed out by Chapman et al. in their review, primary somatosensory cortex receives not only cutaneous input subserving the tactile sense modality but also proprioceptive inputs from joint receptors, Golgi tendon organs, and muscle spindles. In Chapter 17, Jones considers the integration of tactile and proprioceptive information into the perception of position and movement of the digits. She argues that, in combination with a sense of force, these factors are important components of manual dexterity. The evidence she reviews suggests that force perception arises centrally rather than peripherally, depending on neural correlates of descending efferent commands (corollary discharge).

Proprioceptive input and its possible role in shaping motor commands responsible for 8- to 10-Hz oscillations during slow digit movements are the focus of Chapter 18 by Vallbo and Wessberg. They show that muscle spindles respond to the fluctuations in movement kinematics in such movements. To determine whether such responses might drive the muscle through a reflex loop, Vallbo and Wessberg imposed unexpected mechanical perturbations of the digit during slow movements, which would have produced large and synchronized spindle responses. These resulted in smaller fluctuations in EMG than occurred during movement and so the authors conclude that the oscillation in efferent output has a central origin.

Unexpected loading of an object held in a precision grip leads to a reflex increase in grip force that helps stabilize the object with a latency of 70–80 ms, which is consistent with a supraspinal path involving the sensorimotor cortex. In contrast, grip force adjustment for predictable increase in load force takes place in parallel with the load force change and so may be described as anticipatory. In Chapter 19, Johansson describes sensory influences on the anticipatory control of grip force in lift and hold tasks. A core idea is that appropriate setting of the force used in precision grip (to frictional conditions and to object weight) operates on two time scales. On an extended time scale previous experience with the object allows default settings of motor commands—anticipatory parameter control. As the task evolves, somatosensory information may then modify ongoing behavior on a shorter time scale. Mechanical events, sampled under an intermittent control policy, are used to inform the CNS about the completion of successive phases of the task. These may then trigger preprogrammed corrective actions appropriate to the task phase. Simultaneously there is updating of the memory system for the anticipatory parameter control. Consideration of the underlying neural mechanisms and their maturation explains the relatively late development of precision grip in lifting tasks in children.

Perception of object weight, as for perception of force, is considered to be centrally mediated and depend on corollary discharge. In Chapter 20, Flanagan points out that the central drive to the muscles required in holding an object in a pinch grip (thumb and finger on each side) depends not only on its weight but also on the surface friction. A smooth object requires a greater grip force to generate a frictional force to overcome the load force due to gravity than does a rough object. If weight judgments do depend on corollary discharge, a smooth-sided object might be judged heavier than an object of the same weight but having rough sides. Flanagan reviews a series of experiments that support this view.

Weight is just one of a number of attributes that we extract by handling an object. Other aspects include texture, hardness, temperature, shape, and size (volume). Some of these attributes are available through vision (e.g., shape), but in other cases (e.g., hardness) mechanical interaction with the object is essential; for this the hand is ideally suited to extracting information by active exploration. Chapter 21 by Lederman and Klatzky brings this book to a close with a consideration of the perceptual functions of the hand. The authors turn around the concern of the preceding chapters (sensory influences on hand movement) and focus on hand movements and their influence on sensation, or more accurately, on the perception of object attributes. They document a number of purposive, stereotypical hand movement patterns (exploratory procedures) in terms of the information each makes available and the extent to which different exploratory procedures are compatible. These parameters affect the nature of goal-directed manual exploration and, in turn, can either enhance or constrain the quality of object perception.

16

Role of Primary Somatosensory Cortex in Active and Passive Touch

**C. ELAINE CHAPMAN, FRANÇOIS TREMBLAY,
AND STACEY A. AGERANIOTI-BÉLANGER**

1. INTRODUCTION

The sensory and motor capabilities of the hand in humans and other nonhuman primates are highly developed and together confer a special evolutionary advantage to primates whereby they can interact with, and control, their environment. But when the hand is used to manipulate objects, for example, during tool use, the sensory functions become secondary to the goals of the motor acts. Conversely, when the hand is used as a sensory organ, specifically for discriminative touch and stereognosis, then the movements become subsidiary to the goal of obtaining somesthetic feedback. Given this dual role for the hand, it is not surprising that there exist controls within the central nervous system that can regulate the quantity and quality of sensory feedback that gains access to the cortical centers that are intimately involved in these functions. Moreover, it should be stressed that the sensory and motor functions of the hand are intimately interrelated. Thus, primary somatosensory (S1) cortex is a major source of somatosensory input to motor cortex (E. G. Jones, Coulter, & Hendry, 1978), and as such is unique among the primary sensory receiving areas in having direct access to primary motor cortex. The importance of this projection is shown by the observation that discrete, reversible lesions of S1 cortex can produce profound deficits in the hand's manipulative abilities. Thus, inactivation of a portion of the S1 hand representation produced by microinjection of muscimol, an agonist of gamma-aminobutyric acid (GABA, an inhibitory neurotransmitter) results in the temporary loss of the ability to manipulate small objects (Hikosaka, Tanaka, Sakamoto, & Iwamura, 1985).

This chapter provides a brief overview of the major pathway conveying tactile information from the hand to S1 cortex, as well as the physiological properties of S1 cortex as revealed by detailed recording studies carried out in passive, and usually anesthetized, preparations. It is argued that the functional role of S1 cortex can be fully appreciated only when studied in relation to the various behavioral factors that modify the access of sensory information to the central processing centers, including movement, attention, motivation, motor set (or intention to move), and arousal. Movement is used as an example of one such behavioral factor. The importance of movement to touch is underlined by the observation that tactile perception is better when there is movement between the stimulus and the skin, as compared to when the same stimulus is applied statically (reviewed in Chapman, 1994). Paradoxically, however, voluntary movement also reduces the transmission of tactile inputs to S1 cortex, a phenomenon referred to as movement-related gating of sensory transmission, thereby limiting the amount of afferent input that must be processed at higher levels. This chapter describes the conditions under which tactile signals to S1 cortex are diminished, or gated, during movement. The sources of the gating signals, including both movement-related sensory feedback and central signals, are also described. Finally, the influence of the behavioral context within which stimuli are presented on movement-related gating is addressed, with special reference to the cortical representation of surface texture, as an example of one of the types of tactile inputs that S1 is involved in processing.

2. DORSAL COLUMN–MEDIAL LEMNISCAL PATHWAY

Discriminative touch is subserved by a variety of different cutaneous mechanoreceptors (see Table 1 for details), all innervated by large diameter, myelinated afferents (A Beta). As shown in Figure 1, cutaneous afferent signals from the limbs are relayed to S1 cortex through a pathway containing a minimum of three neurons. The primary afferents terminate in the periphery in close association with specialized receptor structures (Table 1), which, together with the anatomical location of the receptors, determine their rate of adaptation to mechanical stimuli (rapidly or slowly adapting). This chapter

TABLE I Cutaneous Mechanoreceptors Involved in Discriminative Touch

Physiological classification	Adaptation rate	Receptor type	RF size	Skin type	Location	Adequate stimulus
SAI	slow	Merkel cells	small	G + H	superficial	light, static touch
SAII	slow	Ruffini corpuscle	large	G + H	deep	moderate, static touch
RA/FAI	rapid	Meissner corpuscle	small	G	superficial	light dynamic touch (flutter)
PC/FAII	rapid	Pacinian corpuscle	large	G + H	deep	light, dynamic touch (vibration)
Hair	rapid	Hair follicles	large	H	receptor endings deep	light, dynamic touch

Note: FAI, fast adapting type I; FAII, fast adapting type II; G, glabrous skin; H, hairy skin; PC, Pacinian corpuscle; RA, rapidly adapting; RF, receptive field; SAI, slowly adapting type I; SAII, slowly adapting type II.

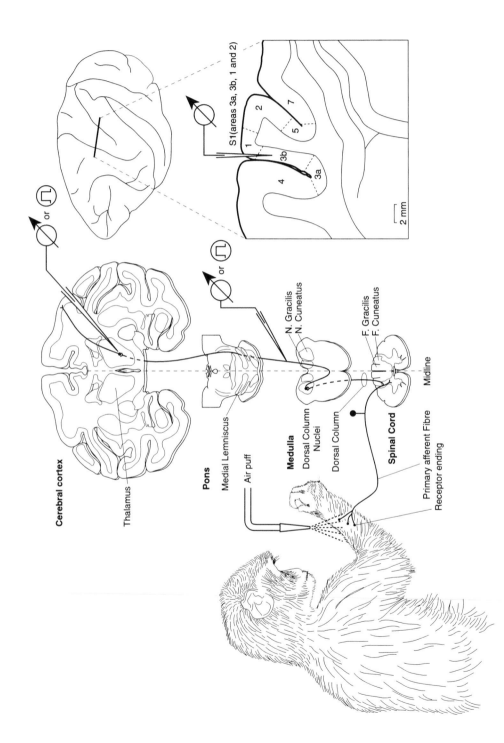

Cerebral cortex

Thalamus

Pons

Medial Lemniscus

Air puff

Medulla

Dorsal Column Nuclei

N. Gracilis
N. Cuneatus

Dorsal Column

F. Gracilis
F. Cuneatus

Spinal Cord

Primary afferent Fibre

Receptor ending

Midline

S1 (areas 3a, 3b, 1 and 2)

2

1

3b

4

3a

5

7

2 mm

follows the convention of referring to the two types of rapidly adapting mechanoreceptors found in the glabrous skin of the hand as RA (rapidly adapting) and PC (Pacinian) afferents. Johansson and colleagues have adopted another classfication (see Table 1), FAI (fast adapting type I, RA) and FAII (PC).

The region of skin from which a primary afferent can be activated by application of the appropriate stimulus, termed its receptive field, is characteristically small and circumscribed for those afferents that terminate in the superficial layers of the skin, SAI (slowly adapting type I) and RA units. Large, diffuse receptive fields are characteristic of units whose receptors are located in the deeper layers of the skin, SAII (slowly adapting type II) and PC units. Centrally, the axons of the primary cutaneous afferents enter the spinal cord through the dorsal roots and ascend in the ipsilateral dorsal column to the medulla; collaterals from the primary afferents synapse in the dorsal horn, and a proportion of these also project rostrally in the dorsal column. The fibers in the dorsal column synapse upon projection neurons in the dorsal column nuclei (cuneate nucleus for the upper limb, gracile nucleus for the lower limb), which in turn send their axons rostrally in the medial lemniscus. The latter fibers cross at the level of the medulla and ascend to the contralateral sensory thalamic relay nucleus, ventral posterior lateral nucleus, caudal division, (VPLc). Subsequently, thalamic relay neurons project through the internal capsule to S1 cortex, with area 3b receiving the densest thalamic projections.

3. ORGANIZATION OF PRIMARY SOMATOSENSORY CORTEX

The classical approach to studying the functional role of the S1 cortex, pioneered by Mountcastle (1957), has been to characterize the neuronal discharge properties of single cells in response to passively applied stimuli.

FIGURE 1 General organization of the dorsal column–medial lemniscal pathway that carries tactile information from the arm to the contralateral primary somatosensory (S1) cortex in the postcentral gyrus of the parietal lobe. Discriminative touch is subserved by large diameter, myelinated primary afferents that innervate a region of skin, generally ending in close association with specialized structures (hair follicles, various other accessory structures such as corpuscles). The primary afferents enter the spinal cord through the dorsal roots and ascend in the dorsal columns (fasciculus cuneatus for the arm; afferents from the leg ascend in the adjacent f. gracilis) to terminate in the dorsal column nuclei (nucleus cuneatus and n. gracilis for, respectively, afferents from the arm and leg). Primary afferents send a collateral into the dorsal horn to make synaptic contact, and a proportion of these neurons also project rostrally in the dorsal columns. From the dorsal column nuclei, second-order neurons project to the contralateral thalamus (nucleus VPLc) through the medial lemniscus. Third-order thalamic neurons subsequently project to the different subfields of S1 cortex. Also shown are the stimulating and recording sites for the results shown in Figure 2.

Such studies, largely performed in anesthetized animals, have led to a number of important observations. The following section is, unless otherwise noted, restricted to studies of the monkey S1 cortex.

First, as described by Mountcastle (1957) for the cat and T. P. S. Powell and Mountcastle (1959) for the monkey, the cerebral cortex is organized in vertical columns within which neurons have similar, although not necessarily identical, peripheral receptive fields. Neurons within an individual column also share the same modality preference, responding specifically to tactile or proprioceptive stimuli (e.g., joint manipulation).

Second, detailed mapping studies of the monkey brain have shown that there are multiple representations of the contralateral half of the body within the postcentral gyrus, with each of the four cytoarchitectonic zones (going from anterior to posterior: 3a, 3b, 1, and 2) containing a complete topographic representation of the body, with the head lateral and the foot medial (Kaas et al., 1979; Pons, Garraghty, Cusick, & Kaas, 1985). The cortical area devoted to each body part reflects the density of the peripheral innervation so that densely innervated regions, specifically the hand and the perioral region, have the largest cortical representations.

Third, the afferent inputs to each of the four cytoarchitectonic areas show some segregation as a function of modality, with tactile inputs predominating in areas 3b and 1, and proprioceptive inputs (joint and muscle) predominating in areas 3a and 2 (Iwamura, Tanaka, Sakamoto, & Hikosaka, 1983a, 1983b, 1985a, 1985b; T. P. S. Powell & Mountcastle, 1959). The hand representation in area 2 is an exception in that tactile inputs predominate here (Iwamura et al., 1985a, 1985b). Modality specificity is the general rule for individual S1 cortical neurons studied in awake monkeys (Hyvärinen & Poranen, 1978b; Iwamura et al., 1985a, 1985b). When convergence from skin and deep inputs is found, however, such neurons are particularly concentrated in the more posterior fields of S1 cortex. The latter studies may, however, have underestimated the frequency of convergence, since Zarzecki and Wiggin (1982) found that 50% of units recorded in cat S1 cortex showed evidence of cross-modal convergence when subthreshold inputs were also considered.

Fourth, for cutaneous mechanoreceptive units (i.e., those activated by touch), there is also a relative segregation as a function of the adaptation rate of the primary afferents (rapidly or slowly adapting: RA, SA), at least as regards the initial processing of the cutaneous signals. Thus, separate clusters or bands of RA and SA neurons are found in the middle, granular layers of area 3b (Sur, Wall, & Kaas, 1984), that is, the layers that are closest to the specific thalamocortical input. SA responses are infrequent in the supra- and infragranular layers of area 3b (Sur et al., 1984); likewise, SA neurons are uncommon in areas 1 and 2 (Ageranioti-Bélanger & Chapman, 1992; Chapman & Ageranioti-Bélanger, 1991; Paul, Merzenich, & Goodman, 1972).

Fifth, receptive field size varies gradually across S1 cortex, with the smallest receptive fields being found in area 3b (which in turn receives the heaviest thalamic projection), and larger receptive fields being found in areas 1 and 2 (Hyvärinen & Poranen, 1978b; Iwamura et al., 1983a, 1983b, 1985a, 1985b, 1993). These changes in receptive field size likely reflect increased convergence, and are consistent with the pattern of cortico-cortical connectivity (3b to 1 to 2) across S1 cortex.

Finally, the posterior region of S1 cortex, area 2, is particularly characterized by the presence of neurons with complex response properties that must represent the result of cortical integration of inputs from a variety of sources, as no individual peripheral afferent carries the necessary information. Thus, area 2 is characterized by the presence of direction-sensitive neurons, movement-sensitive units, orientation-selective units, and neurons receiving convergent tactile and proprioceptive inputs (Costanzo & Gardner, 1980; Hyvärinen & Poranen, 1978a; S. Warren, Hamalainen, & Gardner, 1986; Whitsel, Roppolo, & Werner, 1972). In addition, some neurons are insensitive to passively applied stimuli, and yet discharge in relation to active manipulation of specifically shaped objects (Iwamura et al., 1985b).

Thus, the picture that emerges is one of an orderly progression from relatively simple receptive field properties in area 3b (cutaneous) to more complex receptive field properties in the most posterior areas of the S1 hand representation.

4. FUNCTION OF PRIMARY SOMATOSENSORY CORTEX IN RELATION TO BEHAVIOR

Much of our knowledge of the organization of S1 cortex has been obtained in passive and anesthetized animals and, as recently forcefully argued by Kalaska (1994), this can give only a partial view of the functional role of S1 cortex, since there is a wealth of behavioral factors that can influence both the central processing of sensory stimuli and ultimately their perception. Thus, factors such as attention, motor set (or intention to move), motivation, and arousal need to be taken into consideration. Studies of the central neural mechanisms underlying tactile perception, therefore, need to be performed under conditions in which these various factors are controlled, ideally by having the subject engaged in a perceptual task.

One of the earliest studies of S1 cortex in animals engaged in a perceptual task (vibrotactile detection) was performed by Hyvärinen, Poranen, and Jokinen (1980). They compared neural responses to vibration when the monkeys were performing the task (relevant stimuli) to that seen when the same stimuli were applied outside of the context of the task (irrelevant stimuli). Their results indicated that attention toward the sensory stimuli augments neuronal responsiveness in the postcentral gyrus (16% of the cells in their sample). The attentional influences were differentially distributed across S1 cortex, being most common in area 1 (22%), intermediate in area 2 (15%), and least common in area 3b (8%). Furthermore, the effects were observed primarily in the supra- and infragranular cortical layers. Even more widespread attentional effects have more recently been reported by Hsiao, O'Shaughnessy, and Johnson (1993) who found that one half of their sample of area 3b and 1 units discharged more intensely in response to embossed letters scanned under the digit tips when the monkey was attending, and discriminating, the tactile stimuli as compared to when the animal was performing a visual detection task. The discrepancy between these two reports has yet to be reconciled, although other factors may have contributed to the results of Hyvärinen et al. (1980) including motor set and motivation. In this regard, R. J. Nelson (1988) reported that motor set strongly modulates neuronal responsiveness to vibration (serving as the movement cue) in areas 3a and 1, but not in area 3b. Many cells discharged more intensely when the stimulus served as a movement cue, as compared to when the motor response was withheld.

One factor missing from the preceding studies of attention was movement as the stimuli were passively applied to the immobile animal. We would like to argue that the central mechanisms underlying touch need to be evaluated in a situation that closely resembles the mode whereby touch is employed in everyday life, namely during movements that generate the tactile and proprioceptive inputs we evaluate and act upon. This dependence on movement is such that entire classes of cutaneous mechanoreceptors are specialized to signal transient, and not static, events (e.g., RA afferents from the glabrous skin of the hand, Pacinian afferents, and hair follicle afferents). Furthermore, slowly adapting mechanoreceptive afferents discharge much more intensely during dynamic as opposed to static stimulation. Finally, central cortical neurons in S1 cortex are rapidly adapting in nature (see above): outside of the middle cortical layers of area 3b, relatively few SA cutaneous units are encountered in S1 cortex. These three factors, together, likely contribute to explaining why tactile perception is better with dynamic stimuli than with static stimuli (reviewed in Chapman, 1994).

While the bias of S1 cortical neurons toward dynamic stimuli can be circumvented by applying various types of dynamic stimuli to the immobile limb (e.g., vibration), this approach is limited in that the motor apparatus is not concurrently engaged. The importance of this factor is twofold. First, simple introspection indicates that our richest sensory impressions come from active explorations (referred to here as active touch), be they searching for coins in your pocket or, in a child, putting each new object encountered in its mouth. Stimuli that are applied passively to the body surface (referred to here as passive touch), on the other hand, often elicit incomplete perceptions of the surround (J. J. Gibson, 1962). Second, movement brings an added complication to the central processing of tactile signals, since the act of movement itself can diminish, or gate, the transmission of tactile inputs to the parietal centers that are involved in their decoding (Chapman, Jiang, & Lamarre, 1988; reviewed in Chapman, 1994).

5. MOVEMENT-RELATED GATING OF CUTANEOUS AFFERENT TRANSMISSION

Figure 2 shows, in schematic form, the time course and degree of movement-related gating of cutaneous signals seen at three levels of the dorsal column–medial lemniscal pathway (recording sites shown in Figure 1): the medial

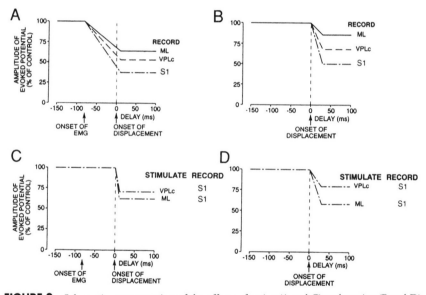

FIGURE 2 Schematic representation of the effects of active (A and C) and passive (B and D) elbow flexion on the amplitude of evoked responses recorded from three levels of the dorsal column–medial lemniscal pathway in response to peripheral (A and B) or central (C and D) stimulation. The stimulation and recording sites are shown, schematically, in Figure 1. Data taken from 16 experiments with 2 monkeys (Chapman et al., 1988) in which simultaneous recordings were made from S1 cortex and either VPLc thalamus or the medial lemniscus (receptive fields, located on the operant forearm, matched for each recording site). Short-latency SEPs were recorded in response to air puffs or percutaneous electrical stimuli applied to the center of the peripheral receptive field. Stimuli were applied at various intervals before, and after, the onset of movement. Data are plotted as a percent of the control values, at rest. Central stimulation was applied at the lemniscal or thalamic recording sites at which movement-related gating of SEPs had been demonstrated; this stimulation elicited short latency EPs in S1. Abbreviations: EMG, electromyographic activity; ML, medial lemniscus. (Reproduced with permission, and some modifications, from Chapman, 1994, Fig. 3, p. 563.)

lemniscus, VPLc thalamus, and S1 cortex (Chapman, 1994; Chapman et al., 1988). The experiments were carried out in monkeys trained to perform a rapid elbow flexion in response to an auditory cue. Microelectrodes were lowered into two of the structures, and sites with matching cutaneous receptive fields on the forearm were first identified. Sensory responsiveness was then assessed by applying a test stimulus (usually a brief air puff) to the center of the common peripheral receptive field (Figure 2, A and B). The air puff stimulus elicited a short latency somatosensory evoked potential (SEP, recorded with a microelectrode), representing the summed activity of the population of afferents (lemniscal recording site) or neurons (thalamic and cortical recording sites) activated by the stimulus. In order to evaluate the influence of movement on sensory responsiveness, test stimuli were applied either with the animal at rest or while the animal performed the motor task. In the latter case, the stimuli were timed so that they were applied either during the reaction time period, as the monkey prepared to initiate the movement, or during the actual movement.

As shown in Figure 2A, the amplitude of the cutaneous SEP declines about 60–80 ms prior to the onset of movement, and the time course is similar at all three levels of the lemniscal pathway (onset at about the same time as electromyographic [EMG] activity in the moving limb). In contrast, the degree of modulation gradually increases at each successive relay, being most pronounced at the cortical level. The latter reflects additional gating influences, and not simply an improvement in the signal-to-noise ratio, because cortical-evoked potentials in response to either lemniscal or thalamic stimulation (Figure 2C) are also decreased during movement. Both central and peripheral influences contribute to this suppression of cutaneous transmission. The decrease that precedes movement onset, and so precedes the arrival of any peripheral feedback from the moving limb, is likely central in origin, and appears to be exerted as early as the level of the first relay in the lemniscal pathway, that is, the dorsal column nuclei. The decrease that follows movement onset, on the other hand, is at least partly peripheral in origin (i.e. attributable to movement-related sensory feedback) because passive movements can produce a similar modulation of the thalamic and cortical SEPs (Figure 2B) and also of centrally evoked thalamic and cortical-evoked potentials (Figure 2D). A variety of peripheral mechanoreceptors are activated in relation to movements (see below), and so may have contributed to the observed modulation.

Movement, per se, is not essential to produce gating, since an equally powerful suppression of S1 cortical SEPs accompanies the dynamic phase of rapid, isometric contractions (Jiang, Lamarre, & Chapman, 1990). The modulation is nonspecific as regards the direction of the movement, flexion versus extension about the elbow, both as regards S1 cortical SEPs and single units recorded in areas 3b and 1 (Jiang, Chapman, & Lamarre, 1991; Jiang, Lamarre, & Chapman, 1990). Motor cortex appears to be a major source of the centrally originating gating signal, since intracortical microstimulation within area 4 also diminishes the amplitude of S1 cortical SEPs (Jiang, Chapman, & Lamarre, 1990). Moreover, these effects are topographically organized in a proximodistal fashion so that the modulation is directed toward gating cutaneous inputs from skin areas overlying or distal to the motor output. To summarize, movement produces a widespread and nonspecific reduction in the transmission of cutaneous inputs to S1 cortex, at least in a situation in which the test stimuli were externally generated and were behaviorally irrelevant for the performance of the motor task.

6. PERIPHERAL MECHANORECEPTIVE DISCHARGE IN RELATION TO DIGIT MOVEMENTS

As recently reviewed by L. A. Jones (1994; see also Jones, Chapter 17), a variety of different peripheral mechanoreceptors are engaged during movement, including both deep (muscle spindles and joint receptors) and cutaneous receptors. What follows is restricted to a discussion of the sensory feedback associated with digital movements.

Much of our knowledge of the discharge properties of peripheral mechanoreceptive afferents during digit movements comes from elegant experiments using the microneurographic technique to record from single afferent fibers in humans. As regards the discharge of proprioceptors, Burke, Gandevia, and Macefield (1988) reported that digital joint afferents are activated during passive digital movements, but often only at the extremes of movement. In addition, 50% of the digital joint units were activated by movements in opposite directions (bidirectional discharge). In contrast, muscle spindle afferents, localized in the intrinsic muscles of the hand, were also activated by passive movements but their discharge patterns were unidirectional, that is, they discharged specifically when their parent muscle was stretched, and fell silent when the muscle was shortened.

In relation to active movements, the discharge pattern of muscle spindle afferents, being under the control of fusimotor activity, cannot easily be predicted from the location of the receptors relative to the active muscles (see Vallbo and Wessberg, Chapter 18, for a discussion of fusimotor discharge during finger movements). Fusimotor discharge may compensate for muscle shortening during movement to maintain spindle discharge under certain conditions (e.g., slow movements or contractions made against an external load), but not under other conditions (rapid, unloaded movements) (Burke, Hagbarth, & Lofstedt, 1978; Hulliger, Nordh, & Vallbo, 1982). More recently, Prochazka

(1989) has argued that, in fact, the fusimotor system acts not simply to compensate for muscle shortening, but rather has a more dynamic role in that it may allow adjustments of length and velocity feedback depending on the state of the animal. In particular, he suggested that fusimotor activity is low at rest and is increased in, for example, novel situations (exploratory movements or learning new motor tasks) or in situations demanding high levels of attention or arousal. Thus, depending on the context or goal of a particular motor act, sensory feedback would be appropriately scaled up or down. Such a gain control system, acting through efferent motor pathways, may also be applicable to feedback from joint receptors, since joint afferent discharge is modulated by the activation of muscles inserting into the joint capsule (Grigg, 1975). While much of this gain control could be accomplished by controlling receptor sensitivity in the periphery, it is possible that controls over transmission within the central nervous system, as seen for the gating of cutaneous transmission, also contribute (e.g., Tsumoto, Nakamura, & Iwama, 1975).

The discharge of cutaneous units, on the other hand, which do not have an efferent control system to modulate their sensitivity, is more predictable during movement. Two approaches have been taken to studying their discharge during movement, using either unrestricted, free movements of the digits, or in relation to the isometric precision grip.

Hulliger, Nordh, Thelin, and Vallbo (1979) reported that all four types of low-threshold cutaneous mechanoreceptive afferents found in the glabrous skin of the hand are activated during active digit movements (77% of their sample), with PC units being the most sensitive, followed by SAII, SAI, and RA afferents. They also stressed that, while all responsive units were activated during movement, only a small proportion of the SA units (mainly SAII units) also discharged during static postures. SA afferents were also more likely to be directionally specific in their discharge, in contrast to the nonspecific activation of PC and RA afferents. Edin and Abbs (1991) and Edin (1992) have argued that the discharge pattern of SAII afferents contributes information about both digit position and the direction of digit movement. In relation to passive movements, Burke et al. (1988) reported very similar patterns of discharge to those seen with active movements.

Johansson and his collaborators (reviewed in Johansson & Cole, 1994; Johansson & Westling, 1991) have characterized the discharge properties of cutaneous mechanoreceptors in the human glabrous skin during the performance of the precision grip, a motor task in which subjects are requested to grasp, lift, and release an object using the thumb and index finger. Their results indicate that the SAI, FAI (or RA), and FAII (or PC) afferents all show transient increases in discharge at the onset and end of the grip. During the static phase of the grip, ongoing activity can be seen in both SAI and SAII afferents.

Although there is considerable cutaneous feedback in association with active movement, this feedback is subject to controls during movement as discussed above, the controls being exerted within the central nervous system rather than peripherally. Cutaneous feedback to higher centers could be selectively enhanced or suppressed by, respectively, inactivating or activating these gating controls (Prochazka, 1989).

7. SOMATOSENSORY CORTICAL DISCHARGE IN RELATION TO DIGIT MOVEMENTS

Several studies have examined the discharge of S1 cortical neurons during movements about more proximal arm joints, including the shoulder and elbow, in relation to their receptive field properties (e.g., Cohen, Prud'homme, & Kalaska, 1994; Prud'homme and Kalaska, 1994; Soso & Fetz, 1980). Their results indicate that S1 cortical neurons receiving proprioceptive, and to a lesser extent tactile, inputs are activated during limb movements, in a manner consistent with their playing a role in signaling information about the direction of limb movements and limb posture. Less is known about the discharge of S1 cortical units in relation to digit movements. Inase, Mushiake, Shima, Aya, and Tanji (1989) reported that units in S1 hand cortex are activated during digit flexion movements, and that their discharge generally follows the onset of movement (defined as the onset of EMG activity in the digit flexor muscles). They suggested that the task-related modulation was peripheral in origin (mean onset 46 ms after EMG onset, an average of 86 ms later than motor cortical [area 4] discharge in one of the same monkeys). Unfortunately, no attempt was made to correlate the receptive field properties of their sample with the task-related discharge.

More recently, Wannier et al. (1991) recorded from S1 cortical neurons during an isometric precision grip task involving the thumb and index finger. The majority of units activated in the task received afferent input from peripheral mechanoreceptors (cutaneous or, less frequently, proprioceptive), and the timing of their discharge was such that activity began at or after the onset of the force increase. Furthermore, S1 cortex neuronal discharge covaried with grip force, in a manner consistent with their discharge reflecting feedback from cutaneous, and possibly deep, mechanoreceptors activated during the performance of the task. To summarize, S1 cortical neurons are activated during movements, and the pattern of discharge of both deep and cutaneous units most likely reflects feedback from peripheral mechanoreceptors activated during the course of the movement. While several authors have argued that some S1 cortical discharge is a reflection of the central motor command (corollary discharge) (e.g., Fromm & Evarts, 1982; R. J. Nelson,

1988; Soso & Fetz, 1980), data from other studies of S1 cortical timing (above) and of S1 cortical discharge properties subsequent to limb deafferentation (Bioulac & Lamarre, 1979) both argue against a central source being responsible for the S1 cortical movement-related discharge.

8. SOMATOSENSORY CORTICAL DISCHARGE DURING ACTIVE TOUCH

In the studies reviewed in the previous section, the digital movements were stereotyped, and performed within the context of a motor task. One of the first studies of a more natural type of movement, mimicking the exploratory movements made during active touch, was that by Darian-Smith and colleagues (I. Darian-Smith, Goodwin, Sugitani, & Heywood, 1985; I. Darian-Smith, Sugitani, Heywood, Karita, & Goodwin, 1982). They trained monkeys to scan their digit tips back and forth over textured surfaces (periodic gratings) within the context of a visuomotor tracking task. All of their units with a digital cutaneous receptive field were activated during the scanning movements, and some of the units varied their discharge as a function of the texture of the underlying surface, discharge frequency increasing when coarser gratings were presented. The pattern of finger movement was, however, incompletely represented within the cortical discharge patterns, with many cells being active only during a part of the cycle of movement (specifically at the turning points), in contrast to the discharge patterns of cutaneous afferents in response to similar sinusoidal movements of gratings (A. W. Goodwin & Morley, 1987). They concluded that S1 cortical neurons do not unambiguously represent surface features, such as texture, because, as in the periphery, discharge also covaries with force and velocity.

More recently, investigators have recorded the discharge of S1 cortical neurons during active touch within the context of texture discrimination tasks. Data from this laboratory (Ageranioti-Bélanger & Chapman, 1992; Chapman & Ageranioti-Bélanger, 1991) and from Sinclair and Burton (1991) indicate that a substantial proportion of S1 cortical neurons sensitive to cutaneous input from the hand (areas 3b, 1, and 2) are activated during active touch, and that many of these signal differences in the scanned textures (respectively, smooth vs. rough, and periodic gratings with varying spatial periods). Furthermore, while the discharge of many of these neurons covaries with peripheral factors such as the velocity of movement or the force exerted on the scanned surfaces, a substantial proportion of the texture-related units are insensitive to variations in, for example, the velocity of movement. Both we and Sinclair and Burton argued that the extraction of an unambiguous texture-related signal must reflect the result of cortical processing, which removes the component of the signal related to movement kinematics and kinetics. To do this, information related to the physical parameters of the movement needs to be available centrally in order to interpret the neural code relayed to S1 cortex, since peripheral mechanoreceptors do not themselves signal texture independently of velocity and force (e.g., I. Darian-Smith & Oke, 1980). A variety of signals might be employed for this feature extraction process, including corollary discharge from the precentral motor areas. As discussed above, however, it is unclear if the latter information is relayed to S1 cortex since S1 cortical discharge in relation to arm movements disappears following limb deafferentation (Bioulac & Lamarre, 1979). Another source of information related to the temporal features of the movement might be a special class of non-texture-related cutaneous units that were encountered throughout S1 cortex and signaled, precisely, the onset and end of movement (Ageranioti-Bélanger & Chapman, 1992; Chapman & Ageranioti-Bélanger, 1991).

9. GATING OF SOMATOSENSORY CORTICAL DISCHARGE IN RELATION TO ACTIVE TOUCH

It is reasonable, however, to ask whether the gating controls over cutaneous afferent transmission to S1 cortex seen during conditioned limb movements also limit the access of cutaneous inputs that are behaviorally relevant. We investigated this by comparing the discharge of neurons recorded during the performance of the texture discrimination task (active touch) with that seen when the digit tips were passively displaced over the surfaces outside of the context of the task, that is, in the absence of behavioral significance (Ageranioti-Bélanger & Chapman, 1992; Chapman & Ageranioti-Bélanger, 1991). In this case, one of the potential sources of the gating signal, movement-related peripheral feedback, was similar, although obviously any centrally originating gating signals linked to the performance of the motor task, including the central motor command (Jiang, Chapman, & Lamarre, 1990), were absent as the monkeys were passive. While many neurons continued to signal the difference in texture even when this was no longer behaviorally relevant, a proportion of neurons localized in area 1 failed to discharge when the inputs were no longer behaviorally relevant. It was suggested that attentional influences likely enhanced the neural responses in area 1 to tactile inputs during the performance of the texture discrimination task, although this conclusion was only tentative since we could not rule out the possibility that other factors (motivation, motor set) may also have contributed. Such an observation is, nevertheless, consistent with the notion that some tactile feedback is spared from gating controls when the signal is behaviorally relevant, and so is consistent with Prochazka's (1989) suggestion of state-dependent gain controls over sensory transmission during movement.

A second approach to the question of gating of relevant inputs was taken by examining the patterns of discharge elicited during the performance of the task of active texture discrimination as a function of the location of the peripheral receptive field, that is, whether or not the cutaneous field included the digit tips used to scan the surfaces. As shown in Figure 3, these two sources of peripheral feedback were clearly treated differently within S1 cortex. Regardless of the location of the receptive field, the majority of area 3b units showed a pattern of increased discharge during the task. On going caudally within S1 cortex, the proportion of units with a receptive field on the digit tips used to scan the surfaces (A) that showed an increase in discharge during the task grew, while the number of unmodulated units declined correspondingly. The opposite trends were seen for units with a cutaneous field not in contact with the discriminanda (B): the proportion of unmodulated units increased in the caudal fields, largely at the expense of a reduction in the proportion of units showing a pattern of increased task-related discharge. These results suggest that the transmission of information across S1 cortex is selective, with relevant inputs (A) being transmitted on for further processing, and irrelevant inputs (B) being suppressed.

The question remains, however, as to whether or not movement gates the transmission of behaviorally relevant tactile signals to S1 cortex. We have addressed this in two ways. First, we found that S1 cortical neurons with appropriate digital receptive fields generally discharged less during the task of active texture discrimination than they did in response to optimal (passive) stimulation of their receptive field outside of the context of the task (Ageranioti-Bélanger & Chapman, 1992; Chapman & Ageranioti-Bélanger, 1991). While this observation suggested that there is indeed gating during active touch, it should be mentioned that the stimuli were not identical in the two situations (optimal, passive stimulation = best response to hand-held probes applied to the peripheral receptive field).

In order to examine responses to identical stimuli, with and without active movement, we have subsequently devised a second behavioral apparatus, essentially a motor-driven drum to which the textured surfaces were affixed, which allows us to present the textured surfaces to the passive animal. Monkeys were then trained to discriminate changes in surface texture (rough vs. smooth) using either active touch or passive touch. While the results are only preliminary so far, we have found that approximately 40% of the S1 cortical units with appropriate digital receptive fields showed evidence of movement-related gating, that is, they signaled the difference in texture during passive touch (no movement) but not during active touch (movement) (Chapman & Ageranioti, 1991). The gating controls are, however, selective in that approximately one quarter of the units signaled the differences in texture equally well during active and passive touch. Thus, it appears that self-generated, and behaviorally relevant, cutaneous feedback is subject to

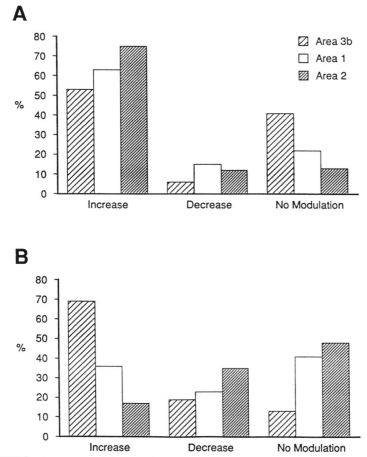

FIGURE 3   Comparison of the sign of modulation shown by cutaneous units in areas 3b, 1, and 2 during performance of an active texture discrimination task as a function of the location of their receptive field. (A) The field included one or more of the digit tips scanned over the surfaces (*n* = 113). (B) The field did not include the scanned digit tips, but was instead located elsewhere on the digits, hand or distal forearm (*n* = 61). (Reproduced with permission from Chapman, 1994, Fig. 5, p. 567.)

movement-related gating controls. Nevertheless, the proportion of neurons that were spared from gating controls during active touch, that is, units that signaled the difference in texture equally well with active and passive touch, was substantially higher (25%) than in our previous study of gating of S1 cortex unitary responses to irrelevant air puff stimuli applied to the forearm or hand during the performance of conditioned elbow movements (10%, Jiang et al., 1991). This suggests that the gating controls were selectively inactivated for some inputs, and supports the hypothesis of the existence of state-related gain controls over the transmission of cutaneous feedback (Prochazka, 1989). This notion receives further support from a recent report from Knecht, Kunesch, Buchner, and Freund (1993) who found that, although the earliest cortical SEPs (up to 25 ms) to median nerve stimulation in humans were diminished during movement (i.e., movement-related gating), an additional negative wave, peaking at 28 ms, appeared during movement or passive tactile stimulation and became most pronounced during active exploratory movements of the hand. They suggested that this new wave reflected the preactivation or "gating-in" of a cortical area, localized to the central sulcus, in association with exploratory movements.

10. CONCLUSIONS

The results of studies of the transmission of tactile inputs to S1 cortex undertaken in a variety of different experimental conditions indicate that even behaviorally relevant tactile inputs to S1 cortex are subject to movement-related gating controls. These controls are, however, differential with some inputs being spared and so faithfully transmitted to S1 cortex. Moreover, gating of relevant inputs is much less widespread than for behaviorally irrelevant inputs. There is a further selection of inputs within S1 cortex, so that tactile signals that are behaviorally relevant, but not those that are irrelevant, are passed on to higher centers, that is, the more posterior S1 cortical fields, for subsequent processing. In addition, influences such as attention, motor set, and motivation may all modify S1 cortical sensory responsiveness.

The existence of movement-related gating controls over behaviorally relevant cutaneous inputs to S1 cortex may appear to be paradoxical and difficult to reconcile with the highly refined tactile abilities associated with active touch. To put things into perspective, however, much of the feedback generated during tactile discrimination with active touch may not contribute directly to sensory perception. Some feedback clearly provides important information about the execution of the exploratory movement. Yet other feedback may be completely irrelevant within the context of a simple discrimination between rough and smooth surfaces, and yet could become relevant within another context, for example, resolving the spatial representation of scanned elements into Braille symbols. Thus, depending on the demands of a particular perceptuomotor task, movement-related gating controls could be reoriented to permit the transmission of relevant feedback and to suppress unnecessary or predictable feedback. Such an approach would optimize the functioning of the central processing centers. Continuing along this line of reasoning, it is interesting to speculate that those neurons whose inputs were spared from gating influences in our experiments with texture discrimination might have been those most directly involved in the sensory decision process, discriminating between rough and smooth textures.

Given that sensory feedback to motor centers is important for guiding movement and given that S1 cortex is an important source of sensory feedback for motor control, it is suggested that the available feedback must be interpreted in the light of the conditions under which it was obtained. Moreover, it should not be forgotten that the motor strategies employed during active touch may, in a variety of ways, optimize sensory feedback by, for example, reducing movement speed at critical moments in an exploratory movement and so minimizing gating influences (Chapman et al., 1988), or by optimally orienting the digits so as to bring the most sensitive skin areas into contact with the object being explored.

ACKNOWLEDGMENTS

The authors thank Dr. Trevor Drew for helpful comments on the manuscript. We also thank Daniel Cyr, Giovanni Filosi, and Claude Gauthier for the preparation of the illustrations. This research was supported by grants from the Medical Research Council of Canada and the Université de Montréal to CEC. C.E. Chapman was supported by a scholarship from the Fonds de la recherche en santé du Québec (FRSQ). F. Tremblay is supported by funds from the University of Ottawa and the Université de Montréal. S.A. Ageranioti-Bélanger was supported by the FRSQ, the Physiotherapy Foundation of Canada, and the Alberta Heritage Foundation.

17

Proprioception and Its Contribution to Manual Dexterity

LYNETTE JONES

1. INTRODUCTION

The proprioceptive or kinesthetic sensory system is involved in processing information that arises both centrally and peripherally about limb movements, changes in limb position, and muscle force (Clark & Horch, 1986; L. A. Jones, 1986; P. B. C. Matthews, 1988). This information is used to control limb movements and to correct for any disturbance encountered during the course of a movement (Hulliger, 1984). In the absence of proprioceptive information, the ability of human subjects to perform a variety of fine manual tasks is impaired (Rothwell et al., 1982), and so it is assumed that normal proprioceptive abilities are a prerequisite for such tasks. As a corollary, it may be hypothesized that the ability to perform highly skilled manual activities is associated with superior proprioceptive capacities. Microsurgery provides an interesting arena to explore this relation, because of its high-precision requirements in terms of the amplitudes of the movements generated and the forces exerted at the tool–tissue interface. In this context, the limiting factors on performance are not those of the proprioceptive system, as defined in terms of thresholds, since movements can be made using an operating microscope that cannot be seen under normal viewing conditions nor perceived kinesthetically. In this chapter psychophysical studies of the perception of limb position, movement, and muscle force are reviewed and then the relation between these studies and manual dexterity, as defined by microsurgical skill, is considered.

2. SENSORY BASIS OF PROPRIOCEPTION

Much of the research on proprioception has been directed toward elucidating which peripheral receptors in the muscles, skin, and joints give rise to kinesthetic sensations. The approach usually adopted to address this question involves eliminating input from one of the receptor populations, for example, by disengaging or reversibly paralyzing the muscles to eliminate input from muscle receptors or by anesthetizing the skin or joints, and then measuring the changes in perception that occur following this temporary loss of sensory input (Clark, Burgess, & Chapin, 1986; Clark, Burgess, Chapin, & Lipscomb, 1985; Ferrell & Smith, 1988; Gandevia & McCloskey, 1976). Sensory performance in the hand is assessed using a number of different tasks including detecting the direction of movements passively imposed on a finger (Clark et al., 1986; Taylor & McCloskey, 1990), matching the positions or forces produced by two corresponding fingers on the left and right hands (Ferrell & Smith, 1988; Gandevia & Kilbreath, 1990), and indicating the static position of a finger by positioning a finger silhouette in the same perceived location (Ferrell & Craske, 1992).

One feature of research in proprioception that distinguishes it from work on the tactile sensory modality (Johnson & Hsiao, 1992) is the absence of the tradition of coupling neurophysiological with psychophysical experimentation (with some exceptions, e.g., Clark, Grigg, & Chapin, 1989). This situation no doubt reflects the considerable problems associated with interpreting peripheral neural activity from muscle spindle receptors whose discharge rates are a complex function of muscle length, the velocity with which the muscle is shortening or lengthening, and the activity of the fusimotor (gamma) system (Burgess, Clark, Simon, & Wei, 1982; Hulliger, 1984).

2.1 Muscle Receptors

Over the past twenty years a consistent body of data has emerged that indicates that no one source of afferent information can be excluded from contributing to the proprioceptive capacities of the human hand (Ferrell & Smith, 1988; P. B. C. Matthews, 1988). The results from early experiments on the effects of muscle tendon vibration on the perception of limb movement clearly demonstrated the importance of feedback from muscle spindle receptors to the perception of limb movement (G. M. Goodwin, McCloskey, & Matthews, 1972). More recent studies have shown that cutaneous and joint receptors also provide kinesthetic information (Clark et al., 1986; Ferrell, Gandevia, & McCloskey, 1987; Macefield, Gandevia, & Burke, 1990), and that optimal proprioceptive performance is achieved when all sources of information (i.e., skin, joint, and muscle) are available (Ferrell & Smith, 1988; Gandevia & McCloskey, 1976).

The results from the initial experiments of G. M. Goodwin et al. (1972) in which the movement illusions evoked by vibration of a muscle tendon in an immobilized and unseen arm were described, led to a reconsideration of the role of muscle receptors in proprioception and a complete reversal of the classic viewpoint that had emphasized the importance of joint receptors to proprioception. The movement illusions were attributed to the intense levels of activity in muscle spindle receptors, which were interpreted centrally as indicating that the muscle was being stretched (for more details of spindle function, see Vallbo and Wessberg's Chapter 18). The subsequent finding that the velocity of the illusory movement evoked by vibration was dependent on both the frequency (Roll & Vedel, 1982) and amplitude (Clark, Matthews, & Muir, 1979) of stimulation was further support for this interpretation.

These results have been replicated and extended in numerous experiments over the past twenty years (see L. A. Jones, 1988, for a review). Two findings of particular interest have emerged from this research. First, during vibration a limb can be perceived to be in an anatomically impossible position, which suggests that perceptually the limits of the sense of position are not set by the anatomical constraints of joint excursion, and that the cortical sensory centers will extrapolate beyond previous experience to interpret incoming afferent signals (Craske, 1977; Lackner & Taublieb, 1983). Second, under degraded viewing conditions, that is, in the dark or without full view of the limb, the visual system interprets these illusory movements as if they are real movements of the limb. Lackner and Taublieb (1984) reported that when subjects are asked to fixate on the position of their unseen index finger during vibration of the biceps tendon, they lower the direction of their gaze. If a light is now affixed to the restrained hand, subjects not only experience movement of their unseen, stationary arm but also see the target light move in the direction of the perceived movement of the arm, even though they have continued to fixate on the stationary target (Lackner & Levine, 1978). With full view of the limb, however, vibration-induced movement illusions disappear, indicating that visual input can dominate proprioceptive signals (G. M. Goodwin et al., 1972). These findings suggest that the sense of limb position is not simply derived from the activity of modality-specific topographic maps, but rather results from interactions between the sensory representations of different body parts that are in turn cross-referenced with representations in other afferent domains such as vision (Lackner & Taublieb, 1984). In addition, they indicate that visual input does not predominate over proprioceptive input under some viewing conditions, and that there is a two-way interaction between these sensory systems.

2.2 Skin and Joint Receptors

The precise contribution of signals arising from joint and cutaneous receptors in the hand to proprioception remains contentious (Proske, Schaible, & Schmidt, 1988). The results from a number of studies do indicate that following a digital nerve block in which both joint and cutaneous afferent input is eliminated, but the muscles in the forearm controlling flexion and extension movements of the fingers are unaffected, there is a loss of proprioceptive acuity (Ferrell & Smith, 1988, 1989; Gandevia, Hall, McCloskey, & Potter, 1983). This is evident in the elevated movement detection thresholds recorded during anesthesia (Ferrell et al., 1987; Gandevia et al., 1983), which are illustrated in Figure 1, and in the increased errors observed when subjects are asked to match the position of the index finger using the contralateral

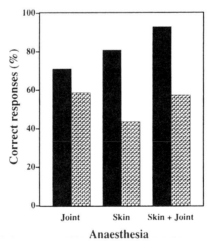

FIGURE 1   The effect of anesthetizing the distal interphalangeal joint of the middle finger (10 subjects), the skin on the tip of the index finger (6 subjects), and both the joint and skin surrounding the distal interphalangeal joint of the middle finger (8 subjects) on the ability to detect 5- (skin anesthesia) or 10-degree (joint and combined anesthesia) displacements imposed on the joint. The solid bars are the results obtained under control conditions (preanesthesia) and the hatched bars are the results during anesthesia. (The data on the effects of joint or skin anesthesia are taken from Clark et al., 1986, and Clark et al., 1989, respectively, and those for combined skin and joint anesthesia are from Gandevia et al., 1983.)

anesthetized finger (Ferrell & Smith, 1989), or to match the position of an anesthetized finger to that of a finger silhouette (Ferrell & Craske, 1992). In the latter experiments, the finger was perceived to be at intermediate joint positions, as if the absence of afferent feedback, and in particular joint receptor activity, was interpreted as indicating that the finger was in the position it would normally occupy for that level of afferent discharge, namely its midrange of movement (Ferrell & Craske, 1992). In the absence of joint and cutaneous feedback, subjects have an awareness of finger position that is described as being clear and sharp, but is in fact incorrect. It is still possible for subjects to match the position of the finger joints and to detect movements under these conditions, however, which shows that muscle receptors are an important source of proprioceptive information. Nevertheless, the proprioceptive impairment evident during cutaneous and joint anesthesia indicates that the perception of finger position does depend on afferent input from receptors other than those in the muscle.

When the proximal interphalangeal joint of the index finger is anesthetized by an intra-articular injection of a local anesthetic, the ability to match the position of the joint deteriorates. The greatest errors are associated with perceiving the location of the finger when it is positioned near the extremes of its range of joint motion (Ferrell & Smith, 1989). This is consistent with electrophysiological recordings of the activity of isolated afferent fibers from finger joints in human subjects, which indicate that over 80% of these fibers discharge at the extremes of the range of joint movement and a much smaller percentage are active when the joint is held in intermediate positions (Burke et al., 1988). The errors in matching finger positions during joint anesthesia are, however, less than those found following both joint and skin anesthesia (Ferrell & Smith, 1988, 1989).

In contrast to the results of Ferrell and Smith (1989), Clark et al. (1986) reported that anesthesia of the proximal interphalangeal joint of the index finger had no effect on subjects' ability to detect 5-degree displacements of the finger from a midrange location. However, they did note a significant reduction in the ability to detect 10-degree displacements made near maximum extension following joint anesthesia (see Figure 1). The discrepancy between the results of Ferrell and Smith (1989) and Clark et al. (1986) may reflect the different tasks assigned to subjects, one of which assessed the sense of position (following movements that were above threshold; 22 deg/s) and the other the perception of movement. In the latter situation subjects were simply required to indicate verbally whether the finger had changed position relative to a starting position (i.e., say higher, lower, or no change). Inputs from muscle and skin receptors appear to be sufficient to perform this task, particularly when the joint is positioned in its midrange of movement, as was the case in this experiment. Matching the position of two fingers is a more difficult task, and subjects probably used movement cues as a source of information about the position of the joint. Edin (1990) has shown that joint afferents in the radial nerve respond during finger movements, although their responses are dramatically affected by muscle activity. The finding that the ability to match the position of two fingers was affected by the velocity of the displacement of the reference finger during anesthesia, but not under normal conditions (Ferrell & Milne, 1989), is consistent with the idea that joint receptor activity was used to provide information about the amplitude of a finger movement, and hence the position of a joint. Nevertheless, studies of the proprioceptive abilities of subjects with prosthetic replacements of the metacarpophalangeal joint in the hand suggest that whatever information is conveyed by joint afferent activity is adequately duplicated by other sensory channels. After surgical removal of the joint, and presumably its complement of receptors, these subjects are not impaired when making judgments about the amplitude of finger movements (Kelso, Holt, & Flatt, 1980) or their direction (Cross & McCloskey, 1973).

Signals arising from cutaneous receptors provide an important input to the central nervous system that can be used both to signal the movement of a limb and to interpret position and movement signals arising from other sources. Edin and Abbs (1991) have shown that cutaneous mechanoreceptors in the dorsal skin of the human hand respond to finger movements that involve deformation of the skin overlying a joint, and typically discharge in response to movements made by several joints. In the absence of such movement signals, Clark et al. (1986) have reported that the ability to detect movements of the proximal interphalangeal (PIP) joint of the index finger is impaired, as shown in Figure 1. The effects of cutaneous anesthesia are not limited to the skin surface overlying the PIP joint, however, but also occur when the skin on the fingertip or the thumb is anesthetized, which is consistent with Edin and Abbs's (1991) data showing that cutaneous mechanoreceptors can respond to skin stimulation applied 70–80 mm away from the actual location of the receptors.

The above results indicate that the influence of signals arising from cutaneous receptors on the perception of movement is not limited to those originating in the skin overlying the joint being moved. These effects appear to be limited to the perception of movement, in that eliminating afferent input from the skin of fingers adjacent to a reference finger has no effect on the ability to match the position of the joint (Ferrell & Craske, 1992; Ferrell & Smith, 1988). However, if the skin of the matching finger itself is anesthetized, then its position is not perceived accurately, and subjects make errors in aligning the positions of the reference and matching digits (Ferrell & Smith, 1988). The largest errors in this situation occur at the extremes of joint motion where lateral skin stretch may be assumed to be maximal. This latter result argues against the idea that cutaneous receptors provide a nonspecific facilitatory input to the proprioceptive sensory system, that is, that they are used only to enhance the effects of other kinesthetic inputs (Marsden, Merton, & Morton, 1977), and instead suggests that for the hand, cutaneous inputs can provide fairly specific information about joint movements.

3. SENSE OF LIMB POSITION AND MOVEMENT

In many of the psychophysical experiments described above there was no attempt to distinguish between the sense of limb position and movement. In some studies (e.g., Ferrell & Smith, 1988) subjects made judgments of limb position after a perceptible movement was imposed on the joint, and in these situations it is not possible to estimate how much their perceptions rely on information about movement as opposed to positional cues. Although a change in the position of a limb is usually experienced as a consequence of limb movement, Clark and his colleagues have shown that it is possible to dissociate these two aspects of proprioception experimentally by imposing extremely slow movements (i.e., 0.004 deg/s) on a joint (Clark et al., 1985, 1986, 1989). Using this procedure, it has been shown that subjects can make independent judgments of the static position and movement of a limb (Clark et al, 1985), and that in contrast to the sense of movement, the sense of position is not influenced by the velocity of the limb movement. As the velocity of a movement imposed on the proximal interphalangeal joint of the index finger decreases from 20 deg/s to 0.5 deg/s, the error in matching its position increases by only 2 degrees (Ferrell & Milne, 1989). In contrast, the threshold (70%) for detecting movement imposed on the distal interphalangeal joint of the middle finger increases from approximately 1 degree at 80 deg/s to 8 degrees at 1.25 deg/s (Gandevia et al., 1983; Hall & McCloskey, 1983). The relation between angular velocity and movement detection thresholds and position matching accuracy is illustrated in Figure 2. Movement velocity influences not only the threshold for detecting a movement but also the perceived amplitude of the movement, with slower movements being perceived as larger than faster movements of the same amplitude (Hollins & Goble, 1988).

It appears that muscle afferent input is very important for detecting changes in static limb position during slow movements of less than 10 deg/min, and that during faster movements feedback from receptors in the joints and skin can compensate for a loss in muscle afferent input, which occurs, for example, when the middle finger is positioned so that the distal interphalangeal joint is effectively disengaged from its muscular attachments (Gandevia & McCloskey, 1976). As the velocity of a movement increases, a

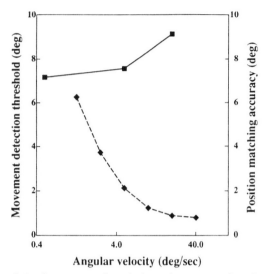

FIGURE 2   The relation between angular velocity and movement detection thresholds (70% correct responses) measured from the distal interphalangeal joint of the middle finger (dashed line). Both extension and flexion movements were imposed randomly on the finger. (The data are taken from Hall and McCloskey, 1983.) The relation between angular velocity and the accuracy with which the position of the proximal interphalangeal joint of the index finger is matched by the contralateral index finger is also shown (solid line). (These data are from Ferrell and Milne, 1989.)

change in limb position can be inferred from sensations of movement (Clark et al., 1985; Ferrell et al., 1987). These findings suggest that movement and position are encoded independently and that movement sensations result from the activation of a number of receptor types, including those found in muscles, skin, and probably the joints.

4. SENSE OF FORCE

The perceived amplitude of forces generated by muscles does not appear to be based on peripheral afferent activity arising from muscle spindle and tendon organ receptors, but seems to be derived from neural correlates (corollary discharges) of the descending efferent command (L. A. Jones, 1986; McCloskey, 1981). This is in contrast to the peripherally based perceptions of limb movement and position, but should not be interpreted as dismissing a contribution from peripheral receptors, such as the Golgi tendon organs, to the awareness of muscle force. Afferent input is required to provide a signal that the force generated by the muscle is adequate for the task being performed (Gandevia & McCloskey, 1978). In addition, reflex inputs from joint, muscle, and skin receptors in the hand can inhibit or facilitate motoneurons in the spinal cord and in so doing influence the magnitude of the centrally generated motor command, and hence the perceived amplitude of weights supported by the hand (Aniss, Gandevia, & Milne, 1988; see Flanagan, Chapter 20, for a discussion of the effects of surface texture and hence gripping force on perceived weight).

The basis for the hypothesis that force perception is centrally mediated comes from experiments in which it has been found that whenever there is an increase in the efferent signal sent to a muscle there is a corresponding increase in the perceived magnitude of the force of contraction. This over-estimation of muscle force occurs even when the force produced by the muscle remains constant. The increase in the motor command may result from a change in the excitability of the muscle due to fatigue or blocking of the neuromuscular junction, of the spinal cord because of cerebellar damage, or the motor cortex following damage to the corticofugal pathways, and in each of these situations the forces generated by the affected muscle are overestimated in magnitude (Gandevia & McCloskey, 1977a, 1977b; L. A. Jones & Hunter, 1983). It has also been shown, however, that under some conditions, subjects can estimate and regulate muscular tension when only intramuscular receptors, presumably the Golgi tendon organs, could be providing the guiding signals (Roland & Ladegaard-Pedersen, 1977). This dissociation between effort and force has not been possible during fatiguing contractions, even when subjects were made aware of the increased effort required to generate the force, and in this situation they continued to overestimate the magnitude of the sustained constant force (L. A. Jones, 1983).

5. SPECIALIZATION OF THE SENSORIMOTOR FUNCTIONS OF THE HAND

The accuracy with which forces produced by the intrinsic or extrinsic muscles of the hand are perceived is not more acute than that achieved by other muscle groups, although recent evidence suggests that the forces produced by muscles acting on the thumb are perceived more accurately than those produced by other muscles controlling finger movements (Kilbreath & Gandevia, 1993). In an earlier study, Gandevia and Kilbreath (1990) reported that when subjects were asked to match the heaviness of two weights, one lifted on the reference side and the other lifted by the corresponding muscle group on the matching side, the ability to match weights at the same relative force level was poorer for the first dorsal interosseous (FDI), an intrinsic hand muscle, than for the elbow flexors. In that study, accuracy was measured in terms of reproducibility of the matching weights. Contrary to what might be expected on the basis of movement control, at a perceptual level muscles were found to operate with greater accuracy at higher rather than lower forces, although in absolute terms variability increased (i.e., accuracy decreased) with force and muscle size. In their more recent study, Kilbreath and Gandevia (1993) compared the ability of subjects to match weights lifted by the thumb and index finger. They found that not only were forces perceived more accurately when generated by the thumb (flexor pollicis longus and adductor pollicis) than by the index finger (flexor digitorum profundus and FDI) muscles, but also unlike the other thumb and index finger muscles, the flexor pollicis longus was equally accurate over a wide range of weights corresponding to 2.5–50% of the maximum force of the muscle. These findings suggest that the neural control of thumb muscles may be more specialized than that of other finger muscles, perhaps reflecting the wide range of forces the thumb must oppose in daily activities (Kilbreath & Gandevia, 1993).

In contrast to the above findings on the perception of force, which suggest that, with the exception of the thumb muscles, the mechanisms involved in sensing force operate in a similar manner for most distal and proximal muscles, it appears that for other aspects of proprioception, namely the perception of limb movement and position, the hand should be considered unique. This observation is based on the differential effects of joint and skin anesthesia on distal and proximal joints. Whereas joint (Clark et al., 1989; Ferrell et al., 1987; Ferrell & Smith, 1988) and cutaneous anesthesia (Clark et al., 1986; Ferrell & Smith, 1988) result in a significant impairment in the ability to detect movements of the fingers and to match finger positions, as shown in Figure 1, joint and/or skin anesthesia has no effect on the perception of knee position (Barrack, Skinner, Brunet, & Haddad, 1983; Clark, Horch, Bach, & Larson, 1979) or the threshold for detecting passive movement of the knee (Barrack et al., 1983). The effect of joint and/or skin anesthesia on the ability to detect changes in knee position is illustrated in Figure 3. A comparison of Figures 1 and 3 clearly reveals the differential effects of anesthesia on the proprioceptive functioning of the hand and knee.

The importance of cutaneous sensory feedback to proprioception in the hand is not surprising given the high density of mechanoreceptor innervation in the skin and the large area of cortex devoted to processing tactile information from the hand. The specialization of the hand for tactile exploration makes it unique in comparison to other parts of the body, and one element of this process is sensing finger positions and movements. Feedback from joint and cutaneous receptors may also be important for proprioception in the hand, because of the inability of muscle receptors to signal accurately which joint has moved. Most muscles in the hand, including the intrinsic hand muscles, act over many joints and therefore identifying which joint has moved on the basis of muscle spindle afferent activity is presumably difficult.

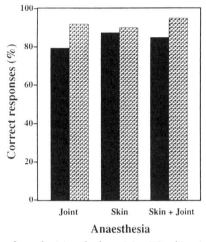

FIGURE 3   The effect of anesthetizing the knee joint (10 subjects), a 150-mm band of skin around the joint (4 subjects), and both the joint and skin (2 subjects) on the ability to detect 5-degree changes in the angle of the knee. The solid bars are the results obtained under control conditions (i.e., pre- and postinjection) and the hatched bars the results during anesthesia. (The data are taken from Clark, Horch, Bach, and Larson, 1979.)

6. PROPRIOCEPTION AND THE NEW PSYCHOPHYSICS

In comparison with other sensory modalities, such as vision and audition, for which there is a vast literature on the sensitivity of the system to different kinds of environmental stimuli, proprioception is still in its infancy. Even very basic properties, such as the proprioceptive tuning curve, have not been calculated, although this tuning curve is considered a fundamental characteristic of the auditory (Berger, 1981) and cutaneous sensory systems (Bolanowski, Gescheider, Verrillo, & Checkosky, 1988). The tuning curve is the function that describes the relation between the just noticeable difference in the amplitude of a sinusoidal stimulus that a subject can detect and the frequency of the imposed displacement. Until recently, psychophysical studies of the proprioceptive system were limited by technological difficulties associated with automating stimulus delivery and rapidly adjusting stimulus intensity, which for many of the variables of interest required sophisticated high-speed actuator servocontrol systems. In addition, classical psychophysical techniques, such as the method of average error or matching technique (Gescheider, 1985), have been used extensively to determine proprioceptive thresholds (L. A. Jones, 1989; Worringham et al., 1987) to the exclusion of the more sensitive and efficient techniques (Green & Swets, 1989; Shelton,

Picardo, & Green, 1982) commonly used in studies of the auditory and visual systems.

7. MANUAL DEXTERITY

It is usually assumed that the highly skilled movements of the hand require a finer degree of control than the gross movements of the forearm or upper arm (De Luca, LeFever, McCue, & Xenakis, 1982a). In absolute terms this does appear to be the case, in that the ability to match forces is superior for distal muscles as compared to those situated more proximally. However, in relative terms, that is, as a percentage of the maximum force generated by the muscle, the converse is true (Gandevia & Kilbreath, 1990). A similar picture emerges with respect to movement, although again it depends on how accuracy is defined. If accuracy is assessed in terms of the fineness of control of the linear displacement of the end point, that is, the fingertip, then movements of distal joints, such as the thumb, are more accurate than those made by proximal joints. However, if accuracy is now evaluated in terms of the fineness of control of angular rotation, then movements of proximal joints such as the elbow are more accurate (De Domenico & McCloskey, 1987).

Normal proprioceptive ability is a prerequisite for the performance of a variety of fine manual tasks, as shown by the motor disturbances seen in patients with impaired peripheral sensory feedback (Rothwell et al., 1982; Sanes, Mauritz, Dalakas, & Evarts, 1985). It would seem reasonable to expect, therefore, that highly skilled manual performance would be associated with superior proprioceptive abilities. Relatively little is known about the relation between proprioception and motor skill, although it is clear that the limits of the proprioceptive sensory system, as defined in terms of absolute and differential thresholds, are not those of the motor system. For example, during microsurgery and in the construction of electronic components it is possible to make movements under visual control (through an operating microscope) that are not perceived kinesthetically. During a microsurgical operation it is not uncommon for a surgeon to perform 150- to 200-μm movements (Charles & Williams, 1989). Under these conditions the motor system can function very effectively beyond the limits imposed by the normal range of vision.

Microsurgery provides an interesting domain for evaluating the relation between manual skill and proprioceptive abilities, because of its high-precision requirements and sophisticated tool use. At present there is no reliable or objective index of surgical proficiency that can be used to evaluate microsurgical skill (Schueneman & Pickleman, 1993). The most commonly used index of surgical performance is the time taken to perform a standard procedure, such as completing a suture, and this appears to be sensitive to the level of experience of the surgeon (Starkes, Payk, Jennen, & Leclair, 1993). Few measurements have been made of the movements generated and forces produced during microsurgery, in part because of the considerable technological difficulties associated with instrumenting microsurgical tools, which are typically small and lightweight (Stangel & Lahr, 1984). Because of this limitation, it has not been possible to specify the movement control parameters that distinguish the performance of novice and experienced surgeons. A number of systems have, however, been developed to measure the grasp forces generated when subjects hold small objects, and to see how these change as a function of the properties of the objects being grasped (Johansson & Westling, 1987a; L. A. Jones & Hunter, 1992; see Flanagan, Chapter 20), and the results from these studies are relevant to understanding tool use during surgery. The limited data available for microsurgery indicate that the forces generated by a surgeon at the tool interface are typically very low (0.1–2 N) as compared to the forces used to grasp an object (4–10 N), and movements can be in the 150- to 200-μm range (Charles & Williams, 1989; Sabatini, Bergamasco, & Dario, 1989).

A set of instrumented surgical tools is being designed and constructed (in collaboration with Ian Hunter) with the objective of providing a system that can be used to measure the movements produced and forces generated during microsurgery. These instruments (an example is shown in Figure 4) will be used to record forces at the tool tip–tissue interface and movements during standard microsurgical procedures such as suturing and cutting. The time taken to perform standard procedures under different operating conditions (e.g., tissues with varying mechanical properties) and the consistency with which these tasks are completed (i.e., the variability in force and displacement) will be used as indices of surgical performance. These will then be evaluated in conjunction with measurements of the subjects' psychophysical thresholds for force and displacement.

The information obtained from analyzing surgical performance will be used to assist in establishing criteria for evaluating surgical competence, for which there is an increasing demand as new procedures are introduced (Soci-

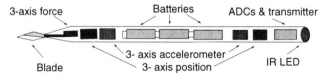

FIGURE 4   A schematic illustration of the instrumented scalpel. ADCs refer to analog-to-digital convertors and the IR LED is the infrared light emitting diode.

ety of American Gastrointestinal Endoscopic Surgeons, 1991). It should also provide information about performance variables that distinguish novice from experienced surgeons, which can then be incorporated into the design of surgical simulators used for training (Hunter, Jones, Sagar, Lafontaine, & Hunter, 1995). In this context it should be noted that manual dexterity appears to be but one of a number of abilities that distinguish proficient from mediocre surgical performance. Schueneman and Pickleman (1993) have shown that perceptual abilities, and in particular the capacity to analyze a situation rapidly and organize one's perceptions so as to distinguish essential from nonessential details, appear to be important predictors of surgical competence. Finally, the analysis of surgical performance should provide a basis for evaluating the performance of microsurgical robotic systems, for which it is essential to know the accuracy and consistency with which various tasks are carried out by their human counterparts (Hunter et al., 1993).

8. CONCLUSION

Considerable progress has been made in our understanding of the sensory basis of proprioception over the past twenty-five years. As this information is applied to other areas, however, the limits to this knowledge become apparent. For example, the relation between proprioceptive acuity (i.e., differential and absolute thresholds) and manual dexterity has not been explored, and yet in many contexts it is of interest to know how sensitive subjects are to changes in force and displacement, and what effect enhancing this feedback would have on performance. The demanding precision requirements of microsurgery make it an interesting field to explore these issues, particularly as microsurgical interventions are often limited by the dexterous capabilities of the human hand. This dexterity can be enhanced by filtering out tremor (Bose et al., 1992) or having a robot perform the surgery under the control of the surgeon (Hunter et al., 1993). In the latter situation tactile and proprioceptive information can be scaled up (amplified) and fed back to the surgeon (using actuators associated with the tool that he or she controls), and here it is essential to know the surgeon's sensitivity to changes in force and the gain and bandwidth required to feed back this information. These data can come only from detailed psychophysical studies of the human proprioceptive system.

ACKNOWLEDGMENTS

This research was supported by grants from the Institute for Robotics and Intelligent Systems (IRIS), and the Office of Naval Research (ONR).

18

Proprioceptive Mechanisms and the Control of Finger Movements

ÅKE B. VALLBO AND JOHAN WESSBERG

1. INTRODUCTION

There are indications that the control of hand and finger movements may be unique in several respects. First, the direct cortico-motoneuronal connections are supposed to be particularly prominent in relation to the hand, suggesting a strong cortical command (Porter & Lemon, 1993). Second, hand muscles are strongly influenced by tactile sense organs in the glabrous skin (Johansson & Westling, 1987a). Whether these features imply that the role of proprioceptive mechanisms is qualitatively different in the control of hand and finger movements compared to other muscular systems remains an open question.

This chapter presents some basic properties of human proprioceptive afference from the finger muscles and it addresses the role of muscular afference in the control of movements. Particularly, proprioceptive mechanisms will be discussed in relation to the pulsatile motor output, which seems to characterize the activation of human finger muscles during voluntary movements.

1.1 Muscle Proprioceptors

Intramuscular proprioceptors are of two kinds, Golgi tendon organs and muscle spindles (Kandel, Schwartz, & Jessel, 1991). The former are partic-

Hand and Brain
Copyright © 1996 by Academic Press, Inc. All rights of reproduction in any form reserved.

ularly sensitive to active contraction and send their afferent message to the central nervous system through nerve fibers denoted group Ib afferents. Muscle spindles consist of bundles of thin and specialized muscle fibers, that is, intrafusal muscle fibers, which are densely innervated. Primarily they code the length and length changes of the intramuscular structures that are parallel to the spindles, that is, the extrafusal muscle fibers. A powerful efferent control is exerted by the gamma system, which allows motor centers to adjust response properties as well as working range of spindles by contraction of intrafusal muscle fibers. In addition, the alpha motor fibers, which innervate the ordinary motor fibers, send branches to many muscle spindles, constituting the beta system (Emonet-Dénand & Laporte, 1975). An interesting functional significance is that the beta system implies an obligate coactivation of intrafusal and extrafusal muscle fibers, whereas the gamma system has the potential of adjusting the functional state of spindles independently of the contraction of the main muscle. The afferent message from muscle spindles is carried in two types of fibers, the large group Ia afferent and the smaller group II afferent (P. B. C. Matthews, 1972).

The general problem of proprioceptive coding may be considered from two different angles. One is to focus on the response characteristics of the sense organs and try to answer the question "What are proprioceptors seeing?" The other is to focus on central mechanisms and consider the question "Which features are extracted by motor centers from the afferent signal?" Although we take it for granted that there is a reliable match between what the sense organs are seeing and what is essential for motor control functions, the problem is not all that simple from an analytical point of view, because researchers may overlook features in the neural message that are essential for motor centers.

This may be illustrated by the history of the physiology of the Golgi tendon organ. For a long time, tendon organs were considered to report when the muscle is approaching the limit of being overstretched and damaged. An important reason for this view was that tendon organs were mainly studied by applying imposed stretch to the muscle.

When physiologists began to analyze the effect of active contractions (Houk & Hennemann, 1967; Jansen & Rudjord, 1964), the view on the function of tendon organs started to change radically. It is now generally accepted that the essential information provided by tendon organs is closely related to the amount of muscle contraction. Actually, it is well established that they are very sensitive to the force produced by a few motor units that are connected to the sense organ. However, we have not yet reached land's end because physiologists are still working further to define the particular features of the self-generated muscular activity that the Golgi tendon organs are responding to (Jami, 1992).

It seems reasonable also to be open to the possibility that the afferent response from muscle spindles may include attributes that deserve more interest than they have attracted so far. The present chapter discusses a particular feature of muscle spindle afference and ties this to a behavioral characteristic of slow finger movements that has not been greatly studied as yet. As a background, a short survey of proprioceptive response to various kinds of movements is presented.

2. METHODS

Much of the presented data are based on recordings of afferent activity from muscles of attending human subjects. Single-unit impulses were recorded from muscle spindles and Golgi tendon organs in the finger extensor muscles, using the microneurography technique (Vallbo, Hagbarth, Torebjörk, & Wallin, 1979). This technique implies that a fine needle electrode, insulated to the tip, is inserted percutaneously into a peripheral nerve. Its position is adjusted until impulses from a single nerve fiber can be discriminated. By various test procedures it is possible to define the location and type of end organ connected to the fiber. Afferent activity was studied in relation to contraction of finger muscles and movements of a single metacarpophalangeal joint. Sense organs in the finger extensor muscles rather than the finger flexor muscles were selected for two reasons. First, the extensor muscles constitute the superficial layer of muscles in this region and therefore lend themselves to adequate recording of their electrical activity by surface electrodes. Second, they are the sole muscles that act to extend the metacarpophalangeal joints and it is therefore particularly relevant to relate the afferent signal from the sense organs in these muscles to the electrical activity of the muscle as well as the forces and movements at the individual metacarpophalangeal joint.

3. PROPRIOCEPTIVE RESPONSES FROM FINGER MUSCLES

3.1 Responses to Imposed Movements

When the finger extensor muscles are passively stretched by an external device, many of them respond as predicted by previous work on animals. An example is shown in Figure 1 displaying the classical type of response from a muscle spindle primary ending to an imposed ramp stretch. It is easy to identify the high dynamic response, the initial burst, the small deceleration response at the end of the ramp stretch, and the immediate stop of firing at the onset of imposed shortening. The torque response seems to be that of a passive viscoelastic system to an imposed ramp displacement. Actually, the time course of the torque is similar to what is reported with linear stretch of an isolated muscle.

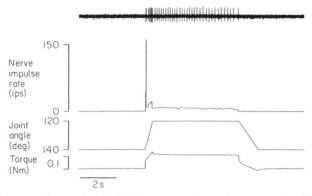

FIGURE 1   Response of a muscle spindle afferent to an imposed ramp stretch exhibiting the classical features of a deafferented primary ending. In this and all other figures, upward deflections of the joint angle record indicate lengthening of the muscle housing the sense organ (Å. B. Vallbo & J. Wessberg, unpublished).

In contrast to most recordings from reduced animals, many spindles in human finger muscles fail to exhibit the classical characteristics to imposed stretch in such a complete and clear form as in Figure 1. The reason is probably a trivial experimental difference because recordings with reduced animals are usually pursued with the muscle close to its maximal length, whereas studies on humans are done with intermediate muscle lengths and it is well known that spindle response is highly dependent on the muscle length (G. M. Goodwin, Hulliger, & Matthews, 1975; Houk, Rymer, & Crago, 1981; P. B. C. Matthews, 1963; P. B. C. Matthews & Stein, 1969).

Figure 2 shows representative responses from the three types of human muscle afferents. The muscle spindle primary afferents (Ia) exhibit a fair dynamic response, the muscle spindle secondary (II) mainly a static response, whereas the tendon organ afferents (Ib) give very little or no response to imposed stretch even when they are continuously firing, as the one illustrated in Figure 2.

3.2 Muscle Spindle Response during Isometric Voluntary Contractions

The records of Figures 1 and 2 were taken while the parent muscle was completely relaxed. There is strong evidence that the fusimotor activity is negligible under these conditions. On the other hand, when the muscle contracts many of its spindles are brought into a totally different state because the skeletomotor activity is associated with an increased fusimotor output, which makes many spindles fire at a higher rate. An example is shown in Figure 3 illustrating a response of a muscle spindle primary afferent to isometric contractions. Although recordings of this kind strongly suggest an increased fusimotor drive, it is obvious that more refined analyses are required to assess the nature of the fusimotor drive, that is, whether it is mainly dynamic or static and whether it is mainly carried in gamma or beta fibers.

When movements are imposed while human subjects voluntarily contract the parent muscle the spindle response is not predictable, because the balance between effects of intramuscular length changes and effects of static and dynamic fusimotor drives seems to vary between spindles and tests as well as from moment to moment.

3.3 Proprioceptive Response to Self-Generated Movements

Although imposed movements have been used a lot in experimental studies of proprioceptive mechanisms there is general agreement that muscle stretch receptors are of utmost importance for the control of self-generated movements, which often involve active shortening of one or several agonist

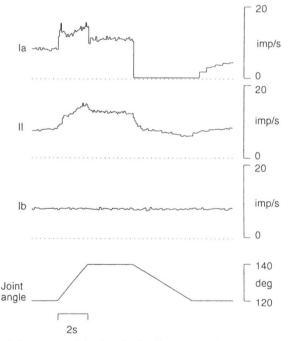

FIGURE 2 Typical responses of the three kinds of human muscle stretch receptors to imposed ramp stretches of identical amplitude and velocity when the parent muscle is relaxed (N. Kakuda, Å. B. Vallbo & J. Wessberg, unpublished).

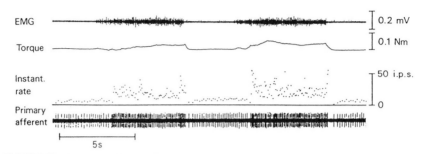

FIGURE 3 Response of a muscle spindle primary ending to isometric contractions. (From Vallbo, 1981, Fig. 1, p. 251.)

muscles and the lengthening of their antagonists, whether relaxed or contracting.

Figure 4 demonstrates the basic response patterns of muscle spindles and Golgi tendon organs during natural and free finger movements unopposed by external forces. In this particular recording, the nerve signal shows impulses, not from one, but from two afferent nerve fibers, which are possible to discriminate because their action potentials clearly differed in size. One fiber originated from a muscle spindle secondary ending (the smaller, low-frequency spike pattern), and the other originated from a Golgi tendon organ

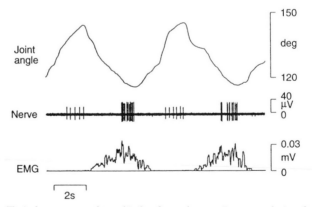

FIGURE 4 Typical responses of two kinds of muscle proprioceptors during free voluntary finger movements unopposed by external forces. The small spikes belong to a muscle spindle secondary afferent and the large spike to a Golgi tendon organ. Upward deflections in the joint angle record represent lengthening of the muscle in this and all other records (N. Kakuda, Å. B. Vallbo, & J. Wessberg, unpublished).

(the larger, higher frequency spike pattern). It may be seen that the spindle fired during lengthening and when the muscle was long, whereas the Golgi tendon organ fired in the opposite phase, that is, when the muscle was short. Of importance, this is the phase when the parent muscle is particularly active because the tendon organs respond to the force exerted by the motor units that insert on the sense organ.

4. KINEMATIC AND MUSCULAR CHARACTERISTICS OF SELF-GENERATED FINGER MOVEMENTS

In analyses of single-joint finger movements it has been found that such movements are not smooth but characterized by speed variations (Vallbo & Wessberg, 1993). When the kinematics are explored in detail it turns out that speed variations tend to recur with a rate of 8–10 Hz. Figure 5 shows EMG and kinematic events in a slow tracking movement. The velocity record as well as the acceleration record demonstrate a series of discontinuities recurring at 8–10 Hz. This phenomenon has not attracted much interest before, although it has been mentioned in passing in a few studies (Marsden, 1984; Young & Hagbarth, 1980), whereas very few actual recordings have been published (Darling, Cole, & Abbs, 1988; Marshall & Walsh, 1956).

On the other hand, other forms of discontinuities during movements have attracted more interest. For instance, Brooks (1974) has described dis-

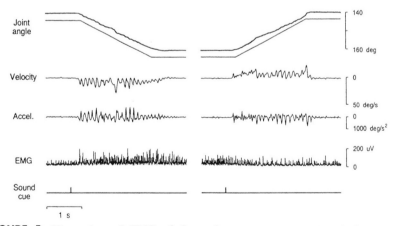

FIGURE 5   Kinematics and EMG of slow voluntary movements at a single metacarpophalangeal joint. The two top traces represent the actual joint angle attained by the subject (thick line) and the demanded joint position in a visual tracking task (thin line, offset a few degrees for clarity). (From Vallbo & Wessberg, 1993, Fig. 1, p. 676.)

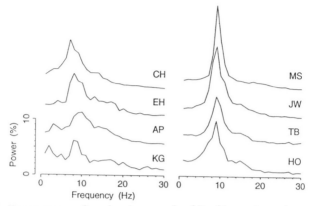

FIGURE 6 Power spectra of acceleration records of 8 subjects who performed nonloaded extension movements with a track speed of 10 deg/s. Curves offset by a distance corresponding to five percentage points on the y-axis. (From Vallbo & Wessberg, 1993, Fig. 3, p. 679.)

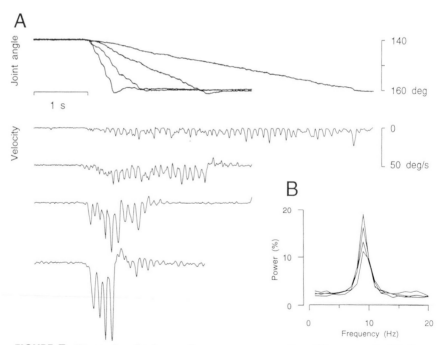

FIGURE 7 Kinematics of voluntary finger movements at four different speeds. (A) shows original recordings of joint angle and angular velocity from visual tracking movements with tracking speeds of 4, 10, 25, and 62 deg/s. (B) shows power spectra of movements with the same tracking speeds calculated from a large number of movements (n = 160). (From Vallbo & Wessberg, 1993, Fig. 4, p. 680.)

continuities in the 3–4 Hz frequency band in the monkey performing flexion and extension movements of the elbow while Navas and Stark (1968) have analyzed 1–2 Hz discontinuities during pronation–supination movements of the forearm in humans. Both groups have presented hypotheses in relation to these phenomena, based on feedback loops of different kinds.

We have found that the amplitude and the amount of 8–10 Hz varies between subjects but it is relatively constant within the same subject. Hence, the velocity pattern appears to be a kind of fingerprint of the individual subject's control system for finger movements. Power spectrum analyses demonstrate a peak in the 8–10 Hz frequency band in all subjects as illustrated in Figure 6.

The 8–10 Hz discontinuities are not vitally dependent on the particular test situation but it has been found that they are present under a variety of conditions, for example, with different size of loads, with multijoint movements as well as single joint movements, with precision movements as well as movements without precision requirements. Moreover, they are present with varying angular speeds, as illustrated in Figure 7, where it may be appreciated that the faster movements are implemented by a series of large steps, whereas the slower movements are implemented by smaller steps repeated at the same rate.

5. WHICH MECHANISMS MIGHT PRODUCE THE 8–10 HZ DISCONTINUITIES DURING FINGER MOVEMENTS?

5.1 Mechanical Resonance

When discussing the mechanisms that may be involved in the generation of the 8–10 Hz discontinuities, it is important to note that mechanical resonance can be ruled out because the resonance frequency of the finger system is in the range of 20–25 Hz (Halliday & Redfearn, 1956; Stiles & Randall, 1967). Thus, it can be inferred that the 8–10 Hz discontinuities are of muscular origin. This was confirmed in EMG recordings showing that the muscular activity was modulated in phase with the speed variations as illustrated in Figure 8. The modulation involves primarily the shortening muscle, that is, the muscle that drives the movement in the desired direction. The antagonist is sometimes silent, sometimes active in these movements, but when it is active it is modulated at 8–10 Hz as well, as illustrated in Figure 8.

Hence analyses of the EMG indicated that the 8–10 Hz discontinuities are produced by a series of motor pulses, either directed to the agonist muscle alone while the antagonist is silent or by a series of double pulses, one driving pulse produced by the agonist and, a few tens of milliseconds later, a braking pulse produced by the antagonist.

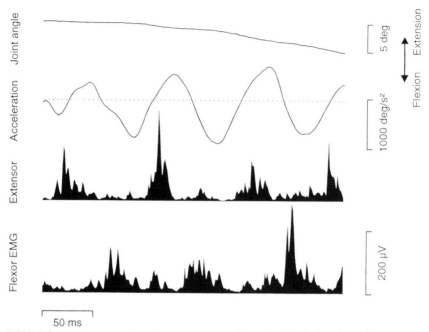

FIGURE 8   EMG activities in relation to 8–10 Hz discontinuities during slow voluntary ramp movements. Traces show from above angular displacement of the third metacarpophalangeal joint, angular acceleration, and root-mean-squared EMG from the finger extensor and flexor muscles. (From Vallbo & Wessberg, 1993, Fig. 8, p. 686.)

5.2 Feedback Oscillations

A reasonable hypothesis is that the 8–10 Hz discontinuities are manifestations of oscillations in a feedback loop. Simple principles say that oscillations of this nature should have a period time that is twice the loop time. Moreover, the oscillations would most likely be essentially sinusoidal in shape.

The short latency stretch reflex loop is an interesting candidate because the timing seems to fit with 8–10 Hz. The loop time of the spinal stretch reflex, including the electrokinematic delay, is in the range of 45–55 ms for finger muscles on the forearm while the period time of the 8–10 Hz discontinuities is 100–120 ms, that is, twice the loop time. (Incidentally, by the same token, it seems reasonable to rule out the supraspinal, long latency stretch reflex because this would produce oscillations at lower frequencies, since the loop time of this reflex is longer, i.e., 80–110 ms in the finger muscles (Capaday et al., 1991; P. B. C. Matthews, Farmer, & Ingram, 1990; E. Palmer & Ashby, 1992b).) On the other hand, it should be noted that the cycle time argument is schematic and there is conflicting evidence that suggests that the spinal stretch reflex would typically sustain oscillations at frequencies below 8 Hz (T. I. H. Brown, Rack, & Ross, 1982; Elble & Randall, 1978; Gottlieb & Lippold, 1983; Jacks, Prochazka, & Trend, 1988; Prochazka & Trend, 1988; Stiles, 1976).

Another argument for considering the monosynaptic stretch reflex emerges from studies of physiological tremor during position holding. When a subject is holding a finger outstretched and the muscles are getting fatigued, an enhanced physiological tremor appears. Its frequency falls in the 8–12 Hz band, while the amplitude is a few tenths of a degree (Bigland & Lippold, 1954; Burne, Lippold, & Pryor, 1984; Elble & Koller, 1990; Hagbarth & Young, 1979; Halliday & Redfearn, 1956; Lippold, 1970; Marsden, 1984; Young & Hagbarth, 1980). It has been suggested that the enhanced physiological tremor is accounted for by oscillations in the spinal stretch reflex. In a few reports it has even been stated in passing that this tremor increases during voluntary movements, implying the tacit assumption that discontinuities during movements may be of the same nature as enhanced physiological tremor during position holding.

In summary, it seems reasonable to explore the possibility that an oscillation in the spinal stretch reflex loop is superimposed on a more smoothly changing motor command from higher centers to produce the 8–10 Hz discontinuities, as described in Figures 5–8.

5.3 Complex Kinematics of Individual Step Movement

On the other hand, there are several findings that challenge the interpretation that the spinal stretch reflex accounts for the 8–10 Hz discontinuities during finger movements. One is that the individual discontinuity has a fairly complex kinematic structure that is not what you would expect with oscillations in a simple feedback loop. This comes out particularly clear in slow movements, as illustrated in Figure 9A. In each cycle of discontinuity two phases may be discriminated on the basis of the velocity record, that is, a phase of standstill and a phase of movement. The acceleration records reveal further kinematic details. Here, three phases may be discerned, that is, a phase of acceleration, a phase of deceleration, and a phase of standstill. Moreover, there is often a close relationship between the size of the peak acceleration and the size of the peak deceleration, the latter being higher than the former. This relation is also evident in Figure 5 during both lengthening and shortening movements. All these kinematic details are not evident in faster movements (Figure 7B) where merely a notch is seen in the acceleration record.

At first sight, the complex kinematic structure of the discontinuities appears as a strong argument against oscillations in a feedback loop because

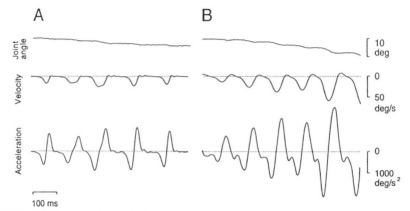

FIGURE 9   Kinematics of individual movement cycles at slow voluntary ramp movements at a single metacarpophalangeal joint. (A) and (B) show sample records from two different subject. (From Vallbo & Wessberg, 1993, Fig. 6, p. 684.)

one would expect more sinusoidal movements. However, it is probably not a tight argument because it is feasible that nonlinear mechanical characteristics might account for complex kinematics in a feedback loop.

5.4 Spindle Response Related to 8–10 Hz Discontinuities

An important question in relation to the hypothesis that the 8–10 Hz discontinuities are due to oscillations in the spinal stretch reflex loop is to what extent muscle spindle afferents respond to the discontinuities. It is well known from animal work that muscle spindle primary afferents may be very sensitive to minute speed variations (Cussons, Hulliger, & Matthews, 1977; Hasan & Houk, 1975a, 1975b; Hulliger, Matthews, & Noth, 1977; P. B. C. Matthews & Stein, 1969). On the other hand, this is not an invariant characteristic but the sensitivity to speed variations is dependent on a number of factors, for example, range of movement, amount of prestretch of the muscle, and fusimotor activity.

When voluntary finger movements were analyzed, it was found that the spindle population responded clearly to the discontinuities. An example with a Ia afferent during a shortening movement is shown in Figure 10. It may be seen that the impulses tended to occur in close relation to the discontinuities and in the phases of movement when the speed attained its local minima. It seems likely that this was the result of a balance between the fusimotor drive, which tends to keep the firing up, and the shortening movement, which tends to silence the afferent. Generally the impulse rates were fairly low, particularly during shortening, but the probability of firing was clearly related to

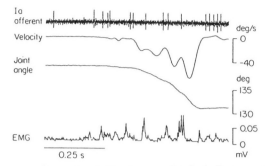

FIGURE 10 Response of a muscle spindle primary ending in the finger extensor muscle during a shortening movement (Å. B. Vallbo & J. Wessberg, unpublished).

the 8–10 Hz discontinuities. Figure 11 shows an example of response of another primary afferent during a lengthening movement where it is particularly obvious that many of the velocity peaks were associated with pairs of impulses at short intervals. Quantitative analyses supported the impression that the majority of spindle primary afferents and a fair proportion of secondary afferents tended to fire in relation to the 8–10 Hz discontinuities.

The examples of Figures 10 and 11 illustrate that the muscle spindle primary afferents often fired in the phase of the discontinuities when the instantaneous kinematic state was most favorable for a stretch receptor to be excited, that is, close to peak velocity of stretch during lengthening voluntary movements and close to minimal velocity during shortening movements. Hence, it was justified to conclude that the population of spindles coded the occurrence of the 8–10 Hz discontinuities.

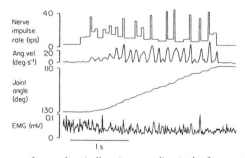

FIGURE 11 Response of a muscle spindle primary ending in the finger extensor muscle during a lengthening movement (Å. B. Vallbo & J. Wessberg, unpublished).

5.5 Strength of the Spinal Stretch Reflex

Considering the response of the population of muscle spindle afferents, it seems reasonable that the monosynaptic stretch reflex might contribute to the 8–10 Hz discontinuities. Another question is whether the reflex is strong enough to account for it all or even contribute significantly.

When the EMG responses to large perturbations were analyzed during these voluntary movements, it was found that the reflex at short latency was quite weak compared to the EMG modulations associated with the self-generated 8–10 Hz discontinuities. It is particularly relevant that the perturbations used represent strong stimuli and it can be safely inferred that they give rise to large and synchronized responses from the population of muscle spindle primary afferents. In contrast, the self-generated discontinuities produce smaller spindle responses, which are also more dispersed in time. Still, the 8–10 Hz modulations of the EMG activity during the self-generated movements were larger than the reflex effects of the perturbations.

The modest response to perturbations seems to reject not only the stretch reflex but, in addition, other kinds of movement-induced reflexes as the main mechanism generating the discontinuities. This is not to deny, however, that spinal reflexes from muscular, joint, or cutaneous receptors that respond to movements may contribute to the occurrence as well as the characteristics of the discontinuities. However, the fact that the reflex effects are very weak strongly suggests that neuronal mechanisms within the central nervous system are essential to generate the basic pattern of speed variations at 8–10 Hz during voluntary finger movements.

5.6 Intrinsic Properties of Motoneurons

Among candidate mechanisms that might promote a pulsatile motor output in the 8–10 Hz frequency range, it seems pertinent to consider the intrinsic properties of the motoneurons. The fact that motoneurons tend to fire at 6–8 Hz when they are just recruited (Freund, Büdingen, & Dietz, 1975) has been advanced to explain nonenhanced physiological tremor, the mechanism being that the last recruited motor units that fire at low rates produce a series of single twitches, whereas higher firing rates yield smooth contractions. However, it seems unlikely that this mechanism is strong enough to account for the large angular steps that occur during voluntary movements of moderate speed, as illustrated in Figure 7, or the large modulations of the gross EMG activity, as illustrated in Figure 8. Moreover, it was demonstrated that the discontinuities during movements involve a subtle coordination between agonist and antagonist activities that is difficult to explain on the basis of the intrinsic properties of the motoneurons alone.

6. PREMOTONEURONAL MECHANISMS

6.1 Simplistic Model

If mechanical resonance, reflexes, and intrinsic motoneuron properties can be excluded as the essential mechanisms producing the 8–10 Hz discontinuities, the generator of the motor pulses must be sought among mechanisms upstream of the motoneurons. Although the studies pursued so far do not allow specific conclusions on which neural circuits might produce 8–10 Hz modulations of the synaptic input to the motoneurons, it may be conjectured, as a framework for further discussions, that the control system for slow finger

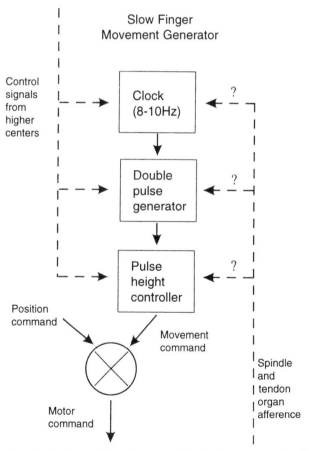

FIGURE 12 Speculative scheme of central generator for slow finger movements (Å. B. Vallbo & J. Wessberg, unpublished).

movements realizes three separate functions (Figure 12). One would be a clock producing pulses that occur with slightly varying intervals in the frequency range of 8–10 Hz. Second, there may be a simple pattern generator producing a series of double pulses, that is, one to the agonist, which drives the movement in the desired direction, and a few tens of milliseconds later, a braking pulse to the antagonist. Incidentally, this pattern is akin to the triphasic pattern produced during fast movements (Cooke & Brown, 1990; Ghez & Gordon, 1987; Hallet, Shahani, & Young, 1975). Finally, one might conceive of a functional unit that sets the size of the pulses and hence the sizes of the individual steps in order to accomplish the desired overall speed of movement.

The idea of a central pulse generator and intermittency in motor control is certainly not new. It has been discussed in several studies on physiological tremor (Burne et al., 1984; Elble & Koller, 1990; Lippold, 1970; Lippold, Redfearns & Vuco, 1957). In particular, it has been proposed that the olivo-cerebellar system constitutes a functional unit that is essential for the generation of intermittent motor integration and output (Llinás, 1991; Llinás & Volkind, 1973). Llinás (1991) has pointed out that the olivocerebellar system has several physiological properties that are consistent with an oscillator function. For instance, the setup of ionic channels in the cells of the inferior olive as well as the connections between the cells tend to make them fire synchronously at low rate. Particularly, the neurons are supplied with calcium channels that are inactivated at resting potential and require hyperpolarization to be deinactivated. In addition, there are calcium-activated potassium channels. Similar ionic mechanisms are present in the thalamic cells, which have been suggesed to be involved in the production of the alpha rhythm in the EEG.

6.2 Proprioceptive Mechanisms in Relation to the Model

If slow movements are implemented by an intermittent controller rather than a continuous one, it seems reasonable to assume that the control system would need information about the occurrence as well as the characteristics of individual movement steps. It was found that the extreme sensitivity of muscle spindle primary afferents is adequate to code these features during natural movements. Moreover, it may be reasonable to speculate whether the afferent signal from intramuscular proprioceptors might have a role in relation to a controller of the type outlined in Figure 12 (broken lines on the right side).

Since the proprioceptor population codes the occurrence of the discontinuities one might ask whether this afference has a conditional role for running the clock, for example, that the afference supports an inherent clock function even though it might not be essential for the basic rhythm of the clock. Moreover, preliminary observations suggest that the proprioceptive input, in addition, may code the characteristics of the individual discontinuity, which could be of significance for the double pulse generator as well as for a size controller.

6.3 Reservations

It should be emphasized that the model proposed above is highly speculative because it is perfectly reasonable that the motor performance described in slow finger movements is implemented by mechanisms that cannot be separated in the three functions outlined above. In addition, it should be pointed out that already the kinematic structure of finger movements suggests that control systems other than a strict 8–10 Hz pulse generator are involved as well, because the 8–10 Hz discontinuities are mixed with a number of other frequencies in most subjects.

7. FUNCTIONAL IMPLICATIONS OF PULSATILE MOTOR CONTROL

It may be asked whether pulsatile control might offer significant functional advantages or if the 8–10 Hz modulations are merely a side effect of the circuit design. Obviously, the material available so far does not answer this question but it may be of interest to speculate about a potential advantage. It is reasonable to assume that the descending motor command for a voluntary action is based on the combination of information from a number of different sources, for example, from visual, proprioceptive, and exteroceptive sensory systems as well as from motor centers within the brain and spinal cord, which contribute separate aspects and specify requisites for muscular activity to attain the desired motor action. The process of synthesizing and balancing the information from a number of rersources is complicated by the fact that the neural conduction times from various origins to any summation point differ considerably. It is reasonable that this problem is more easily dealt with in an intermittent control system than in a continuous control system, as suggested by Llinás (1991). Moreover, it seems that the elaboration of motor commands would require less computational power if the relevant neuronal signals were synthesized intermittently at a relatively low rate rather than continuously. Similar ideas are implicit already in Bernstein's writing from 1967 (Bernstein, 1967) where he conceived of a minimal time interval of about 0.1 second for the coordination of sensory and motor activities.

ACKNOWLEDGMENTS

This study was supported by the Swedish Medical Research Council (Grant 14X-3548), The Bank of Sweden, Tercentenary Foundation, and the Göteborg Medical Society. We would like to thank Naoyuki Kakuda for permission to publish materials from his work in Figures 2 and 4.

19

Sensory Control of Dexterous Manipulation in Humans

ROLAND S. JOHANSSON

1. INTRODUCTION

The remarkable manipulative skills of the human hand are neither the result of rapid sensorimotor processes nor of fast or powerful effector mechanisms. Rather, the secret lies in the way manual tasks are organized and controlled by the nervous system. Successful manipulation requires that the subject selects the appropriate pattern of motor commands based on the manipulative intent, on various constraints imposed by the task, and on the relevant physical properties of the manipulated object(s) (Figure 1). For instance, most tasks require that we stabilize the object within our grasp as we move the object or use it as a tool. To prevent slips and accidental loss of the object we apply adequately large forces normal to the grip surfaces (*grip forces*) in relation to destabilizing forces tangential to the grip surfaces (*load forces*). At the same time, excessive grip forces must be avoided because they cause unnecessary fatigue and may crush fragile objects or injure the hand. Hence, the term grasp stability entails a prevention of accidental slips as well as of excessive fingertip forces. Various types of constraints are imposed by the object. Its location in space and its size and shape may influence the selected grasp configuration (e.g., a precision grip between thumb and index finger, a power grip engaging the palm or a bimanual grasp; for review of grasp classification schemes see MacKenzie & Iberall, 1994), whereas its friction in

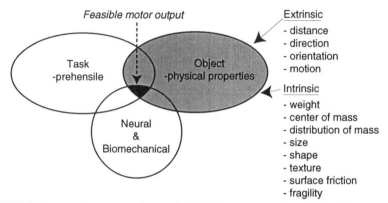

FIGURE 1   During object manipulation, the feasible motor output is constrained by a number of factors. Important constraints are imposed by the task (e.g., grasp stability and required object movements), the neural system and the skeleton-muscular apparatus, and by various intrinsic and extrinsic physical properties of the manipulated object.

relation to the skin, its weight, and distribution of mass determines primarily the magnitudes of the muscle commands.

1.1 Handling of Passive versus Active Objects

Based on the properties of the object, manipulative tasks may be divided into two principal classes (Johansson & Cole, 1994). One concerns the handling of mechanically predictable, passive objects whose relevant physical properties are stable over time. Because the motor output is self-paced and the objects are predictable, the spatiotemporal control of the muscle commands can rely largely on anticipatory mechanisms based on memory information from previous manipulation. The second class of tasks concerns the handling of active objects that are subject to unpredictable loading forces, as in holding a dog's leash, restraining a child by holding her arm, or operating power tools. Anticipatory control strategies are obviously of limited use when the manipulated objects are subjected to unpredictable loading forces, at least with regard to the forces of the grasp.

Figure 2 compares the grip forces employed by a subject while generating load forces on a passive manipulandum (dotted lines) with those employed while identical load force profiles were imposed on the grasp through the same manipulandum (active object; solid lines). In the former case, the subject was asked to pull the passive manipulandum that was immovable to produce various periods of force changes mixed with hold periods (Figure 2A, *left*). The resulting load pattern was recorded and later played back through a servo-controlled force motor while the subject was asked to restrain the active manipulandum from moving (Figure 2A, *right*) (Johansson, Riso, et al., 1992). In both tasks the blindfolded subject grasped the object by the tips of the thumb and index finger.

It is notable that in both tasks the load and grip forces increased and decreased in parallel, ensuring that adequately strong grip forces are used to prevent frictional slippage at any load force (Figure 2B). Furthermore, in both tasks this parallel coordination emerges automatically and it proceeds despite the absence of instructions to respond with grip changes. However,

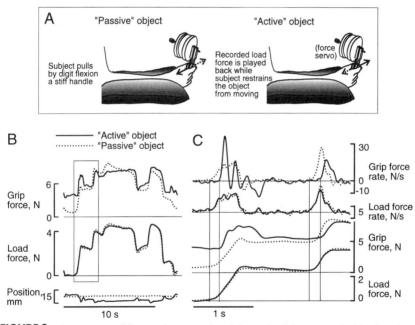

FIGURE 2   Comparison of the grip forces employed during load changes applied by the subject to a passive manipulandum with identical load profiles imposed on the grasp through the same manipulandum that was loaded by a servo-controlled force motor (active object). (A) Schematic drawing of the apparatus and tasks. The blindfolded subject used the tips of the thumb and index finger of the right hand to grasp the manipulandum, which consisted of two parallel grip surfaces (30 mm diameter; spaced 25 mm apart). Solid line arrow indicates the direction of pull; the dotted-line arrow, the corresponding reaction force. (B, C) Load and grip forces during manipulation of a passive object (dotted lines) and an active object producing similar load force profiles (solid lines). The rectangle in (B) marks the period represented at a faster time base in (C) together with the grip and load force rate profiles. Pairs of vertical lines in (C) indicate onset of grip force responses during the passive and active conditions. Single subject. (Adapted from Johansson, Riso, et al., 1992.)

despite the similarity of grip regulation there are differences in the behavior: (1) The change in the grip and load forces are nearly synchronous when the manipulandum is passive, whereas with the active manipulandum the grip force changes lag those of the load force because they are reactively generated (Figure 2C). The correspondence in timing of the grip and load force changes with the passive object indicates that the grip force modulation is programmed in parallel with (rather than as a reaction to) the self-induced movements, for example, a rise in grip force coincides with, or slightly anticipates, the increase in load. (2) The subject generally uses higher grip forces with the active manipulandum than with the passive, in particular at loads close to zero. This is necessary to prevent slips during the latent period between the onset of the increases in load forces and the onset of the grip force response. (3) Finally, with the passive manipulandum the force rate profiles are generally unimodal, indicating that the target forces are determined in advance (see further below). In contrast, with the active object the grip force responses to extended periods of load force increases consist of an initial strong grip force rate pulse followed by a period of slower, often stepwise, grip force increases (Figure 2C).

2. MANIPULATION OF PASSIVE OBJECTS

In the present account I will discuss mainly the sensorimotor control of manipulation while handling passive objects and, in particular, I consider mechanisms for the control of grasp stability. Sensorimotor control of manipulation has been analyzed most extensively in tasks in which subjects grasp an object between a finger and thumb and impose various action forces on it, for example, to lift it from a support table, hold and move it in the air and then replace it on the table (Figure 3A) (for reviews, see Johansson, 1991; Johansson & Cole, 1994; Johansson & Edin, 1993; Johansson & Westling, 1990, 1991). This chapter is focused on the period of actual object manipulation; for discussion of visual factors in reaching preceding the actual manipulation of the object see Chapters 2 and 13 in this volume. For further information on the sensorimotor control during handling of active objects subjected to unpredictable loading forces the reader may refer to a brief overview by Johansson and Cole (1994). More detailed discussions on this topic may be found in original articles by Cole and Abbs (1988), Cole and Johansson (1993), Häger-Ross, Cole, and Johansson (in press), Häger-Ross and Johansson (in press), Johansson, Häger, and Bäckström (1992), Johansson, Häger, & Riso (1992), Johansson et al. (1994), Johansson, Riso, et al. (1992), Johansson and Westling (1988b), L. A. Jones and Hunter (1992), Macefield, Häger-Ross, and Johansson (in press), and Macefield and Johansson (1994, in press).

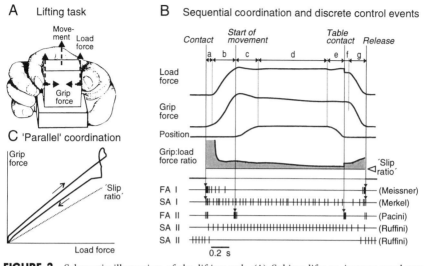

FIGURE 3   Schematic illustration of the lifting task. (A) Subject lifts an instrumented test object from a table, holds it in the air, and then replaces it, using the precision grip. The tangential (load) force applied to the object to overcome gravity and inertia and the normal (grip) force are measured as well as the vertical movement. (B) Shown schematically as a function of time are the grip and load forces, vertical movement, grip:load force ratio, and obligatory afferent responses present in the four types of tactile afferent units in the human glabrous skin. Minimum grip:load force ratio to prevent slips is indicated by slip ratio. The safety margin to prevent slips is indicated by hatching. After contact with the object, demarcated by initial tactile responses, the grip force increases by a short period (a, preload phase) before the command is released for a parallel increase in grip and load force during isometric conditions (load phase; triggered by the initial responses). This increase (b) continues until the start of movement (demarcated by burst responses in FA II afferents) when the load force overcomes the force of gravity. The object is lifted to the intended position (c) by wrist and/or elbow flexion, and a static (hold) phase is reached (d). After the replacement of the object (e) and table contact occurs (also demarcated by burst responses in FA II afferents), there is a short delay (f) before the two forces decline in parallel (g, unload phase) until the object is released (demarcated by tactile release responses). Apart from the transient event-related responses, there also are responses characterized by an ongoing impulse activity in the SA II units and many of the SA I units. Some spontaneously active SA IIs are unloaded during the lift and cease firing. (C) Grip force as a function of the load for a similar lift as in (B). Dotted line indicates the minimum grip:load force ratio to prevent slips. (Adapted from Johansson and Westling, 1991.)

2.1 Sequential Coordination

Most manipulative tasks evolve in a series of phases. Each of these sequential phases is characterized by a particular goal (e.g., to establish contact or to lift the object off the supporting table), unique patterns of muscle activity, and typically a transient mechanical event that marks the goal completion and the transition to the next phase. This certainly applies to lifting tasks (Figure 3B)

(Johansson & Westling, 1984b, 1988a; Westling & Johansson, 1984, 1987).

When we reach out to grasp and lift a small object, the first goal is to adequately position the tips of the digits onto its surfaces such that a stable grasp can be established. The transport and shaping of the hand reflect a precise coordination to achieve the necessary spatiotemporal features for arresting the reach, and for an appropriate closure of the fingers around the object (Iberall et al., 1986; Jeannerod, 1984, 1986). Once the digits contact the object the goal is to generate the necessary fingertip forces to lift it (Figure 3B). The initial contact marks the beginning of the first phase, the *preload phase*. After contact has been established by a small increase in the grip force (normal to the grip surface), the subsequent *load phase* is characterized by the grip force increasing in parallel with the load force (i.e., the lift force tangential to the contact area). When the load force has overcome the weight of the object it starts to move (*transitional phase*) into the desired vertical position (*static(hold)phase*). Similarly, at the end of a lifting task, a parallel decrease in grip and load force begins shortly after the object makes contact with the table (*unload phase*). One specific role of sensory signals from the hand is to link the various phases of the lifting task by informing the CNS that particular mechanical events have occurred, for example, that the digits have made a stable contact with the object, or that the object has started to move (Johansson & Westling, 1991).

2.2 Parallel Coordination and Coordinative Constraints Supporting Grasp Stability

Grasp stability is primarily obtained by the parallel change (increase and decrease) in the grip and load forces applied to each contact surface (Figures 2, 3B, 3C) (Edin, Westling, & Johansson, 1992; Johansson & Westling, 1984b). This coordinative constraint ensures adequate grip forces during the considerable changes in load forces that may occur in many manipulative tasks (see below). Likewise, this way of linking the forces allows considerable flexibility when lifting objects of different weights (cf. Figure 5A). With a heavy object the load force reaches high values before the weight is counterbalanced and the object is lifted, while the proportional increase in grip force ensures appropriate grip forces. Accordingly, with a lightweight object the grip force will be low.

The parallel change in the grip and load forces represents a general control strategy during prehension requiring grasp stability and is not specific to any particular task (e.g., mode of object transport) or grasp configuration. For instance, the grip forces are modulated with the fluctuations in inertial loads that arise from moving a grasped object in space as the object is accelerated and decelerated by the arm (Flanagan et al., 1993; Flanagan &

Wing, 1993; Kinoshita, Kawai, Ikuta, & Teraoka, in press), from the variations in object acceleration when objects are lifted at various speeds (Kinoshita et al, 1993), while operating against spring loads (Johansson & Westling, 1984b) and while applying pushing or pulling forces on immovable objects (Figure 2; passive object). The grip forces modulate approximately in phase with changes in load force also induced by whole body jumping even though the arm's joint angles are fixed (Flanagan & Tresilian, 1994) and during walking and running (Kinoshita et al., in press). This basic coordination of grip and load forces also shows effector invariance in the sense that it applies for a variety of grips, including one- and two-handed grips, "inverted" grips (Burstedt, Westling, Johansson, & Edin, 1992; Flanagan & Tresilian, 1994), and multidigit grips (Kinoshita, Kawai, & Ikuta, 1995). Moreover, this coordinative constraint is expressed in anticipatory adjustments of the grip force in more complex bimanual actions such as when weights are transferred between the hands, for example, by being dropped from one hand into a receptacle held by the other hand (see Figure 6) (Johansson & Westling, 1987b, 1988b). Further accounts of the characteristics of the grip load force coupling are provided by Wing in this volume (Chapter 15).

It is commonly believed that this type of task-related coordinative constraint (or synergy) represents a strategy that simplifies the demands on the control mechanisms by reducing the number of degrees of freedom of the musculoskeletal apparatus that have to be explicitly controlled (Bernstein, 1967; Sporns & Edelman, 1993; Turvey, Shaw, & Mace, 1978). Apparently, in manipulation the coupling of grip and load forces also forms the basis for an efficient sensory control of the motor output to accommodate the physical properties of the object, such as its weight (see above) and the friction in the hand–object interface (Johansson, 1991).

3. PARAMETRIC ADJUSTMENTS OF FINGERTIP FORCES TO PHYSICAL PROPERTIES OF OBJECTS

The approximately proportional relationship between the changes in grip and load force is functional only if appropriately scaled to the friction between the skin and the object: at a given load force (tangential force) there is a minimum grip force (normal force) required to prevent slip. Thus, to prevent slip the grip:load force ratio that is employed must exceed a certain minimum determined by the inverse of the coefficient of friction, termed the slip ratio (Figures 3B and C) (Johansson & Westling, 1984b). In everyday situations there may be substantial changes in friction related to the various surface materials of objects (Figure 4A), objects may be soaked and the sweating rate and so on may vary. Indeed, people automatically adjust the employed grip

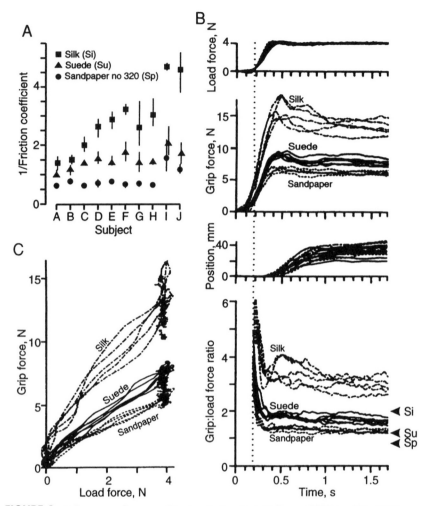

FIGURE 4 Influence on force coordination during the initial part of lifting trials of different surface structures: finely textured silk, most slippery; suede, less slippery; and fine grain sandpaper (no. 320), least slippery. (A) Friction between the surface and fingertip skin for the three surfaces in 10 subjects (A–J) plotted as the inverse coefficient of friction. Symbols represent median values of 5 trials, and bars represent the corresponding range. Note that these materials exhibited different friction but there were large interindividual variations. Some of this variation may be explained by differences in the sweating rate between individuals. Indeed, the two extreme subjects showing the lowest friction were postmenopausal women (subjects I and J). (B) Load force, grip force, vertical position, and ratio between grip and load force as a function of time; 15 trials by single subject superimposed. Arrowheads indicate mean slip ratios for the three structures. A comparison between the force ratios employed for the three materials and the corresponding slip ratios clearly indicates that the force coordination is adapted to the frictional condition. (C) Coordination between grip force and load force during the same trials as in (A) illustrated by displaying the grip force against the load force. (B–C) Illustrations represent standardized conditions in which the previous trials were carried out with the same friction. Weight constant at 400 g. (A, Modified from Johansson and Westling, 1984a; B–C, from Johansson and Westling, 1984b.)

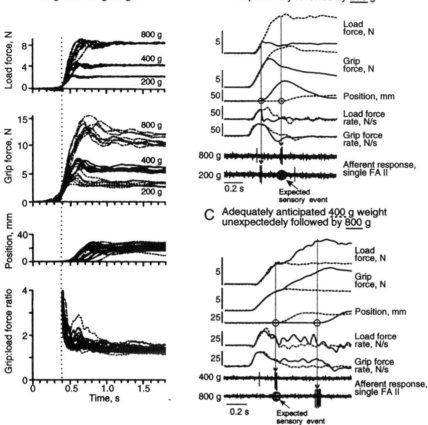

FIGURE 5 Adaptation of the force output to the weight of objects. (A) Force coordination during the initial part of adequately-programmed lifts with three different weights of the object (data from 24 single trials superimposed; single subject). (B) Initial parts of an adequately programmed lift with an 800-g weight and a lift with 200 g that was erroneously programmed for the heavier 800-g weight, which was lifted in the previous trial. The burst responses in the FA II (Pacinian) afferent at the start of movement were recorded using microneurography (Westling & Johansson, 1987). The sensory information about the start of movement at the unexpected point in time for the erroneously programmed 200-g trial is used to terminate the load phase. Note, however, overshoots in position and forces due to the reflex delay. (C) Initial parts of an adequately programmed lift with a 400-g weight and a lift with 800 g that was erroneously programmed for the lighter 400 g weight lifted in the previous trial. The absence of burst responses in the FA II afferents at the expected point in time for the erroneously programmed 800-g trial (see expected sensory event) is used to initiate a new control mode. This involves slow, more discontinuous probing force increases, until terminated by the sensory input at the actual take-off. (A, Adapted from Johansson and Westling, 1984b; B–C, From Johansson and Cole, 1992.)

forces and thereby the grip:load force ratio to these changes in friction, that is, the more slippery the object the higher the employed force ratio (Figure 4) (Edin et al., 1992; Johansson & Westling, 1984b; Westling & Johansson, 1984; also see Cole & Johansson, 1993; Flanagan, Wing, Allison, & Spenceley, 1995; Forssberg, Eliasson, Kinoshita, Westling, & Johansson, 1995). It seems clear that this adaptation is made to the friction per se, rather than on the basis of different texture properties of the touched materials. Thus, for example, Johansson and Westling (1984a) showed that subjects compensate for the drop in friction caused by washing the hands even though there is no change in surface texture of the grasped object. One expression of the safety margin against slip is the difference between the force ratio coordinated by the subject and the slip ratio (Figures 3B, 4B). The safety margin employed while objects are held usually constitutes some 10–40% of the grip force, depending on subject and context.

People parametrically adapt their force output also to the weight of a lifted object. This is most clearly observed during the isometric load phase (A. M. Gordon, Westling, Cole, & Johansson, 1993; Johansson & Westling, 1988a). To get a predictable, smooth, and critically damped vertical lifting movement the lifting drive must be decreased and appropriately adjusted to match the weight of the object before the moment of lift-off. In fact, with an adequately programmed lift, the first time derivative of the grip and load forces have their maximum when the load force matches about half the weight of the object; the force rates are reduced prior to lift-off to harmonize with the expected weight (Figure 5B; trials with adequate weight anticipation). In addition, the desired speed (acceleration) and height of the lifting movement play a significant role in the parameterization of the force output during the isometric load phase (Kinoshita et al., 1993).

4. MEMORY FOR OBJECT PHYSICAL PROPERTIES: ANTICIPATORY PARAMETER CONTROL

There are two important determinants of the parametric changes described in the previous section. In this section I consider the role in anticipatory control of memory information acquired during previous manipulation. In the following section I discuss the role of afferent information about various discrete events in the hand–object interface during execution of the task.

It has been repeatedly shown that the initial forces applied to an object reflect the requirements of the previous lift. The frictional conditions in the preceding lift with an object are reflected in the development of the grip and load forces immediately after the object is touched (see grip forces in Figures 4B and C) (Edin et al., 1992; Forssberg et al., 1995; Johansson & Westling,

1984b). Likewise, the adaptation of force development to an object's weight during the load phase must rely on memory representations of the object's weight acquired during previous lifts because explicit information about object weight is not available until lift-off (A. M. Gordon et al., 1991c, 1993; Johansson & Westling, 1988a). Thus, one must hypothesize that there exist sensorimotor memories that represent both important physical properties of the objects to be manipulated and the appropriate magnitude parameters of the motor commands. Furthermore, the fact that information about both frictional conditions and weight is transferred from one hand to the other hand in subsequent manipulation of the same object further supports the idea that relevant physical properties of objects as such are retained (A. M. Gordon, Forssberg, & Iwasaki, 1994; Johansson & Westling, 1984b, 1988b; also see Flanagan, Wing, et al., 1995).

4.1 Anticipatory Control in Bimanual Manipulative Tasks

Anticipatory control during manipulation is also important in coordinating the hands during bimanual tasks. Consider a task in which a ball is dropped by the subject from one hand into a receptacle held in a precision grip by the other hand (Figure 6A) (Johansson & Westling, 1988b). Whether visual control is allowed or not, there is a task-dependent graded preparatory grip force increase appearing about 150 ms prior to the impact (e.g., Figure 6B). In addition, the target object is simultaneously lifted to meet the impact of the ball. These preparatory actions are precisely scaled to the peak in load force at impact, the former to prevent dropping the target apparatus due to slips, the latter to avoid excessive position deviations. Thus, these preparatory actions are automatically scaled to the magnitude of the perturbation, which is influenced by the weight of the dropped object (Figure 6B), the weight of the target apparatus (not illustrated), and the length of the drop (Figure 6C). In addition, the preparatory grip force responses are also properly adapted to the frictional condition between the skin and the grip surfaces of the receptacle in ways that conform to the principles described above (Figure 6D). The somatosensory information used to adjust the preparatory action is obtained while the ball and target object are handled before the drop by the separate hands, and combined in a predictive feed-forward manner with other task-related information such as height of drop. The anticipatory control of the task and the aforementioned coordinative constraints appear particularly clearly if the preparatory actions are examined in isolation (Figure 7, solid lines).

Electromyographic (EMG) recordings during the ball-drop task reveal that the entire arm-hand system is appropriately stiffened by cocontractions in agonistic and antagonistic hand and arm muscles during the preparatory grip force increases (see Figure 7). Likewise, the impact elicits some reflex coactivation appearing 35–40 ms and 55–65 ms after impact in the proximal arm and distal hand muscles, respectively (cf. Figure 7; dotted EMG curves) (Johansson & Westling, 1988b). Note, however, in Figure 7 that the motor program executing the preparatory actions caused a pronounced depression of the motoneuronal activity specifically during the period at which the triggered EMG responses appear (cf. dotted and solid EMG curves). Indeed, if the ball is dropped unexpectedly (e.g., by the experimenter), in the absence of the preparatory actions there are much stronger triggered responses (Johansson & Westling, 1988b). This is true even though they appear too late to be useful to prevent slips. In the prepared case, however, there is no obvious need for these responses. These findings are reminiscent of patterns of preparatory and triggered actions recently observed when humans catch a freely falling ball (e.g., Lacquaniti et al., 1991, 1992). Evidently, the central nervous

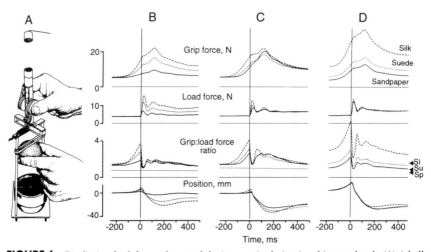

FIGURE 6 Predictive feed-forward control during manipulation in a bimanual task. (A) A ball is dropped by the subject from one hand into a receptacle (400-g weight; instrumented for grip force, load force, and position measurements) held in a precision grip by the other hand. (B) The weight of the ball was randomly varied between trials: 100 g (solid line), 300 g (dotted line), and 500 g (dashed line). (C) The distance the ball fell was randomly varied between trials: 2 cm (solid line), 4 cm (dotted line), and 8 cm (dashed line). Weight of ball, 300 g. (D) The surface material was randomly varied between trials: sandpaper (solid line), suede (dotted line), and silk (dashed line). Arrowheads indicate slip ratios for these grip surfaces, respectively. Weight of ball, 300 g. (B–D) Data averaged from total 22 trials, respectively. Vertical lines indicate the moment the ball hits the receptacle of the grip apparatus. (B–C) Horizontal dotted lines indicate estimated slip ratio. Note that the preparatory force increase is precisely scaled such that the minimum force ratio at the impact is always the same in B–C, and adequately adapted to the frictional condition (B–D). (Adapted from Johansson and Westling, 1988b.)

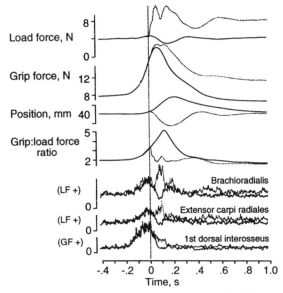

FIGURE 7   Preparatory actions while the subject dropped the ball (400 g) studied in isolation by means of preventing the ball from reaching the target cup (grip apparatus, 400 g). The ball was prevented from hitting the target surface (solid line; averaged data from 24 trials) or the ball hit the target surface (dotted line; averaged data from 56 trials) in the same experimental series. Vertical dotted line indicates the moment the ball hit the target cup during the ordinary trials (time = 0). Grip surface suede, single blindfolded subject. The surface EMG signal was root-mean-square processed (rise and decay time constants of 1 ms and 3 ms). The primary actions of three muscles regarding their influences on the load and grip forces are indicated by LF+ (load force increase) and GF+ (grip force increase). (Adapted from Johansson and Westling, 1988b.)

system (CNS) dynamically regulates both the preparatory muscle activity and spinal and supraspinal reflex pathways in a predictive feed-forward manner. Hence, this control represents an anticipatory adaptation of limb mechanics according to task demands and implies that the CNS entertains global models of relevant object and task properties during manipulation (e.g., Ghez et al., 1991; Johansson & Cole, 1992; Lacquaniti, 1992), including the associated postural control (Hugon et al., 1982; Massion, 1994; Paulignan et al., 1989; for further discussion, see Lacquaniti, Chapter 11).

5. AFFERENT CONTROL DURING TASK EXECUTION: DISCRETE EVENT, SENSORY-DRIVEN CONTROL

Various sensory systems can provide the information that there is a mismatch between the expected and the true properties of an object. Information from such mismatches is used to trigger preprogrammed patterns of corrective responses and to update the relevant sensorimotor memories used in anticipatory parameter control. The most relevant afferent information for the adaptation of the motor commands to the intrinsic physical properties of the object is provided by the mechanoreceptors located close to the interface between the hand and the object, that is, tactile receptors in the glabrous skin of the digits. Indeed, the general importance of sensory input from the digits in the control of finger movements has been extensively documented over decades (e.g., Caccia, McComas, Upton, & Blogg, 1973; Darton, Lippold, Shahani, & Shahani, 1985; Evans, Harrison, & Stephens, 1989; Garnett & Stephens, 1980; Jenner & Stephens, 1982; Marsden, Merton, & Morton, 1985; P. B. C. Matthews, 1989; McCloskey, Gandevia, Potter, & Colebatch, 1983; Mott & Sherrington, 1895; Twitchell, 1954).

5.1 Sequential Phase Coordination and Updating of Weight-Related Memory

Typical responses in the four types of tactile afferents from the glabrous skin of the human digits during a lift are shown in Figure 3B (for reviews of the tactile innervation of the human glabrous skin see Johansson & Vallbo, 1983; Vallbo & Johansson, 1984). At the four points corresponding to phase transitions, there are distinct burst discharges in tactile afferents (Westling & Johansson, 1987): (1) initial responses appear during the preload phase when the object is first contacted, (2) burst responses in the FA II afferents occur both at the start of the vertical movement when the object leaves the table and (3) near the end when contact is again made with the table, and finally (4) responses appear at the end of the unload phase when the object is released.

5.1.1 Tactile Contact and Release Responses

Initial (contact) and release responses occur in slowly adapting (SA) type I and fast adapting (FA) type II afferents but most distinctly and reliably in the FA I afferents (Figure 3B, also see Figure 8A). Due to the curved shape of the fingertip and the viscoelastic properties of the skin and the subjacent tissues, an increase in grip force results in an increase in the area of contact between the fingers and the object. With a flat contact surface this increase is steepest at low grip forces, for example, at 1 N the contact area is about $\frac{2}{3}$ of the area at 10 N. The major determinant of the responses of type I afferents during contact is probably the propagating front of skin deformation across the fingertip as it conforms to the flat surface of the object. It has been estimated that at a grip force of < 1 N approximately 300 FA I and 150 SA I afferents are engaged at each digit (Westling & Johansson, 1987).

The contact responses evidently provide information that a secure contact has been established. Such information must exist for the subsequent release of motor commands that drive further manipulation, that is, in the lifting task a parallel increase in the grip and load forces (Figure 3B). Quite predictably, when sensory information is lacking as a result of nerve damage or an anesthetic block of the digital nerves, the contact force becomes excessive before the parallel increases in load and grip forces commence (Johansson & Westling, 1984b). Release responses, on the other hand, provide information about disengaged parts of the fingers, which are free for further tasks. Or it may be used to forewarn that contact may be lost, which, in turn, may be used to elicit various compensatory responses.

5.1.2 Afferent Responses to Object Lift-Off and Touch-Down

FA II afferents (Pacinian corpuscles) show an exquisite sensitivity to mechanical transients such as those caused by an object's lift-off and by the sudden cessation of the movement at touch-down when an object is replaced on a support (Figure 3B and Figure 5B and C) (Westling & Johansson, 1987).

The parallel increase in the grip and load forces during the load phase terminates shortly after the object starts to move. As discussed above, memory information based on previous experiences with the weight of the current object (or related objects; see below) is used to parameterize the force output in anticipation of the weight of the object. Consequently, with an unexpected change to a lighter weight, the load and grip force rates are excessively high when the load force suddenly overcomes the force of gravity (Figure 5B; solid lines). However, an abrupt triggered termination of the muscle commands driving the load phase takes place some 80–110 ms after lift-off (depending on the muscle) (Johansson & Westling, 1988a). Burst responses in FA II afferents, which effectively indicate that the object has started to move, are most likely used to trigger this (Figure 5B, afferent response during the 200-g lift). But the delays in the control loop (due to receptor and effector delays, axonal conductances, and CNS processing delays) are still long enough to cause a pronounced position overshoot (a common experience when lifting an unexpectedly light object).

If the object is heavier than expected and the lift-off does not occur at the predicted load force (Figure 5C; solid lines), the absence of motion is indicated through the lack of a transient sensory response at the expected moment of lift-off (Figure 5C, afferent signal during the 800-g lift). In this case the CNS uses the absence of the expected sensory signal to quickly initiate a new control mode. This is characterized by slow, discontinuous increases in force that, in effect, probe for the lift-off (see force rate signals in Figure 5C). This control mode continues until somatosensory information confirming movement is eventually obtained (Figure 5C, burst response during the 800-g trial). The motor program thus appears to generate a set of predicted afferent signals, that are compared to the actual afferent signals (cf. Baev &

Shimansky, 1992; Merfeld, Young, Oman, & Shelhamer, 1993; Miall et al., 1993). When a particular situation is sensed, an appropriate motor response appears to be generated in a conditional manner according to a rule-based scheme (see the discussion of Finite state control in Prochazka, 1993). Hence, whether the object's weight is correctly anticipated or not, somatosensory signals apparently trigger the termination of the load phase and presumably simultaneously update the memory system representation of the weight of the object. Indeed, with erroneous weight anticipation, only one lift is typically required to efficiently update the weight-related memory system.

Due to their high sensitivity to various mechanical transients, which may be physically quite remote, FA II afferents whose endings are located in the palm and at the wrist, as well as those in the fingers, show burst responses at lift-off and touch-down. We have estimated that more than 500 FA IIs respond at lift-off (Westling & Johansson, 1987). Thus, even if the digits are anesthetised, FA II afferents still respond and the sensory events at the transition between phases of lifting continue to take place as described. The termination of the load phase will be disrupted during finger anesthesia only if the lifting is too gentle (Johansson & Westling, 1991). The remote (unanesthetized) units may fail to respond to the weak transients. The other three types of tactile afferents in the glabrous skin are virtually indifferent to these type of mechanical events, and so are the musculotendinous receptors (cf. Macefield & Johansson, in press; also see Evarts, 1981; Vallbo, 1985).

5.2 Sensory Signals Updating the Grip:Load Force Ratio for Grasp Stability

It has been demonstrated that tactile receptors in the fingertips are of crucial importance in adapting the relation between grip and load forces to the friction at the digit–object interface (Edin et al., 1992; Johansson & Westling, 1984b, 1987a). The skin receptors play a dual role in this respect. The most important adjustments takes place shortly after the initial contact and can be observed about 0.1 s after contact. If these are inadequate, secondary adjustments take place that always increase the grip:load force ratio. The initial burst responses in subpopulations of excited FA I afferents are markedly influenced by the surface material (Johansson & Westling, 1987a). The more slippery the material, the stronger the response (Figure 8A). Hence, this afferent information most likely accounts for the early adjustment to a new frictional condition (cf. grip force traces in Figure 8A).

In less than 10% of trials in series of lifting trials in which the surface friction is varied in an unpredictable manner, the initial adjustments are inadequate, or leave only a minute safety margin against slips so that the force ratio may approach the critical ratio at a later point. The resulting small slips (which typically occur at one digit only; see below) are rarely felt, but they

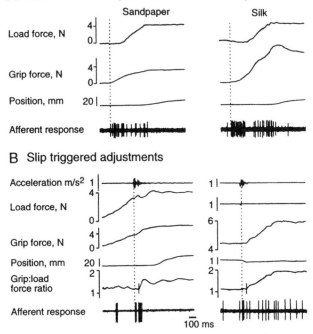

A Initial afferent responses and frictional adjustments

B Slip triggered adjustments

FIGURE 8 Single tactile afferent responses and adjustments to the frictional condition between the object and the digits. (A) Examples of initial afferent responses in a FA I unit, and the influence of the surface structure (single trials). Note the early scaling of the rate of grip force increase to the frictional condition. Vertical lines indicate the initial touch. (B) Examples of afferent slip responses and upgradings of the grip:load force ratio elicited by small but distinct slips. Vertical dotted lines indicate the onset of the slips as revealed by vibrations in the object (acceleration signal; 10–600 Hz). Short vertical lines indicate the onset of the upgrading of the force ratio. (*Left*) Slip during the load phase, FA II unit. The middle burst is the afferent slip response, whereas the third represents dynamic responses to the force changes following the slips, and the first is the result of mechanical events not reflected in our mechanical recordings, respectively. (*Right*) Slip during the static phase, SA I unit. (Adapted from Johansson and Westling, 1987a.)

promptly trigger an automatic increase in the grip force to a higher maintained level (Figure 8B). The slips are encoded as brief burst responses in FA I, FA II, and SA I afferents, which trigger an active upgrading in the grip:load force ratios appearing about 70 ms after the onset of the slip. The new higher and stable ratio restores the safety margin preventing further slips. We consider that the maintained upgrading of the ratio results from updating of a frictional memory, which, in turn, controls the force ratio (Johansson & Westling, 1984b). Small slips localized to only a part of the skin area in contact with the object elicit similar effects, mediated by localized slip responses in FA I and SA I afferents (Johansson & Westling, 1987a).

Slip events during the load phase trigger changes in both the load (decrease) and grip (increase) force rates (Figure 8B, *left*). During the static phase, however, just the grip force is influenced (Figure 8B, *right*). This phase dependence is functional, since gravity restrains the response alternatives preventing efficient load force adjustments during the static phase. A similar dependence on the phase of movement or postural situation has been described with other multiarticulate actions triggered by somatosensory input (for review, see Rossignol, Lund, & Drew, 1988).

With electrical stimulation of tactile afferents it is possible, under certain restricted conditions, to artificially induce an upgrading of the grip:load force ratio similar to that triggered by slips (Johansson & Westling, 1987a). However, after only a few trials subjects completely habituate to this stimulation and the response disappears, but the subject still responds adequately to natural slips. This improved selectivity in the interpretation of the afferent signal points to the highly discriminative nature of sensory information processing that can be displayed by the sensorimotor systems involved.

With local finger anesthesia, the grip and load forces still change in parallel after a prolonged preload phase. However, the frictional adjustment is disrupted (Johansson & Westling, 1984b). When tactile sensory information from the digits is blocked, subjects use strong grip forces that are unnecessarily high during less slippery frictional conditions, yet they may be inadequate with a slippery material. Similar but less pronounced impairments are observed in patients suffering from moderate degradation of tactile signals after median nerve compression (Cole, 1994), as well as after nerve regeneration following laceration (Johansson & Westling, 1991), and also in elderly subjects (Cole, 1991; Cole & Beck, 1994).

5.3 Independent Sensory Control of the Digits for Grasp Stability

By varying the frictional condition independently at each digit (thumb and index finger) engaged in lifting tasks it can be shown that the grip:load force ratios employed at each of the digits engaged are controlled independently (Edin et al., 1992). As illustrated in Figure 9A–C, during the load phase (before the lift-off) the load force is already actively distributed between the digits in a way that reflects the frictional conditions at the separate digits. As a result, the safety margins against slips are similar at the two digits regardless of the surfaces they contact (shaded areas in Figure 9A–C). The observed load distributions are established using tactile information from each digit combined with anticipatory parameter control that is specific for each digit (cf. the scheme outlined above). Accordingly, the initial forces at each dig-

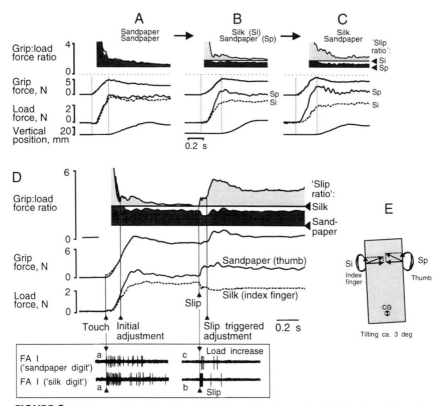

FIGURE 9 Digit-specific adjustments of force coordination to the frictional condition. The subject lifted an instrumented test object (E) with low center of gravity (CG) from a support surface, and held the object still in the air before replacing it. (A–C) Initial parts of three consecutive lifts. The grip:load force ratio and corresponding slip ratios are shown for each digit; the safety margin to prevent slips is indicated by soft shading for the index finger, heavy shading for the thumb. In (A) the index finger and thumb both contacted sandpaper (Sp). The total load force was approximately uniformly distributed between the index finger and thumb. (B) The contact surface at the index finger had been unexpectedly changed to the more slippery silk. An adjustment to the new frictional condition occurs initially during the trial; the tangential (load) forces were distributed so that an adequate safety margin was maintained at each digit (also see D). (C) In the subsequent trial, the index finger which contacted the more slippery surface in (B), already picked up less load force than the thumb at the onset of the load force increase (i.e., reflecting anticipatory parameter control). These frictional adjustments resulted in an adequate safety margin at each digit despite the different friction. Due to the uneven load force distributions (in B–D) the test object tilts a bit while held aloft (E). (D) An initial adjustment to a new frictional condition followed by a secondary adjustment triggered by a slip event. The slip at the index finger, which contacted silk (Si), resulted in a rapid decrease of the tangential (load) force at that digit and a concomitant increase of the load force at the nonslipping digit. About 70 ms later the normal (grip) force increased such that the ratio at the digit that had slipped (Si) increased and the ratio at the nonslipping digit was effectively restored. (D, *below*) signals in examples of tactile sensors: initial responses in a FA I sensor (a) showing influence of the surface structure on the impulse rate; responses in a FA I sensor related to a distinct slip (b) associated with rapid decrease in the load force at that digit; and responses in an FA I sensor to an increase of the load force (c) corresponding to that occurring at the nonslipping digit in (A). (Adapted from Edin et al., 1992.)

it reflect the frictional characteristics present at each digit for the previous lift (cf. Figure 9A vs. B vs. C, which represent three consecutive trials).

The anticipatory partitioning of the forces among the digits seems to relate to a low-level neural controller, operating locally at each digit and reflecting a representation of motor commands used in the previous lift (Edin et al., 1992). However, this low-level control is subordinated to a higher level of anticipatory control related to the total load and grip forces required by the physical properties of the object (weight and average friction). How these two levels of control are integrated remains to be investigated.

Figure 9D illustrates initial adjustments to a new frictional condition (based on sensory information originating from each of the contact areas). Prior to this lift, the contact surface at the index finger was unexpectedly changed from sandpaper to silk, that is, to a more slippery material than the sandpaper experienced in the previous trial. After a period of similar force development, as in the previous trial, less load force is applied to the more slippery silk surface and more to the sandpaper surface of the opposing digit. A somewhat higher grip force is also used compared to that in the previous trial, since on average the object became more slippery (cf. grip forces in Figure 9A and B). With similar frictional conditions at the two digits the force ratio increase upon changing to a more slippery material is realized only by increasing the grip force (Figure 4B).

Slips that may occur later in a lift (Figure 9D), typically at one digit only, result in an abrupt grip:load force ratio increase on the slipping digit (as it suddenly becomes unloaded). Simultaneously, the increase in load force causes the ratio to fall suddenly at the other (nonslipping) digit and it may approach the slip ratio (Figure 9D). The triggered upgrading in the grip force restores an adequate safety margin on the nonslipping digit to the levels that existed before the slip, and increases appropriately the safety margin on the slipping digit. These updated force ratios are not only used to prevent future slips during the current trial but also for anticipatory parameter control employed for future lifts.

Further evidence that the digits are controlled by parallel but independent (digit-specific) mechanisms for grasp stability was provided in experiments where subjects lifted a test object between the fingers of the right and left hand, but also when two subjects shared the task, each subject contributing one finger (Burstedt, et al., 1992). The performance during precision lifting using digits belonging to one hand, two hands, or two subjects was remarkably similar. Except for a slight protraction of the dynamic phases of the lift carried out by two subjects (lifting was synchronized by the experimenter by a verbal countdown), the same basic patterns of spatial and sequential coordination were observed. Importantly, the safety margins at each digit were adjusted adequately to reflect the local frictional conditions.

These findings reinforce our theory that the grip:load force ratio required for a stable grasp is controlled by a lower level controller that is digit specific. Accordingly, important aspects of the distribution of forces among digits in manipulative tasks would be an emergent property of the proposed digit-specific controllers that communicate only through sensory inputs concerning mechanical events at the separate digit–object interfaces. That is, grasp stability as such is not dependent on a mechanism that explicitly coordinates the engaged digits. This notion is particularly attractive, while considering that grasp stability applies to a variety of grips.

5.4 Recall of Relevant Sensorimotor Memories by Vision and Haptics

A variety of sensory-based identification processes, including the retrieval of relevant object properties based on visual or haptic identification, are involved in the mechanisms for anticipatory parameter control. For instance, during everyday activities we commonly handle objects of different shapes, weights, and densities, and often the object is lifted only once. During the very first lift of such objects, and before sensory information related to the object's weight is available, the force rate profiles during the load phase are appropriately targeted for the weight of the current object (Figure 10) (A. M. Gordon et al., 1993). This indicates that physical properties of common objects are indeed represented in memories that are used for anticipatory parameter control of the force output.

Likewise, object size cues acquired both visually and haptically influence the anticipatory parameterization of the forces during the load phase (A. M. Gordon et al., 1991a, 1991b), and weight estimation by size-weight associations is efficiently used for classes of related objects (Gordon et al., 1991c). Such a representation of weight-size relationships obviously makes anticipatory control of similar objects of different size possible without vast amounts of previously stored data.

The ability of humans to learn to identify novel unfamiliar objects in terms of appropriate force parameters has also been investigated (A. M. Gordon et al., 1993). With unfamiliar objects, to initially parameterize force output, subjects apparently use a default, density-related estimate that is in the range of common densities. With novel objects of a density that is unusually high (4.0 kg/l) two to four trials are required to form an adequate memory representation of the weight. When lifting the same object 24 hours later, the force scaling is adapted to the object's weight at the first lift.

That visuomotor mechanisms support grasp is already evident from our ability to reach for an object. Using visual mechanisms we identify relevant intrinsic physical features of the object and employ these to automatically control the reach. We preshape the hand to object shape and position the

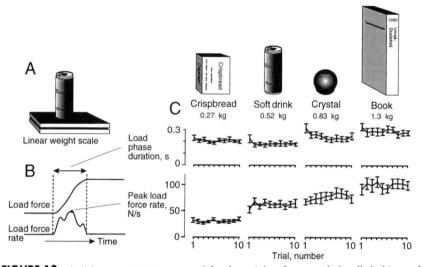

FIGURE 10 Anticipatory parameter control for the weight of commonly handled objects of different shapes, weights, and densities. (A) The isometric lifting force (load force) was recorded while subjects lifted from an analog weight scale a variety of objects, that is, crispbread, soft drink, crystal, and telephone book. (B). Duration of load phase and load force rate were measured from the unloading of the weight scale while subjects lifted the test object. (C) Load phase duration and peak load force rate for each of ten consecutive lifts of each common object (means ±1 *SEM;* data averaged across subjects). Note, during the very first lift, and before sensory information related to the object's weight was available, the load force output was scaled differently for the various objects with force rate profiles targeted for the weight of the current object. Also note the similar performance in the first and last lift. That small changes in these force profiles occurred across ten consecutive lifts indicates that the force output is successfully specified from information in memory related to the weight of the common objects, retrieved by visual identification of the target object prior to the first trial; the subjects had no practice prior to the lift series. (Adapted from A. M. Gordon et al., 1993.)

digits on its surfaces so as to promote grasp stability and the achievement of further action goals (cf. Gentilucci et al., 1991; Jakobson & Goodale, 1991; Jeannerod, 1984, 1986; Paulignan, Jeannerod, et al., 1991; Rosenbaum et al., 1990; Steimach, Stiello, & Jeannerod, 1994; also see Fikes, Klatzky, & Lederman, 1994; Marteniuk et al., 1990). Importantly, the kinematics of these movements are determined largely by the initial view of the object before the movement onset, that is, visual feedback signals seem of little importance during the movement itself (e.g., Jackson, Jackson, & Rosicky, 1995; Jakobson & Goodale, 1991; Servos & Goodale, 1994; also see Goodale, Jakobson, & Keillor, 1994; Jeannerod, 1981, 1984). This further supports the general importance of implicit memory control of relevant motor program parameters in manipulation.

6. ONTOGENETIC DEVELOPMENT OF SENSORIMOTOR CONTROL IN PRECISION LIFTING

Precision grip first emerges around 10 months of age but the mature pattern of grasping, lifting, and holding objects is not observed before the age of about 8 years (Forssberg, Eliasson, Kinoshita, Johansson, & Westling, 1991; Forssberg et al., 1992, 1995; A. M. Gordon et al., 1994; A. M. Gordon, Forssberg, Johansson, Eliasson, & Westling, 1992; for a review, see A. M. Gordon, 1994). The gradual improvement in behavioral aspects of grasping seems to parallel the gradual maturation of central descending and ascending pathways in humans (e.g., Eyre et al., 1991; see also Armand et al., Chapter 7), and takes place in conjunction with qualitative improvements of independent finger movements (Pehoski, 1994). Since motor development is considered to reflect an increased influence by the corticospinal tract over spinal motor networks, including monosynaptic connections to the motoneurones of the distal hand muscles (Lawrence & Hopkins, 1976; Lemon, 1993), it is likely that the control of the lift task largely relies on cerebral processes.

Children up to about 18 months of age do not display the adult grip-lift synergy characterized by a parallel smooth change in the grip and load forces (Figure 11) (Forssberg et al., 1991). Rather, they tend to increase grip force in advance of the load force. The transition from a sequential and nonparallel force coordination to the mature pattern is not completed until several years later (Figure 11B). Furthermore, young children produce comparably slow isometric increases in fingertip forces prior to object lift-off, with stuttering movements involving multiple peaks in the force rate in contrast to the smooth parallel grip and load force increase observed in adults (Figure 11A) (Forssberg et al., 1991). Bernstein (1967) pointed out that when learning a motor task, subjects cocontract many muscles, thus reducing the degrees of freedom (the number of variables requiring active control). This strategy simplifies the control problem, but is inefficient and renders movements stiff and jerky. In children the discontinuous force increase is terminated by somatosensory information related to the take-off, which is reminiscent of the probing strategy used by adults who erroneously parameterized the lift for a too-light weight (cf. Figure 5C, solid lines) (Johansson & Westling, 1988a). In this sense the behavior in children may be viewed as reflecting a feedback strategy in the absence of weight-related anticipatory parameter control (Forssberg et al., 1992). Indeed, it has been argued that sensory input is vital during the learning stages, and becomes less and less important as a skill is learnt, provided that the resultant movements proceed according to plan (e.g., Sakamoto, Arissian, & Asanuma, 1989).

The prolongation of the sequential phases of the lifting task in young children also relate to less precise control at the transitions between succes-

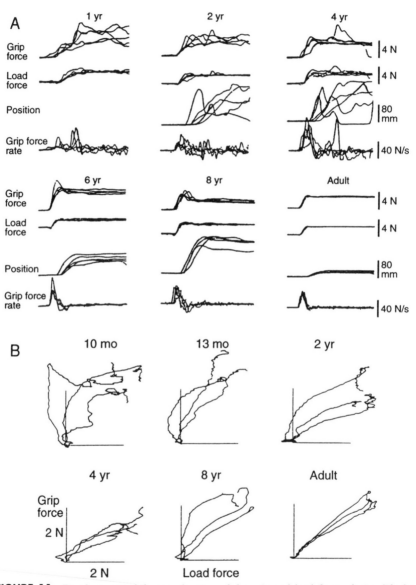

FIGURE 11 Development of the coordination of the grip and load forces during lifts by children and adults. (A) Grip force and load force and grip force rate as a function of time during several consecutive trials (superimposed) for individual children of various ages and an adult. Note the large variability and excessive grip forces used by young children compared to the adults. (B) Grip force as a function of load force during the initial parts of lifting trials by children of various ages and an adult. Note the nonparallel increase in grip and load forces for young children compared to adults. (A–B) Surface material and object's weight constant. (Adapted from Forssberg et al., 1991.)

sive phases of lifting (Forssberg et al., 1991, 1992). For instance, the youngest children exhibit long delays between contact by the index finger and thumb with the object, and the onset of increases in grip and load force. This likely reflects an immature control of hand closure and inefficient triggering of the motor commands by cutaneous afferents (see above). The decrease in the duration of the phases during subsequent years parallels a maturation of cutaneous reflexes of the hand (Issler & Stephens, 1983).

Nevertheless, during the latter part of the second year children already begin to use memory information for anticipatory parameter control pertaining to the somatosensory experiences of the object's weight in the previous lift (Forssberg et al., 1992). However, adult-like lifting performance with adequate control of object acceleration is not seen until 6–8 years of age. Interestingly, there are manual asymmetries in the development of the anticipatory scaling of the force output. The object's weight in the previous trial shows stronger influences at earlier ages with lifts by the left hand than by the right hand (A. M. Gordon et al., 1994). Handedness emerges early in ontogeny, but despite extensive research its mechanisms are largely unknown (Bishop, 1990). Approximately one year later, that is, at about 3 years of age, children begin to use weight information gained in the previous trial for some scaling of the force output in subsequent lifts by the contralateral hand (A. M. Gordon et al., 1994). This slower development may be related to a late maturation of interhemispheric connections (Galin, Johnstone, Nakell, & Herron, 1979; Yakolev & Lecours, 1967). Somatosensory information from active touch and proprioception is lateralized to the contralateral hemisphere and is transferred through the anterior commissure of corpus callosum, which is one of the last structures to be myelinated (Gazzaniga et al., 1963; Semmes & Mishkin, 1965; Wall, 1970).

The use of vision for weight estimation through size-weight associations for classes of related objects (e.g., A. M. Gordon et al., 1991c) also emerges at about 3 years of age, that is, about one year later than the use of somatosensory information for anticipatory control related to object weight (A. M. Gordon et al., 1992). Additional cognitive development is apparently required before the necessary associative size-weight mapping can take place. Moreover, in contrast to adults, once children begin to use visual size cues they are unable to adequately attenuate the effects of those size cues that do not provide accurate weight-related information, that is, in situations in which weight and size do not covary. This is consistent with the view that vision has a particularly strong influence on motor coordination in children (e.g., D. N. Lee & Aronson, 1974). Hence, the context-related selective suppression of visual influences requires even further cognitive development than using size cues for weight estimation.

Young children display a limited capacity to adapt the grip:load force ratio to the frictional conditions of the digit–object interface (Forssberg et al., 1995). As with adults with impaired digital sensibility (see above), children use high grip forces resulting in a large and variable safety margin against slips in trials with high friction. This may reflect a strategy to compensate for an immature tactile control of precision grip and avoid slips with slippery materials. The grip forces and their variability decrease during the first five years, in parallel with a better adaptation to the current frictional condition. However, even the youngest children (1–2 years) show some capacity to adjust grip force to the friction provided that the same surface material is used in series of lifts. The need for repetitive presentation suggests a poor capacity to form a sensorimotor memory representation of the current friction, or an immature capacity to control the grip:load force ratio employed on the basis of this representation. Older children require fewer lifts and adults only one lift, to update their force coordination to new frictional conditions.

It is noteworthy that in all these developmental studies, there were large intertrial variations reported in employed forces and in the temporal aspects of performance for tasks carried out by individual children (cf. Figure 11). Small children show a large variation in the performance of various types of movements (Cioni, Ferrari, & Prechtl, 1989; Forssberg, 1985; Forssberg & Nashner, 1982; Hadders-Algra & Prechtl, 1992), and this large variability probably reflects an important principle for motor development (Touwen, 1978). It may be hypothesized that by monitoring and evaluating the effect of various spatiotemporal patterns, the CNS will eventually be able to select the best pattern (Sporns & Edelman, 1993). This process takes several years of practice; in the case of manipulative capacity a behavior similar to that of adults is not achieved until about 5–10 years of age.

In many respects, impaired coordination of the motor commands underlying grasping in 6- to 8-year-old children with cerebral palsy is similar to the immature coordination seen in young children just beginning to use the precision grip (Eliasson, Gordon, & Forssberg, 1991, 1992, 1995). Likewise, Down's syndrome individuals generate substantially greater grip forces than controls in lifting trials and fail to adapt normally to changes in the frictional properties of the objects (Cole, Abbs, & Turner, 1988). In both cases the results for grasp are consistent with other findings indicating impaired use of somatosensory information for controlling movement and posture in general.

7. COMMENTS ON CENTRAL NEURAL MECHANISMS

Little is yet known about the exact implementation, at the neural network level, of the specific sensorimotor control functions used by humans in manipulative tasks. However, in general terms the control of grasping and manipulation appears to rely on distributed processes in the CNS, engaging most areas known to be involved in sensorimotor control. These parallel processes may to some extent be responsible for specific control functions such as selection of task-related sensorimotor transforms, initiation of motor actions, and specification of various motor command parameters based on memory systems.

7.1 Primary Motor Cortex

Numerous lines of evidence indicate that the primary motor cortex as well as the corticospinal pathways (including the cortico-motoneuronal pathway) are of fundamental importance for the execution of skilled hand tasks in primates, particularly those that involve precision grip (Datta, Harrison, & Stephans, 1989; Evans et al., 1989; Kuypers, 1981; Lawrence & Kuypers, 1968; Porter & Lemon, 1993). Through its descending influences upon the spinal cord, the motor cortex can modulate activity in all of the motoneurone pools involved in reach and grasp (Johansson et al., 1994; Lemon, Johansson, & Westling, 1995). This may take place directly, through the cortico-motoneuronal pathway, or indirectly, through spinal neural networks (Gracies et al., 1994). Indeed, Smith and colleagues (Picard & Smith, 1992a, 1992b) reported that a significant number of neurons active in the hand area of the monkey primary motor cortex were modulated during lifting tasks and could alter their discharge frequency as a function of the object's weight and texture. Afferent activity generated during grasping, particularly of cutaneous origin, exerts a direct influence on motor cortical cells. Tactile inputs exert excitatory effects on some 60% of monkey motor cortex neurones whose activity is related to hand movement (Lemon, 1981; Picard & Smith, 1992a).

Using noninvasive transcranial magnetic brain stimulation (TMS) directed at the hand area of the motor cortex, we recently attempted to assess the influence of the motor cortex on various hand and arm muscles while human subjects reached out, grasped, and lifted an object (Lemon et al., 1995). The results suggest that the intrinsic hand muscles receive their strongest cortical drive as the digits closed around the object, and during the early dynamic phases of the actual manipulation. Because tactile inputs are known to be essential for appropriate coordination of this task and are particularly intense during these phases (Johansson & Westling, 1987a), it is possible that this strong drive partly relates to the central effects of these inputs (cf. Johansson et al., 1994).

In contrast, the extrinsic hand muscles (flexors and extensors), which act to orient the palm and fingertips, appear to be strongly influenced by the motor cortex throughout the reach. Once grip is established after the initial touch of the object, the excitatory drive of these muscles by the motor cortex falls rapidly during the subsequent phases of the lift. The brachioradialis and anterior deltoid muscles, which contribute to transport of the hand, show a similar pattern. Indeed, many studies in monkeys have shown that neurones in the primary motor cortex, whose activity relate to proximal muscles discharge during reaching (Fu, Suarez, & Zebner, 1993; Georgopoulos, Camaniti, Kalaska, & Massey, 1982), are recruited earlier than are neurones with more distal involvement (Kwan, Murphy, & Wong, 1987; Murphy, Kwan, & Wong, 1985).

The cortical drive to arm and hand muscles during the static phase while an object is held still in the air appears much reduced compared to during the dynamic phases of the lift. One possible explanation is that the parameterization of the motor output to suit the physical properties of the object (friction, shape, weight, etc.) is carried out under tight cortical control during the early phases of manipulation (see above). But once adequately parameterized, the cortical influence over the motor output would not be needed and the function of maintaining a stable grasp may thereafter be taken over by subcortical mechanisms.

The weak TMS intensities used in this study (Lemon et al., 1995) did not impair subjects' ability to carry out the task. However, TMS delivered late during the reach significantly delayed the onset of the load phase, that is, the isometric parallel increase in load and grip forces necessary to lift the object. During the late phases of reach cortical control may undergo a critical transition from reach to grasp-related programs, which would be particularly vulnerable to disruption by TMS at this time. TMS might also interfere with the use of tactile information by the cortex, that is, the initial afferent contact responses confirming that the grip has been established (Westling & Johansson, 1987). The observation that TMS can produce delays in the execution of a voluntary task was first made by Day, Rothwell, et al. (1989).

7.2 The Basal Ganglia

The basal ganglia may also be involved in using sensory information to guide the motor commands of precision grip lifting tasks. Parkinsonian subjects manifest a smaller rate and range of lifting, consistent with the clinical observation of bradykinesia (F. Müller & Abbs, 1990; also cf. Wing, 1988). While they adjust their grip force to different weights of objects, they operate with a much higher safety margin. This could not be explained in terms of force production deficits, but rather by impairments in the use of sensory information to guide motor output. Deficits in the use of sensory information are also supported by slower onset latencies, whereby sensory input is used to trigger the next phase of the motor task. Indeed, considerable evidence indicates that the basal ganglia are of importance for the processing of sensory information to control movements (Lidsky, Manetto, & Schneider, 1985; Schultz, 1989). As such, both the basal ganglia and the cerebellum directly influence the hand representation of the primary motor cortex via the ventrolateral thalamus (Holsapple, Preston, & Strick, 1991).

7.3 Cerebellum

As with the primary motor cortex neurons, when monkeys lift an object and hold it in the air the discharge rate in many cerebellar Purkinje cells and unidentified neurons reflects the object's weight and/or friction (as well as the occurrence of load perturbations tending to cause slips) (Dugas & Smith, 1992; Espinoza & Smith, 1990). These effects occur not only during the lifts, but also prior to the application of grip and load forces, suggesting a role of cerebellum in anticipatory parameter control pertaining to object properties. Patients with degenerative cerebellar lesions performing lifting tasks by the precision grip of thumb and index finger are, however, able to adapt their grip force levels to the different object loads (F. Müller & Dichgans, 1994). But they are less efficient than healthy controls in using sensorimotor memory about object weight for anticipatory control. Accordingly, the temporal profile of grip force rate of change featured an irregular pattern characteristic of a lack of sufficient anticipatory parameterization (cf. Johansson & Westling, 1988a). These patients also show prolonged latencies between contact with the object and onset of lift force, and the level of grip force at the start of lift force is elevated.

It is not clear which CNS areas might store or represent weight- and frictional-related somatosensory information acquired during previous lifts. However, the neural computations underlying the use of such memory information for anticipatory parameter control probably take place in CNS areas that are involved in the processing of specific attributes of sensorimotor information. Accordingly, sensorimotor learning is not critically dependent on specific brain regions necessary for episodic and semantic memory operations (Halsband & Freund, 1993; Seitz & Roland, 1992).

7.4 Sensory and Association Cortex

Primary somatosensory cortex (S1) receives and processes somatosensory information used in the regulation of fine grip forces during precision grip, but does not participate in force initiation per se in a visual step-tracking paradigm (Wannier et al., 1991). Integration of somatic sensory information proceeds within the postcentral gyrus in a hierarchical manner (Iwamura, 1993). Many of the caudal neurons that integrate signals from cutaneous and deep afferent sources of the hand respond to specific types of stimulation related to manipulative actions rather than simple somatic stimulation. Indeed, pharmacological inactivation of S1 neurons in area 2 causes deficits in precision grasping but not in visually guided reaching or hand shaping (Hikosaka et al., 1985).

Animal as well as human clinical data implicate the posterior parietal and premotor cortical areas in control of object-oriented manual actions (Goodale & Milner, 1992; Jeannerod, 1994c; Rizzolatti et al., 1988, 1990; Sakata & Taira, 1994; Taira et al., 1990; Viallet, Massion, Massarino, & Khalil, 1992). The anticipatory control related to visual identification of intrinsic physical properties of objects appears to involve the dorsal stream projecting from the striate cortex to the posterior parietal region, while the conscious perception of objects viewed involves the ventral stream of projections from the striate cortex to the inferotemporal cortex (Goodale & Milner, 1992; see Goodale et al., Chapter 2). However, rather than analyze the use of visual cues to retrieve memory information about the intrinsic object properties for control of fingertip forces during actual manipulation, most CNS studies have so far been concerned with the control of hand transport, shaping, and orientation prior to actual manipulation. Nevertheless, a dissociation between perceiving objects and the operation of mechanisms for anticipatory control of finger forces is also evident in lifting tasks. When healthy adults lift objects equal in weight but not in size, they reliably report smaller objects to be heavier (Charpentier, 1891), but still they use a larger force output for larger objects (A. M. Gordon et al., 1991a). Hence, the operation of relating the target object to the information stored in memory needed for parameterizing the motor commands most likely represents an automatic process dissociated from conscious perception.

In general terms, parietal lobe processes apparently keep various egocentric and allocentric spatiotemporal maps in register, allowing the integration of proprioceptive, tactile, and visual cues necessary for object-oriented manual actions (Jeannerod, 1988; Pause, Kunesch, Binkofski, & Freund, 1989). Moreover, separate representations may exist within parietal cortex for pointing, reaching, and grasping movements (Gallese, Murata, Roseda, Niki, & Sakata, 1994; Jeannerod, 1994a; see also Carnahan, Goodale, & Marteniuk, 1993). Similarly, the intermediate cerebellum appears specialized for the control of object-oriented manual actions such as those involving reaching to grasp rather than reach per se (van Kan, Horn, & Gibson, 1994).

7.5 Organizational Principles

The independence of adjustment of fingertip force coordination in providing grasp stability noted earlier is complemented by parallel sensory information processing for the separate digits by the CNS. For example, adjacent digits of the hand are represented discontinuously in multiple sensory maps in various brain areas, but only as long as independent finger actions are possible (cf. artificial syndactyly; Allard et al., 1991). In contrast, similar ordered maps comprising digit-specific representations do not seem to exist in brain areas executing motor commands such as the motor cortex (e.g., Donoghue et al., 1992). Indeed, given anatomical constraints (e.g., muscle-joint organization) and mechanical constraints (e.g., coupling of fingertip forces through the object), it seems inconceivable that the CNS would achieve independent digit control for the force coordination of stable grasp by operating on digit-specific muscles (Maier & Hepp-Reymond, 1995a, 1995b; Schieber, 1995; see also Schieber, Chapter 5 and Hepp-Reymond et al., Chapter 3). Instead, several digit and wrist/forearm movement representation areas of the motor cortex interdigitate in mosaic-like patterns (e.g., Nudo, Jenkins, Merzenich, Prejeon, & Grenda, 1992).

The partitioning of the forces among the digits seems to relate partly to a low-level neural controller ensuring grasp stability at each digit–object interface, operating locally at each digit. This is probably true regardless of grasp configurations, for example, one- and two-handed grips, inverted grips, and multidigit grips (Burstedt et al., 1992; Flanagan & Tresilian, 1994; Kinoshita et al., 1995). However, there is still the need for higher level control related to the overall manipulative intent, choice of grasp configurations, and so on. Although the basic structure of a motor program may not be generated within the cerebellum, it certainly plays an important role for the temporal processing and the distribution of the synergetic activating inputs across muscles. The lack of coordination in cerebellar patients is due to deficits affecting both the programming and the execution of motor activity (for recent reviews, see Dichgans & Fetter, 1993; Rispalpadel, 1993). Synergies that are initiated by external sensory signals are most likely supported by inputs from the dentate and interpositus nuclei and signals transmitted to parietal associative areas 5 and 7. Synergies induced by internal signals or motivational states are likely to involve the dentate nucleus and prefrontal area 9 as well as the supplementary motor and premotor areas (cf. Viallet et al., 1992). The fastigial and dentate nuclei give off projections to PM whereby they activate both axial and proximal muscles via bilateral reticulospinal pathways, and these nuclei therefore seems responsible for synergies that provide for the necessary postural adjustments when limb movements are performed (see Wing, Chapter 15, this volume). When voluntary movements are to be performed, the cerebellar efferents from the three cerebellar nuclei to the motor cortex are able to trigger all the necessary synergies. Since the motor cortex can be subdivided into several representation areas dealing with various elementary movements, activating the requisite coordinations requires particular patterns of cerebello-thalamo-cortical activation.

The rubrospinal and the cortico-motoneuronal systems seem to have a similar and parallel involvement in the control of hand movements. In monkeys, activity in neurones in the magnocellular red nucleus (RNm) is preferentially linked to distal limb muscles, and the primary role of the forelimb zone may be to control coordinated hand-arm functions (Houk, Gibson, Harvey, Kennedy, & van Kan, 1988; Mewes & Cheney, 1991); the RNm becomes highly active when a monkey reaches to grasp an object (Sinkjaer, Miller, Andersen, & Houk, 1995). However, there are marked differences between these two systems in some aspects of output organization. A strong extensor bias and the existence of cofacilitation cells reinforce the importance of the RNm in the control of coordinated, whole-limb movements such as those involving reaching to grasp.

It is clear that the sensorimotor transformations employed during object manipulation are based on prediction models within the CNS that apparently represent the entire dynamics of the entire control process and therefore allow prediction of the appropriate output several steps ahead. Given there are time delays in control loops, it is generally accepted that sensorimotor systems may use internal predictive (memory) models of the body and its motor apparatus (and of external objects) to achieve better control than would be possible by negative feedback (Rack, 1981). Accordingly, a set of predicted afferent signals are considered to be generated by internal models, and are compared to the actual afferent signals (e.g., Baev & Shimansky, 1992; Merfeld et al., 1993; Miall et al., 1993). Several theories have proposed that the cerebellum may form these predictive representations. For instance, inspired by an engineering control model known as a Smith Predictor, Miall et al. (1993) suggest that the cerebellum forms two types of internal models. One model is a forward predictive model of the motor apparatus (e.g., limb and muscle), providing a rapid prediction of the sensory consequences of each movement. The second model is of the time delays in the control loop (due to receptor and effector delays, axonal conductances, and cognitive processing delays). This model delays a copy of the rapid prediction so that it can be compared in temporal register with actual sensory feedback from the movement. The result of this comparison is used both to correct for errors in performance and as a training signal to learn (or update) the first model.

8. CONCLUSIONS

The sensorimotor mechanisms employed in precision grip lifting to adapt force output to frictional condition and to object weight operate according to a predictive feed-forward sensory control policy running on at least two time scales (Johansson, 1991). Contextual, cognitive, and movement phase-dependent interpretations of multisensory input seem to be vital features of the underlying sensorimotor transformations. On an extended time scale, previous experience with the object at hand (or similar objects) is used to adjust the motor commands parametrically in advance of the movement. This ability to parameterize default motor commands has been called anticipatory parameter control (Johansson & Cole, 1992, 1994; Johansson & Edin, 1993). At the heart of this is the need to carry out sensible motor behaviors despite sensory and effector systems subject to large neural conduction and processing delays. Before the relevant physical properties of an object are definitely known (typically via somatosensory mechanisms), action has to be taken on the basis of what can be anticipated. A motor program is thus preshaped on the basis of memory systems pertaining to physical properties of objects gained in previous manipulative experiences and previous tasks of the same or similar nature. Through vision, for instance, common objects can be identified in terms of necessary initial fingertip forces.

While the task evolves, somatosensory as well as other sources of information may then modify the ongoing behavior. This takes place on a shorter time scale: During the actual manipulation discrete mechanical events are encoded in the spatiotemporal pattern of signals in parallel sensory channels, particularly tactile, and this information intervenes intermittently according to what has been called a discrete event, sensory-driven control policy (Johansson & Cole, 1992, 1994; Johansson & Edin, 1993). In this control policy, which is distinguished from continuous feedback or other continuous regulation, task progress is monitored to inform the CNS about completion of the goal for each of subsequent action phases of the task, and for triggering commands for the task's sequential phases. Moreover, disturbances in task execution due to erroneous anticipatory settings of the motor commands are reflected by discrete mechanical events. Afferent information about these, more-or-less expected events immediately triggers preprogrammed corrective or compensatory actions that are appropriate for the task and the current phase of the task. The sensory signals associated with the mechanical events simultaneously mediate the necessary updating of the memory systems that support the anticipatory parameter control policy. Using these two control processes, grasp stability (avoidance of slips but also excessive grip forces) is obtained at each digit by independent control mechanisms. Force coordination across digits is partly an emergent property of these local control mechanisms.

Apparently, the neural processes underlying the employed task-related sensorimotor transformations engage most CNS areas known to be involved in sensorimotor processes pertaining to limb actions. Accordingly, coordinated prehension in humans develops relatively late during ontogeny. The precision grip between the thumb and forefinger does not emerge until around 10 months of age. It does not approximate adult performance in lifting tasks until 6–8 years of age and, even then, subtle improvements continue until adolescence.

ACKNOWLEDGMENTS

This work was supported by the Swedish Medical Research Council (project 08667) and the Office of Naval Research, Arlington, VA (Grant No. N00014-92-J-1919).

20

Action–Perception Coupling in Judgments of Hand-Held Loads

J. RANDALL FLANAGAN

1. INTRODUCTION

The hand serves two fundamental functions: manipulation of objects in the environment and perception of object properties such as weight and texture. These two functions are closely coupled. On one hand, objects may be manipulated in specific ways in order to extract various kinds of information about the object (action for perception). On the other hand, information perceived via the hand is critical in coordinating manipulatory actions with objects (perception for action). From the perspective of movement control, an important object property is mass, which will determine both its weight and its resistance to acceleration. With an accurate estimate of the mass of an object, the motor system can appropriately scale the forces needed to hold and move it. Thus, weight or mass judgment is a key area for understanding action–perception coupling.

In this chapter, a series of recent experiments on the effects of surface texture on perceived weight are described. In these studies, surface texture was varied in order to change the grip force required to grasp the object, and the main interest was in the contribution of muscular activity (i.e., activity related to grip force) that is only indirectly involved in supporting the weight.

These experiments revealed that when lifting with a precision grip, the smoother the surface texture of the object, the greater the perceived weight. The results suggest that a smoother object is judged to be heavier because the grip force required to prevent it from slipping is greater. The implications of these findings for mechanisms underlying weight perception are discussed. In addition, the effects of surface texture on the perception of weight are compared to the effects of other stimulus properties including object size.

2. MUSCLE ACTIVITY AND SENSE OF FORCE

In his early studies on weight discrimination, Weber (1834/1978) observed that the ability to discriminate weight is better when the weights are actively lifted by the hand than when they are passively supported by the hand. This finding suggests that there is a sense of force, associated with voluntary muscular exertion, which contributes to the perception of weight (Bell, 1834) and many subsequent studies have confirmed the role of muscle activation in weight discrimination (L. A. Jones, 1986). The relative contributions of efferent and afferent muscle signals to this sense of force is still a matter of debate (see Jones, Chapter 17, for a discussion of central and peripheral contributions to force and weight perception). However, a number of investigators have suggested that it is likely that both contribute (e.g., Brodie & Ross, 1984).

It is often implicitly assumed that weight perception depends on the activity of only those muscles directly involved in lifting. However, recent results reported by Kilbreath and Gandevia (1991) suggest that perceived weight is sensitive to muscle forces that do not contribute directly to lifting the weight to be judged. In particular, these authors found that the perceived heaviness of a reference weight lifted by one digit increased if a concurrent weight, equal to or greater than the reference, was lifted at the same time by another digit of the same hand. However, Kilbreath and Gandevia also reported that when the concurrent weight was lifted by the ankle, there was no increase in perceived heaviness. Thus, the effect of a concurrent load appears to depend on whether the muscle forces involved are functionally related in everyday tasks, as is presumably the case for forces produced by one hand. It should be kept in mind, however, that the concurrent lifting task studied by these investigators was a laboratory task; it is possible that in well-practiced, functional tasks, concurrent loads are compensated for, perhaps on the basis of experience.

Kilbreath and Gandevia's (1991) results suggest that the sense of force that contributes to weight perception may be more accurately considered as the sense of functionally related forces. This may have functional implications for weight perception of grasped objects. When lifting an object with the tips of the thumb and the index finger at its sides (precision grip), the fingertips must exert vertical forces (tangential to the surface) to counter the load as well as normal forces (into the surface) that allow the development of frictional forces to prevent the object slipping from grasp (see Wing, Chapter 15; Johansson, Chapter 19). The normal or grip force, which stabilizes the object but does not contribute directly to lifting it, may be viewed as a concurrent load that might influence perceived weight.

3. FINGER TIP FORCES IN PRECISION GRIP

Before describing the forces involved in precision grip, it is important to define the terms force, load (or load force), and weight. The load force is the sum or resultant of all forces acting on an object. When lifting an object, the load force is the sum of the gravitation force and the inertial force, which is equal to the mass of the object multiplied by it acceleration due to movement. The gravitational force is equivalent to the weight of the object and is simply the product of the mass and the acceleration due to gravity. Note that when holding a free object in a stationary position, the load force is equal to the weight.

In order to prevent slip when lifting an object with a vertical precision grip (the thumb and index finger contact surfaces on opposite sides of the object, see Figure 1), the limiting friction (f) between the skin and object must exceed the shear force due to the load force. The limiting friction depends on the product of the coefficient of friction (μ) and the grip force (G) such that $f = \mu G$. Thus, for a given object weight, the more slippery the surface texture (i.e., the smaller the value μ), the greater the grip force required to prevent slip.

When lifting an object of unknown weight with a precision grip, subjects will initially employ a large grip force to ensure that the object does not slip. However, the grip force is subsequently relaxed until slip occurs and then increased a little so that the grip force is slightly above the minimum required to prevent slip (Westling & Johansson, 1984). When the weight and surface texture of the object can be predicted by the subject, grip force adjustments are anticipatory. Both the rate of rise of grip force during the initial loading phase (prior to lift-off) and the steady grip force during the subsequent holding phase are scaled to the expected weight and slipperiness of the object (Johansson & Westling, 1984b). The heavier or more slippery the object, the greater the rate of rise of grip force and the greater the grip force during the subsequent holding phase. Knowledge of these object properties may be based on memory from previous lifts and on visual and haptic cues (A. M. Gordon et al., 1991a, 1991b).

Johansson and Westling (1988a) have demonstrated that if the weight of

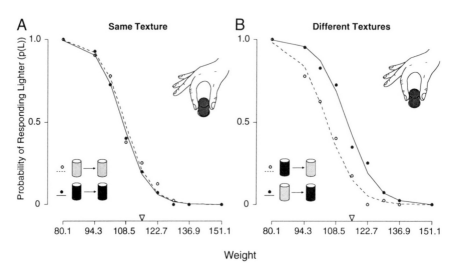

FIGURE 1   Probability ($n = 40$) of responding that the test canister is lighter than the previously lifted reference canister [$p(L)$] when test and reference canisters were the same texture (A) or different textures (B). Open circles and dashed lines code the condition in which the test canister was smooth and the solid circles and solid lines code the condition in which the test canister was rough. The triangle indicates the reference weight. (Points at which the probability was the same in both conditions are half open and half closed.) (From Flanagan et al., 1995)

the object is unexpectedly changed after a series of lifts, the initial rate of rise of grip force may be erroneous. However, in this event, secondary adjustments in grip based on sensory feedback are observed immediately after lift-off (if the object is lighter than expected) or around the expected time of lift-off (if the object is heavier than expected). Moreover, in their earlier experiment Johansson and Westling (1984b) showed that changes in surface texture result in early grip force adjustment (within 60–90 ms of initial contact with the object) so that the appropriate level of grip force may already be set by the time the object is lifted off the table surface. (In elderly subjects, however, full adaptation to an unexpected change in surface texture may be prolonged [Cole, 1991]. Even so, by the second or third lift, grip force is fully adapted.) Thus, regardless of whether or not the initially programmed grip force is appropriate, by the time the object is lifted and held aloft, grip force is precisely scaled for the frictional demands imposed by the object's weight and surface slipperiness. Moreover, if the object is moved vertically after having been lifted aloft, grip force is modulated in anticipation of inertial loads induced by the movement (Flanagan et al., 1993; Flanagan & Wing, 1993).

By varying the surface texture of an object it is possible to manipulate grip force independently of the load force exerted by the fingertips when lifting with a precision grip. The aim of the experiments reviewed in this chapter was to determine whether changes in grip force (related to surface texture) influence perceived heaviness (or load) as revealed in a weight discrimination task. In other words, does grip force act as a concurrent load that affects the perception of the load to be judged? Because grip force is scaled to object weight, it might serve as a useful cue for weight discrimination. On the other hand, because grip force is also scaled to slipperiness, discrimination might be confounded if the objects being discriminated have different surface textures and hence require different grip forces.

4. EXPERIMENTS ON WEIGHT AND LOAD DISCRIMINATION

In this chapter, three experiments on weight and load discrimination are discussed. In the first experiment, subjects compared the weights of a test and a reference object after lifting them successively with the digits at the sides. The objects were covered in either the same texture or different textures. In the second experiment, subjects compared the weights of objects held with the thumb underneath and the index finger on top so that changes in grip force were not required for different surface textures. The aim of this experiment was to determine whether the effect of texture on perceived heaviness, observed in the first experiment, was due to differences in grip force or surface texture per se. The third experiment involved a pulling task rather than a lifting task. In this case, subjects performed a load force discrimination task. However, note that weight discrimination can be viewed as load force discrimination where the load is due to gravity. Visual feedback about grip force was provided and subjects were required to use the same grip force for two different surface textures. If the influence of texture on perceived load is due to grip force, then the effect should be eliminated if grip forces are matched. The first two experiments are described in full in Flanagan, Wing, et al. (1995).

4.1. Effects of Texture When Lifting with a Vertical Precision Grip

In the first experiment, 40 subjects compared the weight of a reference object with the weights of a series of test objects. The objects were 35-mm film canisters (30 mm in diameter and 50 mm high) filled with coins. The canisters were covered in either satin or sandpaper to give a smooth or rough surface. For each surface texture there were 9 test canisters ranging from 80.1 to 151.1 g and a reference canister of weight 115.6 g, which was the central value of the test canisters. In a given trial, the subject lifted a reference canister followed by a test canister with the same, preferred hand using a vertical precision grip with the tips of the thumb and index finger at the sides (see illustrations in Figure 1). The subject had to tell the experimenter whether the test canister was lighter or heavier than the reference or equal in weight. However, subjects were encouraged to respond "lighter" or "heavier" if possible.

Each subject first performed two sets of lifts in which the reference and test canisters were the same texture: smooth–smooth and rough–rough (reference–test). They then performed two more sets of lifts in which the surface textures of the reference and test canisters were different: smooth–rough and rough–smooth. The order of the two "same texture" sets was varied across subjects as was the order of the two "different texture" sets. Subjects were free to move the canisters and no time limit was imposed on the lifts. However, most subjects held each canister in a steady position (after the initial lift) for a second or two before replacing it on the bench.

The results of this experiment are shown in Figure 1. (A) shows the probability of responding that the test canister was lighter, $p(L)$, as a function of the weight of the test canister when both canisters were either smooth (open circles, dashed line) or rough (solid circles, solid line). When the lightest test canister (80.1 g) was lifted, all 40 subjects responded that it was lighter than the reference and $p(L)$ was one. Conversely, none of the subjects responded that the heaviest test canister (151.1 g) was lighter than the reference and $p(L)$ was zero. Note that for both surface textures, when the test canister was equal in weight to the reference, $p(L)$ was less than .5. Thus, there was a bias toward responding that the second, test canister was heavier as has been previously reported (Ross, 1964). Note also that there was essentially no difference between the $p(L)$ curves for the two textures.

Figure 1B shows the $p(L)$ curves obtained when the surface textures of the reference and test canisters were different. As can be seen, the $p(L)$ curve found when the reference canister was smooth and the test was rough (solid circles, solid line) is shifted to the right of the $p(L)$ curve found when the reference canister was rough and the test was smooth (open circles, dashed line). Thus, the probability of responding that the test canister was lighter than the reference was less when the test canister was covered in the smooth (more slippery) texture than when it was covered in the rough texture. Logit analysis revealed that the shift between these $p(L)$ curves was highly significant (see Flanagan, Wing et al., 1995, for details). The shift corresponds to a difference in perceived weight of 9.0 g, 2 g greater than the smallest difference between canisters. There was no significant shift when the textures of the canisters were the same.

In Figure 1 the $p(L)$ curves obtained for the smooth–rough and rough–smooth comparisons fall on either side of the $p(L)$ curves obtained for the same texture comparisons. That is, a smooth test canister was more likely to be judged heavier when the reference was rough than when it was smooth and a rough test canister was more likely to be judged lighter when the reference was smooth than when it was rough. This indicates that the effect of texture on perceived weight did not depend on the order in which textures were presented.

In summary, the results of this experiment reveal that, when lifting with a vertical precision grip, weight perception is influenced by surface texture. Objects covered in the more slippery smooth texture are judged to be heavier than objects covered in a less slippery rough texture. This may be due to the fact that the grip force required to hold the smooth object without slip is greater.

4.2. Effects of Texture When Lifting with a Horizontal Precision Grip

The results of the first experiment are consistent with the hypothesis that the effect of texture on perceived weight is due to changes in grip force. However, another possibility is that the effect is due to texture per se. In order to test this alternative explanation, a second experiment was carried out in which subjects were required to use a horizontal precision grip with the distal pad of the thumb supporting the canister from below and the tip of the index finger on top (see illustration in Figure 2B). In this case, differences in grip force across textures may be assumed to be negligible, since the index finger needs to provide little friction to stabilize the object.

As in the first experiment, subjects ($n = 14$) compared the weights of a series of test canisters to the weight of a reference canister. The same canisters were used; however, only comparisons involving canisters with different textures were made. In this experiment, the subjects held each canister in a stationary position. In each trial, the experimenter first handed the reference canister to the subject and then, after 2–3 seconds, replaced it with the test canister for a further 2–3 seconds. (Subjects were allowed to ask that the trial be repeated if they were uncertain whether the test was lighter or heavier than the reference.) To allow for a direct comparison between the horizontal and vertical grips, this stationary holding procedure was repeated using a vertical precision grip.

The results of this experiment are presented in Figure 2. (A) shows the $p(L)$ curves obtained for rough–smooth (open circles, dashed line) and smooth–rough comparisons (solid circles, solid line) when using a vertical grip. As can be seen, the findings of the first experiment were replicated; a rough test canister compared to a smooth reference was more likely to be judged lighter than a smooth test canister of the same weight compared to a rough reference. Logit analysis revealed that the horizontal shift between these $p(L)$ curves was highly significant. The shift corresponded to a differ-

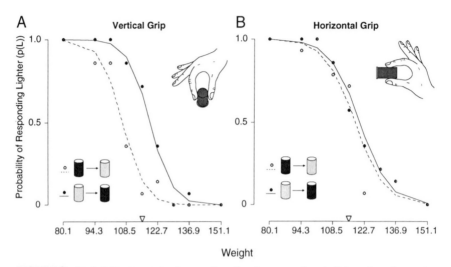

FIGURE 2   Probability ($n = 14$) of responding that the test canister is lighter than the previously lifted reference canister [p(L)] when lifting with a vertical (A) or horizontal (B) precision grip. Open circles and dashed lines code the condition in which the test canister was smooth and the solid circles and solid lines code the condition in which the test canister was rough. The triangle indicates the reference weight. (From Flanagan et al., 1995)

ence in perceived weight of 12.3 g, which is slightly larger than the shift observed in the first experiment.

Figure 2B shows p(L) curves obtained when holding the canisters with a horizontal grip. In this case, there was little difference between the p(L) curves obtained for the smooth–rough and rough–smooth comparisons. Although the p(L) curve for the smooth–rough comparisons was shifted slightly to the right of the curve for the rough–smooth comparisons, the shift was not statistically reliable (see Flanagan, Wing, et al., 1995).

Taken together, the results of the first two experiments suggest that the increase in perceived weight observed when lifting a more slippery object with a vertical grip may be due to the added grip force required to prevent slip and is not due to surface texture per se.

4.3. Effects of Texture When Matching Grip Forces

The hypothesis that grip force, rather than texture, influences perceived weight predicts that if subjects were to employ the same grip force when lifting weights with different surface textures, then texture should not influence perceived heaviness. The objective of the third experiment was to evaluate this prediction. An apparatus was used that measured grip force while generating horizontal loads that subjects were asked to discriminate. Though not strictly weight discrimination, the range of load forces used in this experiment was chosen to correspond to the vertical load forces generated by gravity acting on the masses of the test canisters in the previous experiments. Subjects' ability to discriminate load force in a condition where they themselves selected grip force was compared with their performance in a condition in which they were required to adopt an elevated grip force at the start of the trial.

Twenty-five subjects grasped, with a precision grip, a force transducer attached to a servo-controlled linear motor (see illustrations in Figure 4). The task involved holding the transducer in a fixed position while a pulling force was exerted by the motor. The subject grasped the transducer at one of two locations; one covered in smooth satin and the other covered in rough sandpaper. (The illustrations in Figure 4 show the hand grasping the smooth surface.) The procedure was analogous to that used in the previous experiments. On a given trial, the subject had to indicate verbally whether the force of a test pull was stronger (heavier) or weaker (lighter) than the force of a preceding reference pull. Only comparisons involving different surface textures were examined.

All subjects performed two conditions. In the self-selected condition, which was performed first, no instructions were given about grip force and subjects automatically scaled their grip force for texture and load. In the matching condition, visual feedback about grip force was provided to the subject by means of an oscilloscope. Prior to the onset of the pulling force, the subject was required to increase grip force to a steady high level (marked on the oscilloscope) and to maintain this grip force throughout the pull. The grip force was well above (about 10 N greater) the level employed by the subject when holding the smooth surface in the self-selected condition.

Figure 3 shows grip force (thick line) and load force (thin line) functions obtained for typical trials from one subject in the self-selected and matching conditions. The load force started to increase 1 s after the start of the trial, was maintained at a more-or-less steady level for about 2.5 s, and then started to decrease 4 s after the start. Because of limitations of the servo-controller and interactions between the object and hand, the actual, measured load force fluctuated somewhat both within trials and across trials with the same specified (nominal) load force. In the self-selected trials, grip force increased sharply following load onset. In the matched trials, grip force was elevated at the start and was maintained until the release of load force. In general, subjects successfully maintained a fairly constant grip level in these trials with little or no change in grip force following load force onset.

The difference between the mean measured test load and the mean measured reference load was computed for each trial. (The means were computed for the period from 2 s after the start to 4 s after the start.) On the basis of these load differences, trials were sorted into 9 bins ranging from -2 to 2 N in steps of 0.5 N. The average load force was 6.8 N.

Figure 4A shows the $p(L)$ curve obtained in the self-selected condition. In general, the probability of judging the test pull to be weaker than the reference was greater when the test was rough and the reference was smooth. Thus, when subjects freely selected grip force when resisting pulling loads, an effect of texture on perceived heaviness can be observed. As in the case of lifting, subjects tended to judge the force to be greater when grasping a smooth object. Logit analysis revealed that the $p(L)$ curve for the smooth–rough condition was shifted to the right of the curve for the rough–smooth condition and that this shift was statistically significant ($t = 2.91$; df $= 17$; $p <$ .01). The shift amounted to a difference of 0.58 N. In other words, on average, the pulling force of the rough test object had to be 0.58 N greater than the pulling force of the smooth test object for the force to be perceived as the same.

Linear regression analysis was used to determine, for the test pulls, the

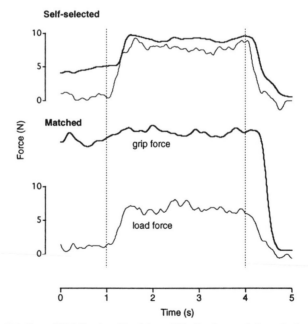

FIGURE 3   Grip force (thick lines) and load force (thin lines) records for a single trial in which grip force was self-selected and a single trial in which grip force was elevated to a target level during the application of the load. The load increased at time $= 1$ s and decreased at time $= 4$ s.

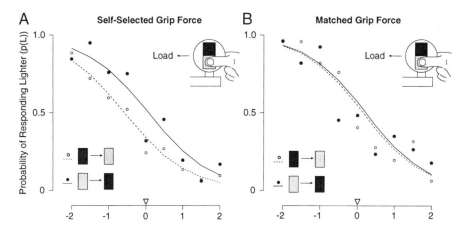

FIGURE 4   Probability ($n = 25$) of responding that the test pull is weaker (lighter) than the previous reference pull [p(L)] when grip force is self-selected (A) or elevated to a constant, high level for both pulls (B). Open circles and dashed lines code the condition in which the surface texture for the test pull was smooth and the solid circles and solid lines code the condition in which the surface texture for the test pull was rough. The triangle indicates the reference weight.

effect of load force, and texture on grip force, while allowing for subject differences in intercept. As expected, the slope of the relation between grip force and load force was significant. The slope was 0.94, indicating an approximately one-to-one correspondence between changes in grip force and changes in load. There was also a reliable difference in the intercept of the best fit relation as a function of texture. On average, for a given load force, grip force was 1.7 N greater for the smooth texture. A similar value was obtained for the average grip forces. The mean grip force, collapsed across subjects and test loads, was 7.9 N for the rough surface and 9.7 N for the smooth surface.

The p(L) curves obtained under the matched grip force condition are shown Figure 4B. In this case, logit analysis revealed that the shift between the two curves was not reliable ($t = 0.346$; df $= 17$; $p > .05$). Thus, when subjects used a constant, elevated grip force while resisting pulling loads, no effect of texture on perceived heaviness was observed. Analysis of the test pulls revealed that there was little difference between the mean grip forces, collapsed across loads and subjects, for the rough (18.7 N) and smooth (18.9 N) surfaces. Thus, the subjects successfully matched grip forces across textures. The results of this experiment are consistent with the hypothesis that the influence of surface texture on weight and load perception, observed under normal conditions, is due to differences in grip force.

5. SENSE OF MUSCLE FORCE IN WEIGHT PERCEPTION

The results of the three experiments described above demonstrate that when lifting or pulling an object with the tips of the thumb and index finger at its sides, the perceived load depends on the surface texture of the object. In particular, the weight or load of a smooth object will be judged to be greater than that of a rough object of the same weight or load. The results suggest that this effect is due to differences in the grip force required to prevent slip. When lifting with a grasp that does not require appreciable grip force an effect of texture on perceived weight is not observed. In addition, under conditions in which grip force is held constant across textures, there is no effect of texture on perceived load.

The hypothesis that grip force influences perceived heaviness is consistent with the view that a sense of muscle force contributes to weight perception. Moreover, the results suggest that grip force and load force may be lumped together to form an overall sense of force. Thus, the sense of force may be considered more precisely as a sense of functionally related muscle forces. Support for this conclusion comes from the recent work of Kilbreath and Gandevia (1991). As noted earlier, these authors have reported that the perceived weight of a reference load lifted by one digit increases if a concurrent load, equal to or greater than the reference, is lifted by another digit on the same hand.

Consideration of the coefficients of friction between the skin and the surfaces used in the experiments described in this chapter reveals that, even for sandpaper, the normal (grip) force exerted by each digit must be roughly twice the tangential force associated with the load in order to prevent slip (see Flanagan, Wing et al., 1995). Moreover, the mean (self-selected) grip forces observed in the pulling task for both textures were greater than the mean load force. Because the tangential force acting at each digit is one half the total load force, the normal force was more than twice as great as the tangential force. Thus, it is reasonable to suppose that the normal forces exerted when lifting or pulling with a precision grip are large enough to influence force perception.

Although the influence of surface texture on perceived weight would appear, on the basis of the current experiments, to result from differences in grip force, the possible contribution of cutaneous afferents cannot be ruled out. Cutaneous afferents in the tips of the thumb and index finger, which are known to be sensitive to surface texture, may provide information that is used in weight perception. The fact that the effect of texture on weight perception is not observed when using a horizontal grip (Experiment 2) does not preclude the possibility that, when lifting with a vertical grip, cutaneous afferents play a role in weight perception. When lifting with the vertical grip, the situation is quite different from the horizontal case because of frictional forces between the skin and object. It is possible that increased microslips at the digit–object interface when holding a smooth object provide cues for weight perception. Future experiments using anesthesia combined with external feedback of grip force may help resolve this issue. Another approach would be to externally induce small slips (perhaps using vibrations) to test whether these influence weight perception.

Although the results described here are consistent with the view that muscles only indirectly involved in resisting a load can contribute to a sense of force, the relative contributions of central and peripheral signals to this sense of force remains an open issue. Evidence for a central contribution comes from studies showing that perceived weight increases when the central drive or effort required to support a given load is increased by fatigue, partial curarization, or neurological disorders resulting in muscular weakness (see L. A. Jones, 1986, for a review). These observations have led to the suggestion that weight perception is based, at least in part, on the sense of effort associated with central motor commands. However, other studies have provided evidence for a strong afferent contribution to the sense of muscle force. For example, Brodie and Ross (1984) have shown that weight discrimination in reflex lifting (produced by tendon vibration) is significantly better than when passively supporting the object with the hand and is nearly as good as in active lifting. This suggests that receptors sensitive to muscular force contribute to weight perception.

The relative contribution of central and peripheral signals to weight perception may also depend on the precise instructions given to the subject. For example, Roland and Ladegaard-Pedersen (1977) reported that when subjects were told to disregard the increased effort required to generate force following partial curarization of one arm, they could accurately match forces produced by the flexor muscles of the forearms. It would be interesting to test whether the effect of surface texture on perceived weight would persist if subjects were informed about the relation between surface texture and grip force or if they were simply instructed to ignore grip force.

6. COMPARISON OF THE TEXTURE EFFECT WITH THE EFFECTS OF SIZE AND COLOR

The mechanism underlying the effect of texture on perceived weight would appear to be very different from the mechanism underlying the size-weight illusion (Charpentier, 1891) whereby smaller objects are judged to be heavier than larger objects of equal weight. According to the expectancy hypothesis of Ross (1969), the size-weight illusion is subserved by cognitive factors. In particular, Ross suggests that subjects judge the larger object to be lighter because it is lighter than expected and judge the smaller object to be heavier because it is heavier than expected. This can be considered as a cognitive effect because it is based on the subject's knowledge about the properties of real-world objects. A similar effect could operate for surface texture only if texture was correlated with weight in the real world. In other words, if it were the case that slippery objects are typically lighter than rough objects, then subjects might judge a slippery object to be heavier than a rough object of equal weight because the former is heavier than expected. However, there do not seem to be any grounds for supposing that slippery objects are typically lighter than rough objects or that subjects believe this to be the case.

The colors of the two textures used in the experiments described in this chapter were different. Specifically, the smooth satin was light blue and the rough sandpaper was black. De Camp (1917) reported that lighter colored objects are judged to be heavier than darker colored objects. This may reflect the fact that subjects expect the darker colored object to be heavier as suggested by experiments in which weight is judged solely on the basis of visual cues (Bullough, 1907; Payne, 1958). However, it might also reflect a verbal confusion, since the word light refers to both weight and color. One wonders whether the effect would be observed in French speakers, since the French words for weight (*léger*, light; *lourd*, heavy) are different from the words for color (*pâle*, light; *foncé*, dark). It may be noted that the texture effects described in this chapter cannot be explained on the basis of color, since there was no effect when lifting with the horizontal grip.

7. PERCEPTION AND ACTION SYSTEMS

A. M. Gordon et al. (1991a, 1991b) recently examined grip forces in a task in which subjects were required to compare the weights of objects of varying size lifted using a precision grip. (The size of the grip aperture was held constant.) These authors found that the initial rate of rise of grip force during the lift depended on size regardless of whether size information was obtained visually (1991a) or haptically (1991b). The initial rate of rise of grip force was greater for larger objects, presumably because subjects expected the larger object to be heavier. However, grip force was quickly recalibrated for the actual weight of the object so that during the subsequent holding phase the grip forces used to grasp large and small objects of equal weight were the same. Thus, despite the fact that subjects perceived a smaller object to be heavier than a larger object of the same weight (as expected), the sensorimotor control mechanisms responsible for updating grip force are not "fooled" by object size. In other words, while the size-weight illusion appeared to operate at a perceptual level, it did not act at the sensorimotor level.

This distinction between perception and action can be related to the distinction between vision for perception and vision for action advocated by Goodale and Milner (1992; see also Goodale et al., Chapter 2). The question is whether the distinct perception and action routes observed in vision are also observed in other modalities subserved by different neural systems. It would be interesting to see whether the influence of surface texture on perceived weight translates into action. For example, if subjects were trained to move a hand-held object covered in coarse sandpaper with a stereotypical acceleration profile, would they overshoot the target acceleration when the texture is switched to satin? In the case of vision, there is some evidence that the action and perception pathways are at least partly dissociated in visual input. It is not known whether a similar dissociation applies to tactile input.

8. GRIP FORCE AND POSTURAL ADJUSTMENTS

Grip force adjustments during lifting may be conceptualized within a more general postural framework (see Wing, Chapter 15). For example, anticipatory postural adjustments (APAs) involving proximal trunk and leg muscles occur just prior to the initiation of arm movements produced while standing (Friedli, Hallett, & Simon, 1984; Horak, Esselman, Anderson, & Lynch, 1984; W. A. Lee, 1984). APAs generate forces that counteract reactive forces produced by the movement, which, if not compensated for, could destabilize posture (Bouisset & Zattara, 1987; Friedli, Cohen, Hallett, Stanhope, & Simon, 1988). Consider, for example, the task of lifting up a load off a table while standing. Just prior to the lift, the activity of the ankle plantarflexors will increase so as to create a backward torque about the ankles to counteract the forward torque generated by the object's weight. Because the ankle muscle activity is functionally related to the arm muscles involved in lifting, one might predict that the perceived weight of the load will be greater than if the body were supported (e.g., when leaning against the table).

9. CONCLUSION

In this chapter, a set of recent experiments are described showing that the surface texture of an object influences its perceived weight when the object is lifted with the tips of the thumb and index fingers at its sides. The results suggest that a smooth (slippery) object is judged to be heavier than a rough object of the same weight because the grip force required to hold it without slipping is greater. This suggests that subjects fail to distinguish between grip and load force when judging object weight. This hypothesis is consistent with the results of Kilbreath and Gandevia (1991) showing that a concurrent load lifted by one digit leads to an increase in the perceived load lifted by another digit of the same hand. According to these authors, one explanation for this finding is that the central nervous system is unable to partition the destination of motor commands to functionally related muscles and that estimates of heaviness are biased by the total command. Another explanation is that the central nervous system is unable to partition the afferent signals of muscular receptors from functionally related muscles.

The findings reported here stress the close coupling between action and perception in the context of hand function and highlight the dual nature of the hand as manipulator and perceiver of objects in the environment. The findings suggest that the tight linkage between grip and load force observed when lifting (e.g., Johansson & Westling, 1984b; see also Johansson, Chapter 19) and transporting objects (e.g., Flanagan & Tresilian, 1994; Flanagan et al., 1993; Wing, Chapter 15) has perceptual consequences. The information that is obtained about an object during manipulation (e.g., weight) appears to be influenced by constraints acting on action (e.g., texture). Of course, it is also the case that the way in which actors manipulate objects depends on the information they wish to extract. Lederman and Klatzky (1987) have shown that when handling objects, subjects select different grasp strategies (or exploratory procedures) depending on the information (weight, texture, shape, etc.) they are required to obtain (see Lederman and Klatzky, Chapter 21). Thus, the links between action and perception work in both directions.

ACKNOWLEDGMENT

I would like to thank Dr. Helen Ross for her helpful and insightful comments on an earlier draft of this chapter.

21

Action for Perception

Manual Exploratory Movements for Haptically Processing Objects and Their Features

SUSAN J. LEDERMAN AND ROBERTA L. KLATZKY

1. INTRODUCTION

The topic of this book is the scientific study of hand and brain, as highlighted by both behavioral and neurophysiological approaches. In practice, research on hand function has tended to remain highly concentrated on either sensory input or motor output with little consideration of the interaction between the two systems. There are numerous scientific studies on planning and control of hand/arm movements for accomplishing motor goals, such as pointing, grasping, and most recently, manipulation. Likewise, there are a number of studies on the sensory side that address psychophysical and higher level issues pertaining to tactile (cutaneous inputs) and haptic (joint cutaneous and kinesthetic inputs) perception. However, there has been considerably less attention devoted to the nature of the interface between the input and output systems: how sensory inputs are used to effect action, and how action is employed in the service of perceptual goals.

   Some of the chapters in the current book have addressed the basis of sensory-guided movements, how vision is used to guide and plan hand and arm movements, and the roles of peripheral cutaneous and proprioceptive feedback. The present chapter also focuses on sensory function in relation to the planning and execution of hand movements, but the emphases are rather different. First, our research program emphasizes the perceptual functions of the hand. It emphasizes purposive exploratory hand movements for achieving perceptual goals, such as detecting object and surface features, discriminating within-feature dimensions, and identifying objects and surface materials. These tasks require action for perception. Second, the perceptual goals we set have been achieved primarily by haptic processing, which depends on the combined use of cutaneous and kinesthetic information.

2. HAND MOVEMENTS FOR PERCEPTION

In keeping with J. J. Gibson's earlier observations (e.g., 1966), much research with humans and other living organisms has highlighted the importance of active exploration for perceptual activities. Our research again confirms this general principle with respect to human haptic object identification.

This program of research began with a simple experiment, which confirmed that humans are remarkably skilled at recognizing common objects (e.g., toothbrush, pencil) using only the sense of touch. We (Klatzky, Lederman, & Metzger, 1985) asked blindfolded, adult subjects to identify 100 common objects via haptic exploration alone, as quickly and accurately as possible. They successfully identified close to 100% of the objects, usually in only 2–3 seconds. Might the manner in which the subjects manually explored objects that varied on multiple dimensions help us understand the basis of such expert haptic performance?

To address this question, we focused on the hand movements people executed in a perceptual match-to-sample task (Lederman & Klatzky, 1987). On each trial, subjects were first presented with a standard followed by three other comparison objects in sequence. Subjects were instructed to select the one comparison object that best matched the standard. Although all objects varied on many dimensions, subjects were told to attend to only one named dimension, such as hardness. Over the full experiment, we used different custom-designed object sets for each of the dimension-matching instructions, which are shown (in underline) in Figure 1.

We videotaped and then analyzed the hand movements subjects used within each trial. These movements proved to be highly systematic. They could be classified into a number of highly stereotypical classes of movement patterns, which we have called *exploratory procedures* (EPs); each of these could be described in terms of necessary and typical features. Subjects freely chose to perform particular EPs in association with specific dimension-matching instructions; the most relevant ones for this chapter are presented in Figure 1.

For texture-matching instructions, subjects executed a Lateral Motion

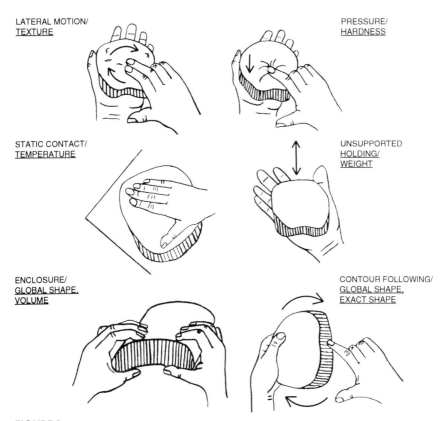

LATERAL MOTION/
TEXTURE

PRESSURE/
HARDNESS

STATIC CONTACT/
TEMPERATURE

UNSUPPORTED
HOLDING/
WEIGHT

ENCLOSURE/
GLOBAL SHAPE,
VOLUME

CONTOUR FOLLOWING/
GLOBAL SHAPE,
EXACT SHAPE

FIGURE 1   Schematic representations of exploratory procedures and the properties with which they are most closely associated. (Reprinted with permission from Lederman, 1991, and revised from Lederman & Klatzky, 1987.)

procedure, involving repetitive, back-and-forth tangential motions on a surface. A Pressure EP was selected to extract information about the compliance or hardness of objects; it involved application of a force normal to the object surface, or a torque about one axis of the object. Static Contact was used to learn about the thermal properties of surfaces; it involved statically resting the palm and/or fingers on the surface. Unsupported Holding was used for weight-matching instructions; in this procedure, subjects lifted the object away from a supporting surface, and typically hefted it. An Enclosure procedure was preferred for extracting both volumetric and global shape (i.e., the low spatial frequency details); here, the fingers and/or palm molded to the contours of the object. Contour Following, or edge following, was used to extract both global and precise shape (i.e., high spatial frequency details).

3. CHARACTERISTICS OF EPs

3.1 Relative Precision, Breadth of Sufficiency, and Duration

A simple change in the match-to-sample experiment above provided valuable information concerning the relative performance capabilities across the set of six EPs discussed here. This time, rather than allowing subjects to freely manually explore, we required them to perform only one named EP in conjunction with a specific dimension-matching instruction. So, for example, the subject might be asked on one trial to make the best texture match using an Unsupported Holding movement pattern. Over the entire experiment, we were able to compare the relative precision of feature information extracted by each EP by combining all possible pairs of EPs and dimension-matching instructions. The results are shown in Table 1 in the form of an EP-property weight matrix.

The entries are based on relative accuracy, and in the case of ties, on speed. A cell entry of 0 indicated that subjects could not perform the dimension-matching task above chance level with the EP shown (e.g., texture matching by Unsupported Holding). An entry of 1 indicated sufficient, though not optimal, performance (e.g., texture matching by Pressure, Static Contact, Enclosure, or Contour Following). An entry of 2 indicated that performance was both optimal and sufficient, but not necessary (e.g., texture matching by Lateral Motion). Finally, a 3 indicated that the particular EP was necessary, as well as optimal and sufficient (i.e., Contour Following). It is evident from Table 1 that the EPs that were spontaneously selected for execution in the earlier free-exploration experiment tended to produce optimal performance in the constrained version.

The data in Table 2 provided further information about the EPs. By summing the number of nonzero cells across a row, we could determine the relative breadth of sufficiency of each EP, shown in Table 2. Thus, Lateral Motion and Pressure each provided sufficient information about several different properties, while Enclosure and Contour Following provided coarse information about most object properties examined in this study. However, the breadth of property information must be weighed against its relatively slow execution time, which is also shown in Table 2. The mean durations were obtained from the initial free-exploration study.

3.2 EP Compatibility

Another issue that is relevant to the selection and implementation of EPs is whether or not they can be coexecuted, that is, carried out concurrently. We have developed a set of four visible static and dynamic kinematic parameters with which we can differentiate EPs. These were derived from an extensive

TABLE I EP-to-Property Weightings

	Texture	Hardness	Temperature	Weight	Volume	Global shape	Exact shape
Lateral motion	2	1	1	0	0	0	0
Pressure	1	2	1	0	0	0	0
Static contact	1	0	2	0	1	1	0
Unsupported holding	0	1	1	2	1	1	0
Enclosure	1	1	1	1	2	2	0
Contour following	1	1	1	1	1	1	3

Note. Reprinted with permission from Klatzky and Lederman, 1993, as adapted from Lederman and Klatzky, 1990a.

TABLE II   Mean Duration and Breadth of Sufficiency for Each EP

	Duration	Breadth of sufficiency
Lateral motion	3.46	3
Pressure	2.24	3
Static contact	0.06	4
Unsupported holding	2.12	5
Enclosure	1.81	6
Contour following	11.20	7

Note. Reprinted with permission from Klatzky and Lederman, 1993, as adapted from Lederman and Klatzky, 1990a.

body of hand-movement data that includes a large number of custom-designed and common objects that vary on many dimensions and that have been tested across a wide domain of experimental conditions. Values for these four parameters occurred reliably for a particular EP across many different conditions. Each of these parameters can be treated as a constraint inherent in an EP when it must be performed to pick up a particular kind of information. The parameters and their typical values are presented in Table 3. They are Movement (static or dynamic), Direction of Movement (normal or tangential to the surface), Region (of the object contacted, i.e., surface, edge, or both), and Workspace Constraint (i.e., whether a supporting surface is necessary or not).

We assume that EP compatibility exists when the parameter values for two EPs, shown in Table 3, can be satisfied simultaneously by means of some form of exploration. Although any pair of EPs must differ on one or more parameters, these differences may be reconciled so that they are capable of being coexecuted. For example, Pressure and Static Contact are considered compatible because Pressure satisfies the need for a dynamic movement pa-

TABLE III   Visible Kinematic and Dynamic Parameters for Distinguishing EPs

Parameter	Parameter values
Movement	Statid/dynamic
Direction	Tangential/normal
Region	Surfaces/edges/surfaces + edges
Workspace constraint	Yes/no

Note. Reprinted with permission from Lederman and Klatzky, 1994, and revised from Klatzky and Lederman, 1993.

TABLE IV Visible Kinematic and Dynamic Parameters for Distinguishing EPs

	Pressure	Lateral motion	Enclosure	Contour following	Unsupported holding
Static contact	+	−	+	−	+
Pressure		+	+	−	+
Lateral motion			−	+	−
Enclosure				−	+
Contour following					−

Note. Reprinted with permission from Lederman and Klatzky, 1994, and revised from Klatzky and Lederman, 1993.

rameter value, while simultaneously satisfying the more inclusive static value required by Static Contact. In contrast, Static Contact and Lateral Motion are considered incompatible because the mismatch between the two movement parameter values cannot be resolved. A set of rules for parameter reconciliation has been developed.

We show such compatibilities and incompatibilities in the form of a binary EP-EP weight matrix table (Table 4). A plus sign indicates that the designated pair of EPs are compatible; a minus sign indicates they are not. Details of the work on EP compatibility are available in Klatzky and Lederman (1993).

3.3 Connectionist Implementation of the EP Decision Rules

The EP characteristics described in Sections 3.1 and 3.2 can be used as decision rules for predicting how people select and order the sequence in which EPs are performed during various perceptual tasks. We (Klatzky & Lederman, 1993) modeled the EP selection/property extraction process as a constraint satisfaction algorithm, using a connectionist approach. We developed a single layer network, in which the nodes were the EPs and properties; the weights on the internodal connections were the EP-property and EP–EP compatibility weights presented in Tables 1 and 4. These weights were viewed as constraints that were progressively relaxed as the activation spread through the network until some maximal level of activation accrued to one of the network elements (EPs). The EP with the highest activation level was selected for execution.

4. PERCEPTUAL CONSEQUENCES OF EP SELECTION

In this section, we show the consequences of the EP selection process for perception given a variety of task goals.

4.1 Cued Object Identification

We have already demonstrated (Lederman & Klatzky, 1987) that EP selection is constrained by the particular goals of the task; in that study, the subject's choice of hand movement pattern was clearly influenced by the object dimension designated in the match-to-sample instructions. The results also highlighted the fact that EP selection constrains the quality of information (precision, speed of access) and the type of information (breadth of sufficiency) available.

On the basis of these earlier results, one would predict that if a person wished to obtain as much information as quickly as possible about a multidimensional object, he or she should initially execute an Enclosure; it is both broadly sufficient and quick to execute. If, however, more precise information about a property were required, one might choose to perform the optimal EP, that is, the one known to provide the most precise information about the desired property. These predictions emerge as well from our network model (Klatzky & Lederman, 1993), which showed that when the full weight matrix was used (Table 1), Enclosure was most active, regardless of what object property was targeted (i.e., activated as input); but, when all nonoptimal EP-Property weights were set to zero, the property-appropriate EP was then selected.

These predictions were confirmed in a cued, object identification task (Lederman & Klatzky, 1990b, Expt. 2). Subjects' knowledge of the most diagnostic properties of common object classes was initially obtained in Experiment 1; it was subsequently used to predict their choice of EPs in Experiment 2. In Experiment 1, subjects were asked a number of questions pertaining to which properties, in order of importance from a closed set, determined that an object belonging to a relatively less inclusive class (e.g., abrasive surface) was also a member of a more specific class (e.g., sandpaper). Subjects selected texture as the most diagnostic property for the preceding example.

In Experiment 2, we designated an EP implicitly for selection by naming the object class for which the property was most diagnostic. (Recall that we had achieved EP selection previously by stating the target property explicitly; Lederman & Klatzky, 1987). Blindfolded subjects were now required to decide whether or not an object that was physically placed in their hands was a member of a named category; as before, the name was either at a relatively inclusive or specific level (for a discussion of object classification taxonomy, see Rosch, 1978). Subjects were permitted to explore the objects haptically. Hand movements were videotaped on each trial.

Each trial was analyzed as a sequence of EPs. The analysis showed that subjects consistently selected a 2-stage sequence of EPs. This is shown schematically in Figure 2, which presents the percent cumulative occurrence of each EP as a function of its position in the EP sequence. Stage 1 (represented by thick, dark lines) involved a grasp-and-lift sequence (Enclosure and Un-

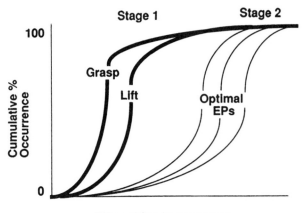

FIGURE 2   The 2-stage sequence of haptic exploration during a constrained object identifica-
tion task. Percent cumulative occurrence of each EP is plotted as a function of its position in the
EP sequence. (Reprinted with permission from Lederman & Klatzky, 1994, and revised from
Lederman & Klatzky, 1990b.)

supported Holding), regardless of the class targeted in the question. From
Table 2, and confirmed by our network model, it is evident that both EPs are
relatively broadly sufficient, providing coarse information about most object
properties; they are also relatively quick to execute. Stage 2 (the thinner,
lighter lines in Figure 2) included EP(s) that provided the most precise
information about the property our earlier experiment had found to be most
diagnostic of the targeted object class.

A separate study in this series (Klatzky & Lederman, 1992) restricted
subjects initially to performing only the grasp-and-lift sequence of Stage 1;
only afterward were they allowed to explore more. Accuracy proved to be
above chance at the end of Stage 1, confirming our assumption that the
grasp/lift routine was broadly useful. When subjects chose to explore beyond
the initial grasp-and-lift, their accuracy and confidence improved. This
second stage mainly elicited EPs associated with the object's geometry, although exploration was also influenced by the property judged to be most
diagnostic of the object class named.

To summarize, the two studies on cued, haptic object identification demonstrate the effects of breadth of EP sufficiency and relative EP precision (as
related to knowledge of property diagnosticity) on haptic perception.

4.2 Sorting Objects by Similarity

EPs vary in the relative efficiency with which they provide information about
object properties, both with respect to each other and to visual exploration.

Lateral Motion and Pressure are relatively quick to execute; in addition, they provide relatively precise information about variation on two object material dimensions, texture and hardness. In contrast, the geometry-extracting EPs are considerably more restricted, either by lengthy execution times and/or by the precision of spatial information they can provide. Thus, while Enclosure is performed relatively fast, the same cannot be said for Contour Following; moreover, neither EP provides high-precision spatial information. A body of research suggests that compared to haptics, vision is often less efficient at extracting the properties of object materials (e.g., Heller, 1989) but considerably better at extracting fine spatial details (e.g., Walk & Pick, 1981).

According to the differences in EP efficiency just described, we predicted that if subjects had to perform tasks that neither explicitly nor implicitly targeted a particular property, they would attend more to object material than to geometric properties when using touch alone. In contrast, we predicted that when vision was also permitted, subjects would emphasize the geometric properties more strongly; in this case, vision should be considerably more efficient than any haptic EP at extracting geometry, but somewhat less effective than touch in extracting material properties. Finally, we predicted that the subjects' manual exploration patterns, that is, the relative frequency of occurrence with which the associated optimal EPs were performed, would reflect the relative cognitive salience of material versus geometric cues. We define cognitive salience as the relative weighting of perceptual dimensions. In this task where no object property has been targeted for further processing (and dimensional variations have been perceptually equated), any differential weighting presumably reflects more general biases. The latter stem from internal representations and processes and/or reflect the nature of constraints imposed by associated forms of manual exploration.

These predictions were confirmed in two studies (Klatzky, Lederman, & Reed, 1987; Lederman et al., submitted). Subjects were asked to sort objects that varied in their material and geometric dimensions (e.g., texture, hardness, thermal conductivity, and weight, the latter being a hybrid of density vs. shape and size, respectively). The objects were factorially manipulated by property; thus, for example, in the Klatzky et al. study, three values each were used for texture, hardness, shape, and size variation. Subjects were required to manually sort the 81 objects into three piles according to perceived object similarity. So, for example, if subjects chose to sort by texture, they would have had to aggregate objects on the other three dimensions (i.e., objects with different hardness, shapes, and sizes would be placed in the same similarity pile). Such a sorting pattern would lead us to conclude that subjects judged texture to be more cognitively salient than the other dimensions. Patterns of manual exploration associated with the sorting responses were also analyzed.

The results of both studies (Klatzky et al., 1987; Lederman et al., submitted) confirmed that the relative cognitive salience of object material versus geometric properties is strongly influenced by a modality encoding bias that favors performance of the most efficient EPs. In each of the four following sorting conditions, subjects manually sorted the objects into piles. When the instructions were neutral ("sort objects into similar piles") or explicitly biased toward haptic encoding ("sort objects into piles that feel most similar"), subjects emphasized object material more strongly than geometry in their sorting. When the instructions biased subjects toward visual encoding ("sort objects into piles in terms of the similarity of your visual images," or "sort objects into similar piles" using vision in addition to touch), subjects' judgments indicated that the geometric properties (particularly shape) were more cognitively salient than any material property.

The influence of modality encoding biases on sorting preferences was likewise reflected in the associated manual exploration patterns. Thus, for example, when given the touch-biasing instructions, people tended to execute Lateral Motion and Pressure EPs most often when variations in texture and hardness were available as material properties. In contrast, when subjects were given vision-biasing instructions, they tended to use Enclosure and Contour Following, reflecting their preference for sorting objects by shape (and less so, by size). Subjects performed these two EPs when they were instructed to sort only by the similarity of their visual images. When real vision was also permitted, they did not manually explore the objects.

4.3 Speeded Object Classification

In another set of studies, we (Klatzky, Lederman, & Reed, 1989; Lederman, Klatzky, & Reed, 1993; Reed, Lederman, & Klatzky, 1990) explored the role served by EPs in constraining the kinds and relative precision of information available for simultaneous haptic object processing. We examined the extent to which variation along one dimension might influence the speed with which subjects learn to classify multidimensional objects. A number of different dimensions were used across the complete set of experiments. However, we will discuss the main results by considering only three: texture, hardness, and shape.

We began this program using the set of planar objects described in the similarity-sorting studies above (Klatzky et al., 1989). Subjects were required to learn to identify a particular set of objects by name (i.e., A, B, C). The objects in any given set were grouped according to different classification rules of which the subjects were unaware. A one-dimensional rule classified multidimensional objects by changes on just one dimension (texture, hardness, or shape). Two-dimensional (texture/hardness; texture/shape; shape/hardness) and three-dimensional (texture/hardness/shape) redundancy rules classified objects by redundant variation on two dimensions (e.g., hard and rough vs. soft and smooth; hard and rough and one-lobed vs. soft and smooth and two-lobed, respectively). Adding redundant information speeded object classification, such that the mean response time averaged across all two-dimensional tasks was shorter than for all one-dimensional tasks, particularly for texture/hardness versus either texture or hardness alone. Following Garner (1974), we call this a redundancy gain effect. However, adding a third redundant dimension had no additional positive effect on response times. We suggested the differences in dimensional integration were due to whether or not subjects could extract the dimensional variations simultaneously, which in turn depends on EP compatibility (see earlier discussion).

We then employed a different experimental paradigm known as redundancy withdrawal to explore this interpretation further. Subjects initially learned a two-dimensional redundancy rule in which one of the two dimensions was targeted; when their performance reached an asymptote, the non-targeted dimension was withdrawn unbeknownst to the subject; that is, it was held constant. The increase in response time following withdrawal of the nontargeted dimension served as a measure of the extent to which the two sources of information were integrated. For example, as above, we found that redundant variation in both texture and hardness was well integrated, regard-less of the dimension withdrawn (i.e., there was an increase in response time). However, there was little or no effect of redundancy withdrawal when either texture or hardness varied redundantly with shape (i.e., no change in response time following withdrawal of information about the nontargeted dimension). This is not surprising, because neither Lateral Motion (optimal for texture) nor Pressure (optimal for hardness) is compatible with Contour Following (optimal for shape, which for these planar objects was available only along the edges).

Haptic integration was also investigated using three-dimensional ellip-soids of revolution that varied in shape (ratio of major to minor axes) and texture (Reed et al., 1990). Unlike the planar objects used previously, infor-mation about both dimensions was potentially available through a local con-tact. Recall that for the planar objects, texture was located on interior sur-faces, whereas shape information was restricted to the outer edges. In this case, unlike the planar objects, there was a redundancy gain across shape and texture.

Finally, the extent of haptic dimensional integration was confirmed using a new orthogonal-insertion paradigm: after subjects learned a one-dimen-sional classification rule (e.g., the target dimension was shape), orthogonal information about the nontargeted dimension (e.g., texture) was introduced (Lederman et al., 1993). The degree of haptic dimensional integration was evaluated in terms of the magnitude of the increase in response time follow-ing the orthogonal-insertion manipulation. In contrast to the results with planar objects, subjects showed strong bidirectional integration effects for both shape and texture. We interpreted these results once again in terms of the consequences of EP compatibility for haptically processing multiple dimensions simultaneously.

4.4 Perceptual Discriminations Involving Vision with Optional Touch

We (Klatzky, Lederman, & Matula, 1993) also investigated the role of manual exploration in a set of perceptual discrimination tasks that involved both object material (texture, hardness, thermal conductivity, weight) and geometric (shape and size) variations. Vision was always available, whereas manual exploration was optional. We wished to determine which constraints on its use apply. Based on the relative efficiency with which haptics and vision extract object material and geometric properties, respectively, we expected that subjects would use vision alone unless precise material information was required, in which case subjects would perform the appropriate haptic EP.

Subjects were presented with pairs of objects, and asked to decide which object was rougher (harder, etc.). For each dimension, subjects were required to perform both easy and difficult discriminations. So, for texture, the subject might be asked: which is rougher: sandpaper or binderpaper? (easy); a marble or a teaspoon? (difficult).

The results are presented in Figure 3. Subjects never used manual explo-

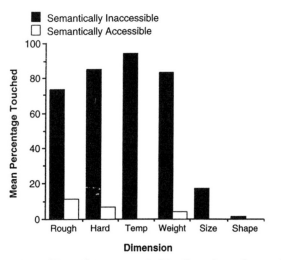

FIGURE 3   Percentage of items that were touched by dimension and semantic accessibility level. Note that there were no semantically accessible items for the temperature dimension. (Reprinted with permission from Klatzky et al., 1993. Copyright © 1993 by the American Psychological Association.)

ration when the discriminations were easy. Presumably these tasks could be solved semantically rather than perceptually, or the perceptual discriminations required were visually apparent. However, haptic exploration was reliably invoked during the difficult material discriminations. Although touch was also used for the difficult size discriminations, the movements in this case seemed to be more in the service of vision than touch. That is, subjects grasped the objects and moved them closer to their eyes, presumably to improve the visual viewing conditions.

The results of the current study confirm those in the similarity-sorting experiments above in emphasizing the relative importance of object material properties for touch. We have argued this is the result of differences in the relative quality of information that is made available by the EP that is most nearly optimal for extracting a targeted property. Even when the tasks did not demand the use of touch, subjects chose to use manual exploration to extract precise information about the material properties of objects. Presumably, this is because the resulting haptic information is of better quality than that obtained visually.

5. ISSUES RAISED

In this final section, we highlight a number of issues that our work on hand movements raises for further consideration.

5.1 Perception for Action versus Action for Perception

Traditionally, researchers have focused on either perception or action in isolation from one another. In studying hand function, we have suggested the importance of understanding the sensory–motor interface between action and perception. The work that relates to this topic has typically examined the role of sensory feedback, particularly visual, in performing movements of the hand and arm. In contrast, the current chapter explores the contribution of exploratory hand movements (and the ensuing sensory feedback that they afford) to haptic perception. Here, the emphasis is on action for perception, rather than on perception for action.

5.2 A Taxonomy of Manual Exploratory Hand Movements for Extracting Object Properties

We have documented the existence of purposive, stereotypical hand movement patterns, known as exploratory procedures or EPs. Empirical and analytic techniques for determining a number of important characteristics about each EP have been described: the relative precision of information each makes available, the relative breadth of multidimensional information that can be extracted, and the extent to which pairs of EPs are compatible. We have argued that these parameters affect the nature of goal-directed manual exploration, and more specifically the selection of EPs and the sequence in which they are performed. These, in turn, can either enhance or constrain the quality of haptic object perception.

5.3 Irrelevance of End Effector and Locus of Skin Contact for EP Implementation

To uncover any strong consistencies between EPs and properties, it was necessary to use a fairly high-level classification system for analyzing hand movements. Thus, our final taxonomy disregarded the particular end effector: the necessary features of each EP can be effected using the foot or the tongue, one versus two hands, one versus multiple fingers, and so forth. The part of the end effector contacted (e.g., fingertips, palm) also mattered little in uncovering the EP-property associations, although given the high density of mechanoreceptors in the fingertips, it is not surprising that they were typically preferred, particularly for high-precision tasks.

Although our EP taxonomy applies equally well to movement planning and control of any of the body's end effectors, we would argue that the hand surely occupies the premier position for at least two reasons. With its dense array of mechanoreceptors and its exceptionally flexible musculature, it is possible for the brain to achieve hand movements that provide greater sensory precision than is possible with other end effectors.

5.4 EPs Need Not Be Manual

The notion of an EP as a systematic form of exploration for extracting one or more specific object properties can be extended to include other nonmanual sensing modes as well. For example, within the conceptual framework provided by our EP analysis, we suggested that, as a first step, vision can be treated as an EP with strong weights on geometric properties, such as size and shape. This led to two predictions: (1) object geometry would be more salient than material properties when subjects were required to use visual images or real visual input to sort multidimensional objects by similarity (Section 4.2); and (2) haptic EPs would be used less often for extracting information about object geometry than about object material, when vision was permitted (Section 4.4). Finer differentiations among visual exploratory EPs may prove helpful; however, for our current purposes, a single EP proved sufficient.

5.5 Other Hand-Movement Classification Systems

The present chapter presents an "exploratory" classification system for classifying regularities in hand movements that pertain to the role of the hand in sensing object properties. Other hand-movement classification systems that extend beyond the contents of this book would also likely benefit from neurophysiological and additional behavioral scrutiny. One example is a "manipulatory" hand-shaping classification system, which focuses on people's knowledge of movements for functional hand–object interactions (Klatzky, Lederman, Pellegrino, Doherty, & McCloskey, 1990). A second involves gestures by speakers of oral language to intensify or illustrate speech (McNeill, 1985). A third involves the study of noncontact gestures as a form of communication for the deaf.

ACKNOWLEDGMENTS

This chapter was prepared with the financial assistance of the Institute of Robotics and Intelligent Systems (IRIS) and the Natural Sciences and Engineering Research Council of Canada (NSERC).

References

Brackets indicate chapter(s) in which the referenced work is cited.

Abbs, J. H., & Cole, K. J. (1987). Neural mechanisms of motor equivalence and goal achievement. In S. P. Wise (Ed.), *Higher brain functions* (pp. 15–43). New York: Wiley. [14]

Abend, W., Bizzi, E., & Morasso, P. (1982). Human arm trajectory formation. *Brain, 105,* 331–348. [10]

Abrams, R. A., Meyer, D. E., & Kornblum, S. (1989). Speed and accuracy of saccadic eye movements: Characteristics of impulse variability in the oculomotor system. *Journal of Experimental Psychology: Human Perception and Performance, 15,* 529–543. [9]

Adams, C. E., Mihailoff, G. A., & Woodward, D. J. (1983). A transient component of the developing corticospinal tract arises in visual cortex. *Neuroscience Letters, 36,* 243–248. [7]

Adolphs, R., Tranel, D., Damasio, H., & Damasio, A. (1994). Impaired recognition of emotional facial expressions following bilateral damage to the human amygdala. *Nature (London), 372,* 669–672. [2]

Ageranioti-Bélanger, S. A., & Chapman, C. E. (1992). Discharge properties of neurones in the hand area of primary somatosensory cortex in monkeys in relation to the performance of an active tactile discrimination task. II. Area 2 as compared to areas 3b and 1. *Experimental Brain Research, 91,* 207–228. [16]

Aizawa, H., Inase, M., Mushiake, H., Shima, K., & Tanji, J. (1991). Reorganization of activity in the supplementary motor area associated with motor learning and functional recovery. *Experimental Brain Research, 84,* 668–671. [6]

Aizawa, H., Mushiake, H., Inase, M., & Tanji, J. (1990). An output zone of the monkey primary motor cortex specialized for bilateral hand movement. *Experimental Brain Research, 82,* 219–221. [6]

447

Akazawa, K., Milner, T. E., & Stein, R. B. (1983). Modulation of reflex EMG and stiffness in response to stretch of human finger muscle. *Journal of Neurophysiology, 49,* 16–27. [11]

Alderson, G. J. K., Sully, D. J., & Sully, H. G. (1974). An operational analysis of a one-handed catching task using high speed photography. *Journal of Motor Behavior, 6,* 217–226. [11]

Alexander, G., & Crutcher, M. D. (1990a). Preparation for movement: Neural representations of intended direction in three motor areas of the monkey. *Journal of Neurophysiology, 64,* 133–150. [6]

Alexander, G., & Crutcher, M. D. (1990b). Neural representations of the target (goal) of visually guided arm movements in three motor areas of the monkey. *Journal of Neurophysiology, 64,* 164–178. [6]

Alexander, R. M. (1991). Optimum timing of muscle activation for simple models of throwing. *Journal of Theoretical Biology, 150,* 349–372. [9]

Alisky, J. M., Swink, T. D., & Tolbert, D. L. (1992). The postnatal spatial and temporal development of corticospinal projections in cats. *Brain Research, 88,* 265–276. [7]

Allard, T., Clark, S. A., Jenkins, W. M., & Merzenich, M. M. (1991). Reorganization of somatosensory area 3b representations in owl monkeys after digital syndactyly. *Journal of Neurophysiology, 66,* 1048–1058. [5, 19]

Alstermark, B., Gorska, T., Johanisson, T., & Lundberg, A. (1987). Hypermetria in forelimb target-reaching after interruption of the inhibitory pathway from forelimb afferents to C3-C4 propriospinal neurones. *Neuroscience Research, 3,* 457–461. [10]

Alstermark, B., Isa, T., Lundberg, A., Pettersson, L. G., & Tantisira, B. (1991). The effect of a low pyramidal transection following previous transection of the dorsal column in cats. *Neuroscience Research, 11,* 215–220. [10]

Alstermark, B., Isa, T., & Tantisira, B. (1991). Pyramidal excitation in long propriospinal neurones in the cervical segments of the cat. *Experimental Brain Research, 84,* 569–582. [10]

Alstermark, B., Lundberg, A., Norrsell, U., & Sybirska, E. (1981). Integration in the descending motor pathways controlling the forelimb in the cat. 9. Differential behavioural defects after spinal cord lesions interrupting defined pathways from higher centers to motoneurones. *Experimental Brain Research, 42,* 299–318. [10]

Anderson, P., Hagan, P. J., Phillips, C. G., & Powell, T. P. S. (1975). Mapping by microstimulation of overlapping projections from area 4 to motor units of the baboon's hand. *Proceedings of the Royal Society of London, Series B, 188,* 31–60. [5]

Andersen, R. A. (1987). Inferior parietal lobule function in spatial perception and visuomotor integration. In V. B. Mountcastle, F. Plum, & S. R. Geiger (Eds.), *Handbook of physiology: Sect. 1. The nervous system.* (Vol. 5, Part 2, pp. 483–518). Bethesda, MD: American Physiological Association. [2]

Andersen, R. A., Asanuma, C., Essick, G., & Siegel, R. M. (1990). Corticocortical connections of anatomically and physiologically defined subdivisions within the inferior parietal lobule. *Journal of Comparative Neurology, 296,* 65–113. [2]

Andersen, R. A., Essick, G. K., & Siegel, R. M. (1985). The encoding of spatial location by posterior parietal neurons. *Science, 230,* 456–458. [2]

Andersen, R. A., & Zipser, D. (1988). The role of posterior parietal cortex in coordinate transformations for visual-motor integration. *Canadian Journal of Physiology and Pharmacology, 66,* 488–501. [8]

Angelaki, D. E., & Hess, B. J. M. (1994). Inertial representation of angular motion in the vestibular system of rhesus monkeys. I. Vestibuloocular reflex. *Journal of Neurophysiology, 71,* 1222–1249. [8]

Aniss, A. M., Gandevia, S. C., & Milne, R. J. (1988). Changes in perceived heaviness and motor commands produced by cutaneous reflexes in man. *Journal of Physiology, (London), 397,* 113–126. [17]

Anner-Baratti, R. E. C., Allum, J. H. J., & Hepp-Reymond, M.-C. (1986). Neural correlates of isometric force in the "motor" thalamus. *Experimental Brain Research, 63*, 567–580. [3]

Arbib, M. A. (1981). Perceptual structures and distributed motor control. In V. B. Brooks, (Ed.), *Handbook of physiology; Sect. 1. The nervous system* (Vol. 2, pp. 1449–1480). Bethesda, MD: American Physiological Society. [13]

Arbib, M. A. (1985). Schemas for the temporal organization of behaviour. *Human Neurobiology, 4*, 63–72. [10]

Arbib, M. A. (1990). Programs, schemas, and neural networks for control of hand movements: Beyond the RS framework. In M. Jeannerod (Ed.), *Attention and performance XIII* (pp. 111–138). Hillsdale, NJ: Erlbaum. [14]

Arbib, M. A., Iberall, T., & Lyons, D. (1985). Coordinated control programs for control of the hands. *Experimental Brain Research, Supplement, 10*, 111–129. [10, 12, 13]

Armand, J. (1982). The origin, course and terminations of corticospinal fibers in various mammals. *Progress in Brain Research, 57*, 330–360. [6, 7]

Armand, J., Edgley, S. A., Lemon, R. N., & Olivier, E. (1994). Protracted postnatal development of corticospinal projections from the primary motor cortex to hand motoneurones in the macaque monkey. *Experimental Brain Research, 101*, 178–182. [7]

Asanuma, C., Andersen, R. A., & Cowan, W. M. (1985). The thalamic relations of the caudal inferior parietal lobule and the lateral prefrontal cortex in monkeys: Divergent cortical projections from cell clusters in the medial pulvinar nucleus. *Journal of Comparative Neurology, 241*, 357–381. [2]

Asanuma, H., & Rosén, I. (1972). Topographical organization of cortical efferent zones projecting to distal forelimb muscles in the monkey. *Experimental Brain Research, 14*, 243–256. [6]

Asatryan, D. G, & Feldman, A. G. (1965). Functional tuning of the nervous system with control of movement or maintenance of a steady posture. 1. Mechanographic analysis of the work of the joint on execution of a postural task. *Biophysics, 10*, 925–935. [9]

Åström, K. J., & Wittenmark, B. (1989). *Adaptive control*, p. 526. Addison-Wesley, MA: Reading. [11]

Atkeson, C. G., & Hollerbach, J. M. (1985). Kinematic features of unrestrained arm movements. *Journal of Neuroscience, 5*, 2318–2330. [10]

Babalian, A., Liang, F., & Rouiller, E. M. (1993). Cortical influences on cervical motoneurons in the rat: Recordings of synaptic responses from motoneurons and compound action potential from corticospinal axons. *Neuroscience Research, 16*, 301–310. [6, 7]

Backhouse, K. M., & Catton, W. T. (1954). An experimental study of the functions of the lumbrical muscles in the human hand. *Journal of Anatomy, 88*, 133–141. [4]

Baev, K. V., & Shimansky, Y. P. (1992). Principles of organization of neural systems controlling automatic movements in animals. *Progress in Neurobiology, 39*, 45–112. [19]

Baizer, J. S., Desimone, R., & Ungerleider, L. G. (1993). Comparison of subcortical connections of inferior temporal and posterior parietal cortex in monkeys. *Visual Neuroscience, 10*, 59–72. [2]

Baker, J. R., Bremner, F. D., Cole, J. D., & Stephens, J. A. (1988). Short-term synchronization of intrinsic hand muscle motor units in 'Deafferented' man. *Journal of Physiology (London), 396*, 155P. [3]

Baker, S. N., Olivier, E., & Lemon, R. N. (1994). Recording an identified pyramidal volley evoked by transcranial magnetic stimulation in a conscious macaque monkey. *Experimental Brain Research, 99*, 529–532. [7]

Baldissera, F., Campadelli, P., & Cavallari, P. (1983). Inhibition from radial group I afferent of H-reflex in wrist flexors. *Electromyography and Clinical Neurophysiology, 23*, 187–193. [11]

Baldissera, F., & Cavallari, P. (1993). Short latency subliminal effects of transcranial magnetic stimulation on forearm motoneurones. *Experimental Brain Research, 96*, 513–518. [7]

Baldissera, F., Hultborn, H., & Illert, M. (1981). Integration in spinal neuronal systems. In V. B. Brooks (Ed.), *Handbook of Physiology: Sect. 1. The nervous system* (Vol 2, Part 1, pp. 509–595). Bethesda, MD: American Physiological Society. [10]

Bàlint, R. (1909). Seelenlähmung des 'Schauens,' optische Ataxie, räumliche Störung der Aufmerksamkeit. *Monatsschrift fuer Psychiatrie und Neurologie, 25*, 51–81. [2]

Barkovich, J. A., Lyon, G., & Evrard, P. (1992). Formation, maturation, and disorders of white matter. *American Journal of Neuroradiology, 13*, 447–461. [7]

Barrack, R. L., Skinner, H. B., Brunet, M. E., & Haddad, R. J. (1983). Functional performance of the knee after intraarticular anesthesia. *American Journal of Sports Medicine, 11*, 258–261. [17]

Barto, A. G., Sutton, R. S., & Anderson, C. W. (1983). Neuron-like adaptive elements that can solve difficult learning control problems. *IEEE Transactions on Systems, Man, and Cybernetics, SMC-5*, 834–846. [12]

Basmajian, J. V. (1978). *Muscles alive. Their functions revealed by electromyography* (4th ed.). Baltimore: Williams & Wilkins. [5]

Bastian, A. J., Mueller, M. J., Martin, T. A., Keating, J. G., & Thach, W. T. (1994). Control of interaction torques during reaching in normal and cerebellar patients. *Society for Neuroscience Abstracts, 20*, 408.5. [10]

Beevor, C. (1904). *The Croonian Lectures on muscular movements and their representation in the central nervous system.* London: Adlard. [3]

Bekey, G. A., Tomovic, R., & Zeljkovic, I. (1990). Control architecture for the Belgrade/USC hand. In T. Venkataraman & T. Iberall (Eds.), *Dextrous robot hands* (pp. 136–149). New York: Springer-Verlag. [12]

Bell, C. (1834). *The hand. Its mechanism and vital endowments as evincing design.* London: Pickering. [20]

Bennett, D. J., Hollerbach, J. M., Xu, Y., & Hunter, I. W. (1992). Time-varying stiffness of human elbow joint during cyclic voluntary movement. *Experimental Brain Research, 88*, 433–442. [11]

Bennett, K. M. B., & Lemon, R. N. (1994). The influence of single monkey cortico-motoneuronal cells at different levels of activity in target muscles. *Journal of Physiology (London), 477*, 291–307. [3]

Berger, E. H. (1981). Re-examination of the low-frequency (50–1000 Hz) normal threshold of hearing in free and diffuse sound fields. *Journal of the Acoustical Society of America, 70*, 1635–1645. [17]

Bernstein, N. (1967). *The co-ordination and regulation of movements.* Oxford: Pergamon. [3, 9, 10, 14, 18, 19]

Berthoz, A., Lacour, M. Soechting, J. F., & Vidal, P. P. (1979). The role of vision in the control of posture during linear motion. *Progress in Brain Research, 50*, 197–209. [11]

Berthoz, A., Pavard, B., & Young, L. R. (1975). Perception of linear horizontal self-motion induced by peripheral vision (linear vection). *Experimental Brain Research, 23*, 471–489. [8]

Biber, M. P., Kneisley, L. W., & LaVail, J. H. (1978). Cortical neurons projecting to the cervical and lumbar enlargements of the spinal cord in young and adult monkeys. *Experimental Neurology, 59*, 492–508. [7]

Bigland, B., & Lippold, O.C.J. (1954). The relation between force, velocity and integrated electrical activity in human muscles. *Journal of Physiology (London), 123*, 214–224. [18]

Bioulac, B., & Lamarre, Y. (1979). Activity of postcentral cortical neurons of the monkey during conditioned movements of a deafferented limb. *Brain Research, 172*, 427–437. [16]

Bishop, D. V. M. (1990). *Handedness and developmental disorders: Clinics in developmental medicine.* London: MacKeith Press. [19]

Bizzi, E., Hogan, N., Mussa-Ivaldi, F. A., & Giszter, S. (1992). Does the nervous system use equilibrium-point control to guide single and multiple joint movements? *Behavioral and Brain Sciences, 15,* 603–613. [9, 11]

Bizzi, E., & Mussa-Ivaldi, F. A. (1989). Geometrical and mechanical issues in movement planning and control. In M. I. Posner (Ed.), *Handbook of cognitive science* (pp. 769–792). Cambridge, MA: MIT Press. [9]

Blake, A. (1992). Computational modelling of hand-eye coordination. *Philosophical Transactions of the Royal Society of London, 337,* 351–360. [2]

Bock, O. (1994). Scaling of joint torque during planar arm movements. *Experimental Brain Research, 101,* 346–352. [9]

Bodine, S. C., Roy, R. R., Eldred, E., & Edgerton, V. R. (1987). Maximal force as a function of anatomical features of motor units in the cat tibialis anterior. *Journal of Neurophysiology, 6,* 1730–1745. [4]

Bolanowski, S. J., Gescheider, G. A., Verrillo, R. T., & Checkosky, C. M. (1988). Four channels mediate the mechanical aspects of touch. *Journal of the Acoustical Society of America, 84,* 1680–1694. [17]

Bootsma, R. J., Marteniuk, R. G., MacKenzie, C. L., & Zaal, F. T. (1994). The speed-accuracy trade-off in manual prehension: Effect of movement amplitude, object size and object width on kinematic characteristics. *Experimental Brain Research, 98,* 535–541. [13]

Bootsma, R. J., & Van Wieringen, P. C. W. (1992). Spatio-temporal organisation of natural prehension. *Human Movement Science, 11,* 205–215. [13]

Bortoff, G. A., & Strick, P. L. (1993). Corticospinal terminations in two New-World primates: Further evidence that corticomotoneuronal connections provide part of the neural substrate for manual dexterity. *Journal of Neuroscience, 13,* 5105–5118. [6, 7]

Bose, B., Kalra, A. K., Thurkral, S., Sood, A., Guha, S. K., & Anand, S. (1992). Tremor compensation for robotics assisted microsurgery. *Proceedings of the Annual International Conference of the IEEE Engineering in Medicine and Biology Society, 14,* (Pt. 3), 1067–1068. [17]

Bouisset, S., & Zattara, M. (1981). A sequence of postural movements precedes voluntary movement. *Neuroscience Letters, 22,* 263–270. [15]

Bouisset, S., & Zattara, M. (1987). Biomechanical study of the programming of anticipatory postural adjustments associated with voluntary movement. *Journal of Biomechanics, 20,* 735–742. [15, 20]

Boussaoud, D. (1995). Primate premotor cortex: Modulation of preparatory neuronal activity by gaze angle. *Journal of Neurophysiology, 73,* 886–890. [6]

Boussaoud, D., Barth, T. M., & Wise, S. P. (1993). Effects of gaze on apparent visual responses of frontal cortex neurons. *Experimental Brain Research, 93,* 423–434. [6]

Boussaoud, D., di Pellegrino, G., & Wise, S. P. (in press). Frontal lobe mechanisms subserving vision for action vs. vision for perception. *Behavioural Brain Research.* [6]

Boussaoud, D., & Wise, S. P. (1993a). Primate frontal cortex: Neuronal activity following attentional versus intentional cues. *Experimental Brain Research, 95,* 15–27. [6]

Boussaoud, D., & Wise, S. P. (1993b). Primate frontal cortex: Effects of stimulus and movements. *Experimental Brain Research, 95,* 28–40. [6]

Brand, P. W., Beach, R. B., & Thompson, D. E. (1981). Relative tension and potential excursion of muscles in the forearm and hand. *Journal of Hand Surgery, 3,* 209–219. [4]

Brandell, B. R. (1970). An electromyographic-cinematographic study of the muscles of the index finger. *Archives of Physical Medicine and Rehabilitation, 51,* 278–285. [5]

Bremner, F. D, Baker, J. R., & Stephens, J. A. (1991a). Correlation between the discharges of motor units recorded from the same and from different finger muscles in man. *Journal of Physiology (London) 432,* 355–380. [3]

Bremner, F. D., Baker, J. R., & Stephens, J. A. (1991b). Effect of task on the degree of synchronization of intrinsic hand muscle motor units in man. *Journal of Neurophysiology, 66,* 2072–2083. [3]

Bremner, F. D., Baker, J. R., & Stephens, J. A. (1991c). Variation in the degree of synchronization exhibited by motor units lying in different finger muscles in man. *Journal of Physiology (London), 432,* 381–399. [3]

Brinkman, C. (1981). Lesions in supplementary motor area interfere with a monkey's performance of a bimanual coordination task. *Neuroscience Letters, 27,* 267–270. [6]

Brinkman, C. (1984). Supplementary motor area of the monkey's cerebral cortex: Short- and long-term deficits after unilateral ablation and the effects of subsequent callosal section. *Journal of Neuroscience, 4,* 918–929. [6]

Brinkman, C., & Porter, R. (1979). Supplementary motor area in the monkey: Activity of neurons during performance of a learned motor task. *Journal of Neurophysiology, 42,* 681–709. [6]

Brodie, E. E., & Ross, H. E. (1984). Sensorimotor mechanisms in weight discrimination. *Perception & Psychophysics, 36,* 477–481. [20]

Brody, B. A., Kinney, H. C., Kloman, A. S., & Gilles, F. H. (1987). Sequence of central nervous system myelination in human infancy. I. An autopsy study of myelination. *Journal of Neuropathology and Experimental Neurology, 46,* 283–301. [7]

Brooks, V. B. (1974). Some examples of programmed limb movements *Brain Research, 71,* 299–308. [18]

Brothers, L., & Ring, B. (1993). Mesial temporal neurons in the macaque monkey with responses selective for aspects of social stimuli. *Behavioural Brain Research, 57,* 53–61. [2]

Brown, J. M. M., & Brinks, R. (1988). The electromyographical basis of inaccurate motor performance. *European Journal of Applied Physiology and Occupational Therapy, 58,* 132–140. [3]

Brown, T. I. H., Rack, P. M. H., & Ross, H. F. (1982). Different types of tremor in the human thumb. *Journal of Physiology (London), 332,* 113–123. [18]

Bruce, C. J. (1990). Integration of sensory and motor signals in primate frontal eye fields. In G. M. Edelman, W. E. Gall, & W. M. Cowan (Eds.), *Signal and sense. Local and global order in perceptual maps* (pp. 261–314). New York: Wiley-Liss. [2]

Bruce, C. J., & Goldberg, M. E. (1984). Physiology of the frontal eye fields. *Trends in Neurosciences, 7,* 436–441. [2]

Bruce, I. C., & Tatton, W. G. (1980). Sequential output-input maturation of kitten motor cortex. *Experimental Brain Research, 39,* 411–419. [7]

Bruce, I. C., & Tatton, W. G. (1981). Descending projections to the cervical spinal cord in the developing kitten. *Neuroscience Letters, 25,* 227–231. [7]

Buchanan, T. S., Almdale, D. P. J., Lewis, J. L., & Rymer, W. Z. (1986). Characteristics of synergic relations during isometric contractions of human elbow muscles. *Journal of Neurophysiology, 56,* 1225–1241. [3]

Buchanan, T. S., Rovai, G. P., & Rymer, W. Z. (1989). Strategies for muscle activation during isometric torque generation at the human elbow. *Journal of Neurophysiology, 62,* 1201–1212. [3]

Buchbinder, S., Dixon, B., Hyang, Y.-W., May, J. G., & Glickstein, M. (1980). The effects of cortical lesions on visual guidance of the hand. *Society for Neuroscience Abstracts, 6,* 675. [2]

Bullock, D., & Grossberg, S. (1988). Neural dynamics of planned arm movements: Emergent invariants and speed-accuracy properties during trajectory formation. *Psychological Review, 95,* 49–90. [9]

Bullock, D., Grossberg, S., & Guenther, F. H. (1993). A self-organizing neural model of motor equivalent reaching and tool use by a multijoint arm. *Journal of Cognitive Neuroscience, 5,* 408–435. [9]

Bullough, E. (1907). On the apparent heaviness of colours. *British Journal of Psychology, 2*, 111–152. [20]

Bülthoff, H. H., & Edelman, S. (1992). Psychophysical support for a two-dimensional view interpolation theory of object recognition. *Proceedings of the National Academy of Sciences of the U.S.A., 89*, 60–64. [2]

Burgess, P. R., Clark, F. J., Simon, J., & Wei, J. W. (1982). Signalling of kinesthetic information by peripheral sensory receptors. *Annual Review of Neuroscience, 5*, 171–187. [17]

Burke, D., Gandevia, S. C., & Macefield, G. (1988). Responses to passive movement of receptors in joint, skin and muscle of the human hand. *Journal of Physiology (London), 402*, 347–361. [16, 17]

Burke, D., Gracies, J. M., Mazevet, D., Meunier, S., & Pierrot-Deseilligny, E. (1992). Convergence of descending and various peripheral inputs onto common propriospinal-like neurones in man. *Journal of Physiology (London), 449*, 655–671. [11]

Burke, D., Gracies, J. M., Meunier, S., & Pierrot-Deseilligny, E. (1992). Changes in presynaptic inhibition of afferents to propriospinal-like neurones in man during voluntary contractions. *Journal of Physiology (London), 449*, 673–687. [3]

Burke, D., Hagbarth, K.-E., & Lofstedt, L. (1978). Muscle spindle activity in man during shortening and lengthening contractions. *Journal of Physiology (London), 277*, 131–142. [16]

Burke, D., Hicks, R., & Stephen, J. (1990). Corticospinal volleys evoked by anodal and cathodal stimulation of the human motor cortex. *Journal of Physiology (London), 425*, 283–300. [7]

Burne, J. A., Lippold, O. C. J., & Pryor, M. (1984). Proprioceptors and normal tremor. *Journal of Physiology (London), 384*, 559–572. [18]

Burstedt, M., Westling, G., Johansson, R. S., & Edin, B. B. (1992, September 10–13). Co-ordinated manipulative behavior can emerge by independent neural systems. In *ENA-Satellite Symposium: Neural Control of Eye, Head and Limb Movements* (p. 4). Ohlstadt, München, Germany. [19]

Buys, E. J., Lemon, R. N., Mantel, G. W. H., & Muir, R. B. (1986). Selective facilitation of different hand muscles by single corticospinal neurones in the conscious monkey. *Journal of Physiology (London), 381*, 529–540. [3, 5]

Cabana, T., & Martin, G. F. (1984). Developmental sequence in the origin of descending spinal pathways. Studies using retrograde transport techniques in the north american opossum (*Didelphis virginiana.*). *Developmental Brain Research, 15*, 247–263. [7]

Cabana, T., & Martin, G. F. (1985). Corticospinal development in the North American opossum: Evidence for a sequence in the growth of cortical axons in the spinal cord and for transient projections. *Developmental Brain Research, 23*, 69–80. [7]

Caccia, M. R., McComas, A. J., Upton, A. R. M., & Blogg, T. (1973). Cutaneous reflexes in small muscles of the hand. *Journal of Neurology, Neurosurgery and Psychiatry, 36*, 960–977. [19]

Caminiti, R., & Johnson, P. B. (1992). Internal representations of movement in the cerebral cortex as revealed by the analysis of reaching. *Cerebral Cortex, 2*, 269–276. [6]

Caminiti, R., Johnson, P. B., Burnod, Y., Galli, C., & Ferraina, S. (1990). Shift of preferred directions of premotor cortical cells with arm movements performed across the workspace. *Experimental Brain Research, 83*, 228–232. [6, 8]

Caminiti, R., Johnson, P. B., Galli, C., Ferraina, S., & Burnod, Y. (1991). Making arm movements within different parts of space: The premotor and motor cortical representation of a coordinate system for reaching to visual targets. *Journal of Neuroscience, 11*, 1182–1197. [6, 8]

Caminiti, R., Johnson, P. B., & Urbano, A. (1991). Making arm movements within different parts of space: Dynamic aspects in the primate motor cortex. *Journal of Neuroscience, 10*, 2039–2058. [6]

Capaday, C., Forget, R., Fraser, R., & Lamarre, Y. (1991). Evidence for a contribution of the motor cortex to the long-latency stretch reflex of the human thumb. *Journal of Physiology (London), 440*, 243–255. [11, 18]

Carnahan, H., Goodale, M. A., & Marteniuk, R. G. (1993). Grasping versus pointing and the differential use of visual feedback. *Human Movement Science, 12*, 219–234. [19]

Carrozzo M., & Lacquaniti, F. (1994). A hybrid frame of reference for visuo-manual coordination. *NeuroReport, 5*, 453–456. [8]

Castiello, U., Bennett, K. M. B., & Stelmach, G. E. (1993). Reach to grasp: The natural response to perturbation of object size. *Experimental Brain Research, 94*, 163–178. [13]

Castiello, U., Paulignan, Y., & Jeannerod, M. (1991). Temporal dissociation of motor responses and subjective awareness: A study in normal subjects. *Brain, 114*, 2639–2655. [13]

Cavada, C., & Goldman-Rakic, P. S. (1989). Posterior parietal cortex in rhesus monkey: II. Evidence for segregated corticocortical networks linking sensory and limbic areas with the frontal lobe. *Journal of Comparative Neurology, 287*, 422–445. [2]

Cavada, C., & Goldman-Rakic, P. S. (1991). Topographic segregation of corticostriatal projections from posterior parietal subdivisions in the macaque monkey. *Neuroscience, 42*, 683–696. [2]

Cavallari, P., & Katz, R. (1989). Pattern of projections of group I afferents from forearm muscles to motoneurones supplying biceps and triceps muscles in man. *Experimental Brain Research, 78*, 465–478. [11]

Chanaud, C. M., Pratt, C. A., & Loeb, G. E. (1991). Functionally complex muscles of the cat hindlimb. V. The roles of histochemical fiber-type regionalization and mechanical heterogeneity in differential muscle activation. *Experimental Brain Research, 85*, 300–313. [5]

Chao, E. Y. S., An, K.-N., Cooney, W. P., & Linscheid, R. L. (1989). *Biomechanics of the hand*. Singapore: World Scientific. [3]

Chapman, C. E. (1994). Active versus passive touch: Factors influencing the transmission of somatosensory signals to primary somatosensory cortex. *Canadian Journal of Physiology and Pharmacology, 72*, 558–570. [16]

Chapman, C. E., & Ageranioti, S. A. (1991). Comparison of the discharge of primary somatosensory cortical (SI) neurones during active and passive tactile discrimination. *Third International Brain Research Organization (IBRO) World Congress of Neuroscience*, p. 317. [16]

Chapman, C. E., & Ageranioti-Bélanger, S. A. (1991). Discharge properties of neurones in the hand area of primary somatosensory cortex in monkeys in relation to the performance of an active tactile discrimination task. I. Areas 3b and 1. *Experimental Brain Research, 87*, 319–339. [16]

Chapman, C. E., Jiang, W., & Lamarre, Y. (1988). Modulation of lemniscal input during conditioned arm movements in the monkey. *Experimental Brain Research, 72*, 316–334. [16]

Charles, S., & Williams, R. (1989). Measurement of hand dynamics in a microsurgery environment: Preliminary data in the design of a bimanual telemicro-operation test bed. *Proceedings of the NASA Conference on Space Telerobotics*, pp. 109–118. [17]

Charpentier, A. (1891). Analyse expérimentale de quelques éléments de la sensation de poids [Experimental study of some aspects of weight perception]. *Archives de Physiologie Normales et Pathologiques, 3*, 122–135. [19, 20]

Chen, D. F., Hyland, B., Maier, V., Palmeri, A., & Wiesendanger, M. (1991). Comparison of neural activity in the supplementary motor cortex and in the primary motor cortex in monkeys performing a choice-reaction task. *Somatosensory and Motor Research, 8*, 27–44. [6]

Cheney, P. D., & Fetz, E. E. (1980). Functional classes of primate corticomotoneuronal cells and their relation to active force. *Journal of Neurophysiology, 44*, 773–791. [5]

Cheney, P. D., & Fetz, E. E. (1985). Comparable patterns of muscle facilitation evoked by individual corticomotoneuronal (CM) cells and by single intracortical microstimuli in primates: Evidence for functional groups of CM cells. *Journal of Neurophysiology, 53,* 786–804. [5]

Cheney, P. D., Fetz, E. E., & Palmer, S. (1985). Patterns of facilitation and suppression of antagonist forelimb muscles from motor cortex sites in the awake monkey. *Journal of Neurophysiology, 53,* 805–820. [5]

Chieffi, S., Fogassi, L., Gallese, V., & Gentilucci, M. (1992). Prehension movements directed to approaching objects: Influence of stimulus velocity on the transport and the grasp components. *Neuropsychologia, 30,* 877–897. [13]

Chieffi, S., & Gentilucci, M. (1993). Coordination between the transport and the grasp component during prehension movements. *Experimental Brain Research, 94,* 471–477. [13]

Churchland, P. S., & Sejnowski, T. J. (1988). Perspectives on cognitive neuroscience. *Science, 242,* 741–745. [12]

Cioni, G., Ferrari, F., & Prechtl, H. F. R. (1989). Posture and spontaneous mobility in full term infants. *Early Human Development, 18,* 247–262. [19]

Clark, F. J., Burgess, R. C., & Chapin, J. W. (1986). Proprioception with the proximal interphalangeal joint of the index finger. *Brain, 109,* 1195–1208. [17]

Clark, F. J., Burgess, R. C., Chapin, J. W., & Lipscomb, W. T. (1985). Role of intramuscular receptors in the awareness of limb position. *Journal of Neurophysiology, 54,* 1529–1540. [17]

Clark, F. J., Grigg, P., & Chapin, J. W. (1989). The contribution of articular receptors to proprioception with the fingers in humans. *Journal of Neurophysiology, 61,* 186–193. [17]

Clark, F. J., & Horch, K. W. (1986). Kinesthesia. In K. Boff, L. Kaufman, & J. P. Thomas (Eds.), *Handbook of perception and human performance* (Vol. 1, chap. 13), New York: Wiley. [17]

Clark, F. J., Horch, K., W., Bach, S. W., & Larson, G. F. (1979). Contribution of cutaneous and joint receptors to static knee-position sense in man. *Journal of Neurophysiology, 42,* 877–888. [17]

Clark, F. J., Matthews, P. B. C., & Muir, R. B. (1979). Effect of the amplitude of muscle vibration on the subjectively experienced illusion of movement. *Journal of Physiology (London), 296,* 14P–15P. [17]

Close, J. R., & Kidd, C. C. (1969). The functions of the muscles of the thumb, the index and the long fingers. *Journal of Bone and Joint Surgery, American Volume, 51-A*(8), 1601–1620. [3, 5]

Close, R. I. (1972). Dynamic properties of mammalian skeletal muscles. *Physiological Reviews, 52,* 129–197. [4]

Cohen, D. A. D., Prud'homme, M. J. L., & Kalaska, J. F. (1994). Tactile activity in primary primary somatosensory cortex during active arm movement: Correlation with receptive field properties. *Journal of Neurophysiology, 71,* 161–172. [16]

Cole, K. J. (1990). Muscle activation patterns and kinetics of human index finger movements. *Journal of Neurophysiology.* [10]

Cole, K. J. (1991). Grasp force control in older adults. *Journal of Motor Behavior, 23,* 251–258. [19, 20]

Cole, K. J. (1994). The effects of graded tactile anesthesia on the control of grip force. *Society for Neuroscience Abstracts, 20,* 4906. [19]

Cole, K. J., & Abbs, J. H. (1986). Coordination of three-joint digit movements for rapid finger-thumb grasp. *Journal of Neurophysiology, 55,* 1407–1423. [3]

Cole, K. J., & Abbs, J. H. (1988). Grip force adjustments evoked by load force perturbations of a grasped object. *Journal of Neurophysiology, 60,* 1513–1522. [15, 19]

Cole, K. J., Abbs, J. H., & Turner, G. S. (1988). Deficits in the production of grip forces in Down syndrome. *Developmental Medicine and Child Neurology, 30,* 752. [19]

Cole, K. J., & Beck, C. L. (1994). The stability of precision grip force in older adults. *Journal of Motor Behavior, 26,* 171–177. [19]

Cole, K. J., & Johansson, R. S. (1993). Friction in the digit-object interface scales the sensorimotor transformation for grip responses to pulling loads. *Experimental Brain Research, 95,* 523–532. [19]

Colebatch, J. G., Deiber, M. P., Passingham, R. E., Friston, K. J., & Frackowiak, R. S. J. (1991). Regional cerebral blood flow during voluntary arm and hand movements in human subjects. *Journal of Neurophysiology, 65,* 1392–1401. [5]

Conway, E. A., Eyre, J. A., Kelly, S., de Kroon, J., & Miller, S. (1992). Is the corticospinal projection to the motoneurones of biceps brachii monosynaptic in the human neonate? *Journal of Physiology (London), 452,* 274P. [7]

Cooke, J. D., & Brown, S. H. (1990). Movement-related phasic muscle activation. II. Generation and functional role of the triphasic pattern. *Journal of Neurophysiology, 63,* 465–472. [18]

Cooper, S. E. (1995). *The cerebellum and interjoint coordination: A kinematic and dynamic analysis of an accurate multijoint mov during reversible inactivation of cerebellar nuclei.* Doctoral thesis, Columbia University, New York. [10]

Cooper, S. E., Martin, J. H., & Ghez, C. (1993). Differential effects of localized inactivation of deep cerebellar nuclei on reaching in the cat. *Society for Neuroscience Abstracts, 19,* 529. [10]

Corcos, D. M., Gottlieb, G. L., & Agarwal, G. C. (1989). Organizing principles for single-joint movements. II. A speed-sensitive strategy. *Journal of Neurophysiology, 62,* 358–368. [10]

Costanzo, R. M., & Gardner, E. P. (1980). A quantitative analysis of responses of direction-sensitive neurons in somatosensory cortex of awake monkeys. *Journal of Neurophysiology, 43,* 1319–1341. [16]

Craig, J. J. (1986). *Introduction to robotics.* Reading, MA: Addison-Wesley. [9]

Craske, B. (1977). Perception of impossible limb positions induced by tendon vibration. *Science, 196,* 71–73. [17]

Cross, M. J., & McCloskey, D. I. (1973). Position sense following surgical removal of joints in man. *Brain Research, 5,* 443–445. [17]

Curfs, M. H. J. M., Gribnau, A. A. M., and Dederen, P. J. W. C. (1994). Selective elimination of transient corticospinal projections in the rat cervical spinal cord gray matter. *Developmental Brain Research, 78,* 182–190. [7]

Cussons, P. D., Hulliger, M., & Matthews, P. B. C. (1977). Effects of fusimotor stimulation on the response of the secondary ending of the muscle spindle to sinusoidal stretching. *Journal of Physiology (London), 270,* 835–850. [18]

D'Amato, C. J., & Hicks, S. P. (1978). Normal development and post-traumatic plasticity of corticospinal neurons in rats. *Experimental Neurology, 60,* 557–569. [7]

Darian-Smith, C., Darian-Smith, I., & Cheema, S. S. (1990). Thalamic projections to sensorimotor cortex in the macaque monkey: Use of multiple retrograde fluorescent tracers *Journal of Comparative Neurology, 299,* 17–46. [6]

Darian-Smith, I., Goodwin, A., Sugitani, M., & Heywood, J. (1985). Scanning a textured surface with the fingers: Events in sensorimotor cortex. *Experimental Brain Research, Supplement, 10,* 17–43. [16]

Darian-Smith, I., & Oke, L. E. (1980). Peripheral neural representation of the spatial frequency of a grating moving across the monkey's finger pad. *Journal of Physiology (London), 309,* 117–133. [16]

Darian-Smith, I., Sugitani, M., Heywood, J., Karita, K., & Goodwin, A. (1982). Touching textured surfaces: Cells in somatosensory cortex respond both to finger movement and to surface features. *Science, 218,* 906–909. [16]

Darling, W. G. (1991). Perception of forearm angles in 3-dimensional space. *Experimental Brain Research, 87,* 445–456. [8]

Darling, W. G., Cole, K. J., & Abbs, J. H. (1988). Kinematic variability of grasp movements as a function of practice and movement speed. *Experimental Brain Research, 73,* 225–235. [18]

Darton, K., Lippold, O. C. J., Shahani, M., & Shahani, U. (1985). Long-latency spinal reflexes in humans. *Journal of Neurophysiology, 53,* 1604–1618. [19]

Datta, A. K., Farmer, S. F., & Stephens, J. A. (1991). Central nervous pathways underlying synchronization of human motor unit firing studied during voluntary contractions. *Journal of Physiology (London)*, *432*, 401–425. [3]

Datta, A. K., Harrison, L. M., & Stephens, J. A. (1989). Task-dependent changes in the size of response to magnetic brain stimulation in human first dorsal interosseous muscle. *Journal of Physiology (London)*, *418*, 13–23. [19]

Datta, A. K., & Stephens, J. A. (1990). Synchronization of motor unit activity during voluntary contractions in man. *Journal of Physiology (London)*, *422*, 397–419. [3]

Davey, N. J., Ellaway, P. H., Friedland, C. L., & Short, D. J. (1990). Motor unit discharge characteristics and short term synchrony in paraplegic humans. *Journal of Neurology, Neurosurgery and Psychiatry*, *53*, 764–769. [3]

Davey, N. J., Ellaway, P. H., & Stein, R. B. (1986). Statistical limits for detecting change in the cumulative sum derivative of the peristimulus time histogram. *Journal of Neuroscience Methods*, *17*, 153–166. [3]

Day, B. L., Dressler, D., Maertens de Noordhout, A., Marsden, C. D., Nakashima, K., Rothwell, J. C., & Thompson, P. D. (1989). Electric and magnetic stimulation of human motor cortex: Surface EMG and single motor unit responses. *Journal of Physiology (London)*, *412*, 449–473. [7]

Day, B. L., Marsden, C. D., Obeso, J. A., & Rothwell, J. C. (1984). Reciprocal inhibition between the muscles of the human forearm. *Journal of Physiology (London)*, *349*, 519–534. [11]

Day, B. L., Rothwell, J. C., Thompson, P. D., Dick, J. P. R., Cowan, A., Berardelli, A., & Marsden, C. D. (1987). Motor cortex stimulation in intact man. II. Multiple descending volleys. *Brain*, *110*, 1191–1209. [7]

Day, B. L., Rothwell, J. C., Thompson, P. D., Maertens de Noordhout, A., Nakashima, K., Shannon, K., & Marsden, C. D. (1989). Delay in the execution of voluntary movement by electrical or magnetic brain stimulation in intact man. Evidence for the storage of motor programs in the brain. *Brain*, *112*, 649–663. [19]

De Camp, J. E. (1917). The influence of color on apparent weight. A preliminary study. *Journal of Experimental Psychology*, *62*, 347–370. [20]

De Domenico, G., & McCloskey, D. I. (1987). Accuracy of voluntary movements at the thumb and elbow joints. *Experimental Brain Research*, *65*, 471–478. [17]

Deiber, M.-P., Passingham, R. E., Colebatch, J. G., Friston, K. J., Nixon, P. D., & Frackowiak, R. S. J. (1991). Cortical areas and the selection of movement: A study with positron emission tomography. *Experimental Brain Research*, *84*, 393–402. [6]

Dekkers, J., Becker, D. L., Cook, J. E., & Navarrete, R. (1994). Early postnatal changes in the somatodendritic morphology of ankle flexor motoneurons in the rat. *European Journal of Neuroscience*, *6*, 87–97. [7]

Delp, S. L., Loan, J. P., Hoy, M. G., Zajac, F. E., Topp, E. L., & Rosen, J. M. (1990). An interactive graphics-based model of the lower extremity to study orthopaedic surgical procedures. *IEEE Transactions on Biomedical Engineering*, *BME-37*, 757–767. [4]

De Luca, C. J., LeFever, R. S., McCue, M. P., & Xenakis, A. P. (1982a). Behaviour of human motor units in different muscles during linearly varying contractions. *Journal of Physiology (London)*, *329*, 113–128. [17]

De Luca, C. J., LeFever, R. S., McCue, M. P., & Xenakis, A. P. (1982b). Control scheme governing concurrently active human motor units during voluntary contractions. *Journal of Physiology (London)*, *329*, 129–142. [3]

Dichgans, J., & Fetter, M. (1993). Compartmentalized cerebellar functions upon the stabilization of body posture. *Revue Neurologique*, *149*, 654–664. [19]

Dietz, V. (1992). Human neuronal control of automatic functional movements: Interaction between central programs and afferent input. *Physiological Reviews*, *72*, 33–69. [11, 15]

Dietz, V., Bischofberger, E., Wita, C., & Freund, H.-J. (1976). Correlation between the discharges of two simultaneously recorded motor units and physiological tremor. *Electroencephalography and Clinical Neurophysiology, 40,* 97–105. [3]

di Pellegrino, G., Fadiga, L., Fogassi, L., Gallese, V., & Rizzolatti, G. (1992). Understanding motor events: A neurophysiological study. *Experimental Brain Research, 91,* 176–180. [6]

Di Stefano, M., Morelli, M., Marzi, C. A., & Berlucchi, G. (1980). Hemispheric control of unilateral and bilateral movements of proximal and distal parts of the arm as inferred from simple reaction time to lateralized light stimuli in man. *Experimental Brain Research, 38,* 197–204. [14]

Doemges, F., & Rack, P. M. H. (1992). Changes in the stretch reflex of the human first dorsal interosseus muscle during different tasks. *Journal of Physiology (London), 447,* 563–573. [11]

Donoghue, J. P., Leibovic, S., & Sanes, J. N. (1992). Organization of the forelimb area in squirrel monkey motor cortex: Representation of digit, wrist, and elbow muscles. *Experimental Brain Research, 89,* 1–19. [6, 19]

Duffy, C. J., & Wurtz, R. H. (1991). Sensitivity of MST neurons to optic flow stimuli. I. A continuum of response selectivity to large-field stimuli. *Journal of Neurophysiology, 65,* 1329–1345. [11]

Dufossé, M., Hugon, M., & Massion, J. (1985). Postural forearm changes induced by predictable in time or voluntary triggered unloading in man. *Experimental Brain Research, 60,* 330–334. [14]

Dugas, C., & Smith, A. M. (1992). Responses of cerebellar Purkinje cells to slip of a hand-held object. *Journal of Neurophysiology, 67,* 483–495. [11, 19]

Duhamel, J.-R., Colby, C. L., & Goldberg, M. E. (1992). The updating of the representation of visual space in parietal cortex by intended eye movements. *Science, 255,* 90–92. [2]

Dum, R. P., & Strick, P. L. (1991). The origin of corticospinal projections from the premotor areas in the frontal lobe. *Journal of Neuroscience, 11,* 667–689. [6]

Dum, R. P., & Strick, P. L. (1992). Medial wall motor areas and skeletomotor control. *Current Opinion in Neurobiology, 2,* 836–839. [6]

Easton, T. A. (1972). On the normal use of reflexes. *American Scientist, 60,* 591–599. [14]

Edgley, S. A., Eyre, J. A., Lemon, R. N., & Miller, S. (1990). Excitation of the corticospinal tract by electromagnetic and electrical stimulation of the scalp in the macaque monkey. *Journal of Physiology (London), 425,* 301–320. [7]

Edgley, S. A., Eyre, J. A., Lemon, R. N., & Miller, S. (1992). Direct and indirect activation of corticospinal neurones by electrical and magnetic stimulation in the anaesthetized macaque monkey. *Journal of Physiology (London), 446,* 224P. [7]

Edin, B. B. (1990). Finger joint movement sensitivity of non-cutaneous mechanoreceptor afferents in the human radial nerve. *Experimental Brain Research, 82,* 417–422. [17]

Edin, B. B. (1992). Quantitative analysis of static strain sensitivity in human mechanoreceptors from hairy skin. *Journal of Neurophysiology, 67,* 1105–1113. [16]

Edin, B. B., & Abbs, J. H. (1991). Finger movement responses of cutaneous mechanoreceptors in the dorsal skin of the human hand. *Journal of Neurophysiology, 65,* 657–670. [8, 16, 17]

Edin, B. B., Westling, G., & Johansson, R. S. (1992). Independent control of fingertip forces at individual digits during precision lifting in humans. *Journal of Physiology (London), 450,* 547–564. [19]

Elble, R. J., & Koller, W. C. (1990). *Tremor.* Baltimore: Johns Hopkins University Press. [18]

Elble, R. J., & Randall, J. E. (1978). Mechanistic components of normal hand tremor. *Electroencephalography and Clinical Neurophysiology, 44,* 72–82. [18]

Eliasson, A. C., Gordon, A. M., & Forssberg, H. (1991). Basic co-ordination of manipulative forces of children with cerebral palsy. *Developmental Medicine and Child Neurology, 33,* 661–670. [19]

Eliasson, A. C., Gordon, A. M., & Forssberg, H. (1992). Impaired anticipatory control of isometric forces during grasping by children with cerebral palsy. *Developmental Medicine and Child Neurology, 34,* 216–225. [19]

Eliasson, A. C., Gordon, A. M., & Forssberg, H. (1995). Tactile control of isometric fingertip forces during grasping in children with cerebral-palsy. *Developmental Medicine and Child Neurology, 37,* 72–84. [19]

Ellaway, P. H., & Murthy, K. S. K. (1985). The origins and characteristics of cross-correlated activity between gamma-motoneurones in the cat. *Quarterly Journal of Experimental Physiology and Cognate Medical Sciences, 70,* 219–232. [3]

Emonet-Dénand, F., & Laporte, Y. (1975). Proportion of muscle spindles supplied by skeletofusimotor axons (beta-axons) in peroneus brevis muscle of the cat. *Journal of Neurophysiology, 38,* 1390–1394. [18]

English, A. W. (1984). An electromyographic analysis of compartments in cat lateral gastrocnemius muscle during unrestrained locomotion. *Journal of Neurophysiology, 52,* 114–125. [5]

English, A. W., & Weeks, O. I. (1987). An anatomical and functional analysis of cat biceps femoris and semitendinosus muscles. *Journal of Morphology, 191,* 161–175. [5]

Erickson, R. P. (1984, May–June). On the neural bases of behavior. *American Scientist, 72,* 233–241. [9]

Ericson, H., & Blomqvist, A. (1988). Tracing of neuronal connections with cholera toxin subunit B: Light and electron microscopic immunohistochemistry using monoclonal antibodies *Journal of Neuroscience Methods, 24,* 225–235. [6]

Eskandar, E. M., Optican, L. M., & Richmond, B. J. (1992). Role of inferior temporal neurons in visual memory. II. Multiplying temporal waveform related to vision and memory. *Journal of Neurophysiology, 68,* 1296–1306. [2]

Eskandar, E. M., Richmond, B. J., & Optican, L. M. (1992). Role of inferior temporal neurons in visual memory. I. Temporal encoding of information about visual images, recalled images, and behavioral context. *Journal of Neurophysiology, 68,* 1277–1295. [2]

Espinoza, E., & Smith, A. M. (1990). Purkinje cell simple spike activity during grasping and lifting objects of different textures and weights. *Journal of Neurophysiology, 64,* 698–714. [19]

Evans, A. L., Harrison, L. M., & Stephens, J. A. (1989). Task-dependent changes in cutaneous reflexes recorded from various muscles controlling finger movement in man. *Journal of Physiology (London), 418,* 1–12. [19]

Evans, A. L., Harrison, L. M., & Stephens, J. A. (1990). Maturation of the cutaneomuscular reflex recorded from the 1st dorsal interosseous muscle in man. *Journal of Physiology (London), 428,* 425–440. [7]

Evarts, E. V. (1968). Relation of pyramidal tract activity to force exerted during voluntary movement. *Journal of Neurophysiology, 31,* 14–27. [6]

Evarts, E. V. (1981). Sherrington's concepts of proprioception. *Trends in Neurosciences, 4,* 44–46. [19]

Eyre, J. A., Miller, S., & Ramesh, V. (1991). Constancy of central conduction delays during development in man: Investigation of motor and somatosensory pathways. *Journal of Physiology (London), 434,* 441–452. [7, 19]

Fagg, A. H., & Arbib, M. A. (1992). A model of primate visual-motor conditional learning. *Journal of Adaptive Behavior, 1,*(1), 3–37. [12]

Fagg, A. H., Lotspeich, D., Hoff, J., & Bekey, G. A. (1994). Rapid reinforcement learning for reactive control policy design in autonomous robots. In *Proceedings of the World Congress on Neural Networks*, San Diego, California (pp. 118–126). [12]

Fagot, J., & Vauclaire, J. (1988). Handedness and bimanual coordination in the lowland gorilla. *Brain, Behavior and Evolution, 32,* 89–95. [14]

Fahy, F. L., Riches, I. P., & Brown, M. W. (1993). Neuronal signals of importance to the performance of visual recognition memory tasks: Evidence from recordings of single neurones in the medial thalamus of primates. *Progress in Brain Research, 95*, 401–416. [2]

Farmer, S. F., Swash, M., Ingram, D. A., & Stephens, J. A. (1993). Changes in motor unit synchronization following central nervous lesions in man. *Journal of Physiology (London), 463*, 83–105. [3]

Faugier-Grimaud, S., Frenois, C., & Stein, D. G. (1978). Effects of posterior parietal lesions on visually guided behavior in monkeys. *Neuropsychologia, 16*, 151–168. [14]

Feldman, A. G. (1974). Change of muscle length due to shift of the equilibrium point of the muscle-load system. *Biofizika, 19*, 749–753. [10]

Feldman, A. G. (1980). Superposition of motor programs. I. Rhythmic forearm movements in man. *Neuroscience, 5*, 81–90. [11]

Feldman, A. G. (1986). Once more on the equilibrium-point hypothesis (lambda model). *Journal of Motor Behavior, 18*, 17–54. [9, 15]

Felix, D., & Wiesendanger, M. (1971). Pyramidal and non-pyramidal motor cortical effects on distal forelimb muscles of monkeys. *Experimental Brain Research, 12*, 81–91. [7]

Felleman, D. J., & Van Essen, D. C. (1991). Distributed hierarchical processing in the primate cerebral cortex. *Cerebral Cortex, 1*, 1–47. [2]

Ferrell, W. R., & Craske, B. (1992). Contribution of joint and muscle afferents to position sense at the human proximal interphalangeal joint. *Experimental Physiology, 77*, 331–342. [17]

Ferrell, W. R., Gandevia, S. C., & McCloskey, D. I. (1987). The role of joint receptors in human kinaesthesia when intramuscular receptors cannot contribute. *Journal of Physiology (London), 386*, 63–71. [17]

Ferrell, W. R., & Milne, S. E. (1989). Factors affecting the accuracy of position matching at the proximal interphalangeal joint in human subjects. *Journal of Physiology, 411*, 575–583. [17]

Ferrell, W. R., & Smith, A. (1988). Position sense at the proximal interphalangeal joint of the human index finger. *Journal of Physiology (London), 399*, 49–61. [17]

Ferrell, W. R., & Smith, A. (1989). The effect of loading on position sense at the proximal interphalangeal joint of the human index finger. *Journal of Physiology (London), 418*, 145–161. [17]

Ferrera, V. P., Nealey, T. A., & Maunsell, J. H. R. (1992). Mixed parvocellular and magnocellular geniculate signals in visual area V4. *Nature (London), 358*, 756–758. [2]

Fetz, E. E. (1992). Are moving parameters recognizably coded in the activity of single neurons? *Behavioral and Brain Sciences, 15*, 679–690. [6]

Fetz, E. E., & Cheney, P. D. (1980). Postspike facilitation of forelimb muscle activity by primate corticomotoneuronal cells. *Journal of Neurophysiology, 44*, 751–772. [3, 5]

Fikes, T. G., Klatzky, R. L., & Lederman, S. J. (1994). Effects of object texture on precontact movement time in human prehension. *Journal of Motor Behavior, 26*, 325–332. [19]

Fitts, P. M. (1954). The information capacity of the human motor system in controlling the amplitude of movement. *Journal of Experimental Psychology, 47*, 381–391. [10, 13]

Flament, D. A., Goldsmith, P., & Lemon, R. N. (1992). The development of corticospinal projections to tail and hindlimb motoneurons studied in infant macaques using magnetic brain stimulation. *Experimental Brain Research, 90*, 225–228. [7]

Flament, D. A., Hall, E. J., & Lemon, R. N. (1992). The development of cortico-motoneuronal projections investigated using magnetic brain stimulation in the infant macaque. *Journal of Physiology, (London), 447*, 755–768. [7]

Flanagan, J. R., Feldman, A. G., & Ostry, D. J. (1992). Equilibrium trajectories underlying rapid target-directed arm movements. In G. E. Stelmach & J. Requin (Eds.), *Tutorials in motor behavior II* (pp. 661–675). Amsterdam: North-Holland. [15]

Flanagan, J. R., Lemon, R. N., & Wing, A. M. (1996). *Role of antagonist muscles of the hand in anticpatory grip force modulation during arm movements.* Unpublished observations manuscript. [15]

Flanagan, J. R., & Ostry, D. J. (1990). Trajectories of human multi-joint arm movements: Evidence of joint level planning. In V. Hayward & O. Khatib (Eds.), *Experimental robotics: 1. Lecture notes in control and information science* (pp. 594–613). New York: Springer-Verlag. [9]

Flanagan, J. R., & Tresilian, J. R. (1994). Grip-load force coupling: A general control strategy for transporting objects. *Journal of Experiment Psychology: Human Perception and Performance*, *20*, 944–957. [15, 19, 20]

Flanagan, J. R., Tresilian, J. R., & Wing, A. M. (1993). Coupling of grip force and load force during arm movements with grasped objects. *Neuroscience Letters*, *152*, 53–56. [15, 19, 20]

Flanagan, J. R., Tresilian, J. R., & Wing, A. M. (1996). Grip force adjustments during rapid hand movements suggest that detailed movement kinematics are predicted. *Behavioral and Brain Sciences*, *18*, 753–754. [15]

Flanagan, J. R., & Wing, A. M. (1993). Modulation of grip force with load force during point to point arm movements. *Experimental Brain Research*, *95*, 131–143. [15, 19, 20]

Flanagan, J. R., & Wing, A. M. (1995). The stability of precision grip forces during cyclic arm movements with a hand-held load. *Experimental Brain Research*, *105*, 455–464. [15]

Flanagan, J. R., & Wing, A. M. (1996). *Anticipatory grip force modulation for inertial, viscous and spring load forces.* Manuscript in preparation. [15]

Flanagan, J. R., Wing, A. M., Allison, S., & Spenceley, A. (1995). Effects of surface texture on weight perception when lifting objects with a precision grip. *Perception & Psychophysics*, *57*, 282–290. [19, 20]

Flanders, M., & Soechting, J. F. (1995). Frames of reference for hand orientation. *Journal of Cognitive Neuroscience*, *7*, 182–195. [8]

Flanders, M., Tillery, S. I. H., & Soechting, J. F. (1992). Early stages in a sensorimotor transformation. *Behavioral and Brain Sciences*, *15*, 309–362. [8, 11]

Flash, T., & Henis, E. (1991). Arm trajectory modification during reaching towards visual targets. *Journal of Cognitive Neuroscience*, *3*, 220–230. [10]

Flash, T., & Hogan, N. (1985). The coordination of arm movements: An experimentally confirmed mathematical model. *Journal of Neuroscience*, *5*, 1688–1703. [9, 15]

Fogassi, L., Gallese, V., di Pellegrino, G., Fadiga, L., Gentilucci, M., Luppino, G., Matelli, M., Pedotti, A., & Rizzolatti, G. (1992). Space coding by premotor cortex. *Experimental Brain Research*, *89*, 686–690. [6]

Forssberg, H. (1985). Ontogeny of human locomotor control. I. Infant stepping, supported locomotion and transition to independent locomotion. *Experimental Brain Research*, *57*, 480–493. [19]

Forssberg, H., Eliasson, A. C., Kinoshita, H., Johansson, R. S., & Westling, G. (1991). Development of human precision grip. I: Basic coordination of force. *Experimental Brain Research*, *85*, 451–457. [19]

Forssberg, H., Eliasson, A. C., Kinoshita, H., Westling, G., & Johansson, R. (1995). Development of human precision grip. IV. Tactile adaptation of isometric finger forces to the frictional condition. *Experimental Brain Research*, *104*, 323–330. [19]

Forssberg, H., Kinoshita, H., Eliasson, A. C., Johansson, R. S., Westling, G., & Gordon, A. M. (1992). Development of human precision grip 2: Anticipatory control of isometric forces targeted for objects weight. *Experimental Brain Research*, *90*, 393–398. [19]

Forssberg, H., & Nashner, L. M. (1982). Ontogenetic development of postural control in man: adaption to altered support and visual conditions during stance. *Journal of Neuroscience*, *2*, 545–552. [19]

Fox, C. (1987). *An introduction to the calculus of variations.* New York: Dover. [9]

Fraser, C., & Wing, A. M. (1981). A case study of reaching by a user of a manually-operated artificial hand. *Prosthetics and Orthotics International, 5*, 151–156. [13]

Freund, H., Büdingen, H. J., & Dietz, V. (1975). Activity of single motor units from human forearm muscle during voluntary isometric contractions. *Journal of Neurophysiology, 38*, 933–946. [18]

Fridén, J., & Lieber, R. L. (1994). Physiological consequences surgical lengthening of human extensor carpi radialis brevis muscle for tennis elbow. *Journal of Hand Surgery, 19A*, 269–274. [4]

Friedli, W. G., Cohen, L., Hallett, M., Stanhope, S., & Simon, S. R. (1988). Postural adjustments associated with rapid voluntary arm movements. II. Biomechanical analysis. *Journal of Neurology, Neurosurgery and Psychiatry, 51*, 232–243. [20]

Friedli, W. G., Hallett, M., & Simon, S. R. (1984). Postural adjustments associated with rapid voluntary arm movements. I. Electromyographic data. *Journal of Neurology, Neurosurgery and Psychiatry, 47*, 611–622. [20]

Fromm, C., & Evarts, E. V. (1982). Pyramidal tract neurons in somatosensory cortex: Central and peripheral inputs during voluntary movements. *Brain Research, 238*, 186–191. [16]

Fu, Q. G., Suarez, J. I., & Ebner, T. J. (1993). Neuronal specification of direction and distance during reaching movements in the superior precentral premotor area and primary motor cortex of monkeys. *Journal of Neurophysiology, 70*, 2097–2116. [19]

Fuchs, A., & Kelso, J. A. S. (1994). A theoretical note on models of interlimb coordination. *Journal of Experimental Psychology: Human Perception and Performance, 20*, 1088–1097. [9]

Fujita, I., Tanaka, K., Ito, M., & Cheng, K. (1992). Columns for visual features of objects in monkey inferotemporal cortex. *Nature (London), 343*, 343–346. [2]

Galin, D., Johnstone, J., Nakell, L., & Herron, J. (1979). Development of the capacity for information transfer between hemispheres in normal children. *Science, 204*, 1330–1332. [19]

Gallese, V., Murata, A., Kaseda, M., Niki, N., & Sakata, H. (1994). Deficit of hand preshaping after muscimol injection in monkey parietal cortex. *NeuroReport, 5*, 1525–1529. [19]

Gandevia, S. C., & Burke, D. (1992). Does the nervous system depend on kinesthetic information to control natural limb movements? *Behavioral and Brain Sciences, 15*, 614–632. [3]

Gandevia, S. C., Hall, L. A., McCloskey, D. I., & Potter, E. K. (1983). Proprioceptive sensation at the terminal joint of the middle finger. *Journal of Physiology (London), 335*, 507–517. [17]

Gandevia, S. C., & Kilbreath, S. L. (1990). Accuracy of weight estimation for weights lifted by proximal and distal muscles of the human upper limb. *Journal of Physiology (London), 423*, 299–310. [17]

Gandevia, S. C., & McCloskey, D. I. (1976). Joint sense, muscle sense and their combination as position sense measured at the distal interphalangeal joint of the middle finger. *Journal of Physiology (London), 260* 387–408. [8, 17]

Gandevia, S. C., & McCloskey, D. I. (1977a). Changes in motor commands as shown by changes in perceived heaviness, during partial curarization and peripheral anaesthesia in man. *Journal of Physiology (London), 272*, 673–689. [17]

Gandevia, S. C., & McCloskey, D. I. (1977b). Sensations of heaviness. *Brain, 100*, 345–354. [17]

Gandevia, S. C., & McCloskey, D. I. (1978). Interpretation of perceived motor commands by reference to afferent signals. *Journal of Physiology (London), 283*, 493–499. [17]

Gans, C. (1982). Fibre architecture and muscle function. *Exercise and Sport Science Reviews, 10*, 160–207. [4]

Garner, W. P. (1974). *The processing of information and structure.* Potomac, MD: Erlbaum. [21]

Garnett, R., & Stephens, J. A. (1980). The reflex responses of single motor units in human first dorsal interosseous muscle following cutaneous afferent stimulation. *Journal of Physiology (London), 303*, 351–364. [3, 19]

Gelfand, I. M., Gurfinkel, V. S., Tsetlin, M. L., & Shik, M. L. (1971). Some problems in the analysis of movements. In I. M. Gelfand et al. (Eds.), *Models of the structural-functional organization of certain biological systems.* Cambridge, MA: MIT Press. [3]

Gentilucci, M., Castiello, U., Corradini, M. L., Scarpa, M., Umiltà, C., & Rizzolatti, G. (1991). Influence of different types of grasping on the transport component of prehension movements. *Neuropsychologia, 29,* 361–378. [13, 19]

Gentilucci, M., Chieffi, S., Scarpa, M., & Castiello, U. (1992). Temporal coupling between transport and grasp components during prehension movements: Effects of visual perturbation. *Behavioural Brain Research, 47,* 71–82. [13]

Gentilucci, M., Fogassi, L., Luppino, G., Matelli, M., Camarda, R., & Rizzolatti, G. (1988). Functional organization of inferior area 6 in the macaque monkey: I. Somatotopy and the control of proximal movements. *Experimental Brain Research, 71,* 475–490. [6]

Gentilucci, M., & Rizzolatti, G. (1990). Cortical motor control of arm and hand movements. In M. A. Goodale (Ed.), *Vision and action: The control of grasping* (pp. 147–162). Norwood, NJ: Ablex. [2]

Georgopoulos, A. P. (1986). On reaching. *Annual Review of Neuroscience, 9,* 147–170. [11]

Georgopoulos, A. P. (1991). Higher order motor control. *Annual Review of Neuroscience, 14,* 361–377. [9]

Georgopoulos, A. P. (1994). New concepts in generation of movement. *Neuron, 13,* 257–268. [6]

Georgopoulos, A. P., Ashe, J., Smyrnis, N., & Taira, M. (1992). The motor cortex and the coding of force. *Science, 256,* 1692–1695. [6]

Georgopoulos, A. P., Caminiti, R., Kalaska, J. F., & Massey, J. T. (1983). Spatial coding of movement: A hypothesis concerning the coding of movement direction by motor cortical populations. *Experimental Brain Research, Supplement, 7,* 327–336. [8]

Georgopoulos, A. P., Kalaska, J. F., Caminiti, R., & Massey, J. T. (1982). On the relations between the direction of two-dimensional arm movements and cell discharge in primate motor cortex. *Journal of Neuroscience, 2,* 1527–1537. [6, 19]

Georgopoulos, A. P., Kalaska, J. F., Crutcher, M. D., Caminiti, R., & Massey, J. T. (1984). The representation of movement direction in the motor cortex: Single cell and population studies. In G. M. Edelman, W. E. Gall, & W. M. Cowan (Eds.), *Dynamical aspects of cortical function* (pp. 453–473). New York: John Wiley. [8]

Georgopoulos, A. P., Kettner, R. E., & Schwartz, A. B. (1988). Primate motor cortex and free arm movements to visual targets in three-dimensional space. II. Coding of the direction of movements by a neuronal population. *Journal of Neuroscience, 8,* 2928–2937. [6]

Gescheider, G. A. (1985). *Psychophysics: Method, theory, and application* (2nd ed.). Hillsdale, NJ: Erlbaum. [17]

Ghez, C. (1979). Contributions of central programs to rapid limb movements in the cat. In H. Asanuma & V. J. Wilson (Eds.), *Integration in the nervous system* (pp. 305–320). Tokyo: Igaku-Shoin. [10]

Ghez, C. (1983). Sensory motor processing of targeted movements in motor cortex. *Advances in Neurology, 39,* 61–92. [10]

Ghez, C. (1991). Voluntary movement. In E. R. Kandel, J. H. Schwartz, & T. M. Jessel (Eds.), *Principles of neural sciences* (3rd ed., pp. 609–625). New York & Amsterdam: Elsevier. [6]

Ghez, C., & Gordon, J. (1987). Trajectory control in targeted force impulses. Role of opposing muscle. *Experimental Brain Research, 67,* 225–240. [18]

Ghez, C., Gordon, J., Ghilardi, M. F. (1995). Impairments of reaching movements in patients without proprioception. II. Effects of visual information on accuracy. *Journal of Neurophysiology.* [10]

Ghez, C., Gordon, J., Ghilardi, M. F., Christakos, C. N., & Cooper, S. E. (1990). Roles of proprioceptive input in the programming of arm trajectories. *Cold Spring Harbor Symposium on Quantitative Biology, 55,* 837–847. [10, 11]

Ghez, C., Gordon, J., Ghilardi, M. F., & Sainburg, R. (1994). Contributions of vision and proprioception to accuracy in limb movements. In M. S. Gazzaniga (Ed.), *The cognitive neurosciences* (pp. 549–564). Cambridge, MA: MIT Press. [10]

Ghez, C., Henning, W., & Gordon, J. (1991). Organization of voluntary movement. *Current Opinion in Neurobiology, 1,* 664–671. [10, 11, 19]

Ghez, C., & Martin, J. (1982). The control of rapid limb movement in the cat. III. Agonist-antagonist coupling. *Experimental Brain Research, 45,* 115–125. [10]

Ghez, C., & Sainburg, R. (1995). Proprioceptive control of interjoint coordination. *Canadian Journal of Physiology and Pharmacology, 73,* 273–294. [10]

Ghez, C., & Vicario, D. S. (1978). The control of rapid limb movement in the cat. II. Scaling of isometric force adjustments. *Experimental Brain Research, 33,* 191–202. [10]

Ghilardi, M. F., Gordon, J., & Ghez, C. (1995). Learning a visuomotor transformation in a local area of workspace produces directional biases in other areas. *Journal of Neurophysiology.* [10]

Gibson, A. R., Houk, J. C., & Kohlerman, N. J. (1985). Relation between red nucleus discharge and movement parameters in trained macaque monkeys. *Journal of Physiology (London), 358,* 551–570. [6]

Gibson, J. J. (1962). Observations on active touch. *Psychological Reviews, 69,* 477–491. [16]

Gibson, J. J. (1966). *The senses considered as perceptual systems.* Boston: Houghton Mifflin. [11, 21]

Gielen, C. C. A. M., Ramaekers, L., & van Zuylen, E. J. (1988). Long-latency stretch reflexes as co-ordinated functional responses in man. *Journal of Physiology (London), 407,* 275–292. [11]

Girard, L., Bleicher, C., & Cabana, T. (1993). Development of skilled locomotion in the kitten: A comparison with the development of the corticospinal tract. *Society for Neuroscience Abstracts, 19,* 63.16. [7]

Glickstein, M., & May, J. G. (1982). Visual control of movement: The circuits which link visual to motor areas of the brain with special reference to the visual input to the pons and cerebellum. In W. D. Neff (Ed.) *Contributions to sensory physiology* (Vol. 7, pp. 103–145). New York: Academic Press. [2]

Glickstein, M., May, J. G., & Mercier, B. E. (1985). Corticopontine projection in the macaque: The distribution of labelled cortical cells after large injections of horseradish peroxidase in the pontine nuclei. *Journal of Comparative Neurology, 235,* 343–359. [2]

Goldstein, L. A., Kurz, E. M., Kalkbrenner, A. E., & Sengelaub, D. R. (1993). Changes in dendritic morphology of rat spinal motoneurons during development and after unilateral target deletion. *Developmental Brain Research, 73,* 151–163. [7]

Goodale, M. A. (1993a). Visual pathways supporting perception and action in the primate cerebral cortex. *Current Opinion in Neurobiology, 3,* 578–585. [2]

Goodale, M. A. (1993b). Visual routes to knowledge and action. *Biomedical Research, 14*(Suppl. 4), 113–124. [2]

Goodale, M. A., Jakobson, L. S., & Keillor, J. M. (1994). Differences in the visual control of pantomimed and natural grasping movements. *Neuropsychologia, 32,* 1159–1178. [2, 19]

Goodale, M. A., Jakobson, L. S., Milner, A. D., Perrett, D. I., Benson, P. J., & Hietanen, J. K. (1994). The nature and limits of orientation and pattern processing supporting visuomotor control in a visual form agnosic. *Journal of Cognitive Neuroscience, 6,* 45–55. [8]

Goodale, M. A., Meenan, J. P., Bülthoff, H. H., Nicolle, D. A., Murphy, K. S., & Racicot, C. I. (1994). Separate neural pathways for the visual analysis of object shape in perception and prehension. *Current Biology, 4,* 604–610. [2]

Goodale, M. A., & Milner, A. D. (1992). Separate visual pathways for perception and action. *Trends in Neurosciences, 15,* 20–25. [2, 19, 20]

Goodale, M. A., Milner, A. D., Jakobson, L. S., & Carey, D. P. (1991). A neurological dissociation between perceiving objects and grasping them. *Nature (London)*, *349*, 154–156. [2, 8]

Goodale, M. A., Murphy, K., Meenan, J.-P., Racicot, C., & Nicolle, D. A. (1993). Spared object perception but poor object-calibrated grasping in a patient with optic ataxia. *Society for Neuroscience Abstracts*, *19*, 775. [2, 13]

Goodale, M. A., & Servos, P. (1992). Now you see it, now you don't: How delaying an action system can transform a theory. *Behavioral and Brain Sciences*, *15*, 335–336. [8]

Goodwin, A. W., & Morley, J. W. (1987). Sinusoidal movement of a grating across the monkey's fingerpad: Representation of grating and movement features in afferent fiber responses. *Journal of Neuroscience*, *7*, 2168–2180. [16]

Goodwin, G. M., Hulliger, M., & Matthews, P. B. C. (1975). The effects of fusimotor stimulation during small amplitude stretching on the frequency-response of the primary ending of the mammalian muscle spindle. *Journal of Physiology (London)*, *253*, 175–206. [18]

Goodwin, G. M., McCloskey, D. I., & Matthews, P. B. C. (1972). The contribution of muscle afferents to kinaesthesia shown by vibration induced illusions of movement and by the effects of paralysing joint afferents. *Brain*, *95*, 705–748. [17]

Gordon, A. M. (1994). Development of the reach to grasp movement. *Advances in Psychology*, *105*, 37–56. [19]

Gordon, A. M., Forssberg, H., & Iwasaki, N. (1994). Formation and lateralization of internal representations underlying motor commands during precision grip. *Neuropsychologia*, *32*, 555–568. [19]

Gordon, A. M., Forssberg, H., Johansson, R. S., Eliasson, A. C., & Westling, G. (1992). Development of human precision grip 3: Integration of visual size cues during the programming of isometric forces. *Experimental Brain Research*, *90*, 399–403. [19]

Gordon, A. M., Forssberg, H., Johansson, R. S. & Westling, G. (1991a). Visual size cues in the programming of manipulative forces during precision grip. *Experimental Brain Research*, *83*, 477–482. [15, 19, 20]

Gordon, A. M., Forssberg, H., Johansson, R. S., & Westling, G. (1991b). The integration of haptically acquired size information in the programming of precision grip. *Experimental Brain Research*, *83*, 483–488. [15, 19, 20]

Gordon, A. M., Forssberg, H., Johansson, R. S., & Westling. G. (1991c). Integration of sensory information during the programming of precision grip: Comments on the contribution of size cues. *Experimental Brain Research*, *85*, 226–229. [15, 19]

Gordon, A. M., Westling, G., Cole, K. J., & Johansson, R. S. (1991). Memory representations underlying motor commands used during manipulation of common and novel objects. *Journal of Neurophysiology*, *69*, 1789–1796. [15]

Gordon, A. M., Westling, G., Cole, K. J., & Johansson, R. S. (1993). Memory representations underlying motor commands used during manipulation of common and novel objects. *Journal of Neurophysiology*, *69*, 1789–1796. [19]

Gordon, J., and Ghez, C. (1987a). Trajectory control in targeted force impulses. II. Pulse height control. *Experimental Brain Research*, *67*, 241–252. [10]

Gordon, J., and Ghez, C. (1987b). Trajectory control in targeted force impulses. III. Compensatory adjustments for initial errors. *Experimental Brain Research*, *67*, 253–269. [10]

Gordon, J., Ghilardi, M. F., Cooper, S. E., & Ghez, C. (1994). Accuracy of planar reaching movements II. Systematic extent errors resulting from inertial anisotropy. *Experimental Brain Research*. [10]

Gordon, J., Ghilardi, M. F., & Ghez, C. (1994). Accuracy of planar reaching movements. I. Independence of direction and extent variability. *Experimental Brain Research*. [10]

Gorska, T., & Sybirska, E. (1980). Effects of pyramidal lesions on forelimb movements in the cat. *Acta Neurobiologiae Experimentalis*, *40*, 843–859. [10]

Gottlieb, S., & Lippold, O. C. J. (1983). The 4-6 Hz tremor during sustained contraction in normal human subjects. *Journal of Physiology (London), 336,* 499–509. [18]

Gould, H. J., III, Cusick, C. G., Pons, T. P., & Kaas, J. H. (1986). The relationship of the corpus callosum connections to electrical simulation maps of motor, supplementary motor and the frontal eye fields in owl monkeys. *Journal of Comparative Neurology, 247,* 297–325. [6]

Gracies, J. M., Meunier, S., & Pierrot-Deseilligny, E. (1994). Evidence for corticospinal excitation of presumed propriospinal neurones in man. *Journal of Physiology (London), 475,* 509–518. [7, 19]

Grafton, S. T., Mazziotta, J. C., Woods, R. P., & Phelps, M. E. (1992). Human functional anatomy of visually guided finger movements. *Brain, 115,* 565–587. [6]

Grafton, S. T., Woods, R. P., & Mazziotta, J. C. (1993). Within-arm somatotopy in human motor areas determined by positron emission tomography imaging of cerebral blood flow. *Experimental Brain Research, 95,* 172–176. [5]

Grafton, S. T., Woods, R. P., Mazziotta, J. C., & Phelps, M. E. (1991). Somatotopic mapping of the primary motor cortex in humans: Activation studies with cerebral blood flow and positron emission tomography. *Journal of Neurophysiology, 66,* 735–742. [6]

Graziano, M. S. A., & Gross, C. G. (1993). A bimodal map of space: Somatosensory receptive fields in the macaque putamen with corresponding receptive fields. *Experimental Brain Research, 97,* 96–109. [2]

Green, D. M., & Swets, J. A. (1989). *Signal detection theory and psychophysics.* Los Altos, CA: Peninsula. [17]

Greenwood, R. G., & Hopkins, A. (1976). Muscle response during sudden falls in man. *Journal of Physiology (London), 254,* 507–518. [11]

Gribnau, A. A. M., De Kort, E. J. M., Dederen, P. J. W. C., & Nieuwenhuys, R. (1986). On the development of the pyramidal tract in the rat. II. An anterograde tracer study of the outgrowth of the corticospinal fibers. *Anatomy and Embryology, 175,* 101–110. [7]

Grigg, P. (1975). Mechanical factors influencing response of joint afferent neurons from cat knee. *Journal of Neurophysiology, 38,* 1473–1483. [16]

Grillner, S., & Wallén, P. (1985). Central pattern generators for locomotion, with special reference to vertebrates. *Annual Review of Neuroscience, 8,* 233–261. [14]

Gross, C. G. (1973). Visual functions of inferotemporal cortex. In R. Jung (Ed.), *Handbook of sensory physiology* (Vol. 7, Part 3B, pp. 451–482). Berlin: Springer-Verlag. [2]

Gross, C. G. (1991). Contribution of striate cortex and the superior colliculus to visual function in area MT, the superior temporal polysensory area and inferior temporal cortex. *Neuropsychologia, 29,* 497–515. [2]

Guiard, Y. (1988). The kinematic chain as a model for human asymmetrical bimanual cooperation. In A. M. Colley & J. R. Beech (Eds.), *Cognition and action in skilled behavior* (pp. 205–228). Amsterdam: Elsevier/North-Holland. [14]

Gurfinkel, V. S., & Levik, Yu. (1979). Sensory complexes and sensorimotor integration. *Human Physiology, 5,* 269–281. [11]

Haas, W. S., & Meyer, M. (1989). An automatic decomposition system for routine clinical examinations and clinical research: ARTMUP -automatic recognition and tracking of motor unit potentials. In J. E. Desmedt (Ed.), *Clinical Neurophysiology updates: Vol. 2, Computer-aided electromyography and expert systems* (pp. 67–81). Amsterdam: Elsevier. [3]

Hadders-Algra, M., & Prechtl, H. F. R. (1992). Developmental course of general movements in early infancy. 1. Descriptive analysis of change in form. *Early Human Development, 28,* 201–213. [19]

Hagbarth, K.-E., & Young, R. R. (1979). Participation of the stretch reflex in human physiological tremor. *Brain, 102,* 509–526. [18]

Häger-Ross, C., Cole, K. J., & Johansson, R. S. (in press). Grip force responses to unanticipated object loading: Load direction reveals body- and gravity-referenced intrinsic task variables. *Experimental Brain Research.* [19]

Häger-Ross, C., & Johansson, R. S. (in press). Non-digital afferent input in reactive control of fingertip forces during precision grip. *Experimental Brain Research.* [19]

Haggard, P. (1994). Perturbations studies of coordinated prehension. In K. M. B. Bennett & U. Castiello (Eds.), *Insights into the reach to grasp movement* (pp. 151 –170). Amsterdam: Elsevier/North-Holland. [13]

Haggard, P., & Wing, A. M. (1991). Remote responses to perturbation in human prehension. *Neuroscience Letters, 122,* 103–108. [9, 13]

Hall, L. A., & McCloskey, D. I. (1983). Detections of movements imposed on finger, elbow and shoulder joints. *Journal of Physiology (London), 335,* 519–533. [17]

Hallet, M., Shahani, B. T., & Young, R. R. (1975). EMG analysis of stereotyped voluntary movements in man. *Journal of Neurology, Neurosurgery and Psychiatry, 38,* 1154–1162. [18]

Halliday, A. M., & Redfearn, J. W. T. (1956). An analysis of the frequency of finger tremor in healthy subjects. *Journal of Physiology (London), 134,* 600–611. [18]

Halsband, U., & Freund, H.-J. (1993). Motor learning. *Current Opinion in Neurobiology, 3,* 940–949. [6, 19]

Halsband, U., Ito, N., Tanji, J., & Freund, H.-J. (1993). The role of premotor cortex and the supplementary motor area in the temporal control of movement in man. *Brain, 116,* 243–266. [6]

Halsband, U., Matsuzaka, Y., & Tanji, J. (1994). Neuronal activity in the primate supplementary, pre-supplementary and premotor cortex during externally and internally instructed sequential movements. *Neurosciences Research, 20,* 149–155. [6]

Hamuy, T. P. (1956). Retention and performance of "skilled movements" after cortical ablations in monkeys. *Bulletin of the Johns Hopkins Hospital, 98,* 417–444. [5]

Harrison, L., Ironton, R., & Stephens, J. A. (1991). Cross-correlation analysis of multi-unit EMG recordings in man. *Journal of Neuroscience Methods, 40,* 171–179. [3]

Hasan, Z., & Houk, J. C. (1975a). Analysis of response properties of deefferented mammalian spindle receptors based on frequency response. *Journal of Neurophysiology, 38,* 663–672. [18]

Hasan, Z., & Houk, J. C. (1975b). Transition in sensitivity of spindle receptors that occurs when muscle is stretched more than a fraction of a millimeter. *Journal of Neurophysiology, 38,* 673–689. [18]

Hasselmo, M. E., Rolls, E. T., Baylis, G. C., & Nalwa, V. (1989). Object-centered encoding by face-selective neurons in the cortex in the superior temporal sulcus of the monkey. *Experimental Brain Research, 75,* 417–429. [2]

He, S.-Q., Dum, R. P., & Strick, P. L. (1993). Topographic organization of corticospinal projections from the frontal lobe: Motor areas on the lateral surface of the hemisphere. *Journal of Neuroscience, 13,* 952–980. [6]

Heald, A., Bates, D., Cartlidge, N. E. F., French, J. M., & Miller, S. (1993). Longitudinal study of central motor conduction time following stroke. 1. Natural history of central motor conduction. *Brain, 116,* 1355–1370. [7]

Hécaen, H. (1978). Les apraxies idéomotrices, essai de dissociation. In H. Hécaen & M. Jeannerod (Eds.), *Du contrôle moteur à l'organisation du geste* (pp. 343–358). Paris: Masson. [14]

Heffner, R. S., & Masterton, R. B. (1975). Variation in form of the pyramidal tract and its relationship to digital dexterity. *Brain, Behavior and Evolution, 12,* 161–200. [7]

Heffner, R. S., & Masterton, R. B. (1983). The role of the corticospinal tract in the evolution of human digital dexterity. *Brain, Behavior and Evolution, 23,* 165–183. [7]

Heller, M. A. (1989). Texture perception in sighted and blind observers. *Perception & Psychophysics, 45,* 49–54. [21]

Hepp-Reymond, M.-C. (1988). Functional organization of motor cortex and its participation in voluntary movements. *Comparative Primate Biology, 4*, 501–624. [3]

Hepp-Reymond, M.-C., Huesler, E. J., Maier, M. A., & Qi, H.-X. (1994). Force-related neuronal activity in two regions of the primate ventral premotor cortex. *Canadian Journal of Physiology and Pharmacology, 72*, 571–579. [3]

Hepp-Reymond, M.-C., & Maier, M. A. (1991). Central and peripheral control of dynamics in finger movements and precision grip. In J. Requin & G. E. Stelmach (Eds.), *Tutorials in motor neuroscience* (pp. 517–527). Netherlands: Kluwer Academic Publishers. [6]

Hepp-Reymond, M.-C., & Wiesendanger, M. (1972). Unilateral pyramidotomy in monkeys: Effect on force and speed of a conditioned precision grip. *Brain Research, 36*, 117–131. [3]

Hepp-Reymond, M.-C., Wyss, U., & Anner, R. E. C. (1978). Neuronal coding of static force in the primate motor cortex. *Journal of Physiology (Paris), 74*, 287–291. [3]

Heuer, H. (in press). Coordination. In H. Heuer & S. W. Keele (Eds.), *Handbook of motor control*. London: Academic Press. [9]

Hietanen, J. K., & Perrett, D. I. (1993). Motion sensitive cells in the macaque superior temporal polysensory area. I. Lack of response to the sight of the monkey's own limb movement. *Experimental Brain Research, 93*, 117–128. [2]

Hietanen, J. K., Perrett, D. I., Oram, M. W., Benson, P. J., & Dittrich, W. H. (1992). The effects of lighting conditions on responses of cells selective for face views in the macaque temporal cortex. *Experimental Brain Research, 89*, 157–171. [2]

Hikosaka, O., Tanaka, M., Sakamoto, M., & Iwamura, Y. (1985). Deficits in manipulative behaviors induced by local injections of muscimol in the first somatosensory cortex of the conscious monkey. *Brain Research, 325*, 375–280. [16, 19]

Hinde, R. A., Rowell, T. E., & Spencer-Booth, Y. (1964). Behaviour of socially living rhesus monkeys in their first six months. *Proceedings of the Zoological Society of London, 143*, 609–649. [7]

Hocherman, S., & Wise, S. P. (1990). Trajectory-selective neuronal activity in the motor cortex of rhesus monkeys. (*Macaca mulatta*). *Behavioral Neuroscience, 104*, 495–499. [6]

Hogan, N. (1984). An organizing principle for a class of voluntary movements. *Journal of Neuroscience, 4*, 2745–2754. [9, 10]

Hogan, N. (1985). The mechanics of multi-joint posture and movement control. *Biological Cybernetics, 52*, 315–331. [3, 11]

Hogan, N. (1988). Planning and execution of multijoint movements. *Canadian Journal of Physiology and Pharmacology, 66*, 508–517. [10]

Hollerbach, J. M. (1988). Fundamentals of motor behavior. In D. Osherson (Ed.), *Invitation to cognitive science* (Chap. 6). Cambridge, MA: MIT Press. [8]

Hollerbach, J. M., & Atkeson, C. G. (1987). Deducing planning variables from experimental arm trajectories: Pitfalls and possibilities. *Biological Cybernetics, 56*, 279–292. [9]

Hollerbach, J. M., & Flash, T. (1982). Dynamic interactions between limb segments during planar arm movement. *Biological Cybernetics, 44*, 67–77. [10, 15]

Hollins, M., & Goble, A. K. (1988). Perception of the length of voluntary movements. *Somatosensory Research, 5*, 335–348. [17]

Holmes, G. (1939). The cerebellum of man. *Brain, 62*, 1–30. [10]

Holsapple, J. W., Preston, J. B., & Strick, P. L. (1991). The origin of thalamic inputs to the hand representation in the primary motor cortex. *Journal of Neuroscience, 11*, 2644–2654. [19]

Holt, A. B., Cheek, D. B., Mellits, E. D., & Hill, D. E. (1975). Brain size and the relation of the primate to the nonprimate. In D. B. Cheek (Ed.), *Fetal and postnatal cellular growth* (pp. 23–44). New York: Wiley. [7]

Hoover, J. E., & Strick, P. L. (1993). Multiple output channels in the basal ganglia. *Science, 259*, 819–821. [6]

Horak, F. B., Esselman, P., Anderson, M. E., & Lynch, M. K. (1984). The effects of movement velocity, mass displaced, and task certainty on associated postural adjustments made by normal and hemiplegic individuals. *Journal of Neurology, Neurosurgery and Psychiatry, 47*, 1020–1028. [20]

Horak, F. B., & Nashner, L. M. (1986). Central programming of postural movements: Adaptation to altered support-surface configurations. *Journal of Neurophysiology, 55*, 1369–1381. [3]

Houk, J. C., Gibson, A. R., Harvey, C. F., Kennedy, P. R., & van Kan, P. L. (1988). Activity of primate magnocellular red nucleus related to hand and finger movements. *Behavioural Brain Research, 28*, 201–206. [19]

Houk, J. C., & Hennemann, E. (1967). Responses of Golgi tendon organs to active contraction of the soleus muscle of the cat. *Journal of Neurophysiology, 30*, 466–488. [18]

Houk, J. C., & Rymer, W. Z. (1981). Neural control of muscle length and tension. In J. M. Brookhart & V. B. Mountcastle (Eds.), *Handbook of physiology: Sect. 1. The nervous system* (Vol. 2, Part 1, pp. 257–324). Bethesda, MD: American Physiological Society. [11]

Houk, J. C., Rymer, W. Z., & Crago, P. E. (1981). Dependence of dynamic response of spindle receptors on muscle length and velocity. *Journal of Neurophysiology, 46*, 143–166. [18]

Hoy, M. G., Zajac, F. E., & Gordon, M. E. (1990). A musculoskeletal model of the human lower extremity: The effect of muscle, tendon, and moment arm on the moment-angle relationship of musculotendon actuators at the hip, knee, and ankle. *Journal of Biomechanics, 23*, 157–169. [4]

Hoy, M. G., & Zernicke, R. F. (1985). Modulation of limb dynamics in the swing phase of locomotion. *Journal of Biomechanics, 18*, 49–60. [10]

Hoy, M. G., & Zernicke, R. F. (1986). The role of intersegmental dynamics during rapid limb oscillations. *Journal of Biomechanics, 19*, 867–877. [10]

Hsiao, S. S., O'Shaughnessy, D. M., & Johnson, K. O. (1993). Effects of selective attention on spatial form processing in monkey primary and secondary somatosensory cortex. *Journal of Neurophysiology, 70*, 444–447. [16]

Huesler, E. J., Maissen, G. C., Maier, M. A., & Hepp-Reymond, M.-C. (1995). Motor unit synchronization during the precision grip. In A. Taylor, M. H. Gladden, & R. Durbaba, (Eds.), *Alpha and Gamma motor systems* (pp. 106–108). New York: Plenum Press. [3]

Hugon, M., Massion, J., & Wiesendanger, M. (1982). Anticipatory postural changes induced by active unloading and comparison with passive unloading in man. *Pfluegers Archiv, 393*, 292–296. [14, 19]

Hulliger, M. (1984). The mammalian muscle spindle and its central control. *Reviews of Physiology, Biochemistry and Pharmacology, 101*, 1–110. [17]

Hulliger, M., Matthews, P. B. C. & Noth, J. (1977). Static and dynamic fusimotor action on the response of IA fibres to low frequency sinusoidal stretching of widely ranging amplitude. *Journal of Physiology (London), 267*, 811–838. [18]

Hulliger, M., Nordh, E., Thelin, A.-E., & Vallbo, Å. B. (1979). The responses of afferent fibres from the glabrous skin of the hand during voluntary finger movements in man. *Journal of Physiology (London), 291*, 233–249. [16]

Hulliger, M., Nordh, E., & Vallbo, Å. B. (1982). The absence of position response in spindle afferent units from human finger muscles during accurate position holding. *Journal of Physiology (London), 322*, 167–179. [16]

Hultborn, H., & Illert, M. (1991). How is motor behavior reflected in the organization of spinal systems? In D. R. Humphrey & H.-J. Freund (Eds.), *Dahlem workshop on motor control: Concepts and issues*, (pp. 49–73). Chichester, UK: Wiley. [3]

Humphrey, D. R. (1986). Representation of movements and muscles within the primate precentral motor cortex: Historical and current perspectives. *Federation Proceedings, 45*, 2687–2699. [5, 6]

Humphrey, D. R., & Corrie, W. S. (1978). Properties of pyramidal tract neuron system within a functionally defined subregion of primate motor cortex. *Journal of Neurophysiology, 41,* 216–243. [7]

Humphrey, D. R., & Tanji, J. (1990). What features of voluntary motor control are incoded in the neuronal discharge of different cortical motor areas? In D. R. Humphrey & H.-J. Freund (Eds.), *Dahlem workshop on motor control: Concepts and issues* (pp. 413–443). Chichester, UK: Wiley. [6]

Humphrey, T. (1960). The development of the pyramidal tracts in human fetuses, correlated with cortical differentiation. In D. B. Tower & J. P. Schadé (Eds.), *Structure and function of the cerebral cortex* (pp. 93–103). Amsterdam: Elsevier. [7]

Hunter, I. W., Doukoglou, T. D., Lafontaine, S. R., Charette, P. G., Jones, L. A., Sagar, M. A., Mallinson, G. D., & Hunter, P. J. (1993). A teleoperated microsurgical robot and associated virtual environment for eye surgery. *Presence, 2,* 265–280. [17]

Hunter, I. W., Jones, L. A., Sagar, M. A., Lafontaine, S. R., & Hunter, P. J. (1995). Ophthalmic microsurgical robot and associated virtual environment. *Computers in Biology and Medicine, 25,* 173–182. [17]

Huntley, G. W., and Jones, E. G. (1991). Relationship of intrinsic connections to forelimb movement representations in monkey motor cortex: A correlative anatomic and physiological study. *Journal of Neurophysiology, 66,* 390–413. [5]

Hutchins, K. D., Martino, A. M., & Strick, P. L. (1988). Corticospinal projections from the medial wall of the hemisphere. *Experimental Brain Research, 71,* 667–672. [6]

Hyvärinen, J., & Poranen, A. (1974). Function of the parietal associative area 7 as revealed from cellular discharges in alert monkeys. *Brain, 97,* 673–692. [2]

Hyvärinen, J., & Poranen, A. (1978a). Movement-sensitive and direction and orientation- selective cutaneous receptive fields in the hand area of the post-central gyrus in monkeys. *Journal of Neurophysiology, 283,* 523–537. [16]

Hyvärinen, J., & Poranen, A. (1978b). Receptive field integration and submodality convergence in the hand area of the post-central gyrus of the alert monkey. *Journal of Neurophysiology, 283,* 539–556. [16]

Hyvärinen, J., Poranen, A., & Jokinen, Y. (1980). Influence of attentive behavior on neuronal responses to vibration in primary somatosensory cortex of the monkey. *Journal of Neurophysiology, 43,* 870–883. [16]

Iberall, T. (1988, June). A neural network for planning hand shapes in human prehension. In *Proceedings of the 1988 Automatic Controls Conference,* Atlanta, Georgia, USA (pp. 2288–2293). [12]

Iberall, T., Bingham, G., & Arbib, M. A. (1986). Opposition space as a structuring concept for the analysis of skilled hand movements. *Experimental Brain Research, 15,* 158–173. [2, 12, 13, 19]

Iberall, T., Preti, M. J., & Zemke, R. (1989). Task influence on timing and grasp patterns in human prehension. *Society for Neuroscience Abstracts, 15*(1), 397. [12]

Ikeda, A., Lüders, H. O., Burgess, R. C., & Shibasaki, H. (1992). Movement-related potentials recorded from supplementary motor area and primary motor cortex. *Brain, 115,* 1017–1043. [6]

Ikeda, A., Lüders, H. O., Burgess, R. C., & Shibasaki, H. (1993). Movement-related potentials associated with single and repetitive movements recorded from human supplementary motor area. *Electroencephalography and Clinical Neurophysiology: Electromyography and Motor Control, 89,* 269–277. [6]

Inase, M., Mushiake, H., Shima, K., Aya, K., & Tanji, J. (1989). Activity of digital area neurons of the primary somatosensory cortex in relation to sensorially triggered and self-initiated digital movements of monkeys. *Neuroscience Research, 7,* 219–234. [16]

Inase, M., & Tanji, J. (1995). Thalamic distribution of projection neurons to the primary motor cortex relative to afferent terminal fields from the globus pallidus in the macaque monkey. *Journal of Comparative Neurology, 353*, 415–426. [6]

Issler, H., & Stephens, J. A. (1983). The maturation of cutaneous reflexes studied in the upper limb in man. *Journal of Physiology (London), 335*, 643–654. [19]

Iwamura, Y. (1993). Dynamic and hierarchical processing in the monkey somatosensory cortex. *Biomedical Research, 14*, 107–111. [19]

Iwamura, Y., Tanaka, M., Sakamoto, M., & Hikosaka, O. (1983a). Functional subdivisions representing different finger regions in area 3 of the first somatosensory cortex of the conscious monkey. *Experimental Brain Research, 51*, 315–326. [16]

Iwamura, Y., Tanaka, M., Sakamoto, M., & Hikosaka, O. (1983b). Converging patterns of finger representation and complex response properties of neurons in area 1 of the first somatosensory cortex of the conscious monkey. *Experimental Brain Research, 51*, 327–337. [16]

Iwamura, Y., Tanaka, M., Sakamoto, M., & Hikosaka, O. (1985a). Diversity in receptive field properties of vertical neuronal arrays in the crown of the postcentral gyrus of the conscious monkey. *Experimental Brain Research, 58*, 400–411. [16]

Iwamura, Y., Tanaka, M., Sakamoto, M., & Hikosaka, O. (1985b). Vertical neuronal arrays in the postcentral gyrus signalling active touch: A receptive field study in the conscious monkey. *Experimental Brain Research, 58*, 412–420. [16]

Iwamura, Y., Tanaka, M., Sakamoto, M., & Hikosaka, O. (1993). Rostrocaudal gradients in the neuronal receptive field complexity in the finger region of the alert monkey's postcentral gyrus. *Experimental Brain Research, 92*, 360–368. [16]

Jacks, A., Prochazka, A., & Trend, P. S. J. (1988). Instability in human forearm movements studied with feed-back-controlled electrical stimulation of muscles. *Journal of Physiology (London), 402*, 443–461. [18]

Jackson, S. R., Jackson, G. M., & Rosicky, J. (1995). Are non-relevant objects represented in working-memory—The effect of nontarget objects on reach and grasp kinematics. *Experimental Brain Research, 102*, 519–530. [19]

Jacobson, M. D., Raab, R., Fazelli, B. M., Abrams, R. A., & Botte, M. J. (1992). Architectural design of the human intrinsic hand muscles. *Journal of Hand Surgery, 17A*, 804–809. [4]

Jakobson, L. S., Archibald, Y. M., Carey, D. P., & Goodale, M. A. (1991). A kinematic analysis of reaching and grasping movements in a patient recovering from optic ataxia. *Neuropsychologia, 29*, 803–809. [2]

Jakobson, L. S., & Goodale, M. A. (1991). Factors affecting higher-order movement planning: A kinematic analysis of human prehension. *Experimental Brain Research, 86*, 199–208. [10, 13, 19]

Jakobson, L. S., & Goodale, M. A. (1994). The neural substrates of visually guided prehension: The effects of focal brain damage. In K. M. B. Bennett & U. Castiello (Eds.), *Insights into the reach to grasp movement* (pp. 199–214). Amsterdam: Elsevier. [2, 13]

Jami, L. (1992). Golgi tendon organs in mammalian skeletal muscle: Functional properties and central actions. *Physiological Reviews, 72*, 623–666. [18]

Jankowska, E. (1992). Interneuronal relay in spinal pathways from proprioceptors. *Progress in Neurobiology, 38*, 335–378. [11]

Jansen, J. K. S., & Rudjord, T. (1964). On the silent period and the Golgi tendon organs of the soleus muscle of the cat. *Acta Physiologica Scandinavica, 62*, 364–379. [18]

Jeannerod, M. (1981). Intersegmental coordination during reaching at natural visual objects. In J. Long & A. Baddeley (Eds.), *Attention and performance IX* (pp. 153–168). Hillsdale, NJ: Erlbaum. [13, 19]

Jeannerod, M. (1984). The timing of natural prehension movements. *Journal of Motor Behavior, 16*, 235–254 [11, 13, 19]

Jeannerod, M. (1986). The formation of finger grip during prehension. A cortically mediated visuomotor pattern. *Behavioural Brain Research, 19*, 99–116. [13, 19]

Jeannerod, M. (1988). *The neural and behavioral organization of goal-directed movements.* Oxford: Clarendon Press. [2, 10, 19]

Jeannerod, M. (1991). The interaction of visual and proprioceptive cues in controlling reaching movements. In D. R. Humphrey & H.-J. Freund (Eds.), *Dahlem workshop on motor control: Concepts and issues* (pp. 277–291). Chichester, UK: Wiley. [11]

Jeannerod, M. (1994a). The hand and the object—The role of posterior parietal cortex in forming motor representations. *Canadian Journal of Physiology and Pharmacology, 72*, 535–541. [19]

Jeannerod, M. (1994b). Object oriented action. In K. M. B. Bennett & U. Castiello (Eds.), *Insights into the reach to grasp movement* (pp. 3–15) Elsevier/North-Holland: Amsterdam. [13]

Jeannerod, M. (1994c). The representing brain—Neural correlates of motor intention and imagery. *Behavioral and Brain Sciences, 17*, 187–202. [19]

Jeannerod, M., Arbib, M. A., Rizzolatti, G., & Sakata, H. (1995). Grasping objects: The cortical mechanisms of visuomotor transformation. *Trends in Neurosciences, 18*, 314–320. [10, 13]

Jeannerod, M., & Biguer, B. (1982). Visuomotor mechanisms in reaching within extrapersonal space. In D. Ingle, M. A. Goodale, & R. Mansfield (Eds.), *Advances in the analysis of visual behavior* (pp. 387–409). Boston: MIT Press. [13]

Jeannerod, M., Decety, J., & Michel, F. (1994). Impairement of grasping movements following a bilateral posterior parietal lesion. *Neuropsychologia, 32*,(4), 369–380. [13]

Jeannerod, M., & Rossetti, Y. (1993). Visuomotor coordination as a dissociable visual function: Experimental and clinical evidences. In C. Kennard (Ed.), *Visual perceptual defects, Baillière's Clinical Neurology* (Vol. 2, No. 2, pp. 439–460). London: Baillière Tindall. [13]

Jenkins, I. H., Brooks, D. J., Nixon, P. D., Frackowiak, R. S. J., & Passingham, R. E. (1994). Motor sequence learning: A study with positron emission tomography. *Journal of Neuroscience, 14*, 3775–3790. [6]

Jenner, J. R., & Stephens, J. A. (1982). Cutaneous reflex responses and their central nervous pathways studied in man. *Journal of Physiology (London), 333*, 405–419. [19]

Jenny, A. B., & Inukai, J. (1983). Principles of motor organization of the monkey cervical spinal cord. *Journal of Neuroscience, 3*, 567–575. [6, 7]

Jiang, W., Chapman, C. E., & Lamarre, Y. (1990). Modulation of somatosensory evoked responses in the primary somatosensory cortex produced by intracortical microstimulation of the motor cortex in the monkey. *Experimental Brain Research, 80*, 333–344. [16]

Jiang, W., Chapman, C. E., & Lamarre, Y. (1991). Modulation of the cutaneous responsiveness of neurones in the primary somatosensory cortex during conditioned arm movements in the monkey. *Experimental Brain Research, 84*, 342–354. [16]

Jiang, W., Lamarre, Y., & Chapman, C. E. (1990). Modulation of cutaneous cortical evoked potentials during isometric and isotonic contractions in the monkey. *Brain Research, 536*, 69–78. [16]

Jinnai, K., Nambu, A., Tanibuchi, I., Yoshida, S. (1993). Cerebello- and pallido-thalamic pathways to areas 6 and 4 in the monkey. *Stereotactic Functional Neurosurgery 60*, 70–79. [6]

Johansson, R. S. (1991). How is grasping modified by somatosensory input? In D. R. Humphrey & H.-J. Freund, (Eds.), *Dahlem workshop on motor control: Concepts and issues* (pp. 331–355). Chichester, UK: Wiley. [11, 15, 19]

Johansson, R. S., & Cole, K. J. (1992). Sensory-motor coordination during grasping and manipulative actions. *Current Opinion in Neurobiology, 2*, 815–823. [19]

Johansson, R. S., & Cole, K. J. (1994). Grasp stability during manipulative actions. *Canadian Journal of Physiology and Pharmacology, 72*, 511–524. [16, 19]

Johansson, R. S., & Edin, B. B. (1993). Predictive feedforward sensory control during grasping and manipulation in man. *Biomedical Research, 14*, 95–106. [19]

Johansson, R. S., Häger, C., & Bäckström, L. (1992). Somatosensory control of precision grip during unpredictable pulling loads. III. Impairments during digital anesthesia. *Experimental Brain Research, 89*, 204–213. [19]

Johansson, R. S., Häger, C., & Riso, R. (1992). Somatosensory control of precision grip during unpredictable pulling loads. II. Changes in load force rate. *Experimental Brain Research, 89*, 192–203. [19]

Johansson, R. S., Lemon, R. N., & Westling, G. (1994). Time-varying enhancement of human cortical excitability mediated by cutaneous inputs during precision grip. *Journal of Physiology (London), 481*, 761–775. [3, 19]

Johansson, R. S., Riso, R., Häger, C., & Bäckström, L. (1992). Somatosensory control of precision grip during unpredictable pulling loads. I. Changes in load force amplitude. *Experimental Brain Research, 89*, 181–191. [15, 19]

Johansson, R. S., & Vallbo, Å. B. (1983). Tactile sensory coding in the glabrous skin of the human hand. *Trends in Neurosciences, 6*, 27–31. [19]

Johansson, R. S., & Westling, G. (1984a). Influences of cutaneous sensory input on the motor coordination during precision manipulation. In C. von Euler, O. Franzen, U. Lindblom, & D. Ottoson (Eds.), *Somatosensory mechanisms* (pp. 249–260). London: Macmillan. [19]

Johansson, R. S., & Westling, G. (1984b). Roles of glabrous skin receptors and sensorimotor memory in automatic control of precision grip when lifting rougher or more slippery objects. *Experimental Brain Research, 56*, 550–564. [3, 15, 19, 20]

Johansson, R. S., & Westling, G. (1987a). Signals in tactile afferents from the fingers eliciting adaptive motor responses during precision grip. *Experimental Brain Research, 66*, 141–154. [15, 17, 18, 19]

Johansson, R. S., & Westling, G. (1987b). Tactile afferent input influencing motor coordination during precision grip. In A. Struppler & A. Weindl (Eds.), *Clinical aspects of sensory motor integration* (pp. 3–13). Berlin: Springer-Verlag. [19]

Johansson, R. S., & Westling, G. (1988a). Coordinated isometric muscle commands adequately and erroneously programmed for the weight during lifting task with precision grip. *Experimental Brain Research, 71*, 59–71. [15, 19, 20]

Johansson, R. S., & Westling, G. (1988b). Programmed and triggered actions to rapid load changes during precision grip. *Experimental Brain Research, 71*, 72–86. [15, 19]

Johansson, R. S., & Westling, G. (1990). Tactile afferent signals in the control of precision grip. In M. Jeannerod (Ed.), *Attention and performance XIII* (pp. 677–713). Hillsdale, NJ: Erlbaum. [19]

Johansson, R. S., & Westling, G. (1991). Afferent signals during manipulative tasks in man. In O. Franzen & J. Westman (Eds.), *Somatosensory mechanisms*, (pp. 25–48). London: Macmillan. [16, 19]

Johnson, K. O., & Hsiao, S. S. (1992). Neural mechanisms of tactual form and texture perception. *Annual Review of Neuroscience, 15*, 227–250. [17]

Jones, E. G., Coulter, J. D., & Hendry, S. H. C. (1978). Intracortical connectivity of architectonic fields in the somatic sensory, motor and parietal cortex of monkeys. *Journal of Comparative Neurology, 181*, 291–348. [16]

Jones, L. A. (1983). Role of central and peripheral signals in force sensation during fatigue. *Experimental Neurology, 81*, 497–503. [17]

Jones, L. A. (1986). Perception of force and weight: Theory and research. *Psychological Bulletin, 100*, 29–42. [17, 20]

Jones, L. A. (1988). Motor illusions: What do they reveal about proprioception? *Psychological Bulletin, 103*, 72–86. [17]

Jones, L. A. (1989). Matching forces: Constant errors and differential thresholds. *Perception, 18,* 681–687. [17]

Jones, L. A. (1994). Peripheral mechanisms of touch and proprioception. *Canadian Journal of Physiology and Pharmacology, 72,* 484–487. [16]

Jones, L. A., & Hunter, I. W. (1983). Effect of fatigue on force sensation. *Experimental Neurology, 81,* 640–650. [17]

Jones, L. A., & Hunter, I. W. (1992). Changes in pinch force with bidirectional load forces. *Journal of Motor Behavior, 24,* 157–164. [17, 19]

Joosten, E. A. J., Gribnau, A. A. M., & Dederen, P. J. W. C. (1987). An anterograde tracer study of the developing corticospinal tract in the rat: Three components. *Developmental Brain Research, 36,* 121–130. [7]

Jordan, M. I., & Rosenbaum, D. A. (1989). Action. In M. I. Posner (Ed.), *Foundations of cognitive science* (pp. 727–767). Cambridge, MA: MIT Press. [9]

Jürgens, U. (1984). The efferent and afferent connections of the supplementary motor area. *Brain Research, 300,* 63–81. [6]

Kaas, J. H., Nelson, R. J., Sur, M., Lin, C.-S., & Merzenich, M. M. (1979). Multiple representations of the body within the primary somatosensory cortex of primates. *Science, 204,* 521–523. [5, 16]

Kalaska, J. F. (1991). Parietal cortex area 5: A neuronal representation of movement kinematics for kinaesthetic perception and movement control. In J. Paillard (Ed.), *Brain and space* (pp. 133–146). Oxford: Oxford University Press. [15]

Kalaska, J. F. (1994). Central neural mechanisms of touch and proprioception. *Canadian Journal of Physiology and Pharmacology, 72,* 542–545. [16]

Kalaska, J. F., & Crammond, D. J. (1992). Cerebral cortical mechanisms of reaching movements. *Science, 255,* 1517–1523. [6]

Kalil, K. (1985). Development and plasticity of the sensorimotor cortex and pyramidal tract. In *Development, organization and processing in somatosensory pathways* (pp. 87–96). New York: Liss. [7]

Kaluzny, P., Palmeri, A., & Wiesendanger, M. (1994). The problem of bimanual coupling: A reaction time study of simple unimanual and bimanual finger responses. *Electroencephalography and Clinical Neurophysiology, 93,* 450–458. [14]

Kaluzny, P., & Wiesendanger, M. (1992). Feedforward postural stabilization in a distal bimanual unloading task. *Experimental Brain Research, 92,* 173–182. [14]

Kandel, E. R., Schwartz, J. H., & Jessel, T. M. (1991). *Principles of neural science.* New York: Elsevier. [18]

Katz, R., Penicaud, A., & Rossi, A. (1991). Reciprocal Ia inhibition between elbow flexors and extensors in the human. *Journal of Physiology (London), 437,* 269–286. [11]

Kawashima, R., Roland, P. E., & O'Sullivan, B. T. (1994). Fields in human motor areas involved in preparation for reaching, actual reaching, and visuomotor learning: A positron emission tomography study. *Journal of Neuroscience, 14,* 3462–3474. [6]

Kawato, M. (1992). Optimization and learning in neural networks for formation and control of coordinated movement. In D. E. Meyer & S. Kornblum (Eds.), *Attention and performance XIV* (pp. 821–849). Cambridge, MA: MIT Press. [15]

Kawato, M., Furukawa, K., & Suzuki, R. (1987). A hierarchical neural-network model for control and learning of voluntary movement. *Biological Cybernetics, 59,* 161–177. [15]

Kawato, M., & Gomi, H. (1992). A computational model of four regions of the cerebellum based on feedback-error learning. *Biological Cybernetics, 68,* 95–103. [15]

Kazennikov, O., Wicki, U., Corboz, M., Babalian, A., Rouiller, E. M., and Wiesendanger, M. (1996). In preparation. [14]

Kazennikov, O., Wicki, U., Corboz, M., Hyland, B., Palmeri, A., Rouiller, E. M., & Wiesendanger, M. (1994). Temporal structure of a bimanual goal-directed movement sequence in monkeys. *European Journal of Neuroscience, 6*, 203–210. [14]

Kearney, R. E., & Hunter, I. W. (1990). System identification of human joint dynamics. *CRC Critical Reviews in Biomedical Engineering, 18*, 55–87. [11]

Keenan, M. E. (1987). The orthopaedic management of spasticity. *Journal of Head Trauma Rehabilitation, 12*, 62–71. [4]

Kelso, J. A. S., Holt, K. G., & Flatt, A. E. (1980). The role of proprioception in the perception and control of human movement: Toward a theoretical reassessment. *Perception & Psychophysics, 28*, 45–52. [17]

Kelso, J. A. S., Putnam, C. A., & Goodman, D. (1983). On the space-time structure of human interlimb co-ordination. *Quarterly Journal of Experimental Psychology, 35A*, 347–375. [14]

Kelso, J. A. S., Southard, D. L., & Goodman, D. (1979). On the nature of human interlimb coordination. *Science, 203*, 1029–1031. [9, 14]

Kelso, J. A. S., & Tuller, B. (1981). Toward a theory of apratic syndromes. *Brain and Language, 12*, 224–245. [14]

Keshner, E. A., Baker, J. F., Banovetz, J., & Peterson, B. W. (1992). Patterns of neck muscle activation in cats during reflex and voluntary head movements. *Experimental Brain Research, 88*, 361–374. [3]

Khater-Boidin, J., & Duron, B. (1991). Postnatal development of descending motor pathways studied in man by percutaneous stimulation of the motor cortex and the spinal cord. *International Journal of Developmental Neuroscience, 9*, 15–26. [7]

Kilbreath, S. L., & Gandevia, S. C. (1991). Independent digit control: Failure to partition perceived heaviness of weights lifted by digits of the human hand. *Journal of Physiology (London), 442*, 585–599. [20]

Kilbreath, S. L., & Gandevia, S. C. (1993). Neural and biomechanical specializations of human thumb muscles revealed by matching weights and grasping objects. *Journal of Physiology (London) 472*, 537–556. [3, 17]

Kimura, D., & Archibald, Y. (1974). Motor functions of the left hemisphere. *Brain, 97*, 337–350. [14]

Kinoshita, H., Ikuta, K., Kawai, S., & Udo, M. (1993). Effects of lifting speed and height on the regulation of forces during lifting tasks using a precision grip. *Journal of Human Movement Studies, 25*, 151–175. [15, 19]

Kinoshita, H., Kawai, S., & Ikuta, K. (1995). Contributions and co-ordination of individual fingers in multiple finger prehension. *Ergonomics, 38*, 1212–1230. [19]

Kinoshita, H., Kawai, S., Ikuta, K., & Teraoka, T. (in press). Individual finger forces acting on a grasped object during shaking actions. *Ergonomics.* [19]

Kirkwood, P. A., & Road, J. D. (1995). On the functional significance of long monosynaptic descending pathways to spinal motoneurones. In A. Taylor, M. H. Gladden, & R. Durbaba (Eds.), *Alpha and Gamma motor systems* (pp. 589–592). New York: Plenum. [3]

Kirkwood, P. A., & Sears, T. A. (1978). The synaptic connexions to intercostal motoneurones as revealed by the average common excitation potential. *Journal of Physiology (London), 275*, 103–134. [3]

Klatzky, R. L., & Lederman, S. J. (1992). Stages of manual exploration in haptic object identification. *Perception & Psychophysics, 52*, 661–670. [21]

Klatzky, R. L., & Lederman, S. J. (1993). Toward a computational model of constraint-driven exploration and haptic object identification. *Perception 22*, 597–621. [21]

Klatzky, R. L., Lederman, S. J., & Matula, D. E. (1993). Haptic exploration in the presence of vision. *Journal of Experimental Psychology: Human Perception and Performance, 19*, 726–743. [21]

Klatzky, R. L., Lederman, S. J., & Metzger, V. (1985). Identifying objects by touch: An "expert system." *Perception & Psychophysics, 37*, 299–302. [21]

Klatzky, R. L., Lederman, S. J., Pellegrino, J. W., Doherty, S., & McCloskey, B. P. (1990). Procedures for haptic object exploration vs. manipulation. In M. A. Goodale (Ed.), *Vision and action: The control of grasping* (pp. 110–127). Norwood: NJ: Ablex. [21]

Klatzky, R. L., Lederman, S. J., & Reed, C. (1987). There's more to touch than meets the eye: Relative salience of object dimensions for touch with and without vision. *Journal of Experimental Psychology: General*, 116, 356–369. [21]

Klatzky, R. L., Lederman, S. J., & Reed. C. L. (1989). Haptic integration of object properties: Texture, hardness, and planar contour. *Journal of Experimental Psychology: Human Perception of Performance*, 15, 45–47. [21]

Kling, A., & Brothers, P. C. (1992). The amygdala and social behavior. In J. Aggleton (Ed.), *The amygdala: Neurobiological aspects of emotion, memory, and mental dysfunction* (pp. 353–377). New York: Wiley-Liss. [2]

Klüver, H., & Bucy, P. C. (1939). Preliminary analysis of functions of the temporal lobes of monkeys. *Archives of Neurological Psychiatry, 42*, 979–1000. [2]

Knecht, S., Kunesch, E., Buchner, H., & Freund, H.-J. (1993). Facilitation of somatosensory evoked potentials by exploratory finger movements. *Experimental Brain Research*, 95, 330–338. [16]

Koenderink, J. J. (1986). Optic flow. *Vision Research*, 26, 161–180. [11]

Koh, T. H. H. G., & Eyre, J. A. (1988). Maturation of corticospinal tract from birth to adulthood measured by electromagnetic stimulation of the motor cortex. *Archives of Disease in Childhood*, 63, 1347–1352. [7]

Koshland, G. F., Gerilovsky, L., & Hasan, Z. (1991). Activity of wrist muscles elicited during imposed or voluntary movements about the elbow joint. *Journal of Motor Behavior, 23*, 91–100. [11]

Koshland, G. F., & Smith, J. L. (1989a) Mutable and immutable features of paw-shake responses after hindlimb deafferentation in the cat. *Journal of Neurophysiology*, 62, 162–173. [10]

Koshland, G. F., & Smith, J. L. (1989b). Paw-shake response with joint immobilization: EMG changes with atypical feedback. *Experimental Brain Research*, 77, 361–373. [10]

Kots, Y. M., & Syrovegnin, A. V. (1966). Fixed set of variants of interactions of the muscles of two joints in the execution of simple volutantry movements. *Biophysics*, 11, 1212–1219. [9]

Kristeva, R., Cheyne, D., & Deecke, L. (1991). Neuromagnetic fields accompanying unilateral and bilateral voluntary movements: Topography and analysis of cortical sources. *Electroencephalography and Clinical Neurophysiology*, 81, 284–298. [6]

Kudo, N., Furukawa, F., Okado, N. (1993). Development of descending fibers to the rat embryonic spinal cord. *Neuroscience Research*, 16, 131–141. [7]

Kugler, P. N., Kelso, S., & Turvey, M. T. (1980). On the concept of coordinative structures as dissipative structures: I. Theoretical lines of convergence. In G. E. Stelmach & J. Requin (Eds.), *Tutorials in motor behavior* (pp. 3–47). Amsterdam: North-Holland. [9, 14]

Künzle, H. (1978). An autoradiographic analysis of the efferent connections from premotor and adjacent prefrontal regions (areas 6 and 9) in *Macaca fascicularis*. *Brain, Behavior and Evolution*, 15, 185–234. [6]

Kurata, K. (1989). Distribution of neurons with set- and movement-related activity before hand and foot movements in the premotor cortex of rhesus monkeys. *Experimental Brain Research*, 77, 245–256. [6]

Kurata, K. (1991). Corticocortical inputs to the dorsal and ventral aspects of the premotor cortex of macaque monkeys. *Neuroscience Research*, 12, 263–280. [6]

Kurata, K. (1992). Somatotopy in the human supplementary motor area. *Trends in Neurosciences*, 15, 159–160. [6]

Kurata, K. (1994). Information processing for motor control in primate premotor cortex. *Behavioural Brain Research*, 61, 135–142. [6]

Kurata, K., & Hoffman, D. S. (1994). Differential effects of muscimol microinjection into dorsal and ventral aspects of the premotor cortex of monkeys. *Journal of Neurophysiology, 71*, 1151–1164. [6]

Kurata, K., & Tanji, J. (1986). Premotor cortex neurons in macaques: Activity before distal and proximal forelimb movements. *Journal of Neuroscience, 6*, 403–411. [6]

Kuypers, H. G. J. M. (1958). Cortico-bulbar connexions to the pons and lower brain stem in man. *Brain, 81*, 364–388. [7]

Kuypers, H. G. J. M. (1962). Corticospinal connections: Postnatal development in the rhesus monkey. *Science, 138*, 678–680. [7]

Kuypers, H. G. J. M. (1981). Anatomy of descending pathways. In V. B. Brooks (Ed.), *Handbook of physiology: Sect. I: The nervous system* (Vol. 2, Part 1, pp. 597–666). Bethesda, MD: American Physiological Society. [6, 7, 14, 19]

Kwan, H. C., MacKay, W. A., Murphy, J. T., & Wong, Y. C. (1978). Spatial organization of precentral cortex in awake primates. II. Motor outputs. *Journal of Neurophysiology, 41*, 1120–1131. [5]

Kwan, H. C., Murphy, J. T., & Wong, Y. C. (1987). Interactions between neurons in precentral cortical zones controlling different joints. *Brain Research, 400*, 259–269. [19]

Laabs, G. J. (1973). Retention characteristics of different reproduction cues in motor short-term memory. *Journal of Experimental Psychology 100*, 168–177. [9]

Lackner, J. R. (1990). Sensory-motor adaptation to high force levels in parabolic flight maneuvers. In M. Jeannerod (Ed.), *Attention and performance XIII* (pp. 527–548). Hillsdale, NJ: Erlbaum. [15]

Lackner, J. R., & Graybiel, A. (1981). Illusions of postural, visual and aircraft motion elicited by deep kneebends in the increased gravitoinertial force phase of parabolic flight. *Experimental Brain Research, 44*, 312–316. [8]

Lackner, J. R., & Levine, M. S. (1978). Visual direction depends on the operation of spatial constancy mechanisms: The oculobrachial illusion. *Neuroscience Letters, 7*, 207–212. [17]

Lackner, J. R., & Taublieb, A. B. (1983). Reciprocal interactions between the position sense representations of the two forearms. *Journal of Neuroscience, 3*, 2280–2285. [17]

Lackner, J. R., & Taublieb, A. B. (1984). Influence of vision on vibration-induced illusions of limb movement. *Experimental Neurology, 85*, 97–106. [17]

Lacquaniti, F. (1992). Automatic control of limb movement and posture. *Current Opinion in Neurobiology, 2*, 807–814. [19]

Lacquaniti, F., Borghese, N. A., & Carrozzo, M. (1991). Transient reversal of the stretch reflex in human arm muscles. *Journal of Neurophysiology, 66*, 939–954. [11, 19]

Lacquaniti, F., Borghese, N. A., & Carrozzo, M. (1992). Internal models of limb geometry in the control of hand compliance. *Journal of Neuroscience, 12*, 1750–1762. [11, 19]

Lacquaniti, F., Carrozzo, M., & Borghese, N. A. (1993a). The role of vision in tuning anticipatory motor responses of the limbs. In A. Berthoz et al. (Eds.), *Multisensory control of movement* (pp. 379–393). Oxford: Oxford University Press. [11]

Lacquaniti, F., Carrozzo, M., & Borghese, N. A. (1993b). Time-varying mechanical behavior of multi-jointed arm in man. *Journal of Neurophysiology, 69*, 1443–1464. [11]

Lacquaniti, F., & Maioli, C. (1989a). The role of preparation in tuning anticipatory and reflex responses during catching. *Journal of Neuroscience, 9*, 134–148. [11]

Lacquaniti, F., & Maioli, C. (1989b). Adaptation to suppression of visual information during catching. *Journal of Neuroscience, 9*, 149–159. [11]

Lacquaniti, F., & Maioli, C. (1992). Distributed control of limb position and force. In G. E. Stelmach & J. Requin (Eds.), *Tutorials in motor behavior II* (pp. 31–54). Amsterdam: Elsevier. [11]

Lacquaniti, F., & Soechting, J. F. (1982). Coordination of arm and wrist motion during a reaching task. *Journal of Neuroscience*, 2, 399–408. [9]

Lacquaniti, F., & Soechting, J. F. (1986). Responses of mono- and bi-articular muscles to load perturbations of the human arm. *Experimental Brain Research*, 65, 135–144. [11]

Lacquaniti, F., Soechting, J. F., & Terzuolo, C. (1982). Some factors pertinent to the organization and control of arm movements. *Brain Research*, 252, 394–397. [11]

Lacquaniti, F., Terzuolo, C., & Viviani, P. (1983). The law relating the kinematic and figural aspects of drawing movements. *Acta Psychologica*, 54, 115–130. [10]

Lamotte, R. H., & Acuna, C. (1978). Defects in accuracy of reaching after removal of posterior parietal cortex in monkeys. *Brain Research*, 139, 309–326. [14]

Landsmeer, J. M. F. (1962). Power grip and precision handling. *Annuals of the Rheumatic Diseases*, 21, 164–169. [3]

Landsmeer, J. M. F., & Long, C. (1965). The mechanism of finger control, based on electromyograms and location analysis. *Acta Anatomica*, 60, 330–347. [5]

Lang, W., Cheyne, D., Kristeva, R., Beisteiner, R., Lindinger, G., & Deecke, L. (1991). Three-dimensional localization of SMA activity preceding voluntary movement. A study of electric and magnetic fields in a patient with infarction of the right supplementary motor area. *Experimental Brain Research*, 87, 688–695. [6]

Lang, W., Cheyne, D., Kristeva, R., Lindinger, G., & Deecke, L. (1991). Functional localisation of motor processes in the human cortex. *Event Related Brain Research*, 42, 97–115. [6]

Lang, W., Obrig, H., Lindinger, G., Cheyne, D., & Deecke, L. (1990). Supplementary motor area activation while tapping bimanually different rhythms in musicians. *Experimental Brain Research*, 79, 504–514. [6]

Langworthy, O. R. (1933). Development of behavior patterns and myelinization of the nervous system in the human fetus and infant. *Contributions to Embryology*, 24, 1–58. [7]

Lashley, K. S. (1930). Basic neural mechanisms in behavior. *Psychological Review*, 37, 1–24. [14]

Lawrence, D. G. (1994). Central neural mechanisms of prehension. *Canadian Journal of Physiology and Pharmacology*, 72, 580–582. [6]

Lawrence, D. G., & Hopkins, D. A. (1976). The development of motor control in the rhesus monkey: Evidence concerning the role of corticomotoneuronal connections. *Brain*, 99, 235–254. [7, 19]

Lawrence, D. G., & Kuypers, H. G. J. M. (1968). The functional organization of the motor system in the monkey: I. The effects of bilateral pyramidal lesions. *Brain*, 91, 1–14. [5, 19]

Lawrence, D. G., Porter, R., & Redman, S. J. (1985). Corticomotoneuronal synapses in the monkey:light microscopic localization upon motoneurons of intrinsic muscles of the hand. *Journal of Comparative Neurology*, 232, 499–510. [6]

Lederman, S. J. (1991). Skin and touch. In R. Delbucco (Ed.), *Encyclopedia of human biology* (pp. 51–63). San Diego, CA: Academic Press. [21]

Lederman, S. J., & Klatzky, R. L. (1987). Hand movements: A window into haptic object recognition. *Cognitive Psychology*, 19, 342–368. [20, 21]

Lederman, S. J., & Klatzky, R. L. (1990a). Flexible exploration by human and robotic haptic systems. *Proceedings of the 12th Annual International Conference of the IEEE/Engineering in Medicine and Biology Society*, 12, 1915–1916. [21]

Lederman, S. J., & Klatzky, R. L. (1990b). Haptic classification of common objects: Knowledge-driven exploration. *Cognitive Psychology*, 22, 421–459. [21]

Lederman, S. J., & Klatzky, R. L. (1994). The intelligent hand: An experimental approach to human object recognition and implications for robotics and AI. *AI Magazine*, 15, 26–38. [21]

Lederman, S. J., Klatzky, R. L., & Reed, C. (1993). Constraints on haptic integration of spatially shared object dimensions. *Perception*, 22, 723–743. [21]

Lederman, S. J., Summers, C., & Klatzky, R. (1996). Haptic object similarity with and without vision: Geometric versus material properties. Manuscript under revision. [21]

Lee, D. N. (1980). Visuo-motor coordination in space-time. In G. E. Stelmach & J. Requin (Eds.), *Tutorials in motor behavior* (pp. 281–295). Amsterdam: North-Holland. [11]

Lee, D. N., & Aronson, E. (1974). Visual proprioceptive control of standing in human infants. *Perception & Psychophysics, 15*, 529–532. [19]

Lee, D. N., Lishman, J. R., & Thomson, J. A. (1982). Regulation of gait in long jumping. *Journal of Experimental Psychology: Human Perception and Performance, 8*, 448–459. [11]

Lee, D. N., Young, D. S., Reddish, P. E., Lough, S., & Clayton, T. M. H. (1983). Visual timing in hitting an accelerating ball. *Quarterly Journal of Experimental Psychology, 35A*, 333–346. [11]

Lee, W. A. (1984). Neuromotor synergies as a basis for coordinated intentional action. *Journal of Motor Behavior, 16*, 135–170. [3, 20]

Leenen, L., Meek, J., & Nieuwenhuys, R. (1982). Unmyelinated fibers in the pyramidal tract of the rat: A new view. *Brain Research, 246*, 297–301. [7]

Leenen, L., Meek, J., Postjuyma, P. R., & Nieuwenhuys, R. (1985). A detailed morphometrical analysis of the pyramidal tract of the rat. *Brain Research, 359*, 65–80. [7]

Leichnetz, G. R. (1986). Afferent and efferent connections of the dorsolateral precentral gyrus (area 4, hand/arm region) in the macaque monkey, with comparison to area 8. *Journal of Comparative Neurology, 254*, 460–492. [6]

Leijnse, J. N. A. L., Bonte, J. E., Landsmeer, J. M. F., Kalker, J. J., Van Der Meulen, J. C., & Snijders, C. J. (1992). Biomechanics of the finger with anatomical restrictions-the significance for the exercising hand of the musician. *Journal of Biomechanics, 25*, 1253–1264. [5]

Lemon, R. N. (1981). Functional properties of monkey motor cortex neurones receiving afferent input from the hand and fingers. *Journal of Physiology (London), 311*, 497–519. [19]

Lemon, R. N. (1988). The output map of the primate motor cortex. *Trends in Neurosciences, 11*, 501–506. [6]

Lemon, R. N. (1993). Cortical control of the primate hand. The 1992 G. L. Brown Prize Lecture. *Experimental Physiology, 78*, 263–301. [3, 6, 7, 19]

Lemon, R. N., Johansson, R. S., & Westling. G. (1995). Corticospinal control during reach, grasp and precision lift in man. *Journal of Neuroscience, 15*, 6145–6156. [19]

Lemon, R. N., Mantel, G. W. H., & Muir, R. B. (1986). Corticospinal facilitation of hand muscles during voluntary movement in the conscious monkey. *Journal of Physiology (London), 381*, 497–527. [3, 5, 7]

Leong, S. K. (1983). Localizing the corticospinal neurons in neonatal, developing and mature albino rat. *Brain Research, 265*, 1–9 [7]

Leyton, A. S. F., & Sherrington, C. S. (1917). Observations on the excitable cortex of the chimpanzee orang-utan and gorilla. *Quarterly Journal of Experimental Physiology, 11*, 137–222. [5]

Liang, F., Moret, V., Wiesendanger, M., & Rouiller, E. M. (1991). Corticomotoneuronal connections in the rat: Evidence from double-labeling of motoneurons and corticospinal axon arborizations. *Journal of Comparative Neurology, 311*, 356–366. [6]

Liang, F., & Wan, X. S. T. (1989). Improvement of the tetramethyl benzidine reaction with ammonium molybdate as a stabilizer for light and electron microscopic ligand-HRP neurohistochemistry, immunocytochemistry and double-labeling. *Journal of Neuroscience Methods, 28*, 155–162. [6]

Lidsky, T. I., Manetto, C., & Schneider, J. S. (1985). A consideration of sensory factors involved in motor functions of the basa ganglia. *Brain Research Reviews, 9*, 133–146. [19]

Lieber, R. L., & Blevins, F. T. (1989). Skeletal muscle architecture of the rabbit hind limb: Functional implications of muscle design. *Journal of Morphology, 199*, 93–101. [4]

Lieber, R. L., & Boakes, J. L. (1988). Sarcomere length and joint kinematics during torque production in the frog hind limbs *American Journal of Physiology*, *254*, C759–C768. [4]

Lieber, R. L., & Brown, C. C. (1992). Quantitative method for comparison of skeletal muscle architectural properties. *Journal of Biomechanics*, *25*, 557–560. [4]

Lieber, R. L., Fazeli, B. M., & Botte, M. J. (1990). Architecture of selected wrist flexor and extensor muscles. *Journal of Hand Surgery*, *15*, 244–250. [4]

Lieber, R. L., Jacobson, M. D., Fazeli, B. S., Abrams, R. A., & Botte, M. J. (1992). Architecture of selected muscles of the arm and forearm: Anatomy and implications for tendon transfer. *Journal of Hand Surgery*, *17A*, 787–798. [4]

Lieber, R. L., Loren, G. J., & Fridén, J. (1994). In vivo-measurement of human wrist extensor muscle sarcomere length changes. *Journal of Neurophysiology*, *70*, 874–881. [4]

Liepmann, H. (1920). Apraxie. In T. Brugsch & A. Entenburg (Eds.), *Real-Enzyklopädie der gesamten Heilkunde. Ergebnisse der gesamten Medizin* (pp. 116–143). Berlin: Urban & Schwarzenberg. [14]

Lippold, O. C. J. (1970). Oscillation in the stretch reflex arc and the origin of the rhythmical, 8–12 c/s component of physiological tremor. *Journal of Physiology (London)*, *206*, 359–382. [18]

Lippold, O. C. J., Redfearn, J. W. T., & Vuco, J. (1957). The rhythmical activity of groups of motor units in the voluntary contraction of muscle. *Journal of Physiology (London)*, *137*, 473–487. [18]

Livingstone, M. S., & Hubel, D. H. (1988). Segregation of form, color, movement, and depth: Anatomy, physiology, and perception. *Science*, *240*, 740–749. [2]

Llinás, R. R. (1991). The noncontinuous nature of movement execution. In D. R. Humphrey & H.-J. Freund (Eds.), *Dahlem workshop on motor control: Concepts and Issues* (pp. 223–242). Chichester, UK: Wiley. [18]

Llinás, R. R., & Volkind, R. A. (1973). The olivo-cerebellar system: Functional properties as revealed by harmaline-induced tremor. *Experimental Brain Research*, *18*, 69–87. [18]

Loeb, G. E. (1989). The functional organization of muscles, motor units, and tasks. In M. D. Binder & L. M. Mendell, (Eds.), *The segmental motor system* (pp. 23–35). Oxford: Oxford University Press. [5]

Long, C. (1968). Intrinsic-extrinsic muscle control of the fingers. *Journal of Bone and Joint Surgery, American Volume*, *50-A*, 973–984. [4, 5]

Long, C., & Brown, M. E. (1964). Electromyographic kinesiology of the hand: Muscles moving the long finger. *Journal of Bone and Joint Surgery*, *46*, 1683–1706. [5]

Long, C., Conrad, P. W., Hall, E. A., & Furler, S. L. (1970). Intrinsic-extrinsic muscle control of the hand in power grip and precision handling. *Journal of Bone and Joint Surgery, American Volume*, *52-A*, 853–867. [3, 5]

Ludolph, A. C., Hugon, J., & Spencer, P. S. (1987). Non-invasive assessment of the pyramidal tract and motor pathway of primates. *Electroencephalography and Clinical Neurophysiology*, *67*, 63–67. [7]

Lundberg, A. (1979). Multisensory control of spinal reflex pathways. *Progress in Brain Research*, *50*, 11–28. [7]

Luppi, P. H., Sakai, K., Salvert, D., Fort, P., & Jouvet, M. (1987). Peptidergic hypothalamic afferents to the cat raphe pallidus as revealed by a double immunostaining technique using unconjugated cholera-toxin as retrograde tracer. *Brain Research*, *402*, 339–345. [6]

Luppino, G., Matelli, M., Camarda, R. M., Gallese, V., & Rizzolatti, G. (1991). Multiple representations of body movements in mesial area 6 and the adjacent cingulate cortex: An intracortical microstimulation study in the macaque monkey. *Journal of Comparative Neurology*, *311*, 463–482. [6]

Luppino, G., Matelli, M., Camarda, R., & Rizzolatti, G. (1993). Corticocortical connections of area F3 (SMA-proper) and area F6 (pre-SMA) in the macaque monkey. *Journal of Comparative Neurology, 338*, 114–140. [6]

Lynch, J. C., Graybiel, A. M., & Lobeck, L. J. (1985). The differential projection of two cytoarchitectural subregions of the inferior parietal lobule of macaque upon the deep layers of the superior colliculus. *Journal of Comparative Neurology, 235*, 241–245. [2]

Macefield, V. G., Gandevia, S. C., & Burke, D. (1990). Perceptual responses to microstimulation of single afferents innervating joints, muscles and skin of the human hand. *Journal of Physiology (London), 429*, 113–130. [17]

Macefield, V. G., Häger-Ross, C., & Johansson, R. S. (in press). Control of grip force during restraint of an object held between finger and thumb: Responses of cutaneous afferents from the digits. *Experimental Brain Research.* [19]

Macefield, V. G., & Johansson, R. S. (1994). Electrical signs of cortical involvement in the automatic-control of grip force *NeuroReport, 5*, 2229–2232. [19]

Macefield, V. G., & Johansson, R. S. (in press). Control of grip force during restraint of an object held between finger and thumb: Responses of muscle and joint afferents from the digits. *Experimental Brain Research.* [19]

MacKenzie, C. L., & Iberall, T. (1994). *The grasping hand.* Amsterdam: North-Holland. [3, 12, 19]

MacNeilage, P. F. (1990). *Grasping in modern primates: The evolutionary context.* Norwood, NJ: Ablex. [14]

Macpherson, J. M. (1988). Strategies that simplify the control of quadrupedal stance. II. Electromyographic activity. *Journal of Neurophysiology, 60*, 218–231 [3]

Macpherson, J. M. (1991). How flexible are muscle synergies? In D. R. Humphrey & H.-J. Freund (Eds.), *Dahlem workshop on motor control: Concepts and issues* (pp. 33–47). Chichester, UK: Wiley. [3]

Macpherson, J. M., Marangoz, C., Miles, T. S., & Wiesendanger, M. (1982). Microstimulation of the supplementary motor area (SMA) in the awake monkey. *Experimental Brain Research, 45*, 410–416. [6]

Macpherson, J. M., Wiesendanger, M., Marangoz, C., & Miles, T. S. (1982). Corticospinal neurones of the supplementary motor area of monkeys: A single unit study. *Experimental Brain Research, 48*, 81–88. [6]

Maier, M. A., Bennett, K. M. B., Hepp-Reymond, M.-C., & Lemon, R. N. (1993). Contribution of the monkey corticomotoneuronal system to the control of force in precision grip. *Journal of Neurophysiology, 69*, 772–785. [3, 6]

Maier, M. A., de Luca, F., Herrmann, P., & Hepp-Reymond, M.-C. (1992). Motor responses to microstimulation in the periarcuate region in the alert monkey. *Abstract of the 15th annual meeting of the European Neuroscientific Association,* p. 205. [6]

Maier, M. A., & Hepp-Reymond, M.-C. (1995a). EMG activation patterns during force production in precision grip. I. Contribution of 15 finger muscles to isometric force. *Experimental Brain Research, 103*, 108–122. [3, 19]

Maier, M. A., & Hepp-Reymond, M.-C. (1995b). EMG activation patterns during force production in precision grip. II. Muscular synergies in the spatial and temporal domain. *Experimental Brain Research, 103*, 123–136. [3, 19]

Mark, R. F., & Sperry, R. W. (1968). Bimanual coordination in monkeys. *Experimental Neurology, 21*, 92–104. [14]

Marr, D. (1982). *Vision.* San Francisco: Freeman. [2]

Marsden, C. D. (1984). Origins of normal and pathological tremor. In L. J. Findley & R. Capildeo (Eds.), *Movement disorders: Tremor* (pp. 37–84). London: Macmillan. [18]

Marsden, C. D., Merton, P. A., & Morton, H. B. (1977). The sensory mechanisms of servo action in human muscle. *Journal of Physiology (London)*, *265*, 521–535. [17]

Marsden, C. D., Merton, P. A., & Morton, H. B. (1981). Human postural responses. *Brain*, *104*, 513–534. [15]

Marsden, C. D., Merton, P. A., & Morton, H. B. (1985). New observations on the human stretch reflex. *Journal of Physiology (London)*, *360*, 51P. [19]

Marshall, J., & Walsh, E. G. (1956). Physiological tremor. *Journal of Neurology, Neurosurgery and Psychiatry*, *19*, 260–267. [18]

Marteniuk, R. G., Leavitt, J. L., MacKenzie, C. L., & Athenes, S. (1990). Functional relationships between grasp and transport components in a prehension task. *Human Movement Science*, *9*, 149–176. [13, 19]

Marteniuk, R. G., MacKenzie, C. L., & Baba, D. M. (1984). Bimanual movement control: Information processing and interaction effects. *Quarterly Journal of Experimental Psychology*, *36A*, 335–365. [14]

Marteniuk, R. G., MacKenzie, C. L., Jeannerod, M., Athenes, S., & Dugas, C. (1987). Constraints on human arm movement trajectories. *Canadian Journal of Psychology*, *41*, 365–378. [13]

Martin, J. H., Cooper, S. E., & Ghez, C. (1995). Kinematic characteristics of prehension in the cat. *Experimental Brain Research*, *102*, 379–392. [10]

Martin, J. H., Cooper, S. E., Hacking, A., & Ghez, C. (1994). Spatial organization of kinematic and dynamic changes during prehension in the cat. *Society for Neuroscience Abstracts*, *20*, 1410. [10]

Martin, J. H., & Ghez, C. (1993). Differential impairments in reaching and grasping produced by local inactivation within the forelimb representation of the motor cortex in the cat. *Experimental Brain Research*, *94*, 429–443. [10]

Martino, A. M., & Strick, P. L. (1987). Corticospinal projections originate from the arcuate premotor area. *Brain Research*, *404*, 307–312. [6]

Massion, J. (1992). Movement, posture and equilibrium: Interaction and coordination. *Progress in Neurobiology*, *38*, 35–56. [15]

Massion, J. (1994). Postural control-system. *Current Opinion in Neurobiology*, *4*, 877–887. [19]

Matelli, M., Luppino, G., Fogassi, L., & Rizzolatti, G. (1989). Thalamic input to inferior area 6 and area 4 in the macaque monkey. *Journal of Comparative Neurology*, *280*, 468–488. [6]

Matelli, M., Luppino, G., & Rizzolatti, G. (1991). Architecture of superior and mesial area 6 and the adjacent cingulate cortex in the macaque monkey. *Journal of Comparative Neurology*, *311*, 445–462. [6]

Matelli, M., Rizzolatti, G., Bettinardi, V., Gilardi, M. C., Perani, D., Rizzo, G., & Fazio, F. (1993). Activation of precentral and mesial motor areas during the execution of elementary proximal and distal arm movements: A PET study. *NeuroReport*, *4*, 1295–1298. [6]

Matsuzaka, Y., Aizawa, H., & Tanji, J. (1992). A motor area rostral to the supplementary motor area (presupplementary motor area) in the monkey: Neuronal activity during a learned motor task. *Journal of Neurophysiology*, *68*, 653–662. [6]

Matthews, M. A., & Duncan, D. (1971). A quantitative study of morphological changes accompanying the initiation and progress of myelin production in the dorsal funiculus of the rat spinal cord. *Journal of Comparative Neurology*, *142*, 1–22. [7]

Matthews, P. B. C. (1963). The response of de-efferented muscle spindle receptors to stretching at different velocities. *Journal of Physiology (London)*, *68*, 660–678. [18]

Matthews, P. B. C. (1972). *Mammalian muscle receptors and their central actions*. London: Arnold. [18]

Matthews, P. B. C. (1984). The contrasting stretch reflex responses of the long and short flexor muscles in the human thumb. *Journal of Physiology (London)*, *348*, 545–558. [15]

Matthews, P. B. C. (1988). Proprioceptors and their contribution to somatosensory mapping: Complex massages require complex processing. *Canadian Journal of Physiology and Pharmacology, 66*, 430–438. [17]

Matthews, P. B. C. (1989). Long-latency stretch reflexes of two intrinsic muscles of the human hand analysed by cooling the arm. *Journal of Physiology, 419*, 519–538. [19]

Matthews, P. B. C. (1991). The human stretch reflex and the motor cortex. *Trends in Neurosciences, (London), 14*, 87–91. [11]

Matthews, P. B. C., Farmer, S. F., & Ingram, D. A. (1990). On the localization of the stretch reflex of intrinsic hand muscles in a patient with mirror movements. *Journal of Physiology (London), 428*, 561–577. [18]

Matthews, P. B. C., & Stein, R. B. (1969). The sensitivity of muscle spindle afferents to small sinusoidal changes of length. *Journal of Physiology (London), 200*, 723–743. [18]

McCloskey, D. I. (1978). Kinesthetic sensibility. *Physiological Review, 58*, 763–820. [8]

McCloskey, D. I. (1981). Corollary discharges: Motor commands and perception. In V. B. Brooks (Ed.), *Handbook of physiology: Sect. 1. The nervous system* (Vol. 2, pp. 1415–1447). Bethesda, MD: American Physiological Society. [17]

McCloskey, D. I., Gandevia, S., Potter, E. K., & Colebatch, J. G. (1983). Muscle sense and effort: Motor commands and judgments about muscular contractions. In J. E. Desmedt (Ed.), *Motor control mechanisms in health and disease* (pp. 151–167). New York: Raven Press. [19]

McDonald, P. V., van Emmerik, R. E., & Newell, K. M. (1989). The effects of practice on limb kinematics in a throwing task. *Journal of Motor Behavior, 21*, 245–264. [9]

McDonald, W. I., & Sears, T. A. (1970). The effects of experimental demyelination on conduction in the central nervous system. *Brain, 93*, 583–598. [7]

McGraw, M. B. (1943). *Neuro-muscular maturation of the infant.* New York: Columbia University Press. [9]

McGuire, P. K., Bates, J. F., & Goldman-Rakic, P. S. (1991). Interhemispheric integration: II. Symmetry and convergence of the corticostriatal projections of the left and the right pricipal sulcus (PS) and the left and the right supplementary motor area (SMA) of the rhesus monkey. *Cerebral Cortex, 1*, 408–417. [6]

McKinley, P. A., Smith, J. L., & Gregor, R. J. (1983). Responses of elbow extensors to landing forces during jump downs in cats. *Experimental Brain Research, 49*, 218–228. [11]

McMahon, T. A. (1984). *Muscles, reflexes, and locomotion.* Princeton, NJ: Princeton University Press. [9]

McNeill, D. (1985). So you think gestures are non-verbal? *Psychological Review, 92*, 350–371. [21]

Meissirel, C., Dehay, C., & Kennedy, H. (1993). Transient cortical pathways in the pyramidal tract of the neonatal ferret. *Journal of Comparative Neurology, 338*, 193–213. [7]

Melvill Jones, G., & Watt, D. G. D. (1971). Observations on the control of stepping and hopping movements in man. *Journal of Physiology (London), 219*, 709–727. [11]

Merfeld, D. M., Young, L. R., Oman, C. M., & Shelhamer, M. J. (1993). A Multidimensional model of the effect of gravity on the spatial orientation of the monkey. *Journal of Vestibular Research, 3*, 141–161. [19]

Meulenbroek, R. G. J., Rosenbaum, D. A., Thomassen, A. J. W. M., & Loukopoulos, L. (1994). A model of limb segment coordination in drawing behaviour. In C. Faure, P. Keuss, G. Lorette, & A. Vinter (Eds.), *Advances in handwriting and drawing: A multidisplinary approach* (pp. 349–362). Paris: Europia. [9]

Meulenbroek, R. G. J., Rosenbaum, D. A., Thomassen, A. J. W. M., Loukopoulos, L. D., & Vaughan, J. (in press). Adaptation of a reaching model to handwriting: How different effectors can produce the same written output, and other results. *Psychological Research.*

Meunier, S., & Pierrot-Deseilligny, E. (1989). Gating of afferent volley of the monosynaptic stretch reflex during movement in man. *Journal of Physiology (London)*, *419*, 753–763. [3]

Mewes, K., & Cheney, P. D. (1991). Facilitation and suppression of wrist and digit muscles from single rubromotoneuronal cells in the awake monkey, *Journal of Neurophysiology*, *66*, 1965–1977. [3, 19]

Miall, R. C., Weir, D. J., Wolpert, D. M., & Stein, J. F. (1993). Is the cerebellum a Smith predictor. *Journal of Motor Behavior*, *25*, 203–216. [15, 19]

Mihailoff, G. A., Adams, C. E., & Woodward, D. J. (1984). An autoradiographic study of the postnatal development of sensorimotor and visual components of the corticopontine system. *Journal of Comparative Neurology*, *222*, 116–127. [7]

Milner, A. D., & Goodale, M. A. (1993). Visual pathways to perception and action. *Progress in Brain Research*, *95*, 317–338. [2]

Milner, A. D., & Goodale, M. A. (1995). *The visual brain in action.* Oxford: Oxford University Press. [2]

Milner, A. D., Perrett, D. I., Johnston, R. S., Benson, P. J., Jordan, T. R., Heeley, D. W., Bettucci, D., Mortara, F., Mutani, R., Terazzi, E., & Davison, D. L. W. (1991). Perception and action in visual form agnosia. *Brain*, *114*, 405–428. [2]

Mitz, A. R., & Wise, S. P. (1987). The somatotopic organization of the supplementary motor area: Intracortical microstimulation mapping. *Journal of Neurophysiology*, *7*, 1010–1021. [6]

Moore, S. P., Rushmer, D. S., Windus, S. L., & Nashner, L. M. (1988). Human automatic postural responses: Responses to horizontal perturbations of stance in multiple directions. *Experimental Brain Research*, *73*, 648–658. [3]

Morasso, P. (1981). Spatial control of arm movements. *Experimental Brain Research*, *42*, 223–227. [9, 10, 13]

Morecraft, R. J., & Van Hoesen, G. W. (1992). Cingulate input to the primary and supplementary motor cortices in the rhesus monkey: Evidence for somatotopy in areas 24c and 23c. *Journal of Comparative Neurology*, *323*, 471–489. [6]

Mott, F. W., & Sherrington, C. S. (1895). Experiments upon the influence of sensory nerves upon movement and nutrition of the limbs. Preliminary communication. *Proceedings of the Royal Society of London, Series B 57*, 481–488. [19]

Mountcastle, V. B. (1957). Modality and topographic properties of single neurons of cat's somatic sensory cortex. *Journal of Neurophysiology*, *20*, 408–434. [16]

Mountcastle, V. B., Lynch, J. C., Georgopoulos, A., Sakata, H., & Acuña, C. (1975). Posterior parietal association cortex of the monkey: Command functions for operations within extrapersonal space. *Journal of Neurophysiology*, *38*, 871–908. [2]

Mountcastle, V. B., Motter, B. C., Steinmetz, M. A., & Duffy, C. J. (1984). Looking and seeing: The visual functions of the parietal lobe. In G. Edelman, W. E. Gall, & W. M. Cowan (Eds.), *Dynamic aspects of neocortical function* (pp. 159–193). New York: Wiley. [2]

Muakkassa, K. F., & Strick, P. L. (1979). Frontal lobe inputs to primate motor cortex: Evidence for four somatotopically organized "premotor" areas. *Brain Research*, *177*, 176–182. [6]

Müller, F., & Abbs, J. H. (1990). Precision grip in Parkinsonian patients. In M. B. Streifler, A. D. Korezyn, E. Melamed, & M. B. H. Youdim (Eds.), *Advances in neurology* (pp. 191–195). New York: Raven Press. [19]

Müller, F., & Dichgans, J. (1994). Dyscoordination of pinch and lift forces during grasp in patients with cerebellar lesions. *Experimental Brain Research*, *101*, 485–492. [15, 19]

Müller, K., Ebner, B., & Hömberg, V. (1994). Maturation of fastest afferent and efferent central and peripheral pathways: No evidence for a constancy of central conduction delays. *Neuroscience Letters*, *166*, 9–12. [7]

Müller, K., & Hömberg, V. (1992). Development of speed of repetitive movements in children is determined by structural changes in corticospinal efferents. *Neuroscience Letters, 144,* 57–60. [7]

Müller, K., Hömberg, V., & Lenard, H. G. (1991). Magnetic stimulation of motor cortex and nerve roots in children. Maturation of corticomotoneuronal projections. *Electroencephalography and Clinical Neurophysiology, 81,* 63–70. [7]

Murphy, J. T., Kwan, H. C., & Wong, Y. C. (1985). Sequential activation of neurons in primate motor cortex during unrestrained forelimb movements. *Journal of Neurophysiology, 53,* 435–445. [19]

Mushiake, H., Inase, M., & Tanji, J. (1990). Selective coding of motor sequence in the supplementary motor area of the monkey cerebral cortex. *Experimental Brain Research, 82,* 208–210. [6]

Mushiake, H., Inase, M., & Tanji, J. (1991). Neuronal activity in the primate premotor, supplementary, and precentral motor cortex during visually guided and internally determined sequential movements. *Journal of Neurophysiology, 66,* 705–716. [6]

Mussa-Ivaldi, F. A., Hogan, N., & Bizzi, E. (1985). Neural, mechanical and geometric factors subserving arm posture in humans. *Journal of Neuroscience, 5,* 2732–2743. [8, 10, 11]

Nambu, A., Yoshida, S., Jinnai, K. (1988). Projection on the motor cortex of thalamic neurons with pallidal input in the monkey. *Experimental Brain Research, 71,* 658–662. [6]

Nambu, A., Yoshida, S., Jinnai, K. (1991). Movement-related activity of thalamic neurons with input from the globus pallidus and projection to the motor cortex in the monkey. *Experimental Brain Research, 84,* 279–284. [6]

Napier, J. R. (1955). Form and function of the carpo-metacarpal joint of the thumb. *Journal of Anatomy, 89,* 362–369. [13]

Napier, J. R. (1956). The prehensile movements of the human hand. *Journal of Bone and Joint Surgery, British Volume, 38B,* 902–913. [3, 12, 13]

Napier, J. R. (1960). Studies of the hands of living primates. *Proceedings of the Zoological Society of London, 134,* 647–657. [3]

Nashner, L. M. (1981). Analysis of stance posture in humans. In A. Towe & E. S. Luschei (Eds.), *Handbook of behavioral neurobiology* (Vol. 5, pp. 527–565). [3]

Navas, F., & Stark, L. (1968). Sampling and intermittency in hand control system dynamics. *Biophysical Journal, 8,* 253–302. [18]

Nelson, R. J. (1988). Set related and premovement related activity of primate primary somatosensory cortical neurons depends upon stimulus modality and subsequent movement. *Brain Research Bulletin, 21,* 411–424. [16]

Nelson, W. L. (1983). Physical principles for economies of skilled movements. *Biological Cybernetics, 46,* 135–147. [9]

Newell, K. M., Scully, D. M., Tenebaum, F., & Hardinman, S. (1989). Body scale and the development of prehension. *Developmental Psychobiology, 22,*(1), 1–13. [12]

Newsome, W. T., Wurtz, R. H., & Komatsu, H. (1988). Relation of cortical areas MT and MST to pursuit eye movements. II. Differentiation of retinal from extraretinal inputs. *Journal of Neurophysiology, 60,* 604–620. [2]

Nielsen, J., & Kagamihara, Y. (1992). The regulation of disynaptic reciprocal Ia inhibition during co-contraction of antagonistic muscles in man. *Journal of Physiology (London), 456,* 373–691. [3]

Nishijo, H., Ono, T., Tamura, R., & Nakamura, K. (1993). Amygdalar and hippocampal neuron response related to recognition and memory in monkey. *Progress in Brain Research, 95,* 339–358. [2]

Nordstrom, M. A., Fuglevand, A. J., & Enoka, R. M. (1992). Estimating the strength of common input to human motoneurons from the cross-correlogram. *Journal of Physiology (London), 453,* 547–574. [3]

Nordstrom, M. A., Miles, T. S., & Türker, K. S. (1990). Synchronization of motor units in human masseter during a prolonged isometric contraction. *Journal of Physiology (London)*, *426*, 409–421. [3]

Nudo, R. J., Jenkins, W. M., Merzenich, M. M., Prejean, T., Grenda, R. (1992). Neurophysiological correlates of hand preference in primary motor cortex of adult Squirrel-Monkeys. *Journal of Neuroscience, 12*, 2918–2947. [19]

Nudo, R. J., & Masterton, R. B. (1988). Descending pathways to the spinal cord: A comparative study of 22 mammals. *Journal of Comparative Neurology, 277*, 53–79. [7]

Oka, H., Samejima, A., & Yamamoto, T. (1985). Post-natal development of pyramidal tract neurones in kittens. *Journal of Physiology (London), 363*, 481–499. [7]

Okano, K., & Tanji, J. (1987). Neuronal activities in the primate motor fields of the agranular frontal cortex preceding visually triggered and self-paced movement. *Experimental Brain Research, 66*, 155–166. [6]

Oldfield, R. C. (1971). The assessment and analysis of handedness. The Edinburgh inventory. *Neuropsychologia, 9*, 97–113. [14]

Olivier, E., Lemon, R., Edgley, S., & Armand, J. (1994). Development of the primate corticospinal tract:changes in the conduction velocity of corticospinal fibres in anaesthetized neonatal and infant macaque monkeys. *Journal of Physiology (London), 476*, 27P–28P. [7]

Paintal, A. S. (1978). Conduction properties of normal peripheral mammalian axons. In S. G. Waxman (Ed.), *Physiology and pathobiology of axons* (pp. 131–144). New York: Raven Press. [7]

Palmer, E., & Ashby, P. (1992a). Corticospinal projections to upper limb motoneurones in humans. *Journal of Physiology (London), 448*, 397–412. [7]

Palmer, E., & Ashby, P. (1992b). Evidence that a long latency stretch reflex in humans is transcortical. *Journal of Physiology (London), 449*, 429–440. [11, 18]

Palmer, S., Rosch, E., & Chase, P. (1981). Canonical perspective and the perception of objects. In J. Long & A. Baddeley (Eds.), *Attention and performance IX* (pp. 135–151). Hillsdale, NJ: Earlbaum. [2]

Pascual, R., Fernandez, V., Ruiz, S., & Kuljis, R. O. (1993). Environmental deprivation delays the maturation of motor pyramids during the early postnatal period. *Early Human Development, 33*, 145–155. [7]

Passingham, R. E. (1985). Rates of brain development in mammals including man. *Brain, Behavior and Evolution, 26*, 167–175. [7]

Paul, R. L., Merzenich, M. M., & Goodman, H. (1972). Representation of slowly and rapidly adapting cutaneous mechanoreceptors of the hand in Brodmann's areas 3 and 1 of *Macaca mulatta. Brain Research, 36*, 229–249. [16]

Paulignan, Y., Dufossé, M., Hugon, M., & Massion, J. (1989). Acquisition of coordination between posture and movement in a bimanual task. *Experimental Brain Research, 77*, 337–348. [14, 19]

Paulignan, Y., & Gentilucci, M. (1996). Manuscript in preparation.

Paulignan, Y., Jeannerod, M., MacKenzie, C. L., & Marteniuk, R. G. (1991). Selective perturbation of visual input during prehension movements. 2. The effects of changing object size. *Experimental Brain Research, 87*, 407–420. [13, 19]

Paulignan, Y., MacKenzie, C. L., Marteniuk, R. G., & Jeannerod, M. (1990). The coupling of arm and finger movements during prehension. *Experimental Brain Research, 79*, 431–435. [10, 13]

Paulignan, Y., MacKenzie, C. L., Marteniuk, R. G., & Jeannerod, M. (1991). Selective perturbation of visual input during prehension movements. 1. The effects of changing object position. *Experimental Brain Research, 83*, 502–512. [10, 13]

Paus, T., Petrides, M., Evans, A. C., & Meyer, E. (1993). Role of the human anterior cingulate cortex in the control of oculomotor, manual, and speech responses: A positron emission tomography study. *Journal of Neurophysiology, 70*, 453–469. [6]

Pause, M., Kunesch, E., Binkofski, F., & Freund, H. J. (1989). Sensorimotor disturbances in patients with lesions of the parietal cortex. *Brain, 112*, 1599–1625. [19]

Payne, M. C. (1958). Apparent weight as a function of colour. *American Journal of Psychology, 71*, 725–730. [20]

Penfield, W., & Boldrey, E. (1937). Somatic motor and sensory representation in the cerebral cortex of man as studied by electrical stimulation. *Brain, 37*, 389–443. [5]

Penfield, W., & Jasper, H. (1954). *Epilepsy and the functional anatomy of the human brain*. Boston: Little, Brown. [6]

Penfield, W., & Rasmussen, T. (1950). *The cerebral cortex of man*. New York: Macmillan. [5]

Perenin, M.-T., & Vighetto, A. (1988). Optic ataxia: A specific disruption in visuomotor mechanisms. I. Different aspects of the deficit in reaching for objects. *Brain, 111*, 643–674. [2]

Perrett, D. I., Oram, M. W., Harries, M. H., Bevan, R., Hietanen, J. K., Benson, P. J., & Thomas, S. (1991). Viewer-centred and object-centred coding of heads in the macaque temporal cortex. *Experimental Brain Research, 86*, 159–173. [2]

Perrig, et al. (1996). Manuscript in preparation.

Petrides, M., & Pandya, D. N. (1984). Projections to the frontal cortex from the posterior parietal region in the rhesus monkey. *Journal of Comparative Neurology, 228*, 105–116. [2]

Phillips, C. G. (1971). Evolution of the corticospinal tract in primates with special reference to the hand. *Proceedings of the 3rd International Congress of the Primatological Society*, Zurich, Vol. 2, pp. 2–23. [7]

Phillips, C. G., & Porter, R. (1977). *Corticospinal neurones: Their role in movement*. London & New York: Academic Press. [7]

Picard, N., & Smith, A. M. (1992a). Primary motor cortical activity related to the weight and texture of grasped objects in the monkey. *Journal of Neurophysiology, 68*, 1867–1881. [19]

Picard, N., & Smith, A. M. (1992b). Primary motor cortical responses to perturbations of prehension in the monkey. *Journal of Neurophysiology, 68*, 1882–1894. [19]

Plassman, B. L., & Gandevia, S. C. (1989). High voltage stimulation over the human spinal cord: Sources of error latency. *Journal of Neurology, Neurosurgery and Psychiatry, 52*, 213–217. [7]

Polit, A., & Bizzi, E. (1979). Characteristics of motor programs underlying arm movements in monkey. *Journal of Neurophysiology, 42*, 183–194. [10]

Pons, T. P., Garraghty, P. E., Cusick, C. G., & Kaas, J. H. (1985). The somatotopic organization of area 2 in macaque monkeys. *Journal of Comparative Neurology, 241*, 445–466. [16]

Pons, T. P., Wall, J. T., Garraghty, P. E., Cusick, C. G., & Kaas, J. H. (1987) Consistent features of the representation of the hand in area 3b of macaque monkeys. *Somatosensory Research, 4*, 309–331. [5]

Porter, R. (1990). The Kugelberg lecture. Brain mechanisms of voluntary motor commands—A review. *Electroencephalography and Clinical Neurophysiology, 76*, 282–293. [6]

Porter, R., & Lemon, R. (1993). *Corticospinal function and voluntary movement*. Oxford: Clarendon Press. [6, 7, 18, 19]

Poulton, E. C. (1981). Human manual control. In J. M. Brookhart & V. B. Mountcastle (Eds.), *Handbook of Physiology: Sect. 1. The nervous system* (Vol. 2, pp. 1337–1389). Bethesda, MD: American Physiological Society. [11]

Powell, P. L., Roy, R. R., Kanim, P., Bello, M., & Edgerton, V. R. (1984). Predictability of skeletal muscle tension from architectural determinations in guinea pig hind limbs. *Journal of Applied Physiology, 57*, 715–1721. [4]

Powell, T. P. S., & Mountcastle, V. B. (1959). Some aspects of the functional organization of the cortex of the postcentral gyrus of the monkey: A correlation of findings obtained in a single unit analysis with cytoarchitecture. *Bulletin of the Johns Hopkins Hospital, 105*, 108–131. [16]

Pozzo, T., Berthoz, A., & Lefort, L. (1990). Head stabilization during various locomotor tasks in humans. *Experimental Brain Research, 82,* 97–106. [8]

Preilowski, B. (1975). Bilateral motor interaction: Perceptual-motor performance of partial and complete "split-brain" patients. In K. S. Zülch, O. Creutzfeldt, & G. C. Galbraith (Eds.), *Cerebral localization* (pp. 115–132). Berlin: Springer-Verlag. [6]

Press, W. H., Flannery, B. P., Teukolsky, S. A., & Vetterling, W. T. (1988). *Numerical recipes in C.* Cambridge, UK: Cambridge University Press. [3]

Pribram, K. H. (1967). Memory and the organization of attention. *UCLA Forum in Medical Sciences, 6,* 79–122. [2]

Prochazka, A. (1989). Sensorimotor gain control: A basic strategy of motor systems? *Progress in Neurobiology, 33,* 281–307. [16]

Prochazka, A. (1993). Comparison of natural and artificial control of movement. *IEEE Transactions on Rehabilitation Engineering, 1,* 7–17. [19]

Prochazka, A., & Trend, P. S. J. (1988). Instability in human forearm movements studied with feed-back-controlled muscle vibration. *Journal of Physiology (London), 402,* 421–442. [18]

Proske, U., Schaible, H.-G., & Schmidt, R. F. (1988). Joint receptors and kinaesthesia. *Experimental Brain Research, 72,* 219–224. [17]

Prud'homme, M. J. L., & Kalaska, J. F. (1994). Proprioceptive activity in primary somatosensory cortex during active arm reaching movements. *Journal of Neurophysiology, 72,* 2280–2301. [16]

Pujol, J., Vendrell, P., Junque, C., Marti-Vilalta, J. L., & Capdevila, A. (1993). When does human brain development end? Evidence of corpus callosum growth up to adulthood. *Annals of Neurology, 34,* 71–75. [7]

Rack, P. M. H. (1981). Limitations of somatosensory feedback in control of posture and movement. In J. M. Brookhart & V. B. Mountcastle (Eds.), *Handbook of physiology: Sect. 1. The nervous system* (pp. 229–256). Bethesda, MD: American Physiological Society. [19]

Ralston, D. D., Milroy, A. M., & Ralston, H. J. (1987). Non-myelinated axons are rare in the medullary pyramids of the macaque monkey. *Neuroscience Letters, 73,* 215–219. [7]

Ralston, D. D., & Ralston, J. H. (1985). The terminations of corticospinal tract axons in the macaque monkey. *Journal of Comparative Neurology, 242,* 325–337. [7]

Ranney, D., & Wells, R. (1988). Lumbrical muscle function as revealed by a new and physiological approach. *Anatomical Record, 222,* 110–114. [3]

Ratcliff, G., & Davies-Jones, G. A. B. (1972). Defective visual localization in focal brain wounds. *Brain, 95,* 49–60. [2]

Reed, C. L., Lederman, S. J., & Klatzky, R. L. (1990). Haptic integration of planar size with hardness, texture and plan contour. *Canadian Journal of Psychology, 44,* 522–545. [21]

Reh, T., & Kalil, K. (1981). Development of the pyramidal tract in the hamster. I. A light microscopic study. *Journal of Comparative Neurology, 200,* 55–67. [7]

Reh, T., & Kalil, K. (1982). Development of the pyramidal tract in the hamster. II. An electron microscopic study. *Journal of Comparative Neurology, 205,* 77–88. [7]

Relova, J. L., & Padel, Y. (1991). Conduction velocities of pyramidal tract and corticospinal neurons in the primary motor cortex of the cat. *European Journal of Neuroscience, Supplement, 4,* 312. [7]

Remy, P., Zilbovicius, M., Leroy-Willig, A., Syrota, A., & Samson, Y. (1994). Movement-and task-related activations of motor cortical areas: A positron emission tomographic study. *Annals of Neurology, 36,* 19–26. [5]

Richmond, B. J., & Sato, T. (1987). Enhancement of inferior temporal neurons during visual discrimination. *Journal of Neurophysiology, 58,* 1292–1306. [2]

Riddoch, G. (1935). Visual disorientation in homonymous half-fields. *Brain, 58,* 376–382. [2]

Rispalpadel, L. (1993). Contribution of cerebellar efferents to the organization of motor synergies. *Revue Neurologique, 149,* 716–727. [19]

Rizzolatti, G. (1987). Functional organization of inferior area 6. *Ciba Foundation Symposium, 132,* 171–186. [12]

Rizzolatti, G., Camarda, R., Fogassi, L., Gentilucci, M., Luppino. G., & Matelli, M. (1988). Functional organization of inferior area 6 in the macaque monkey: II. Area F5 and the control of distal movements. *Experimental Brain Research, 71,* 491–507. [6, 12, 13, 19]

Rizzolatti, G., Gentilucci, M., Camarda, R. M., Gallese, V., Luppino, G., Matelli, M., & Fogassi, L. (1990). Neurons related to reaching-grasping arm movements in the rostral part of area 6 (area 6a beta). *Experimental Brain Research, 82,* X337–X350. [19]

Rizzolatti, G., Gentilucci, M., Fogassi, L., Luppino, G., Matelli, M., & Ponzoni-Maggi, S. (1987). Neurons related to goal-directed motor acts in inferior area 6 of the macaque monkey. *Experimental Brain Research, 67,* 220–224. [6]

Rizzolatti, G., Scandolara, C., Matelli, M., & Gentilucci, M. (1981a). Afferent properties of periarcuate neurons in macaque monkeys. I. Somatosensory responses. *Behavioural Brain Research, 2,* 125–146. [6]

Rizzolatti, G., Scandolara, C., Matelli, M., & Gentilucci, M. (1981b). Afferent properties of periarcuate neurons in macaque monkeys. II. Visual responses. *Behavioural Brain Research, 2,* 147–163. [6]

Robinson, D. A. (1981). The use of control systems analysis in the neurophysiology of eye movements. *Annual Review of Neuroscience, 4,* 463–503. [8]

Robinson, D. A. (1985). The coordinates of neurons in the vestibulo-ocular reflex. *Review of Oculomotor Research, 1,* 297–312. [8]

Roland, P. E., & Ladegaard-Pedersen, H. (1977). A quantitative analysis of sensations of tensions and of kinaesthesia in man. *Brain, 100,* 671–692. [17, 20]

Roland, P. E., Larsen, B., Lassen, N. A., & Skinhoj, E. (1980). Supplementary motor area and other cortical areas in organization of voluntary movements in man. *Journal of Neurophysiology, 43,* 118–136. [6]

Roland, P. E., Meyer, E., Shibasaki, T., Yamamoto, Y. L., & Thompson, C. J. (1982). Regional cerebral blood flow changes in cortex and basal ganglia during voluntary movements in normal human volunteers. *Journal of Neurophysiology, 48,* 467–480. [6]

Roll, J. P., & Vedel, J. P. (1982). Kinaesthetic role of muscle afferents in man, studied by tendon vibration and microneurography. *Experimental Brain Research, 47,* 177–190. [17]

Rosch, E. (1978). Principles of categorization. In E. Rosch & B. Lloyd (Eds.), *Cognition and categorization* (pp. 27–48). New York: Erlbaum. [21]

Rosenbaum, D. A. (1991). *Human motor control.* San Diego, CA: Academic Press. [9]

Rosenbaum, D. A., & Engelbrecht, S. E., Bushe, M. M., & Loukopoulos, L. D. (1993) Knowledge model for selecting and producing reaching movements. *Journal of Motor Behavior, 25,* 217–227. (Special issue edited by T. Flash & A. Wing: Modeling the control of upper limb movement). [9]

Rosenbaum, D. A., & Krist, H. (in press). Antecedents of action. In H. Heuer & S. W. Keele (Eds.), *Handbook of motor control.* London: Academic Press. [9]

Rosenbaum, D. A., Loukopoulos, L. D., Meulenbroek, R. G. M., Vaughan, J., & Engelbrecht, S. E. (1995). Planning reaches by evaluating stored postures. *Psychological Review 102,* 28–67. [9]

Rosenbaum, D. A., Marchak, F., Barnes, H. J., Vaughan, J., Slotta, J. D., & Jorgensen, M. J. (1990). Constraints for action selection: Overhand versus underhand grips. In M. Jeannerod (Ed.), *Attention and performance XIII* (pp. 321–342). Hillsdale, NJ: Erlbaum. [19]

Rosenbaum, D. A., Vaughan, J., Jorgensen, M. J., Barnes, H. J., & Stewart, E. (1993). Plans for object manipulation. In D. E. Meyer & S. Kornblum (Eds.), *Attention and performance XIV* (pp. 803–820). Cambridge, MA: MIT Press, Bradford Books. [9]

Ross, H. E. (1964). Constant errors in weight judgements as a function of the differential threshold. *British Journal of Psychology, 55*, 133–141. [20]

Ross, H. E. (1969). When is a weight not illusory? *Quarterly Journal of Experimental Psychology, 21*, 346–355. [20]

Ross, H. E., Brodie, E. E., & Benson, A. J. (1986). Mass-discrimination in weightlessness and readaptation to earth's gravity. *Experimental Brain Research, 64*, 358–366. [11]

Rossignol, S., Lund, J. P., & Drew, T. (1988). The role of sensory inputs in regulating patterns of rhythmical movements in higher vertebrates. In A. H. Cohen, S. Rossignol, & S. Grillner, (Eds.), *Neural control of rhythmic movements* (pp. 201–283). New York: Wiley. [19]

Rothwell, J., Burke, D., Hicks, R., Stephen, J., Woodforth, I., & Crawford, M. (1994). Transcranial electrical stimulation of the motor cortex in man: Further evidence for the site of activation. *Journal of Physiology (London), 481*, 243–250. [7]

Rothwell, J. C., Thompson, P. D., Day, B. L., Boyd, S., & Marsden, C. D. (1991). Stimulation of the human motor cortex through the scalp. *Experimental Physiology, 76*, 159–200. [7]

Rothwell, J. C., Traub, M. M., Day, B. L., Obeso, J. A., Thomas, P. K., & Marsden, C. D. (1982). Manual motor performance in a deafferented man. *Brain, 105*, 515–542. [17]

Rouiller, E. M., Babalian, A., Kazennikov, O., Moret, V., Yu, X. H., & Wiesendanger, M. (1994). Transcallosal connections of the distal forelimb representations of the primary and supplementary motor cortical areas in macaque monkeys. *Experimental Brain Research, 102*, 227–243. [6]

Rouiller, E. M., Liang, F., Babalian, A., Moret, V., & Wiesendanger, M. (1994). Cerebellothalamocortical and pallidothalamocortical projections to the primary and supplementary motor cortical areas: A multiple tracing study in macaque monkeys. *Journal of Comparative Neurology, 345*, 185–213. [6]

Rouiller, E. M., Liang, F., Moret, V., & Wiesendanger, M. (1991). Trajectory of redirected corticospinal axons after unilateral lesion of the sensorimotor cortex in neonatal rat; A phaseolus vulgaris-leucoagglutinin (PHA-L) tracing study. *Experimental Neurology 114*, 53–65. [6]

Rouiller, E. M., Moret, V., & Liang, F. (1993). Comparison of the connectional properties of the two forelimb areas of the rat sensorimotor cortex: Support for the presence of a premotor or supplementary motor cortical area. *Somatosensory and Motor Research, 10*, 269–289. [6]

Roy, R. R., Bello, M. A., Powell, P. L., & Simpson, D. R. (1984). Architectural design and fibre type distribution of the major elbow flexors and extensors of the monkey (*Cynomolgus*). *Journal of Morphology, 171*, 285–293. [4]

Rufener, E. A., & Hepp-Reymond, M.-C. (1988). Muscle coactivation patterns in the precision grip. *Advances in the Biosciences, 70*, 169–172. [3]

Rumelhart, D. E., Hinton, G. E., & Williams, R. J. (1986). Learning internal representations by error propagation. In D. Rumelhart & J. McClelland (Eds.), *Parallel distributed processing: Explorations in the microstructure of cognition* (pp. 318–62). Cambridge, MA: Bradford Books/MIT Press. [12]

Sabatini, A. M., Bergamasco, M., & Dario, P. (1989). Force feedback-based telemanipulation for robot surgery on soft tissues. *Proceedings of the Annual International Conference of the IEEE Engineering in Medicine and Biology Society, 3*, 890–891. [17]

Sacks, R. D., & Roy, R. R. (1982). Architecture of hind limb muscles of cats: Functional significance. *Journal of Morphology, 173*, 185–195. [4]

Sainburg, R. L., & Ghez, C. (1994). Learning and generalization of limb dynamics. *Society for Neuroscience Abstracts, 20*. [10]

Sainburg, R. L., & Ghez, C. (in press). Limitations in the learning and generalization of multijoint dynamics. *Neuroscience Abstracts.* [10]

Sainburg, R. L., Ghilardi, M. F., Poizner, H., & Ghez, C. (1995). The control of limb dynamics in normal subjects and patients without proprioception. *Journal of Neurophysiology, 73,* 820–835. [10]

Sainburg, R. L., Poizner, H., & Ghez, C. (1993). Loss of proprioception produces deficits in interjoint coordination. *Journal of Neurophysiology, 70,* 2136–2147. [10, 15]

Saito, H., Yukie, M., Tanaka, K., Hikosaka, D., Fukada, Y., & Iwai, E. (1986). Integration of direction signals of image motion in the superior temporal sulcus of the macaque monkey. *Journal of Neuroscience, 6,* 145–157. [2]

Sakai, K., & Miyashita, Y. (1992). Neural organization for the long-term memory of paired associates. *Nature (London), 354,* 152–155. [2]

Sakamoto, T., Arissian, K., & Asanuma, H. (1989). Functional role of the sensory cortex in learning motor skills in cat. *Brain Research, 503,* 258–264. [19]

Sakata, H., & Taira, M. (1994). Parietal control of hand action. *Current Opinion in Neurobiology, 4,* 847–856. [19]

Sakata, H., Taira, M., Mine, S., & Murata, A. (1992). Hand-movement-related neurons of the posterior parietal cortex of the monkey: Their role in visual guidance of hand movements. In R. Caminiti, P. B. Johnson, & Y. Burnod (Eds.), *Control of arm movement in space: Neurophysiological and computational approaches* (pp. 185–198). Berlin: Springer-Verlag, [2]

Saltzman, C. D., & Newsome, W. T. (1994). Neural mechanisms for forming a perceptual decision. *Science, 264,* 231–237. [9]

Saltzman, E. (1979). Levels of sensorimotor representation. *Journal of Mathematical Psychology, 20,* 91–163. [9]

Sanes, J. N., Mauritz, K. H., Dalakas, M. C., & Evarts, E. V. (1985). Motor control in humans with large-fiber sensory neuropathy. *Human Neurobiology, 4,* 101–114. [17]

Sato, K. C., & Tanji, J. (1989). Digit-muscle responses evoked from multiple intracortical foci in monkey precentral motor cortex. *Journal of Neurophysiology, 62,* 959–970. [5, 6]

Savelsbergh, G. J. P., Whiting, H. T. A., & Bootsma, R. J. (1991). Grasping tau. *Journal of Experimental Psychology: Human Perception and Performance, 17,* 315–322. [11]

Savelsbergh, G. J. P., Whiting, H. T. A., Burden, A. M., & Bartlett, R. M. (1992). The role of predictive visual temporal information in the coordination of muscle activity in catching. *Experimental Brain Research, 89,* 223–228. [11]

Schell, G. R., & Strick, P. L. (1984). The origin of thalamic inputs to the arcuate premotor and supplementary motor areas. *Journal of Neuroscience, 4,* 539–560. [6]

Schieber, M. H. (1990). How might the motor cortex individuate movements? *Trends in Neurosciences, 13,* 440–445. [5]

Schieber, M. H. (1991). Individual finger movements of rhesus monkeys: A means of quantifying the independence of the digits. *Journal of Neurophysiology, 65,* 1381–1391. [5]

Schieber, M. H. (1993). Electromyographic evidence of two functional subdivisions in the rhesus monkey's flexor digitorum profundus. *Experimental Brain Research, 95,* 251–260. [3, 5]

Schieber, M. H. (1995). Muscular production of individuated finger movements: The roles of extrinsic finger muscles. *Journal of Neuroscience, 15,* 284–297. [5, 19]

Schieber, M. H., & Hibbard, L. S. (1993). How somatotopic is the motor cortex hand area? *Science, 261,* 489–492. [5]

Schlesinger, G. (1919) *Der mechanische Aufbau der künstlichen Glieder* [The Mechanical Structure of Artificial Limbs]. In G. Schlesinger (Ed.), *Ersatzglieder und Arbeitshilfen.* Berlin: Springer-Verlag. [3, 12]

Schmahmann, J. D., & Pandya, D. N. (1993). Prelunate, occipitotemporal, and parahippocampal projections to the basis pontis in rhesus monkey. *Journal of Comparative Neurology, 337*, 94–112. [2]

Schmidt, E. M., Porter, R., & McIntosh, J. S. (1992). The effects of cooling supplementary motor area and midline cerebral cortex on neuronal responses in area 4 of monkeys. *Electroencephalography and Clinical Neurophysiology: Electromyography and Motor Control, 85*, 71–71. [6]

Schmidt, R. A. (1988). *Motor control and learning*. Champaign, IL: Human Kinetics Publishers. [14]

Schmidt, R. A., Zelaznik, H. N., & Frank, J. S. (1979). Sources of inaccuracy in rapid movement. In G. E. Stelmach (Ed.), *Information processing in motor control and learning* (pp. 183–203). New York: Academic Press. [13]

Schmied, A., Ivarsson, C., & Fetz, E. E. (1993). Short-term synchronization of motor units in human extensor digitorum communis muscle: Relation to contractile properties and voluntary control. *Experimental Brain Research, 97*, 159–172. [3]

Schmied, A., Vedel, J.-P., & Pagni, S. (1994). Human spinal lateralization assessed from motorneurone synchronization: Dependence on handedness and motor unit type. *Journal of Physiology (London), 480*, 369–387. [3]

Schöner, G., & Kelso, J. A. S. (1988). Dynamic pattern generation in behavioral and neural systems. *Science, 239*, 1513–1520. [9]

Schreyer, D. J., & Jones, E. G. (1982). Growth and target finding by axons of the corticospinal tract in prenatal and postnatal rats. *Neuroscience, 7*, 1837–1853. [7]

Schreyer, D. J., & Jones, E. G. (1988a). Topographic sequence of outgrowth of corticospinal axons in the rat: A study using retrograde axonal labeling with fast blue. *Developmental Brain Research, 38*, 89–101. [7]

Schreyer, D. J., & Jones, E. G. (1988b). Axon elimination in the developing corticospinal tract of the rat. *Developmental Brain Research, 38*, 103–119. [7]

Schueneman, A., & Pickleman, J. (1993). Neuropsychological analyses of surgical skill. In J. L. Starkes & F. Allard (Eds.), *Cognitive issues in motor expertise* (pp. 189–199). New York: Elsevier. [17]

Schultz, A. H. (1968). Form und Funktion der Primatenhände. In B. Rensch (Ed.), *Handgebrauch bei Affen und Frühmenschen* (pp. 9–25). Berne: Huber. [3]

Schultz, M. (1989). Neurophysiology of basal ganglia. In D. B. Calne (Ed.), *Handbook of Experimental Pharmacology* (pp. 1–45). Berlin & Heidelberg: Springer-Verlag. [19]

Schwartz, A. B., Kettner, R. E., & Georgopoulos, A. P. (1988). Primate motor cortex and free arm mouvements to visual targets in three-dimensional space. I. Relations between single cell discharge and direction of movement. *Journal of Neuroscience, 8*, 2913–2927. [6]

Sears, T. A., & Stagg, D. (1976). Short-term synchronization of intercostal motoneurone activity. *Journal of Physiology (London), 263*, 357–381. [3]

Seitz, R. J., & Roland, P. E. (1992). Learning of sequential finger movements in man: A combined kinematic and positron emission tomography (PET) study. *European Journal of Neuroscience, 4* 154–165. [6, 19]

Semmes, J., & Mishkin, M. (1965). Somatosensory loss in monkeys after ipsilateral cortical ablation. *Journal of Neurophysiology, 28*, 473–486. [19]

Serlin, D. M., & Schieber, M. H. (1993). Morphologic regions of the multitendoned extrinsic finger muscles in the monkey forearm. *Acta Anatomica, 146*, 255–266. [5]

Servos, P., & Goodale, M. A. (1994). Binocular vision and the on-line control of human prehension. *Experimental Brain Research, 98*, 119–127. [13, 19]

Servos, P., Goodale, M. A., & Jakobson, L. S. (1992). The role of binocular vision in prehension: A kinematic analysis. *Vision Research, 32*(8), 1513–1521. [13]

Sessle, B. J., & Wiesendanger, M. (1982). Structural and functional definition of the motor cortex in the monkey (*Macaca fascicularis*). *Journal of Physiology (London)*, *323*, 245–265. [6]

Shadmehr, R. (1993). Control of equilibrium position and stiffness through postural modules. *Journal of Motor Behavior, 25*, 228–241. [9]

Shadmehr, R., & Mussa-Ivaldi, F. A. (1994). Adaptive representation of dynamics during learning of a motor task. *Journal of Neuroscience, 14*, 3208–3224. [10]

Sharp, R. H., & Whiting, H. T. A. (1974). Exposure and occluded duration effects in a ball catching skill. *Journal of Motor Behavior, 6*, 139–147. [11]

Sharp, R. H., & Whiting, H. T. A. (1975). Information-processing and eye movement behavior in a ball catching skill. *Journal of Human Movement Studies, 1*, 124–131. [11]

Shelton, B. R., Picardi, M. C., & Green, D. M. (1982). Comparison of three adaptive psychophysical procedures. *Journal of the Acoustical Society of America, 71*, 1527–1533. [17]

Sherrington, C. S. (1906). *The integrative action of the nervous system*. New Haven, CT: Yale University Press. [15]

Sherrington, C. S. (1947). *The integrative action of the nervous system.* (2nd ed.). New Haven, CT: Yale University Press. [3]

Shibasaki, H., Sadato, N., Lyshkow, H., Yonekura, Y., Honda, M., Nagamine, T., Suwazono, S., Magata, Y., Ikeda, A., Miyazaki, M., Fukuyama, H., Asato, R., & Konishi, J. (1993). Both primary motor cortex and supplementary motor area play an important role in complex finger movement. *Brain, 116*, 1387–1398. [6]

Shima, K., Aya, K., Mushiake, H., Inase, M., Aizawa, H., & Tanji, J. (1991). Two movement-related foci in the primate cingulate cortex observed in signal-triggered and self-paced forelimb movements. *Journal of Neurophysiology, 65*, 188–202. [6]

Shinoda, Y., Yokata, J., & Futami, T. (1981). Divergent projection of individual corticospinal axons to motoneurons of multiple muscles in the monkey. *Neuroscience Letters, 23*, 7–12. [3, 5]

Simpson, J. I., & Graf, W. (1985). The selection of reference frames by nature and its investigation. *Review of Oculomotor Research, 1*, 3–20. [8]

Sinclair, R. J., & Burton, H. (1991). Neuronal activity in the primary somatosensory cortex in monkeys (*Macaca mulatta*) during active touch of textured surface gratings: Responses to groove width, applied force and velocity of motion. *Journal of Neurophysiology, 66*, 153–169. [16]

Sinkjaer, T., Miller, L., Andersen, T. & Houk, J. C. (1995). Synaptic linkages between red nucleus cells and limb muscles during a multijoint motor task. *Experimental Brain Research, 102*, 546–550. [19]

Sirin, A. V., & Patla, A. E. (1987). Myoelectric changes in the triceps surae muscle under sustained contractions. *European Journal of Applied Physiology, 56*, 238–244. [3]

Skoglund, S. (1973). Joint receptors and kinaesthesis. In A. Iggo (Ed.), *Handbook of sensory physiology* (pp. 111–136). New York: Springer. [8]

Smeets, J. B. J., & Erkelens, C. J. (1991). Dependence of autogenic and heterogenic stretch reflexes on pre-load activity in the human arm. *Journal of Physiology (London), 440*, 455–465. [11]

Smith, A. M. (1981). The coactivation of antagonist muscles. *Canadian Journal of Physiology and Pharmacology, 59*, 733–747. [3, 11]

Smith, A. M., & Bourbonnais, D. (1981). Neuronal activity in cerebellar cortex related to control of prehensile force. *Journal of Neurophysiology, 45*, 286–303. [3]

Smith, A. M., Hepp-Reymond, M.-C., & Wyss, U. R. (1975). Relation of activity in precentral cortical neurons to force and rate of force change during isometric contractions of finger muscles. *Experimental Brain Research, 23*, 315–332. [3]

Smith, J. L., & Zernicke, R. F. (1987). Predictions for neural control based on limb dynamics. *Trends in Neurosciences, 10*, 123–128. [10]

494   References

Smyth, M. M. (1984). Memory for movements. In M. M. Smyth & A. M. Wing (Eds.), *The psychology of human movement* (pp. 83–117). London: Academic Press. [9]

Society of American Gastrointestinal Endoscopic Surgeons. (1991). Guidelines on privileging and credentialling: Standards of practice and continuing medical education of laparoscopic cholecystectomy. *American Journal of Surgery, 161*, 324–325. [17]

Soechting, J. F. (1982). Does position sense at the elbow reflect a sense of elbow joint angle or one of limb orientation? *Brain Research, 248*, 392–395. [8]

Soechting, J. F., & Flanders, M. (1989). Sensorimotor representations for pointing to targets in three-dimensional space. *Journal of Neurophysiology 62*, 582–594. [8]

Soechting, J. F., & Flanders, M. (1991). Deducing central algorithms of arm movement control from kinematics. In D. R. Humphrey & H.-J. Freund (Eds.), *Dahlem workshop on motor control: Concepts and issues* (pp. 293–306). Chichester, UK: Wiley. [8]

Soechting, J. F., & Flanders, M. (1992). Moving in three-dimensional space: Frames of reference, vectors, and coordinate systems. *Annual Review of Neuroscience, 15*, 167–191. [11]

Soechting, J. F., & Flanders, M. (1993). Parallel, interdependent channels for location and orientation in sensorimotor transformations for reaching and grasping. *Journal of Neurophysiology, 70*, 1137–1150. [8]

Soechting, J. F., & Lacquaniti, F. (1981). Invariant characteristics of a pointing movement in man. *Journal of Neuroscience, 1*, 710–720. [8, 9]

Soechting, J. F., & Lacquaniti, F. (1989). An assessment of the existence of muscle synergies during load perturbations and intentional movements of the human arm. *Experimental Brain Research, 74*, 535–548. [3]

Soechting, J. F., & Ross, B. (1984). Psychophysical determination of coordinate representation of human arm orientation. *Neuroscience, 13*, 595–604. [8]

Soechting, J. F., & Terzuolo, C. A. (1986). An algorithm for the generation of curvilinear wrist motion in an arbitrary plane in three-dimensional space. *Neuroscience, 19*, 1395–1405. [8]

Soso, M. J., & Fetz, E. E. (1980). Responses of identified cells in postcentral cortex of awake monkeys during comparable active and passive joint movements. *Journal of Neurophysiology, 43*, 1090–1110. [16]

Spoor, C. W. (1983). Balancing a force on the fingertip of a two-dimensional finger model without intrinsic muscles. *Journal of Biomechanics, 16*, 497–504. [5]

Sporns, O., & Edelman, G. M. (1993). Solving Bernstein's problem: A proposal for the development of coordinated movement by selection. *Child Development, 664*, 960–969. [19]

Stanfield, B. B., & Asanuma, C. (1993). The distribution of corticospinal axons within the spinal gray of infant rhesus monkeys. *Society for Neuroscience Abstracts, 19*, 281.6. [7]

Stanfield, B. B., & O'Leary, D. D. M. (1985). The transient corticospinal projection from the occipital cortex during the postnatal development of the rat. *Journal of Comparative Neurology, 238*, 236–248. [7]

Stanfield, B. B., O'Leary, D. D. I., & Fricks, C. (1982). Selective collateral elimination in early postnatal development restricts cortical distribution of rat pyramidal tract neurones. *Nature (London), 298*, 371–373. [7]

Stangel, J. J., & Lahr, D. Y. (1984). Microsurgery, microinstruments, and microsutures. In W. L. Olszewski (Ed.), *CRC Handbook of microsurgery* (pp. 5–12). Boca Raton, FL: CRC Press. [17]

Starkes, J. L., Payk, I., Jennen, P., & Leclair, D. (1993) A stitch in time: Cognitive issues in microsurgery. In J. L. Starkes & F. Allard (Eds.) *Cognitive issues in motor expertise* (pp. 225–240). New York: Elsevier. [17]

Stein, R. B., Oguztoreli, M. N., & Capaday, C. (1986). What is optimized in muscular movements? In N. L. Jones, N. McCartney, & A. J. McComas (Eds.), *Human muscle power* (pp. 131–150). Champaign, IL: Human Kinetics Publishers. [9]

Stelmach, G. E., Castiello, U., & Jeannerod, M. (1994). Orienting the finger opposition space during prehension movements. *Journal of Motor Behavior, 26,* 178–186. [19]

Stevens, S. S. (1975). *Psychophysics,* p. 329. New York: Wiley. [11]

Stiles, R. N. (1976). Frequency and displacement amplitude relation for normal hand tremor. *Journal of Applied Physiology, 40,* 44–54. [18]

Stiles, R. N., & Randall, J. E. (1967). Mechanical factors in human tremor frequency. *Journal of Applied Physiology, 23,* 324–330. [18]

Strick, P. L., & Preston, J. B. (1982). Two representations of the hand in Area 4 of a primate. II. Somatosensory input organization. *Journal of Neurophysiology, 48,*(1), 150–159. [12]

Sur, M., Wall, J. T., & Kaas, J. H. (1984). Modular distribution of neurons with slowly adapting and rapidly adapting responses in area 3b of somatosensory cortex in monkeys. *Journal of Neurophysiology, 51,* 724–744. [16]

Sutton, R. S. (1988). Learning to predict by the methods of temporal differences. *Machine Learning, 3,* 9–44. [12]

Suzuki, W., & Amaral, D. G. (1994). Perirhinal and parahippocampal cortices of the macaque monkey: Cortical afferents. *Journal of Comparative Neurology, 350,* 497–533. [2]

Taira, M., Mine, S., Georgopoulos, A. P., Murata, A., & Sakata, H. (1990). Parietal cortex neurons of the monkey related to the visual guidance of hand movement. *Experimental Brain Research, 83,* 29–36. [2, 12, 19]

Tanji, J. (1994). The supplementary motor area in the cerebral cortex. *Neuroscience Research, 19,* 251–268. [6]

Tanji, J., Okano, K., & Sato, K. C. (1988). Neuronal activity in cortical motor areas related to ipsilateral, contralateral, and bilateral digit movements of the monkey. *Journal of Neurophysiology, 60,* 325–343. [6]

Tanji, J., & Shima, K. (1994). Role for supplementary motor area cells in planning several movements ahead. *Nature (London), 371,* 413–416. [6]

Taylor, J. L., & McCloskey, D. I. (1990). Ability to detect angular displacements of the fingers made at an imperceptibly slow speed. *Brain, 113,* 157–166. [17]

Thaler, D. E., Rolls, E. T., & Passingham, R. E. (1988). Neuronal activity of the supplementary motor area (SMA) during internally and externally triggered wrist mouvements. *Neuroscience Letters, 93,* 264–269. [6]

Thelen, E., Kelso, J. A. S., & Fogel, A. (1987). Self-organizing systems and infant motor development. *Developmental Review, 7,* 39–65. [9]

Theriault, E., & Tatton, W. G. (1989). Postnatal redistribution of pericruciate motor cortical projections within the kitten spinal cord. *Developmental Brain Research, 45,* 219–237. [7]

Thilmann, A. F., Schwarz, M., Tipper, R., Fellows, S. J., & Noth, J. (1991). Different mechanisms underlie the long-latency stretch reflex response of active human muscle at different joints. *Journal of Physiology (London), 444,* 631–643. [11]

Thomas, A., Westrum, L. E., Devito, J. L., & Biedenbach, M. A. (1984). Unmyelinated axons in the pyramidal tract of the cat. *Brain Research, 301,* 162–165. [7]

Touwen, B. (1978). Variability and stereotypy in normal and deviant development. In B. Touwen (Ed.), *Neurological development in infancy* (pp. 99–110). London: SIMP & Heinemann Med Books. [19]

Traub, M. M., Rothwell, J. C., & Marsden, C. D. (1980). A grab reflex in the human hand. *Brain, 103,* 869–884. [15]

Travis, A. M. (1955a). Neurological deficiencies after ablation of the precentral motor area in *Macaca mulatta. Brain, 78,* 155–173. [5]

Travis, A. M. (1955b). Neurological deficiencies following supplementary motor area lesions in *Macaca mulatta. Brain, 78,* 174–198. [6]

Tsumoto, T., Nakamura, S., & Iwama, K. (1975). Pyramidal tract control over cutaneous and kinesthetic sensory transmission in the cat thalamus. *Experimental Brain Research, 22,* 281–294. [16]

Tubiana, R. (1981). Architecture and function of the hand. In R. Tubiana (Ed.), *The hand* (Vol. 1, pp. 19–93). Philadelphia: Saunders. [3]

Tuller, B., Turvey, M. T., & Fitch, H. L. (1982). The Bernstein perspective: II. The concept of muscle linkage or coordinative structure. In J. A. S. Kelso (Ed.), *Human motor behavior* (pp. 253–281). Hillsdale, NJ: Erlbaum. [9]

Turvey, M. T. (1977). Preliminaries to a theory to action with reference to vision. In R. A. Shaw & J. Bransford (Eds.), *Perceiving, acting, and knowing: Toward an ecological psychology* (pp. 211–265). Hillsdale, NJ: Erlbaum. [14]

Turvey, M. T. (1990). Coordination. *American Psychologist, 45,* 938–953. [9]

Turvey, M. T., Fitch, H. L., & Tuller, B. (1982). The Bernstein perspective: I. The problems of degrees of freedom and context-conditioned variability. In J. A. S. Kelso (Ed.), *Human motor behavior* (pp. 239–252). Hillsdale, NJ: Erlbaum. [9]

Turvey, M. T., Shaw, R. E., & Mace, W. (1978). Issues in the theory of action. Degrees of freedom, coordinative structures and coalitions. In J. Requin & N. J. Hillsdale (Eds.), *Attention and performance VII* (pp. 557–595). London: Erlbaum. [19]

Twitchell, T. E. (1951). The restoration of motor function following hemiplegia in man. *Brain, 74,* 443–480. [5]

Twitchell, T. E. (1954). Sensory factors in purposive movements. *Journal of Neurophysiology, 17,* 239–252. [19]

Tyszka, J. M., Grafton, S. T., Chew, W., Woods, R. P., & Coletti, P. M. (1994). Parceling of mesial frontal motor areas during ideation and movement using functional magnetic resonance imaging at 1.5 Tesla. *Annals of Neurology, 35,* 746–749. [6]

Uematsu, S., Lesser, R., Fisher, R. S., Gordon, B., Hara, K., Krauss, G. L., Vining, E. P., & Webber, R. W. (1992). Motor and sensory cortex in humans: Topography studied with chronic subdural stimulation. *Neurosurgery, 31,* 59–72. [5]

Ungerleider, L. G., & Mishkin, M. (1982). Two cortical visual systems. In D. J. Ingle, M. A. Goodale, & R. J. W. Mansfield (Eds.), *Analysis of visual behavior* (pp. 549–586). Cambridge, MA: MIT Press. [2]

Uno, Y., Fukumura, N., Suzuki, R., & Kawato, M. (1993). Integration of visual and somatosensory information for preshaping hand in grasping movements. *Advances in Neural Information Processing Systems, 5,* 311–318. [12]

Uno, Y., Kawato, M., & Suzuki. R. (1989). Formation and control of optimal trajectory in human multijoint arm movement: Minimum torque-change model. *Biological Cybernetics, 61,* 89–101. [9]

Vallbo, Å. B. (1981). A critique of the papers by Loeb and Hoffer, and Prochazka and Wand. Differences in muscle spindle discharge during natural movements in cat and man. In A. Taylor & A. Prochazka (Eds.), *Muscle receptors and movement* (pp. 249–255). London: Macmillan.

Vallbo, Å. B. (1985). Proprioceptive activity from human finger muscles. In W. J. P. Barnes & M. H. Gladden (Eds.), *Feedback and motor control in invertebrates and vertebrates* (pp. 411–430). London: Croom Helm. [19]

Vallbo, Å. B., Hagbarth, K. E., Torebjörk, H. E., & Wallin, B. G. (1979). Somatosensory, proprioceptive, and sympathetic activity in human peripheral nerves. *Physiological Reviews, 59,* 919–57. [18]

Vallbo, Å. B., & Johansson, R. S. (1984). Properties of cutaneous mechanoreceptors in the human hand related to touch sensation. *Human Neurobiology, 3,* 3–14. [19]

Vallbo, Å. B., & Wessberg, J. (1993). Organization of motor output in slow finger movements. *Journal of Physiology (London) 469,* 673–691. [18]

van Kan, P. L. E., Horn, K. M., & Gibson, A. R. (1994). The importance of hand use to discharge of interpositus neurons of the monkey. *Journal of Physiology (London), 480,* 171–190. [19]

Vaughan, J., Rosenbaum, D. A., Loukopoulos, L. D., & Engelbrecht, S. E. (1995). *Finding final postures.* Manuscript in preparation. [9]

Vaughan, J., Rosenbaum, D. A., Moore, C., & Diedrich, F. (1995). Cooperative selection of movements: The optimal selection model. *Psychological Research, 58,* 254–273.

Veenman, C. L., Reiner, A., & Honig, M. G. (1992). Biotinylated dextran amine as an anterograde tracer for single- and double-labeling studies. *J. Neuroscience Methods, 41,* 239–254. [6]

Verhaart, W. (1950). Hypertrophy of pes pedunculi and pyramid as result of degeneration of contralateral corticofugal fiber tracts. *Journal of Comparative Neurology, 92,* 1–15. [7]

Viallet, F., Massion, J., Massarino, R., & Khalil, R. (1992). Coordination between posture and movement in a bimanual load lifting task: Putative role of a medial frontal region including the supplementary motor area. *Experimental Brain Research, 88,* 674–684. [19]

Vicario, D. S., & Ghez, C. (1984). The control of rapid limb movement in the cat. IV. Updating of ongoing isometric responses. *Experimental Brain Research, 55,* 134–144. [10]

Viviani, P., & Cenzato, M. (1985). Segmentation and coupling in complex movements. *Journal of Experimental Psychology: Human Perception and Performance, 11,* 828–845. [10]

Viviani, P., & McCollum, G. (1983). The relation between linear extent and velocity in drawing movements. *Neuroscience, 10,* 211–218. [10]

Viviani, P., & Schneider, R. A. (1991). Developmental study of the relation between gerometry and kinematics in drawing movements. *Journal of Experimental Psychology: Human Perception and Performance, 17,* 198–218. [10]

von Hofsten, C., & Rönnqvist, L. (1988). Preparation for grasping an object: A developmental study. *Journal of Experimental Psychology: Human Perception and Performance, 14,* 610–621. [13]

von Holst, E. (1939). Die relative Koordiatnion als Phänomenon und als Methode zentralnervöse Funktionsanalyze. *Ergebnisse der Physiologie, Biologischen Chemie und Experimentellen Pharmakologie, 42,* 228–306. [English translation in von Holst, E. (1973). Relative coordination as a phenomenon and as a method of analysis of central nervous functions. In (R. Martin, Trans.), *The behavioural physiology of animal and man: The collected papers of Erich von Holst* (Vol. 1) London: Methuen. [9]

von Monakow, C. (1914). *Die Lokalisation im Grosshirn und der Abbau der Funktion durch kortikale Herde.* Wiesbaden: Bergmann. [14]

Walk, R. D., & Pick, H. L., Jr. (1981). *Intersensory perception and sensory integration.* New York: Plenum. [21]

Wall, P. D. (1970). The sensory and motor role of impulses travelling in the dorsal columns toward cerebral cortex. *Brain, 93,* 505–524. [19]

Wallace, A. (1964). *Culture and personality.* New York: Random House. [9]

Wallace, S. A., & Weeks, D. L. (1988). Temporal constraints in the control of prehensive movements. *Journal of Motor Behavior, 20,* 81–105. [13]

Wallace, S. A., Weeks, D. L., & Kelso, J. A. S. (1990). Temporal constraints in reaching and grasping behavior. *Human Movement Science, 9,* 69–93. [13]

Wannier, T. M. J., Maier, M. A., & Hepp-Reymond, M.-C. (1991). Contrasting properties of monkey somatosensory and motor cortex neurons activated during the control of force in precision grip. *Journal of Neurophysiology, 65,* 572–587. [3, 6, 16, 19]

Warren, S., Hamalainen, H. A., & Gardner, E. P. (1986). Objective classification of motion- and direction-sensitive neurons in primary somatosensory cortex of awake monkeys. *Journal of Neurophysiology, 56,* 598–622. [16]

Warren, W. H., Young, D. S., & Lee, D. N. (1986). Visual control of step length during running over irregular terrain. *Journal of Experimental Psychology: Human Perception and Performance, 12,* 259–266. [11]

Watts, C., Eyre, J. A., Kelly, S., & Ramesh, V. (1992). Development of the pincer grasp and its relationship to the development of adult corticospinal delays in man. *Journal of Physiology, (London), 452,* 273P. [7]

Waxman, S. G. (1978). Variations in axonal morphology and their functional significance. In S. G. Waxman (Ed.), *Physiology and pathobiology of axons* (pp. 169–190). New York: Raven Press. [7]

Weber, E. H. (1978). *The sense of touch* (H. E. Ross & D. J. Murray, Eds., and Trans.). London: Academic Press. (Original work published 1834) [20]

Weidenheim, K. M., Kress, Y., Isaak Epshteyn, M. S., Rashbaum, W. K., & Lyman, W. D. (1992). Early myelination in the human fetal lumbosacral spinal cord: characterization by light and electron microscopy. *Journal of Neuropathology and Experimental Neurology, 51,* 142–149. [7]

Weiss, P. A. (1969). The living system: Determinism stratified. In A. Koestler & J. R. Smythies (Eds.), *Beyond reductionism* (pp. 3–55). London: Hutchinson. [14]

Weitzenfeld, A. (1991). *NSL—Neural Simulation Language Version 2.1* (TR No. CNE-91-05). Los Angeles: University of Southern California, Center for Neural Engineering. [12]

Welford, A. T. (1968). *Fundamentals of skill.* London: Methuen. [14]

Westling, G., & Johansson, R. S. (1984). Factors influencing the force control during precision grip. *Experimental Brain Research, 53,* 277–284. [15, 19, 20]

Westling, G., & Johansson, R. S. (1987). Responses in glabrous skin mechanoreceptors during precision grip in humans. *Experimental Brain Research, 66,* 128–140. [19]

Whiting, H. T. A., & Sharp. R. H. (1974). Visual occlusion factors in a discrete ball-catching task. *Journal of Motor Behavior, 6,* 11–16. [11]

Whitsel, B. L., Roppolo, J. R., & Werner, G. (1972). Cortical information processing of stimulus motion on primate skin. *Journal of Neurophysiology, 35,* 691–717. [16]

Wickiewicz, T. L., Roy, R. R., Powell, P. J., & Edgerton, V. R. (1983). Muscle architecture of the human lower limb. *Clinical Orthopaedics and Related Research, 179,* 317–325. [4]

Wiesendanger, M. (1986). Recent developments in studies of the supplementary motor area of primates. *Review of Physiology, Biochemistry and Pharmacology, 103,* 1–59. [6]

Wiesendanger, M. (1990). The motor cortical areas and the problem of hierarchies. In M. Jeannerod (Ed.), *Attention and performance XIII* (pp. 59–75). Hillsdale, NJ: Erlbaum. [14]

Wiesendanger, M. (1993). The riddle of supplementary motor area function. In N. Mano, I. Hamada, & M. R. DeLong (Eds.), *Role of the cerebellum and basal ganglia in voluntary movement* (pp. 253–266). Amsterdam: Elsevier. [6]

Wiesendanger, M., Rouiller, E. M., Kazennikov, O., & Perrig, S. (in press). Is the supplementary motor area a bilaterally organized system? In Hans O. Lüders (Ed.), *The supplementary sensorimotor area.* Raven Press.

Wiesendanger, M., Wicki, U., & Rouiller, E. (1994). Are there unifying structures in the brain responsible for interlimb coordination? In S. P. Swinnen, H. Heuer, J. Massion, & P. Casaer (Eds.), *Interlimb coordination: Neural, dynamical and cognitive constraints* (pp. 179–207). San Diego, CA: Academic Press. [6, 14]

Wiesendanger, M., & Wise, S. P. (1992). Current issues concerning the functional organization of motor cortical areas in nonhuman primates. *Advances in Neurology, 57,* 117–134. [6, 14]

Wiesendanger, R., & Wiesendanger, M. (1985). Cerebello-cortical linkage in the monkey as revealed by transcellular labeling with the lectin wheat germ agglutinin conjugated to the marker horseradish peroxidase. *Experimental Brain Research, 59,* 105–117. [6]

Williams, P. E., & Goldspink, G. (1973). The effect of immobilization on the longitudinal growth of striated muscle fibres. *Journal of Anatomy, 116,* 45–55. [4]

Wing, A. M. (1988). A comparison of the rate of pinch grip force increases and decreases in parkinsonian bradykinesia. *Neuropsychologia, 26,* 479–482. [19]

Wing, A. M. (1992). The uncertain motor system: Perspectives on the variability of movement. In D. E. Meyer & S. Kornblum (Eds.), *Attention and performance XIV* (pp. 708–744). Cambridge, MA: MIT Press. [3, 15]

Wing, A. M., & Fraser, C. (1983). The contribution of the thumb to reaching movements. *Quarterly Journal of Experimental Psychology, 35A,* 297–309. [13]

Wing, A. M., Flanagan, J. R., & Richardson, J. (1996). *Anticpatory postural synergies in posture and grip.* Manuscript in preparation. [15]

Wing, A. M., Flanagan, J. R., & Tresilian, J. (1996). *Object dynamics and the anticpatory modulation of grip force.* Manuscript in preparation. [15]

Wing, A. M., Turton, A., & Fraser, C. (1986). Grasp size and accuracy of approach in reaching. *Journal of Motor Behavior, 18,* 245–260. [11, 13]

Wise, S. P. (1985). The primate premotor cortex: Past, present, and preparatory. *Annual Review of Neuroscience, 8,* 1–19. [6]

Wise, S. P., di Pellegrino, G., & Boussaoud, D. (1992). Primate premotor cortex: Dissociation of visuomotor from sensory signals. *Journal of Neurophysiology, 68,* 969–972. [6]

Withworth, R. H., LeDoux, M. S., & Gould H. J. (1991). Topographic distribution of connections from the primary motor cortex to the corpus striatum in *Aotus trivirgatus. Journal of Comparative Neurology, 307,* 177–188. [6]

Wolpert, D. M., Ghahramani, Z., & Jordan, M. I. (1994). Perceptual distortion contribute to the curvature of human reaching movements. *Experimental Brain Research, 98,* 153–156. [9]

Woolsey, C. N., Erickson, T. C., & Gilson, W. E. (1979). Localization in somatic sensory and motor areas of human cerebral cortex as determined by direct recording of evoked potentials and electrical stimulation. *Journal of Neurosurgery, 51,* 476–506. [5]

Woolsey, C. N., Settlage, P. H., Meyer, D. R., Sencer, W., Hamuy, T. P., & Travis, A. M. (1951). Patterns of localization in precentral and "supplementary" motor areas and their relation to the concept of a premotor area. *Research Publications of the Association for Research in Nervous and Mental Disorders, 30,* 238–264. [5]

Worringham, C. J., Stelmach, G. E., & Martin, Z. E. (1987). Limb segment inclination sense in proprioception. *Experimental Brain Research, 66,* 653–658. [8, 17]

Yakolev, P. I., & Lecours, A. R. (1967). The myelogenetic cycles of regional maturation of the brain. In A. Minkowski (Ed.), *Regional development of the brain in early life* (pp. 3–70). Oxford: Blackwell. [7, 19]

Young, R. R., & Hagbarth, K.-E. (1980). Physiological tremor enhanced by maneuvers affecting the segmental stretch reflex. *Journal of Neurology, Neurosurgery and Psychiatry, 43,* 248–256. [18]

Zaal, F. T., & Bootsma, R. J. (1993). Accuracy demands in natural prehension. *Human Movement Science, 12,* 339–345. [13]

Zarzecki, P., & Wiggin, D. M. (1982). Convergence of sensory inputs upon projection neurons of somatosensory cortex. *Experimental Brain Research, 48,* 28–42. [16]

Zecevic, N., Bourgeois, J.-P., & Rakic, P. (1989). Changes in synaptic density in motor cortex of rhesus monkey during fetal and postnatal life. *Developmental Brain Research, 50,* 11–32. [7]

Zeki, S. (1993). *A vision of the brain.* Oxford: Blackwell. [2]

Glossary

The following selective glossary is intended to explain terms that are widely used in research on hand function, appear in a number of the chapters in this volume, but which may not be familiar to all readers. (*Compiled by the editors.*)

Active touch   Sensory information based on cutaneous, muscle, and joint receptors obtained when the hand manipulates or moves over an object. (cf. Passive touch)

Adaptive control   A method of control that monitors the behavior of the controlled system and adjusts the control strategy to achieve better performance.

Afferent   Carrying neural information (usually sensory) toward a given structure. (cf. Efferent)

Affordance   The set of possible actions allowed by the form of an object and given a set of effector capabilities.

Agonist   Muscle acting in the direction of motion. (cf. Antagonist)

Antagonist   Muscle tending to produce movement contrary to the desired direction of motion. (cf. Agonist)

Anterograde   Following a neural pathway in the direction normally taken by nervous impulses. (cf. Retrograde)

Antidromic   Electrical stimulation of a neuron in the direction normally taken by nervous impulses. (cf. Orthodromic)

Coactivation   Simultaneous activation of opposing (agonist and antagonist) muscles acting around the same joint. (cf. Reciprocal inhibition)

Compliance   The change in an object's extent when it is subjected to external force. In general terms, the softness of an object. (The inverse of Impedance)

Coordinative structure   A set of joints that the motor system groups together in a single functional element as a control strategy for reducing the degrees of freedom. (See also Muscle synergy)

Cortico-motoneuronal tract   Cortical neurons whose axons synapse directly onto motoneurons in the spinal cord.

Corollary discharge   A copy of the neural commands that the brain issues to the muscles (also referred to as efference copy).

Degree of freedom   A muscle or joint whose activity the motor system must control when carrying out an action.

Dexterity   The ability to make fine, coordinated movements of the hand.

Distal   Far from the body. (cf. Proximal)

Dorsal stream   The set of visual pathways projecting from primary visual cortex to other visual areas, especially those in the parietal lobe, concerned with the motion of objects and with object-oriented actions.

Double-labeling   Anatomical method for identifying a set of neurons using injections of both retrograde tracers in areas to which the neurons project, and also anterograde tracers in areas from which the neurons receive projections.

Dynamics   The study of motions and the forces that bring about motion (includes Kinematics and Kinetics).

Efferent   Carrying neural information (usually motor) away from a given structure. (cf. Afferent)

Electromyography (EMG)   Recording of the electrical activity of muscles made with surface electrodes (which yield a complex interference trace reflecting the activity of many units) or needle electrodes (which can be more selective and may yield information on the activity of single motor units).

Equilibrium point hypothesis   Theory of aimed movement that takes the balance of agonist and antagonist activity around a joint as the basic representation used in the motor control system.

Extrinsic attributes   Features of an object that are determined in relation to other objects, for example, location. (cf. Intrinsic attributes)

Extrinsic hand muscles   Those muscles that move the digits and that are situated in the forearm. (cf. Intrinsic hand muscles)

Feedback   Sensory information about the progress of an action; usually used in control to modify subsequent action.

Forward kinematics   Calculation of the position in space of the hand from the joint angles of the segments of the arm.

Frame of reference   The coordinate system used to specify the location of an object.

Friction   Resistance to motion (tangential to the surfaces in contact) that depends on normal force (at right angles to the contact surfaces); if the resistance is proportional to the normal force and does not depend on contact area it is termed Coulomb friction.

Gating   Process whereby a brain structure can control the extent to which it does or does not receive afferent input.

Goal invariance   Attaining a goal by a variety of different movement patterns (also termed motor equivalence).

Grip force   The force generated between the contact points of the hand and a grasped object that acts to keep the object in the hand. (cf. Load force)

Haptic perception   Appreciation of object-related attributes based on active touch.

Impedance   The force that must be applied to an object to produce a given change in its length or extent; stiffness. (The inverse of Compliance)

Inertia   Resistance to motion dependent on acceleration.

Intracortical microstimulation (ICMS)   Use of a small electrode to induce activity of a single neuron in the cortex.

Intrinsic attributes   Those features of an object that depend on the basic qualities of an object in isolation, for example, diameter. (cf. Extrinsic attributes)

Intrinsic hand muscles   Muscles that move the digits and that are situated in the hand. (cf. Extrinsic hand muscles)

Kinematics The geometry of motion of parts of the body, specifically their positions and derivatives with respect to time (first, velocity; second, acceleration; third, jerk, etc.).

Kinesthesis The sense of movement of a part of the body.

Kinetics The forces and torques underlying kinematics.

Load force The resultant or net force acting on an object; usually excludes grip force.

Minimum jerk hypothesis Theory of aimed movement that assumes limb movements are represented in terms of hand kinematics, selected so that the cumulated jerk (rate of change of acceleration) is minimized.

Motor program Set of commands to the muscles required for coordinated action.

Motor unit A neuron in the spinal cord that projects to the muscle (motoneuron) and the group of muscle fibers it innervates (which therefore exhibit synchronous activity).

Muscle spindle A structure in parallel with the main muscle fibers, which carries primary and secondary receptors that respond to the rate of change of muscle length and to muscle length respectively.

Muscle synergy A group of distinct muscles whose activity is coordinated to produce a desired action. (See also Coordinative structure)

Orthodromic Electrical stimulation of a neuron resulting in an impulse traveling in the direction normally taken by nervous impulses. (cf. Antidromic)

Passive touch Sensory information derived from contact with an object in the absence of self-initiated movement. (cf. Active touch)

Population coding Representation of an event in terms of activity patterns distributed across several neurons rather than by the firing pattern of a single neuron.

Posture Geometric arrangement of a set of body segments; often used to refer to the whole body.

Precision grip A grip in which the object is grasped by the tip of the thumb opposing the tip of one or more fingers, typically the index finger.

Prehension The act of reaching out and grasping an object.

Projection Efferent connections between neurons in one region of the nervous system and those in another.

Proprioception   Information derived from sensory input from skin, muscle, and joint receptors about the state, movement, and activity of parts of one's own body.

Proximal   Near the body (cf. Distal)

Reach   Arm movements taking the hand to a target.

Reciprocal inhibition   Inhibition between agonist and antagonist muscles so that the two are not active simultaneously. (cf. Coactivation)

Retrograde   Following a neural pathway in the opposite direction to that normally taken by nervous impulses. (cf. Anterograde)

Reversible inactivation   Temporary inactivation of brain tissue achieved by injecting chemicals that reduce neural transmission.

Safety margin   Grip force applied to an object that is in excess of that required to develop frictional force to oppose load force and stop the object from slipping.

Sense of effort   The sense of muscle contraction hypothesized to exist in the absence of peripheral feedback, and thought to arise from corollary discharge.

Sensorimotor transformations   When the location of an object is specified using different frames of reference for sensation and action, the relation between the two may be specified by a transformation that maps points in one frame of reference onto points in the other.

Somatotopic   Having a body-like shape. Used specifically to describe the arrangement of groups of neurons into a map in which neurons in distinct areas code sensory or motor events in distinct parts of the body.

Stretch reflex   Muscle stretch elicits contraction in that muscle which is mediated, at the shortest latencies (20–30 ms) by spinal circuitry, or at longer latencies (60–80 ms) by supraspinal pathways thought to include sensorimotor cortex.

Tracing   Anatomical method of studying neural pathways by injecting chemicals that are transported along nerve fibers.

Trajectory   The kinematics of an action; usually refers to (angular) position as a function of time. Sometimes it is equated with the position trace swept out over the full course of the action (as in handwriting).

Transcranial magnetic stimulation (TMS)   A noninvasive method of stimulating neurons in superficial layers of cortex; a brief, powerful magnetic field from an electromagnet positioned over the scalp induces electrical currents in a relatively large volume of underlying brain tissue.

Index